# Longman Annotated English Poets

GENERAL EDITORS : F. W. BATESON & JOHN BARNARD

LONGMAN ANNOTATED ENGLISH POETS
General Editors: F.W. Bateson & John Barnard

*Published titles in the series:*

* Spenser: The Faerie Queene
  *A.C. Hamilton*

* Milton: The Complete Shorter Poems
  *John Carey*

* Milton: Paradise Lost
  *Alastair Fowler*

* The Poems of Gray, Collins and Goldsmith
  *Roger Lonsdale*

* William Blake: The Complete Poems
  *W.H. Stevenson*

* John Keats: The Complete Poems
  *Miriam Allott*

* Matthew Arnold: The Complete Poems
  *Kenneth Allott; second edition edited by Miriam Allot*

* Tennyson: A Selected Edition
  *Christopher Ricks*

The Poems of Shelley: Volume I 1809–1817
*Geoffrey Matthews and Kelvin Everest*

The Poems of Browning:
  Volume I 1826-1840
  Volume II 1841-1846
*John Woolford and Daniel Karlin*

* available in paperback.

# JOHN MILTON

# COMPLETE
# SHORTER POEMS

### EDITED BY

### JOHN CAREY

**LONGMAN**
**London and New York**

**Longman Group UK Limited**
Longman House, Burnt Mill, Harlow,
Essex CM20 2JE, England
*and Associated Companies throughout the world.*

Published in the United States of America
*by Longman Inc., New York*
© *Longman Group Limited 1968, 1971*

The Complete Poems of Milton
*first issued in one volume in the
Longman Annotated English Poets series 1968.
This edition of the* Complete Shorter Poems
*first published separately in paperback 1971.
Fourth impression, with corrections 1981
Eighth impression 1992*

ISBN 0-582-48456-1

*Printed in Malaysia by CL*

# Contents

## THE MINOR POEMS
## AND SAMSON AGONISTES

## PARADISE REGAINED

# Preface

In preparing the text I have throughout this volume followed a somewhat unusual plan. I have modernized old spelling, but have reproduced old punctuation with diplomatic faithfulness. Usually a different, even an opposite, plan is followed. A modernized text is commonly modernized throughout; and it is even possible to find cases where an editor has retained old spelling but modernized the punctuation. But if the matter is considered in the light of linguistic theory the plan adopted in the present edition will normally appear preferable. Of course some readers need freely modernized texts, just as scholars for certain purposes need texts scrupulously diplomatic. In general, however, it is best to modernize only the spelling.

Spelling and punctuation present quite separate problems to an editor for the good reason that they have quite different functions linguistically. Punctuation, like word order, inflection and function words, is a class of grammatical symbols. It is an organic part of the grammatical system, and as such its mode of operation is subtle and complex. Not only does it obey conventions of logic but also others whereby it renders the pauses and junctures and tones of spoken language (see the emphasis laid in, e.g., D. W. Brown, W. C. Brown, and D. Bailey, *Form in Modern English* (1958) or H. Whitehall, *Structural Essentials of English* (New York 1956)). Consequently we ought to be almost as reluctant to alter the punctuation of an old text as we would be to alter, say, its word order. Moreover, punctuation is less standardized than the other types of grammatical symbol; which means that the gain from modernizing is reduced, while the difficulty of finding exactly equivalent modern conventions is increased. And unless he finds exact equivalents the modernizing editor must continually falsify the meaning (not to mention the rhythm) of the text. With subtle complex poetry like Milton's, decisions will have to be made about tone, juncture and logical structure for which there is no basis in the punctuation of the early editions, and distinctions introduced that the poet himself may have taken care to exclude. Time and again ambiguities will have to be removed and enhancing suggestions lost. Yet even these are not all the problems with which the modernizing editor is faced. For he has next to maintain a sensible rank-ordering or relative frequency among the modern punctuation points he uses. He could make some sort of version of the meaning of *Paradise Lost*, for example, if he allowed himself a very high relative incidence of dashes or of commas. But this he may not do; since the overall effect would be breathy and talkative in the one instance, unrhythmical and pedantic in the other.

My aim, then, has been to provide a text that retains evidential value with respect to punctuation, equally with word order and the other grammatical symbols. The cost that has to be paid for this (a relatively low cost) is that the reader may at first experience an occasional temporary difficulty in making out Milton's syntax. But when he overcomes the difficulty it will at least be Milton's syntax he has understood, and not the editor's.

The linguistic function of spelling is by comparison much cruder and simpler. It is not a grammatical symbol but a vocabulary symbol. That is to say, all that can generally be expected of orthographic signals is that they should enable the reader to make the right vocabulary selection. Now modern spelling is perfectly well able to do this for a seventeenth-century text. It is usually easy to find exact modern equivalents for old spellings, because orthographic signals are essentially simple binary signals. True, spelling also conveys some information about how words sound. But in English the relation between orthography and the phonetic reality it renders is remote. Certainly with our knowledge of the pronunciation of the seventeenth century in its present state there can be few instances where the old spelling indicates the sound to a modern reader better than the new. The typical case, on which editorial practice must be based, is instead exemplified by *eternity*, *PL* viii 406, where the early editions have *eternitie*. It is probable that Milton intended a pronunciation something like *etarnity*: or perhaps even *etarrnity*, since (according to Aubrey) 'he pronounc'd the letter R very hard'. But how are we to tell this from the old spelling?

As for the special orthographic rules and preferences (the distinction between *hee* and *he*, *mee* and *me*, etc.), which some editors have ascribed to Milton, the case for accepting these as Milton's even in *Paradise Lost* now looks desperate (see R. M. Adams, *Ikon: John Milton and the Modern Critics*. Ithaca, N.Y. 1955, and J. T. Shawcross, 'One aspect of Milton's spelling: idle final "E"', *PMLA* lxxviii (1963) 501–10). Although the so-called 'emphatic' pronoun spellings occur in the poems printed after *Paradise Lost* (*Paradise Regained* has 5 and *Samson Agonistes* 8), no one has even pretended that their incidence in these poems is other than random.

Accordingly I have paid no attention in the present edition to spelling variants in the early editions. The early punctuation, on the other hand, for reasons explained above, is reproduced with diplomatic faithfulness; though this should not be taken to imply that it is necessarily Milton's punctuation. In the few instances where a clear misprint in the early editions had to be corrected, a note calls attention to the emendation.

For the rest, I have retained the early spelling of words that have changed their form in a way that might have a bearing on sound or sense (e.g. *highth*), even if the obsolete form is probably only a spelling variant. A very few obsolete words and words intended by Milton as archaisms are also inevitably given in old spelling; but the forms are those selected as commonest in *OED*, and have no evidential value. Similarly with obsolete verb terminals, which for uniformity and intelligibility are given in standard spelling, regardless of contractions and elisions, unless the modern spelling is likely to confuse the reader by suggesting an extra-metrical syllable: thus 'winged' is printed for 'wing'd' (*Comus* 729); but *Bless'd* (*Psalm* i 1). Similarly 'the' is printed for 'th''. Old hyphenated words now amalgamated are given their new form. Italicization of proper names is not retained: it is a typographical accidental not found in the MSS. But a note is given where its presence or absence may have a bearing on, for example, personification.

(The above refers only to the text, and to quotations from M.'s poems. In the notes generally, the spelling and italicization of the edition cited are retained, with *v, u, i, j, s*, and *∫* normalized in the usual way.)

This textual policy may seem an oversimplification. But editorial policy is bound to be decided in terms of broad simple issues; even though it is a different matter with editorial practice in individual cases. And if the policy seems a compromise, this too is inevitable. For no text is completely modern unless the editor is prepared to change word order and vocabulary; and none is completely diplomatic unless he resorts to photographic facsimile (perhaps not even then). I have tried to arrive at the best practicable compromise between the demand for evidential value and the demand for readability.

In the headnotes and footnotes, the titles of works cited fairly frequently have been abbreviated to the author's or editor's surname. Where similar abbreviation has been needed for a second, third or fourth work by the same author or editor, I have used the surname followed by the appropriate arabic numeral above the line. A list of these abbreviations will be found at pp. 1168–75.

Reference-books used include: D. H. Stevens, *A Reference Guide to Milton* (Chicago, Ill. 1930); Harris F. Fletcher, *Contributions to a Milton Bibliography 1800–1930*, University of Illinois Studies in Language and Literature xvi (1931); Calvin Huckabay, *John Milton. A Bibliographical Supplement 1929–1957*, Duquesne Studies Philological Series i (1960); John Bradshaw, *A Concordance to the Poetical Works of John Milton* (1894); Lane Cooper, *A Concordance of the Latin, Greek, and Italian Poems of*

*Milton* (Halle 1923); A. H. Gilbert, *A Geographical Dictionary of Milton*
(New Haven, Conn. 1919); E. S. Le Comte, *A Milton Dictionary* (1961); J.
Milton French, *The Life Records of John Milton* (New Brunswick, N.J.
1949–58); and Harris F. Fletcher, *The Intellectual Development of John
Milton*, Vols. i and ii (Urbana, Ill. 1956–61).

In preparing my edition I have greatly profited from the pertinent
observations of Mr F. W. Bateson, general editor of the series of Anno-
tated English Poets. I have received generous assistance from Professor
Richard Beck of the Royal University of Malta, who placed his un-
published edition of *Paradise Regained* at my disposal. My notes to that
poem are repeatedly indebted to Professor Beck's mastery of his subject.
Learned advice as well as kindly interest was offered by Mrs E. E. Duncan-
Jones of Birmingham University, and Mr J. C. Maxwell of Balliol College.
For instruction on some points in Milton's Greek and Italian poems and
translations from Hebrew I applied to Mr W. S. Barrett of Keble College,
Professor C. Grayson of Magdalen and the Revd L. H. Brockington of
Wolfson. I should like to express my gratitude to each. The remaining
errors, needless to say, are mine.

*St. John's College*                                                    J. C.
*Oxford*
*August 1966*

# Abbreviations

The following abbreviations will be found, in addition to standard abbreviations for books of the Bible, classical works and literary periodicals.

*1637* = *A Maske Presented at Ludlow Castle* (1637).
*1645* = *Poems of Mr John Milton* (1645).
*1671* = *Paradise Regain'd. A Poem in IV Books. To which is added Samson Agonistes* (1671).
*1673* = *Poems, &c. Upon Several Occasions* (1673).
*Trin. MS* = The Trinity Manuscript.

*Ad Pat* = *Ad Patrem.*
*Dam* = *Epitaphium Damonis*
*Id Plat* = *De Idea Platonica quemadmodum Aristoteles intellexit.*
*Leon* = *Ad Leonoram Romae canentem.*
*Natur* = *Naturam non pati senium.*
*PL* = *Paradise Lost.*
*PR* = *Paradise Regained.*
*Prae E* = *In obitum Praesulis Eliensis.*
*Proc Med* = *In obitum Procancellarii medici.*
*Prod Bomb* = *In Proditionem Bombardicam.*
*Prol* = *Prolusion.*
*Q Nov* = *In quintum Novembris.*
*SA* = *Samson Agonistes.*
*Salsill* = *Ad Salsillum poetam Romanum aegrotantem. Scazontes.*

Columbia = *The Works of John Milton,* ed. F. A. Patterson *et al.* (New York 1931–8).
*FQ* = *The Faerie Queene.*
Migne = *Patrologia Latina,* ed. J. P. Migne (Paris 1844–55).
Migne *P. G.* = *Patrologia Graeca,* ed. J. P. Migne (Paris 1857–66).
Yale = *The Complete Prose Works of John Milton,* ed. Douglas Bush *et al.* (New Haven 1953– ).

xiii

# Selected Journal Abbreviations

| | |
|---|---|
| *AR* | *American Review* |
| *CQ* | *Classical Quarterly* |
| *E & S* | *Essays and Studies by Members of the English Association* |
| *EC* | *Essays in Criticism* |
| *ELH* | *A Journal of English Literary History* |
| *EM* | *English Miscellany* |
| *HLQ* | *Huntington Library Quarterly* |
| *JEGP* | *Journal of English and Germanic Philology* |
| *JHI* | *Journal of the History of Ideas* |
| *JWI* | *Journal of the Warburg and Courtauld Institutes* |
| *KR* | *Kenyon Review* |
| *MLN* | *Modern Language Notes* |
| *MLQ* | *Modern Language Quarterly* |
| *MLR* | *Modern Language Review* |
| *N & Q* | *Notes and Queries* |
| *PMLA* | *PMLA: Publications of the Modern Language Association of America* |
| *PQ* | *Philological Quarterly* |
| *RES* | *Review of English Studies* |
| *SP* | *Studies in Philology* |
| *TLS* | *The Times Literary Supplement* |
| *TRSL* | *Transactions of the Royal Society of Literature* |
| *UTQ* | *University of Toronto Quarterly* |
| *UTSE* | *University of Texas Studies in English* |

# Chronological Table of Milton's Life and Chief Publications

1608   (*9 December*) Born at his father's house, The Spreadeagle, Bread St, London.

1615   (*24 November*) Brother Christopher born.

1618   Portrait painted by Cornelius Janssen.

1620   Enters St Paul's School, under Alexander Gill. The date is uncertain: some would put it as early as 1615, but see *Defensio Secunda* 'after I was 12 years old I rarely retired to bed from my studies till midnight' (Columbia viii 119). Friendship with Charles Diodati begins. Either now, or earlier, begins to receive tuition at home from, among others, Thomas Young.

1625   (*12 February*) Admitted to Christ's College, Cambridge, under tutorship of Chappell.

1626   Perhaps rusticated temporarily. Removed to tutorship of Tovell.

1627   Unpopular with fellow-students: dissatisfied with Cambridge syllabus (see *Prolusions* i, iii and iv, Columbia xii 118–49, 158–99 Yale i 218–33, 240–56).

       (*11 June*) Lends future father-in-law, Richard Powell, £500.

1628   (*June*) Writes verses for one of his College fellows (*Id Plat?*).

1629   So-called Onslow-portrait painted, also portrait painted by unknown artist (now in Christ's College).

       (*26 March*) Takes B.A.

1630   Portrait, said to be M., painted by Daniel Mytens (now in St Paul's School: the date is uncertain).

       (*16 April*) Charles Diodati matriculates at Geneva.

       (*10 June*) Edward King given a fellowship which it has been assumed (without evidence) M. expected or desired.

1631   (*November*) Brother Christopher admitted to Inner Temple.

1632   *On Shakespeare* published.

       (*3 July*) Takes M.A.

       Retires to Horton for life of study; see *Defensio Secunda* 'I left with most of the fellows of the College, by whom I had been cultivated with more than indifference, a regretful desire for my presence. At my father's house in the country, to which he had gone to pass his old age, I gave myself up with the most complete leisure to reading through the Greek and Latin writers; with this proviso, however, that I occasionally exchanged the country for the town, for the sake of buying books or of learning something new in mathematics or music, in which I then delighted' (Columbia viii 120).

1634   (*29 September*) *Comus* acted.

1637   *Comus* published.

.(*3 April*) Mother dies.

(*September*) Thinking of entering an Inn of Court (see letter to Diodati dated 29 September, Columbia xii 28, Yale i 327).

1638   *Lycidas* printed in *Justa Edouardo King Naufrago*.

(*1 February*) Lends Sir John Cope and others £150 at 8 per cent.

(*April*) Meets Sir Henry Wotton; is kindly treated (see Wotton's letter to M., Columbia i 476–7, Yale i 339–43).

(*May*) Sails for France; meets John, Viscount Scudamore, in Paris; calls on Hugo Grotius.

(*June-July*) To Nice, Genoa, Leghorn, Pisa.

(*27 August*) Charles Diodati buried.

(*August-September*) Arrives in Florence; makes friends (see *Defensio Secunda* 'There I quickly contracted intimacy with many truly noble and learned men. I also assiduously attended their private academies, an institution which is most highly to be praised there ... Time shall never efface the memory of you, James Gaddi, Charles Dati, Frescobaldi, Cultellino, Bonmatthei, Clementillo, Francini, and numerous others', Columbia viii 122). Visits Galileo (see *Areopagitica*, Columbia iv 329–30).

(*October*) To Siena, Rome. Meets Lucas Holstein, one of the Vatican librarians. Attends Barberini concert. Entertained in English College.

(*December*) To Naples. Meets Manso.

1639   Receives news of Diodati's death. Gives up plan of crossing to Sicily and Greece (see *Defensio Secunda* 'The sad news of the English civil war recalled me; for I thought it shameful, while my countrymen were fighting for their liberty at home, that I should be peacefully travelling for culture', Columbia viii 124).

(*January-February*) Revisits Rome.

(*March*) Returns to Florence. Again reads poems at Svogliati academy.

(*April*) Excursion to Lucca (home of Diodati family). To Bologna, Ferrara, Venice (stays a month, and ships parcel of books home).

(*May*) To Verona and Milan. Travels through Lombardy.

(*June*) Visits theologian John Diodati in Geneva (uncle of Charles)

(*July*) Returns home.

1640   Moves to St Bride's churchyard: begins tutoring nephews. Takes 'a large house' to contain self, books and pupils, who include 'the Earl of Barrimore ... Sir Thomas Gardiner of Essex, and others' (Darbishire 24–5).

Occasionally leaves this secluded 'pretty Garden-House ... in Aldersgate-Street, at the end of an Entry' and drops 'into the society of some young sparks of his acquaintance, the chief whereof were Mr Alphry, and Mr Miller, two Gentlemen of Gray's-Inn, the Beaus of those times,' with whom he likes to 'keep a Gawdy-day' (Darbishire 62).

Poem on Hobson printed in *A Banquet of Jests*.

*Epitaphium Damonis* printed? The first edition is undated but probably belongs to 1640.

(*30 June*) Takes Powell's lands in Wheatley by mortgage.

1641   (*May*) *Of Reformation* published.

*Of Prelatical Episcopacy* published.

(*July*) *Animadversions* published.

1642   (*February*) *The Reason of Church Government* published.

(*May?*) *Apology For Smectymnuus* published. Marries Mary Powell ('At Whitsuntide it was, or a little after, that he took a Journey into the Country; no body about him certainly knowing the Reason: ... after a Month's stay, home he returns a Married-man, that went out a Batchelor', Darbishire 63).

(*July?*) Mary returns home.

(*October?*) M. sends for her without success.

(*21 October*) Brother Christopher's name on Reading muster-roll: supporting Royal cause.

1643   Brother-in-law Richard Powell doing intelligence work for Royalists.

(*1 August*) *Doctrine and Discipline of Divorce* published.

1644   (*2 February*) *Doctrine and Discipline of Divorce* (second edition) published.

(*5 June*) Tract *Of Education* published. About this time M.'s attempts to seize the Powell property for debt begin: they continue till 16 July 1647, when he obtains the writ he requires.

(*6 August*) *Judgment of Martin Bucer Concerning Divorce* published.

(*13 August*) Divorce books attacked by Herbert Palmer in sermon before Parliament.

(*24–26 August*) Stationers petition against his divorce books.

(*September*) Begins to notice failure of sight (cp. letter to Philaras, 28 September 1654, Columbia xii 66).

(*23 November*) *Areopagitica* published.

(*28 December*) Summoned before the House of Lords for examination: 'soon dismissed' (Darbishire 24).

1645 Plans to marry 'one of Dr Davis's Daughters, a very Handsome and Witty Gentlewoman' (Darbishire 66). Wife returns.

(*4 March*) *Tetrachordon* and *Colasterion* published.

(*September?*) Moves to larger house at Barbican.

(*6 October*) *Poems of Mr John Milton, Both English and Latin . . . 1645* registered for publication.

1646 (*2 January*) *Poems . . . 1645* published.

(*29 July*) Daughter Anne born.

1647 (*1 January*) Father-in-law Richard Powell dies.

(*13 March*) Father dies, leaving M. the Bread St house and a 'moderate Estate' (Darbishire 32–3).

(*16 July*) Obtains extent on Powell's property in Oxfordshire.

(*September–October*) Moves from Barbican to a smaller house in High Holborn 'among those that open backward into Lincolns-Inn Fields, here he liv'd a private and quiet Life, still prosecuting his Studies and curious Search into Knowledge' (Darbishire 68).

(*20 November*) Takes possession of Powell property at Wheatley.

1648 (*25 October*) Daughter Mary born.

1649 (*13 February*) *Tenure of Kings and Magistrates* published.

(*13 March*) Invited to be Secretary for the Foreign Tongues by the Council of State.

(*15 March*) Appointed Secretary (at £288 p.a.). Ordered to answer *Eikon Basilike*.

(*11 May*) Salmasius's *Defensio Regia* appears in England.

(*16 May*) *Observations on the Articles of Peace* published.

(*6 October*) *Eikonoklastes* published.

(*19 November*) Given lodgings for official work in Scotland Yard.

1650 (*8 January*) Ordered by Council of State to reply to Salmasius.

1651 (*24 February*) *Defensio pro populo Anglicano* published.

(*16 March*) Son John born.

(*17 December*) Moves, for the sake of health, to 'a pretty Garden-house in Petty-France in Westminster . . . opening into St James's Park' (Darbishire 71).

1652 (*28 February*) Becomes totally blind at about this date.

(*2 May*) Daughter Deborah born.

(*5 May*) Wife dies.

(*16 June*) Son John dies on or about this date.

(*August*) Pierre du Moulin's *Regii Sanguinis Clamor* published, in reply to M.'s *Defensio*. M. ordered to reply by Council of State.

1653 (*21 February*) Writes letter recommending Andrew Marvell to John Bradshaw (this is the first evidence of M.'s acquaintance with Marvell).

(*3 September*) Salmasius dies.

1654 (*30 May*) *Defensio Secunda* published.

1655 Allowed substitute in Secretaryship (Darbishire 28). Takes up private studies again. Starts compiling Latin dictionary and Greek lexicon; works on *De Doctrina*, and possibly on *Paradise Lost* (Darbishire 29).

(*17 April*) Salary reduced from £288 to £150, but made pension for life.

(*8 August*) *Defensio Pro Se* published.

1656 (*12 November*) Marries Katherine Woodcock.

1657 (*19 October*) Daughter Katherine born.

1658 (*14 January*) Lends Thomas Maundy £500 and takes mortgage on property in Kensington as security.

(*3 February*) Wife dies.

(*17 March*) Daughter Katherine dies.

(*May?*) Edits and publishes his MS of Sir Walter Raleigh's *Cabinet Council*.

1659 (*16 February?*) *A Treatise of Civil Power* published.

(*August*) *The Likeliest Means to Remove Hirelings out of the Church* published.

(*20 October*) Writes *Letter to a Friend, Concerning the Ruptures of the Commonwealth* (not published until 1698).

1660 (*3 March*) *Ready and Easy Way to Establish a Free Commonwealth* published.

(*April*) Publishes *Brief Notes Upon a late Sermon* in reply to Matthew Griffith's *Fear of God and the King*.

(*May*) Goes into hiding in friend's house in Bartholomew Close to escape retaliation (Darbishire 74).

(*16 June*) Parliament takes steps to have M. arrested and *Defensio pro populo Anglicano* and *Eikonoklastes* burned.

(*27 August*) Copies of M.'s books burned by hangman in London.

(*29 August*) Act of Indemnity does not exclude M.

(*September*) Takes house in Holborn, near Red Lion Fields. Moves from there to Jewin St (Darbishire 74-5).

(*October?*) Arrested, and imprisoned.

(*15 December*) Parliament orders that M. should be released.

(*17 December*) Andrew Marvell protests in Parliament about M.'s excessive jail fees (£150).

1662 Becomes acquainted with Thomas Ellwood: begins tutoring him (see *The History of the Life of Thomas Ellwood*, ed. C. G. Crump (1900) 88–90).

(*June?*) Sonnet to Sir Henry Vane published.

1663    On bad terms with children: 'a former Maidservant of his told Mary one of the deceased's [M.'s] Daughters ... that shee heard the deceased was to be marryed, to which the said Mary replyed ... that that was noe News to Heare of his wedding but if shee could heare of his death that was something, – and further told this Respondent that all his said Children did combine together and counsell his Maidservant to cheat him ... in her Markettings, and that his said children had made away some of his bookes and would have sold the rest of his bookes to the Dunghill women' (from Elizabeth Fisher's deposition on M.'s will, 15 December 1674, French iv 374–5).

(*24 February*) Marries Elizabeth Minshull.

(*February?*) Moves from Jewin St to 'a House in the Artillery-walk leading to Bunhill Fields' (Darbishire 75). New wife allegedly severe to M.'s daughters, 'the two eldest of whom she bound prentices to Workers in Gold-Lace, without his knowledge; and forc'd the younger to leave his Family' (from a letter of Thomas Birch, 17 November 1750, French iv 388).

1665    (*June?*) Thomas Ellwood takes house for M. in Chalfont St Giles, to avoid plague.

1666    (*2–6 September*) House in Bread St destroyed by fire.

1667    (*August?*) *Paradise Lost* published.

1669    (*June*) *Accedence Commenced Grammar* published.

1670    Portrait by William Faithorne.

(*November?*) *History of Britain* published.

1671    *Paradise Regained* and *Samson Agonistes* published.

1672    (*May?*) *Art of Logic* published.

1673    (*May?*) *Of True Religion* published.

(*November?*) *Poems, &c. upon Several Occasions ... 1673* published.

1674    (*May*) *Epistolae Familiares* and *Prolusiones* published.

(*6 July?*) Second edition of *Paradise Lost* published.

(*8–10 November*) Dies in Bunhill house. The exact date is not known.

(*12 November*) Buried in St Giles, Cripplegate.

# The Minor Poems
# and *Samson Agonistes*

# Textual Introduction: the Minor Poems, *Samson Agonistes* and *Paradise Regained*

There were two editions of M.'s collected minor poems in his lifetime: *1645* and *1673*. In *1673* thirty-two poems were added: 6 (*Apologus de Rustico et Hero*), 7 (*Fair Infant*), 23 (*Vacation Exercise*), 33 (*The Fifth Ode of Horace*), 70 (*Sonnet XIII*), 71 (*Sonnet XII*), 72 (*On the New Forcers of Conscience*), 73 (*Sonnet XIV*), 74 (*Ad Joannem Rousium*), 75 (*Sonnet XI*), 76 (*Psalms lxxx–lxxxviii*), 83 (*Sonnet XVI*), 85 (*Psalms i–viii*), 87 (*Sonnet XVII*), 88 (*Sonnet XV*), 89 (*Sonnet XVIII*), 91 (*Sonnet XIX*). For these poems *1673* is the only authoritative text, and has been followed.

The other poems in *1673* appeared also in *1645*. In twenty-three of them (1, 10, 12–16, 19, 21, 25, 28, 29, 35, 37, 38, 49, 51, 52, 55–57, 59, 69) the two texts do not vary significantly. There remain, however, thirty-six poems in which significant differences between the *1645* and *1673* texts occur. Which should be followed? The differences are not numerous, and usually involve punctuation, not words. It is clear that the poems in *1673* which are common to both editions were set up from a copy of *1645*. This would be a reason for following *1645*. There are variants, however, which indicate that at some time the copy of *1645* used was corrected by M. or under his direction (the most obvious are at *Nativity Ode* 143–4 and *Solemn Music* 6). If some of *1673*'s divergences from *1645* are evidently M.'s, it would appear unsafe to assume, without evidence to the contrary, that all are not.

It has been claimed that such evidence is particularly strong in *L'Allegro* 104, and in *Comus* 166–8 and 546. In the first of these instances *1645* introduces a new subject after the 'She' of l. 103, reading 'And he by friar's lantern led', where *1673* reads 'And by the friar's lantern led' making the girl tell the story of Robin Goodfellow and his cream-bowl, as well as that about Fairy Mab and the junkets. Perhaps the kitchen-detail of the cream-bowl made the tale seem more suitable for a girl; and Jonson, in a passage M. may have remembered, associated Robin Goodfellow's 'drudgerie' with country maids (see l. 105*n*). At any rate there seems as much to be said for the *1673* reading as for that of *1645*, and I have retained it. It seems possible, too, to defend the *1673* version of *Comus* 166–8 (see note), as representing M.'s final intention, particularly in view of the attitude he had developed towards 'the jingling sound of like endings'. In *Comus* 546, however, where *1645*'s 'meditate' becomes

3

'meditate upon', it seems likely that the *1673* printer has automatically followed English idiom, though M., as at *Lycidas* 66 (see note) is imitating Latin. Here I have adopted the *1645* reading.

Some have argued that since M. was blind in *1673* he could not have supervised the printing efficiently, and so *1645* should always be followed except in cases of indisputably Miltonic emendation. This objection to *1673* is weakened by the fact that at *In Quintum Novembris* 149–50 (where *1673* reads *Perpetuoque leves per muta silentia Manes / Exululat, tellus & sanguine conscia stagnat.*) the *1673 Errata* calls for 'a Comma after *Manes*, none after *Exululat*'. *1645* had read *Exululant* at the beginning of 150. The change to the singular *Exululat* in *1673* means that *Manes*, which had been the subject of this verb, becomes one of the subjects of a previous verb, *videntur* (l. 147), and *tellus* becomes the subject of *Exululat* (as of *stagnat*). The *Errata* removes the comma before *tellus* which would otherwise separate the new subject from its verb. One way of explaining these alterations would be to say that *1645*'s *Exululant* was the correct reading, that the *1673* compositor misprinted *Exululat*, and that some hasty reader undirected by M., perhaps Edward Phillips, getting together a list of *Errata*, noticed *tellus* divided from the nearest singular verb by a comma, assumed it was the subject of that verb, and shifted the comma. The trouble with this explanation is that whoever got together the *1673 Errata* list must surely have had the *1645* copy from which *1673* was set up, or at any rate some copy of *1645*, at hand. A quick glance at this would have shown him that there was no need to move the comma: all he had to do in the *Errata* list was restore the *1645* reading. That no such action was in fact taken makes it difficult to believe that anyone but M. was originally responsible for the change from plural to singular in the verb, and consequent change of meaning, in *1673*. Since the punctuation given in the *1673 Errata* list supports this change, the inference is that the compiler of the list was acting in accordance with M.'s wishes, and this suggests that M. was too closely connected with the production of *1673* for any editor to jettison *1673* variants even when there is superficially little to choose between *1645* and *1673* readings.

For these reasons I have adopted *1673* as copy text for all poems appearing in it, but have abandoned it for *1645* in the few places where the arguments for that text seem conclusive, as, for example, when a word has obviously been garbled by the *1673* compositor (e.g. 14 l. 4, where *1673* prints the impossible *corona* for *1645*'s *cornua*). I have also left *1673* on a few occasions when its punctuation, compared with that of *1645*, seriously hampers the modern reader's understanding of M.'s meaning (e.g. 17 l. 43, where *1673*'s full stop after *possunt* divides the subject from the rest of the sentence). Any such divergences from the copy text are clearly indicated in the *Publication* section of the headnote of each poem.

In the same section of the headnote I have listed all *1645* variants. In each case the reading adopted in the text is given first, and then the variant in the edition under discussion. For example, in the headnote to 2:

*Publication. 1645 (10.* Who]That *similarly 13, 17, 21 and 25)* means that *1645* reads 'That' in the lines specified where my text (following *1673*) reads 'Who'.

Of the poems in both *1645* and *1673* five had appeared in print before 1645: 37 (*On Shakespeare*), 39 (the second Hobson poem), 50 (*Comus*), 53 (*Lycidas*) and 60 (*Epitaphium Damonis*). The pre-*1645* text of the second of these (see headnote) is incomplete and of no authority. For the others I have listed in the *Publication* section of each headnote all verbal variants of the pre-*1645* texts, and summarized the punctuation variants (of which full details may be found in Fletcher[3]).

Of the minor poems in neither *1645* nor *1673*, four (3, 4, 45 and 54) were not printed in the seventeenth century, and are printed here from M.'s autograph. Ten (61–63, 67, 68, 78–80, 86, 92) were first printed in various of M.'s prose works, and the text followed here is that of the first editions of those works. Three (77, 81, 90) were first printed, in poor versions, in Edward Phillips's edition of the *Letters of State* (1694). They also exist, however, in fair copies in the Trinity MS, which the present text follows. The remaining poem (82) was first printed in George Sikes's *Life and Death of Sir Henry Vane* (1662), which the present text follows.

Several of M.'s early poems are found, some in more than one version, in the Trinity MS, either in his own hand or that of an amanuensis. *Comus* is also in the Bridgewater MS. The footnotes of the present edition give full details of the verbal variants of each MS version (though not of punctuation variants, since the punctuation of the MSS is so sparse that this would multiply footnotes excessively), and also of all MS corrections and deletions. In doing this, the following conventions have been used: *italics* denote that the item italicized is crossed out in the MS; SMALL CAPITALS denote that the crossed-out item has later been reinstated in the MS; insertion marks ' ' denote that the item between them has been inserted in the MS; square brackets and dots [. . .] denote that a section has been cut or torn away from the MS. E.g. *Comus* 4–5:

*Trin.* MS: Amidst the '*gardens*' Hesperian gardens, ON WHOSE BANKS '*where the banks*'

means that 'gardens' has been inserted into the line, then deleted; and that 'on whose banks' has been deleted and 'where the banks' substituted, then 'where the banks' deleted and 'on whose banks' reinstated. In *Comus* 79:

*Trin. MS*: adventu ` ` 'rous
means that the 'u' of 'adventurous' has been deleted in the MS and an
apostrophe inserted.

*Samson Agonistes* and *Paradise Regained* were published together in 1671.
This was the only edition in M.'s lifetime. The present text follows it.

J.C.

# 1 A Paraphrase on Psalm cxiv

*Date.* 1624. Headnote in *1645* reads: 'This and the following Psalm were
done by the Author at fifteen years old.'
*Publication.* *1645* and *1673* (no significant variants).
*Modern criticism.* Metrical versions of the psalms became so common in
the late sixteenth and early seventeenth centuries (206 versions of the
complete psalter were published between 1600 and 1653) that something
approaching a traditional phraseology grew up. M. H. Studley, *PQ* iv
(1925) 364–72, examines the effect of this on M. (see headnote to *Psalms
lxxx–lxxxviii* p. 306 below). M.'s ignorance of Hebrew in 1624 forced him
to depend on previous translations, among them, probably, Buchanan's
Latin metrical psalter (1566). For M.'s translation of this psalm into Greek
see p. 229 below.

When the blest seed of Terah's faithful son,
After long toil their liberty had won,
And passed from Pharian fields to Canaan land,
Led by the strength of the Almighty's hand,
5   Jehovah's wonders were in Israel shown,
His praise and glory was in Israel known.
That saw the troubled sea, and shivering fled,
And sought to hide his froth-becurled head
Low in the earth, Jordan's clear streams recoil,
10   As a faint host that hath received the foil.
The high, huge-bellied mountains skip like rams
Amongst their ewes, the little hills like lambs.

¶ 1. *1. faithful son*] Abraham–an example of faith in *Heb.* xi 8–9: *faithful*
has particular force–Terah was an idolater.
*3. Pharian*] Egyptian. Sylvester (Du Bartas 14) coined the adj. from Pharos,
the island off Alexandria. Buchanan's Latin has *arva Phari* here.
*8–9.* Echoing Sylvester (Du Bartas[2] 954): 'Cleer Jordan's Selfe . . . was fain
to hide his head.'
*10. foil*] defeat.

Why fled the ocean? And why skipped the mountains?
Why turned Jordan toward his crystal fountains?
15  Shake earth, and at the presence be aghast
Of him that ever was, and ay shall last,
That glassy floods from rugged rocks can crush,
And make soft rills from fiery flint-stones gush.

## 2 Psalm cxxxvi

*Date.* 1624: see headnote to previous poem.
*Publication.* *1645* (*10.* Who] That *similarly 13, 17, 21 and 25*), and *1673* (the text followed here, except in *65* where *1673* misprints a full stop after 'host').
*Modern criticism.* W. B. Hunter observes, *PQ* xxviii (1949) 141, that though each line should contain four iambic feet the unstressed syllable in the first foot is frequently lacking. This is also found in *L'Allegro* and *Il Penseroso* but, Hunter remarks, there are no comparable examples in the Puritan psalters.

Let us with a gladsome mind
Praise the Lord, for he is kind
  For his mercies ay endure,
  Ever faithful, ever sure.

5  Let us blaze his name abroad,
For of gods he is the God;
  For, *&c.*

O let us his praises tell,
10  Who doth the wrathful tyrants quell.
  For, *&c.*

Who with his miracles doth make
Amazed heaven and earth to shake.
15  For, *&c.*

Who by his wisdom did create
The painted heavens so full of state.
20  For, *&c.*

*14.* Echoing Sylvester (Du Bartas 61): 'Toward the Crystall of his double source / Compelled Jordan to retreat.'
*17.* Sylvester has 'glassie' (Du Bartas 59) as epithet for water, and 'crush/ gush' rhyme (Du Bartas 38) in a description of rain.

Who did the solid earth ordain
To rise above the watery plain.
　　For, &c.

25   Who by his all-commanding might,
Did fill the new-made world with light.
　　For, &c.

And caused the golden-tressed sun,
30   All the day long his course to run.
　　For, &c.

The horned moon to shine by night,
Amongst her spangled sisters bright.
35   　　For, &c.

He with his thunder-clasping hand,
Smote the first-born of Egypt land.
40   　　For, &c.

And in despite of Pharaoh fell,
He brought from thence his Israel.
　　For, &c.

45   The ruddy waves he cleft in twain,
Of the Erythraean main.
　　For, &c.

The floods stood still like walls of glass,
50   While the Hebrew bands did pass.
　　For, &c.

¶ 2. *22. watery plain*] Found in Spenser, *F.Q.* IV xi 24, Drayton, *Polyolbion*
xv 110, and Phineas Fletcher, *Purple Island* iii 28.

*29. golden-tressed*] Sylvester gives the sun 'golden tresses' (Du Bartas 107,
452). Buchanan's Latin translation has *solem auricomum* here.

*33-4.* In Sylvester the moon is frequently 'horned' (Du Bartas 51, 103)
and the stars 'spangles' (Du Bartas 17, 91). Shakespeare has stars which
'spangle heaven' (*Taming of Shrew* IV v 31) and 'spangled starlight'
(*Midsummer Night's Dream* II i 29). 'Horned moone' occurs in Spenser,
*F.Q.* IV vi 43.

*41-2.* Sylvester calls Pharaoh's hands 'fell' (Du Bartas 453), and rhymes
'fell / Israel' (Du Bartas 447, 473, 598).

*46. Erythraean*] Adjective from Greek, ἐρυθρός (red), used by Herodotus,
i 180, ii 8 and 158, to denominate the Red Sea. Sylvester makes God's voice
'cleave the bottom of th' *Erythraean* Deepe' (Du Bartas 61), and refers
to 'the *Erythraean* ruddy Billowes' (Du Bartas[2] 967).

*49.* In Sylvester the Red Sea divides to form 'Two Walls of Glass' (Du
Bartas 454)

But full soon they did devour
The tawny king with all his power.
55    For, &c.

His chosen people he did bless
In the wasteful wilderness.
60    For, &c.

In bloody battle he brought down
Kings of prowess and renown.
For, &c.

65  He foiled bold Seon and his host,
That ruled the Amorean coast.
For, &c.

And large-limbed Og he did subdue,
70  With all his over-hardy crew.
For, &c.

And to his servant Israel,
He gave their land therein to dwell.
75  For, &c.

He hath with a piteous eye
Beheld us in our misery.
80  For, &c.

And freed us from the slavery
Of the invading enemy.
For, &c.

85  All living creatures he doth feed,
And with full hand supplies their need.
For, &c.

Let us therefore warble forth
90  His mighty majesty and worth.
For, &c.

53–4. Echoing Sylvester's 'But contrarie the Red-sea did devower / The barbrous tyrant with his mighty power' (Du Bartas 21).
54. *tawny king*] Fairfax's translation of Tasso iii 38 has 'Affrikes tawnie kings'.
65–6. Buchanan's Latin translation has *Amorrhaeum ... Seonem* here and *Quique Amorrhaeis Seon regnavit in oris* in *Ps.* cxxxv. Sylvester uses 'Ammorrean' for Amorite (Du Bartas 372).
89. Sylvester has 'warble forth' (Du Bartas 1).

That his mansion hath on high
Above the reach of mortal eye.
95   For his mercies ay endure,
Ever faithful, ever sure.

# 3 *Carmina Elegiaca*
[Elegiac Verses]

*Date.* 1624? The verses were discovered *c.* 1874 by A. J. Horwood at Netherby Hall, Longtown, Cumberland. The MS leaf on which they are written bears M.'s name and contains also *Ignavus satrapam* . . . (p. 11) and the prose theme on early rising (Columbia xii 288–91). Horwood found the leaf among the papers of Sir Frederick Graham, loose in the same box as M.'s Commonplace Book. H. C. H. Candy has argued that the leaf is autograph in *Library* xv (1934–5) 330–9 and prints a reproduction of part of it. There is an autotype reproduction in the Public Record Office (Autotypes Milton &c./Fac. 6/Library/Shelf 156a), and a photograph of this autotype in the BM (Add. MS 41063 I, ff 84–5).

Reasons for regarding the contents of the leaf as grammar-school exercises, belonging to M.'s St Paul's days, are given by Clark (178–80, 230–7), and by Maurice Kelley and D. C. Mackenzie (Yale i 1034–6).

*Publication.* First printed in Horwood 62–3. The text printed below follows M.'s autograph. Note the scanty punctuation.

Surge, age surge, leves, iam convenit, excute somnos,
    Lux oritur, tepidi fulcra relinque tori
Iam canit excubitor gallus praenuntius ales
    Solis et invigilans ad sua quemque vocat
5   Flammiger Eois Titan caput exserit undis
    Et spargit nitidum laeta per arva iubar
Daulias argutum modulatur ab ilice carmen
    Edit et excultos mitis alauda modos
Iam rosa fragrantes spirat silvestris odores
10   Iam redolent violae luxuriatque seges

¶ 3. *1. excute*] M. first wrote *arcere*, then inserted *excute* over the top, without deleting *arcere*.

*7. Daulias*] The swallow, which Ovid calls *Daulias ales* (*Her.* xv 154) because Daulis, a city of Phocis, was celebrated as the scene of the fable of Tereus, Philomela and Progne (*Met.* vi 438–674), at the end of which Progne is turned into a swallow.

Ecce novo campos Zephyritis gramine vestit
    Fertilis, et vitreo rore madescit humus
Segnes invenias molli vix talia lecto
    Cum premat imbellis lumina fessa sopor
15  Illic languentes abrumpunt somnia somnos
    Et turbant animum tristia multa tuum
Illic tabifici generantur semina morbi
    Qui pote torpentem posse valere virum
Surge age surge, leves, iam convenit, excute somnos
20  Lux oritur, tepidi fulcra relinque tori.

Get up, come on, get up! It's time! Shake off these worthless slumbers: it's
getting light. Come on out from between the posts of that warm bed. The
cock's crowing already: the guardsman cock: the bird that forewarns us
of sunrise. He's wide awake and calling everyone to work. Fiery Titan is
rearing his head above the eastern waves, and flinging bright sunlight over
the gay fields. From her oak-tree perch the Daulian bird[7] trills a piercing song,
and the gentle lark is pouring forth exquisite harmonies. Now the wild
rose breathes out sweet perfumes; now violets scent the air, and the standing
corn frisks and dances. Look, fruit-bringing Venus[11] is decking out the
fields in fresh turf, and watering the ground with dew as bright as glass.
You sluggard, you're not likely to find such sights as these in that downy
bed of yours, where feeble lethargy closes your tired eyes. There your idle
slumbers are racked by dreams, and a host of griefs troubles your spirit. That
is where the germs of corroding disease are bred! How can an inactive man
be healthy? Get up, come on, get up! It's time! Shake off these worthless
slumbers: it's getting light. Come on out from between the posts of that
warm bed.


# 4 *Ignavus satrapam . . .*
## [Kings should not oversleep]

*Date.* 1624? See headnote to previous poem: these lines appear on the MS
leaf directly beneath *Carmina Elegiaca*, without a separate heading. The
metre is the Lesser Asclepiad.

*Publication.* First printed in Horwood 63. The text printed below follows
M.'s autograph.


*11. Zephyritis*] Venus. Arsinoe, Ptolemy II's queen, was deified, identified
with Aphrodite, and given a temple on the promontory of Zephyrium
east of Alexandria, from which she took the title Aphrodite Zephyritis.
M. probably found the name in Catullus lxvi 57 (a translation from Calli-
machus's *Aetia* IV cx), where Zephyrus, the west wind, appears as Aphro-
dite-Arsinoe's attendant.

*15. somnos*] M. first wrote, in error, *somnum*.

*19. excute*] M. first wrote *arcere*, then deleted it and inserted *excute*.

Ignavus satrapam dedecet inclytum
Somnus qui populo multifido praeest.
Dum Dauni veteris filius armiger
Stratus purpureo procubuit strato
5    Audax Euryalus, Nisus et impiger
Invasere cati nocte sub horrida
Torpentes Rutilos castraque Volscia
Hinc caedes oritur clamor et absonus.

To a famous governor, who is responsible for the many and various concerns
of a nation, idle slumber is a disgrace. While old Daunus's soldier son[3] lay
stretched in his luxurious bed, bold Euryalus and energetic Nisus craftily
attacked the Volscian camp and the drowsy Rutilians, under cover of
thick darkness. The result: slaughter and a confused clamour.

## 5 *Philosophus ad regem quendam qui eum ignotum et insontem inter reos forte captum inscius damnaverat* τὴν ἐπὶ θανάτῳ πορευόμενος, *haec subito misit.*

[A philosopher on his way to execution sent these impromptu
verses to a certain king who had unknowingly condemned
him to death when he happened to be taken prisoner—unrecog-
nized and innocent—in the company of some criminals]

*Date.* 1624? There is no certain evidence. Clark 206 suggests that this
epigram may have been written to 'fulfill the requirements of a moral
theme in Greek verse, if such an assignment were imposed on M. in the
Eighth Form' at St Paul's. If not written at school the epigram must be
post-1634 (see *Psalm cxiv* headnote, p. 229). W. R. Parker (Taylor² 128–9)
dates between Dec. 1634 and 1638 (on the assumption that the order of
poems in *1645* corresponds to the order of composition). He adds 'the
poem could indirectly allude to Gill's unfortunate clash with Laud and the
Star Chamber, and his subsequent pardon by King Charles (Nov. 30, 1630)'.
*Publication. 1645* (4. Μαψιδίως] Μὰψ αὔτως    τεὸν πρὸς θυμὸν ὀδυρῇ]

¶ 4. *3. Dauni ... filius*] Turnus, whose camp is attacked by Nisus and
Euryalus in *Aen.* ix 176–449.

χρόνῳ μάλα πολλὸν ὀδύρῃ 5. πόλιος] πόλεως) 1673 (the text followed
here).

> Ὦ ἄνα εἰ ὀλέσῃς με τὸν ἔννομον, οὐδέ τιν' ἀνδρῶν
> Δεινὸν ὅλως δράσαντα, σοφώτατον ἴσθι κάρηνον
> Ῥηϊδίως ἀφέλοιο, τὸ δ' ὕστερον αὖθι νοήσεις,
> Μαψιδίως δ' ἄρ' ἔπειτα τεὸν πρὸς θυμὸν ὀδύρῃ,
> 5 Τοιόνδ' ἐκ πόλιος περιώνυμον ἄλκαρ ὀλέσσας.

King, if you destroy me, a law-abiding man who has done no harm to
anybody at all, you may easily, let me tell you, take away a head of great
wisdom, but afterwards you will realize what you have done, and you
will lament, then, in vain to your own heart [*1645*: and in time then you
lament very greatly, all in vain] that you have deprived your city of a
bulwark of such renown.

## 6 Apologus De Rustico et Hero
[The Fable of the Peasant and the Landlord]

*Date.* 1624? Harris Fletcher has demonstrated, *JEGP* lv (1956) 230-3, that
M.'s fable is a close imitation of one in Mantuan's *Opera* (Paris 1513) 194v.
Fletcher considers the *Apologus* a grammar school exercise.
*Publication.* First printed in *1673* (the text followed here).

> Rusticus ex malo sapidissima poma quotannis
>     Legit, et urbano lecta dedit domino:
> Hic incredibili fructus dulcedine captus
>     Malum ipsam in proprias transtulit areolas.
> 5 Hactenus illa ferax, sed longo debilis aevo,
>     Mota solo assueto, protinus aret iners.
> Quod tandem ut patuit domino, spe lusus inani,
>     Damnavit celeres in sua damna manus.

¶ *5. 4.* ὀδύρῃ] M. must have intended the future, 'you will lament'.
In *1645* he accents as present, ὀδύρῃ; in *1673* as future, ὀδύρῇ.
5. Cp. *Prov.* xxiv 3-6: 'Through wisdom is a house builded; and by under-
standing it is established. . . A wise man is strong; yea, a man of knowledge
increaseth strength. For by wise counsel thou shalt make war; and in
multitude of counsellors there is safety'; also Comenius, *Didactica Magna*
tr. M. W. Keatinge (1896) p. 453, 'With truth did the sainted Luther
write . . . "Where one ducat is expended in building cities, fortresses,
monuments and arsenals, one hundred should be spent in educating one
youth aright. . . For a good and wise man is the most precious treasure
of a state, and is of far more value than . . . gates of bronze and bars of iron."'

Atque ait, Heu quanto satius fuit illa coloni
10     (Parva licet) grato dona tulisse animo!
Possem ego avaritiam frenare, gulamque voracem:
Nunc periere mihi et foetus et ipsa parens.

A peasant had an apple-tree from which he picked, each year, fruit of really
exquisite flavour. He presented the choicest specimens to his landlord, who
lived in the city. The landlord, fascinated by the unbelievable sweetness of
the apples, transplanted the tree to his own little pleasure-gardens. Although
it had borne fruit up till now, the tree was really very old and weak, and
once moved from its accustomed soil it withered and became barren. Even-
tually, when the landlord realised what had happened, and saw that he
had been deluded by a vain hope, he cursed himself for being so swift in
his own undoing.

'Alas!' he said, 'how much better it was to accept my tenant's gifts with
gratitude, small though they were! If only I could have kept my avarice
and my ruinous gluttony under control! Now I have lost both the fruit
and the tree.'

# 7 On the Death of a Fair Infant Dying of a Cough

*Date.* Winter 1625–6. Headed *Anno aetatis 17* in *1673* (i.e. Dec. 1625–Dec.
1626). Edward Phillips, writing in 1694, confirms that *Fair Infant* was written
at seventeen, but also claims that its occasion was 'the Death of one of his
Sister's Children (a Daughter), who died in her Infancy' (Darbishire 62).
W. R. Parker, *TLS* (17 Dec. 1938) 802, taking Phillips at his word, concludes
that the only child of M.'s sister who could have been the poem's subject
was Anne (baptized 12 Jan. 1626, buried 22 Jan. 1628–when M. was
nineteen, not seventeen). However, two-year-old Anne cannot have been
the poem's subject, since the 'infant' of whom M. writes did not outlast
even a single winter (*3–4*). If, then, we accept Phillips's and M.'s dating,
there is one piece of corroboratory evidence: M.'s references to the horrors
of the plague (*64–70*). The great plague year was 1625 (see *Elegia III 6–7n*,
p. 49 below). As F. P. Wilson says (*The Plague in Shakespeare's London*
(Oxford 1927) p. 174), the next London plague of any importance did
not occur until 1636.

*Publication.* First printed in *1673* (the text followed here, but emended in
these instances: *3*. outlasted]outlasted,     *12*. blot]blot,     *40*. were)]
were.) *49*. head?]head.     *53*. youth?]youth!     *54*. crowned]cown'd
*56*. good?]good.     *63*. aspire?]aspire.     *69*. smart?]smart ).

*Modern criticism.* Allen 47–52 examines *Fair Infant* and finds it 'a vivid
indication of the poet's mature technique. . . Pagan myth, with Christian
undertones, leads to universal philosophical abstractions that open the door
to Christian legend.' Following up Allen's analysis, H. N. Maclean, *ELH*

xxiv (1957) 296–305, finds that from the viewpoint of the Pagan-Christian antithesis *Fair Infant* marks an intermediate stage in M.'s development between *Elegia III* and *Prae E* on the one hand and *Nativity Ode* on the other.

**I**

O fairest flower no sooner blown but blasted,
Soft silken primrose fading timelessly,
Summer's chief honour if thou hadst outlasted
Bleak winter's force that made thy blossom dry;
5   For he being amorous on that lovely dye
    That did thy cheek envermeil, thought to kiss
But killed alas, and then bewailed his fatal bliss.

**II**

For since grim Aquilo his charioteer
By boisterous rape the Athenian damsel got,
10  He thought it touched his deity full near,
If likewise he some fair one wedded not,
Thereby to wipe away the infamous blot
    Of long-uncoupled bed, and childless eld,
Which 'mongst the wanton gods a foul reproach
    was held.

**III**

15  So mounting up in icy-pearled car,
Through middle empire of the freezing air
He wandered long, till thee he spied from far,
There ended was his quest, there ceased his care.
Down he descended from his snow-soft chair,
20     But all unwares with his cold-kind embrace
Unhoused thy virgin soul from her fair biding-place.

¶ 7. *1–2.* Probably echoing the pseudo-Shakespearean *Passionate Pilgrim* x 1–4: 'Sweet rose, fair flower, untimely pluck'd, soon vaded, / Pluck'd in the bud and vaded in the spring! / Bright orient pearl, alack too timely shaded! / Fair creature kill'd too soon by death's sharp sting!'
*2. timelessly*] unseasonably; the first recorded occurrence of the adverb in *OED*.
*6–7.* In Shakespeare's *Venus and Adonis* 1110 the boar 'thought to kiss him, and hath kill'd him so'.
*8–9.* Ovid *Met.* vi 682–710 describes how Boreas (also called Aquilo), the north wind, carried off Orithyia, daughter of King Erechtheus of Athens.
*15. icy-pearled*] Sylvester calls hail 'Ice-pearls' and 'Bals of Ice-pearl' (Du Bartas 389 and Du Bartas² 1096).

IV

Yet art thou not inglorious in thy fate;
For so Apollo, with unweeting hand
Whilom did slay his dearly-loved mate
25   Young Hyacinth born on Eurotas' strand
Young Hyacinth the pride of Spartan land;
   But then transformed him to a purple flower
Alack that so to change thee winter had no power.

V

Yet can I not persuade me thou art dead
30   Or that thy corse corrupts in earth's dark womb,
Or that thy beauties lie in wormy bed,
Hid from the world in a low-delved tomb;
Could heaven for pity thee so strictly doom?
   O no! for something in thy face did shine
35   Above mortality that showed thou wast divine.

VI

Resolve me then O soul most surely blest
(If so it be that thou these plaints dost hear)
Tell me bright spirit where'er thou hoverest
Whether above that high first-moving sphere
40   Or in the Elysian fields (if such there were)
   O say me true if thou wert mortal wight
And why from us so quickly thou didst take thy flight.

VII

Wert thou some star which from the ruined roof
Of shaked Olympus by mischance didst fall;
45   Which careful Jove in nature's true behoof
Took up, and in fit place did reinstall?

23-7. Ovid, *Met.* x 162–216 tells how Apollo accidentally killed Hyacinthus, son of Oebalus, king of Sparta (which stands on the river Eurotas), with a discus, and made a flower of bright colour (*purpureus color*) spring from his blood. Allen 49 notes that in Servius' commentary on Virgil, *Ecl.* iii Boreas, not the more usual Zephyrus, is blamed for diverting the discus. Thus these lines are linked with ll. 8–9.

25-6. Probably echoing Spenser, *Astrophel* 7–8: 'Young Astrophel, the pride of shepheards praise, / Young Astrophel, the rusticke lasses love.'

31. Shakespeare, *Midsummer Night's Dream* III ii 384 has 'wormy beds'.

39. *high first-moving sphere*] The *primum mobile* of the Ptolemaic universe (see *Vacation Exercise* 34–5n, p. 77).

40. *Elysian fields*] The abode of the blessed in Greek myth, described by Homer, *Od.* iv 563–8. See p. 225 ll. 980–1n.

Or did of late Earth's sons besiege the wall
Of sheeny heaven, and thou some goddess fled
Amongst us here below to hide thy nectared head?

### VIII

50 Or wert thou that just maid who once before
Forsook the hated earth, O tell me sooth
And cam'st again to visit us once more?
Or wert thou that sweet smiling youth?
Or that crowned matron sage white-robed Truth?
55    Or any other of that heavenly brood
Let down in cloudy throne to do the world some good?

### IX

Or wert thou of the golden-winged host,
Who having clad thyself in human weed,
To earth from thy prefixed seat didst post,
60 And after short abode fly back with speed,
As if to show what creatures heaven doth breed,
   Thereby to set the hearts of men on fire
To scorn the sordid world, and unto heaven aspire?

### X

But O why didst thou not stay here below
65 To bless us with thy heaven-loved innocence,
To slake his wrath whom sin hath made our foe
To turn swift-rushing black perdition hence,
Or drive away the slaughtering pestilence,
   To stand 'twixt us and our deserved smart?
70 But thou canst best perform that office where thou art.

47. *Earth's sons*] The giants, sons of Ge (Earth): see Q *Nov* 174*n* (p. 43).
48. *sheeny*] having a shiny surface; the first recorded occurrence of the word in *OED*.
50. *that just maid*] Astraea (Justice): see *Elegia IV* 81 *n* (p. 57).
53. The line lacks two syllables. John Heskin in the mid-eighteenth century suggested the emendation 'wert thou Mercy' (following *Nativity Ode* 141-4). J. A. Himes, *MLN* xxxv (1920) 441-2 and xxxvi (1921) 414-19, opposes any emendation and reads the line as a reference to Ganymede. The sex of the child ('Her' 72) is against this. H. N. Maclean, *ELH* xxiv (1957) 302-3 takes the 'youth' to be Peace, pointing out that Astraea is linked with Peace and Truth in *Prolusion IV*. Allen 51 suggests 'Virtue'.
54. *white robed*] One of the representations of Truth (*Verità*) in Cesare Ripa's *Iconologia* (Padua 1611) p. 530 is white-robed (*vestita di color bianco*).
57. *golden-winged*] Spenser's 'bright Cherubins' in *Hymn of Heavenly Beauty* 93-4 have 'golden wings'.

### XI

Then thou the mother of so sweet a child
Her false imagined loss cease to lament,
And wisely learn to curb thy sorrows wild;
Think what a present thou to God hast sent,
75    And render him with patience what he lent;
This if thou do he will an offspring give,
That till the world's last end shall make thy name
to live.

## 8 *Elegia prima ad Carolum Diodatum*
### [Elegy I, to Charles Diodati]

*Date.* April 1626? This elegy was apparently written from London (*9*),
early in M.'s Cambridge career, before he had become reconciled to the
university (*14–16, 90*), and in the spring (*48*). He matriculated at Cambridge
9 Apr. 1625. In 1626 the Lent Term ended 31 Mar. and the Easter Term
began 19 Apr.

Charles Diodati (*c.* 1609–38), to whom the elegy is addressed, was a
schoolfellow of M.'s at St Paul's. He matriculated from Trinity College,
Oxford 7 Feb. 1623, took his B.A. 10 Dec. 1625 and remained in residence
to work for his M.A. which he took 28 Jul. 1628 (Dorian 102, 111 and 118).
Two undated Greek letters from Diodati to M. survive (BM Add. MS
5016, ff 5 and 71: printed in French i 98–9 and 104–5). Dorian 112–13 thinks
that the second of these may have been written in spring 1626, while Diodati
was holidaying in Cheshire, and that this elegy may be a reply to it.

On the evidence of the reference to 'forbidden rooms' and 'exile'
(*12, 17–20*), it has sometimes been assumed that M. was temporarily rusti-
cated from Cambridge, but corroboration is lacking (French i 106): M.'s
'exile' is probably merely the university vacation.

*Publication.* 1645 (*54*. possit]posset     ) and *1673* (the text followed here).

*Modern criticism.* R. W. Condee, *PQ* xxvii (1958) 498–502 detects in this
elegy a 'cross-comparison' of M. with Ovid: M.'s exile to London is as
happy as Ovid's to Tomis was miserable: the Ovid/Homer collocation
(*21–3*) is a cross-development of that in *Tristia* I i 47–8: M.'s books in London
(*25–6*) balance the booklessness of Tomis, *Tristia* III xiv 37–8: M.'s theatre-
visits (*27–46*) are the counterpart of Ovid's regretful memories of Roman
theatres, *Tristia* III xii 23–4 and *Ex Ponto* I viii 35: the barren marshy land-
scape of Cambridge (*11, 13, 89*) recalls Ovid's complaints about Tomis,
*Tristia* III x 71–8, xii 13–16; *Ex Ponto* I iii 51–2, II vii 74, III i 11–13, viii
13–16, IV x 61–2.

Tandem, care, tuae mihi pervenere tabellae,
    Pertulit et voces nuntia charta tuas,
Pertulit occidua Devae Cestrensis ab ora

Vergivium prono qua petit amne salum.
5  Multum crede iuvat terras aluisse remotas
    Pectus amans nostri, tamque fidele caput,
    Quodque mihi lepidum tellus longinqua sodalem
    Debet, at unde brevi reddere iussa velit.
    Me tenet urbs reflua quam Thamesis alluit unda,
10  Meque nec invitum patria dulcis habet.
    Iam nec arundiferum mihi cura revisere Camum,
    Nec dudum vetiti me laris angit amor.
    Nuda nec arva placent, umbrasque negantia molles,
    Quam male Phoebicolis convenit ille locus!
15  Nec duri libet usque minas perferre magistri
    Caeteraque ingenio non subeunda meo.
    Si sit hoc exilium patrios adiisse penates,
    Et vacuum curis otia grata sequi,
    Non ego vel profugi nomen, sortemve recuso,
20  Laetus et exilii conditione fruor.
    O utinam vates nunquam graviora tulisset
    Ille Tomitano flebilis exul agro,
    Non tunc Ionio quicquam cessisset Homero
    Neve foret victo laus tibi prima Maro.
25  Tempora nam licet hic placidis dare libera Musis,
    Et totum rapiunt me mea vita libri.

¶ 8. 4. Vergivium ... salum] A fairly common name for the Irish Sea
in the sixteenth and seventeenth centuries, deriving from Ptolemy's
'Ωκεανὸς Οὐεργιόνιος (Geographia II ii 5 and II iii 2). M. may have found it
in Drayton, who uses the form Vergivian in Polyolbion i 24 and v 317, or
in Camden, who discusses the name in Britannia (1586) 490 and suggests
a derivation from the Welsh Mor Iwerydd or the Irish fairge (open sea).

15-16. These lines are frequently associated with the two words inserted
by Aubrey into a passage (Darbishire 10) of his MS life of M., which allege
that M. was whipped by his tutor William Chappell. The insertion
suggests that the information was not, like that contained in the sur-
rounding passage, received by Aubrey from M.'s brother Christopher,
but picked up later from some gossip who was, perhaps, merely
elaborating imaginatively upon the hint of these lines. However, among
the information which Aubrey claims to have received from Christopher
is the fact that M. received 'some unkindness' from Chappell, and was
afterwards transferred to the tuition of Nathaniel Tovey.

21. vates] Ovid, banished to Tomis on the north-west shore of the Black
Sea by Augustus in 8 A.D.

23. Ionio] Of the seven or more cities usually recorded as claiming to be
Homer's birthplace Chios and Smyrna are the most commonly mentioned:
Smyrna is in Ionia.

Excipit hinc fessum sinuosi pompa theatri,
Et vocat ad plausus garrula scena suos.
Seu catus auditur senior, seu prodigus haeres,
30    Seu procus, aut posita casside miles adest,
Sive decennali foecundus lite patronus
Detonat inculto barbara verba foro,
Saepe vafer gnato succurrit servus amanti,
Et nasum rigidi fallit ubique patris;
35    Saepe novos illic virgo mirata calores
Quid sit amor nescit, dum quoque nescit, amat.
Sive cruentatum furiosa Tragoedia sceptrum
Quassat, et effusis crinibus ora rotat,
Et dolet, et specto, iuvat et spectasse dolendo,
40    Interdum et lacrymis dulcis amaror inest:
Seu puer infelix indelibata reliquit
Gaudia, et abrupto flendus amore cadit,
Seu ferus e tenebris iterat Styga criminis ultor
Conscia funereo pectora torre movens,
45    Seu maeret Pelopeia domus, seu nobilis Ili,
Aut luit incestos aula Creontis avos.
Sed neque sub tecto semper nec in urbe latemus,
Irrita nec nobis tempora veris eunt.
Nos quoque lucus habet vicina consitus ulmo
50    Atque suburbani nobilis umbra loci.
Saepius hic blandas spirantia sidera flammas
Virgineos videas praeteriisse choros.

27. *sinuosi pompa theatri*] Recalls Propertius IV i 15 *sinuosa cavo pendebant
vela theatro* (rippling awnings hung over the hollow theatre).

29–36. The stock characters mentioned suggest Roman comedy, not
English. Warton took ll. 31–2 as a reference to a Latin play *Ignoramus* by
George Ruggle, Fellow of Clare, but there is no evidence that this was
acted in London.

36. Cp. Ovid's Hermaphroditus, *Met.* iv 330 *nescit enim, quid amor.*

37–8. Ovid similarly describes *violenta Tragoedia* with her sceptre in *Am.*
III i 11–13.

40. *dulcis amaror*] Catullus lxviii 18 says that love *dulcem curis miscet amaritiem*
(mingles sweet bitterness with cares).

45–6. Pelops was father of Atreus and grandfather of Agamemnon. His
descendants appear in the *Oresteia* trilogy of Aeschylus, the *Electra* of
Sophocles, and the *Orestes*, *Electra* and two *Iphigenia* plays of Euripides.
Euripides' *Hecuba* and *Trojan Women* deal with the house of Ilus founder
of Troy. It is Creon, brother of Jocasta, who offers her hand to Oedipus,
actually her son: the tragic after-events are seen in Sophocles' two *Oedipus*
plays and his *Antigone*, Aeschylus' *Seven against Thebes*, and Euripides'
*Phoenician Maidens* and *Suppliants*.

Ah quoties dignae stupui miracula formae
  Quae possit senium vel reparare Iovis;
55 Ah quoties vidi superantia lumina gemmas,
  Atque faces quotquot volvit uterque polus;
Collaque bis vivi Pelopis quae brachia vincant,
  Quaeque fluit puro nectare tincta via,
Et decus eximium frontis, tremulosque capillos,
60  Aurea quae fallax retia tendit Amor.
Pellacesque genas, ad quas hyacinthina sordet
  Purpura, et ipse tui floris, Adoni, rubor.
Cedite laudatae toties Heroides olim,
  Et quaecunque vagum cepit amica Iovem.
65 Cedite Achaemeniae turrita fronte puellae,
  Et quot Susa colunt, Memnoniamque Ninon.
Vos etiam Danaae fasces submittite Nymphae,
  Et vos Iliacae, Romuleaeque nurus.
Nec Pompeianas Tarpeia Musa columnas
70  Iactet, et Ausoniis plena theatra stolis.

57. Pelops was killed by his father Tantalus and served as a feast for the gods.
Only Demeter ate any (part of one shoulder), and when Pelops was restored
to life the missing part was made good with ivory. Ovid retells the story,
*Met.* vi 403–11.

58. *via*] The Milky Way. Ovid refers to the milk of sheep as *nectar, Met.*
xv 117.

62. *tui floris, Adoni*] Ovid, *Met.* x 731–9, tells how Venus caused the anemone
to spring from Adonis' blood.

63. The reference is to Ovid's *Heroides.*

65. *Achaemeniae turrita fronte puellae*] The *Achaimenidai* (from *Achaemenes,*
ancestor of the Persian kings) are named by Herodotus (i 125) as the royal
clan of the Persians. The *tiara* or felt headdress of the Persians assumed
different shapes according to the rank of the wearer: only royalty could
wear it upright (see Aeschylus, *Persae* 662), in which case it became a high,
sharp-pointed cap. M.'s *turrita* suggests that he associated this with the high
headdress worn by women in the seventeenth century (*OED* Tower *sb.*[1]
6 b), which is first mentioned in Sylvester (Du Bartas[2] 1151); perhaps also
with the towered crown of Cybele (Ovid, *Fast.* iv 219, vi 321; Virgil,
*Aen.* vi 785).

66. *Susa . . . Memnoniamque Ninon*] Strabo XV iii 2 says that Susa was
supposedly founded by Tithonus, Memnon's father, and that its acropolis
was called the Memnonium: also that Memnon was buried in Syria, by
the river Badas. Perhaps this is why M. calls Nineveh (founded by Ninos,
Strabo II i 31) 'Memnonian', since it was the capital city of Syria.

69–70. The 'Tarpeian Muse' is Ovid, who lived near the Tarpeian Rock
(*Tristia* I iii 29–30). He recommends Pompey's colonnade and the Roman

Gloria virginibus debetur prima Britannis,
  Extera sat tibi sit foemina posse sequi.
Tuque urbs Dardaniis Londinum structa colonis
  Turrigerum late conspicienda caput,
75 Tu nimium felix intra tua moenia claudis
  Quicquid formosi pendulus orbis habet.
Non tibi tot caelo scintillant astra sereno
  Endymioneae turba ministra deae,
Quot tibi conspicuae formaque auroque puellae
80  Per medias radiant turba videnda vias,
Creditur huc geminis venisse invecta columbis
  Alma pharetrigero milite cincta Venus,
Huic Cnidon, et riguas Simoentis flumine valles,
  Huic Paphon, et roseam posthabitura Cypron.
85 Ast ego, dum pueri sinit indulgentia caeci,
  Moenia quam subito linquere fausta paro;
Et vitare procul malefidae infamia Circes
  Atria, divini Molyos usus ope.
Stat quoque iuncosas Cami remeare paludes,
90  Atque iterum raucae murmur adire Scholae.
Interea fidi parvum cape munus amici,
  Paucaque in alternos verba coacta modos.

At last, dear friend, your letter has reached me. Messenger-like its paper
has carried your words to me from the western bank of Chester's river, the
Dee, where it flows down towards the Irish Sea.[4] It is, believe me, a great
joy to know that distant lands have bred a heart that loves me and a head
so true: that a faraway place owes me a charming companion and is, more-
over, ready to repay that debt soon, at my request.

I am still in the city which the Thames washes with its tides: still in the
delightful place where I was born. Nor am I reluctant to be here. At present
I am not anxious to revisit the reedy Cam. I am not pining away for my
rooms, recently forbidden to me. Bare fields which offer no gentle shades do

theatres as likely places for meeting girls (*Ars Am.* i 67–8, 89–90; iii 387–8,
394).

73. The earliest record of the theory that the Britons are descended from
Brutus and his Trojan fugitives is found in Nennius's eighth-century *Historia
Brittonum*. The tradition is traced by G. S. Gordon in *E & S* ix (1924) 9–30.

77–80. M. is mimicking the claim Ovid made for Rome (*Ars Am.* i 59–60).

83–4. Cnidos and Paphos (a town in Cyprus) were both sacred to Venus
(see Horace, *Odes* I xxx 1–2, III xxviii 13–15). The Simois rises on Mount
Ida where, according to Ovid, Paris awarded the prize for beauty to Venus
(*Her.* xvi 53–88).

88. *Molyos*] In Homer it is the herb Moly (*Od.* x 305) which makes Odysseus
proof against the charms of Circe.

92. *alternos ... modos*] The alternate hexameters and pentameters of the
elegiac couplet, which Ovid refers to in a similar phrase (*Tristia* III vii 10).

not attract me. How badly that place suits the worshippers of Phoebus! I do not like having always to stomach the threats of a stern tutor, and other things which my spirit will not tolerate.[15] If this be exile–to have come home, to live in welcome leisure free from care–then I do not object to the name or fate of an exile, but gladly enjoy my banishment. Ah! If only that poet[21] who was once a tearful exile in the land of Tomis had never had to put up with anything worse than this: then he would have been a match for Ionian Homer,[23] and you, Virgil, outdone, would not enjoy the supreme glory.

For here I can devote my leisure hours to the mild Muses: here books, which are my life, quite carry me away. When I am tired the pageantry of the rounded theatre[27] attracts me, and the play's babbling speeches claim my applause. Sometimes the speaker is a crafty old man,[29] sometimes a spendthrift heir; sometimes a lover appears, or a soldier (minus his helmet). Sometimes a barrister, with pockets well lined by a ten-year-old case, thunders out his barbarous jargon to an ignorant courtroom. Often there is a wily slave who comes to the rescue of some love-struck son, and tricks the stern father at every turn, under the old man's very nose. Often, too, there is a young girl who is surprised by a warmth of feeling she never felt before, and falls in love without knowing what love is.[36]

Sometimes raging Tragedy, with streaming hair and rolling eyes, brandishes her bloody sceptre.[37] It makes me sad to watch, yet watch I do, and find a pleasure in the sadness. Sometimes there is a sweet bitterness even in weeping,[40] as when some poor lad leaves joys untasted and dies, his love snuffed out, a fit subject for tears; or when a fierce avenger of crime returns from the darkness of death, recrosses the Styx, and perturbs conscience-stricken souls with his dismal firebrand; or when the house of Pelops[45] or of noble Ilus mourns, or Creon's[46] palace atones for incestuous ancestors.

But I do not always hide myself away indoors, or stay in the city: the spring does not pass by me unnoticed. A dense elm grove nearby, and a magnificently shady spot just outside the city are my haunts. Here you can often see parties of young girls walking by–stars which breathe forth seductive flames. Ah, how often have I been struck dumb by the miraculous shapeliness of a figure which might well make even old Jove young again! Ah, how often have I seen eyes brighter than jewels, brighter than all the stars which wheel round both the poles; necks which excel twice-living Pelops's shoulders,[57] or that flowing Way which is drenched in pure nectarous milk;[58] a forehead of exceptional loveliness, light-blown hair–a golden net spread by deceitful Cupid, and enticing cheeks beside which the flush of the hyacinth, and even the blushing red of your flower, Adonis,[62] seem dull. Admit defeat, you heroines so often praised:[63] admit defeat, all you girls who have caught the eye of inconstant Jove. Admit defeat, you Achaemenian girls in your turreted hats,[65] and you who live in Susa and Memnonian Nineveh.[66] Surrender, you maidens of Greece and of Troy and of Rome. Let the Tarpeian Muse[69] stop boasting about Pompey's colonnade, or about theatres crowded with the noblewomen of Italy. The first prize goes to the British girls: be content, foreign woman, to take second place! And you, London, a city built by Trojan settlers,[73] a city whose towery head can be seen for miles, you are more than fortunate for you enclose within your walls whatever beauty there is to be found in all this pendent world. The stars which spangle the calm sky above you[77]–those hosts of handmaidens who wait on Endymion's goddess—are fewer in number than the host which can be seen all a-glitter in your streets: girls whose good looks and golden trinkets catch the eye. There is a story that kindly Venus came to this city, drawn by her twin doves and escorted by her quivered soldiery, and that she preferred it to Cnidos,[83] and to the valleys which the Simois waters, and to Paphos and rosy Cyprus.[84]

But for my part I intend to quit this pampered town as quickly as possible, while the blind boy's indulgence permits, and, with the help of divine moly,[88] to leave far behind the infamous halls of faithless Circe. I am to return to the Cam's reedy marshes and face the uproar of the noisy University again. Meanwhile accept this little gift from a loyal friend—one or two words forced into elegiac metre.[92]

## 9 *In Obitum Praesulis Eliensis*
### [On the Death of the Bishop of Ely]

*Date.* Oct. 1626. Headed *Anno aetatis 17* in *1645* and *1673.* Dr Nicholas Felton, Bishop of Ely, died 5 Oct. 1626. He had been a great friend of Lancelot Andrewes (commemorated in *Elegia III*); like him he was scholar, fellow (1583) and master (1617) of Pembroke College, Cambridge, and one of the translators of the Authorized Version.

*Publication.* *1645* (2. lumina;]lumina ) and *1673* (the text followed here).

>      Adhuc madentes rore squalebant genae,
>           Et sicca nondum lumina;
>      Adhuc liquentis imbre turgebant salis,
>           Quem nuper effudi pius,
> 5    Dum maesta charo iusta persolvi rogo
>           Wintoniensis praesulis.
>      Cum centilinguis Fama (proh semper mali
>           Cladisque vera nuntia)
>      Spargit per urbes divitis Britanniae,
> 10       Populosque Neptuno satos,
>      Cessisse morti, et ferreis sororibus
>           Te generis humani decus,
>      Qui rex sacrorum illa fuisti in insula
>           Quae nomen Anguillae tenet.
> 15   Tunc inquietum pectus ira protinus
>           Ebulliebat fervida,
>      Tumulis potentem saepe devovens deam:
>           Nec vota Naso in Ibida

¶ 9. *10. Neptuno*] See Q *Nov* 27–30*n* (p. 37).
*11. sororibus*] The fates, Clotho, Lachesis and Atropos.
*14. Anguillae*] Ely (O.E. Elig) means eel-isle.
*18. Ibida*] Ovid's *Ibis* is the example usually cited by Renaissance critics of the curse or *dira* as a literary form.

Concepit alto diriora pectore,
20   Graiusque vates parcius
Turpem Lycambis execratus est dolum,
Sponsamque Neobolen suam.
At ecce diras ipse dum fundo graves,
Et imprecor neci necem,
25 Audisse tales videor attonitus sonos
Leni, sub aura, flamine:
Caecos furores pone, pone vitream
Bilemque et irritas minas,
Quid temere violas non nocenda numina,
30   Subitoque ad iras percita.
Non est, ut arbitraris elusus miser,
Mors atra Noctis filia,
Erebove patre creta, sive Erinnye,
Vastove nata sub Chao:
35 Ast illa caelo missa stellato, Dei
Messes ubique colligit;
Animasque mole carnea reconditas
In lucem et auras evocat:
Ut cum fugaces excitant Horae diem
40   Themidos Iovisque filiae;
Et sempiterni ducit ad vultus patris;
At iusta raptat impios
Sub regna furvi luctuosa Tartari,
Sedesque subterraneas
45 Hanc ut vocantem laetus audivi, cito
Foedum reliqui carcerem,

20. *Graiusque vates*] Archilochus of Paros, a Greek iambic and elegiac poet of the seventh or eighth centuries B.C. The story that, when an unsuccessful suitor for the hand of Lycambes' daughter Neobule, he avenged himself with such biting satires that father and daughter hanged themselves, is alluded to by Horace, *Epist.* I xix 23–31. As Starnes and Talbert (239) point out, the story is summarized three times in Stephanus: under *Archilocus, Lycambes* and *Neobule.*

27–8. *vitream Bilemque*] Black bile or melancholy was supposed to look shiny; cp. Persius iii 8 : *vitrea bilis.*

32. *Noctis filia*] Hesiod, *Theog.* 758–9, makes Death daughter of Night.

33. *Erebove*] See Q *Nov* 69n (p. 39). *Erinnye*] Virgil, *Aen.* vii 447, and Ovid, *Met.* i 241, iv 490 use the name Erinnys to mean a Fury.

37–8. M.'s Christian-Platonic view of death as release from the body is derived partly from Socrates's discussion of it in *Phaedo* 64–8.

39–40. *Horae ... filiae*] Hesiod, *Theog.* 901 says that the Hours were daughters of Zeus and Themis.

Volatilesque faustus inter milites
Ad astra sublimis feror:
Vates ut olim raptus ad coelum senex
50    Auriga currus ignei,
Non me Bootis terruere lucidi
Sarraca tarda frigore, aut
Formidolosi Scorpionis brachia,
Non ensis Orion tuus.
55 Praetervolavi fulgidi solis globum,
Longeque sub pedibus deam
Vidi triformem, dum coercebat suos
Fraenis dracones aureis.
Erraticorum siderum per ordines,
60    Per lacteas vehor plagas,
Velocitatem saepe miratus novam,
Donec nitentes ad fores
Ventum est Olympi, et regiam crystallinam, et
Stratum smaragdis atrium.
65 Sed hic tacebo, nam quis effari queat
Oriundus humano patre
Amoenitates illius loci, mihi
Sat est in aeternum frui.

My cheeks were still wet, still begrimed with tears, and my eyes, not yet dry, were still swollen with the shower of streaming salt water that I, tender-hearted, had just spilt as I paid my sad respects beside the dear grave of Winchester's bishop; when hundred-tongued Fame–always, alas, a trust-worthy messenger where evil and disaster are concerned–spread through rich Britain's cities and among the race of Neptune's descendants[10] the news that you, the glory of humanity, you who reigned over holy men in that

49. *Vates*] Elijah is whirled up to heaven in a chariot of fire in *2 Kings* ii 11.
51–2. *Bootis . . . Sarraca*] The constellation of the Bear (cp. Juvenal v 23 *serraca Bootae*). The lateness of its setting is commented on by Homer, *Od.* v 272, and Ovid therefore calls it *tardus*, *Met.* ii 176. It is 'cold' because of its northern situation. The words *tarda* and *sarraca* occur, Starnes and Talbert (241–2) note, in Stephanus, under *Bootes*.
53–4. *Scorpionis . . . Orion*] It was the constellation of the Scorpion which terrified Phaëthon (Ovid, *Met.* ii 195–200). Ovid, Lucan, Seneca, Manilius and Claudian all give Orion a spear, but he has a sword which 'frightens the stars' in Statius, *Silv.* I i 44–5.
56–8. *deam*] Hecate, the moon goddess, 'triform' because she was called Luna or Cynthia in heaven, Diana on earth and Proserpina in hell. The attribution of dragons to her derives from Ovid, *Met.* vii. 218–9, where a dragon-drawn chariot descends in answer to Medea's prayer to Hecate.
63–4. Cp. the vision of new Jerusalem in *Rev.* xxi 10–27, in the Vulgate version of which *crystallum* and *smaragdus* both appear.

island which is called Eel Isle,[14] had succumbed to death and to the iron-hearted sisters.[11] At once my anxious heart began to seethe with fierce anger: again and again I cursed that goddess who has power over the tomb. The curses upon Ibis[18] which Ovid gave vent to from the depths of his heart were not more dreadful than mine: more restrained than I was the Greek poet[20] who heaped abuse upon Lycambes' low trickery and upon his fiancée Neobule. But look what happened! While I was pouring forth these terrible curses and calling down death upon Death, I seemed to my amazement to hear, breathed gently beneath the breeze, syllables like these: 'Stop your blind raging, your melancholy,[27] your useless threats. Why are you so rashly violent against powers which cannot be harmed—powers which are quickly moved to anger themselves? Death is not, as you, poor fool, imagine, the dark daughter of Night.[32] She is not the daughter of Erebus[33] or of a Fury, nor was she born in the gulf of Chaos. On the contrary, she is sent down from the starry heavens to gather in God's harvests in every land. Just as the fleeting Hours,[39] daughters of Themis and Jove, rouse up the dawn, so she calls up into the light and the air souls which were buried beneath a mass of flesh:[37] she leads them up until they are before the face of the eternal Father. But since she is just she carries the wicked off towards the mournful realms of dusky Tartarus, and to his dens under ground. Glad when I heard her calling, I swiftly left my loathsome prison and was carried up in blessedness to the stars amidst winged warriors, as once that ancient prophet[49] was snatched up to the sky, riding in a chariot of fire. The Wain[51] of twinkling Boötes, crawling along because of the cold, did not frighten me, nor did the Scorpion's[53] fearful claws, nor, Orion, did your sword. I flew past the blazing globe of the sun and saw, far away beneath my feet, the triform goddess[56] steering her dragon-team[58] with golden reins. I was carried past the courses of the wandering planets, and through the expanses of the Milky Way, often marvelling at my extraordinary speed, until I reached the gleaming gates of Olympus, the palace of crystal[63] and the forecourt paved with emerald. But now I will hold my tongue: for who of mortal seed could describe the bliss of that place? For me it is enough to enjoy it eternally.'

## 10 *In Obitum Procancellarii Medici*
### [On the Death of the Vice-Chancellor, a Doctor]

*Date.* Oct.-Nov. 1626. The Vice-Chancellor, Dr John Gostlin, died 21 Oct. 1626; he had been appointed Regius Professor of Medicine in 1623.
*Publication.* *1645* and *1673* (no significant variants). In both editions the poem is headed *Anno aetatis 16*. This is clearly an error: when Dr Gostlin died M. was almost eighteen.

> Parere fati discite legibus,
> Manusque Parcae iam date supplices,

¶ 10. 2. *Parcae*] The goddesses of Fate (Nona, Decuma and Morta).

Qui pendulum telluris orbem
Iäpeti colitis nepotes.
5   Vos si relicto mors vaga Taenaro
Semel vocarit flebilis, heu morae
Tentantur incassum dolique;
Per tenebras Stygis ire certum est.
Si destinatam pellere dextera
10  Mortem valeret, non ferus Hercules
Nessi venenatus cruore
Aemathia iacuisset Oeta.
Nec fraude turpi Palladis invidae
Vidisset occisum Ilion Hectora, aut
15   Quem larva Pelidis peremit
Ense locro, Iove lacrymante.
Si triste fatum verba Hecatëia
Fugare possint, Telegoni parens
Vixisset infamis, potentique
20      Aegiali soror usa virga.
Numenque trinum fallere si queant

4. *Iäpeti ... nepotes*] Japetus was father of Prometheus who, as Ovid relates in *Met.* i 80–6, created man out of the earth.

5. *Taenaro*] There was supposed to be a mouth of hell at Taenarum, a promontory in Laconia: Ovid calls Tartarus 'the Taenarian vale' in *Fast.* iv. 612.

*10–12.* When the centaur Nessus was killed by Hercules he gave his blood-stained shirt to Deianira, saying that it would revive her husband's failing love. In fact, as Ovid relates in *Met.* ix 101–272, its burning poison drove Hercules to suicide on *Oeta*, the moutain range between Aetolia and Thessaly (M.'s *Aemathia* = Thessalian).

*13–14.* In *Il.* xxii 224–46 Homer makes Athene disguise herself as Hector's brother, Deïphobus, in order to persuade Hector to fight his fatal combat with Achilles. During the combat she retrieves Achilles's spear for him when he has thrown and missed (xxii 276–7).

*15–16.* In *Il.* xvi 426–505 Sarpedon is killed by Patroclus, a Locrian, who wears the armour of Achilles, son of Peleus. Zeus weeps because Sarpedon was his son by Laodamia. *Pelidis* is M.'s error for *Pelidae*.

*17. Hecatëia*] associated with Hecate, who presides over enchantments. Ovid's Circe uses *Hecatëia carmina*, *Met.* xiv 44.

*18. Telegoni parens*] Circe; the tradition that she was mother of Telegonus is found in Hesiod, *Theog.* 1011–14. Ovid calls her *Telegoni parens*, *Ex Ponto* III i 123.

*20. Aegiali soror*] Medea. Her brother, whom she murdered, is usually called Absyrtus. The alternative name, Aegialeus, is given by Cicero, *De Deorum Natura* iii 48.

*21. Numenque trinum*] See l. 2*n*.

Artes medentum, ignotaque gramina,
Non gnarus herbarum Machaon
Eurypyli cecidisset hasta.
25 Laesisset et nec te Philyreie
Sagitta echidnae perlita sanguine,
Nec tela te fulmenque avitum
Caese puer genitricis alvo.
Tuque O alumno maior Apolline,
30 Gentis togatae cui regimen datum,
Frondosa quem nunc Cirrha luget,
Et mediis Helicon in undis,
Iam praefuisses Palladio gregi
Laetus, superstes, nec sine gloria,
35 Nec puppe lustrasses Charontis
Horribiles barathri recessus.
At fila rupit Persephone tua

23–4. Machaon was a surgeon, the son of Aesculapius, and one of the Greeks at Troy (*Il.* xi 514, 614). His death at the hand of Eurypylus is not related by Homer but by Quintus Smyrnaeus in his *Posthomerica* vi 390–429, a work which according to Edward Phillips (Darbishire 60) was used by M. in educating his two nephews. Starnes and Talbert (234) think it more likely that M. was indebted to Stephanus, who mentions Eurypylus as Machaon's killer.

25–6. *Philyreie*] Chiron, the centaur, son of the nymph Philyra and tutor of Aesculapius. Ovid, who calls him *Phillyrides* and *Philyreius heros*, relates how he was killed when one of Hercules' arrows, poisoned with the blood of the Lernean hydra, dropped from its quiver and struck him (*Fast.* v 379–414). Starnes and Talbert (234–5) note that Stephanus's account of the incident also uses the word *perlita* and perhaps suggested it to M.

27–8. *te . . . puer*] Aesculapius. Ovid, *Met.* ii 596–648, tells how he was cut from the womb of his dead mother, Coronis, by his father, Apollo. He became so expert a physician that he could raise the dead, so Jupiter killed him with a thunderbolt.

29. *alumno*] The usual meaning of *alumnus* is pupil, and it may be that M. is paying a hyperbolical compliment to Dr Gostlin by pretending that he was Apollo's tutor. However, *alumnus* can also mean, in late Latin, 'nourisher, one who brings up or educates'.

31–2. *Cirrha*] An ancient town near Delphi which, like Mount Helicon, was sacred to Apollo.

33. *Palladio gregi*] Cambridge University. Pallas was goddess of wisdom.

37. *Persephone*] Ovid tells (*Met.* v 385–424 and *Fast.* iv 420–54) how she was carried off by Pluto and made queen of the Underworld. M. gives her her Latin name *Proserpina* 46 and calls her *Aetnaea* (an adj. used by Ovid, *Met.* viii 260 to mean 'Sicilian') because it was from the meadows of Enna in Sicily that Pluto took her.

  Irata, cum te viderit artibus
  Succoque pollenti tot atris
40   Faucibus eripuisse mortis.
  Colende praeses, membra precor tua
  Molli quiescant cespite, et ex tuo
  Crescant rosae, calthaeque busto,
   Purpureoque hyacinthus ore.
45 Sit mite de te iudicium Aeaci,
  Subrideatque Aetnaea Proserpina,
  Interque felices perennis
   Elysio spatiere campo.

Learn to obey the laws of fate. Lift up your hands now in prayer to the goddess of destiny,[2] all you sons of Japetus[4] who live on this pendent orb, the earth. If that dismal visitor, Death, once leaves Taenarus[5] and calls you, ah! then all your tricks and turns will do you no good: down you will have to go through the Stygian darkness. If strength of arm could push back death, once fated, then fierce Hercules[10] would not have lain lifeless on Emathian Oeta, poisoned by Nessus' blood: Troy would not have seen Hector cut down by envious Athene's low trickery,[13] nor Sarpedon killed, while Jove wept, by a man disguised as Achilles[15] but wielding a Locrian sword. If the spells of witchcraft[17] could chase sad fate away, Telegonus' ill-famed mother[18] would have survived: so, too, would Aegialeus' sister,[20] by the aid of her powerful wand. If medical skill and recondite drugs could cheat the three goddesses,[21] then Machaon,[23] who knew all about herbs, would not have fallen a prey to Eurypylus' spear; nor would you, son of Philyra,[25] have been wounded by that arrow smeared with the Hydra's blood; and neither your grandfather's weapons nor his thunderbolt would have done you[27] any harm—you who, as a baby, were cut from your mother's womb.

And you, also, greater than your foster-father,[29] Apollo, you to whom the government of our gowned society was given, you for whom leafy Cirrha[31] is now in mourning, and Helicon, too, amidst its streams—you would still be alive, would still be the happy and glorious shepherd of Pallas' flock:[33] you would not have crossed the dreadful deeps of the Underworld in Charon's boat. But Persephone[37] snapped the thread of your life, angry because she saw that you had rescued so many patients from the black jaws of death by your skill and by your potent medicine. I pray, reverend master, that your limbs may rest peacefully in the soft turf: from your grave may roses and marigolds and the crimson-lipped hyacinth spring. May the judgment Aeacus[45] passes upon you be mild, may Aetnean Proserpina smile, and may you walk for ever among the blessed in the Elysian fields.

38-40. Starnes and Talbert (235-6) suggest M. has taken the reason for Dr Gostlin's death—that his cures were emptying the underworld—from Stephanus's account of the death of Aesculapius.

45. Aeaci] Aeacus was made one of the judges in the Underworld. Ovid mentions him in this capacity, Met. xiii 25-6: Virgil gives only Minos and Rhadamanthus, Aen. vi 432, 566.

# 11 *Elegia secunda. In Obitum Praeconis Academici Cantabrigiensis*

## [Elegy II. On the Death of the University of Cambridge Beadle]

*Date.* Oct.-Nov. 1626. Richard Ridding, the subject of this elegy, matriculated from St John's in 1587, took his B.A. in 1591 and his M.A. in 1594, and became Esquire Beadle in 1596. As such one of his duties, referred to by M. (*1*), was to carry the mace before the Vice-Chancellor on public occasions. Ridding died between 19 Sept. 1626, when his will was signed, and 28 Nov. 1626, when it was proved. In both *1645* and *1673* the poem is headed *Anno aetatis 17*, which must mean 'At seventeen years of age' not 'In the seventeenth year of his age': M. was almost eighteen in Nov. 1626.

*Publication. 1645* (*12.* tuo,]tuo ), *1673* (the text followed here).

> Te, qui conspicuus baculo fulgente solebas
>     Palladium toties ore ciere gregem,
> Ultima praeconum praeconem te quoque saeva
>     Mors rapit, officio nec favet ipsa suo.
> 5  Candidiora licet fuerint tibi tempora plumis
>     Sub quibus accipimus delituisse Iovem,
> O dignus tamen Haemonio iuvenescere succo,
>     Dignus in Aesonios vivere posse dies,
> Dignus quem Stygiis medica revocaret ab undis
> 10   Arte Coronides, saepe rogante dea.
> Tu si iussus eras acies accire togatas,
>     Et celer a Phoebo nuntius ire tuo,
> Talis in Iliaca stabat Cyllenius aula
>     Alipes, aetherea missus ab arce patris.

¶ 11. *2. Palladium . . . gregem*] See *Proc Med* 33*n* (p. 29).

*5-6.* Ovid, as he grows old, compares the hair of his own temples to the plumage of a swan (*Tristia* IV viii 1). In his *Her.* viii 67-8 Hermione refers to Jove's transformation to a swan and rape of Leda, using the same words (*plumis delituisse Iovem*) as M. here.

*7-8.* In Ovid, *Met.* vii 251-93, Medea rejuvenates Jason's father, Aeson, with a brew of herbs, juices (*sucos*) and roots gathered in *Haemonia . . . valle* (a vale of Thessaly).

*9-10.* In *Fast.* vi 743-56 Ovid tells how Coronides (i.e. Aesculapius, who was son of Apollo by Coronis) restored Hippolytus to life, pitying Diana's grief. Starnes and Talbert (233) think M. indebted to the version of the story in Stephanus, which mentions Diana's prayers.

*12. Phoebo . . . tuo*] The Vice-Chancellor.

*13-14.* In Homer, *Il.* xxiv 336-467, Mercury (frequently called *Cyllenius*

15   Talis et Eurybates ante ora furentis Achillei
       Rettulit Atridae iussa severa ducis.
     Magna sepulchrorum regina, satelles Averni
       Saeva nimis Musis, Palladi saeva nimis,
     Quin illos rapias qui pondus inutile terrae,
20     Turba quidem est telis ista petenda tuis.
     Vestibus hunc igitur pullis Academia luge,
       Et madeant lachrymis nigra feretra tuis.
     Fundat et ipsa modos querebunda Elegëia tristes,
       Personet et totis naenia moesta scholis.

Fierce Death, the last of beadles, shows no favour even to her own profession.
She seizes you, a fellow-beadle—you who, resplendent with your glittering
mace, used to rouse Pallas' flock[2] so often with your call. Though your
brows were whiter than the swan's down[5] beneath which, so the story goes,
Jove hid himself, yet you deserved to be made young again with a Haemo-
nian[7] medicine. You deserved to live on, Aeson-like; you deserved to be
called back from the waters of Styx,[9] in answer to the insistent prayer of a
goddess, by Coronides and his medical skill. If your Apollo[12] ordered you
to carry his swift message and call together the gowned assembly, you were
like wing-footed Cyllenius,[13] when he was sent from his father's heavenly
citadel and stood in the Trojan court. You were like Eurybates[15] when,
face to face with furious Achilles, he delivered the uncompromising com-
mands of his chief, Atrides.

Great queen of tombs, accomplice of Avernus,[17] too cruel to the Muses,
too cruel to Pallas, why not carry off those who are a useless burden to the
earth?[19] There are crowds of them for you to aim your arrows at!

Grieve then, University, for this man, and wear mourning. May his
black hearse be wet with your tears. May plaintive Elegy herself pour
sorrowful harmonies forth, and may all the schools resound with a song of
lamentation.

in Latin poetry because he was born on Mount Cyllene in Arcadia), is
sent by his father, Jupiter, to guide Priam to Achilles. He meets Priam not,
as M. implies, in the Trojan court, but outside the walls of Troy.

*15–16.* In Homer, *Il.* i 318–44, Eurybates and Talthybius, the heralds of
Agamemnon (son of Atreus, hence called *Atrides* by M.), are sent to Achilles
to demand the return of Briseïs. M.'s reference is inaccurate: the heralds
were too frightened to say anything, and Achilles guessed why they had
come from their silence.

*17. satelles Averni*] Cp. Horace, *Odes* II xviii 34 where Charon is called
*satelles Orci.* Avernus, used poetically to mean the Underworld (as in Ovid
*Am.* III ix 27), is a lake near Naples: close to it was located the cave by which
Aeneas descended to the nether world (*Aen.* vi 106–7).

*19. pondus inutile terrae*] The phrase is taken from Achilles' description of
himself in *Il.* xviii 104.

## 12 *In Proditionem Bombardicam*
### [On the Gunpowder Plot]

*Date.* Nov. 1626? There is no evidence to show when M.'s four epigrams on the Gunpowder Plot or his epigram on the inventor of gunpowder were written. Because of their subject-matter they are generally assumed to be contemporary with *Q Nov* (p. 36 below).
*Publication.* 1645 and 1673 (no significant variants).

> Cum simul in regem nuper satrapasque Britannos
> Ausus es infandum perfide Fauxe nefas,
> Fallor? an et mitis voluisti ex parte videri,
> Et pensare mala cum pietate scelus;
> 5 Scilicet hos alti missurus ad atria caeli,
> Sulphureo curru flammivolisque rotis.
> Qualiter ille feris caput inviolabile Parcis
> Liquit Iordanios turbine raptus agros.

Treacherous Fawkes, when, not long ago, you dared to plot that unutterable wickedness against the King and the English nobles, did you—or am I mistaken?—intend to appear, in a way, merciful? Did you intend to make up for your crime by a sort of evil piety? It was, I take it, to the halls of high heaven that you meant to blow them up in their sulphurous chariot with its wheels of whirling flame: you meant to blow them up just as that man[7] whose life the fierce Parcae could not harm was swept up from Jordan's banks in a whirlwind.

## 13 *In Eandem*
### [On the Same]

*Date.* Nov. 1626? See headnote to previous poem. This epigram must be dated later than Mar. 1625 because of its allusion to James's death.
*Publication.* 1645 and 1673 (no significant variants).

> Siccine tentasti caelo donasse Iacobum
> Quae septemgemino Belua monte lates?
> Ni meliora tuum poterit dare munera numen,
> Parce precor donis insidiosa tuis.
> 5 Ille quidem sine te consortia serus adivit
> Astra, nec inferni pulveris usus ope.

¶12. 7. *ille*] Elijah is swept up from Jordan's banks by a whirlwind, riding in a chariot of fire, in *2 Kings* ii 11.
¶ 13. 2. *Belua*] The Protestants commonly identified the seven-headed beast of *Rev.* xiii 1 with the Roman Church.
5. James I died 27 Mar. 1625.

Sic potius foedos in caelum pelle cucullos,
   Et quot habet brutos Roma profana deos,
Namque hac aut alia nisi quemque adiuveris arte,
10      Crede mihi caeli vix bene scandet iter.

So you tried to send James to heaven did you, you skulking Beast on your
seven hills?[2] Traitor! Unless your godship can give better gifts do us the
favour of keeping your presents to yourself. James has now gone to join the
starry brotherhood,[5] at a ripe old age, without the help of you or your
infernal gunpowder. Use it instead to blow up to heaven your filthy monks[7]
and all the brutish gods in profane Rome. For believe me, unless you give
each of them an upward shove by this means or some other, not one will
have an easy climb up the heavenly path.

## 14 *In Eandem*
### [On the Same]

*Date.* Nov. 1626? See headnote to *Prod Bomb* (p. 33).
*Publication.* *1645* and *1673* (no significant variants: in l. *4 1673* misprints
*corona* for *cornua*).

Purgatorem animae derisit Iacobus ignem,
   Et sine quo superum non adeunda domus.
Frenduit hoc trina monstrum Latiale corona
   Movit et horrificum cornua dena minax.
5  Et nec inultus ait temnes mea sacra Britanne,
   Supplicium spreta relligione dabis.
Et si stelligeras unquam penetraveris arces,
   Non nisi per flammas triste patebit iter.
O quam funesto cecinisti proxima vero,
10      Verbaque ponderibus vix caritura suis!
Nam prope Tartareo sublime rotatus ab igni
   Ibat ad aethereas umbra perusta plagas.

James joked about the purgatorial fire,[1] without which the soul cannot
reach the home of the blessed. At this the triple-crowned monster of Latium[3]
gnashed its teeth and lowered its ten horns[4] in a horribly menacing way.
'Briton', it said, 'your contempt for what is sacred to me will not go
unpunished. You will pay the penalty for scorning religion. And if ever

7–10. Cp. *PL* iii 474–93.
¶ 14. *1.* As W. MacKellar points out in *MLR* xviii (1923) 472–3, James
referred to the idea of purgatory as 'trash' in the *Premonition* prefaced to
the second edition (1609) of his *Apology for the Oath of Allegiance*.
*3. Latiale]* Roman (from *Latium*, the part of Italy in which Rome was
situated).
*4. cornua dena]* The beast of *Rev.* xiii 1 has ten horns.

you get inside the starry citadels it will be only after a fearful journey through the flames.' Oh how near your prophetic words came to being deadly truth! How little they lacked of fulfilment! For he was almost whirled up to the heavenly regions by Tartarean fire, a burnt-up ghost.

## 15 *In Eandem*
### [On the Same]

*Date.* Nov. 1626? See headnote to *Prod Bomb* (p. 33).
*Publication. 1645* and *1673* (no significant variants).

> Quem modo Roma suis devoverat impia diris,
> Et Styge damnarat Taenarioque sinu,
> Hunc vice mutata iam tollere gestit ad astra,
> Et cupit ad superos evehere usque Deos.

Impious Rome once cursed this man with horrid imprecations[1] and con-demned him to Styx and the Taenarian gulf.[2] Now, going to the opposite extreme, she longs to raise him to the stars and desires to lift him up to the gods above.

## 16 *In Inventorem Bombardae*
### [On the Inventor of Gunpowder]

*Date.* Nov. 1626? See headnote to *Prod Bomb* (p. 33).
*Publication. 1645* and *1673* (no significant variants).

> Iapetionidem laudavit caeca vetustas,
> Qui tulit aetheream solis ab axe facem;
> At mihi maior erit, qui lurida creditur arma,
> Et trifidum fulmen surripuisse Iovi.

¶ 15. *1.* When James came to the throne Clement VIII did not excommu-nicate him (as Pius V had Elizabeth in 1570); indeed he had high hopes of his conversion, and James's relations with Rome were good up to 1605. Perhaps M. is alluding to the anger felt by English Catholics when the king permitted the fines payable by them under the Elizabethan code to be collected in May 1603. It was this anger which led to William Watson's abortive plot to kidnap the king (see D. H. Willson, *King James VI and I* (1956) 218–23).
*2. Taenarioque sinu*] See *Proc Med* 5n (p. 28).
¶ 16. *1. Iapetionidem*] Prometheus, son of Japetus. Hesiod, *Theog.* 562–9, relates how when Jupiter, in anger, denied fire to men Prometheus stole it and brought it to earth hidden in a hollow fennel stalk.
*4.* Drummond has an epigram on the invention of the cannon (*Madrigals and Epigrams* (1616) xviii) in which Jove, on hearing a cannon for the first time, wonders 'What mortall Wight had stollen from him his Thunder'.

In their blindness the ancients praised Japetus's son[1] for bringing down heavenly fire from the sun's axle. But I think this man greater who, we may well believe, has snatched from Jove his ghastly weapons and three-forked thunderbolt.[4]

# 17 *In Quintum Novembris*
## [On the Fifth of November]

*Date.* Nov.? 1626. The closing lines suggest that the poem was written for an actual celebration of 5 Nov., but this is not certain. The heading *Anno aetatis 17*, which appears in *1645* and *1673*, could mean either 'In the seventeenth year of his age' or 'At seventeen years of age' (i.e. 1625 or 1626). The same heading, however, is used for *Elegia II* and *Elegia III*, and in both these cases it must refer to 1626.

*Publication.* *1645 (84.* salaces.]salaces,      *86.* Talis]Talis,      *92.* artus?]artus      *93.* tuorum!]tuorum,      *96.* Britanni:]Britanni;      *125.* casumque]casumque      *143.* praeruptaque]semifractaque      *146.* fauces.]fauces,      *148.* timor,] Timor,      *149.* Manes,]Manes      *150.* Exululat]Exululant, ) *1673* (the text followed here, but emended in these instances: *13.* unanimes] unamimes      *43.* tentamina]tantamina      possunt,]possunt. )

*Modern criticism.* E. K. Rand, *SP* xix (1922) 121-2, considers that 'the little epic on Guy Fawkes, the work of the author's seventeenth year, shows greater poise and firmness than the little epic on the *Gnat* which Virgil wrote at sixteen'. M. Cheek, *SP* liv (1957) 172-84, demonstrates the Virgilian nature of *Q Nov*: the aerial survey and dream visitation are prefigured in Virgil's epic: M.'s *Fama* derives from *Aen.* iv 173-97 with additions from ix 473-5 and xi 139-41: Satan's mission of destruction parallels Allecto's, *Aen.* vii 335-8. The Satan of *Q Nov*, claims Cheek, is the Satan of *PL* in embryo, as is shown by his numbering of his followers (*10*, cp. *PL* i 571), his sighs of envy (*34*, cp. *PL* iv 31), his character as 'artificer of fraud' (*17*, cp. *PL* iv 121) etc. Tillyard 22-3 suggests the influence of Giles Fletcher's *Locustae* (not published till 1627).

> Iam pius extrema veniens Iacobus ab arcto
> Teucrigenas populos, lateque patentia regna
> Albionum tenuit, iamque inviolabile foedus
> Sceptra Caledoniis coniunxerat Anglica Scotis:
> 5   Pacificusque novo felix divesque sedebat
> In solio, occultique doli securus et hostis:
> Cum ferus ignifluo regnans Acheronte tyrannus,

¶ 17. 1. James came from Scotland in 1603. The date finally planned for the blowing up of Parliament by the plotters was 5 Nov. 1605.
2. *Teucrigenas populos*] See *Elegia I* 73n (p. 22).
7. *ignifluo ... Acheronte*] Of the infernal rivers in Virgil Phlegethon, not Acheron, was the river of fire (see *Aen.* vi 295-7 and 550-1).

Eumenidum pater, aethereo vagus exul Olympo,
Forte per immensum terrarum erraverat orbem,
10   Dinumerans sceleris socios, vernasque fideles,
Participes regni post funera moesta futuros;
Hic tempestates medio ciet aere diras,
Illic unanimes odium struit inter amicos,
Armat et invictas in mutua viscera gentes;
15   Regnaque olivifera vertit florentia pace,
Et quoscunque videt purae virtutis amantes,
Hos cupit adiicere imperio, fraudumque magister
Tentat inaccessum sceleri corrumpere pectus,
Insidiasque locat tacitas, cassesque latentes
20   Tendit, ut incautos rapiat, seu Caspia tigris
Insequitur trepidam deserta per avia praedam
Nocte sub illuni, et somno nictantibus astris.
Talibus infestat populos Summanus et urbes
Cinctus caeruleae fumanti turbine flammae.
25   Iamque fluentisonis albentia rupibus arva
Apparent, et terra Deo dilecta marino,
Cui nomen dederat quondam Neptunia proles
Amphitryoniaden qui non dubitavit atrocem
Aequore tranato furiali poscere bello,
30   Ante expugnatae crudelia saecula Troiae.
At simul hanc opibusque et festa pace beatam
Aspicit, et pingues donis Cerealibus agros,

---

*8. Eumenidum pater*] Virgil names Pluto as father of the Furies in *Aen.* vii
327.     *exul Olympo*] Echoes *Aen.* viii 319–20 where Saturn is *Olympo . . .
exsul.*

*10. vernas*] Specifically 'slaves by birth'. Though in *De doctrina* I iv
(Columbia xiv 129–30) M. denies that any men are predestined to damnation
he admits that some men are, by nature and disposition, more alienated
from the grace of God than others.

*12. medio . . . aere*] The theory of the three regions of the air, current in the
seventeenth century, is explained by Du Bartas 35–6, who points out that
the middle region is characterized by cold and that from it hail comes.

*23. Summanus*] Pliny II liii 138 says that Summanus was originally a Tuscan
deity, taken over by the Romans as the god of nocturnal thunderbolts.

*27–30.* In the *History of Britain* M. recounts the legend of Albion, a giant
son of Neptune, who reigned in England '44 years. Till at length passing
over into *Gaul*, in aid of his brother *Lestrygon*, against whom *Hercules* was
hasting out of *Spain* into *Italy*, he was there slain in fight' (Columbia x 4).
*Amphitryoniaden*] Hercules, whose real father was Jove, but whose mother,
Alcmena, was married to Amphitryon.

*31–5.* Satan's grief and noxious sighs are borrowed from Ovid's description
of Envy coming into sight of Athens (*Met.* ii 790–6).

Quodque magis doluit, venerantem numina veri
Sancta Dei populum, tandem suspiria rupit
35   Tartareos ignes et luridum olentia sulphur.
Qualia Trinacria trux ab Iove clausus in Aetna
Efflat tabifico monstrosus ab ore Tiphoeus.
Ignescunt oculi, stridetque adamantinus ordo
Dentis, ut armorum fragor, ictaque cuspide cuspis.
40   Atque pererrato solum hoc lacrymabile mundo
Inveni, dixit, gens haec mihi sola rebellis,
Contemtrixque iugi, nostraque potentior arte.
Illa tamen, mea si quicquam tentamina possunt,
Non feret hoc impune diu, non ibit inulta,
45   Hactenus; et piceis liquido natat aere pennis;
Qua volat, adversi praecursant agmine venti,
Densantur nubes, et crebra tonitrua fulgent.
    Iamque pruinosas velox superaverat alpes,
Et tenet Ausoniae fines, a parte sinistra
50   Nimbifer Appenninus erat, priscique Sabini,
Dextra veneficiis infamis Hetruria, nec non
Te furtiva Tibris Thetidi videt oscula dantem;
Hinc Mavortigenae consistit in arce Quirini.
Reddiderant dubiam iam sera crepuscula lucem,
55   Cum circumgreditur totam Tricoronifer urbem,
Panificosque Deos portat, scapulisque virorum
Evehitur, praeeunt submisso poplite reges,

*35. luridum . . . sulphur*] Echoes Ovid, *Met.* xiv 791: *lurida . . . sulphura.*

*36–7.* Ovid, *Met.* v 346–53, explains how Jove pinned the giant Tiphoeus down by placing the island of Sicily upon him, with Mount Aetna resting upon his head, through which he spouts flame and ash.

*38. Ignescunt oculi*] Cp. *PL* i 193–4.

*47. Densantur*] Cp. *PL* i 226–7.

*48.* Echoing Lucan i 183: *Iam gelidas Caesar cursu superaverat Alpes.*

*51. veneficiis*] M. apparently uses the word loosely: the inhabitants of Etruria (modern Tuscany) were, as Livy remarks (V i 6), more devoted to the pagan religious rites than any other nation; they were particularly noted for divination and augury.

*52. Thetidi*] M. uses the name of Thetis, a sea nymph, to mean the sea, as does Virgil, *Ecl.* iv 32.

*53. Mavortigenae . . . Quirini*] Romulus, son of Mars, was called Quirinus after his deification (cp. Ovid, *Fast.* i 199 *Martigenam . . . Quirinum*).

*54. dubiam . . . crepuscula lucem*] Echoes Ovid, *Met.* xi 596 *dubiaeque crepuscula lucis.*

*56. Panificosque Deos*] the Host.

Et mendicantum series longissima fratrum;
Cereaque in manibus gestant funalia caeci,
60 Cimmeriis nati in tenebris, vitamque trahentes.
Templa dein multis subeunt lucentia taedis
(Vesper erat sacer iste Petro)fremitusque canentum
Saepe tholos implet vacuos, et inane locorum.
Qualiter exululat Bromius, Bromiique caterva,
65 Orgia cantantes in Echionio Aracyntho,
Dum tremit attonitus vitreis Asopus in undis,
Et procul ipse cava responsat rupe Cithaeron.
 His igitur tandem solenni more peractis,
Nox senis amplexus Erebi taciturna reliquit,
70 Praecipitesque impellit equos stimulante flagello,
Captum oculis Typhlonta, Melanchaetemque ferocem,
Atque Acherontaeo prognatam patre Siopen
Torpidam, et hirsutis horrentem Phrica capillis.
Interea regum domitor, Phlegetontius haeres
75 Ingreditur thalamos (neque enim secretus adulter
Producit steriles molli sine pellice noctes)
At vix compositos somnus claudebat ocellos,
Cum niger umbrarum dominus, rectorque silentum,
Praedatorque hominum falsa sub imagine tectus
80 Astitit, assumptis micuerunt tempora canis,

60. *Cimmeriis ... tenebris*] In *Od.* xi 13–22 Odysseus sails to the land of the
Cimmerians who live on the edge of the world in perpetual darkness.
64. *Bromius*] Literally, 'the noisy one', Bacchus.
65–7. *Echionio Aracyntho*] Echion, one of the heroes who sprang from the
dragon's teeth sown by Cadmus, founded the citadel of Thebes: thus
*Echionius* may mean Theban or, since Thebes was chief city of Boeotia,
Boeotian. *Aracynthus*: a mountain between Boeotia and Attica. *Asopus*:
a river in Boeotia flowing near Mount *Cithaeron*, which is mentioned as
the scene of Bacchic orgies by Ovid, *Met.* iii 702, and Virgil, *Aen.* iv 303.
Propertius III xv 25–42, names Aracynthus, Asopus and Cithaeron
together in the story of Dirce.
69. *Nox ... Erebi*] Hesiod, *Theog.* 123–5, tells how Night, sister of Erebus,
bore his children Ether and Day.
70–3. Virgil, *Aen.* v 721, mentions Night's chariot and Spenser gives it
'cole blacke steedes' (*F.Q.* I v 20), but M. invents names for them from
the Greek words τυφλός, blind; μέλαν, black and χαίτη, long hair; σιωπή,
silence; and φρίξ, shuddering.
72–4. *Acherontaeo ... Phlegetontius*] See l. 7n.
80–5. Cp. Satan's disguise in *PR* i 314–20 and 497–8. In Buchanan's Latin
poem *Franciscanus* 19–20 St Francis is *cannabe cinctus* and has *obrasum ...
caput duro velante cucullo,* and the description of a friar in the same poem

Barba sinus promissa tegit, cineracea longo
Syrmate verrit humum vestis, pendetque cucullus
Vertice de raso, et ne quicquam desit ad artes,
Cannabeo lumbos constrinxit fune salaces.

85 Tarda fenestratis figens vestigia calceis.
Talis uti fama est, vasta Franciscus eremo
Tetra vagabatur solus per lustra ferarum,
Sylvestrique tulit genti pia verba salutis
Impius, atque lupos domuit, Libicosque leones.

90 Subdolus at tali Serpens velatus amictu
Solvit in has fallax ora execrantia voces;
Dormis nate? Etiamne tuos sopor opprimit artus?
Immemor O fidei, pecorumque oblite tuorum!
Dum cathedram venerande tuam, diademaque triplex

95 Ridet Hyperboreo gens barbara nata sub axe,
Dumque pharetrati spernunt tua iura Britanni:
Surge, age, surge piger, Latius quem Caesar adorat,
Cui reserata patet convexi ianua caeli,
Turgentes animos, et fastus frange procaces,

100 Sacrilegique sciant, tua quid maledictio possit,
Et quid Apostolicae possit custodia clavis;
Et memor Hesperiae disiectam ulciscere classem,
Mersaque Iberorum lato vexilla profundo,
Sanctorumque cruci tot corpora fixa probrosae,

(45-8) includes *longo sub syrmate rasum . . . caput*. The friar who appears to Buchanan in his *Somnium* 5-9 (printed among the *Fratres Fraterrimi*) wears *fenestratus calceus*.

*86-9.* Among the anecdotes about St Francis of Assisi preserved in the *Fioretti*, one (xvi) records his preaching to the birds (M.'s 'woodland folk') and another (xxi) his taming of the wolf of Gubbio. St Bonaventure's *Life of St Francis* tells how, after his conversion, he left the city and wandered through the woods chanting praises to God (ii 5), how later he spent Lent in the solitudes of Alverna (viii 10), and how he was able to tame wild beasts (viii 11).

*92-3.* M. recalls Mercury's rousing speeches to Aeneas, *Aen.* iv 267 and 560, and the Dream's to Agamemnon, *Il.* ii 22-34.

*95. Hyperboreo . . . axe*] See *Mansus 26n* (p. 262).

*97.* Echoing the words of Aeneas' Penates, appearing to him in a dream: *surge age* (*Aen.* iii 169).

*101. Apostolicae . . . custodia clavis*] Refers to the Catholic doctrine by which succeeding Popes inherit the keys of the kingdom of heaven given to Peter by Christ, *Matt.* xvi 19.

*102-3* Referring to the Spanish Armada of 1588.

*104-5.* Referring to the persecution of Catholics during Elizabeth's reign.

105 Thermodoontea nuper regnante puella.
At tu si tenero mavis torpescere lecto
Crescentesque negas hosti contundere vires,
Tyrrhenum implebit numeroso milite pontum,
Signaque Aventino ponet fulgentia colle:
110 Relliquias veterum franget, flammisque cremabit,
Sacraque calcabit pedibus tua colla profanis,
Cuius gaudebant soleis dare basia reges.
Nec tamen hunc bellis et aperto Marte lacesses,
Irritus ille labor, tu callidus utere fraude,
115 Quaelibet haereticis disponere retia fas est;
Iamque ad consilium extremis rex magnus ab oris
Patricios vocat, et procerum de stirpe creatos,
Grandaevosque patres trabea, canisque verendos;
Hos tu membratim poteris conspergere in auras,
120 Atque dare in cineres, nitrati pulveris igne
Aedibus iniecto, qua convenere, sub imis.
Protinus ipse igitur quoscunque habet Anglia fidos
Propositi, factique mone, quisquamne tuorum
Audebit summi non iussa facessere Papae.
125 Perculsosque metu subito, casumque stupentes
Invadat vel Gallus atrox, vel saevus Iberus.
Saecula sic illic tandem Mariana redibunt,
Tuque in belligeros iterum dominaberis Anglos.
Et nequid timeas, divos divasque secundas
130 Accipe, quotque tuis celebrantur numina fastis.
Dixit et adscitos ponens malefidus amictus
Fugit ad infandam, regnum illaetabile, Lethen.
Iam rosea Eoas pandens Tithonia portas
Vestit inauratas redeunti lumine terras;
135 Maestaque adhuc nigri deplorans funera nati
Irrigat ambrosiis montana cacumina guttis;
Cum somnos pepulit stellatae ianitor aulae
Nocturnos visus, et somnia grata revolvens.

---

*Thermodoontea*: Amazonian: the adjective is formed by M. from *Thermodon*, a river at the mouth of which, according to Strabo I iii 7, the Amazons lived.
*109. Aventino . . . colle*] The Aventine, one of Rome's seven hills, extends from the Palatine to the Coelian Mount.
*127. Saecula . . . Mariana*] the reign of Mary (1553–58) with its burning of Protestants, as recorded, for example, in Foxe's *Acts and Monuments* XI-XII.
*132.* Lethe is the river of forgetfulness in the infernal regions.
*133–5. Tithonia*] Aurora, the dawn, wife of Tithonus. Her son Memnon fought for the Trojans and was killed by Achilles; Ovid, *Met.* xiii 576–622, tells of her inconsolable grief.
*136. montana cacumina*] The phrase is from Ovid, *Met.* i 310.

Est locus aeterna septus caligine noctis
*140* Vasta ruinosi quondam fundamina tecti,
Nunc torvi spelunca Phoni, Prodotaeque bilinguis
Effera quos uno peperit discordia partu.
Hic inter caementa iacent praeruptaque saxa,
Ossa inhumata virum, et traiecta cadavera ferro;
*145* Hic dolus intortis semper sedet ater ocellis,
Iurgiaque, et stimulis armata calumnia fauces.
Et furor, atque viae moriendi mille videntur
Et timor, exanguisque locum circumvolat horror,
Perpetuoque leves per muta silentia manes,
*150* Exululat tellus et sanguine conscia stagnat.
Ipsi etiam pavidi latitant penetralibus antri
Et Phonos, et Prodotes, nulloque sequente per antrum
Antrum horrens, scopulosum, atrum feralibus umbris
Diffugiunt sontes, et retro lumina vortunt,
*155* Hos pugiles Romae per saecula longa fideles
Evocat antistes Babylonius, atque ita fatur.
Finibus occiduis circumfusum incolit aequor
Gens exosa mihi, prudens natura negavit
Indignam penitus nostro coniungere mundo:
*160* Illuc, sic iubeo, celeri contendite gressu,
Tartareoque leves difflentur pulvere in auras
Et rex et pariter satrapae, scelerata propago
Et quotquot fidei caluere cupidine verae
Consilii socios adhibete, operisque ministros.
*165* Finierat, rigidi cupide paruere gemelli.

*139–54.* M.'s cave with its personified inhabitants is based on Virgil's description of hell-gate (*Aen.* vi 273–81) and Spenser's imitation of it (*F.Q.* II vii 21–5).

*143. praeruptaque*] altered from *1645*'s *semifractaque*, which Salmasius in his *Responsio* (1660) had picked on as a false quantity.

*146. calumnia*] As C. Symmons points out, *CJ* ix (1814) 344, this word is never used in classical Latin poetry: it is found only in prose.

*148.* Horror similarly flies about in Spenser's Cave of Mammon, *F.Q.* II vii 23.

*149. per muta silentia*] The phrase is from Ovid, *Met.* vii 184.

*156. Babylonius*] In English Protestant literature of the sixteenth and seventeenth centuries the Babylon of *Rev.* xiv 8 and xvii 5 is frequently identified with Rome. Coverdale praises Henry VIII, in the epistle prefaced to his translation of the Bible, for 'delyverynge us out of oure olde Babylonycall captivyte'.

*158. prudens*] In Horace, *Odes* I iii 22, the division of lands by oceans is ascribed to *deus . . . prudens*.

*165. paruere*] The short first syllable is a false quantity.

Interea longo flectens curvamine coelos
Despicit aetherea dominus qui fulgurat arce,
Vanaque perversae ridet conamina turbae,
Atque sui causam populi volet ipse tueri.
*170*     Esse ferunt spatium, qua distat ab Aside terra
Fertilis Europe, et spectat Mareotidas undas;
Hic turris posita est Titanidos ardua Famae
Aerea, lata, sonans, rutilis vicinior astris
Quam superimpositum vel Athos vel Pelion Ossae
*175*     Mille fores aditusque patent, totidemque fenestrae,
Amplaque per tenues translucent atria muros;
Excitat hic varios plebs agglomerata susurros;
Qualiter instrepitant circum mulctralia bombis
Agmina muscarum, aut texto per ovilia iunco,
*180*     Dum Canis aestivum coeli petit ardua culmen
Ipsa quidem summa sedet ultrix matris in arce,
Auribus innumeris cinctum caput eminet olli,
Queis sonitum exiguum trahit, atque levissima captat
Murmura, ab extremis patuli confinibus orbis.
*185*     Nec tot Aristoride servator inique iuvencae
Isidos, immiti volvebas lumina vultu,

*166. longo . . . curvamine coelos*] Echoes Ovid, *Met.* vi 64: *longum curvamine caelum.*

*170–93.* The sources for M.'s description of Fame and her tower are Ovid, *Met.* xii 39–63, Virgil, *Aen.* iv 173–88, and possibly Chaucer *House of Fame* iii. The borrowings from Ovid and Virgil are reviewed in Harding 50–3.

*171. Mareotidas*] Lake Mareotis is in Egypt, near Alexandria. It was Lake Maeotis (the Sea of Azof) which was considered as part of the boundary between Europe and Asia. Both Ovid and Chaucer place Fame's tower at a central point in the world. Thus possibly M., having mentioned Europe and Asia, meant Lake Mareotis to stand for the third continent, Africa (as A. H. Gilbert suggests, *MLN* xxviii (1913) 30), or possibly *Mareotidas* should be emended to *Maeotidas* (as D. T. Starnes argues, *N & Q* cxcvi (1951) 515–12, quoting Lucan iii 271–8 as evidence for the centrality of Lake Maeotis).

*172. Titanidos*] Virgil's Fame is sister of the Titans Coeus and Enceladus (*Aen.* iv 178–80).

*174. Athos*] A mountain at the southern tip of the Hagion Oros peninsula in eastern Greece, given first place in Ovid's list of mountains, *Met.* ii 217. *Pelion* and *Ossa* are mountains in Thessaly. When the giants made war on the gods they piled Ossa on Olympus and Pelion on Ossa in an attempt to climb to heaven, as Homer relates, *Od.* xi 313-16 and Ovid, *Met.* i 151-5.

*178–80.* The simile of the flies and milking pails is from Homer who uses it to describe the Greeks before Troy, *Il.* ii 469–73, and the Greeks and Trojans fighting over Sarpedon's body, xvi 641–3.

*185-6. Aristoride . . . Isidos*] According to Ovid, *Met.* i 624-31, Argus, son

Lumina non unquam tacito nutantia somno,
Lumina subiectas late spectantia terras.
Istis illa solet loca luce carentia saepe
*190* Perlustrare, etiam radianti impervia soli.
Millenisque loquax auditaque visaque linguis
Cuilibet effundit temeraria, veraque mendax
Nunc minuit, modo confictis sermonibus auget.
Sed tamen a nostro meruisti carmine laudes
*195* Fama, bonum quo non aliud veracius ullum,
Nobis digna cani, nec te memorasse pigebit
Carmine tam longo, servati scilicet Angli
Officiis vaga diva tuis, tibi reddimus aequa.
Te Deus aeternos motu qui temperat ignes,
*200* Fulmine praemisso alloquitur, terraque tremente:
Fama siles? an te latet impia Papistarum
Coniurata cohors in meque meosque Britannos,
Et nova sceptrigero caedes meditata Iacobo:
Nec plura, illa statim sensit mandata Tonantis,
*205* Et satis ante fugax stridentes induit alas,
Induit et variis exilia corpora plumis;
Dextra tubam gestat Temesaeo ex aere sonoram.
Nec mora iam pennis cedentes remigat auras,
Atque parum est cursu celeres praevertere nubes,
*210* Iam ventos, iam solis equos post terga reliquit:
Et primo Angliacas solito de more per urbes
Ambiguas voces, incertaque murmura spargit,
Mox arguta dolos, et detestabile vulgat
Proditionis opus, nec non facta horrida dictu,

of Arestor, had a hundred eyes of which only one pair closed in sleep at
any one time, and Juno therefore set him to guard Io, whom Jove had
turned into a heifer. M. calls him 'unjust' because he forced Io away from
her father, Inachus (*Met.* i 664–5). Io became identified with the Egyptian
goddess Isis: Herodotus (ii 41) draws attention to the similarity between
the two, and in the *Mythologiae* (1612) Conti has a chapter (VIII xix) *De Ione
sive Iside*.

*194–8.* The plot was discovered because Lord Monteagle received a letter
from his brother-in-law Francis Tresham on 26 Oct. 1605, warning him
not to attend the opening of Parliament: he immediately informed the
Government.

*195.* Echoing Virgil, *Aen.* iv 174: *Fama, malum qua non aliud velocius ullum.*

*207. Temesaeo ex aere*] Temese, on the southern tip of Italy, was famous
for its copper mines in Homeric times (see *Od.* i 184). Ovid has *Temesaea
. . . aera, Met.* vii 207–8 and *Fast.* v 441.

*212. Ambiguas voces . . . spargit*] Echoes Virgil, *Aen.* ii 98–9: *spargere voces . . .
ambiguas.*

215 Authoresque addit sceleris, nec garrula caecis
  Insidiis loca structa silet; stupuere relatis,
  Et pariter iuvenes, pariter tremuere puellae,
  Effaetique senes pariter, tantaeque ruinae
  Sensus ad aetatem subito penetraverat omnem
220 Attamen interea populi miserescit ab alto
  Aethereus pater, et crudelibus obstitit ausis
  Papicolum; capti poenas raptantur ad acres;
  At pia thura Deo, et grati solvuntur honores;
  Compita laeta focis genialibus omnia fumant;
225 Turba choros iuvenilis agit: quintoque Novembris
  Nulla dies toto occurrit celebratior anno.

Now came good King James[1] from the far north and began his reign over that nation which traces its origins to Troy,[2] and over the extensive domains of the English people. Now an inviolable treaty had united the Scots of Caledonia under English rule. James, the peace-bearer, sat on his new throne. Wealth and good fortune were his: he was not worried about any enemy or secret plot. It happened at that time that the fierce tyrant who controls Acheron's[7] flaming currents, the tyrant who is father to the Furies[8] and a wandering exile from heavenly Olympus, had gone roaming over this huge globe. He was counting up his companions in crime, his faithful slaves by birth,[10] who, after their miserable deaths, were going to share his kingdom. Here and there he stirs up frightful storms in the middle air,[12] or sows hatred between close friends. He arms invincible nations for deadly war one against the other, and overturns kingdoms hitherto flourishing under the olive-branch of peace. He is especially eager to add to his empire any lovers of pure virtue that he comes across: a past-master of trickery, he does his best to corrupt the soul which is locked against sin. Silently he sets his traps, and stretches hidden nets to catch the unwary, just as the Caspian tigress stalks her trembling prey through trackless wastes while the stars wink drowsily in the moonless night: just as Summanus,[23] wrapped in a smoking whirlwind of blue flame, falls upon peoples and cities.

Presently white cliffs and rocks with roaring breakers come into view. It is the land dear to the god of the sea; the land which, long ago, Neptune's son[27] gave his name to: that son who, when he had crossed the ocean, did not shrink from challenging Amphitryon's fierce son to fearful combat, before the cruel days of Troy's downfall.[30]

As soon as he catches sight of this island, blessed with wealth and joyful peace,[31] with its fields cram-full of Ceres's gifts and—what pained him even more—its people worshipping the sacred powers of the true God, he breaks into sighs that stink of hellish flames and yellow sulphur;[35] sighs like those which the savage monster Tiphoeus, imprisoned under Sicilian Aetna by Jove,[36] breathes out from his decaying mouth. His eyes flash fire,[38] his rows of teeth, hard as steel, gnash with a noise like the clash of weapons, like spear crashing against spear. 'I have wandered over the whole world', he says, 'and this is the only thing that brings tears to my eyes; this is the only nation I have found which rebels against me, spurns my government and is mightier than my crafts. But if my efforts have any effect, these people

221. *crudelibus obstitit ausis*] The phrase is from Ovid, *Her.* xiv 49.

will not get away with it for long: they will not go unpunished.' His speech finished, he glides through the calm air on wings as black as pitch. Wherever he flies opposing winds rush in a crowd before him, clouds grow dense,[47] and flashes of lightning come thick and fast. He flew swiftly and had soon crossed the frosty Alps[48] and reached the north of Italy. To his left were the cloud-capped Apennines and the ancient Sabine land; to his right, Etruria, notorious for its sorceries.[51] Now he can see the place where you, Tiber, steal kisses from the sea.[52] Presently he alighted on the citadel of Quirinus,[53] son of Mars. The shades of evening had fallen, bringing twilight,[54] and now the wearer of the Triple Crown is making his tour of the city. He is carried shoulder-high, and with him he bears his gods, made of bread.[56] Kings crawl before him on their knees, and there is a long, long procession of beggarly friars. The blind fools carry wax tapers in their hands, for they were all born in Cimmerian[60] darkness and are dragging out their lives in it still. The procession winds its way into churches which are ablaze with innumerable candles (for it was St Peter's Eve), and again and again the wailing of the chanters fills the empty domes and void spaces. They make a noise like Bromius[64] and his mob howling and singing orgiastic songs on Echionian Aracynthus[65] while startled Asopus shudders beneath his glassy waves and even Cithaeron, far, far away, sends back an echo from its hollow cliff.[67]

When the rites had eventually been performed in the time-honoured way, Night silently slipped from old Erebus's embrace[69] and, with her smarting whip, set her team galloping at a headlong pace–blind Typhlon,[71] fierce Melanchaetes, numb Siope, a mare sired by an Acherontean[72] steed, and shaggy Phrix with his bristling mane.[73]

Meanwhile the king-tamer, the heir of Hell,[74] goes into his bridal apartments (for this secret adulterer does not drag out barren nights without the company of a soft whore). But just as slumber was closing his peaceful eyes the dark lord of shadows, the ruler of the silent dead who preys upon men, appeared at his bedside in disguise. His temples gleamed with white hair, put on for the occasion;[80] a long beard covers his chest; his ash-coloured gown sweeps the floor with its trailing hem; a cowl hangs back from his tonsured head, and to complete his crafty disguise he has bound a hempen rope round his lustful loins and tied latticed sandals to his slow old feet.[85] Francis,[86] so the story goes, looked like this when he wandered alone in the desolate wilderness and through the filthy dens of wild animals and (though unredeemed himself), carried the redeeming words of salvation to woodland folk, and tamed the wolves and Libyan lions.[89]

Disguised in this way the crafty, lying serpent opened his foul lips and spoke these words: 'Are you asleep, my son?[92] Are your limbs heavy with slumber? O forgetful of the faith, neglectful of your flocks,[93] while a barbarous nation born beneath the northern sky[95] is laughing at your throne and triple diadem; while the British archers are spurning your rights–you, who should be revered! Get up, come on, get up, sluggard![97] You whom the Holy Roman Emperor worships: you for whom the locked gate of heaven's vault lies open–break their vaunting spirits, their insolent pride, and let these sacrilegious sinners know the power of your curse, the power which control of the Apostolic key gives you.[101] Remember the past! Avenge the scattered Spanish fleet![102] Avenge the Iberian standards overwhelmed in the deep[103] and the bodies of so many saints nailed to the shameful cross[104] during the Amazonian virgin's recent reign.[105] If you choose, instead, to lie like a dolt in your soft bed, and refuse to crush your enemy's growing strength, he will fill the Tyrrhenian Sea with his swarming battalions and plant his glittering standards on the Aventine hill.[109] He will smash your ancient relics and throw them on the fire and trample your holy neck beneath his profane feet – you whose shoes kings were once glad to kiss! But do not challenge him to war or open combat: that would be a waste of time. Be cunning: use trickery – no trap is too base to use against heretics. At the present moment their great king is summoning the ruling classes to parliament from the furthest corners of their country: the heirs of the nobility and their aged fathers, venerable for their robes of state and their white hair. If you explode gunpowder under the foundations of the building in which they are assembled you will be able to tear them limb from limb, scatter them in the air and burn them to cinders. So inform any of the faithful who are still left in England of this plan of action immediately. Will any of your followers dare to ignore the supreme Papal commands? Afterwards let the fierce Frenchman or the cruel Spaniard invade the Britons while they are still panic-stricken, still wondering at the catastrophe. Thus the Marian regime[127] will at last be re-established in that land, and you will have the warlike English under your thumb again. And in case you should be nervous let me tell you that all the gods and goddesses are on your side, all those deities you worship on your various feast-days.'

When he had finished speaking the deceitful creature abandoned his disguise and fled to Lethe,[132] his unspeakable, joyless kingdom.

Now rosy dawn[133] is opening the eastern gates and clothing the gilded earth with returning light and, still weeping for the sad death of her dark-skinned son,[135] is sprinkling the mountain summits[136] with ambrosial drops. The doorkeeper of the starry court has shaken off slumber and rolled away the sweet dreams and visions of night.

There is a place, shut up in eternal darkness and night,[139] which once formed the giant foundations of a now-ruined building. This place has become the cavernous den of fierce-eyed Murder and double-tongued Treachery, savage Discord's twin children. Here among heaps of rubble and jagged rocks lie unburied skeletons, and corpses thrust through with steel. Here Guile, black and cross-eyed, sits for ever: here are Strife and Calumny,[146] armed with fangs. Here is Rage: Fear and a thousand kinds of death are seen, and bloodless Horror[148] flitting around, and wispy ghosts moving unceasingly through the voiceless silences.[149] The conscious earth shrieks and rots with blood. Murder and Treachery themselves cower terrified into the deepest recesses of that cavernous place and, though no one pursues them through the cave – a horrible cave, jagged with rocks and black with deathly shadows – they flee away guiltily, and keep looking back.[154] The Babylonian priest[156] summons these champions of Rome who have been loyal to her for centuries past, and says: 'By the sea which flows round the western horizon there lives a nation which I detest. Prudent Nature[158] refused to join it up with our continent because it was unworthy. Go there with all speed – that is my command – and let the King and all his nobles, the whole wicked brood, be blown to the four winds by hellish powder. Use all those who are fired with enthusiasm for the true faith as your fellow-conspirators and fellow-workers.' When he had finished speaking the cruel pair eagerly obeyed him.[165]

Meanwhile the Lord who sends the lightning from his skyey citadel and bends the heavens in their wide arc[166] looks down and laughs at the vain attempts of the evil mob, intending to defend His people's cause Himself.

There is, men say,[170] an expanse fronting Lake Mareotis,[171] which separates the Asian continent from fertile Europe. Here the high tower of Fame, daughter of the Titaness,[172] is built–brazen, broad, reverberating, and reaching up nearer to the twinkling stars than Athos[174] or Pelion piled upon Ossa. A thousand doors and entrances gape wide, and a thousand windows too, and the spacious halls inside gleam through thin walls. The crowd which swarms here sends up a mingled murmur, like swarms of flies[178] humming and buzzing around the milking pails or through the wattled sheepfolds when the Dog Star is climbing the steeps of heaven to its summer height.[180] Fame herself, her mother's avenger, is seated at the very top of her citadel, and lifts her head high. Innumerable ears stick out all round it, and with these she can intercept even the tiniest sounds and catch the faintest whisper from the remotest corners of the wide world. You, Arestor's son,[185] unjust guardian of the heifer Isis, did not have as many eyes rolling in your harsh face as she–eyes which never close in silent sleep, eyes which keep watch, far and wide, over the lands below. With these Fame often scans unlighted places, where even the sun's rays do not penetrate. Then, blabbing with her thousand tongues, the inconsiderate creature pours out all she has heard and seen to anyone she comes across. She is a liar, too: sometimes she speaks less than the truth, and sometimes more, adding her own invented tales.[193]

But still, Fame, you have deserved praise in my song[194] for one good deed, and there was never a deed more truly good.[195] You deserve to be sung about by me, and I shall never regret having commemorated you at such length in my verse. We English, who were plainly saved by your good offices, wandering goddess, render to you your just dues.[198] God who guides the eternal fires in their wheeling hurled down a thunderbolt and then, as the earth still trembled, said: 'Are you silent, Fame? Is this godless mob of Papists hidden from your sight–this mob which has conspired against me and my Englishmen? Is this new kind of murder which has been planned for sceptred James hidden from you?' He said no more, but the Thunderer's commands had an instant effect on Fame who, though swift of flight before, now puts on creaking wings and covers her thin body with parti-coloured feathers. She takes a blaring trumpet of Temesaean brass[207] in her right hand and, without delay, wings her way through the yielding air. Not content to outstrip the rushing clouds, she soon leaves the winds and the sun's horses behind. As usual she first spreads contradictory rumours[212] and vague murmurings through the English cities, and then in a clear voice she makes public the plots and foul working of treason, its deeds horrible to speak of and, lastly, the instigators of the crime. Chattering away, she makes no secret of the places which have been prepared for the performance of this secret treachery. Her reports caused utter amazement. Young men, girls and weak old men all shuddered. People of all ages were suddenly struck to the heart by the sense of so great a disaster.

But meanwhile our Heavenly Father looked down on his people with pity and put a stop to the Papists' cruel venture.[221] They are captured and hurried off to sharp punishments. Pious incense is burned and grateful honours paid to God. There is merrymaking at every crossroads and smoke rises from the festive bonfires: the young people dance in crowds: in all the year there is no day more celebrated than the fifth of November.

# 18 *Elegia tertia. In Obitum Praesulis Wintoniensis*

[Elegy III. On the Death of the Bishop of Winchester]

*Date.* Sept.-Dec. 1626. Headed *Anno actatis 17* in *1645* and *1673*. Lancelot Andrewes, for whom this elegy was written, died 25 Sept. 1626. If Ernst von Mansfeld is one of the leaders mentioned in *9* the poem cannot have been completed until after news of his death (20 Nov. 1626) reached England. In *Prae E* 1–6 M. says that his eyes were hardly dry from weeping for Andrewes when news of Felton's death (6 Oct. 1626) reached him. Douglas Bush, *HLB* ix (1955) 392–6, takes this to mean that the present elegy must have been completed by 5 Oct., and that *9* cannot, therefore, refer to Mansfeld's death, but there is no need to equate the weeping of *Prae E* 1–6 with the composition of this elegy.

M.'s view of Andrewes had changed by 1641 when he devoted half of *Reason of Church Government* v to a refutation of his 'shallow reasonings' in defence of episcopacy (Columbia iii 201–5; Yale i 768–74).
*Publication.* *1645* (*34*. Phoebus,]Phoebus ) and *1673* (the text followed here).

> Moestus eram, et tacitus nullo comitante sedebam,
>   Haerebantque animo tristia plura meo,
> Protinus en subiit funestae cladis imago
>   Fecit in Angliaco quam Libitina solo;
> 5 Dum procerum ingressa est splendentes marmore turres
>   Dira sepulchrali mors metuenda face;
> Pulsavitque auro gravidos et iaspide muros,
>   Nec metuit satrapum sternere falce greges.
> Tunc memini clarique ducis, fratrisque verendi
> 10   Intempestivis ossa cremata rogis.

¶ 18. *4. Libitina*] Goddess of corpses.
*6–7. mors ... Pulsavitque*] Echoes Horace, *Odes* I iv 13 *Mors ... pulsat.* B. Whitelocke, *Memorials* (1682) 2–3, records that in 1625 over 35,000 people died of the plague in London and its suburbs, 5,000 of them in one week, and that so many people fled from the city that in Westminster the streets were deserted and overgrown with grass.
*9–10. ducis*] Probably Ernst von Mansfeld, a mercenary general of a marauding army in the early years of the Thirty Years War, who championed the Protestant cause and was appointed general of Frederick V's army in Bohemia in 1621. He visited London in 1624 to raise an army for the relief of Breda, and was hailed as a hero (see John Chamberlain, *Letters* ed. N.E. McClure (Philadelphia 1939) ii 590: 'all the world here running after Mansfeld and wondering at him like an owle'). He was finally defeated by Wallenstein at Dessau, Apr. 1626.     *fratrisque*] Probably Christian of

Et memini heroum quos vidit ad aethera raptos,
    Flevit et amissos Belgia tota duces.
At te praecipue luxi dignissime praesul,
    Wintoniaeque olim gloria magna tuae;
*15*  Delicui fletu, et tristi sic ore querebar,
    Mors fera Tartareo diva secunda Iovi,
Nonne satis quod sylva tuas persentiat iras,
    Et quod in herbosos ius tibi detur agros,
Quodque afflata tuo marcescant lilia tabo,
*20*    Et crocus, et pulchrae Cypridi sacra rosa,
Nec sinis ut semper fluvio contermina quercus
    Miretur lapsus praetereuntis aquae?
Et tibi succumbit liquido quae plurima coelo
    Evehitur pennis quamlibet augur avis,
*25*  Et quae mille nigris errant animalia sylvis,
    Et quod alunt mutum Proteos antra pecus.
Invida, tanta tibi cum sit concessa potestas;
    Quid iuvat humana tingere caede manus?

Brunswick, who allied himself to Frederick's cause early in 1622 and, with Mansfeld, defeated the Spaniards at Fleurus, Aug. 1622. He was defeated by Tilly at Stadtlohn in 1623, but came back into the war on the Protestant side in 1625, along with Christian IV of Denmark. He died 16 Jun. 1626.

*11. heroum*] Probably those killed in the operations around Breda, which fell to the Catholic general Spinola in May 1625. They included Henry Vere, Earl of Oxford, who died at the Hague after taking part in the unsuccessful assault on Terheiden, and, says John Chamberlain, *Letters* ii 618, 'Sir Thomas Winne, Sir Walter Devreux, Captain Tubbe, Captain Dakers and I know not how many more'.

*12. duces*] Probably Maurice of Nassau, Prince of Orange, the great adversary of the Catholic armies in the Netherlands, who died 23 Apr. 1625 after failing to relieve Breda, and Johan van Oldenbarneveldt who, as leading statesman of the Netherlands, had worked with Maurice to drive the Spaniards out of Holland during the 1590s, but who quarrelled with Maurice in 1609 over the truce with Spain, and was finally executed in May 1619.

*16. Tartareo . . . Iovi*] Pluto, ruler of the underworld; cp. Virgil, *Aen.* iv 638 *Iovi Stygio.*

*20. Cypridi*] Venus, to whom Cyprus was sacred.

*21. contermina quercus*] The phrase is from Ovid, *Met.* viii 620.

*22. praetereuntis aquae*] The phrase is from Buchanan, *Elegy* ii 60.

*25. nigris . . . sylvis*] The phrase is from Horace, *Odes* I xxi 7–8.

*26. pecus*] Neptune's seals, among which Odysseus and his companions hide (*Od.* iv 388–460) in order to seize their herdsman Proteus.

Nobileque in pectus certas acuisse sagittas,
30    Semideamque animam sede fugasse sua?
Talia dum lacrymans alto sub pectore volvo,
    Roscidus occiduis Hesperus exit aquis,
Et Tartessiaco submerserat aequore currum
    Phoebus, ab eoo littore mensus iter.
35    Nec mora, membra cavo posui refovenda cubili,
    Condiderant oculos noxque soporque meos.
Cum mihi visus eram lato spatiarier agro,
    Heu nequit ingenium visa referre meum.
Illis punicea radiabant omnia luce,
40    Ut matutino cum iuga sole rubent.
Ac veluti cum pandit opes Thaumantia proles,
    Vestitu nituit multicolore solum.
Non dea tam variis ornavit floribus hortos
    Alcinoi, Zephyro Chloris amata levi.
45    Flumina vernantes lambunt argentea campos,
    Ditior Hesperio flavet arena Tago.
Serpit odoriferas per opes levis aura Favoni,
    Aura sub innumeris humida nata rosis.
Talis in extremis terrae Gangetidis oris
50    Luciferi regis fingitur esse domus.

32. *Roscidus . . . Hesperus*] The evening star (an echo of Ovid, *Fast.* ii 314 *Hesperos . . . roscidus*).

33. *Tartessiaco . . . aequore*] M. probably took his adjective from Silius Italicus, *Punica* vi 1 where the Sun pastures his team by the Tartessian ocean (*Tartessiaco . . . aequore*). Herodotus iv 152 tells of a Greek sailing ship from Samos which was driven far to the west through the pillars of Hercules to the ancient port of Tartessus on Spain's Atlantic coast, previously unknown to the Greeks.

41. *Thaumantia proles*] Iris, the rainbow, daughter of Thaumas and Electra.

44. *Chloris*] The Greek name of Flora, Roman goddess of flowers. Ovid tells of her marriage with Zephyrus, *Fast.* v 197–206. *Alcinoi*] The miraculous gardens of Alcinous, king of the Phaeacians, in which trees bear fruit and flowers bloom all the year round, are described by Homer, *Od.* vii 112–32.

46. *Hesperio . . . Tago*] The river Tagus, which flows through Spain and Portugal to Lisbon, was famed for its golden sands.

47. *Favoni*] Favonius ('the favourable one') was a name for the west wind.

49–50. Lucifer ('light-bearer') means here the Sun. Ovid represents Phaëthon as reaching the palace of the Sun after crossing Ethiopia and India (*Met.* i 778–9): India is M.'s *terra Gangetis* (a term he found in Ovid, *Am.* I ii 47). There is no garden in Ovid's description of the Sun's palace (*Met.* ii 1–18), but Claudian has a vivid description of the garden of the Sun (whom he refers to as Lucifer) in *De Consulatu Stilichonis* ii 467–76.

Ipse racemiferis dum densas vitibus umbras
   Et pellucentes miror ubique locos,
Ecce mihi subito praesul Wintonius astat,
   Sydereum nitido fulsit in ore iubar;
55   Vestis ad auratos defluxit candida talos,
   Infula divinum cinxerat alba caput.
Dumque senex tali incedit venerandus amictu,
   Intremuit laeto florea terra sono.
Agmina gemmatis plaudunt caelestia pennis,
60   Pura triumphali personat aethra tuba.
Quisque novum amplexu comitem cantuque salutat,
   Hosque aliquis placido misit ab ore sonos;
Nate veni, et patrii felix cape gaudia regni,
   Semper ab hinc duro, nate, labore vaca.
65   Dixit, et aligerae tetigerunt nablia turmae,
   At mihi cum tenebris aurea pulsa quies.
Flebam turbatos Cephaleia pellice somnos,
   Talia contingant somnia saepe mihi.

I was sad, and sat alone and silent. A host of sorrows perturbed my thoughts. All at once there arose before me a vision of the dismal carnage which Libitina[4] caused on English soil, when ghastly death[6] with her sepulchral torch—a fearsome sight—made her way into the gleaming marble palaces of the nobility, beat upon the walls massy with jasper and gold, and did not shrink from mowing down troops of princes with her scythe. Then I called to mind that famous general and his well-respected brother in arms,[9] whose bones were burned on untimely pyres,[10] and I remembered the heroes[11] that all Belgia had seen snatched up to the skies—Belgia, who wept for her lost leaders.[12] But I mourned above all for you, worthiest of bishops, once the great glory of your beloved Winchester. I burst into tears and my voice, filled with grief, made this complaint: 'Pitiless Death, goddess second in power only to Tartarean Jove,[16] is it not enough that the woods are made to feel your rage, that you are given power over the grassy fields, that the lilies, the crocus and the rose sacred to lovely Cypris[20] wither at the touch of your putrid breath? Is it not enough to forbid the oak-tree that grows by the river's brim[21] to gaze for ever upon the water flowing by it?[22] The countless birds that glide through the bright sky on their pinions succumb to you, for all their gift of prophecy, and so do the thousand wild beasts that wander through the black forests,[25] and the silent herd[26] that feeds in Proteus' grottoes. Envious Death, when such great power has been granted to you, what pleasure is there in staining your hands with human blood?

59. *gemmatis . . . pennis*] Ovid includes these in Cupid's equipment, *Rem.* 39.
67. *Cephaleia pellice*] Aurora, the dawn, whose love for Cephalus is narrated by Ovid, *Met.* vii 700–13.
68. An adaptation of the last line of *Am.* I v where Ovid, having made love to Corinna one sultry noon, exclaims 'May my lot bring many a midday like this!'

Where is the pleasure in sharpening your unerring darts to pierce a noble breast, or in driving a spirit that was half divine out of its body?'

As I weep and ponder these things in my heart of hearts, dewy Hesperus[32] rises from the western sea and Phoebus, after tracing his course from the eastern strand, sinks his chariot beneath the Tartessian ocean.[33] Without delay I stretched out on my hollowed bed to refresh my limbs. Night and sleep had closed my eyes, when it seemed to me that I was strolling over a wide plain—alas! I have not enough talent to describe what I saw. There everything glowed with a rosy light, like mountain tops flushed by the morning sun. The ground shone, tricked out in a thousand colours, as when Thaumas's daughter[41] spreads her riches to the view. Chloris,[44] the goddess beloved by gentle Zephyrus, did not deck the gardens of Alcinous with flowers as various as these. Silver streams wash the blossoming meadows, and their sands gleam more golden than the sands of Hesperian Tagus.[46] Favonius'[47] light breath steals through the rich, scented foliage—dewy breath, born beneath countless roses. Such[49] is the imagined home of royal Lucifer on the farthest shores of the land of Ganges. As I gaze all around me in wonder at the shining spaces and the thick shadows under the clustering vines, suddenly the Bishop of Winchester appears, close by me. A star-like radiance shone from his bright face, a white robe flowed down to his golden feet and his god-like head was encircled by a white band. As the reverend old man walked forward, dressed in this way, the flowery earth quivered with a joyful sound. The heavenly hosts clap their jewelled wings:[59] the pure upper air rings with the blast of a triumphal trumpet. Each spirit embraces his new companion and greets him with a song, and one of them, with peaceful lips, uttered these syllables: 'Come, my son, and receive in happiness the joys of your Father's kingdom; henceforth be free from cruel toil, my son, for ever.'

When he had spoken the winged squadrons touched their harps. But my golden repose was dispelled with the night, and I wept for the sleep which Cephalus' mistress[67] had disturbed.

May I often be lucky enough to have dreams like this![68]

# 19 *Elegia Quarta*

*Ad Thomam Junium praeceptorem suum, apud mercatores Anglicos Hamburgae agentes, Pastoris munere fungentem*

[Elegy IV. To Thomas Young, his tutor, at present performing the office of chaplain among the English merchants living in Hamburg]

*Date.* Mar.–Apr. 1627. Headed *Anno aetatis 18* in *1645* and *1673*, which according to M.'s usual method of dating (see headnote to *Q Nov*, p. 36) should mean that it was written between Dec. 1626 and Dec. 1627. Harris Fletcher, *TLS* (21 Jan. 1926) 44, argues, however, that this elegy should be dated 1625, on the assumption that it is the *Epistolium quoddam numeris metricis elucubratum* mentioned in the first of M.'s *Epistolae Familiares*. But it seems more likely that the date (26 Mar. 1625) given for this letter in the 1674 *Epistolae* is itself incorrect and that both letter and elegy should be dated 1627, the latter probably, thinks W. R. Parker, *MLN* liii (1938) 399–407, between 21 Mar. and 28 Apr.

Thomas Young (1587?–1655) was a Scotsman with strong Puritan leanings. Some time between his arrival in London, in or before 1618, and his departure for Hamburg, which he reached in 1620, he was one of M.'s private tutors. In 1628 he returned to England and was presented to the living of St Peter and St Mary, Stowmarket, where M. visited him. His *Dies Dominica*, a treatise on Sabbath-observance, appeared in 1639. When Hall published his *Humble Remonstrance* (1640), upholding the divine right of episcopacy, an *Answer* was printed, of which Young was part author, his initials, with those of the four other contributors, forming the pseudonym 'Smectymnuus'. In 1641 M. joined this pamphlet war on the side of his old tutor. Young was nominated to the Westminster Assembly in 1643 and made Master of Jesus College, Cambridge in 1644. M.'s relations with him are examined by A. Barker, *MLR* xxxii (1937) 517–26 and Clark 22–32.

*Publication. 1645* and *1673* (no significant variants: in *123 1673* misprints *miseri* for *miseris*).

> Curre per immensum subito mea littera pontum,
>    I, pete Teutonicos laeve per aequor agros,
> Segnes rumpe moras, et nil, precor, obstet eunti,
>    Et festinantis nil remoretur iter.
> 5  Ipse ego Sicanio fraenantem carcere ventos
>    Aeolon, et virides sollicitabo deos;
> Caeruleamque suis comitatam Dorida nymphis,
>    Ut tibi dent placidam per sua regna viam.
> At tu, si poteris, celeres tibi sume iugales,
> 10  Vecta quibus Colchis fugit ab ore viri.
> Aut queis Triptolemus Scythicas devenit in oras
>    Gratus Eleusina missus ab urbe puer.

¶ 19. *1–4.* M.'s initial instructions to his letter are imitated from Ovid, *Tristia* III vii 1–2.

*3. Segnes rumpe moras*] The phrase is from Virgil, *Georg.* iii 42–3.

*5. Sicanio*] Sicilian. Lipara, fabled home of Aeolus, god of the winds, is an island thirty miles N.E. of Sicily. Virgil couples the 'Sicanian coast' and 'Aeolian Lipara' in *Aen.* viii 416–17.     *fraenantem . . . Aeolon*] Cp. Ovid, *Met.* xiv 224: *Aeolon . . . cohibentem carcere ventos.*

*7. Dorida*] Doris, wife of Nereus, was mother of the fifty Nereids or sea nymphs.

*10. Colchis*] The Colchian, i.e. Medea; for her team see *Prae E* 56–8n (p. 26).

*11–12.* Ovid, *Met.* v 642–61, describes how Ceres sent Triptolemus to

Atque ubi Germanas flavere videbis arenas
    Ditis ad Hamburgae moenia flecte gradum,
15 Dicitur occiso quae ducere nomen ab Hama,
    Cimbrica quem fertur clava dedisse neci.
Vivit ibi antiquae clarus pietatis honore
    Praesul Christicolas pascere doctus oves;
Ille quidem est animae plusquam pars altera nostrae,
20     Dimidio vitae vivere cogor ego.
Hei mihi quot pelagi, quot montes interiecti
    Me faciunt alia parte carere mei!
Charior ille mihi quam tu doctissime Graium
    Cliniadi, pronepos qui Telamonis erat.
25 Quamque Stagirites generoso magnus alumno,
    Quem peperit Libyco Chaonis alma Iovi.
Qualis Amyntorides, qualis Philyreius heros
    Myrmidonum regi, talis et ille mihi.
Primus ego Aonios illo praeeunte recessus
30     Lustrabam, et bifidi sacra vireta iugi,
Pieriosque hausi latices, Clioque favente,
    Castalio sparsi laeta ter ora mero.

Scythia in a chariot drawn by dragons. In *Tristia* III viii 1–4 he links, as does M. here, the dragon-teams of Medea and Triptolemus.

*15–16.* The story of the fight between the Saxon Hama and the Dane Starcaterus is first found in Saxo Grammaticus, *Danish History* vi, and is repeated by the historian Albert Krantz in his *Saxonia* (1520) with the additional information that Hama gave his name to Hamburg. Both Saxo and Krantz say Starcaterus's weapon was a sword. In Stephanus (*s.v. Hamburg*) the derivation from Hama is given and the story of the fight retold, but without specification of weapon. Probably M.'s source was Stephanus, and the *clava* his own invention.

*19–20.* Horace, *Odes* I iii 8, calls Virgil *animae dimidium meae*.

*23–4. doctissime Graium*] Socrates, shown as the intimate friend of Alcibiades, son of Clinias, in Plato's *Symposium*. Alcibiades claims descent from Eurysaces, grandson of Telamon, in Plato's *Alcibiades* 121A; Ovid calls him *Cliniades* in *Ibis* 633.

*25–6. Stagirites*] Aristotle, born at Stageira, was tutor to Alexander the Great, son of Olympias (called *Chaonis* from Chaonia, the district of Epirus where she was born), who was fathered, according to Plutarch, *Alexander* 2–3, by Jupiter Ammon (called 'Libyan Jove' because he had a shrine in the Libyan desert).

*27–8.* Achilles, king of the Myrmidons, had two tutors: Phoenix, son of Amyntor (called *Amyntorides* by Ovid, *Ibis* 259), and Chiron, son of the nymph Philyra (called *Philyreius heros* by Ovid, *Met.* ii 676).

*29–32.* The Parnassus range, with its forked mountain sacred to Apollo and the Muses (born on Mount Pierus in Macedonia: Hesiod, *Theog.* 52–3)

Flammeus at signum ter viderat arietis Aethon,
  Induxitque auro lanea terga novo,
35 Bisque novo terram sparsisti Chlori senilem
  Gramine, bisque tuas abstulit Auster opes:
Necdum eius licuit mihi lumina pascere vultu,
  Aut linguae dulces aure bibisse sonos.
Vade igitur, cursuque Eurum praeverte sonorum,
40   Quam sit opus monitis res docet, ipsa vides.
Invenies dulci cum coniuge forte sedentem,
  Mulcentem gremio pignora chara suo,
Forsitan aut veterum praelarga volumina patrum
  Versantem, aut veri biblia sacra Dei.
45 Caelestive animas saturantem rore tenellas,
  Grande salutiferae religionis opus.
Utque solet, multam, sit dicere cura salutem,
  Dicere quam decuit, si modo adesset, herum.
Haec quoque paulum oculos in humum defixa
    modestos,
50   Verba verecundo sis memor ore loqui:
Haec tibi, si teneris vacat inter praelia Musis
  Mittit ab Angliaco littore fida manus.
Accipe sinceram, quamvis sit sera, salutem;

is in Aonia. At its foot is the sacred Castalian spring at which, according
to a fragment of Simonides quoted by Plutarch, *Oracles at Delphi* 402,
Clio, Muse of History, was the 'holy guardian of lustration'.

*33–4. Aethon*] Named by Ovid, *Met.* ii 153, as one of the horses of the Sun,
which enters Aries at the vernal equinox (approximately 21 Mar.).

*35–6.* Chloris was the Greek name for Flora, goddess of flowers, whose
festival was at the end of April. There had been three vernal equinoxes
since M. saw Young, but Chloris had only twice 'spread fresh turf'. The
date of composition must therefore be late March or early April. Since
Auster, the South Wind (named as a winter wind in Virgil, *Georg.* iv 261)
had only twice carried away Chloris's wealth since that meeting, it must
have taken place at the end of winter 1624–5.

*41–4.* M. is imitating Ovid, who tells his letter to Perilla, *Tristia* III vii
3–4: *aut illam invenies dulci cum matre sedentem, / aut inter libros Pieridasque
suas.*

*49. oculos . . . modestos*] Echoes Ovid, *Am.* III vi 67: *oculos in humum deiecta
modestos.*

*51. praelia*] Hamburg was not attacked in the Thirty Years War. However,
when Mansfeld (see *Elegia III* 9–10*n*) advanced to his defeat at Dessau
(1626) it was from positions about Lübeck, only thirty miles from Hamburg.
Dessau itself and Lutter-am-Barenberge (where Christian IV was defeated
in August 1626 by Tilly) are both within a hundred and fifty miles of
Hamburg.

Fiat et hoc ipso gratior illa tibi.
55  Sera quidem, sed vera fuit, quam casta recepit
    Icaris a lento Penelopeia viro.
    Ast ego quid volui manifestum tollere crimen,
    Ipse quod ex omni parte levare nequit.
    Arguitur tardus merito, noxamque fatetur,
60  Et pudet officium deseruisse suum.
    Tu modo da veniam fasso, veniamque roganti,
    Crimina diminui, quae patuere, solent.
    Non ferus in pavidos rictus diducit hiantes,
    Vulnifico pronos nec rapit ungue leo.
65  Saepe sarissiferi crudelia pectora Thracis
    Supplicis ad moestas delicuere preces.
    Extensaeque manus avertunt fulminis ictus,
    Placat et iratos hostia parva deos.
    Iamque diu scripsisse tibi fuit impetus illi,
70  Neve moras ultra ducere passus Amor.
    Nam vaga Fama refert, heu nuntia vera malorum!
    In tibi finitimis bella tumere locis,
    Teque tuamque urbem truculento milite cingi,
    Et iam Saxonicos arma parasse duces.
75  Te circum late campos populatur Enyo,
    Et sata carne virum iam cruor arva rigat.
    Germanisque suum concessit Thracia Martem,
    Illuc Odrysios Mars pater egit equos.
    Perpetuoque comans iam deflorescit oliva,
80  Fugit et aerisonam Diva perosa tubam,
    Fugit io terris, et iam non ultima virgo

55-6. In Homer, *Od.* xxiii 1-208, Penelope, daughter of Icarius, delays her welcome because she is not convinced that Odysseus has really returned.

61. *da veniam fasso*] The phrase is from Ovid, *Ex Ponto* IV ii 23.

72. *bella*] See l. 51n.

73. *milite*] The armies of Tilly and Wallenstein were not disbanded after Lutter-am-Barenberge. They lived on the country, and in the winter of 1626-7 pressure was being put on Hamburg and other Hanse towns to join Wallenstein against Christian.

74. *Saxonicos . . . duces*] Probably the sons of Duke John of Saxe-Weimar, Dukes Frederick, William and Bernard, who had served with Mansfeld against the imperialists, and were shortly to join Gustavus Adolphus.

75. *Enyo*] Goddess of war, called 'sacker of cities' by Homer, *Il.* v 333.

77-8. Odrysia (see *Met.* vi 490) is an Ovidian name for Thrace. Statius locates Mars' temple on Mount Haemus in Thrace, *Theb.* vii 40-63.

80. *Diva*] Eirene, goddess of peace.

81. *virgo*] The virgin Astraea who, according to Ovid, *Met.* i 149-50, was the last of the immortals to leave the earth.

Creditur ad superas iusta volasse domos.
Te tamen interea belli circumsonat horror,
  Vivis et ignoto solus inopsque solo;
85 Et, tibi quam patrii non exhibuere penates
  Sede peregrina quaeris egenus opem.
Patria dura parens, et saxis saevior albis
  Spumea quae pulsat littoris unda tui,
Siccine te decet innocuos exponere faetus;
90 Siccine in externam ferrea cogis humum,
Et sinis ut terris quaerant alimenta remotis
  Quos tibi prospiciens miserat ipse Deus,
Et qui laeta ferunt de caelo nuntia, quique
  Quae via post cineres ducat ad astra, docent?
95 Digna quidem Stygiis quae vivas clausa tenebris,
  Aeternaque animae digna perire fame!
Haud aliter vates terrae Thesbitidis olim
  Pressit inassueto devia tesqua pede,
Desertasque Arabum salebras, dum regis Achabi
100  Effugit atque tuas, Sidoni dira, manus.
Talis et horrisono laceratus membra flagello,
  Paulus ab Aemathia pellitur urbe Cilix.
Piscosaeque ipsum Gergessae civis Iesum
  Finibus ingratus iussit abire suis.
105 At tu sume animos, nec spes cadat anxia curis
  Nec tua concutiat decolor ossa metus.
Sis etenim quamvis fulgentibus obsitus armis,
  Intententque tibi millia tela necem,
At nullis vel inerme latus violabitur armis,
110  Deque tuo cuspis nulla cruore bibet.
Namque eris ipse Dei radiante sub aegide tutus,
  Ille tibi custos, et pugil ille tibi;
Ille Sionaeae qui tot sub moenibus arcis

---

*87–94.* M. is referring to the gradual migration of non-conforming ministers to Holland, Germany and New England. Young, however, cannot have been an extreme Puritan as he returned to England in 1628 and held the living of Stowmarket throughout the Laudian regime.

*97–100. vates*] Elijah who, in 1 *Kings* xix 1–18, flees from Ahab and from Jezebel, daughter of Ethbaal King of Sidon.

*101–2.* In *Acts* xvi 9–40 Paul and Silas are scourged by order of the magistrates of Philippi in Macedonia. M.'s reference is inaccurate: they are not driven out but asked to leave by magistrates who are anxious because they realize they have scourged Roman citizens.

*103–4.* Cp. *Matt.* viii 28–34.

*113–14.* In 2 *Kings* xix 35–6 the angel of the Lord destroys Sennacherib's army before the walls of Jerusalem.

Assyrios fudit nocte silente viros;
115  Inque fugam vertit quos in Samaritidas oras
Misit ab antiquis prisca Damascus agris,
Terruit et densas pavido cum rege cohortes,
Aere dum vacuo buccina clara sonat,
Cornea pulvereum dum verberat ungula campum,
120  Currus arenosam dum quatit actus humum,
Auditurque hinnitus equorum ad bella ruentum,
Et strepitus ferri, murmuraque alta virum.
Et tu (quod superest miseris) sperare memento,
Et tua magnanimo pectore vince mala.
125  Nec dubites quandoque frui melioribus annis,
Atque iterum patrios posse videre lares.

Make haste, my letter, run across the wide ocean.[1] Off you go! Seek out the
lands of Germany over the smooth sea. Put an end to this idle delay![3] Do
not let anything prevent your going, I beg you, or check the speed of your
journey. I, for my part, will importune Aeolus (who keeps the winds pent
up in their Sicanian[5] den), and the green sea-gods and sky-blue Doris[7]
(with her attendant nymphs), to grant you an undisturbed passage through
their kingdoms. And you, if you can, get hold of that swift team which
Medea[10] drove when she ran away from her husband, or the one which
drew that nice lad Triptolemus[11] to the shores of Scythia when he was
sent from the city of Eleusis. And when you catch sight of the yellow sands
on the shore of Germany, make for the walls of Hamburg, a wealthy city
which, according to tradition, takes its name from Hama,[15] who is supposed
to have been killed by a Danish club. A pastor lives there, well known for
the way he esteems the primitive faith and an expert at the job of tending
his Christian flock. That man is more to me than one half of my soul:[19]
I am forced, now, to live only a half-life. Ah! How many seas and mountains
are thrust between us, to keep me apart from the other half of myself! He is
dearer to me than you, most learned of the Greeks,[23] were to Alcibiades,
Telamon's descendant:[24] dearer than the great Stagirite[25] was to his noble
pupil, the son whom that bountiful girl from Chaonia bore to Libyan Jove.[26]
To me he is as Amyntor's son[27] and the heroic son of Philyra were to the
Myrmidons' king[28] I was the first to wander under his guidance through the
Aonian retreats[29] and over the forked mountain's sacred, grassy slopes.
There I drank Pieria's waters and, through the goodness of Clio, three
times I made my happy mouth wet with Castalian wine.[32] But three times
had flaming Aethon[33] looked upon the sign of the ram and gilded his
woolly back with fresh gold, and twice, Chloris,[35] you spread fresh turf
over the ageing ground, and twice Auster[36] carried your wealth away:
and all this time I have not been allowed to feed my eyes upon his face or
to drink in at my ears the sweet sound of his voice.

115–22. In 2 Kings vii 6–7 the Lord makes the Syrian army under King
Ben-hadad flee from their camp by causing them to hear the noise of
chariots and horses, 'even the noise of a great host'.
119. An attempt to vie with Virgil's famous *quadrupedante putrem sonitu
quatit ungula campum, Aen.* viii 596.

Be off, then, and outstrip the shrill east wind in your flight; you can see from the state of affairs how necessary it is for me to spur you on. Perhaps you will find him sitting with his sweet wife,[41] fondling on his lap the dear tokens of their love; or perhaps thumbing through the huge tomes of the Church fathers, or the Holy Bible, the word of the true God;[44] or perhaps watering delicate souls with heavenly dew, the great work of redemptive religion. Make it your business to give him a hearty greeting, according to the custom of the country, and say whatever it would become your master to say if only he were there. And remember to speak these words, too, modestly, having first fixed your bashful eyes on the ground for a little while:[49] A devoted hand sends these verses from the shores of England to you—if there is any time for the gentle Muses when you are surrounded by battles.[51] Accept a sincere, though delayed greeting: may it be all the more welcome to you because of the delay. That greeting which chaste Penelope, Icarius's daughter, received from her long-absent husband was late,[55] it is true, but sincere. But stop! Why try to make nothing of what is manifestly a crime—a crime which the culprit himself is quite unable to mitigate? He is justly accused of delay; he confesses the fault and is ashamed to have failed in his duty. Only forgive him,[61] now he has confessed and begs for pardon: sins are always lessened when they are openly acknowledged. If its victims are quivering with terror a wild beast refrains from drawing wide its gaping jaws: the lion does not seize with rending claws those who lie motionless. The cruel hearts of Thracian spearmen have often melted at a suppliant enemy's tearful prayers. Outstretched hands can turn aside the stroke of the thunderbolt, and even a small sacrifice placates the angry gods.

He has felt the urge to write to you for a long time, and Love would not allow him to delay any longer, for wandering Rumour—a trustworthy bearer, alas, of evil tidings—reports that wars are breaking out in the lands which border yours,[72] that you and your city are surrounded by cruel-looking soldiers,[73] and that the Saxon leaders[74] have already prepared their weapons for battle. All around you Enyo[75] is ravaging the fields and blood is soaking into ground sown with human flesh. Thrace[77] has surrendered Mars to the Germans, and father Mars has driven his Odrysian[78] warhorses onto German soil. The olive tree, always leafy, is withering now, and the goddess[80] who detests the blaring trumpet has fled—look! she has fled from the earth —and no one believes any longer that Astraea[81] was the last to fly for safety to mansions in the sky. But you are living among strangers, in poverty and loneliness, while all around you echoes the horrifying noise of war. In your need you seek in a foreign land the sustenance which your ancestral home denied you. O native country, hard-hearted parent,[87] more cruel than the white cliffs of your coastline, battered by foaming waves, is it fitting that you should expose your innocent children in this way? Is this the way you treat them, iron-hearted land, driving them onto foreign soil and allowing them to search for their food on distant shores, when God Himself has sent them to you in His providence; when they bring joyful news to you from heaven and teach the way which leads beyond the grave to the stars?[94] You really deserve to live shut up in hellish darkness and to die of a never-ending hunger of the soul! Once, long ago, the Tishbite prophet[97] sought refuge, in a similar way, from the hands of King Ahab and from your hands, too, beastly woman of Sidon:[100] with unaccustomed foot he trod the remote wastes and rough desert of Arabia. In a similar way Paul,[101] the Cilician, was driven from the Emathian city, his flesh torn by the whining scourge; and the ungrateful citizens of the fishing port of Gergessa ordered Jesus[103] himself to leave their coasts.

But take heart. Do not let anxieties quench your hope, even if they make you uneasy, and do not allow pale fear to send shudders through your limbs. Though you are hedged in by flashing arms, though a thousand swords threaten you with death, no weapon shall harm your weaponless body, no spear-point suck out your blood. For you will be kept safe beneath God's gleaming shield. He will be your preserver, your champion; He who beat down[113] so many Assyrian soldiers one silent night beneath the walls of Zion;[114] He who routed those troops[115] which the age-old city of Damascus sent out from her ancient territories against the frontiers of Samaria, and spread panic among the battalions close-packed around their trembling king, when the clear-noted war-trumpets shrilled through the empty air, and horny hooves beat the dusty plain,[119] and hard-driven chariots shook the sandy earth, and the whinnying of charging cavalry was heard, and the clash of steel and the deep, distant roar of shouting men.[122]

And for your part, remember to hope: hope remains even for the wretched. Triumph over your misfortunes with sheer greatness of spirit. Do not doubt that some day you will enjoy happier times and be able to see your home again.

## 20 *Naturam non pati senium*
### [That Nature does not suffer from old age]

*Date.* 1627? There is no evidence for dating these verses: they have some-times been identified as the *leviculas . . . nugas* (trivial jokes) mentioned in M.'s letter to Gill of 2 Jul. 1628 (Columbia xii 8–13; Yale i 313–15), but this description fits *Id Plat* far better than *Natur*, which is serious in tone. Possibly the subject and attitude of *Natur* were suggested by George Hakewill's *Apology of the Power and Providence of God* (1627), a contribution to the debate about the decay of nature–for an account of which see V. Harris, *All Coherence Gone* (Chicago 1949)–which had been reopened by Godfrey Goodman's *Fall of Man* (1616). Hakewill's *Apology* contained the first published account of a famous phlebotomy carried out by Theodore Diodati, Charles's father. It might have been this which attracted M.'s attention to the book and led to *Natur*. But if so the poem would have to be dated in or after 1630, as it was not until Hakewill's second edition, published in that year, that the phlebotomy-account appeared.

*Publication.* *1645* (*38*. Raptat]Raptat, ) and *1673* (the text followed here).

Heu quam perpetuis erroribus acta fatiscit
Avia mens hominum, tenebrisque immersa profundis
Oedipodioniam volvit sub pectore noctem!

¶ 20. *3. Oedipodioniam*] Self-inflicted, like the blindness of Oedipus.

Quae vesana suis metiri facta deorum
5　Audet, et incisas leges adamante perenni
Assimilare suis, nulloque solubile saeclo
Consilium fati perituris alligat horis.
　　Ergone marcescet sulcantibus obsita rugis
Naturae facies, et rerum publica mater
10　Omniparum contracta uterum sterilescet ab aevo?
Et se fassa senem male certis passibus ibit
Sidereum tremebunda caput? num tetra vetustas
Annorumque aeterna fames, squalorque situsque
Sidera vexabunt? an et insatiabile Tempus
15　Esuriet caelum, rapietque in viscera patrem?
Heu, potuitne suas imprudens Iupiter arces
Hoc contra munisse nefas, et temporis isto
Exemisse malo, gyrosque dedisse perennes?
Ergo erit ut quandoque sono dilapsa tremendo
20　Convexi tabulata ruant, atque obvius ictu
Stridat uterque polus, superaque ut Olympius aula
Decidat, horribilisque retecta Gorgone Pallas.
Qualis in Aegaeam proles Iunonia Lemnon
Deturbata sacro cecidit de limine caeli.
25　Tu quoque Phoebe tui casus imitabere nati
Praecipiti curru, subitaque ferere ruina

5. *incisas . . . perenni*] In Ovid, *Met.* xv 813, Jove tells Venus that fate is *incisa adamante perenni.*

9. *mater*] Ge, Earth, who according to Hesiod, *Theog.* 117–63, brought forth Heaven, and was thus common ancestor of gods and men.

15. *patrem*] E. Reiss, *MLN* lxxii (1957) 410–12, believes that the usual explanation of this line by reference to the confusion of Chronos (Time) with Cronos (the child-devourer in Hesiod) is unsatisfactory because Time is here thought of as devouring his father, not his children. Reiss directs attention to the doctrine expounded by M. in *De doctrina* I vii, that God created all things out of Himself. In this sense Time could be called a child of God, and the situation M. imagines his opponents looking forward to is the destruction of God Himself by Time. This seems rather forced.

19–20. *sono . . . tremendo*] Cp. *2 Peter* iii 10: 'The heavens shall pass away with a great noise'.

22. *Gorgone*] According to Homer, *Il.* v 741–2, Pallas Athene wears the Gorgon Medusa's head on her shield.

23. *proles Iunonia*] Hephaestus, thrown out of heaven by Zeus, as Homer tells, *Il.* i 590–4.

25. *tui . . . nati*] Phaëthon. Ovid, *Met.* ii 19–328, tells how when driving his father's chariot he lost control of its horses and was struck down by Jove with a thunderbolt, lest he should destroy the earth.

Pronus, et extincta fumabit lampade Nereus,
Et dabit attonito feralia sibila ponto.
Tunc etiam aerei divulsis sedibus Haemi
30 Dissultabit apex, imoque allisa barathro
Terrebunt Stygium deiecta Ceraunia Ditem
In superos quibus usus erat, fraternaque bella.
At pater omnipotens fundatis fortius astris
Consuluit rerum summae, certoque peregit
35 Pondere fatorum lances, atque ordine summo
Singula perpetuum iussit servare tenorem.
Volvitur hinc lapsu mundi rota prima diurno;
Raptat et ambitos socia vertigine caelos.
Tardior haud solito Saturnus, et acer ut olim
40 Fulmineum rutilat cristata casside Mavors.
Floridus aeternum Phoebus iuvenile coruscat,
Nec fovet effoetas loca per declivia terras
Devexo temone deus; sed semper amica
Luce potens eadem currit per signa rotarum,
45 Surgit odoratis pariter formosus ab Indis
Aethereum pecus albenti qui cogit Olympo
Mane vocans, et serus agens in pascua coeli,
Temporis et gemino dispertit regna colore.
Fulget, obitque vices alterno Delia cornu,
50 Caeruleumque ignem paribus complectitur ulnis.
Nec variant elementa fidem, solitoque fragore
Lurida perculsas iaculantur fulmina rupes.
Nec per inane furit leviori murmure Corus,
Stringit et armiferos aequali horrore Gelonos

27. *Nereus*] The Old Man of the Sea in Hesiod, *Theog.* 233–6 and Homer, *Il.* xviii 141. Ovid, *Met.* ii 268, makes him hide in a cave while Phaëthon's drive is drying up the sea.

29. *Haemi*] A mountain between Thrace and Thessaly: one of those which Ovid mentions as burned by Phaëthon's drive (*Met.* ii 219).

31. *Ceraunia*] The Ceraunian mountains are between Epirus and Thessaly. *Ditem*] Hades, ruler of the lower world and brother of the other Olympian gods whose war against the older gods, the Titans, is described by Hesiod, *Theog.* 617–731. Hesiod mentions rocks but not mountains as ammunition.

37–51. M. adopts the Ptolemaic cosmogony, and the spheres he mentions are given in their Ptolemaic order, reading inwards from the *primum mobile*: Saturn, Mars, Sun, Venus, Moon, Earth.

45–8. The star referred to is Venus, called Hesperus as evening- and Lucifer as morning-star.    *odoratis ... Indis*] Echoes Silius Italicus xvii 647: *odoratis descendens ... ab Indis.*

49. *Delia*] Diana, the moon-goddess, born on the island of Delos.

53. *Corus*] The north-west wind.

55   Trux Aquilo, spiratque hyemem, nimbosque volutat.
      Utque solet, Siculi diverberat ima Pelori
      Rex maris, et rauca circumstrepit aequora concha
      Oceani tubicen, nec vasta mole minorem
      Aegaeona ferunt dorso Balearica cete.
60   Sed neque Terra tibi saecli vigor ille vetusti
      Priscus abest, servatque suum Narcissus odorem,
      Et puer ille suum tenet et puer ille decorem
      Phoebe tuusque et Cypri tuus, nec ditior olim
      Terra datum sceleri celavit montibus aurum
65   Conscia, vel sub aquis gemmas. Sic denique in aevum
      Ibit cunctarum series iustissima rerum,
      Donec flamma orbem populabitur ultima, late
      Circumplexa polos, et vasti culmina caeli;
      Ingentique rogo flagrabit machina mundi.

Ah! How perpetual are the errors which drive man's restless mind to exhaustion! How deep the darkness which swallows him when he harbours in his soul the blind night of Oedipus![3] In his madness he dares to measure the deeds of Gods by his own, to make those laws which are cut in everlasting adamant[5] of no more account than his own laws, and to link that decree of fate which no age will ever wear away to his own dwindling hours.

Will the face of Nature really wither away and be furrowed all over with wrinkles? Will our common mother[9] really contract her all-producing womb and totter along wagging her starry head? Will loathsome old age, and the

55. *Aquilo*] The north-east wind.

56. *Pelori*] Pelorus is a promontory on the north-east coast of Sicily, the modern Capo di Faro.

58. *tubicen*] Triton, Neptune's son. He and his trumpet are vividly described by Ovid, *Met.* i 330–42.

59. *Aegaeona*] Aegaeon was a name for the hundred-handed giant Briareus, son of Uranus and Ge (Earth). Homer, *Il.* i 403–4 says he was called Briareus by gods, Aegaeon by men. In Ovid, *Met.* ii 9–10, Aegaeon is a sea god who leans on the backs of two whales. It is not clear why M. associates him with the Balearic Islands, unless he is glancing at the huge Catholic power of Spain, another monster, like Aegaeon, overhanging the Balearic Islands as he does his whales.

61. *Narcissus*] Ovid, *Met.* iii 402–510, tells the story of his transformation into a flower.

62–3. *puer*] Hyacinthus, loved by Apollo, accidentally killed by him with a discus, and transformed to a flower, as Ovid tells in *Met.* x 162–219. *Cypri tuus*] Adonis, loved by Venus (called Cypris because Cyprus was sacred to her). When he was killed by the boar Venus, according to Ovid, *Met.* x 728–39, made the anemone spring from his blood.

67–9. M. has biblical authority for prophesying a final conflagration: 2 Peter iii 10.

years' insatiable hunger, and filth and rust really do any damage to the stars? Will ravenous Time gobble up heaven itself and cram his own father into his stomach?[15] Ah, was Jove so improvident? Couldn't he have fortified his own citadels against this evil thing, and exempted them from Time's depredation, and let them go on whirling round for ever? As it is, there will come a day when the floors of the vaulted universe will collapse with a terrifying crash:[19] the poles of the earth will shriek when they feel the shock: the Olympian will fall headlong from his hall in the skies and Pallas, too, will fall—a horrifying sight with her Gorgon shield uncovered[22]—just as Juno's son[23] fell down on the Aegean island of Lemnos when he was flung from heaven's sacred threshold. You, Phoebus, will also share the fate of your son[25] in your rushing chariot: suddenly you will fall head-first: Nereus[27] will belch steam as he quenches your lamp and the astounded sea will hiss horribly. Then even the peak of skyey Haemus[29] will fly to pieces as its foundations are torn apart, and the Ceraunian[31] heights which Stygian Dis once used against the Titans in wars where brothers banded together, will be dashed down and hurled to the depths of the abyss to terrify him.

No! The Almighty Father has taken thought for the universe, and set the stars more firmly in their place. He has poised the scales of destiny with a sure weight and commanded each thing to keep its course for ever in a supremely ordered whole. So the *primum mobile*[37] turns with daily rotation and drags the enclosed spheres round with it. Saturn is no slower than he used to be, and Mars, as swift and keen as ever, flashes lightning from his crested helmet. Phoebus is always bright with the bloom of youth: he does not steer his chariot downhill to warm a worn-out earth, but ever strong with friendly light speeds along the same marks as his chariot wheels left before. The star[45] which gathers the heavenly flock together as the sky whitens, and calls them home as morning breaks, and which drives them out again at evening into the pastures of heaven, dividing the realms of time with two colours, rises as beautiful as ever from the spicy Indies. Delia[49] alternately waxes and wanes, her horns pointing now this way, now that, and as always she clasps the fire of heaven in her arms. The elements, too, remain true to type: yellow lightning strikes and shatters the rocks with a crashing noise as it always did: Corus[53] rages through the empty air with a voice no more gentle than before: wild Aquilo[55] huddles the armed Scythians together, shivering as much as ever, and breathes winter upon them, and tumbles the clouds about overhead. The sea-king batters at the base of Pelorus[56] the Sicilian promontory, as he always did, and the ocean-trumpeter[58] surrounds the seas with the blare of his hollow-sounding shell, and the Balearic whales bear on their backs an Aegaeon[59] no less vast in bulk than before. Nor, Earth, do you lack that primitive strength which you had in bygone ages: Narcissus[61] keeps his fragrance still: that boy of yours, Phoebus,[62] is as beautiful as ever and so, Cypris, is that boy of yours.[63] The earth was no richer in days gone by when, conscious of wrong, she hid beneath her mountains and seas the gold and gems which were destined to foster crime.

In fact, then, the process of the universe will go on for ever, worked out with scrupulous justice, until the last flames[67] destroy the globe, enveloping the poles and the summits of vast heaven, and the frame of the world blazes on one huge funeral pyre.[69]

## 21 *De Idea Platonica quemadmodum Aristoteles intellexit*

[Of the Platonic Ideal Form as understood by Aristotle]

*Date*. June 1628? In M.'s letter to Alexander Gill of 2 Jul. 1628 (see headnote to *Natur*, p. 61 above) he refers to some verses he has been writing for the use of a Fellow of his College chosen to act as Respondent in the philosophical disputation at the Cambridge Commencement (which took place 1 Jul. in 1628). The term *leviculas nugas* used to describe these verses fits the semi-serious *Id Plat* better than *Natur*. It is possible that the verses have not survived at all, but M.'s apparent thoroughness in gathering up even his trifling compositions in Latin verse suggests that he would not have omitted from *1645* a poem he had thought worth sending to Gill on the day after its publication. If the *leviculas nugas* are in *1645* at all, they are probably *Id Plat*.

*Publication*. M. enclosed in his letter to Gill a printed copy (*typis donata*) of the verses: the Respondent's verses were customarily printed and distributed by the beadles at the Commencement ceremony. Of this printing no copies have survived. Also printed in *1645* and *1673* (no significant variants: in *23 1673* misprints *iis* for *diis*, and in *36 induxit* for *induxti*).

*Id Plat* is a burlesque of Aristotle's criticisms of Plato's doctrine of ideal forms (outlined, for example, in *Republic* x 596–7, *Cratylus* 389, 439–40, *Phaedo* 75–6, *Parmenides* 135 and *Sophist* 246–7). For Aristotle's attack see *Metaphysics* I ix, VII viii. M. speaks as a literal-minded Aristotelian, demanding where the ideal or archetypal form of man is to be found.

> Dicite sacrorum praesides nemorum deae,
> Tuque O noveni perbeata numinis
> Memoria mater, quaeque in immenso procul
> Antro recumbis otiosa Aeternitas,
> 5  Monumenta servans, et ratas leges Iovis,

¶ *21. 1. deae*] Possibly the Muses, identified in Latin poetry with the Italian Camenae to whom, as Livy I xxi 3 relates, Numa dedicated a grove outside the Porta Capena. Or perhaps Diana (called *nemorum . . . custos*, Virgil, *Aen*. ix 405) and her nymphs. MacKellar 303 suggests that M. calls on Diana because, as moon-goddess, she is sometimes identified with Lucina, goddess of childbirth, and should therefore know about the being who served as pattern for the human race.

*3. mater*] According to Hesiod, *Theog*. 52–3 the Muses were daughters of Zeus and Mnemosyne (Memory).

*4–6*. M.'s cave of Eternity is based on the cave of Time in Claudian, *De Consulatu Stilichonis* ii 424–8, where Time, an old man, writes immutable laws and fixes the revolutions of the planets.

Caelique fastos atque ephemeridas Deum,
Quis ille primus cuius ex imagine
Natura sollers finxit humanum genus,
Aeternus, incorruptus, aequaevus polo,
10    Unusque et universus, exemplar Dei?
Haud ille Palladis gemellus innubae
Interna proles insidet menti Iovis;
Sed quamlibet natura sit communior,
Tamen seorsus extat ad morem unius,
15    Et, mira, certo stringitur spatio loci;
Seu sempiternus ille syderum comes
Caeli pererrat ordines decemplicis,
Citimumve terris incolit Lunae globum:
Sive inter animas corpus adituras sedens
20    Obliviosas torpet ad Lethes aquas:
Sive in remota forte terrarum plaga
Incedit ingens hominis archetypus gigas,
Et diis tremendus erigit celsum caput
Atlante maior portitore syderum.
25    Non cui profundum caecitas lumen dedit
Dircaeus augur vidit hunc alto sinu;
Non hunc silenti nocte Pleiones nepos
Vatum sagaci praepes ostendit choro;
Non hunc sacerdos novit Assyrius, licet

9. *aequaevus polo*] Probably echoing Claudian, *De Bello Gothico* 54 (of Rome) *aequaeva polo*.

*11–12.* Pallas Athene sprang fully armed from the head of Zeus.

*19–20.* The doctrine of metempsychosis is outlined by Plato, *Phaedo* 70–2, *Republic* x 617–18. In Virgil, *Aen.* vi 710–15, Aeneas, in the underworld, is thrilled by the sight of souls, destined to go back to the world, thronging on the banks of Lethe to drink the waters of forgetfulness.

*24. Atlante*] Atlas, according to Hesiod, *Theog.* 507–20, carries the heavens on his head and shoulders.

*26. Dircaeus augur*] Tiresias, see *Elegia VI* 68*n* (p. 116). Dircaean (from Dirce, a fountain near Thebes in Boeotia) means Boeotian or Theban.

*27. Pleiones nepos*] This title for Mercury is from Ovid, *Her.* xvi 62: he was son of Maia, one of the Pleiades–the seven daughters of Atlas and Pleione, a sea nymph.

*29. sacerdos ... Assyrius*] Probably Hierombalus, priest of the god Ieuo. It was from him, according to a fragment of Porphyry preserved in Eusebius, *Praeparationis Evangelicae* I ix–a work on which M. draws in his outlines for tragedies in the Trinity MS (Columbia xviii 235)–and quoted in Selden 111, that Sanchuniathon drew the material for his *Phoenician*

30    Longos vetusti commemoret atavos Nini,
    Priscumque Belon, inclytumque Osiridem.
    Non ille trino gloriosus nomine
    Ter magnus Hermes (ut sit arcani sciens)
    Talem reliquit Isidis cultoribus.
35    At tu perenne ruris Academi decus
    (Haec monstra si tu primus induxti scholis)
    Iam iam poetas urbis exules tuae
    Revocabis, ipse fabulator maximus,
    Aut institutor ipse migrabis foras.

Tell me, goddesses[1] who keep watch over the sacred groves; tell me, Memory, most blessed mother of the nine Muses;[3] tell me, Eternity,[4] you who lie at ease in some vast cave far away, looking after the records of the past, the unshakeable laws of Jove, the calendars of heaven and the diaries of the gods[6]–tell me, who was that first being in whose image skilful Nature has modelled the human race: that first, eternal, incorrupt, single yet universal being, as old as the heavens,[9] the pattern used by God? He is not twin brother to the virgin Athene:[11] he does not live like an unborn child inside Jove's mind.[12] Although he is by nature common to all, he has a separate existence just like a normal individual and, extraordinarily enough, is confined within definite spatial limits. Perhaps he wanders about eternally[16] through the ten concentric spheres of the heavens, keeping the stars company, or perhaps he lives next door to the earth in the globe of the moon. Perhaps he sits on Lethe's banks among the souls who are waiting to get into human bodies,[19] and dozes off beside the waters of forgetfulness,[20] or perhaps in

*History*. Eusebius' work contains the only extant portions of a translation made ostensibly from Sanchuniathon by Philo of Byblos.

*30.* Philo claims that Sanchuniathon lived at or before the time of the Trojan War, in the reign of Queen Semiramis and King Ninus, founders of the Assyrian empire. Of the passages which Eusebius I x quotes from Philo's translations of the *Phoenician History*, the first deals with the origin of life on earth.

*31. Priscumque Belon*] Selden devotes a chapter (II i) to Bel or Baal, and quotes (105) from Philo's translation of Sanchuniathon a passage asserting that Bel was thought the only god in the sky by the Phoenicians. Sandys 207 mentions 'Belus Priscus, (reputed a God and honoured with Temples, called *Bel* by the Assyrians, and *Baal* by the Hebrewes)'.    *Osiridem*] see *Nativity Ode* 213n (p. 111).

*33. Hermes*] Hermes Trismegistus, identified with the Egyptian Thoth, god of wisdom, to whom the Alexandrian neo-Platonists of the third and fourth centuries A.D. attributed various of their writings. According to Philo (quoted by Eusebius I ix), Sanchuniathon based his *History* on Hermes, the inventor of writing.

*34. Isidis*] See *Nativity Ode* 211–12n (p. 111).

*35. Academi decus*] Plato, who excluded poets from his ideal state (*Republic* x 595–607).

some faraway land this archetypal man strides along like an enormous giant, taller than star-bearing Atlas,[24] and rears up his towering head to frighten the gods. The visionary Tiresias,[26] whose blindness gave him piercing sight, never saw this man even in the depths of his heart. Pleione's swift-heeled grandson[27] never showed this man to the crowd of prophetic sages in the silence of the night. The Assyrian priest[29] had never heard of this man, although he could remember the remote ancestors of ancient Ninus,[30] primitive Belus,[31] and famous Osiris. Nor did that seer who glories in a triple name, Hermes Trismegistus,[33] although he knew a lot about erudite things, ever leave word to the worshippers of Isis[34] of a man like this. But you, the immortal glory of the Academy,[35] if you are responsible for introducing these monsters into philosophical discussions, must either hurry up and call home the poets whom you exiled from your Republic or else banish yourself from it, although you were its founder, as the greatest fictional writer of them all.

## 22 *Elegia septima*
[Elegy VII]

*Date.* Summer? 1628. Headed in *1645*, *Anno aetatis undevigesimo* [In his nineteenth year]. This heading is singular because of its use of the ordinal: M. normally employs arabic figures. Thus it might be correct to take his dating literally in this case and place the elegy between Dec. 1626 and Dec. 1627. It would be more in keeping with M.'s normal practice, however, to take his heading to mean 'When he was nineteen' (i.e. Dec. 1627–Dec. 1628). There is no need to date *Elegia VII* in May, as do Masson i 268, MacKellar 33 and French i 153–7. 1 May (*14*) is merely given as the date of Cupid's visit. The reference to the London summertime, when citizens promenade (*51*) and the concept of M. being torn between two places (*79*) might suggest that *Elegia VII* was written when M. had returned to Cambridge in the summer vacation of 1628: cp. his sixth *Prolusion*, delivered at this time, where he tells how he has just returned from London 'stuffed, I might almost say, to corpulence with all the pleasures in which that place overflows beyond measure' (Columbia xii 204–5; Yale i 266). W. R. Parker (Taylor 119–21), anxious to prove that the *1645* order of printing represents the order of composition, dates *Elegia VII* May 1630 and conjectures that *undevigesimo* is an error for *uno & vigesimo* [twenty-first]. M. uses the ordinal, he explains, to make the date of his coming-of-age conspicuous. E. Sirluck, *JEGP* lx (1961) 783–4, pertinently objects that, if this was M.'s intention in using the ordinal, it is inconceivable that a printer's error such as Parker postulates, would have escaped his notice.

In *1645* M. presumably printed *Elegia VII* after *Elegiae V* and *VI* (both later in date), because he felt that the retraction, *Haec ego mente* . . . (p. 231 below) which he wished to append to *Elegia VII*, would fit more easily at the end of the numbered elegies, rather than inserted into the run.

*Publication.* *1645* (*8.* tuae:]tuae.    *50.* erat,]erat.    *59.* misi]misi, *88.* loqui!]loqui; ), *1673* (the text followed here).

Nondum blanda tuas leges Amathusia noram,
    Et Paphio vacuum pectus ab igne fuit.
Saepe cupidineas, puerilia tela, sagittas,
    Atque tuum sprevi maxime, numen, Amor.
5   Tu puer imbelles dixi transfige columbas,
    Conveniunt tenero mollia bella duci.
Aut de passeribus tumidos age, parve, triumphos,
    Haec sunt militiae digna trophaea tuae:
In genus humanum quid inania dirigis arma?
10   Non valet in fortes ista pharetra viros.
Non tulit hoc Cyprius, (neque enim deus ullus ad iras
    Promptior) et duplici iam ferus igne calet.
Ver erat, et summae radians per culmina villae
    Attulerat primam lux tibi Maie diem:
15   At mihi adhuc refugam quaerebant lumina noctem
    Nec matutinum sustinuere iubar.
Astat Amor lecto, pictis Amor impiger alis,
    Prodidit astantem mota pharetra deum:
Prodidit et facies, et dulce minantis ocelli,
20   Et quicquid puero, dignum et Amore fuit.
Talis in aeterno iuvenis Sigeius Olympo
    Miscet amatori pocula plena Iovi;
Aut qui formosas pellexit ad oscula nymphas
    Thiodamantaeus Naiade raptus Hylas;
25   Addideratque iras, sed et has decuisse putares,
    Addideratque truces, nec sine felle minas.
Et miser exemplo sapuisses tutius, inquit,
    Nunc mea quid possit dextera testis eris.

¶ **22.** *1–2. Amathusia*] Venus, who had a temple at Amathus in Cyprus, and another at Paphos (hence *Paphio . . . igne*).

*11. Cyprius*] Not a classical name for Cupid. M. uses it because Venus, Cupid's mother, is frequently called *Cypria* (the Cyprian).

*17. pictis . . . alis*] Cp. Cupid's *purpureas alas* in Ovid, *Rem.* 701.

*21. iuvenis Sigeius*] Ganymede, the youth whom, as Ovid relates, *Met.* x 155–61, Jove, in the shape of an eagle, stole away from Mt Ida to be his cup-bearer. *Sigeum* was the name of a promontory in Troas, thus *Sigeius* could be used, by transference, to mean 'Trojan'. In Homer's account of the rape of Ganymede, *Il.* xx 230–5, his father is given as Tros, the eponym of Troy.

*24. Hylas*] Son of Theodamas, king of the Dryopes, was dragged down to the depths of a fountain by a nymph captivated by his beauty. M. follows Propertius I xx 6 *Theiodamanteo . . . Hylae.*

Inter et expertos vires numerabere nostras,
30   Et faciam vero per tua damna fidem.
Ipse ego si nescis strato pythone superbum
     Edomui Phoebum, cessit et ille mihi;
Et quoties meminit Peneidos, ipse fatetur
     Certius et gravius tela nocere mea.
35   Me nequit adductum curvare peritius arcum,
     Qui post terga solet vincere Parthus eques.
Cydoniusque mihi cedit venator, et ille
     Inscius uxori qui necis author erat.
Est etiam nobis ingens quoque victus Orion,
40   Herculeaeque manus, Herculeusque comes.
Iupiter ipse licet sua fulmina torqueat in me,
     Haerebunt lateri spicula nostra Iovis.

*31–4.* Cp. Ovid, *Met.* i 452–64: 'Now the first love of Phoebus was
Daphne, daughter of Peneus, the river god. It was no blind chance that
gave this love, but the malicious wrath of Cupid. Delian Apollo, while still
exulting over his conquest of the Python, had seen him bending his bow
with tight-drawn string, and had said: "What hast thou to do with the
arms of men, thou wanton boy?" . . . And to him Venus' son replied:
"Thy dart may pierce all things else, Apollo, but mine shall pierce thee."'
When in love Apollo admits: 'My arrow is sure of aim, but oh, one arrow,
surer than my own, has wounded my heart.' This episode is the basis for
the first part of M.'s poem. Apollo's scornful speech is echoed in ll. 5–10,
and Apollo's love is snatched from him as is M.'s.
*37–8. Cydoniusque . . . venator*] The inhabitants of Cydon (modern Canea),
a port in Crete, were famous as archers. Virgil, *Aen.* xii 858, couples
Parthians and Cydonians.    *ille Inscius*] Cephalus who, as Ovid relates,
*Met.* vii 835–62, heard a rustling sound in a bush when he was out hunting,
flung his javelin at the place, and killed his wife, Procris, who was hiding
there.
*39. ingens . . . Orion*] Orion pursued the Pleiades, the seven daughters of
Atlas. Ovid portrays him love-sick, *Ars Amatoria* i 731: 'Pale did Orion
wander in Dirce's glades.'
*40.* Deianira, Hercules' wife, upbraids him in Ovid, *Her.* ix 47 for his
*peregrinos . . . amores* and, 53–118, for his subjection to Omphale, who
dressed him as a waiting-maid and made him spin for her. M.'s concen-
tration on Hercules' hands is Deianira's: 'Do you not shrink, Alcides,
from laying to the polished wool-basket the hand that has triumphed over
a thousand toils; do you draw off with stalwart thumb the coarsely spun
strands? . . . Ah, how often, while with dour finger you twisted the thread,
have your too strong hands crushed the spindle!'    *comes*] probably
Jason, leader of the Argonauts, of whom Hercules was one. Jason abandoned
Medea in favour of Glauce, daughter of Creon, king of Corinth.
*42.* The loves of Jove were notorious: Ovid lists them, *Met.* vi 103–14.

    Caetera quae dubitas melius mea tela docebunt,
      Et tua non leviter corda petenda mihi.
45  Nec te stulte tuae poterunt defendere musae,
      Nec tibi Phoebaeus porriget anguis opem.
    Dixit, et aurato quatiens mucrone sagittam,
      Evolat in tepidos Cypridos ille sinus.
    At mihi risuro tonuit ferus ore minaci,
50    Et mihi de puero non metus ullus erat,
    Et modo qua nostri spatiantur in urbe quirites
      Et modo villarum proxima rura placent.
    Turba frequens, facieque simillima turba dearum
      Splendida per medias itque reditque vias.
55  Auctaque luce dies gemino fulgore coruscat,
      Fallor? an et radios hinc quoque Phoebus habet.
    Haec ego non fugi spectacula grata severus,
      Impetus et quo me fert iuvenilis, agor.
    Lumina luminibus male providus obvia misi
60    Neve oculos potui continuisse meos.
    Unam forte aliis supereminuisse notabam,
      Principium nostri lux erat illa mali.
    Sic Venus optaret mortalibus ipsa videri,
      Sic regina deum conspicienda fuit.
65  Hanc memor obiecit nobis malus ille Cupido,
      Solus et hos nobis texuit ante dolos.
    Nec procul ipse vafer latuit, multaeque sagittae,
      Et facis a tergo grande pependit onus.

---

46. *anguis*] Symbol of Aesculapius, god of medicine, son of Apollo. Ovid tells how in the form of a snake (*Phoebeius anguis*) he came to Rome to put an end to a plague, *Met.* xv 626–744. Captivated by Daphne, Apollo laments 'The art of medicine is my discovery . . . and all the potency o herbs is given unto me. Alas that love is curable by no herbs, and the arts which heal all others cannot heal their lord!' *Met.* i 521–4, see ll. 31–4*n*.

47. *aurato . . . mucrone*] In the Daphne story (see ll. 31–4*n*) Ovid gives Cupid golden arrows to kindle love and leaden to repel it, *Met.* i 468–72.

51. Favourite places for promenading in early seventeenth-century London were Lincoln's Inn Fields, Gray's Inn Fields, the Temple Garden and Moorfields. They were frequented on summer evenings: cp. Jonson, *Bartholomew Fair* I ii 5–7: 'Shee would not ha' worne this habit. I challenge all *Cheapside*, to shew such another: *Moorfields, Pimlico* path, or the *Exchange*, in a sommer evening.'

52. Possibly M. is referring to the same 'magnificently shady spot just outside the city' which he had mentioned to Diodati in *Elegia I* 50.

61. *aliis*] *superemineo*, which here governs the dative, always governs the accusative in the Roman poets.

Nec mora, nunc ciliis haesit, nunc virginis ori,
70     Insilit hinc labiis, insidet inde genis:
Et quascunque agilis partes iaculator oberrat,
    Hei mihi, mille locis pectus inerme ferit.
Protinus insoliti subierunt corda furores,
    Uror amans intus, flammaque totus eram.
75 Interea misero quae iam mihi sola placebat,
    Ablata est oculis non reditura meis.
Ast ego progredior tacite querebundus, et excors,
    Et dubius volui saepe referre pedem.
Findor, et haec remanet, sequitur pars altera votum,
80     Raptaque tam subito gaudia flere iuvat.
Sic dolet amissum proles Iunonia coelum,
    Inter Lemniacos praecipitata focos.
Talis et abreptum solem respexit, ad Orcum
    Vectus ab attonitis Amphiaraus equis.
85 Quid faciam infelix, et luctu victus, amores
    Nec licet inceptos ponere, neve sequi.
O utinam spectare semel mihi detur amatos
    Vultus, et coram tristia verba loqui!
Forsitan et duro non est adamante creata,
90     Forte nec ad nostras surdeat illa preces.
Crede mihi nullus sic infeliciter arsit,
    Ponar in exemplo primus et unus ego.
Parce precor teneri cum sis deus ales amoris,
    Pugnent officio nec tua facta tuo.
95 Iam tuus O certe est mihi formidabilis arcus,
    Nate dea, iaculis nec minus igne potens:
Et tua fumabunt nostris altaria donis,
    Solus et in superis tu mihi summus eris.
Deme meos tandem, verum nec deme furores,

---

*81–2.* Vulcan (Hephaestus) son of Juno (Hera) was thrown from heaven by Jove (Zeus). Homer, *Il.* i 590–3, makes him relate to his mother how, after falling for a whole day, he landed on the island of Lemnos.

*83–4. Orcum*] Orcus was a name for the world of the dead. *Amphiaraus:* one of the seven against Thebes: he was swallowed up by the earth along with his chariot and horses. Statius, *Theb.* vii 690–823, has a dramatic account of the event which mentions, as does M., Amphiaraus' backward glance: 'And as he sank he looked back at the heavens and groaned to see the plain meet above him.'

*89.* Cp. Theocritus iii 39: 'It may be she'll look upon me then, being she's no woman of adamant.'

*90. surdeat*] An incorrect form; there is no verb *surdeo.*

*97.* Cp. Lucretius vi 752: *fumant altaria donis.*

*100*    Nescio cur, miser est suaviter omnis amans:
       Tu modo da facilis, posthaec mea siqua futura est,
       Cuspis amaturos figat ut una duos.

I was still ignorant of your laws, seductive Amathusia,[1] and my breast contained no Paphian[2] fire. I often made fun of Cupid's arrows, calling them childish weapons, and above all I scorned your godhead, Love. 'Go and shoot doves, lad; they can't hurt you', I said, 'a tender campaigner like you is only fit for soft wars. Or go and boast about the triumphs you've won over sparrows, little boy: those are the sort of trophies which your warfare deserves. Why do you aim your stupid darts at human beings? Your quiver's no good against grown-up men.' Cupid[11] could not bear this (not one of the gods is more easily irritated than he), and he grew twice as angry as before.

It was spring, and the dawn shining over the gables of the tall farmhouse had brought your first day, May. But my eyes still longed for the vanishing night, and could not bear the bright morning sunshine. Love stood by my bed, agile Love with his brightly coloured wings.[17] His swinging quiver and his face and his sweetly threatening eyes gave him away, and so did all those other signs which distinguish the boy Cupid. This is what the Trojan lad[21] looks like, while he mixes brimming goblets for infatuated Jove on ageless Olympus' top; and this is what Hylas,[24] Theodamas' son, looked like –Hylas, who lured the beautiful nymphs to his kisses and was stolen away by a Naiad. Cupid was angry, unlike them (though you'd have thought anger made him even lovelier), and what is more he was full of fierce and bitter threats: this is what he said: 'You miserable creature, you would have been wiser and safer if you had learned by the example of others. Now you will yourself witness what my right hand can do. You shall be numbered among those who have felt my strength: by your suffering I shall make people believe the truth about me. It was I, in case you don't know it, who tamed proud Phoebus when he had vanquished the Python.[31] Even he yielded to me, and whenever he remembers Daphne he confesses that my arrows are more accurate and more painful than his own.[34] The Parthian horseman, who is trained to win a fight by shooting behind his back, cannot draw his taut bow more skilfully than I. The Cydonian hunter[37] gives me best too, and so does that hunter who hit his own wife and killed her without knowing who it was.[38] Even the giant Orion[39] was conquered by me; so were the hands of Hercules,[40] and Hercules's comrade as well. Even if Jove himself throws his whirling thunderbolts at me, my little arrows will stick in his side.[42] Whatever other doubts you may have will be resolved by my arrows better than by words, and also by your own heart, which must be my target–and I shall not shoot half-heartedly. Your muses will not be able to protect you, you fool, and Apollo's serpent[46] will not provide you with any cure.' When he had finished speaking he shook a gold-tipped arrow[47] at me and then flew away to nestle between the warm breasts of Cypris. But I was inclined to smile at the threats which this furious little lad thundered at me: I had no fear of the boy. Sometimes the city promenades[51] provided me with entertainment, sometimes the countryside near the outlying houses.[52] A whole host of girls, with faces just like goddesses, go to and fro along the walks, resplendently beautiful. And the day is twice as bright as usual because of the light they add to it. Am I mistaken, or is it from them that the sun borrows his beams? I was not puritanical: I did not run away from such delicious sights. I let myself be driven wherever the impulse of youth carried me. Heedlessly I let my eyes meet theirs: I was unable to keep my eyes in check. Then, by chance, I caught sight of one girl who was far more beautiful than all the rest:[61] that day was the beginning of my downfall. Venus herself, when she appeared to mortals, might have chosen to look like this girl: this is what the queen of the gods must have looked like. That wretch Cupid bore me a grudge and threw her in my way: it was he alone who had woven these nets for me in advance. The artful boy was hiding close at hand with a good supply of arrows and a huge load of torches hung behind his back. Losing no time he swung on the girl's eyelashes, then on her mouth, then jumped between her lips, then perched on her cheek—and wherever the nimble archer landed (alas for me!) he hit my defenceless breast in a thousand places. In an instant passions I had never felt before entered my heart—I burned inwardly with love: my whole being was aflame.

Meanwhile the only girl who could give me relief was taken away from me, never to be seen again. But I went on, madly in love, complaining to myself and irresolute, often wanting to retrace my steps. I am torn apart: one half of me stays here, and the other follows my desire and takes pleasure in weeping for joys so suddenly snatched away. So Juno's son[81] wept for the heaven he had lost, after he had been flung down among the houses of Lemnos:[82] so Amphiaraus,[83] carried down to Hades by his panic-stricken horses, looked back at the sun which was being snatched from his eyes.[84] Luckless, overwhelmed with grief, what am I to do? I am powerless either to stop loving, now I have begun, or to follow my love any further. O if only I may be allowed to see those beloved features once again, and to tell the story of my grief in her presence! Perhaps she is not made of unyielding adamant:[89] it is possible that she may not be deaf[90] to my prayers. Believe me, no one has ever fallen in love in such an unlucky way: I may be chronicled as the first and only example! Spare me, I beg you. After all, you are the winged god of tender love, so do not let your actions be at odds with your office. Child of the goddess, you may be sure that I dread your bow now: you are mighty with your arrows, and no less so with your fire. Your altars shall smoke with my offerings,[97] and you alone shall be supreme to me among the gods. Take away my madness, then—but no, do not take it away! I don't know why, but every lover is miserable in a way which is somehow delightful. Only be gracious enough to grant that, if any girl is ever to be mine in the future, one arrow may pierce both our hearts and make them love.

# 23 At a Vacation Exercise in the College, part Latin, part English

*Date.* Aug.? 1628. The Latin part of this entertainment consists of an *Oratio* on the theme *Exercitationes nonnunquam ludicras philosophiae studiis non obesse* (That sometimes light-hearted entertainments are not prejudicial to philosophic studies), and a *Prolusio*, full of dirty jokes and personal references to members of the audience. *Oratio* and *Prolusio* were printed together as *Prolusio VI* (Columbia xii 204–47; Yale i 265–86) in the 1674 volume of *Epistolae Familiares* and *Prolusiones*. The heading of the *Oratio–In feriis aestivis Collegii* (In the summer vacation of the College), and the words *Anno aetatis 19* prefixed to *Vacation Exercise* in *1673*, show that the performance was in the summer vacation of 1628, which extended from July until early October.

*Publication.* First printed in *1673* (which misprints 'daintest' for 'daintiest' in *14* and 'hollowed' for 'hallowed' in *98*): there is a note in the *1673 Errata* to the effect that *Vacation Exercise* is misplaced and 'should have come in' between *Fair Infant* and *Passion*.

*Modern criticism.* Allen 14–16 points out the remarkable similarity between *Vacation Exercise 29–52* and a passage in *Prolusio III* (Columbia xii 169–71; Yale i 246–7), and derives both from M.'s reading of the *Corpus Hermeticum* xi 20b.

### *The Latin Speeches ended, the English thus began*

Hail native language, that by sinews weak
Didst move my first endeavouring tongue to speak,
And mad'st imperfect words with childish trips,
Half unpronounced, slide through my infant lips,
5    Driving dumb silence from the portal door,
Where he had mutely sat two years before:
Here I salute thee and thy pardon ask,
That now I use thee in my latter task:
Small loss it is that thence can come unto thee,
10   I know my tongue but little grace can do thee.
Thou need'st not be ambitious to be first,
Believe me I have thither packed the worst:
And, if it happen as I did forecast,
The daintiest dishes shall be served up last.
15   I pray thee then deny me not thy aid
For this same small neglect that I have made;
But haste thee straight to do me once a pleasure,
And from thy wardrobe bring thy chiefest treasure;
Not those new-fangled toys, and trimming slight

¶ 23. *1. Hail*] M. greets his native language because he is now turning from the Latin part of the entertainment to the English.

*5.* Sylvester has 'dumb silence' (Du Bartas 16).

*12. thither*] into the Latin part.

*14.* Cp. *Richard II* I iii 68.

*18. wardrobe*] M. continues the conceit of language as supplier of clothes in 'trimming' (19), 'robes . . . attire' (21), 'naked . . . array' (23–6) and 'clothe' (32).

20  Which takes our late fantastics with delight,
    But cull those richest robes, and gayest attire
    Which deepest spirits, and choicest wits desire:
    I have some naked thoughts that rove about
    And loudly knock to have their passage out;
25  And weary of their place do only stay
    Till thou hast decked them in thy best array;
    That so they may without suspect or fears
    Fly swiftly to this fair assembly's ears;
    Yet I had rather, if I were to choose,
30  Thy service in some graver subject use,
    Such as may make thee search thy coffers round,
    Before thou clothe my fancy in fit sound:
    Such where the deep transported mind may soar
    Above the wheeling poles, and at heaven's door
35  Look in, and see each blissful deity
    How he before the thunderous throne doth lie,
    Listening to what unshorn Apollo sings
    To the touch of golden wires, while Hebe brings
    Immortal nectar to her kingly sire:
40  Then passing through the spheres of watchful fire,
    And misty regions of wide air next under,

*20. late fantastics*] W. J. Harvey, *N & Q* n.s. iv (1957) 523–4 thinks this refers to M.'s poetic contemporaries at Cambridge like Thomas Randolph, who mingled metaphysical and Jonsonian strains in their verse. M., in opposing 'richest robes' (a style opulent, decorative and probably Spenserian) to a style which delights in 'new-fangled toys' (i.e. 'new turns of wit'–allowing for the literary sense of 'toy', *OED* sb. 3) but has 'slight' trimming (i.e. is comparatively bare), is perhaps glancing at the cult of 'strong lines'.

*29–52.* See headnote. Du Bartas 166–7 has a similar passage on the soul's flight, probably also deriving from Hermes.

*34–5. wheeling poles*] As in *PL*, M. represents heaven as above the ten spheres of the Ptolemaic universe: the 'poles' are the extremities of the axis of each sphere in this universe. In Du Bartas 658 Urania tells of her ability to transport human-kind 'above the *Poles*' to see 'All th'entercourse of the *Celestiall Court*'.

*37. unshorn*] A classical epithet for Apollo, used by Homer, *Il.* xx 39, Ovid, *Tristia* III i 60 and Horace, *Odes* I xxi 2.

*38. Hebe*] daughter of Zeus and Hera, cup-bearer to the gods, and goddess of youth.

*40. watchful fire*] Plato, *Timaeus* 38c says that sun, moon and planets were created to guard the numbers of time. Ovid has *vigiles flammas, Ars Am.* iii 463.

And hills of snow and lofts of piled thunder,
May tell at length how green-eyed Neptune raves,
In heaven's defiance mustering all his waves;
45  Then sing of secret things that came to pass
When beldam Nature in her cradle was;
And last of kings and queens and heroes old,
Such as the wise Demodocus once told
In solemn songs at king Alcinous' feast,
50  While sad Ulysses' soul and all the rest
Are held with his melodious harmony
In willing chains and sweet captivity.
But fie my wandering Muse how thou dost stray!
Expectance calls thee now another way,
55  Thou knowest it must be now thy only bent
To keep in compass of thy predicament:
Then quick about thy purposed business come,
That to the next I may resign my room.

*Then* ENS *is represented as Father of the Predicaments his
ten Sons, whereof the eldest stood for* SUBSTANCE *with his
Canons, which* ENS *thus speaking, explains.*

Good luck befriend thee Son; for at thy birth
60  The faëry ladies danced upon the hearth;
Thy drowsy nurse hath sworn she did them spy
Come tripping to the room where thou didst lie;

*42.* Cp. Sylvester (Du Bartas 354): 'Cellars of winde, and Shops of Sulphury Thunder'.

*43. green-eyed*] The eyes of Proteus in Virgil, *Georg.* iv 451 are 'ablaze with grey-green light'.

*48-52.* In Homer, *Od.* viii 521-2 Odysseus weeps as he listens to the bard Demodocus sing of the Trojan war at the court of Alcinous, king of the Phaeacians.

*52.* An echo of Sylvester (Du Bartas[2] 997) 'The willing Chaines of my Captivitie'.

*53.* Cp. Horace, *Odes* III iii 70: *quo, Musa, tendis?*

*59. Son*] Towards the end of the Latin *Prolusio* (see headnote) M. as 'father' of the ceremonies gives to his ten 'sons' (fellow-students taking part in the entertainment) names corresponding to the Categories or Predicaments of Aristotle: Substance, Quantity, Quality, Relation, Place, Time, Posture, State, Action and Passivity. The first he addresses is Substance. To Aristotle Primary Substance is exemplified by a visible, individual man (see *Categories* 3b 10), but to M., the Platonist, the visible world is removed from the reality of eternal Forms, which cannot be seen (cp. *Republic* v 474-510). He therefore mocks Aristotle's Substance by declaring it invisible.

And sweetly singing round about thy bed
Strew all their blessings on thy sleeping head.
65 She heard them give thee this, that thou shouldst still
From eyes of mortals walk invisible,
Yet there is something that doth force my fear,
For once it was my dismal hap to hear
A Sibyl old, bow-bent with crooked age,
70 That far events full wisely could presage,
And in time's long and dark prospective glass
Foresaw what future days should bring to pass,
Your son, said she, (nor can you it prevent)
Shall subject be to many an accident.
75 O'er all his brethren he shall reign as king,
Yet every one shall make him underling,
And those that cannot live from him asunder
Ungratefully shall strive to keep him under,
In worth and excellence he shall outgo them,
80 Yet being above them, he shall be below them;
From others he shall stand in need of nothing,
Yet on his brothers shall depend for clothing.
To find a foe it shall not be his hap,
And peace shall lull him in her flow'ry lap;
85 Yet shall he live in strife, and at his door
Devouring war shall never cease to roar:
Yea it shall be his natural property
To harbour those that are at enmity.
What power, what force, what mighty spell, if not
90 Your learned hands, can loose this Gordian knot?

*69. Sibyl*] prophetess.

*71. prospective glass*] Magic crystal for foreseeing events.

*74. accident*] Playing on the senses, 'calamity' and 'one of the nine Categories after Substance'.

*75–6.* Substance is first of the Categories (hence 'king'), but 'the primary substances most of all merit that name, since they underlie all other things,' Aristotle, *Categories* 2b 15.

*77.* Cp. 'And were there no primary substance, nought else could so much as exist', *Categories* 2b 5.

*83.* Cp. 'Substances never have contraries', *Categories* 3b 25.

*85–8.* Cp. 'But what is most characteristic of substance appears to be this: that, although it remains notwithstanding, numerically one and the same, it is capable of being the recipient of contrary qualifications', *Categories* 4a 10.

*90. loose this Gordian knot*] untangle Aristotle's theory. The knot was tied by the Phrygian king Gordius: the oracle declared that whoever undid it would rule Asia. Alexander cut it.

*The next* QUANTITY *and* QUALITY, *spake in prose, then*
RELATION *was called by his name.*

Rivers arise; whether thou be the son,
Of utmost Tweed, or Ouse, or gulfy Dun,
Or Trent, who like some earth-born giant spreads
His thirty arms along the indented meads,
95   Or sullen Mole that runneth underneath,
Or Severn swift, guilty of maiden's death,
Or rocky Avon, or of sedgy Lea,
Or coaly Tyne, or ancient hallowed Dee,
Or Humber loud that keeps the Scythian's name,
100  Or Medway smooth, or royal towered Thame.

*The rest was prose.*

## 24 *Elegia quinta. In adventum veris*
### [Elegy V. On the Coming of Spring]

*Date.* Spring 1629. Headed *Anno aetatis 20* in *1645.*
*Publication. 1645 (30.* perennis]quotannis   *66.* Tenario]Taenario   *106.*
Litus]Littus   *110.* Virgineos]Virgineas ) and *1673* (the text followed here,
but corrected in these instances:   *74.* titulos]ticulos   *115.* Navita]
Natvia ).

*91. Rivers*] The two sons of Sir John Rivers of Chafford, Kent, were
admitted to Christ's College 10 May 1628. One of them plays the part of
Relation.
*92. gulfy*] full of eddies or whirlpools.
*93–4.* Drayton, *Polyolbion* xii 546–54, affirms that the Trent has thirty
tributaries and that its name means 'thirty'.   *earth-born giant*] See
*Natur* 59*n* (p. 64 above).
*92–100.* M.'s catalogue of rivers imitates those in Drayton's *Polyolbion*
and Spenser, *F.Q.* IV xi 20–47.
*95.* The subterranean course of the Mole, in Surrey, is described by Drayton,
*Polyolbion* xvii 59 and Spenser, *F.Q.* IV xi 32.
*96. maiden's*] Sabrina's (see *Comus* 825–30*n*, p. 218).
*98. coaly*] In *Polyolbion* xxix 122–5 Drayton's Tyne boasts of its coal trade.
*hallowed*] Drayton refers to the 'hallowed *Dee*' (x 215) and explains (iv
201–4) that it was thought to change its fords, and that this was regarded
as a prophetic omen.
*99. Scythian's name*] Geoffrey of Monmouth relates (*British History* II ii)
that the Humber takes its name from the Scythian king, Humber, who
was drowned in it after being defeated by Locrine and his brother Camber.
M. (*History of Britain*, Columbia x 15), Drayton (*Polyolbion* viii 45–6) and
Spenser (*F.Q.* II x 16 and IV xi 38) repeat the story.

The subject is a very common one among neo-Latin poets of the Renaissance. For other examples see *Delitiae CC Italorum Poetarum* (Frankfurt 1608) i 330 [Balbi], 468 [Buonamico], 1118 [Frascatoro], ii 116 [Navagero], 714 [Sannazaro], 990 [Tito Strozi], 1459 [Zanchi]; *Delitiae C Poetarum Gallorum* (Frankfurt 1609) i 505 [Beaucaire], ii 401 [Lect]; Buchanan *Poemata* (Leyden 1628) 315; Joannes Secundus, *Opera* (Leyden 1619) 58.

> In se perpetuo Tempus revolubile gyro
>     Iam revocat zephyros vere tepente novos.
> Induiturque brevem Tellus reparata iuventam,
>     Iamque soluta gelu dulce virescit humus.
> 5   Fallor? an et nobis redeunt in carmina vires,
>     Ingeniumque mihi munere veris adest?
> Munere veris adest, iterumque vigescit ab illo
>     (Quis putet) atque aliquod iam sibi poscit opus.
> Castalis ante oculos, bifidumque cacumen oberrat,
> 10  Et mihi Pyrenen somnia nocte ferunt.
> Concitaque arcano fervent mihi pectora motu,
>     Et furor, et sonitus me sacer intus agit.
> Delius ipse venit, video Peneide lauro
>     Implicitos crines, Delius ipse venit.
> 15  Iam mihi mens liquidi raptatur in ardua coeli,
>     Perque vagas nubes corpore liber eo.
> Perque umbras, perque antra feror penetralia vatum,
>     Et mihi fana patent interiora Deum.
> Intuiturque animus toto quid agatur Olympo,
> 20  Nec fugiunt oculos Tartara caeca meos.
> Quid tam grande sonat distento spiritus ore?
>     Quid parit haec rabies, quic sacer iste furor?
> Ver mihi, quod dedit ingenium, cantabitur illo;
>     Profuerint isto reddita dona modo.
> 25  Iam Philomela tuos foliis adoperta novellis
>     Instituis modulos, dum silet omne nemus.
> Urbe ego, tu sylva simul incipiamus utrique,
>     Et simul adventum veris uterque canat.

¶ 24. *9. Castalis . . . cacumen*] Cp. *Elegia IV* 29–32n (p. 55).

*10. Pyrenen*] Pirene, a fountain in the citadel of Corinth which sprang from Pegasus' hoof-mark, was sacred to the Muses.

*13. Peneide lauro*] Ovid, *Met.* i 452–559, tells how Apollo loved Daphne, daughter of the river-god Peneus, and how when her lover pursued her she prayed for help to her father and was turned into a laurel. Apollo vowed to wear laurel leaves in his hair from then on.

*25-6. Philomela . . . nemus*] Cp. *Sonnet I* 1–2 (p. 90). The rape of Philomela by Tereus and her transformation into a nightingale are described by Ovid, *Met.* vi 424–674.

Veris io rediere vices, celebremus honores
30    Veris, et hoc subeat Musa perennis opus.
Iam sol Aethiopas fugiens Tithoniaque arva,
Flectit ad Arctoas aurea lora plagas.
Est breve noctis iter, brevis est mora noctis opacae
Horrida cum tenebris exulat illa suis.
35    Iamque Lycaonius plaustrum caeleste Bootes
Non longa sequitur fessus ut ante via,
Nunc etiam solitas circum Iovis atria toto
Excubias agitant sydera rara polo.
Nam dolus, et caedes, et vis cum nocte recessit,
40    Neve Giganteum Dii timuere scelus.
Forte aliquis scopuli recubans in vertice pastor,
Roscida cum primo sole rubescit humus,
Hac, ait, hac certe caruisti nocte puella
Phoebe tua, celeres quae retineret equos.
45    Laeta suas repetit sylvas, pharetramque resumit
Cynthia, Luciferas ut videt alta rotas,
Et tenues ponens radios gaudere videtur
Officium fieri tam breve fratris ope.
Desere, Phoebus ait, thalamos Aurora seniles,
50    Quid iuvat effoeto procubuisse toro?
Te manet Aeolides viridi venator in herba,
Surge, tuos ignes altus Hymettus habet.

30. *perennis*] Salmasius, *Responsio* (1660) 5, picked on the false quantity in
1645 (*quotannis*, with last syllable short) and M. altered the word in *1673*.
31–2. *Aethiopas . . . Tithoniaque arva . . . Arctoas*] The Ethiopians here
represent the equator and Tithonus' fields the east (Tithonus was husband
to Aurora, the dawn-goddess). After the vernal equinox the sun rises north
of east. *Arctos* is the constellation of the Bear, hence the adjective *arctous*,
northern.
35–6. *Lycaonius*] northern. An Ovidian adjective (cp. *Tristia* III ii 2) formed
from Lycaon, king of Arcadia, whose daughter, Callisto, was changed to
a she-bear by Juno and raised to heaven by Jove as the constellation of the
Great Bear. *Bootes*, another northern constellation, was called the Bear-
keeper and also the Waggoner, since another name for the Great Bear was
the Waggon (*plaustrum*). Starnes and Talbert 262 note that in Calepine's
*Dictionarium* (1609 edn), *s.v. Bootes*, he is given as the son of Jove by Callisto.
40. *Giganteum . . . scelus*] See Q *Nov* 174*n* (p. 43).
46. *Cynthia*] The moon-goddess Diana, called Cynthia from Mount
Cynthus on the island of Delos where she was born.
49–52. Aurora's husband Tithonus was granted immortality by the gods,
but not eternal youth: hence his old age and impotence, and Aurora's love
for Cephalus, son of Aeolus (called *Aeolides* by Ovid, *Met.* vii 672), whom

Flava verecundo dea crimen in ore fatetur,
Et matutinos ocyus urget equos.
55 Exuit invisam Tellus rediviva senectam,
Et cupit amplexus Phoebe subire tuos;
Et cupit, et digna est, quid enim formosius illa,
Pandit ut omniferos luxuriosa sinus,
Atque Arabum spirat messes, et ab ore venusto
60 Mitia cum Paphiis fundit amoma rosis.
Ecce coronatur sacro frons ardua luco,
Cingit ut Idaeam pinea turris Opim;
Et vario madidos intexit flore capillos,
Floribus et visa est posse placere suis.
65 Floribus effusos ut erat redimita capillos
Tenario placuit diva Sicana Deo.
Aspice Phoebe tibi faciles hortantur amores,
Mellitasque movent flamina verna preces.
Cinnamea Zephyrus leve plaudit odorifer ala,
70 Blanditiasque tibi ferre videntur aves.
Nec sine dote tuos temeraria quaerit amores
Terra, nec optatos poscit egena toros,
Alma salutiferum medicos tibi gramen in usus
Praebet, et hinc titulos adiuvat ipsa tuos.
75 Quod si te pretium, si te fulgentia tangunt
Munera, (muneribus saepe coemptus Amor)
Illa tibi ostentat quascunque sub aequore vasto,
Et superiniectis montibus abdit opes.
Ah quoties cum tu clivoso fessus Olympo
80 In vespertinas praecipitaris aquas,
Cur te, inquit, cursu languentem Phoebe diurno
Hesperiis recipit caerula mater aquis?

she first saw spreading nets for deer on Mount Hymettus, as Ovid describes,
*Met.* vii 700–13.
60. *Paphiis*] Paphian, from Paphos, a city in Cyprus sacred to Venus.
62. *Idaeam . . . Opim*] Cybele, a Phrygian goddess (*Idaeus* means Phrygian,
from Ida, a mountain in Phrygia near Troy), was worshipped in Rome as
Ops, goddess of plenty. Ida was crowned with pines (Virgil, *Aen.* x 230)
and the pine was sacred to Cybele because, as Ovid relates, *Met.* x 103–5,
her love, Attis, was turned into a pine. Ovid explains that Cybele wears
a turreted crown because she first gave towers to cities (*Fast.* iv 219–21).
65–6. *Tenario . . . Deo*] Pluto, so called because one of the mouths of hell
was a cave in the promontory of Taenarus in Laconia. His rape of Proserpina
when she was gathering flowers near Enna, a city in Sicily (called *Sicania*
by Ovid) is described in *Met.* v 385–408.
74. *titulos . . . tuos*] Phoebus was god of healing and father of Aesculapius.
79. *clivoso . . . Olympo*] Echoes Ovid, *Fast.* iii 415: *clivosum . . . Olympum.*

Quid tibi cum Tethy? Quid cum Tartesside lympha,
    Dia quid immundo perluis ora salo?
85   Frigora Phoebe mea melius captabis in umbra,
    Huc ades, ardentes imbue rore comas.
Mollior egelida veniet tibi somnus in herba,
    Huc ades, et gremio lumina pone meo.
Quaque iaces circum mulcebit lene susurrans
90    Aura per humentes corpora fusa rosas.
Nec me (crede mihi) terrent Semeleia fata,
    Nec Phaetonteo fumidus axis equo;
Cum tu Phoebe tuo sapientius uteris igni,
    Huc ades et gremio lumina pone meo.
95   Sic Tellus lasciva suos suspirat amores;
    Matris in exemplum caetera turba ruunt.
Nunc etenim toto currit vagus orbe Cupido,
    Languentesque fovet solis ab igne faces.
Insonuere novis lethalia cornua nervis,
100   Triste micant ferro tela corusca novo.
Iamque vel invictam tentat superasse Dianam,
    Quaeque sedet sacro Vesta pudica foco.
Ipsa senescentem reparat Venus annua formam,
    Atque iterum tepido creditur orta mari.
105  Marmoreas iuvenes clamant Hymenaee per urbes,
    Litus io Hymen, et cava saxa sonant.
Cultior ille venit tunicaque decentior apta,
    Puniceum redolet vestis odora crocum.
Egrediturque frequens ad amoeni gaudia veris
110   Virgineos auro cincta puella sinus.

---

83. *Tethy*] Tethys (the *caerula mater* of l. 82), a sea goddess; Hesiod explains (*Theog.* 337–62) that she was mother of the rivers. The form of the line is Ovidian; see e.g. *Her.* vi 47–8: *Quid mihi cum Minyis, quid cum Dodonide pinu? | quid tibi cum patria, navita Tiphy, mea?*

91. *Semeleia fata*] Semele was daughter of Cadmus. She was seduced by Jupiter and tricked by the jealous Juno into asking him to come to her in his divine glory: when he did so she was consumed by fire. Ovid tells the story, *Met.* iii 253–315.

92. *Phaetonteo . . . equo*] See *Natur* 25n (p. 62).

101–2. Diana, the moon goddess, was patroness of virginity. Vesta was goddess of the household; the Vestal virgins were her priestesses.

105–6. Hymen was god of marriage. The refrains of two of Catullus's marriage songs (lxi and lxii) are *io Hymen Hymenaee* and *Hymen o Hymenaee, Hymen ades o Hymenaee!*

108. *Puniceum . . . crocum*] Hymen's colour was yellow. Ovid introduces him clad in *croceo . . . amictu* (*Met.* x 1–2) and has *punicei . . . croci* (*Fast.* v 318).

Votum est cuique suum, votum est tamen omnibus
unum,
Ut sibi quem cupiat, det Cytherea virum.
Nunc quoque septena modulatur arundine pastor,
Et sua quae iungat carmina Phyllis habet.
*115* Navita nocturno placat sua sidera cantu,
Delphinasque leves ad vada summa vocat.
Iupiter ipse alto cum coniuge ludit Olympo,
Convocat et famulos ad sua festa Deos.
Nunc etiam Satyri cum sera crepuscula surgunt,
*120* Pervolitant celeri florea rura choro,
Sylvanusque sua cyparissi fronde revinctus,
Semicaperque Deus, semideusque caper.
Quaeque sub arboribus Dryades latuere vetustis
Per iuga, per solos expatiantur agros.
*125* Per sata luxuriat fruticetaque Maenalius Pan,
Vix Cybele mater, vix sibi tuta Ceres,
Atque aliquam cupidus praedatur Oreada Faunus,

---

*114. Phyllis*] A common name for shepherdesses in pastoral, used by Virgil,
*Ecl.* iii 78.
*116.* Pliny IX viii 24–8 holds that dolphins are susceptible to music and
can be charmed by singing: he tells several anecdotes to prove the point.
*119. sera crepuscula*] The phrase is Ovid's, *Met.* i 219.
*121. Sylvanusque . . . revinctus*] Sylvanus, the Roman god of uncultivated
land, was identified with the Greek satyrs. Servius, in his note to Virgil,
*Georg.* i 20, tells how Sylvanus loved a boy called Cyparissus, who died
of grief at the loss of a pet hind. The god turned the dead boy into a cypress,
and wears leaves of this tree in remembrance.
*122.* An imitation of Ovid, *Ars Am.* ii 24 *semibovemque virum, semivirumque
bovem.* F. R. B. Godolphin, *MP* xxxvii (1940) 356, points to the story in
Seneca's *Controversiae* II ii 12, of Ovid being asked by his friends to cancel
three lines from his poems which they will name. He agrees on condition
that he may first name three lines which shall not be cancelled. It turns out
that Ovid and his friends have the same three lines in mind, of which
*Ars Am.* ii 24 is one. Godolphin calls M.'s line 'the most striking example
of wit' in his Latin poems. J. Goode, *TLS* (13 Aug. 1931) 621, quotes from
Sannazaro's Latin elegies *semideusque caper, semicaperque Deus.* Ovid has
*semicaperque deus, Fast.* iv 752.
*123. Dryades*] wood nymphs.
*125. Maenalius*] Maenalus is a mountain in Arcadia, which was sacred to
Pan.
*126. Cybele*] See l. *62n.* Her daughter *Ceres* was goddess of agriculture.
*127. Oreada*] An Oread was a mountain nymph.     *Faunus*] protecting
deity of agriculture and shepherds.

Consulit in trepidos dum sibi nympha pedes,
Iamque latet, latitansque cupit male tecta videri,
*130*    Et fugit, et fugiens pervelit ipsa capi.
Dii quoque non dubitant caelo praeponere sylvas,
Et sua quisque sibi numina lucus habet.
Et sua quisque diu sibi numina lucus habeto,
Nec vos arborea dii precor ite domo.
*135*  Te referant miseris te Iupiter aurea terris
Saecla, quid ad nimbos aspera tela redis?
Tu saltem lente rapidos age Phoebe iugales
Qua potes, et sensim tempora veris eant.
Brumaque productas tarde ferat hispida noctes,
*140*    Ingruat et nostro serior umbra polo.

Time, turning back upon his own tracks in a never-ending circuit, is now
calling the fresh zephyrs once again as the spring grows warm. The Earth
has recovered and is decking herself in her brief youth, and now that the
frost has melted away the ground is growing pleasantly green. Am I imagining
things, or are my powers of song coming back as well? Is inspiration here
again as a gift from the spring? It *is* here again as a gift from the spring!
With the spring it is beginning to bloom again (who would have thought it?)
and already it is clamouring for something to do. The Castalian fountain
and the forked peak[9] swim before my eyes, and at night my dreams bring
Pirene[10] to me. My soul is deeply stirred and glows with its mysterious
impulse, and I am driven on by poetic frenzy and the sacred sound which
fills my brain. Apollo himself is coming–I can see his hair wreathed in
Penean laurel[13]–Apollo himself is coming. Now my mind is whirled up to
the heights of the bright, clear sky: freed from my body, I move among the
wandering clouds. I am carried through shadows and caves, the secret
haunts of the poets, and the innermost sanctuaries of the gods are open to
me. I see in my mind's eye what is going on all over Olympus, and the
unseen depths of Tartarus do not escape my eyes. What song is my spirit
singing so loudly with wide-open mouth? What is being born of this madness,
this sacred frenzy? The spring, which gave me inspiration, shall be the
theme of the song it inspires: in this way her gifts will be repaid with interest.

You are already beginning your warbling song, Philomela,[25] hidden
among the unfolding leaves, while all the grove is silent.[26] I in the city,
you in the woods, let us both begin together and both together sing the
coming of the spring. Hurrah! the springtime is here again! Let us hymn
the praises of spring; let the never-dying[30] Muse take up the task. Now the
sun is running away from the Ethiopians[31] and from Tithonus' fields, and
is turning his golden reins towards the northern regions.[32] The course
of the night is short, short is the night's dark stay; wild night and his darkness
are banished. Now Lycaonian Boötes[35] does not plod wearily down a long
road behind his skyey waggon, as once he did. Now in the whole sky there

*129–30.* The nymph's behaviour is based on that of Galatea in Virgil, *Ecl.*
iii 65, who runs off to hide from Damoetas in the willows, but hopes to
be seen first.

are now only a few stars to patrol and keep the usual watch around Jove's halls. For fraud, murder and violence have gone away with the night, and the gods are not afraid of the giants' wickedness.[40]

Perhaps some shepherd, stretched out on the top of a crag while the dewy earth grows red in the light of the dawn, exclaims: 'You certainly did not have your girl with you tonight, Phoebus, to delay your swift horses!' When from on high Cynthia[46] sees the wheels of the sun's chariot, she goes back joyfully to her woods and takes up her quiver again, and seems to be glad as she lays her weak moonbeams aside that her own job is made so short by her brother's help. 'Come out of that old man's[49] bedroom, Aurora,' shouts Phoebus, 'what's the use of lying in bed with someone who's impotent? Aeolides, the hunter, is waiting for you on the green grass. Get up! The man you love is on high Hymettus.'[52] The golden-haired goddess acknowledges her guilt by her blushing face, and urges on the horses of dawn to greater speed.

The reviving Earth casts off her detested old age and yearns, Phoebus, for your embraces. She yearns for them, and she deserves them too, for what is more beautiful than she as she voluptuously bares her breasts, mother of all things, and breathes out Arabian spice-harvests and pours Paphian[60] roses and mild perfume from her lovely lips. Look! Her high forehead is crowned with a sacred grove, just as Idaean Ops is ringed with a turret of pine-trees;[62] she has twined many-coloured flowers among her dewy hair, and with her flowers she seems fit to attract the Taenarian god[65] as the Sicanian goddess once attracted him when her flowing hair was plaited with flowers. Look, Phoebus, easily won love is calling to you, and the spring breezes bear honied appeals. Fragrant Zephyrus lightly claps his cinnamon-scented wings and the birds seem to carry blandishments to you. The Earth is not so indiscreet as to seek your love without offering a dowry in return: she is no beggar-maid, praying for a desirable match. She is bountiful, and supplies you with health-giving herbs for use in medicine, and so does something on her own account to increase your glory.[74] If money and glittering gifts touch your heart (love is often bought with gifts), she lays before your eyes all the worth she keeps hidden away under the huge ocean and the heaped-up mountains. Ah, how often she cries out when you plunge into the sea at sunset, tired out by heaven's steep path,[79] 'Phoebus, why should the sky-blue mother take you into her western waves when you are exhausted by your daily journey? What have you got to do with Tethys[83] or the waters of Tartessus? Why do you wash your heavenly face in dirty salt water? It will be more pleasant for you to seek coolness in my shades, Phoebus; come here, and bathe your gleaming hair in dew. You will find softer sleep on the cool grass: come here, and lay your eyes against my breast. The breeze, murmuring gently around you where you lie, will soothe our bodies, stretched out on dewy roses. Semele's fate[91] does not frighten me, I assure you, nor does the chariot which Phaëthon's horses[92] caused to smoke. Come here, and lay your eyes against my breast, and you will put your fire to better use.'

This is the way lascivious Earth breathes out her passion, and all the other creatures are quick to follow their mother's example. For now wandering Cupid speeds through the whole world and renews his dying torch in the flames of the sun. His deadly bow twangs with new strings and his bright arrows, freshly tipped, gleam balefully. Now he tries to subdue even the unconquerable Diana,[101] and chaste Vesta[102] as she sits by her holy hearth. Venus herself, having lasted out the year, is restoring her waning beauty, and seems to have risen again from the warm sea. Through marble cities the young men are shouting 'Hymenaeus!'[105]–the sea-shore and the hollow rocks resound with 'Io Hymen!'[106] Hymen arrives, all decked out and very spruce in his traditional costume; his fragrant gown has the scent of tawny saffron.[108] The girls, with their virgin breasts bound about with gold, run out in crowds to the joys of the lovely springtime. Each one has her own prayer, but all their prayers are the same: that Cytherea will give her the man of her desire. And now the shepherd plays on his pipe of seven reeds, and Phyllis[114] has songs of her own to add to his. At night the sailor sings to his stars to make them gentle, and calls up nimble dolphins[116] to the surface of the sea. Jupiter himself frolics on high Olympus with his wife, and summons even the gods who wait on him to his feast. Now, as the evening twilight[119] falls, the satyrs flit through the flowery meadows in a swift band, and with them Sylvanus,[121] a god half-goat, a goat half-god,[122] crowned with leaves from his favourite tree, the cypress. And the Dryads[123] who lay hidden beneath the ancient trees now wander about on hill-tops and through lonely fields. Maenalian[125] Pan skips through grain-fields and thickets, mother Cybele and Ceres[126] are hardly safe from him. Lustful Faunus catches one of the Oreads,[127] but the nymph saves herself on trembling feet: now she hides, but not very well, and even as she hides she hopes to be seen;[129] she runs away, but as she runs she is anxious to be overtaken.[130] The gods, too, unhesitatingly prefer these woods to their heavens, and each grove has its own particular deities.

Long may each grove have its own particular deities: do not leave your homes among the trees, gods, I beseech you. May the golden age bring you back, Jove, to this wretched world! Why go back to your cruel weapons in the clouds? At any rate, Phoebus, drive your swift team as slowly as you can, and let the passing of the springtime be gradual. May rough winter be tardy in bringing us his dreary nights, and may it be late in the day when shadows assail our sky.

# 25 Sonnet I

*Date.* Spring 1629? There is no firm evidence for dating, but the similarity between *Sonnet I* 1–2 and *Elegia V* 25–6 suggests nearness in date.
*Publication.* 1645 and 1673 (no significant variants).
*Modern criticism.* J. L. Lievsay, *Renaissance Papers* (1959) 36–45, suggests that M., in his repeated references to the nightingale (*Elegia V* 25–8, *Il Penseroso* 55–64, *Comus* 233–5, 566, *PL* iii 37–40, etc.), came to consider this bird–with its associations of chastity (Philomela), opposition to brute force (Tereus), loneliness and nocturnal song–as the symbol of his own poetic voice.

*M.'s sonnets: style and versification.* M. wrote twenty-three sonnets. The first six (25 'O nightingale', and 27, 28 and 30–32, the Italian sonnets) are love poems and were written in 1629, by which time the vogue of the sonnet in England had been over for thirty years. Most of the other sonnets belong to the period 1642–55. Three of them—77, to Fairfax (1648), 81, to Cromwell (1652) and 82 to Vane (1652)—are addressed to great political figures of M.'s day. Probably Tasso's *Sonneti Eroici* gave M. the idea of celebrating contemporary leaders in sonnets of epic grandeur. However, the tone of these sonnets, like that of the three sonnets to young friends—87, to Edward Lawrence (1653) and 89–90, to Cyriack Skinner (1655)—is markedly Horatian (see the notes to these poems).

In Dec. 1629 M. bought a copy of Giovanni Della Casa's *Rime e Prose* (1563), now in the New York Public Library (French i 205). Marginal notes and text corrections in M.'s hand bear witness to the thoroughness of his reading: he also copied into it another Della Casa sonnet from the 1623 edition. Della Casa, like Bembo, from whose experiments he profited, gave his sonnets a complex and artificial word-order by devices such as inversion, interpolation and suspension of grammar, in order to create the impression of an intricate syntax akin to Latin. By multiplying pauses within the lines–manipulating clauses and sentences to chop across the verse divisions–he made his sonnets sound abrupt, uncompromising and densely meaningful. To allow opportunities for more elongated syntactical intricacies he planned the development of ideas within the sonnet so that it struck through the formal limits of quatrains and tercets and flowed across the octave-sestet boundary, where Petrarch and his followers had always observed a pause. At the same time, beneath this elaborately irregular surface, he retained an effect of inner balance by frequent pairing of adjectives, nouns and verbs, by antithesis and parallelism, and by other duplex structures. M.'s sonnets imitate these techniques, and at times, as Prince (106) remarks, citing 88 *On the late Massacre in Piedmont* (1655), they carry Della Casa's innovations further than any poet had done in Italian. In these later sonnets M. is clearly developing his epic style.

M.'s versification follows the Italian metrical scheme (as opposed to the English or Shakespearean) of two quatrains and two tercets. His quatrains always rhyme abba abba: this was called the 'enclosed order' and was favoured by Petrarch who, however, along with other Italian poets, sometimes used alternate rhymes in his quatrains. The rhyming of M.'s tercets, as in the Italian poets, is much more varied. Most frequently he uses well-established Petrarchan schemes: cdc dcd in seven sonnets, cde cde in five, and cde dce in four. In four sonnets he employs a couplet-ending, which Petrarch never does unless there is a rhyme with the first line of the sestet: cdc dee in 28, 30 and 31 (a scheme preferred by Wyatt, but previously used, as Smart (17–19) notes, by the fourteenth century Italian poet Fazio degli Uberti, and mentioned in Minturno's *Arte Poetica*); and cdd cee in 81 (a scheme used by Uberti and also by Tasso). In two of the remaining three sonnets M. introduces a couplet in lines 10 and 11: 77, to Fairfax, has tercets rhyming cdd cdc; and 71 'I did but prompt', a sonnet with only three rhymes, has a variant of this, cbb cbc. 87, to Lawrence, introduces a couplet in lines *12* and *13*, rhyming its tercets cdc eed.

O nightingale, that on yon bloomy spray
Warblest at eve, when all the woods are still,
Thou with fresh hope the lover's heart dost fill,
While the jolly hours lead on propitious May,
5    Thy liquid notes that close the eye of day,
First heard before the shallow cuckoo's bill
Portend success in love; O if Jove's will
Have linked that amorous power to thy soft lay,
Now timely sing, ere the rude bird of hate
10    Foretell my hopeless doom in some grove nigh:
As thou from year to year hast sung too late
For my relief; yet hadst no reason why,
Whether the Muse, or Love call thee his mate,
Both them I serve, and of their train am I.

# 26 Song. On May Morning

*Date.* Spring 1629? There is no firm evidence for dating. *Song. On May Morning* has obvious similarities with *Elegia V* and may, like it, belong to spring 1629. If the order of poems in *1673* is chronologically significant (as the transference of *Vacation Exercise* to a position after *Fair Infant* in the *1673 Errata* implies), it is worth noting that *Song. On May Morning* is placed after the *Winchester Epitaph* (Apr.-May 1631) and before *Shakespeare* (of which the date, '1630', means strictly before 25 Mar. 1631). This suggests May 1631 as a possible date.

*Publication. 1645* (6. youth]youth,    7. groves]groves,    8 dale]dale, ) and *1673* (the text followed here).

Now the bright morning Star, Day's harbinger,
Comes dancing from the east, and leads with her

¶ 25. 1. Echoing Bembo, *Rime* (Venice 1564) 45: *O rosignuol, che'n queste verdi fronde*. . . .
4. *hours*] the Horae, daughters of Jupiter and Themis.
9. *bird of hate*] the cuckoo. M. probably read of the belief that it is a good omen for a lover to hear the nightingale before the cuckoo, and a bad to hear the cuckoo before the nightingale, in *The Cuckoo and the Nightingale*, printed among Chaucer's works in Speght's edition (1598) 333.
¶ 26. 1. *Day's harbinger*] Cp. Shakespeare, *Midsummer Night's Dream* III ii 380 'Aurora's harbinger'; but the exact phrase is found in R. Niccolls, *The Cuckow* (1607) p. 13: 'Daies herbinger, the bloody crested cocke'.
2. *dancing from the east*] In Spenser's dawn scene *F.Q.* I v 2, Phoebus 'came dauncing forth', and in Niccolls's *Cuckow* p. 12: 'Daies bright king came dauncing out.'

The flowery May, who from her green lap throws
The yellow cowslip, and the pale primrose.
5    Hail bounteous May that dost inspire
Mirth and youth and warm desire,
Woods and groves are of thy dressing,
Hill and dale doth boast thy blessing.
Thus we salute thee with our early song,
10  And welcome thee, and wish thee long.

# 27 Sonnet II

*Date.* Nov.–Dec. 1629? The Italian sonnets are so closely related in subject that they are probably of similar date. In *1645* and *1673* they are printed as a group before *Sonnet VII* (Dec. 1631). If the proposed interpretation of *Elegia VI* 89–90 (see p. 117) is correct; the Italian sonnets can be dated (probably late) in 1629 (see *RES* n.s. xiv (1963) 383–6).
*Publication.* *1645* (3. Bene]Ben    6. sui]suoi ) *1673* (the text followed here, but corrected in 7 where *1673* misprints a full stop after 'arco').

Donna leggiadra il cui bel nome honora
L'herbosa val di Rheno, e il nobil varco,
Bene è colui d'ogni valore scarco
Qual tuo spirto gentil non innamora,
5    Che dolcemente mostra si di fuora
De sui atti soavi giamai parco,
E i don', che son d'amor saette ed arco,
La onde l' alta tua virtù s'infiora.
Quando tu vaga parli, o lieta canti
10    Che mover possa duro alpestre legno,

*3. May . . . throws*] A probable echo of Spenser, *F.Q.* VII vii 34: 'Then came faire May, the fayrest mayd on ground, / Deckt all with dainties of her seasons pryde, / And throwing flowers out of her lap around' and of Shakespeare, *Rich. II* III iii 47 where England has a 'green lap'.
*4. pale primrose*] Cp. *Winter's Tale* IV iv 122: 'pale primroses'.
¶ 27. *1–2.* Smart 137–44 explains that these lines mean the lady was called Emilia. Emilia (deriving its name from the Via Emilia) was one of the regions into which Augustus divided Italy. In its eastern part is the 'famous ford' (*nobil varco*) of the Rubicon. Smart cites a close verbal parallel in a sonnet by the sixteenth century Italian poet Gandolfo Porrino, where the name disclosed is Lucia: *O, d'ogni riverenza e d'onor degna, / Alma mia luce, il cui bel nome onora / L'aria, la terra, e le campagne infiora, / E di salir al ciel la via c'insegna, / Luce gentil.*
*8. La*] in her eyes.

> Guardi ciascun a gli occhi, ed a gli orecchi
> L'entrata, chi di te si truova indegno;
> Gratia sola di sù gli vaglia, inanti
> Che'l disio amoroso al cuor s'invecchi.

My lady fair, whose lovely name[1] honours the grassy Reno valley and the famous ford,[2] that man must be utterly worthless who does not fall in love with your gentle spirit, which sweetly shows itself (never niggardly in bestowing soft glances or those favours which are the bows and arrows of love) there[3] where your lofty virtue blossoms. When, graceful lady, you speak or sing for joy (singing that might bring gnarled trees down from the mountains), let every man who is unworthy of you guard the approaches to his eyes and ears. Only grace from above can save him from having desire rooted in his heart for ever.

# 28 Sonnet III

*Date.* Nov.–Dec. 1629? See headnote to *Sonnet II.*
*Publication.* *1645* and *1673* (no significant variants).

> Qual in colle aspro, al imbrunir di sera
> L'avezza giovinetta pastorella
> Va bagnando l'herbetta strana e bella
> Che mal si spande a disusata spera
> 5  Fuor di sua natia alma primavera,
> Cosi amor meco insù la lingua snella
> Desta il fior novo di strania favella,
> Mentre io di te, vezzosamente altera,
> Canto, dal mio buon popol non inteso
> 10  E'l bel Tamigi cangio col bel Arno.
> Amor lo volse, ed io a l'altrui peso
> Seppi ch' Amor cosa mai volse indarno.
> Deh! foss' il mio cuor lento e'l duro seno
> A chi pianta dal ciel si buon terreno.

As on some rugged mountain at dusk a young shepherdess, used to the climate herself, waters an exotic little plant which can hardly spread its leaves in such unfamiliar surroundings, far from the mild springtime which gave it life, so on my nimble tongue love raises up the new flower of a foreign language as I sing to you, charming in your pride, and exchange the beautiful

¶ 28. *10.* M. means that he is changing from English to the Tuscan dialect of Italy. Bembo's *Prose della Volgar Lingua* (1525) had established the Tuscan writers of the fourteenth century as the source of correct literary usage (see Prince 4–13). M. again uses the Arno to represent the Tuscan language in his letter to Benedetto Buonmattei (Columbia xii 34; Yale i 30).

Thames for the beautiful Arno[10] (without my worthy fellow-countrymen understanding me at all). Love willed it, and I knew at other people's expense that Love never willed anything in vain. Ah that my sluggish heart and stony breast were as good a soil for him who sows his seed from heaven!

# 29 Canzone

*Date.* Nov.–Dec. 1629? See headnote to *Sonnet II.*
*Publication. 1645* and *1673* (no significant variants).

Prince 101, who considers this, from the point of view of the mastery of the medium, the most successful of M.'s Italian poems, remarks: 'That his technical insight was not yet complete may be gathered from his calling a *canzone* a poem which, however accomplished in achieving its desired effect, is not a *canzone*'. It is true that M.'s poem, which has only one stanza, is not a *canzone* in the strict sense in which Dante defined it in the *De Vulgar Eloquentia*, since this needs several stanzas of similar structure and rhyme scheme. But, as Dante admits (II viii), Italian poets frequently used the term more loosely, as M. does here, to cover sonnets, *ballate* and any lyrics written for music.

> Ridonsi donne e giovani amorosi
> M' accostandosi attorno, e perche scrivi,
> Perche tu scrivi in lingua ignota e strana
> Verseggiando d'amor, e come t'osi?
> 5 Dinne, se la tua speme sia mai vana,
> E de pensieri lo miglior t' arrivi;
> Cosi mi van burlando, altri rivi
> Altri lidi t' aspettan, ed altre onde
> Nelle cui verdi sponde
> 10 Spuntati ad hor, ad hor a la tua chioma
> L'immortal guiderdon d'eterne frondi
> Perche alle spalle tue soverchia soma?
> Canzon dirotti, e tu per me rispondi
> Dice mia Donna, e'l suo dir, è il mio cuore
> 15 Questa è lingua di cui si vanta Amore.

Girls and boys in love press about me, laughing, and say 'Why, O why do you write your love poems in an odd and unknown language? How do you dare to do it? Tell us, then we'll wish that you may never hope in vain, and that your dreams may come true.' They tease me and say 'There are

¶ 29. *7–12.* The boys and girls, like M. in *Sonnet III* 10, refer to languages as rivers. The *altri rivi* are presumably Latin and English, and the *soverchia soma* the difficulty of writing in Italian. His knowledge of that language was evidently imperfect, as Masson (iii 277–8) and others have noticed.

other rivers[7] and river-banks, and other waters for you, rivers by whose grassy brinks the immortal reward, the crown of unfading leaves, is already sprouting for your head. Why take this excessive load[12] upon your shoulders?'

Canzone, I will tell you, and you can answer for me. My lady says – and her word is my heart – 'This is the language on which Love prides himself'.

## 30 Sonnet IV

*Date.* Nov.–Dec. 1629? See headnote to *Sonnet II.*
*Publication.* *1645* (4. s'impiglia.]s'impiglia, ) and *1673* (the text followed here).

> Diodati, e te'l dirò con maraviglia,
>    Quel ritroso io ch'amor spreggiar soléa
>    E de suoi lacci spesso mi ridéa
>    Gia caddi, ov'huom dabben talhor s'impiglia.
> 5   Ne treccie d'oro, ne guancia vermiglia
>    M' abbaglian sì, ma sotto nova idea
>    Pellegrina bellezza che'l cuor bea,
>    Portamenti alti honesti, e nelle ciglia
> Quel sereno fulgor d' amabil nero,
> 10      Parole adorne di lingua piu d'una,
>    E'l cantar che di mezzo l'hemispero
> Traviar ben può la faticosa Luna,
>    E degli occhi suoi auventa si gran fuoco
>    Che l'incerar gli orecchi mi fia poco.

Diodati, I'll tell you something which absolutely amazes me: I, the coy creature who used to scorn love, I who made a habit of laughing at his snares, have now fallen into his trap (which sometimes does catch a good man). It is not golden tresses or rosy cheeks which have dazzled me like this, but a foreign beauty, modelled on a new idea of loveliness, which fills my heart with joy: a proud, yet modest bearing;[8] and that calm radiance of lovely blackness in her eyes and lashes; her speech which is graced by more than one language, and her singing[11] which might well draw down the labouring moon from mid-air.[12] And such bright fire flashes from her eyes that it would not be much good for me to seal up my ears.[14]

¶ 30. *8. Portamenti alti honesti*] Emilia's mixture of pride and modesty, which fascinates M. (cp. *Sonnet III* 8), is reminiscent of a similar fascination which Petrarch found in Laura (ccxiii 4 *e'n umil donna altà belta divina*). In the same sonnet Petrarch, like M., praises his lady's singing – *e'l cantar che ne l'anima si sente* – and the light of her eyes – *possenti a rischiarar abisso e notti.*
*11–12.* Cp. Virgil, *Ecl.* viii 69, where Alphesiboeus declares that 'songs can even draw the moon down from heaven'.
*14. incerar gli orecchi*] In Homer, *Od.* xii Odysseus, on Circe's advice, puts wax in the ears of his crew so that they will not be able to hear the song of the sirens as they row by.

# 31 Sonnet V

*Date.* Nov.–Dec. 1629? See headnote to *Sonnet II.*
*Publication.* 1645 (1. occhi,]occhi    2. fian]sian ) and *1673* (the text followed here, but corrected in *12* where *1673* misprints 'e trovar').

> Per certo i bei vostr'occhi, Donna mia
>   Esser non puo che non fian lo mio sole
>   Si mi percuoton forte, come ei suole
>   Per l'arene di Libia chi s'invia,
> 5 Mentre un caldo vapor (ne sentì pria)
>   Da quel lato si spinge ove mi duole,
>   Che forse amanti nelle lor parole
>   Chiaman sospir; io non so che si sia:
>   Parte rinchiusa, e turbida si cela
> 10 Scosso mi il petto, e poi n'uscendo poco
>   Quivi d' attorno o s'agghiaccia, o s'ingiela;
> Ma quanto a gli occhi giunge a trovar loco
>   Tutte le notti a me suol far piovose
>   Finche mia Alba rivien colma di rose.

Believe me, lady, your beautiful eyes cannot help but be my sun: their power beats down upon me just as the sun's does on a traveller in the Libyan desert; and at the same time a hot cloud of steam (a thing I never felt before) gushes from that side of my body[6] where I feel my pain. What this is, I don't know: perhaps in lovers' language it is called 'a sigh'. Part of it gets shut in and hides itself away, shuddering. Then, when it has thoroughly shaken my breast, a little of it escapes, whereupon it freezes or congeals in the air round about. But that part of it which manages to get into my eyes makes every night a rainy one for me, until my Dawn returns with roses in her hair.

# 32 Sonnet VI

*Date.* Nov.–Dec. 1629? See headnote to *Sonnet II.*
*Publication.* 1645 (8. se, d'intero]se, e d'intero ) and *1673* (the text followed here).

> Giovane piano, e semplicetto amante
>   Poi che fuggir me stesso in dubbio sono,
>   Madonna a voi del mio cuor l'humil dono

¶ 31. 6. *quel lato*] the left, where his heart is.
¶ 32. 2. The lover's wish to escape from himself and his thoughts is found in Petrarch, ccxxxiv 9–10: *Né pur il mio secreto, e'l mio riposo, | fuggo, ma più me stesso, e'l mio pensero.*

Farò divoto; io certo a prove tante
5   L'hebbi fedele, intrepido, costante,
De pensieri leggiadro, accorto, e buono;
Quando rugge il gran mondo, e scocca il tuono,
S'arma di se, d' intero diamante,
Tanto del forse, e d' invidia sicuro,
10  Di timori, e speranze al popol use
Quanto d'ingegno, e d' alto valor vago,
E di cetra sonora, e delle muse:
Sol troverete in tal parte men duro
Ove amor mise l'insanabil ago.

Since I am a young, unassuming and artless lover, and do not know how to escape from myself,[2] I will make you, lady, in my devotion, the humble gift of my heart. I have proved it in many a trial, faithful, brave and constant, graceful, wise and good in its thoughts. When the whole world roars and the lightning flashes[7] my heart arms itself in itself, in perfect adamant, as safe from chance and envy and from vulgar hopes and fears as it is eager for distinction of mind and real worth, for the sounding lyre and for the Muses.[12] You will find it less hard only in that spot where love stuck its incurable sting.

# 33 The Fifth Ode of Horace, *Lib*. I

*Date*. Late 1629? Suggested dates for this translation range from 1626 to 1655. The subject, deliberate rejection of love, may, however, indicate a date of composition near to that of *Elegia VI*.

*Publication*. First printed in *1673* where M. subjoins a Latin text of Horace's ode, differing in three particulars from modern versions (*munditie* for *munditiis* 5, *quoties* for *quotiens* 5, *intentata* for *intemptata* 13) and headed *Horatius ex Pyrrhae illecebris tanquam e naufragio enataverat, cuius amore irretitos, affirmat esse miseros* (Horace, having escaped from Pyrrha's charms, as from a shipwreck, declares that those who are ensnared by her love are in a wretched state). The text below follows *1673*, except in *12* where it substitutes a question mark for a *1673* full stop.

*Quis multa gracilis te puer in rosa*

*Rendered almost word for word without rhyme according to the Latin measure, as near as the language will permit.*

What slender youth bedewed with liquid odours
Courts thee on roses in some pleasant cave,
Pyrrha for whom bind'st thou
In wreaths thy golden hair,

7–12. Finley (34) notices the Horatian quality of these lines, comparing *Odes* III iii 1–8 and xxix 53–9.

5  Plain in thy neatness; O how oft shall he
   On faith and changed gods complain: and seas
        Rough with black winds and storms
        Unwonted shall admire:
   Who now enjoys thee credulous, all gold,
10 Who always vacant always amiable
        Hopes thee; of flattering gales
        Unmindful? Hapless they
   To whom thou untried seem'st fair. Me in my vowed
   Picture the sacred wall declares t' have hung
15      My dank and dropping weeds
        To the stern god of sea.

# 34 On the Morning of Christ's Nativity

*Date.* 25 Dec. 1629. Headed 'Compos'd 1629' in *1645*. M. tells Diodati
(*Elegia VI* 88) that he began the poem before dawn on Christmas Day.
*Publication. 1645* (*23.* sweet,]sweet:    *55.* hung,]hung;    *82.* new
enlightened]new-enlightened    *143–4.* Orbed in a rainbow; and like glories
wearing / Mercy will sit]Th'enamelled arras of the rainbow wearing, / And
Mercy set    *156.* deep.]deep,    *185.* pale,]pale.    *193.* drear]drear,
*207.* hue;]hue,    *210.* blue;]blue,    *231.* wave,]wave.    *239.* ending:]
ending,    *241.* car,]car.    *242.* attending:]attending. ) and *1673* (the
text followed here).

¶ 33. *8. shall admire*] Latin *emirabitur*: shall be very surprised at.
*9. enjoys ... gold*] enjoys you, believing that you are pure and beautiful:
Horace uses Latin *aurea* figuratively.
*10–12. Who ... Unmindful?*] Who, unmindful of deceitful (Latin *fallacis*)
gales, hopes that you will always be without other lovers (Latin *vacuam*)
and lovable.
*13–16. Me ... sea*] The sacred wall shows that I, whose picture hangs
there, have hung up my sea-clothes as a thank-offering to the sea-god.
Horace here returns to the shipwreck/love analogy suggested in ll. 6–8:
shipwrecked by his love for Pyrrha, he has escaped through Neptune's
help, on the wall of whose temple he has hung up, as a thank-offering, his
wet sea-clothes (for this practice see Virgil, *Aen.* xii 766–9), with a votive
tablet (*tabula ... votiva*: M.'s 'vowed Picture'), presumably showing the
circumstances of his escape.
*16. stern*] M.'s addition: Latin *potenti ... maris deo*, to the god who is
master of the sea.

*Sources, style, versification.* Christian literature before M. contains innumerable examples of nativity poems, in both neo-Latin and the various vernaculars, and the combination of babe-in-the-manger and hymning angels with the flight of the pagan gods and the cessation of oracles was not uncommon. M.'s poem is more distinctive for the elements of the traditional story which it omits than for those it includes (see Tuve[2] and Broadbent, below). However since M.'s interest in Italian poetry towards the end of 1629, and in the development of a particular style through Bembo, Della Casa and Tasso, is well attested (see headnote to *Sonnet I* on *M.'s sonnets: style and versification*, p. 88 above), it seems likely that what appeared to him as inspiration on Christmas morning 1629 (see *Elegia VI* 87–8) was in some part a memory of Tasso's *Nel giorno della Natività* (*Rime* (Venice 1621) viii 63–7). Tasso, like M., contrasts the 'courts of everlasting day' and their 'harmony' with the 'darksome house' to which Christ comes (*mille, e mille / Corone, e fiamme, e lampi / D'angelico splendor l'han fatto adorno. / Mà da le parti lucide, e tranquille, / Di quei celesti campi / Sparsi d'un bel candor, che vince il giorno / E da quell'armonia, che gira intorno, / La rozza turba a contemplare inchina, / . . . E quell'humile albergo, ov'è nascosa . . . ne la notte ombrosa*: thousands and thousands of crowns and flames and lights of angelic splendour adorned him. But from the bright and tranquil regions of those celestial fields, spread with a lovely whiteness that outshines the day, and from that wheeling harmony, he bowed down to look at the rough crowd, . . . And that lowly inn where he was born . . . in the dark night). He also mentions Nature's awe, the world-wide peace, Apollo and the dumb oracles (*Già divien muto Apollo e l'antro, e l'onde, / E gli Dei falsi, e vani / . . . Ne Dafne ne la quercia altrui risponde / Più con accenti humani*: Already Apollo is mute, and cave and fountain, and the false, vain gods . . . No longer do the laurel or oak give replies in human voices), Lybic Hammon (*giace Amon ne la deserta arena*: Ammon lies in the desert sand), Osiris's 'lowings' and the barking Anubis (*E da gli altari suoi dolente fugge / Api, ed Anubi, e più non latra, o mugge*: Apis and Anubis flee lamenting from their altars, and bark and bellow no more), and concludes his *canzone*, as M. concludes his introductory stanzas, by offering his 'humble' (*humil*) poem, comparing it with the 'odours sweet' (*odori*) that the wise men bring. The similarities between M.'s poem and some passages in the *Apotheosis* of Prudentius–the most remarkable of the early-Christian Latin poets–are hardly less striking (see ll. *173–80n*), though there is no definite evidence that Prudentius was a set author at St Paul's (Clark 125).

No exact precedent for M.'s stanza-form in the *Hymn* (a6a6b10c6c6b10 d8d12) has been found,'but its pattern and movement, and the idea of using such a stanza for a solemn ode, derive from the tradition of the *canzone*. No doubt, as Prince 60 suggests, M. found the liberties taken with the *canzone* by Spenser in *Epithalamion* and *Prothalamion* instructive–his final alexandrine has a Spenserian ring. It seems likely that Drummond's experiments in Italian verse forms were useful to M. too. Of his predecessors

Drummond was the most widely read in Italian literature, and his madrigal 'To the delightful green' (*Works*, ed. L. E. Kastner (Manchester 1913) i 22) starts with a verse pattern (a6a6b10c6c6b10) identical with that of the *Hymn*, which is more than can be said for Chiabrera's *Per S. Agata* (a7b7c11 a7b7c11d7d11) – see Fletcher, below.

The introductory stanzas are in a form M. had used before in *Fair Infant* – decasyllables with a final alexandrine, rhyming ababbcc. It is a modification of the Spenserian stanza which Phineas Fletcher, who certainly influenced the young M. elsewhere, had used twice in his *Poetical Miscellanies* and again in *Elisa*, but since neither was published until 1633 one cannot be sure that this stanza form was not M.'s own idea too.

Although there is one striking debt to Petrarch (see *32–4n*), the most potent stylistic influences are not Italian but Elizabethan. Forms like 'wont' (*10*) and 'ychained' (*155*) give a Spenserian flavour, and the elaborate prosopopoeias, culminating in the beautiful baroque image of the sun in bed, which Tillyard 36 finds 'grotesque', are reminiscent of Sidney's rhetorical habits in the *Arcadia*. Even when doubtful likenesses have been discarded, five echoes of the *Faerie Queene* and two of the *Shepheards Calender* remain (see notes), contributing to the poem's ringing first line, and becoming particularly distinct in the Elizabethan pastoral scene of Pan and the shepherds (*85–92*). Shakespeare comes close behind with six apparent echoes, three of them from *A Midsummer Night's Dream* which provides the spirits and fays of lines *232–6*, as well as the moonlight for them. Sylvester's translation of Du Bartas, M.'s earliest English literary model (see notes to Nos. 1 and 2, pp. 6–9 above), still accounts for two or three oddly vivid touches, like the 'lep'rous sin' of line *138*; the leading Spenserian, Giles Fletcher, makes one probable donation to the diction (*110*); Chapman's 'burning axletree' (*84*) sticks in M.'s mind, as later in Eliot's; and M.'s mourning wood-nymphs (*188*) may come from Fairfax's translation (1600, second edition 1624) of Tasso's epic – they are not in the original. Sandys's imaginative account of human sacrifice, with its shrieks and searing flesh, and his illustrations of the 'brutish gods of Nile', supply local colour (see notes to *205–10, 211, 212* etc.); so does Selden's treatise on comparative religion (republished in the year the poem was written). Classical influence is, by contrast, scant. Possibly *84* recalls the description of the sun's throne in M.'s favourite, Ovid; and the light flooding into Virgil's hell probably accounted for *139–40*. Twice there are faint echoes of Horatian phrases (*136, 185*). But in the main M. hails his native language and its authors.

*Modern criticism.* The poem's structure was first attacked by Warton, who called it 'a string of affected conceits' Wilson Knight 64 agrees that 'though it offers a satisfying lyric integrity' it 'remains somewhat fluid in its addition of stanza to stanza: there is no complex inter-knitting, that is, of central action with design'. On the other side Tillyard 37–8 claims that it displays 'architectonic grasp' in that at the beginning M. is hurrying to offer his poem before the wise men arrive, whereas at the end the star

over the stable shows that their arrival is imminent. An abler defence of
the structure is that of A. Barker, *UTQ* x (1941) 167–81, who points out
that the poem has three sections: the first (i–viii) describing the setting of
the nativity and characterized by the reduction of light and sound to a
minimum; the second (ix–xvii) devoted largely to the angelic choir, and
dominated by light, harmony and order (which start to be dissipated in
xvi and xvii); and the third (xviii–xxvi) describing the flight of the pagan
gods, full of discordant sounds and shadows. Light and order return in
xxvii, which thus balances the second section. In the centre of the poem
(xiii) the angelic choir and the music of the spheres are placed in close
association, transcending the conflict between the pagan and Christian
traditions. A. S. P. Woodhouse, *UTQ* xiii (1943) 66–101, endorses Barker's
analysis. Allen 24–9 argues that the poem is based on three vital oppositions,
each of which is not reconciled but transcended. The first is that between
the past (the last hour of the pre-Christian era) and the time of the poem's
composition. From this opposition M. evolves the solution of timelessness,
by pressing towards the eternal consequences of the incarnation. The
second (i–vii) is that between wanton Nature and Nature ashamed, and
is resolved by the sending down of Peace (iii). The third is that between the
harmony of the Church Militant (viii–xii) and the harmony of the pagan
gods (xix–xxviii), which is transcended by M.'s anticipation of the harmony
of the Church Triumphant (xiii–xv).

Tuve[2] (37–72) maintains that the poem's real subject is the incarnation,
not the nativity. Her main endeavour is to clarify the tradition that lies
behind the 'great ancient images' that M. employs. This approach is
brilliantly questioned by J. B. Broadbent (Kermode[3] 12–31) who insists
that Tuve's delight in the traditional materials makes her overestimate
M.'s use of them. M.'s treatment of the nativity is only partially traditional.
Though writing about the incarnation he avoids the flesh and fights shy
of Christ's fleshly life. The direction he takes – and traditionally need not
have taken – is away from the incarnate towards the ideate. Alone, even
among classical and patristic authors, he ignores the central naturalness of
motherhood. The poem represents 'the conquest by hard-edged right
reason of the soft dim liquid allures of passion'.

Both A. S. Cook, *MLR* ii (1907) 121–4, and Tuve[2] 56 attempt to prove
the influence of Mantuan. L. Stapleton, *UTQ* xxiii (1954) 217–26, shows
that Clement of Alexandria's *Exhortation to the Greeks* presents an analogous
pattern of ideas, particularly the connection of the flight of the pagan
gods with the coming of the 'new music' (the discovery of the Logos
in Christ), and the identification of this music with the principle of harmo-
nious order in the universe.

Fletcher (ii 496–7), following Prince (60), suggests the influence of Italian
metrical patterns and compares the stanza form of the *Hymn* with the
first strophe of Chiabrera's *Per S. Agata*.

Røstvig[2] (44–58) examines the poem from the viewpoint of neo-Platonic
numerical theory, detecting the influence of Francesco Giorgio's *De Harmo-*

*nia Mundi* (1525), and pointing out that whereas the numbers of the intro-
duction (four stanzas of seven lines) are earthly, those of the *Hymn* (twenty-
seven stanzas of eight lines) are expressive of perfection.

### I

This is the month, and this the happy morn
Wherein the Son of heaven's eternal King,
Of wedded maid, and virgin mother born,
Our great redemption from above did bring;
5  For so the holy sages once did sing,
    That he our deadly forfeit should release,
And with his Father work us a perpetual peace.

### II

That glorious form, that light unsufferable,
And that far-beaming blaze of majesty,
10  Wherewith he wont at heaven's high council-table,
To sit the midst of trinal unity,
He laid aside; and here with us to be,
    Forsook the courts of everlasting day,
And chose with us a darksome house of mortal clay.

### III

15  Say heavenly Muse, shall not thy sacred vein
Afford a present to the infant God?
Hast thou no verse, no hymn, or solemn strain,
To welcome him to this his new abode,
Now while the heaven by the sun's team untrod,
20      Hath took no print of the approaching light,
    And all the spangled host keep watch in squadrons
        bright?

¶ 34.  *1. happy morn*] Cp. Spenser *F.Q.* IV ii 41: 'Borne . . . in one happie
morne.'
*5. holy sages*] Hebrew prophets.
*10. wont*] was accustomed. Strictly speaking a past participle (O.E. ge-
wunod) but used by M. as the preterite of the vb *won* (to be accustomed).
Spenser has 'wonned' (*Shep. Cal.* Feb. 119) and 'did won' (*F.Q.* III
ix 21) in this sense.
*14. house of mortal clay*] Cp. Marston, *Scourge of Villany* viii 194, where the
body which the soul leaves is called a 'smoakie house of mortall clay'.
*15. heavenly Muse*] Urania, originally the Muse of astronomy, but elevated
by Du Bartas in *La Muse Chrétienne* (1574) to the position of Muse of
Christian poetry. Lily B. Campbell discusses her history, *HLB* viii (1935)
29–70.
*21. spangled . . . bright*] See *Psalm cxxxvi* 33–4n (p. 8). In Spenser, *F.Q.*

### IV

See how from far upon the eastern road
The star-led wizards haste with odours sweet,
O run, prevent them with thy humble ode,
25    And lay it lowly at his blessed feet;
Have thou the honour first, thy Lord to greet,
    And join thy voice unto the angel quire,
From out his secret altar touched with hallowed fire.

### The Hymn

### I

It was the winter wild,
30    While the heaven-born-child
    All meanly wrapped in the rude manger lies;
Nature in awe to him
Had doffed her gaudy trim,
    With her great master so to sympathize:
35    It was no season then for her
To wanton with the sun her lusty paramour.

### II

Only with speeches fair
She woos the gentle air
    To hide her guilty front with innocent snow,
40    And on her naked shame,
Pollute with sinful blame,

II viii 2 the angels 'their bright Squadrons round about us plant' and
'watch', and in Sylvester (Du Bartas 17) 'Heav'ns glorious Hoast in
nimble squadrons flyes'.

*23. star-led wizards*] Cp. Spenser, *F.Q.* V Prologue 8: 'Aegyptian wisards
old, / Which in Star-read were wont have best insight.'

*24. prevent*] anticipate.

*25. blessed feet*] Cp. Shakespeare, *I Hen. IV* I i 25–7: 'Those blessed feet /
Which fourteen hundred years ago were nail'd / For our advantage on the
bitter cross'.

*28. From ... altar*] Qualifies 'fire' (the line is inverted). In *Isa.* vi 6–7
one of the seraphim takes a live coal from the altar and touches the prophet's
lips with it.

*32–4.* Echoing Petrarch, *Sonnet* 3, of the eclipse on Good Friday: *Era il
giorno ch'al sol si scoloraro / per la pietà del suo fattore i rai* (It was the day when
the rays of the sun darkened in pity for their creator).

*35–6.* Cp. *Elegia V* 55–95 (pp. 83–4).

*41. Pollute*] polluted.    *blame*] The Fall (cp. *PL* x 649–719).

The saintly veil of maiden white to throw,
Confounded, that her maker's eyes
Should look so near upon her foul deformities.

### III

45    But he her fears to cease,
Sent down the meek-eyed Peace,
    She crowned with olive green, came softly sliding
Down through the turning sphere
His ready harbinger,
50    With turtle wing the amorous clouds dividing,
And waving wide her myrtle wand,
She strikes a universal peace through sea and land.

### IV

No war, or battle's sound
Was heard the world around
55    The idle spear and shield were high up hung,
The hooked chariot stood
Unstained with hostile blood,
    The trumpet spake not to the armed throng,
And kings sat still with awful eye,
60    As if they surely knew their sovran Lord was by.

### V

But peaceful was the night
Wherein the Prince of Light
    His reign of peace upon the earth began:
The winds with wonder whist,

---

48. *turning sphere*] The Ptolemaic spheres revolving round the earth. Sylvester has 'turning Spheres' (Du Bartas 95).

50. *turtle*] Of a turtle dove, symbol of harmlessness in *Matt.* x 16.    *amorous*] Clinging to Peace as if in love with her: cp. Shakespeare, *Antony and Cleopatra* II ii 201 where the water follows the oars 'as amorous of their strokes'.

51. *myrtle*] The tree of Venus, as Virgil says (*Ecl.* vii 62), hence of love.

52–60. Aquinas, *Summa* III xxxv 8, points out that it was fitting for Christ to be born in the *pax Romana*, as this fulfilled the prophecy in *Isa.* ii 4.

56. *hooked*] Cp. the chariots 'armed with hooks' in *2 Macc.* xiii 2, taken over by Spenser, *F.Q.* V viii 28.

64. *whist*] silent. Cp. Shakespeare, *Tempest* I ii 379–80: 'and kiss'd / The wild waves whist.'

65    Smoothly the waters kissed,
         Whispering new joys to the mild ocean,
     Who now hath quite forgot to rave,
     While birds of calm sit brooding on the charmed wave.


                              VI
     The stars with deep amaze
70   Stand fixed in steadfast gaze,
         Bending one way their precious influence,
     And will not take their flight,
     For all the morning light,
         Or Lucifer that often warned them thence;
75   But in their glimmering orbs did glow,
     Until their Lord himself bespake, and bid them go.


                             VII
     And though the shady gloom
     Had given day her room,
         The sun himself withheld his wonted speed,
80   And hid his head for shame,
     As his inferior flame,
         The new enlightened world no more should need;
     He saw a greater sun appear
     Than his bright throne, or burning axle-tree could bear.


68. *birds of calm*] halcyons (kingfishers). The belief that calm always pre-
vailed during the fourteen midwinter days when they were laying and
sitting ('brooding') on their floating nests, is recorded in Aristotle, *Historia
Animalium* v 8, and Pliny x 47.

71. *influence*] The power exerted upon men by the heavenly bodies; cp.
*Job* xxxviii 31: 'the sweet influences of the Pleiades.'

74. *Lucifer*] A name for the morning star (really Venus).

75. *in . . . orbs*] Cp. Shakespeare, *Midsummer Night's Dream* III ii 61: 'Venus
in her glimmering sphere'.

80–4. Echoing Spenser, *Shep. Cal.* Apr. 73–8: 'I sawe Phoebus thrust
out his golden hedde, / Upon her to gaze: / But, when he sawe how broade
her beames did spredde, / It did him amaze. / He blusht to see another
Sunne belowe, / Ne durst againe his fyrye face out showe.'

83. *sun*] Cp. the prophesied rising of the 'Sun of righteousness' in
*Malachi* iv 2.

84. *throne*] In Ovid, *Met.* ii 24 the throne of the sun gleams with brilliant
emeralds.    *burning axle-tree*] Echoes Chapman, *Bussy D'Ambois* V iii
151–2: 'Fly where men feel / The burning axletree.'

### VIII

85　The shepherds on the lawn,
　　　Or ere the point of dawn,
　　　　　Sat simply chatting in a rustic row;
　　　Full little thought they then,
　　　That the mighty Pan
90　　　Was kindly come to live with them below;
　　　Perhaps their loves, or else their sheep,
　　　Was all that did their silly thoughts so busy keep.

### IX

　　　When such music sweet
　　　Their hearts and ears did greet,
95　　　As never was by mortal finger strook,
　　　Divinely-warbled voice
　　　Answering the stringed noise,
　　　　　As all their souls in blissful rapture took:
　　　The air such pleasure loth to lose,
100　With thousand echoes still prolongs each heavenly close.

### X

　　　Nature that heard such sound
　　　Beneath the hollow round
　　　　　Of Cynthia's seat, the airy region thrilling,

85-92. I. L. Myhr, *Explicator* iv (1945) 16, sees viii as a link between the images of light (v–vii) and music (ix–xiv) and explains that Pan is an appropriate link because Renaissance tradition associated him with Christ, giver of spiritual light, as well as with music.

88. *then*] For the sake of rhyme *1645* and *1673* have 'than': the two forms were interchangeable throughout most of the seventeenth century.

89. *Pan*] Spenser calls Christ 'great Pan' (*Shep. Cal.* May 54), and E.K. s gloss repeats the famous story from Plutarch (*De Defect. Orac.* 418) about the voice which, at the time of the crucifixion, cried that the great Pan was dead. The identification of Christ and Pan arose partly from Christ's role as 'good shepherd' and partly from the idea of Christ as 'All' (the meaning of Greek *pan*).

90. *kindly*] Both 'according to his nature' (as a shepherd he was coming to live with shepherds) and 'benevolently'.

92. *silly*] The senses 'foolish' and 'feeble-minded' had developed in the last quarter of the sixteenth century, but M. presumably intends the older sense 'unlearned, unsophisticated', which was still current in poetry.

98. *took*] captivated.

100. *close*] The conclusion of a musical phrase; a cadence.

102-3. *hollow round . . . seat*] The sphere of the moon.

103. *region*] On the regions of the air see *Q Nov* 12*n* (p. 37).

Now was almost won
*105*　To think her part was done,
　　And that her reign had here its last fulfilling;
　She knew such harmony alone
　Could hold all heaven and earth in happier union.

### XI

At last surrounds their sight
*110*　A globe of circular light,
　　That with long beams the shame-faced night
　　　arrayed,
　The helmed cherubim
　And sworded seraphim,
　　Are seen in glittering ranks with wings displayed,
*115*　Harping in loud and solemn quire,
　With unexpressive notes to heaven's new-born heir.

### XII

Such music (as 'tis said)
Before was never made,
　But when of old the sons of morning sung,
*120*　While the creator great
　His constellations set,
　　And the well-balanced world on hinges hung,
　And cast the dark foundations deep,
　And bid the welt'ring waves their oozy channel keep.

### XIII

*125*　Ring out, ye crystal spheres,
　Once bless our human ears,
　　(If ye have power to touch our senses so)
　And let your silver chime

*110. globe*] Latin *globus* can mean 'troop', and 'globe' has this sense
in *PL* ii 512 and *PR* iv 581–a meaning first recorded in Giles Fletcher's
*Christ's Triumph* (1610).
*116. unexpressive*] inexpressible; first used in this sense by Shakespeare,
*As You Like It* III ii 10.
*119–24.* Cp. *Job* xxxviii 4–8: 'Where wast thou when I laid the foundations
of the earth ... When the morning stars sang together, and all the sons
of God shouted for joy? Or who shut up the sea with doors?', and *Isa.*
xiv 12: 'Lucifer, son of the morning'.
*122. hinges*] Cp. Spenser, *F.Q.* I xi 21: 'To move the world from off his
stedfast henge.'
*125–35.* The idea that each sphere of the universe produced a note as it
revolved (making up M.'s 'ninefold harmony') was Pythagorean in

Move in melodious time;
*130*    And let the base of heaven's deep organ blow,
And with your ninefold harmony
Make up full consort to the angelic symphony.

### XIV

For if such holy song
Enwrap our fancy long,
*135*    Time will run back, and fetch the age of gold,
And speckled vanity
Will sicken soon and die,
And lep'rous sin will melt from earthly mould,
And hell itself will pass away,
*140*    And leave her dolorous mansions to the peering day.

### XV

Yea Truth, and Justice then
Will down return to men,
Orbed in a rainbow; and like glories wearing
Mercy will sit between,

---

origin. See *Arcades* 63–72*n* (p. 159 below). *The Music of the Spheres* was
the topic of M.'s second *Prolusion* (Columbia xii 149–57; Yale i 234–9),
in which he subscribes to the idea that 'Pythagoras alone among mortal
men' was able to hear this music. The rest of mankind cannot, he explains,
because of the Fall, as a result of which we are 'buried in sin and degraded
by brutish desires'. If our souls were pure, our ears would 'be filled with
that exquisite music of the stars in their orbits; then would all things turn
back to the Age of Gold'.

*130. the base*] The Earth, which has not, since the Fall, shared in the nine-
fold harmony.    *organ*] This instrument was thought of as including all
others, and therefore as representing universal harmony, as L. Spitzer
demonstrates, *Traditio* ii (1944) 442–5.

*135.* As Tuve[2] (60) points out, the Messianic interpretation of Virgil, *Ecl.*
iv, common since Constantine's time, made it the *locus classicus* for the
idea of the Nativity as the birth of a restorer of Saturn's Golden Age.

*136. speckled vanity*] Cp. Horace, *Odes* IV v 22: *maculosum . . . nefas.*

*138. lep'rous sin*] Sylvester (Du Bartas 232) has 'leprosie of Sin'.

*139–40.* An echo either of Homer, *Il.* xx 62–5, or Virgil, *Aen.* viii 243–6,
where the light of day is imagined flooding into hell.

*141–4.* Cp. *Ps.* lxxxv 10: 'Mercy and truth are met together, righteousness
and peace have kissed each other.' For the departure of Astraea (Justice)
from the earth see *Elegia IV* 81*n* (p. 57).

*145*    Throned in celestial sheen,
        With radiant feet the tissued clouds down steering,
    And heaven as at some festival,
    Will open wide the gates of her high palace hall.

### XVI

    But wisest fate says no,
*150*    This must not yet be so,
        The babe lies yet in smiling infancy,
    That on the bitter cross
    Must redeem our loss;
        So both himself and us to glorify:
*155*    Yet first to those ychained in sleep,
    The wakeful trump of doom must thunder through
        the deep.

### XVII

    With such a horrid clang
    As on Mount Sinai rang
        While the red fire, and smould'ring clouds out brake:
*160*    The aged earth aghast
    With terror of that blast,
        Shall from the surface to the centre shake;
    When at the world's last session,
    The dreadful judge in middle air shall spread his
        throne.

### XVIII

*165*    And then at last our bliss
    Full and perfect is,
        But now begins; for from this happy day
    The old dragon under ground
    In straiter limits bound,

*146. tissued*] Minsheu (1617) defines *tissu* as 'cloth of silke and silver, or of silver and gold woven together'; cp. *Isa.* lii 7: 'How beautiful upon the mountains are the feet of him . . . that publisheth peace.'

*149.* Cp. *PL* vii 173 where God says 'and what I will is Fate'.

*152. bitter cross*] See 25*n.*

*155. ychained*] M.'s retention of the O.E. prefix 'ge-' (M.E. 'y-') is a Spenserian affectation. See E.K.'s gloss to Spenser, *Shep. Cal.* Apr. 155 ('Y is a poeticall addition').

*158-9.* Cp. *Exod.* xix 16 where God descends upon Sinai with 'thunder and lightnings and a thick cloud . . . and the voice of the trumpet' (Vulgate *clangorque buccinae*).

*163-4.* M.'s concept of the Last Judgment is drawn from *Matt.* xxiv 30: 'the Son of man coming in the clouds of heaven'.

*168. old dragon*] Cp. *Rev.* xx 2: 'the dragon, that old serpent, which is the

*170*     Not half so far casts his usurped sway,
And wroth to see his kingdom fail,
Swinges the scaly horror of his folded tail.

### XIX

The oracles are dumb,
No voice or hideous hum
*175*     Runs through the arched roof in words deceiving.
Apollo from his shrine
Can no more divine,
With hollow shriek the steep of Delphos leaving.
No nightly trance, or breathed spell,
*180*     Inspires the pale-eyed priest from the prophetic cell.

### XX

The lonely mountains o'er,
And the resounding shore,
A voice of weeping heard, and loud lament;
From haunted spring, and dale
*185*     Edged with poplar pale,
The parting genius is with sighing sent,
With flower-inwoven tresses torn
The nymphs in twilight shade of tangled thickets mourn.

Devil', and xii 3–4: 'a great red dragon . . . And his tail drew the third part of the stars of heaven'.

*172. Swinges . . . tail*] Sylvester's lion is depicted 'often swindging, with his sinnewy train' (Du Bartas 155).

*173–80.* The passage on the cessation of the oracles at the birth of Christ in Prudentius *Apotheosis* 438–43 mentions the silence of the caves at Delphi (M.'s 'Delphos', where Apollo had an oracle on the steep slope of Parnassus), the fanatic priest panting and foaming at the mouth, and the silencing of Hammon in Libya (203). In the same poem Apollo is tormented with pain by the words of exorcism, and shrieks (*heiulat*) (402–3, 412–13); at the heathen sacrifice (460–502) the priest breaks off because he senses that a Christian is present, and he sees Persephone fleeing in dread; his spells (*carmina*) are of no effect; the flames go out and the laurel falls from the flamen's head.

*183.* Cp. the slaughter of the innocents in *Matt.* ii 18, quoting *Jerem.* xxxi 15: 'In Rama was there a voice heard, lamentation and weeping and great mourning.'

*185. poplar pale*] Cp. Horace, *Odes* II iii 9: *albaque poplus.*

*186. genius*] A strictly local deity in classical mythology.

*188.* Cp. Fairfax's translation of Tasso iii 75, where a wood is felled at Godfrey's command and 'The weeping Nymphes fled from their bowres exilde'.

### XXI

In consecrated earth,
*190*    And on the holy hearth,
   The lars, and lemures moan with midnight plaint,
In urns, and altars round,
A drear and dying sound
   Affrights the flamens at their service quaint;
*195*    And the chill marble seems to sweat,
While each peculiar power forgoes his wonted seat.

### XXII

Peor, and Baalim,
   Forsake their temples dim,
     With that twice battered god of Palestine,
*200*    And mooned Ashtaroth,
   Heaven's queen and mother both,
     Now sits not girt with tapers' holy shine,
   The Libyc Hammon shrinks his horn,
In vain the Tyrian maids their wounded Thammuz
     mourn.

*191. lars, and lemures*] Augustine, *City of God* ix 11, denies Apuleius' theory that men's souls become lars (deities presiding over private houses) if good and lemures (goblins) if bad.

*194. flamens*] priests    *quaint*] elaborate.

*195. marble . . . sweat*] Virgil, *Georg.* i 480, mentions ivory weeping and bronzes sweating among the prodigies seen at the murder of Caesar, as does Ovid, *Met.* xv 792.

*197. Peor*] Peor was the name of a mountain (*Num.* xxiii 28) and thence of the local deity Baal-Peor, one of the titles under which Baal, the Phoenician sun-god was worshipped (*Num.* xxv 3). Selden has a chapter (I v) on Baal-Peor.    *Baalim*] the plural of Baal, stands for other manifestations of Baal, e.g. Baal-Berith, Baal-Zebub. Cp. *Judges* x 6: 'The children of Israel . . . served Baalim and Ashtaroth.' Selden (II i) discusses these manifestations.

*199. twice battered god*] Dagon, the Philistine god who is twice overturned during the night in *1 Sam.* v 3-4.

*200. mooned Ashtaroth*] The plural form (standing for her collective manifestations) of Ashtoreth, supreme goddess of the Phoenicians and identical with the Syrian Astarte. Selden II ii attests her supremacy ('Heaven's queen'), discusses her relationship to the moon and her consequent assumption of horns ('mooned'), and proves her right to the title *Mater Deum* ('Heaven's . . . mother').

*203. Hammon*] One of the manifestations of Jove, worshipped in Libya (at the Siwah oasis) in the form of a ram.

*204. Thammuz*] Identical with the Greek Adonis, slain, like him, by a boar

## XXIII

205    And sullen Moloch fled,
    Hath left in shadows dread,
      His burning idol all of blackest hue;
    In vain with cymbals' ring,
    They call the grisly king,
210        In dismal dance about the furnace blue;
    The brutish gods of Nile as fast,
    Isis and Orus, and the dog Anubis haste.

## XXIV

    Nor is Osiris seen
    In Memphian grove, or green,
215        Trampling the unshowered grass with lowings loud:
    Nor can he be at rest
    Within his sacred chest,

and mourned annually at his festival at Byblos in Phoenicia ('Tyrian' because Tyre was the principal city of Phoenicia), where the waters of the stream were said to turn red with his blood. Selden devotes a chapter (II x) to him. Cp. *Ezek*. viii 14: 'There sat women weeping for Tammuz.'

*205–10.* Moloch was an idol worhipped by the Ammonites at Rabbah, their capital. Sandys 186 tells how 'the *Hebrews* sacrificed their children to *Molech*, an Idoll of brasse, having the head of a calfe, the rest of a kingly figure, with armes extended to receive the miserable sacrifice, seared to death with his burning embracements. For the Idoll was hollow within, and filled with fire. And lest their lamentable shrieks should sad the hearts of their parents, the Priests of *Molech* did deafe their eares with the continuall clangs of trumpets and timbrels.' Selden I vi gives these and other details. Cp. *2 Kings* xxiii 10: 'that no man might make his son or his daughter pass through the fire to Molech'.

*211. brutish gods of Nile*] Sandys 133 in his section on Egypt illustrates several of these, and describes others 'with the heads of sheepe, haukes, dogs etc. . . . cats, beetles, monkies, and such like', quoting Virgil, *Aen*. viii 698: *omnigenum deum monstra et latrator Anubis*.

*212. Isis*] Egyptian goddess of the earth. Herodotus ii 41 says she is horned like a cow. Sandys 133–4 has an illustration with the caption: 'a lion; under which shape they adored Isis'.    *Orus*] Egyptian sun god, son of Isis.    *Anubis*] son of Osiris, represented with jackal's or dog's head. Sandys 133–4 illustrates 'Anubis . . . figured with the head of a dog', and adds: 'the dog throughout Egypt was universally worshipped'.

*213. Osiris*] Chief Egyptian god, worshipped, as Herodotus describes (iii 27–9) in the shape of the Apis, a black bull with a white star on its forehead, (hence his 'lowings'). Cp. Sandys 132 'In this [Memphis] was the Temple of *Apis* (which is the same with *Osiris*)'. Selden I iv discusses Osiris and the Apis in his chapter on the golden calf.

Nought but profoundest hell can be his shroud,
In vain with timbrelled anthems dark
220  The sable-stoled sorcerers bear his worshipped ark.

### XXV

He feels from Juda's land
The dreaded infant's hand,
The rays of Bethlehem blind his dusky eyn;
Nor all the gods beside,
225  Longer dare abide,
Not Typhon huge ending in snaky twine:
Our babe to show his Godhead true,
Can in his swaddling bands control the damned crew.

### XXVI

So when the sun in bed,
230  Curtained with cloudy red,
Pillows his chin upon an orient wave,
The flocking shadows pale,
Troop to the infernal jail,
Each fettered ghost slips to his several grave,
235  And the yellow-skirted fays,
Fly after the night-steeds, leaving their moon-loved
maze.

220. *ark*] Cp. Herodotus ii 63: 'The image of the god, in a little wooden
gilt casket, is carried . . . from the temple by the priests.'
226. *Typhon*] The Greek Typhon was a hundred-headed monster, son of
Earth and Tartarus, described by Apollodorus, I vi 3. He was serpent below
the waist. Zeus killed him with a thunderbolt. The Egyptian Typhon, or
Set, was slayer of Osiris, cp. Sandys 103: 'By *Osiris* they prefigured *Nilus*;
. . . by *Typhon* the Sea.'
227–8. Hercules who, as D. C. Allen comments, *JEGP* lx (1961) 619–21,
was a common type of Christ, strangled snakes in his cradle. Theocritus
xxiv 1–63 tells the story. For other Hercules–Christ references see M. Y.
Hughes, *Études anglaises* vi (1953) 193–213.
231. *Pillows*] *OED* has no previous example of the use of 'pillow' as a verb.
233. *Troop*] Cp. Shakespeare, *Midsummer Night's Dream* III ii 382–3:
'ghosts, wandering here and there, / Troop home to churchyards.'
234. *fettered*] i.e. to the body, cp. *Comus* 464–74n (p. 199).
235. *fays*] Selden 163 associates the 'fays' with Lucina and Eileithyia,
the Roman and Greek goddesses of childbirth. Their flight is particularly
significant in this nativity poem and is therefore placed last.
236. *night-steeds*] Cp. Q *Nov* 70–3n (p. 39).    *maze*] Cp. Shakespeare,
*Midsummer Night's Dream* II i 99: 'the quaint mazes in the wanton green'
where the fairies dance their 'moonlight revels' (II i 141).

XXVII

But see the virgin blest,
Hath laid her babe to rest.
    Time is our tedious song should here have ending:
240 Heaven's youngest teemed star,
Hath fixed her polished car,
    Her sleeping Lord with handmaid lamp attending:
And all about the courtly stable,
Bright-harnessed angels sit in order serviceable.

## 35 *Elegia sexta*
### [Elegy VI]

*Date.* Dec. 1629. The composition of *Nativity Ode* (Christmas 1629) is referred to (*79–88*) as recent and (presumably) incomplete. M.'s prose heading shows that *Elegia VI* is a reply to a letter of Diodati's dated 13 Dec. *Publication.* *1645* and *1673* (no significant variants: *1673* misprints *13 quereris* as *queretis*, and in *22* it misprints a comma after *modis*). *Modern criticism.* Hanford[2] 369–70 views *Elegia VI* as a deliberate self-consecration, bracketing it with M.'s recollection of his decision to dedicate himself to the 'the experience and the practice of all that which is praiseworthy' for his poetry's sake (Columbia iii 303–4; Yale i 890). W. R. Parker, however, *MLN* lv (1940) 216–17, reads the poem as an academic exercise, 'a rhetorical "debate" discussing each side learnedly from a single point of view'. Z. S. Fink, *English Studies* xxi (1939) 164–5, gives instances of the same debate in J. C. Scaliger and others.

*Ad Carolum Diodatum ruri commorantem*

*Qui cum idibus Decemb. scripsisset, et sua carmina excusari postulasset si solito minus essent bona, quod inter lautitias quibus erat ab amicis exceptus, haud satis felicem operam musis dare se posse affirmabat, hunc habuit responsum.*

Mitto tibi sanam non pleno ventre salutem,
    Qua tu distento forte carere potes.
At tua quid nostram prolectat musa camoenam,
    Nec sinit optatas posse sequi tenebras?
5 Carmine scire velis quam te redamemque colamque,
    Crede mihi vix hoc carmine scire queas.
Nam neque noster amor modulis includitur arctis,

240. *youngest teemed*] latest born.
244. *Bright-harnessed*] bright-armoured.
¶ 35. *3. camoenam*] Latin equivalent of the Greek μοῦσα, a muse.

Nec venit ad claudos integer ipse pedes.
Quam bene sollennes epulas, hilaremque Decembrim
10    Festaque coelifugam quae coluere Deum,
Deliciasque refers, hiberni gaudia ruris,
Haustaque per lepidos Gallica musta focos.
Quid quereris refugam vino dapibusque poesin?
Carmen amat Bacchum, carmina Bacchus amat.
15   Nec puduit Phoebum virides gestasse corymbos,
Atque hederam lauro praeposuisse suae.
Saepius Aoniis clamavit collibus Euoe
Mista Thyoneo turba novena choro.
Naso Corallaeis mala carmina misit ab agris:
20    Non illic epulae non sata vitis erat.
Quid nisi vina, rosasque racemiferumque Lyaeum
Cantavit brevibus Teia musa modis?
Pindaricosque inflat numeros Teumesius Euan,
Et redolet sumptum pagina quaeque merum.

8. M.'s joke about the elegiac couplet 'limping', because its second line
was a foot shorter than its first, is borrowed from Ovid, *Tristia* III i 11–12.
*13–14.* Z. S. Fink, *English Studies* xxi (1939) 164–5, points out that Scaliger,
in the *Poetics*, distinguishes between 'divinely possessed' poets like Homer
and Hesiod, and poets inspired by wine, like Horace, Ennius, Alcaeus and
Aristophanes. Later M. contrasts the kind of poem he wants to write with
that raised from 'the vapours of wine' (Columbia iii 241; Yale i 820).
*15–16. corymbos . . . hederam*] Bacchus was traditionally crowned with ivy
berries and wreathed with ivy.
*17–18. Aoniis . . . collibus*] Cp. *Elegia IV* 29–32*n* (p. 55)    *Thyoneo*]
*Thyoneus* was a name for Bacchus because, according to one tradition,
preserved by Cicero, *Nat. Deor.* III xxiii 58, he was son of Nisus and Thyone
(Semele).    *Euoe*] the shout of the Bacchic revellers.
*19–20.* Ovid was exiled in A.D. 8 to Tomis on the Black Sea, where he
wrote the *Tristia*, the *Ex Ponto* and the *Ibis*. In *Ex Ponto* IV ii 15–22 he admits
that the quality of his poems has suffered from his new surroundings, and
in I iii 49–52 complains of the absence from Tomis of fruit and the vine.
The Coralli were a tribe of Geats from the Danube of whom he saw a
good deal at Tomis: he complains, IV ii 37, 'in this place who is there to
whom I can read my compositions except the yellow-haired Coralli?'
*21. racemiferumque*] The same adjective is used of Bacchus by Ovid, *Met.*
xv 413.
*22. Teia musa*] Anacreon, born at Teos on the Aegean. Ovid calls him by
the same name, *Tristia* ii 364.
*23–6. Teumesius Euan*] Boeotian Bacchus (*Teumesius* from *Teumesus*, a
mountain in Boeotia, and *Euan* from *Euoe*, the Bacchic revellers' cry).
There is a copy of Pindar, possibly M.'s, at Harvard, with the purchase date
15 Nov. 1629 on its flyleaf (French i 204–5): the connection of this volume

25  Dum gravis everso currus crepat axe supinus,
        Et volat Eleo pulvere fuscus eques.
    Quadrimoque madens lyricen Romanus iaccho
        Dulce canit Glyceran, flavicomamque Chloen.
    Iam quoque lauta tibi generoso mensa paratu,
30      Mentis alit vires, ingeniumque fovet.
    Massica foecundam despumant pocula venam,
        Fundis et ex ipso condita metra cado.
    Addimus his artes, fusumque per intima Phoebum
        Corda, favent uni Bacchus, Apollo, Ceres.
35  Scilicet haud mirum tam dulcia carmina per te
        Numine composito tres peperisse deos.
    Nunc quoque Thressa tibi caelato barbitos auro
        Insonat arguta molliter icta manu;
    Auditurque chelys suspensa tapetia circum,
40      Virgineos tremula quae regat arte pedes.
    Illa tuas saltem teneant spectacula musas,
        Et revocent, quantum crapula pellit iners.
    Crede mihi dum psallit ebur, comitataque plectrum
        Implet odoratos festa chorea tholos,
45  Percipies tacitum per pectora serpere Phoebum,
        Quale repentinus permeat ossa calor,
    Perque puellares oculos digitumque sonantem
        Irruet in totos lapsa Thalia sinus.
    Namque elegia levis multorum cura deorum est,
50      Et vocat ad numeros quemlibet illa suos;
    Liber adest elegis, Eratoque, Ceresque, Venusque,
        Et cum purpurea matre tenellus Amor.
    Talibus inde licent convivia larga poetis,
        Saepius et veteri commaduisse mero.

with M. has, however, been questioned by M. Kelley and S. D. Atkins,
*Studies in Bibliography* xvii (1964) 77–82. M. is thinking here of *Olymp.*
ii–iv, odes in honour of charioteers who took part in the Olympic games
held near Elis.
*27–8. lyricen Romanus*] Horace, who sings the charms of Glycera in *Odes*
I xix and woos Chloe (called 'golden-haired', III ix 19) in I xxiii.     *Quad-*
*rimoque . . . iaccho*] Echoes *Odes* I ix 7–8 *quadrimum . . . merum.*
*31. Massica*] Mt Massicus was famous for its wine: M. is echoing Horace,
*Odes* I i 19: *veteris pocula Massici.*
*37. Thressa . . . barbitos*] Cp. Ovid, *Am.* II xi 32 *Threiciam . . . lyram*; the
lyre is called Thracian because Orpheus was of Thrace.
*48. Thalia*] One of the muses; Horace, *Odes* IV vi 25, refers to her as the
muse of lyric poetry.
*51. Erato*] The muse of love poetry, according to Ovid, *Ars Am.* ii 16.
*53. licent*] M.'s construction here has no classical precedent.

55  At qui bella refert, et adulto sub Iove caelum,
        Heroasque pios, semideosque duces,
    Et nunc sancta canit superum consulta deorum,
        Nunc latrata fero regna profunda cane,
    Ille quidem parce Samii pro more magistri
60      Vivat, et innocuos praebeat herba cibos;
    Stet prope fagineo pellucida lympha catillo,
        Sobriaque e puro pocula fonte bibat.
    Additur huic scelerisque vacans, et casta iuventus,
        Et rigidi mores, et sine labe manus.
65  Qualis veste nitens sacra, et lustralibus undis
        Surgis ad infensos augur iture deos.
    Hoc ritu vixisse ferunt post rapta sagacem
        Lumina Tiresian, Ogygiumque Linon,
    Et lare devoto profugum Calchanta, senemque
70      Orpheon edomitis sola per antra feris;
    Sic dapis exiguus, sic rivi potor Homerus
        Dulichium vexit per freta longa virum,

55. *adulto . . . Iove*] As opposed to the youthful and amorous Jove.
58. *cane*] The dog is Cerberus, guardian of the underworld.
59. *Samii . . . magistri*] Pythagoras–'the first', as Ovid remarks, *Met.*
xv 72–3, 'to decry the placing of animal food upon our tables'. Iamblichus,
*Life of Pythagoras* iii, records that the philosopher entirely abstained from
wine and animal food.
68. *Tiresian*] Tiresias was a Theban prophet, blinded by Juno and given
prophetic powers by Jove. His water-drinking is given prominence by
Stephanus (*s.v.* Tiresias): *Author est Strabo lib. 9 Tiresiae monumentum fuisse
sub Tilphosso monte Boeotiae, iuxta fontem eiusdem nominis, ubi profugus diem
suum obiit, cum iam senex gelidissimam Tilphossae aquam hausisset, ibidemque
Thebanos sepulto divinos honores tribuisse* (According to Strabo Book 9
Tiresias' monument was at the foot of Mount Tilphossus in Boeotia, near
the fountain of the same name; he took refuge there and, already advanced
in age, died from drinking the freezing water of Tilphossa; the Thebans
buried him there and honoured him as a god). Actually all Strabo says
(IX ii 27) is that the tomb is near Tilphossus.    *Ogygiumque Linon*] Linus,
son of Apollo and Terpsichore, instructed Orpheus. *Ogygius* means Theban,
from Ogyges, mythical founder of Thebes.
69. *Calchanta*] Calchas is a Greek in Homer. It was Guido delle Colonne
who first made him a Trojan, substituting him for Homer's Chryses. Thus
in Chaucer's *Troilus and Criseyde* i 64–84 Calchas leaves Troy when he
foresees its fall. There is some emphasis in Chaucer on his ensuing poverty
(iv 85–91), but no mention of his simple mode of life. Guido merely says
that Calchas lives *in paupertate et exilio* among the Greeks.
71. M. here is deliberately contradicting Horace, *Epist.* I xix 1–6, who
argues that no good poet is ever a water-drinker, and that the way Homer

Et per monstrificam Perseiae Phoebados aulam,
　　Et vada femineis insidiosa sonis,
75　Perque tuas rex ime domos, ubi sanguine nigro
　　Dicitur umbrarum detinuisse greges.
Diis etenim sacer est vates, divumque sacerdos,
　　Spirat et occultum pectus, et ora Iovem.
At tu si quid agam, scitabere (si modo saltem
80　Esse putas tanti noscere siquid agam)
Paciferum canimus caelesti semine regem,
　　Faustaque sacratis saecula pacta libris,
Vagitumque Dei, et stabulantem paupere tecto
　　Qui suprema suo cum patre regna colit.
85　Stelliparumque polum, modulantesque aethere turmas,
　　Et subito elisos ad sua fana deos.
Dona quidem dedimus Christi natalibus illa
　　Illa sub auroram lux mihi prima tulit.
Te quoque pressa manent patriis meditata cicutis,
90　Tu mihi, cui recitem, iudicis instar eris.

*To Charles Diodati, staying in the country. He had written on 13 Dec. and asked
that his poems should be excused if they had been less good than usual. The reason he
gave was that the magnificent reception which his friends had given him had prevented
him from paying proper attention to the muses. This was the answer he received.*

I, with my empty stomach, wish you health which you, with your full one,
may need. But why does your muse lure mine[3] out into the open, and not
allow her to seek the obscurity which she desires? Perhaps you want my
poem to tell you how warmly I return your love, and how I cherish you.
You could scarcely learn that from this poem, believe me, because my
love cannot be shut up in tight-fitting metres, and being sound refuses to
limp[8] along in elegiac couplets. How well you describe the splendid feasts,
the December merry-making, the festal days in honour of the God who
came down from heaven, and the charms and delights of the winter country-
side, with French wines drunk beside friendly fires. But why complain that

writes about wine shows he was not one.　　*dapis exiguus*] The pseudo-
Herodotean life of Homer presents him wandering from town to town
and living on alms. Stephanus (*s.v.* Homer) also draws attention to his
poverty (*rebusque omnibus egentem*).
*72-6. Dulichium . . . virum*] Ulysses; the island of Dulichium formed part
of his kingdom.　　*Perseiae Phoebados*] Circe, daughter of Phoebus and
Perseis, who turned Ulysses' followers into swine (*Od.* x 274-574).
*femineis . . . sonis*] The sirens' song, described *Od.* xii 184-92.　　*tuas . . .
domos*] The descent to the underworld is narrated *Od.* xi, and the libation
of 'dark blood' in xi 34-6.
*89-90.* The poems which await Diodati along with *Nativity Ode* are,
argues J. Carey, *RES* n.s. xiv (1963) 383-6, the Italian sonnets. M. was
presumably expecting to see Diodati soon: the latter was in Geneva by
Apr. 1630, when he was matriculated at the Academy to read theology.

banquet and bottle frighten poetry away?[13] Song loves Bacchus, and Bacchus loves songs.[14] Phoebus was not ashamed to wear green clusters of ivy-berries,[15] or to prize ivy-leaves more than his own laurel.[16] The troop of nine muses has often mingled with Thyoneus's throng and shrieked 'Euoe!' across the Aonian hills.[17] Ovid sent back poems from the land of the Coralli,[19] but they did not have banquets or cultivate the vine there, so the poems were no good.[20] What did the poet from Teos[22] sing about in his neat little verses but wines and roses and Bacchus with bunches and bunches of grapes?[21] It was Teumasian Bacchus who inspired Pindar's odes,[23] and every page smells of the wine he has been drinking–as the heavy chariot crashes over with its axle in the air and the horseman flashes by, black with Olympia's dust.[26] The Roman lute-player[27] was drunk with four-year-old wine when he sang his sweet songs about Glycera and about Chloe with her golden hair.[28] And now a sumptuous table strengthens *your* mind and warms *your* genius with its rich array. Your goblets of Massic[31] wine foam with poetic power, and you pour out the verses which were stored up inside the bottle. Then again, you have artistry, and Phoebus is present in your heart of hearts. Bacchus, Apollo and Ceres are on your side, and only yours. No wonder you are the mouthpiece for such lovely poems: three gods have combined their godheads and speak through you! Now, too, the Thracian lyre,[37] with its gold engraving, plays for you, as a skilled hand softly plucks it. In rooms hung round with tapestry the harp is heard, and its trembling strings direct the feet of the dancing girls. Let these sights, at any rate, catch your muse's attention, and call back whatever powers sluggish drunkenness drives away. Believe me, while the ivory plectrum dances over the strings and the crowd of merry-makers, keeping time with it, fills the perfumed ballroom, you will notice Phoebus creeping silently into your heart, like a sudden warmth flowing through your bones. Girls' eyes and girls' fingers playing will make Thalia[48] dart into your breast and take command of it. For there are a lot of gods who look after light-footed elegy, and she calls anyone she pleases to her tune. Bacchus aids elegies, and so does Erato[51] and Ceres and Venus and tender little Cupid beside his rosy mother. So grand banquets are quite all right[53] for elegiac poets, and they can get drunk on old wine as often as they like. But the poet who writes about wars, and about a heaven ruled over by a Jove who has outgrown his boy-hood,[55] about heroes who stick to their duty and princes who are half gods; the poet whose subject is, one minute, the holy counsels of the gods above, and the next, those deep-buried kingdoms where a savage dog[58] barks–let this poet live frugally, like the philosopher from Samos,[59] and let herbs provide his harmless diet. Let a bowl of beech-wood, filled with clear water, stand by him, and may he drink soberly from a pure spring. In addition his youth must be chaste and free from crime, his morals strict and his hand unstained. He must be like you, priest, when, bathed in holy water and gleaming in your sacred vestment, you rise to go and face the angry gods. In this way, so it is said, wise Tiresias[68] lived after the loss of his sight, and Theban Linus, and Calchas,[69] when he had fled from his doomed home, and old Orpheus, when he tamed wild beasts among lonely caves. In this way, sparing of food, and drinking water from the brook, Homer[71] guided Ulysses[72] across great oceans and through Circe's hall, where men were turned to monsters, and over the shallows made treacherous by the sirens' song, and through your dwellings, infernal king, where he detained the troops of ghosts, or so the story goes, with a libation of dark blood.[76] For the poet is sacred to the gods: he is their priest: his innermost heart and his mouth are both full of Jove.

But if you want to know what I am doing–if, that is, you think it worth while to know whether I am doing anything at all–I am writing a poem about the king who was born of heavenly seed, and who brought peace to men. I am writing about the blessed ages promised in Holy Scripture, about the infant cries of God, about the stabling under a poor roof of Him who dwells with His Father in the highest heavens, about the sky's giving birth to a new star, about the hosts who sang in the air, and about the pagan gods suddenly shattered in their own shrines. These are the gifts I have given for Christ's birthday: the first light of the dawn brought them to me.

Some terse little poems which I have composed on your native country's pipes[89] are also waiting for you. You shall be, as it were, my judge, when I recite them to you.[90]

# 36 The Passion

*Date.* Mar. 1630? The opening lines clearly refer to the *Nativity Ode*, so the poem must be dated after Christmas 1629. Its subject suggests that it was an Easter poem (Easter day fell on 28 Mar. in 1630). The metre and rhyme scheme are those of the introductory stanzas of the *Nativity Ode*.
*Publication.* 1645 (22. latest]latter    45. up lock,]up-lock, ) 1673 (the text followed here except in 42 where 1673 misprints a comma after 'fit').
*Modern criticism.* Louis Martz, *The Poetry of Meditation* (New Haven 1954) pp. 167–8, suggests that in this poem M. is trying to employ the uncongenial devices of the Catholic meditation upon a subject which was itself generally unattractive to the Puritans.

I

    Erewhile of music, and ethereal mirth,
    Wherewith the stage of air and earth did ring,
    And joyous news of heavenly infant's birth,
    My muse with angels did divide to sing;
5   But headlong joy is ever on the wing,
      In wintry solstice like the shortened light
    Soon swallowed up in dark and long out-living night.

¶ 36. *4. divide*] execute 'divisions', or rapid melodic passages. Elsewhere in M.'s poetry 'divide' means either 'share' or 'separate': it is nowhere else used intransitively, as here.
*6. wintry solstice*] The day is shortest at the winter solstice (22 Dec.). The line is inverted.

II

For now to sorrow must I tune my song,
And set my harp to notes of saddest woe,
10    Which on our dearest Lord did seize ere long,
Dangers, and snares, and wrongs, and worse than so,
Which he for us did freely undergo.
     Most perfect hero, tried in heaviest plight
Of labours huge and hard, too hard for human wight.

III

15    He sovran priest, stooping his regal head
That dropped with odorous oil down his fair eyes,
Poor fleshly tabernacle entered,
His starry front low-roofed beneath the skies;
O what a mask was there, what a disguise!
20        Yet more; the stroke of death he must abide,
Then lies him meekly down fast by his brethren's side.

IV

These latest scenes confine my roving verse,
To this horizon is my Phoebus bound,
His godlike acts; and his temptations fierce,
25    And former sufferings otherwhere are found;
Loud o'er the rest Cremona's trump doth sound;
     Me softer airs befit, and softer strings
Of lute, or viol still, more apt for mournful things.

V

Befriend me night best patroness of grief,
30    Over the pole thy thickest mantle throw,

14. *labours*] Suggesting Hercules, see *Nativity Ode* 227–8n (p. 112).
15. *priest*] Christ is called a 'high priest' in *Heb.* ii 17.
16. The name *Christ*, as M. points out in *De doctrina* I v (Columbia xiv 184–5), means 'anointed' in Greek.
17. The body is referred to as a 'tabernacle' in *2 Cor.* v 1 and *2 Pet.* i 13–14.
21. *brethren's*] Cp. Christ's references to his 'brethren', *Matt.* xii 48–9 and xxv 40; also *Heb.* ii 14–17: 'that through death he might destroy him that had the power of death. . . . Wherefore in all things it behoved him to be made like unto his brethren.'
26. *Cremona's trump*] The *Christiad*, a Latin poem, largely a pastiche of Virgil, in six books on the life of Christ, written at the instigation of Pope Leo X by Marco Girolamo Vida and published in Cremona, Vida's birthplace, in 1535.
28. *still*] quiet.
30. *pole*] sky.

And work my flattered fancy to belief,
That heaven and earth are coloured with my woe;
My sorrows are too dark for day to know:
  The leaves should all be black whereon I write,
35 And letters where my tears have washed a wannish
    white.

### VI

See see the chariot, and those rushing wheels,
That whirled the prophet up at Chebar flood,
My spirit some transporting cherub feels,
To bear me where the towers of Salem stood,
40 Once glorious towers, now sunk in guiltless blood;
  There doth my soul in holy vision sit
In pensive trance, and anguish, and ecstatic fit.

### VII

Mine eye hath found that sad sepulchral rock
That was the casket of heaven's richest store,
45 And here though grief my feeble hands up lock,
Yet on the softened quarry would I score
My plaining verse as lively as before;
  For sure so well instructed are my tears,
That they would fitly fall in ordered characters.

34-5. Sylvester's *Lachrimae Lachrimarum* (1612), a funeral elegy on Prince
Henry, has a title page printed black with the letters left white. M. may,
however, have in mind the more common practice of edging the page
on which a funeral elegy was printed with a thick band of black, and thus
be distinguishing between his page, which should be 'all' black, and the
usual page, which is only edged.
36-40. Ezekiel's vision of the chariot of God was 'by the river of Chebar'
(i 1).    *rushing wheels*] Cp. 'the noise of the wheels . . . and a noise of
a great rushing' (iii 13).    *whirled . . . up*] Cp. 'the spirit lifted me up'
(iii 14).    *cherub*] The 'living creatures' which bear the chariot are later
identified as cherubim (x 8-22).    *Salem*] Jerusalem, to which Ezekiel
was sent with the message 'Thou art become guilty in thy blood that
thou hast shed' (xxii 4).
43. *rock*] Sandys 166-7 uses this word frequently in his description of the
Holy Sepulchre: 'the naturall rocke . . . hewne into the forme of a Chappell
. . . the selfe same rocke . . . a passage through the midst of the rocke . . .
a compass roofe of the solid rocke'.

### VIII

50     Or should I thence hurried on viewless wing,
     Take up a weeping on the mountains wild,
     The gentle neighbourhood of grove and spring
     Would soon unbosom all their echoes mild,
     And I (for grief is easily beguiled)
55        Might think the infection of my sorrows loud,
     Had got a race of mourners on some pregnant cloud.

*This subject the author finding to be above the years he had when he wrote it, and nothing satisfied with what was begun, left it unfinished.*

## 37 On Shakespeare

*Date.* 1630: added to title in *1645* and *1673*.

*Publication.* First printed 1632, anonymously, among prefatory material to the Shakespeare Second Folio, headed *An Epitaph on the admirable Dramatic Poet, W. Shakespeare*, with five verbal variants from *1673* (1. needs]need 6. weak]dull 8. live-long]lasting 10. heart]part 13. itself]herself ). In one state of the Second Folio – surviving in eight exemplars, listed by R. M. Smith, *The Variant Issues of Shakespeare's Second Folio and M.'s First Published English Poem* (Lehigh University 1928) – there is an additional verbal variant (4. star-ypointing]star-ypointed ). Printed for the second time, with the same heading as that in the Second Folio, in *Poems: Written by Wil. Shakespeare, Gent* (1640) with M.'s initials and four verbal variants from *1673* (1. needs]need 6. need'st]needs 13. itself]yourself 15. dost]doth ).

Next printed *1645* (no significant variants from *1673*, but in 9 *1645* misprints 'toth' shame' for 'to th' shame'). Next printed 1664 in Shakespeare Third Folio (heading and five verbal variants as in 1632). Next printed *1673* (the text followed here).

*Modern criticism.* Fletcher ii 506 suggests that M. knew Robert Allot, the bookseller to whom Edward Blount's share in the First Folio was assigned 26 Jun. 1630, and thus wrote *Shakespeare* in 1630 knowing that a second edition of Shakespeare's works was afoot. There were, however, four other booksellers who had shares in the First Folio.

H. W. Garrod, *E & S* xii (1926) 7–23, discusses the textual variants. He also suggests as sources for *Shakespeare* Massinger and Field's *Fatal Dowry*

50. *viewless*] invisible; cp. *Comus* 92.
51. Cp. *Jer.* ix 10: 'For the mountains will I take up a weeping.'
56. Pindar, *Pyth.* ii 21–48, tells how Ixion, when a guest on Olympus, tried to rape Hera; but she substituted a cloud for herself, on which he begot Centaurus, father of the Centaurs.

II i 69–72 and Thomas Tomkins's *Albumazar* I iv 3–4. To these H. Mutsch-
mann (*Further Studies Concerning the Origin of Paradise Lost* (Tartu 1934)
47–55) adds the verses *To the memory of my beloved, The Author* which Ben
Jonson prefixed to the First Folio, and the anonymous epitaph on Stanley
('Ask who lies here . . .') attributed in some seventeenth century MSS to
Shakespeare. The Stanley lines were first proposed as a source by F. Town-
send (Todd vi 84–5) and the claim is repeated by T. Spencer, *MLN* liii
(1938) 366–7.

> What needs my Shakespeare for his honoured bones,
> The labour of an age in piled stones,
> Or that his hallowed relics should be hid
> Under a star-ypointing pyramid?
> 5 Dear son of memory, great heir of fame,
> What need'st thou such weak witness of thy name?
> Thou in our wonder and astonishment
> Hast built thyself a live-long monument.
> For whilst to the shame of slow-endeavouring art,
> 10 Thy easy numbers flow, and that each heart
> Hath from the leaves of thy unvalued book,
> Those Delphic lines with deep impression took,
> Then thou our fancy of itself bereaving,
> Dost make us marble with too much conceiving;

¶ 37. *4. star-ypointing*] Cp. Propertius III ii 19: *Pyramidum sumptus ad
sidera ducti*, quoted by Sandys 127–9 in his description of the pyramids,
some phrases from which may have influenced M. here ('the labours of
the *Jewes* . . . No stone so little throughout the whole, as to be drawne by
our carriages . . . Twenty years it was a-building'). The retention of the
Middle English 'y-' prefix before the past participle was a common feature
of the archaistic language of Spenser and his imitators. Spenser never uses
this prefix before a present participle: M.'s 'ypointing' is a false archaism.
*5. son of memory*] M. makes Shakespeare brother to the Muses, see *Id Plat*
3*n* (p. 66). Browne (i 226) calls the English poets 'sons of Memory'
in a passage where he is regretting that no 'pyramis' whose top should
'seem the stars to kiss' has been built to commemorate Spenser. M. may
be alluding to this passage and contrasting the needs of Spenser with those
of Shakespeare.
*10. easy numbers*] Cp. the epistle *To the great Variety of Readers* prefaced by
Heming and Condell to the First Folio: 'His mind and hand went together:
And what he thought, he uttered with that easinesse, that wee have scarse
received from him a blot in his papers.'
*11. unvalued*] invaluable.
*12. Delphic lines*] Apollo, god of poetry, had his oracle at Delphi.
*14.* Cp. for the conceit *Il Penseroso* 42*n* (p. 141).

15  And so sepulchred in such pomp dost lie,
    That kings for such a tomb would wish to die.

# 38 On the University Carrier

who sickened in the time of his vacancy, being forbid to go to
London, by reason of the Plague

*Date.* Jan. 1631. Thomas Hobson, who died 1 Jan. 1631, aged eighty-six,
was a well-known Cambridge figure. According to Steele (*Spectator* 509;
14 Oct. 1712) the expression 'Hobson's choice' originated in his practice,
when he hired out hackney horses, of making each customer take the
horse which stood nearest the stable door. His death was commemorated
in numerous poems, of which some are printed from seventeenth-century
MSS and miscellanies by G. Blakemore Evans, *MLQ* iv (1943) 281–90
and ix (1948) 10, 184, and by W. Evans, *PQ* xxvi (1947) 321–7.
*Publication.* *1645* (2 And]A ). Next printed *Wit Restor'd* (1658), a garbled
version, of which the textual variants are discussed by W. R. Parker, *MLR*
xxxi (1936) 395–402. *1673* (the text followed here).

      Here lies old Hobson, Death hath broke his girt,
      And here alas, hath laid him in the dirt,
      Or else the ways being foul, twenty to one,
      He's here stuck in a slough, and overthrown.
  5   'Twas such a shifter, that if truth were known,
      Death was half glad when he had got him down;
      For he had any time this ten years full,
      Dodged with him, betwixt Cambridge and the Bull.
      And surely, Death could never have prevailed,
 10   Had not his weekly course of carriage failed;
      But lately finding him so long at home,
      And thinking now his journey's end was come,
      And that he had ta'en up his latest inn,
      In the kind office of a chamberlain
 15   Showed him his room where he must lodge that night,
      Pulled off his boots, and took away the light:
      If any ask for him, it shall be said,
      Hobson has supped, and 's newly gone to bed.

¶ 38. *1. girt*] Variant form of 'girth', current in seventeenth century.
*5. shifter*] trickster.
*8. Dodged with him*] Dodged about in an attempt to catch him. According
to *OED* this is the first occurrence of 'dodge' in this sense.     *the Bull*]
The Bull Inn in Bishopsgate, Hobson's stopping-place in London.
*14. chamberlain*] An attendant at an inn in charge of the bedchambers.

# 39 Another on the Same

*Date.* Jan. 1631: see headnote to previous poem.

*Publication.* An incomplete version was printed in *A Banquet of Jests* (1640, reprinted 1657). *1645* (4. on]on,      8. time:]time;      16. quickened,] quickn'd; ). *Wit Restor'd* (1658), a garbled version. *1673* (the text followed here). There is no evidence to connect the printings of 1640, 1657 or 1658 with M. W.R.Parker discusses the textual variants of 1640 and 1658, *MLR* xxxi (1936) 395–402, and suggests that a third Hobson poem which appears in these miscellanies–'Hobson lies here amongst his many betters . . .' (Columbia xviii 359, 590–1)–may be by M.

> Here lieth one who did most truly prove,
> That he could never die while he could move,
> So hung his destiny never to rot
> While he might still jog on and keep his trot,
> 5 Made of sphere-metal, never to decay
> Until his revolution was at stay.
> Time numbers motion, yet (without a crime
> 'Gainst old truth) motion numbered out his time:
> And like an engine moved with wheel and weight,
> 10 His principles being ceased, he ended straight,
> Rest that gives all men life, gave him his death,
> And too much breathing put him out of breath;
> Nor were it contradiction to affirm
> Too long vacation hastened on his term.
> 15 Merely to drive the time away he sickened,
> Fainted, and died, nor would with ale be quickened,
> Nay, quoth he, on his swooning bed outstretched,
> If I may not carry, sure I'll ne'er be fetched,
> But vow though the cross doctors all stood hearers,

¶ 39. 5. *sphere-metal*] Aristotle discusses the indestructibility of the substance of which the spheres of the universe are made in *De Coelo* I iii.

7. *Time numbers motion*] Aristotle calls time the 'number of motion' in *Physics* iv 11–12, and M. quotes from this discussion of the inter-dependence of time and motion in *De doctrina* I xiii (Columbia xv 240).

10. *principles*] motive forces.

12. *breathing*] respite.

14. *vacation . . . term*] M. plays on two meanings of 'term': 'University Term', 'limit in time' (i.e. death). There is a similar pun on 'vacation' in the University sense, and in the sense 'freedom from work'.

18. *carry . . . fetched*] A play on the phrase 'fetch and carry', and the seventeenth-century sense of 'fetch', 'to restore to consciousness'.

19. *cross doctors*] The Doctors of the University who are opposing (*OED* Cross, *a.* 5. a) Hobson's journeys to and fro.

20    For one carrier put down to make six bearers.
      Ease was his chief disease, and to judge right,
      He died for heaviness that his cart went light,
      His leisure told him that his time was come,
      And lack of load, made his life burdensome,
25    That even to his last breath (there be that say't)
      As he were pressed to death, he cried more weight;
      But had his doings lasted as they were,
      He had been an immortal carrier.
      Obedient to the moon he spent his date
30    In course reciprocal, and had his fate
      Linked to the mutual flowing of the seas,
      Yet (strange to think) his wain was his increase:
      His letters are delivered all and gone,
      Only remains this superscription.

# 40 An Epitaph on the Marchioness of Winchester

*Date.* Apr.–May 1631. Jane Savage, who had married Lord John St John
Paulet, fifth Marquis of Winchester in 1622, died 15 Apr. 1631. Both she
and her husband were Roman Catholics. Sir John Pory wrote to Sir Thomas
Puckering that she 'had an impostume upon her cheek lanced; the humour
fell down into her throat, and quickly despatched her', adding that her
death was lamented 'as well in respect of other her virtues, as that she was
inclining to become a Protestant' (*Court and Times of Charles I*, ed. T.

20. *put down*] brought into disuse.      *bearers*] of coffin.
22. *heaviness*] sadness.
26. *pressed to death*] Cp. *Harrison's Description of England*, ed. F. J. Furnivall
(1876) p. 228: 'Such fellons as stand mute, and speake not at their arraign-
ment, are pressed to death by huge weights [laid upon a boord, that lieth
over their brest, and a sharpe stone under their backs] and these commonlie
hold their peace, thereby to save their goods unto their wives and children,
which, if they were condemned, should be confiscated to the prince.'
*cried*] implored.
30. *In course reciprocal*] He went backwards and forwards between London
and Cambridge as regularly as the ebbing and flowing of the tide.
32. *wain*] Play on 'wain' meaning 'waggon' and 'wane' meaning
'decrease'.
34. *superscription*] Play on two senses of the word – 'the address on a letter'
and 'an inscription above a grave'.

Birch (1894) ii 106). No personal connection between M. and the Paulets is known: probably the poem was intended as a contribution to a proposed volume of Cambridge elegies. Numerous poems on Jane's death survive, including elegies by Jonson, Davenant and Strode, and several in BM MS Sloane 1446, which also contains (37v.–38) a version of M.'s elegy which substitutes for *15–24*: 'Seven times had the yearly star / In every sign set up his car, / Since for her they did request / The god that sits at marriage feast, / When first the early Matrons run / To greet her of her lovely son.' W. R. Parker, *MLR* (1949) 547–50, points out that these lines contain one accurate piece of biographical information not in the published version, and suggests that they represent an authentic early draft which was allowed to circulate.

*Publication. 1645* (*52.* lease;]lease, *53.* Here,]Here ). *1673* (the text followed here, except in *61* where *1673* misprints a full stop after 'glory'). *Modern criticism.* Sprott 16–20 argues, on metrical grounds, that the first half of *L'Allegro* may have been written earlier; A. Oras, *N & Q* cxcviii (1953) 332–3, opposes this view. M. F. Moloney, *MLN* lxxii (1957) 174–8, traces M.'s handling of the octosyllabic here to the 'funerary art of Jonson, made familiar by the Folio of 1616'.

> This rich marble doth inter
> The honoured wife of Winchester,
> A viscount's daughter, an earl's heir,
> Besides what her virtues fair
> 5  Added to her noble birth,
> More than she could own from earth.
> Summers three times eight save one
> She had told, alas too soon,
> After so short time of breath,
> 10  To house with darkness, and with death.
> Yet had the number of her days
> Been as complete as was her praise,
> Nature and fate had had no strife
> In giving limit to her life.
> 15  Her high birth, and her graces sweet,
> Quickly found a lover meet;
> The virgin choir for her request
> The god that sits at marriage-feast;
> He at their invoking came
> 20  But with a scarce-well-lighted flame;

¶ 40. *11–14.* I.e. if she had enjoyed as full a measure of life as she has of praise, her death would be perfectly natural.

*17. virgin choir*] bridesmaids.    *request*] invoke.

*18. god*] Hymen.

*20.* In Ovid, *Met.* x 6–7, Hymen appears at another ill-fated marriage,

And in his garland as he stood,
Ye might discern a cypress bud.
Once had the early matrons run
To greet her of a lovely son,
25    And now with second hope she goes,
And calls Lucina to her throes;
But whether by mischance or blame
Atropos for Lucina came;
And with remorseless cruelty,
30    Spoiled at once both fruit and tree:
The hapless babe before his birth
Had burial, yet not laid in earth,
And the languished mother's womb
Was not long a living tomb.
35    So have I seen some tender slip
Saved with care from winter's nip,
The pride of her carnation train,
Plucked up by some unheedy swain,
Who only thought to crop the flower
40    New shot up from vernal shower;
But the fair blossom hangs the head
Sideways as on a dying bed,

that of Orpheus and Eurydice, with a spluttering and smoky torch that will not catch fire properly.

22. *cypress*] Called 'funeral' by Virgil, *Aen.* vi 216, and by Horace, *Epod.* v 18; the tree of mourning in Elizabethan poetry.

23. *early matrons*] midwives.

24. *greet her of* ] M. seems to be using 'greet' in a sense otherwise peculiar to Spenser, 'offer congratulations upon'. But Spenser does not use this verb with the preposition 'of' (here equivalent to 'on account of').

24. *son*] Charles, born 1629, created first Duke of Bolton, 1689.

26. *Lucina*] Roman goddess of childbirth.

28. *Atropos*] One of the Parcae, whose function it was to cut the thread of life.

31. Jane, as the Duchess of Buckingham informed her father in a letter written 16 Apr. 1631, 'was delivered before shee died of a deed boye' (*Rutland MSS*, Hist. MSS Com., 12th report, part iv (1888) i 490).

33. *languished*] reduced to languor. Browne i 190 rhymes 'mother's womb' and 'living tomb', and Sylvester (Du Bartas 616) also rhymes 'womb' and 'living Toomb'.

35. *slip*] A cutting taken from a plant. In M.'s simile Jane is this precious cutting which has survived winter (twenty-three years of life) but is plucked by death (the 'swain'), who meant to take only the baby ('the flower / New shot up').

37. *her carnation train*] her retinue of carnations (clove-pinks).

And those pearls of dew she wears,
Prove to be presaging tears
45   Which the sad morn had let fall
On her hastening funeral.
Gentle lady may thy grave
Peace and quiet ever have;
After this thy travail sore
50   Sweet rest seize thee evermore,
That to give the world increase,
Shortened hast thy own life's lease;
Here, besides the sorrowing
That thy noble house doth bring,
55   Here be tears of perfect moan
Wept for thee in Helicon,
And some flowers, and some bays,
For thy hearse to strew the ways,
Sent thee from the banks of Came,
60   Devoted to thy virtuous name;
Whilst thou bright saint high sit'st in glory,
Next her much like to thee in story,
That fair Syrian shepherdess,
Who after years of barrenness,
65   The highly favoured Joseph bore
To him that served for her before,
And at her next birth much like thee,
Through pangs fled to felicity,
Far within the bosom bright
70   Of blazing majesty and light,
There with thee, new welcome saint,
Like fortunes may her soul acquaint,
With thee there clad in radiant sheen,
No marchioness, but now a queen.

56. *Helicon*] A mountain in Boeotia, sacred to the Muses.

59. *Came*] The river Cam, which flows through Cambridge.

63. *shepherdess*] Rachel, Jacob's wife; cp. *Gen.* xxix 9: 'Rachel came with her father's sheep: for she kept them.'     *fair*] Cp. *Gen.* xxix 17: 'Rachel was beautiful and well-favoured'.

65. *bore*] Cp. *Gen.* xxx 22–4.

66. *him*] Jacob; cp. *Gen.* xxix 20: 'And Jacob served seven years for Rachel.'

68. *pangs*] Cp. *Gen.* xxxv 17–18: 'She was in hard labour.' Rachel's son lived and 'as her soul was in departing' she called him Ben-oni.

# 41 L'Allegro

*Date.* Summer 1631? There is no certain evidence for dating *L'Allegro*
or *Il Penseroso*. Bateson 155 would place them in the late summer of 1629,
and Fletcher ii 480–3 agrees, but Bateson's argument rests on a questionable
interpretation of *Elegia VI* 89–90 (see note to these lines). Tillyard[2] 1–28
contends that the twin poems grew out of the debate about night and day
in M.'s first *Prolusion*, and were written for an academic audience at Cam-
bridge in M.'s last long vacation (1631), thus the opening of *L'Allegro* is
academic burlesque (a view opposed by Whiting (136–41) who favours a
dating in the Horton period). The absence of the poems from the Trinity
MS is usually taken to indicate a date earlier than Horton, though Grierson
i xix points out that the art of the two poems is akin to that of the descriptive
passages in *Comus*, than which they may therefore be later. The various
attempts to locate the poems' scenery in Cambridge, Horton, Stanton St
John or near London are all suspect (see, for example, A. H. J. Baines,
*N & Q* clxxxviii (1945) 68–71, who recognizes it as that of the Chiltern
summits, about two hours' ride from Horton). Rather more trustworthy
is A. Oras's argument that the prosody is later than that of the *Winchester
Epitaph* (*N & Q* cxcviii (1953) 332–3).
*Publication.* *1645* (*33.* you]ye      *53.* horn]horn,      *62.* dight,]dight.
*104.* And by the]And he by      *108.* corn,]corn      *122.* prize,]prize ),
*1673* (the text followed here, except in *3*, where *1673* misprints a full stop
after 'forlorn' (see note), in *18*, where it misprints a full stop after 'spring',
and in *124*, where it misprints a comma after 'commend').
*Metre and style.* *L'Allegro* and *Il Penseroso* are metrically almost identical.
No precedent has been found in English for such a combination of intricate
prelude with couplet continuation. Each poem begins with a prelude of
ten lines rhyming *abbacddeec*, with the number of syllables per line, excluding
feminine endings, alternately six and ten. This 6/10 pattern of line-lengths
presumably derives from the seven and eleven syllable lines of the *canzone*,
just as the rhyme scheme reflects the Italian sonnet. See also Fletcher, below.
From line *11* onwards both poems are in nominal octosyllabic (iambic)
couplets, but vividly diversified with frequent trochaic (seven-syllable)
lines (32 per cent of the lines in *L'Allegro* and 16 per cent in *Il Penseroso*)
occurring indiscriminately among the octosyllables, which are themselves
sometimes trochaic (e.g. *L'Allegro 19–20, 69–70*) and have a scattering of
extrametrical final syllables (e.g. *L'Allegro 46, 85–6, 141–2*; *Il Penseroso
21–2, 48–9*). Sprott has noticed that the percentage of catalectic lines in
*L'Allegro 11–100* inclusive is 50, but in *101–152* it is only 15.4, and in *Il
Penseroso* 16.9. This change in prosody may, he conjectures, mean that M.

*Title.* John Florio's *Dictionary* (1598) defines *Allegro* as 'joyfull, merie,
jocond, sportfull, pleasant, frolike'.

wrote the first two-thirds of *L'Allegro* at an earlier period than the rest of the poem and *Il Penseroso*. He may be right, but the accelerated pace of the catalectic lines is more evidently suited to the subject matter of *L'Allegro*'s daylight scenes than to any others in the two poems, and this seems a likelier explanation for the change.

Stylistically, as the footnotes demonstrate, the principal model in *L'Allegro* is Shakespeare (fourteen echoes, four from *A Midsummer Night's Dream*, eight of the others from the early plays). Spenser and the Spenserians come next in importance (twelve instances, five from Sylvester). The long sentences differentiate the couplets from those of Jonson and his 'sons'. *Il Penseroso* has noticeably fewer literary echoes than *L'Allegro*, Shakespeare contributing only five (three from *Romeo and Juliet*, but none from *A Midsummer Night's Dream*), and Sylvester three. In both poems there are only two or three echoes of classical poetry, in spite of the parade of mythological figures.

*Modern criticism.* J. B. Leishman, *E & S* n.s. iv (1951) 1–36, thinks that the starting-point for *L'Allegro* and *Il Penseroso* was the song, perhaps by Strode, in Fletcher's *The Nice Valour* ('Hence, all you vain delights . . .'), and Strode's reply to it. This suggestion was originally made by Seward (see Beaumont and Fletcher, *Works* (1750) 336). Leishman also examines the relationship, first indicated by Warton 94, between the twin poems and *The Author's Abstract of Melancholy* prefixed to the third edition of Burton's *Anatomy* (1628). Connections with the *Anatomy* itself are explored by Whiting 136–41 and W. J. Grace, *SP* lii (1955) 578–83. F. M. Padelford, *MLN* xxii (1907) 200, proposes as source for the morning-scene in *L'Allegro* the anonymous narrative lyric 'The sun when he had spread his rays . . .', printed in the second edition of Tottel's *Miscellany*. Another possible source for *L'Allegro*, pointed out by Warton (40) and supported by S. Foster Damon, *PMLA* xlii (1927) 873–4, is Marston's *Scourge of Villainy* (*Proëmium in librum primum* 9–11 and xi 3–8). N. C. Carpenter, *N & Q* cci (1956) 289–92, argues that M. was influenced in the musical passages of both poems by Spenser's *Epithalamion*.

L. Babb, *SP* xxxvii (1940) 257–73, distinguishes between two opposed Renaissance attitudes to melancholy: the first, originating in Galenic medicine, viewed it as a source of stupidity, fearfulness and illusions; the second, originating in Aristotle's *Problemata* xxx 1, and adopted by Ficino in *De Studiosorum Sanitate Tuenda*, stressed that all who have become eminent in philosophy, poetry or the arts have been of melancholy temperament. At the beginning of *L'Allegro* M. exorcises the Galenic melancholy: in *Il Penseroso* he celebrates the Aristotelian. Babb's explanation is supplemented by I. Samuel, *N & Q* cciii (1958) 430–1, who traces the distinction between a 'divine' and a 'damned' melancholy through Erasmus' *Encomium Moriae* to Socrates' division of righthanded from lefthanded madness in the *Phaedrus*.

Allen 3–23 distinguishes between *L'Allegro*, which represents 'common experience', and *Il Penseroso*, which represents 'intellectual experience':

the poet must graduate from one to the other, and thus the two poems are
the 'rising steps' of M.'s poetic plans. Similarly D. C. Dorian, *MP* xxxi
(1933) 175–8, regarded the poems as the 'autobiographical record of an
important step in M.'s development–his consideration of the question
whether he should suppress either the lighter or the more serious side of
his nature, as man and as poet, for the fuller development of the other'.
F. M. Darnall, *MLN* xxxi (1916) 56–8, had previously suggested that the
poems grew out of the contrast, as M. saw it, between Diodati and himself,
and that this might explain the Italian titles. (Darnall's theory is attacked
by A. Thaler, *MLN* xxxi (1916) 437–8, and reasserted, *MLN* xxxii (1917)
377–9.)

Cleanth Brooks, in his examination of the light imagery (Brooks and
Hardy 131–44), demonstrates that both poems are dominated by half-light,
and that this similarity tends to bring the 'patterns of opposites' together.
The progressive emphasis, in both poems, on images of sound and music,
culminating in the Anglican ritual at the end of *Il Penseroso*, is traced by
K. Svendsen, *Explicator* viii (1950) 49.

S. R. Watson, *PMLA* lvii (1942) 404–20, takes the poems as representations
of the 'ideal day' theme, traceable from Theocritus, through Horace,
*Epod.* ii, to Drayton and the Spenserians. The central personifications of
Mirth and Melancholy, as they had figured in the literary environment of
the sixteenth and seventeenth centuries, are discussed by Tuve² (15–36),
who utilizes some of the valuable information about the neo-Platonic
theories of melancholy contained in Erwin Panofsky's *Albrecht Dürer*
(Princeton 1943) i 157–71.

R. M. Lumiansky, *MLN* lv (1940) 591–4, draws attention to the pre-
dominance of the native element in M.'s vocabulary in the poems, and
Fletcher ii 485–9 gives reasons for thinking that their versification was
influenced by Italian models.

> Hence loathed Melancholy
>     Of Cerberus, and blackest Midnight born,
>     In Stygian cave forlorn
>       'Mongst horrid shapes, and shrieks, and sights
>         unholy,
> 5  Find out some uncouth cell,
>       Where brooding Darkness spreads his jealous
>         wings,

¶ 41. *3. cave*] Cerberus' cave on the bank of the Styx is mentioned by
Virgil, *Aen.* vi 418. The mythological parentage is M.'s invention, (cp.
*Q Nov* 69*n*, p. 39 above.) The 'shrieks' of l. 4 are heard by Aeneas as
he passes the cave (vi 426–7) and come from the souls of dead children. They
connect ll. 3 and 4, and so call for an emendation of the *1673* full stop
after 'forlorn'.

*5. uncouth*] unfrequented, desolate.

And the night-raven sings;
   There under ebon shades, and low-browed
      rocks,
   As ragged as thy locks,
10   In dark Cimmerian desert ever dwell.
But come thou goddess fair and free,
In heaven yclept Euphrosyne,
And by men, heart-easing Mirth,
Whom lovely Venus at a birth
15  With two sister Graces more
To ivy-crowned Bacchus bore;
Or whether (as some sager sing)
The frolic wind that breathes the spring,
Zephyr with Aurora playing,
20  As he met her once a-Maying,
There on beds of violets blue,
And fresh-blown roses washed in dew,
Filled her with thee a daughter fair,
So buxom, blithe, and debonair.
25  Haste thee nymph, and bring with thee

7. *night-raven*] The name given, from Anglo-Saxon times on, to a bird heard to croak or cry in the night and supposedly of evil omen: probably an owl or night-heron.

9. *ragged*] The word occurs nowhere else in M.'s poetry. Cp. *Isa.* ii 21, 'ragged rocks', and *Titus Andronicus* II iii 230: 'the ragged entrails of the pit'.

10. *Cimmerian*] See Q *Nov* 60n (p. 39).

11. *fair and free*] A common formula, found in Drayton, *Eclogue* iv 127 and Sylvester (Du Bartas 17).

12. *yclept*] A Spenserian form (*F.Q.* III v 8) not found elsewhere in M's. poetry.   *Euphrosyne*] Mirth, whose sisters were Aglaia (Brightness) and Thalia (Bloom). Servius, in his note to *Aen.* i 720, records the tradition which makes Venus and Bacchus parents of the Graces: they were usually considered to be daughters of Zeus and Hera or Eurynome.

16. *ivy-crowned*] See *Elegia VI* 15–16n, p. 114 above.

17. *as some sager sing*] M. seems to have invented this parentage. Aurora appears as companion of Zephyrus in Jonson's *Entertainment at Highgate*, and their song (93–4) has M.'s rhymes, 'a-Maying' and 'playing'.

22. Echoing *Taming of the Shrew* II i 174: 'morning roses newly wash'd with dew'.

24. J. B. Leishman, *E & S* n.s. iv (1951) 30 shows that these three adjectives were habitually connected in the early seventeenth century, and follows Todd v 77 in quoting Randolph's *Aristippus* (1630) 'blithe, buxome and deboneer'.   *buxom*] yielding, compliant.   *debonair*] of gentle disposition.

    Jest and youthful Jollity,
    Quips and cranks, and wanton wiles,
    Nods, and becks, and wreathed smiles,
    Such as hang on Hebe's cheek,
30   And love to live in dimple sleek;
    Sport that wrinkled Care derides,
    And Laughter holding both his sides.
    Come, and trip it as you go
    On the light fantastic toe,
35   And in thy right hand lead with thee,
    The mountain nymph, sweet Liberty;
    And if I give thee honour due,
    Mirth, admit me of thy crew
    To live with her, and live with thee,
40   In unreproved pleasures free;
    To hear the lark begin his flight,
    And singing startle the dull night,
    From his watch-tower in the skies,
    Till the dappled dawn doth rise;
45   Then to come in spite of sorrow,

*27. Quips*] smart or witty sayings.     *cranks*] jokes which depend upon twisting or changing the form or meaning of a word.

*28. becks*] P. B. Tillyard, *TLS* (25 Jul. 1952) 485 draws attention to Burton's translation (III ii 2 iv) of *nutibus* ('with nods') in a passage from Musaeus as 'With becks and nods and smiles', and deduces that, though *OED* interprets M.'s 'becks' here as 'gestures expressive of salutation or respect', they are in fact upward nods–'coming-on' gestures. E. B. C. Jones, *TLS* (8 Aug. 1952) 517, agrees.

*29. Hebe's*] Cp. *Vacation Exercise* 38n (p. 77).

*31–2.* S. R. Watson, *N & Q* clxxx (1941) 258, anticipated by Warton (46) compares Fletcher's *Purple Island* iv 13: 'Sportful laughter . . . Defies . . . wrinkled care.'

*33. trip it*] Echoes *Tempest* IV i 46: 'Each one tripping on his toe.'

*34. fantastic*] According to *OED* M. is here using this word in a new sense: 'making fantastic or extravagantly conceived movements'; cp. Drayton, *Nimphidia* 29, 'light fantastick mayde'.

*36. mountain nymph*] Oread. In associating Liberty with mountainous districts M. may be referring to Greece, Switzerland or Calvin's Geneva, which lies between the Jura and the Alps.

*42. dull night*] Probably echoes *Henry V* IV Prologue 11: 'Piercing the night's dull ear.'

*44. dappled*] Echoes *Much Ado* V iii 25–7: 'the gentle day . . . Dapple the drowsy east with spots of grey'.

*45–6.* There has been some argument whether it is L'Allegro or the lark that comes to the window and bids good morrow. Adherents of the latter

And at my window bid good morrow,
Through the sweet-briar, or the vine,
Or the twisted eglantine.
While the cock with lively din,
50   Scatters the rear of darkness thin,
And to the stack, or the barn door,
Stoutly struts his dames before,
Oft list'ning how the hounds and horn
Cheerly rouse the slumb'ring morn,
55   From the side of some hoar hill,
Through the high wood echoing shrill.
Sometime walking not unseen
By hedgerow elms, on hillocks green,
Right against the eastern gate,
60   Where the great sun begins his state,
Robed in flames, and amber light,
The clouds in thousand liveries dight,
While the ploughman near at hand,
Whistles o'er the furrowed land,
65   And the milkmaid singeth blithe,

quote Sylvester (Du Bartas 87) 'cheerfull Birds, chirping him sweet
Good-morrows, / With Natures Musick do beguile his sorrows', but
grammar and the habits of larks make decisively for the former, as B. A.
Wright argues, TLS (8 Nov. 1934) 775, supported by E. M. W. Tillyard,
TLS (15 Nov. 1934) 795, and by J. L. Brereton, MLN xli (1926) 533, who
refers to the custom of bidding good-morrow to the sun, common in
Elizabethan and Jacobean drama (see Cymbeline III iii 7 and Volpone I i 1).
47–8. Sweet-briar and eglantine are names for the same plant (a species
of Rosa rubiginosa); 'twisted' suggests M. thought eglantine a plant that
climbs by its twining stem, like honeysuckle (which, it has been conjectured,
he really meant). G. G. Loane, N & Q clxxvi (1939) 225, thinks M. was
misled by Spenser, F.Q. III vi 44 where ivy, caprifole (honeysuckle) and
eglantine are combined. But C. A. Knapp, N & Q clxxvi (1939) 276,
insists that since 'eglantine' derives from Latin aculentus ('prickly') M.
must have known it was a plant with thorns.
52. Cp. the peacock in Sylvester (Du Bartas 96) 'To woo his Mistress,
strowting stately by her.'
55. hoar] H. H. Hoeltje, PMLA xlv (1930) 201–3, points out that in seven-
teenth century England hunting was common in the summer and that
'hoar' has no connection with hoar frost here but is used to designate
colour, referring to the mist-covered hills of a dewy summer morning.
59. Echoes Midsummer Night's Dream III ii 391: 'the eastern gate, all
fiery-red', in Oberon's description of sunrise.
60. state] stately progress.
62. dight] arrayed.

And the mower whets his scythe,
And every shepherd tells his tale
Under the hawthorn in the dale.
Straight mine eye hath caught new pleasures
70 Whilst the landscape round it measures,
Russet lawns, and fallows grey,
Where the nibbling flocks do stray,
Mountains on whose barren breast
The labouring clouds do often rest:
75 Meadows trim with daisies pied,
Shallow brooks, and rivers wide.
Towers, and battlements it sees
Bosomed high in tufted trees,
Where perhaps some beauty lies,
80 The cynosure of neighbouring eyes.
Hard by, a cottage chimney smokes,
From betwixt two aged oaks,
Where Corydon and Thyrsis met,

*67. tells his tale*] The argument about whether this means 'counts the tally of his sheep' or 'tells his story (of love)' goes back to Warton and beyond. The former seems more likely in a catalogue of early-morning phenomena, but J. W. Rankin, *MLN* xxvii (1912) 230, argues that in *Nativity Ode* 85–92 the shepherds in the early morning are 'simply chatting'. J. M. Hart, *MLN* xxviii (1913) 159–60, replies that the shepherds are abnormal there because biblical. Cp. *III Henry VI* II v 42–3: 'Gives not the hawthorn-bush a sweeter shade / To shepherds looking on their silly sheep.'
*71–2.* Bateson 159 calls this couplet 'a masterpiece of concentrated observation. The sheep have broken through the temporary fence round the parish's fallow field, no doubt because the common pastures are "russet", the short-rooted grass having been "burned", as farmers say, in the hot dry weather. "Russet" is decidedly not the epithet one would have expected for "lawns" . . . nor is "grey" what one would have expected for "fallows". M. must have had his eye on a real field. Most fallows after the summer ploughing are brown, but this field, perhaps because the subsoil was chalk, was grey.'
*72. nibbling*] Cp. *Tempest* IV i 62: 'nibbling sheep'.
*73–4.* The 'barren' mountains are contrasted with the 'labouring' clouds (bringing forth rain), cp. *Passion* 56n (p. 122).
*75. pied*] variegated, echoing *Love's Labour's Lost* V ii 882: 'daisies pied'.
*78. tufted*] Sylvester uses the same adjective to describe plane trees (Du Bartas 555).
*80. cynosure*] The constellation of the Lesser Bear, containing the Pole Star, hence, as here, an object of special attention.
*83–8.* The names M. chooses for his rustics are common in Renaissance pastoral.

Are at their savoury dinner set
85   Of herbs, and other country messes,
     Which the neat-handed Phillis dresses;
     And then in haste her bower she leaves,
     With Thestylis to bind the sheaves;
     Or if the earlier season lead
90   To the tanned haycock in the mead,
     Sometimes with secure delight
     The upland hamlets will invite,
     When the merry bells ring round,
     And the jocund rebecks sound
95   To many a youth, and many a maid,
     Dancing in the chequered shade;
     And young and old come forth to play
     On a sunshine holiday,
     Till the livelong daylight fail,
100  Then to the spicy nut-brown ale,
     With stories told of many a feat,
     How Faëry Mab the junkets eat,
     She was pinched, and pulled she said,
     And by the friar's lantern led
105  Tells how the drudging goblin sweat,

85. Sylvester also rhymes 'messes' and 'dresses' (Du Bartas 218).

91. *secure*] carefree (the Latin meaning).

94. *rebecks*] fiddles.

96. *chequered shade*] Echoes *Titus Andronicus* II iii 14–15: 'The green leaves
. . . make a chequer'd shadow on the ground.'

102. *Mab*] The subject of Mercutio's famous speech (*Romeo and Juliet* I
iv 54–95); her fondness for 'junkets' (i.e. cream cheeses, or other prepara-
tions of cream) may be deduced from Jonson, *Entertainment at Althorp* 47,
53–4 where she runs 'about the creame-bowles sweet' and 'doth nightly
rob the dayrie'.

103. It is Mab in Jonson's *Entertainment at Althorp* 58–9 'that pinches
countrey wenches, / If they rub not cleane their benches', and this habit
of fairies is noted both by Drayton, *Nimphidia* 65–6, and Browne i 61.

104. *friar's*] Perhaps a reference to the house-spirit Friar Rush, but M. is
probably influenced by the apparent identification of 'Robin good-fellow'
and 'the Frier' in Samuel Harsnet's *Declaration of Popish Impostures* 134,
where the 'bowle of curds, & creame' is 'duly set' as in l. 106. Robin
Goodfellow tells how he leads travellers astray disguised as a fire in
*Midsummer Night's Dream* III i 11–12.

105. *drudging goblin*] Robin Goodfellow is called 'Hobgoblin' in *Mid-
summer Night's Dream* II i 40, and in Jonson's *Love Restored* 58–9 he 'riddles
for the countrey maides, and does all their other drudgerie'.

To earn his cream-bowl duly set,
When in one night, ere glimpse of morn,
His shadowy flail hath threshed the corn,
That ten day-labourers could not end;
110 Then lies him down the lubber fiend.
And stretched out all the chimney's length,
Basks at the fire his hairy strength;
And crop-full out of doors he flings,
Ere the first cock his matin rings.
115 Thus done the tales, to bed they creep,
By whispering winds soon lulled asleep.
Towered cities please us then,
And the busy hum of men,
Where throngs of knights and barons bold,
120 In weeds of peace high triumphs hold,
With store of ladies, whose bright eyes
Rain influence, and judge the prize,
Of wit, or arms, while both contend
To win her grace, whom all commend.
125 There let Hymen oft appear
In saffron robe, with taper clear,
And pomp, and feast, and revelry,
With mask, and antique pageantry,
Such sights as youthful poets dream
130 On summer eves by haunted stream.
Then to the well-trod stage anon,
If Jonson's learned sock be on,
Or sweetest Shakespeare fancy's child,
Warble his native wood-notes wild,
135 And ever against eating cares,

106. *cream–bowl*] Cp. Burton I ii 1 ii: 'Hobgoblins, and Robin Goodfellows
that would . . . grind corn for a mess of milk, cut wood, or do any manner
of drudgery work.'
110. *lubber*] Robin Goodfellow is called 'lob of spirits' in *Midsummer
Night's Dream* II i 16.
111. *chimney*] fireplace.
120. Echoing *Troilus and Cressida* III iii 239: 'great Hector in his weeds of
peace'.
122. *Rain influence*] The eyes are star-like; 'influence' in astrology was
the flowing from the stars of an etherial fluid which affected the destiny of
men.
132. *sock*] low-heeled slipper, mark of the comic actor on the Greek and
Roman stage. The tragic actor wore buskins.
133. *fancy's child*] Echoes *Love's Labour's Lost* I i 171: 'child of fancy.'
135. *eating cares*] A translation of Horace, *Odes* II xi 18: *curas edaces*.

Lap me in soft Lydian airs,
Married to immortal verse
Such as the meeting soul may pierce
In notes, with many a winding bout
140 Of linked sweetness long drawn out,
With wanton heed, and giddy cunning,
The melting voice through mazes running;
Untwisting all the chains that tie
The hidden soul of harmony.
145 That Orpheus' self may heave his head
From golden slumber on a bed
Of heaped Elysian flowers, and hear
Such strains as would have won the ear
Of Pluto, to have quite set free
150 His half-regained Eurydice.
These delights, if thou canst give,
Mirth with thee, I mean to live.

## 42 Il Penseroso

*Date.* Summer 1631? See headnote to previous poem.
*Publication.* 1645 (21. offended,]offended.    170. spell]spell, ), 1673 (the text

*136. Lydian airs*] Plato, *Republic* iii 398–9, condemns the 'lax' Lydian mode, though as James Hutton points out, *EM* ii (1951) 45–6, Cassiodorus, in his letter to Boethius (*Variae* ii 40), speaks of it approvingly as providing 'relaxation and delight, being invented against excessive cares and worries'. Plato's attitude survived in the English Renaissance, e.g. Guilpin, *Skialetheia* Satyre Preludium 1–2: 'Fie on these *Lydian* tunes which blunt our sprights / And turne our gallants to *Hermaphrodites.*'
*139. bout*] circuit, orbit. Nan C. Carpenter, *UTQ* xxii (1953) 354–67, suggests that in ll. 139–44 M. has in mind the Italian aria as it was developing in the early seventeenth century. She points out that his father associated for some years with a London colony of Italian musicians, headed by Ferrabosco and Coperario.
*145–50.* Virgil, *Georg.* iv 453–527 and Ovid, *Met.* x 11–63 both have the story. Virgil's is the earliest surviving version in which Orpheus looks back at his wife as he is leading her from the underworld and loses her. See C. M. Bowra, *CQ* new ser. ii (1952) 113–22.
*146.* Cp. Dekker, *Patient Grissil* IV ii 99: 'Golden slumbers kisse your eyes.
*151–2.* Echoing the conclusion of Marlowe's popular lyric ('Come live with me and be my love'): 'If these delights thy mind may move, / Then live with me, and be my love.'
*Title.* M.'s *Penseroso* ('pensive') is not the modern spelling, but W. H. David, *N & Q* 7th ser. viii (1889) 326, justifies it by reference to a French-Italian dictionary published by Chouet at Geneva in 1644.

followed here, except in *49*, where *1673* misprints a semi-colon after 'Lei-
sure', and in *81, 88, 143* and *156*, where it misprints full stops after 'mirth',
'unsphere', 'sing' and 'pale').

For modern criticism see headnote to previous poem.

> Hence vain deluding Joys,
>    The brood of Folly without father bred,
> How little you bestead,
>    Or fill the fixed mind with all your toys;
> 5  Dwell in some idle brain,
>    And fancies fond with gaudy shapes possess,
> As thick and numberless
>    As the gay motes that people the sunbeams,
> Or likest hovering dreams
> 10    The fickle pensioners of Morpheus' train.
> But hail thou goddess, sage and holy,
> Hail divinest Melancholy,
> Whose saintly visage is too bright
> To hit the sense of human sight;
> 15  And therefore to our weaker view,
> O'erlaid with black staid wisdom's hue.
> Black, but such as in esteem,
> Prince Memnon's sister might beseem,

¶ 42. *1–2*. Perhaps an echo of Sylvester (Du Bartas[2] 1084): 'Hence, hence
false Pleasures, momentary Joyes; / Mock us no more with your illuding
Toyes.'

*2. brood of Folly*] The same phrase occurs in Jonson, *Love Freed from Ignorance*
274.

*3. bestead*] help.

*6–10*. Cp. Sylvester's description of the Cave of Sleep (Du Bartas 396)
where Morpheus sleeps and 'fantastick', 'gawdy' swarms of dreams
hover like 'Th' unnumbred Moats which in the Sun do play'.

*10. pensioners*] members of royal bodyguard.      *Morpheus*] son of Sleep
and god of dreams.

*14. hit*] suit, fit.

*16. black*] Melancholy is black bile, and the type of melancholy caused by
the influence of Saturn (l. 24) was traditionally associated with a black
face as Z. S. Fink, *PQ* xix (1940) 309–13, points out, referring to the same
idea in Burton I iii 1 iii and I iii 2 iii.

*18. Memnon's sister*] called Himera by Dictys Cretensis, *Ephemeris Belli
Troiani* vi, as E. Venables, *N & Q* 8th ser. i (1892) 149–50, notes. M. Day,
*MLR* xii (1917) 496–7, adds that her beauty is commented on by Guido
delle Colonne, *Historia Destructionis Troiae* viii.

Or that starred Ethiop queen that strove
20   To set her beauty's praise above
The sea-nymphs, and their powers offended,
Yet thou art higher far descended,
Thee bright-haired Vesta long of yore,
To solitary Saturn bore;
25   His daughter she (in Saturn's reign,
Such mixture was not held a stain)
Oft in glimmering bowers, and glades
He met her, and in secret shades
Of woody Ida's inmost grove,
30   Whilst yet there was no fear of Jove.
Come pensive nun, devout and pure,
Sober, steadfast, and demure,
All in a robe of darkest grain,
Flowing with majestic train,
35   And sable stole of cypress lawn,
Over thy decent shoulders drawn.
Come, but keep thy wonted state,
With even step, and musing gait,
And looks commercing with the skies,
40   Thy rapt soul sitting in thine eyes:
There held in holy passion still,
Forget thyself to marble, till
With a sad leaden downward cast,

19. *queen*] Cassiopea who, as Hyginus, *Astronomica* II x records, was changed into a constellation because she claimed to be more beautiful than the Nereids. D. T. Starnes (Taylor[2] 44–5) points out that Hyginus' account of the matter, as opposed to the more usual classical version which makes her boast not her own beauty but that of her daughter Andromeda, is given in Conti and in Stephanus.

23. Vesta's motherhood is M.'s invention: she was virgin daughter of Saturn, goddess of flocks and herds and of the household; cp. Hesiod, *Theog.* 454.

25–6. It was common for both classical and Renaissance authors to present the Golden Age, when Saturn reigned on Mount Ida, as a time of sexual licence. See Propertius III xiii 25–46, Tibullus II iii 69–74.

33. *grain*] dye.

35. *cypress*] dark, gloomy. See *Winchester Epitaph* 22n, p. 128 above.
     *lawn*] fine linen.

42. Cp. *Shakespeare* 14 (p. 123). A possible source for both is Thomas Tomkins's *Albumazar* I iv 4: 'Marvel thyself to Marble.' The idea originates in the Niobe legend, employed in an epitaph by Browne ii 294: 'Some kind woman . . . / Reading this, like Niobe / Shall turn marble, and become / Both her mourner and her tomb.'

43. *sad*] serious.

Thou fix them on the earth as fast.
45  And join with thee calm Peace, and Quiet,
Spare Fast, that oft with gods doth diet,
And hears the Muses in a ring,
Ay round about Jove's altar sing.
And add to these retired Leisure,
50  That in trim gardens takes his pleasure;
But first, and chiefest, with thee bring,
Him that yon soars on golden wing,
Guiding the fiery-wheeled throne,
The cherub Contemplation,
55  And the mute Silence hist along,
'Less Philomel will deign a song,
In her sweetest, saddest plight,
Smoothing the rugged brow of night,
While Cynthia checks her dragon yoke,
60  Gently o'er the accustomed oak;
Sweet bird that shunn'st the noise of folly,
Most musical, most melancholy!
Thee chauntress oft the woods among,
I woo to hear thy even-song;
65  And missing thee, I walk unseen
On the dry smooth-shaven green,
To behold the wandering moon,
Riding near her highest noon,
Like one that had been led astray
70  Through the heaven's wide pathless way;

47–8.  M.'s second *Prolusion* (Columbia xii 154–5, Yale i 237) alludes to the dance of the Muses around Jove's altar, as described by Hesiod, *Theog.* 1–10.

53. See *Passion* 36–40n (p. 121).

54. *cherub Contemplation*] C. B. Mount, *N & Q* 7th ser. ii (1886) 323–4, notes that in the pseudo-Dionysian *Celestial Hierarchy* VII i 31–7 the cherubim are distinguished by their 'faculty of seeing God, and of contemplating the beauty of the Supreme Being'.

55. *hist*] First recorded occurrence of the word in the sense 'summon with the exclamation "hist!"'

56. *Philomel*] See *Sonnet I* headnote (p. 88).

57. *plight*] state of mind.

58. *brow*] Cp. *Romeo and Juliet* III ii 20: 'black-brow'd night'.

59. *Cynthia*] The moon.    *dragon*] See *Prae E* 56–8n (p. 26).

62. *Most musical*] M. refers in the seventh *Prolusion* (Columbia xii 283, Yale i 303–4) to Aristotle, *Hist. Nat.* IV ix 536b, where the nightingale is said to teach her chicks music.

66. *smooth-shaven*] Echoes Sylvester (Du Bartas 539), 'new-shav'n Fields', which comes eight lines after a reference to the nightingale.

And oft, as if her head she bowed,
Stooping through a fleecy cloud.
Oft on a plat of rising ground,
I hear the far-off curfew sound,
75  Over some wide-watered shore,
Swinging slow with sullen roar;
Or if the air will not permit,
Some still removed place will fit,
Where glowing embers through the room
80  Teach light to counterfeit a gloom,
Far from all resort of mirth,
Save the cricket on the hearth,
Or the bellman's drowsy charm,
To bless the doors from nightly harm:
85  Or let my lamp at midnight hour,
Be seen in some high lonely tower,
Where I may oft outwatch the Bear,
With thrice great Hermes, or unsphere
The spirit of Plato to unfold
90  What worlds, or what vast regions hold
The immortal mind that hath forsook
Her mansion in this fleshly nook:
And of those demons that are found
In fire, air, flood, or under ground,
95  Whose power hath a true consent
With planet, or with element.
Sometime let gorgeous Tragedy
In sceptred pall come sweeping by,
Presenting Thebes, or Pelops' line,
100  Or the tale of Troy divine.
Or what (though rare) of later age,
Ennobled hath the buskined stage.

73. *plat*] plot.
76. *sullen*] Cp. *II Henry IV* I i 102: 'sullen bell'.
83–4. For an example of the kind of 'charm' recited by bellmen see Herrick 121 *The Bell-man*.
87. *outwatch the Bear*] the Bear, symbolizing perfection in Hermes (Allen 13), never sets. 'Outwatch' is first used in Jonson vii 709, by a melancholy student.
93. *demons*] E. C. Baldwin, *MLN* xxxiii (1918) 184–5, points out that these element-inhabiting spirits are found in Hermes.
98. *pall*] robe. Pall (*palla*) and sceptre occur in Ovid's description of tragedy, *Am.* III i 11–13.
99–100. See *Elegia I* 45–6n. p. 20 above.
102. *buskined*] See *L'Allegro* 132n, p. 138 above.

But, O sad virgin, that thy power
Might raise Musaeus from his bower,
*105*   Or bid the soul of Orpheus sing
Such notes as warbled to the string,
Drew iron tears down Pluto's cheek,
And made hell grant what love did seek.
Or call up him that left half-told
*110*   The story of Cambuscan bold,
Of Camball, and of Algarsife,
And who had Canace to wife,
That owned the virtuous ring and glass,
And of the wondrous horse of brass,
*115*   On which the Tartar king did ride;
And if aught else, great bards beside,
In sage and solemn tunes have sung,
Of tourneys and of trophies hung;
Of forests, and enchantments drear,
*120*   Where more is meant than meets the ear,
Thus Night oft see me in thy pale career,
Till civil-suited Morn appear,
Not tricked and frounced as she was wont,
With the Attic boy to hunt,
*125*   But kerchieft in a comely cloud,
While rocking winds are piping loud,

*104. Musaeus*] Mythical seer and priest, pupil of Orpheus and founder of priestly poetry in Attica.

*105–8.* See *L'Allegro* 145–50*n* (p. 139).

*109. him*] Chaucer: the 'story' is the unfinished *Squire's Tale*. F. W. Emerson, *MLN* xlvii (1932) 153–4, suggests that M. derived the forms 'Cambuscan' and 'Cabmall' (as opposed to the Chaucerian 'Cambynskan' and 'Camballo') from his father's friend John Lane's continuation of the *Squire's Tale* (written in 1615).

*113. virtuous*] endowed with magical power. Allen 12 suggests that M. refers to the *Squire's Tale* here because he saw ring, glass and brass horse as symbols of intellectual power.

*116–20.* Referring probably to 'our sage and serious Poet *Spencer*' (Columbia iv 311, Yale ii 516) and perhaps to Ariosto and Tasso as well, whose epics had been allegorized by Renaissance critics.

*120.* Cp. Seneca, *Epist.* cxiv 1: *In quibus plus intelligendum esset quam audiendum* (in which more was to be understood than heard).

*122. civil-suited*] Echoes *Romeo and Juliet* III ii 10–11: 'Come, civil night, / Thou sober-suited matron.'

*123. tricked and frounced*] decked out and with curled hair.

*124. Attic boy*] See *Elegia V* 49–52*n* (p. 82).

Or ushered with a shower still,
When the gust hath blown his fill,
Ending on the rustling leaves,
*130*   With minute drops from off the eaves.
And when the sun begins to fling
His flaring beams, me goddess bring
To arched walks of twilight groves,
And shadows brown that Sylvan loves
*135*   Of pine, or monumental oak,
Where the rude axe with heaved stroke,
Was never heard the nymphs to daunt,
Or fright them from their hallowed haunt.
There in close covert by some brook,
*140*   Where no profaner eye may look,
Hide me from day's garish eye,
While the bee with honied thigh,
That at her flowery work doth sing,
And the waters murmuring
*145*   With such consort as they keep,
Entice the dewy-feathered Sleep;
And let some strange mysterious dream,
Wave at his wings in airy stream,
Of lively portraiture displayed,
*150*   Softly on my eyelids laid.
And as I wake, sweet music breathe
Above, about, or underneath,

*127. still*] quiet.
*130. minute*] Falling at intervals of a minute; M. is first to use the word in this sense.
*131. fling*] Probably echoing Drayton, *Muses' Elizium* i 1-2: 'When Phoebus with a face of mirth / Had flung abroad his beams'; cp. also Beaumont and Fletcher, *Maid's Tragedy* I i: 'the day that flings his light':
*132. flaring beams*] Marlowe uses the same phrase, *Hero and Leander* ii 332.
*134. Sylvan*] The Roman wood god.
*141. garish eye*] Echoes *Romeo and Juliet* III ii 25: 'the garish sun'.
*142-4.* Echoing Drayton, *The Owl* 117-21: 'the small brookes . . . murmuring. / Each *Bee* with Honey on her laden thye.'
*145. consort*] musical harmony.
*148. his*] Sleep's: cp. the address to 'Phant'sie' in Jonson's *Vision of Delight* 45-54: 'Spread thy purple wings; / Now all thy figures are allow'd, / and various shapes of things; / Create of ayrie formes, a streame; / . . . And though it be a waking dreame; / Yet let it like an odour rise / . . . And fall like sleep upon their eies, / or musick in their eare.'
*152.* M. is probably remembering the magic music in Shakespeare's

Sent by some spirit to mortals good,
Or the unseen genius of the wood.
155    But let my due feet never fail,
To walk the studious cloister's pale,
And love the high embowed roof,
With antique pillars' massy proof,
And storied windows richly dight,
160    Casting a dim religious light.
There let the pealing organ blow,
To the full-voiced choir below,
In service high, and anthems clear,
As may with sweetness, through mine ear,
165    Dissolve me into ecstasies,
And bring all heaven before mine eyes.
And may at last my weary age
Find out the peaceful hermitage,
The hairy gown and mossy cell,
170    Where I may sit and rightly spell
Of every star that heaven doth shew,
And every herb that sips the dew;
Till old experience do attain
To something like prophetic strain.
175    These pleasures Melancholy give,
And I with thee will choose to live.

# 43 Sonnet VII

*Date.* Dec. 1631. In the Trinity MS after *Solemn Music* and before *Time* there are two drafts in M.'s hand of an undated letter to an unnamed friend, perhaps Thomas Young, (Columbia xii 320–25, Yale i 319–21). The first draft contains this sonnet as an example of 'my nightward thoughts some while since'. M.'s twenty-third year ended 9 Dec. 1631. W. R. Parker, *RES* xi (1935) 276–9, argues from M.'s method of dating some of his Latin

*Tempest*, particularly I ii 390 : 'Where should this music be? i' th' air or th' earth?'

154. *genius*] See *Arcades* 26n (p. 157).
156. *pale*] enclosure.
157. *embowed*] arched.
158. *massy*] made of great blocks of masonry    *proof*] impenetrability.
159. *storied*] ornamented with scenes from (biblical) history.
165–6. See *Solemn Music* 5n (p. 163).
170–1. *spell Of*] find out about.
175–6. See *L'Allegro* 151–2n (p. 139).

poems (see headnote to *Q Nov*) that 'my three and twentieth year' should be interpreted 'the year in which I was twenty-three': he thus dates *Sonnet VII* on or soon after 9 Dec. 1632. For objections to Parker's re-dating see E. Sirluck, *JEGP* lx (1961) 781–4.

*Publication. 1645 (11.* mean]mean, ) and *1673* (the text followed here, except in *2* where *1673* misprints 'Soln' for 'Stol'n'). The Trinity MS draft has no verbal variants but is, with the exception of a comma after 'me' (*12*), entirely unpunctuated.

*Modern criticism.* R. M. Smith, *MLN* lx (1945) 394–8, suggests that the octave may have been influenced by a passage in a Latin verse letter from Spenser to Gabriel Harvey, published in 1580.

P. M. Withim, *Bucknell Review* vi (1957) 29–34, offers a prosodic analysis, noting how the cdedce rhyme scheme in the sestet (also used by M. in 27, 32 and 70) throws special weight on 'heaven' (*12*). By concentrating on prosody Withim evades the question of the sestet's meaning. Three alternative explanations are given by K. Svendsen, *Explicator* vii (1949) 53, who would paraphrase *13–14* 'All that matters is whether I have grace to use my ripeness in accordance with the will of God as one ever in His sight'. D. C. Dorian, *Explicator* viii (1949) 10, suggests a quasi-substantive use of 'ever' (*14*) and paraphrases 'All time is, if I have grace to use it so, as eternity in God's sight'. A. S. P. Woodhouse, *UTQ* xiii (1943) 96, proposes the substitution of a colon for the first comma in *13*, and paraphrases 'All [that matters] is: whether I have grace to use it so, as ever [conscious of being] in my great taskmaster's [enjoining] eye'. Since the Trinity MS draft has not even a comma at this point, Woodhouse's proposal seems dubious.

> How soon hath time the subtle thief of youth,
> Stol'n on his wing my three and twentieth year!
> My hasting days fly on with full career,
> But my late spring no bud or blossom sheweth.
> 5 Perhaps my semblance might deceive the truth,
> That I to manhood am arrived so near,
> And inward ripeness doth much less appear,
> That some more timely-happy spirits endueth.
> Yet be it less or more, or soon or slow,

¶ 43. *5. semblance*] appearance. Cp. M.'s statement in the *Defensio Secunda* (Columbia viii 60–1): 'Though [I am] turned of forty, there is scarcely anyone who would not think me younger by nearly ten years.'

*8. more timely-happy spirits*] Smart 54 suggests Thomas Randolph, M.'s contemporary at Cambridge and already well known as a wit, as one of these.

*9–12.* L. Campbell, *Classical Review* viii (1894) 349, was the first to point out the apparent debt to Pindar, *Nem.* iv 41–3: 'But, whatsoever excellence

10      It shall be still in strictest measure even,
        To that same lot, however mean or high,
    Toward which time leads me, and the will of heaven;
    All is, if I have grace to use it so,
    As ever in my great task-master's eye.

# 44 *Ad Patrem*
## [To My Father]

*Date.* 1632? The date is much disputed and there is no firm evidence.
Tradition has assigned *Ad Patrem* to the early Horton years (see e.g.
Masson i 296) on grounds of its similarity to the letter to an unknown friend
(cp. *Sonnet VII* headnote, p. 146). But Grierson I xxii believes that the
publication of *Comus* lies behind the conflict felt in *Ad Patrem*, which he
dates 1637-8. J. T. Shawcross, *N & Q* cciv (1959) 358-9, agrees. Shawcross
suggests that the order of poems in *1645* was dictated by typographical
convenience: he contradicts W. R. Parker's claim (Taylor² 125-8) that
the *1645* order represents chronology, and that *Ad Patrem* should thus
be dated after the performance of *Comus* (29 Sept. 1634) and before the
Greek *Psalm cxiv* (Nov. 1634). E. Sirluck, *JEGP* lx (1961) 784-5, accepts
Grierson's dating, as does Tillyard (384) who connects lines *82-4* with
a passage in M.'s letter to Diodati dated 23 Sept. 1637 (Columbia xii 23-9,
Yale i 325-8). Harris Fletcher (Scott 199-205) feels that *Ad Patrem* may
well have been written as late as 1640. H. A. Barnett, *MLN* lxxiii (1958)
82-3, takes *38-40* literally and concludes that the star positions indicate a
date in spring (Mar.-Apr.). D. Bush, *MP* lxi (1964) 204-8, questions the
linking of *Ad Patrem* with *Comus* and repeats some of the reasons offered
by A. S. P. Woodhouse, *UTQ* xiii (1943) 88-92, for dating *Ad Patrem* in
M.'s last Cambridge year (1631-2): Bush comments on the present tenses
in *71-6*: 'If he were writing *circa* 1637, or even *circa* 1634, it would be
hard to imagine his using present tenses about an attitude his father must
have taken before or soon after he left Cambridge.' This, and Bush's
other reasons for an early date are convincing, but his suggestion that the
*secessibus* of *74* are Cambridge seems dubious, since *Abductum* (*75*) must
surely imply that M.'s father is himself in the 'seclusion' referred to,
which can therefore only be Horton, to which M. probably moved in
the summer of 1632 (French i 272-3).
*Publication. 1645* (*8.* possunt]possint        *13.* ista,]ista ) *1673* (the text
followed here).

Lord Destiny assigned me, well I know that the lapse of time will bring it
to its appointed perfection.'
*10. still*] always.
*10-11. even, To*] level with.

*Modern criticism.* M. Little, *JEGP* xlix (1950) 354–51, claims that there is a
note of banter in M.'s *apologia* which links it with Alexander Gill's *In
Natalem Mei Parentis.* The *Familiar Letters* show that M. and Gill were in
the habit of exchanging verses, so probably M. saw Gill's poem before its
publication (1632): the subject is uncommon in neo-Latin verse, and it
may well have been Gill's poem which suggested *Ad Patrem.*

> Nunc mea Pierios cupiam per pectora fontes
> Irriguas torquere vias, totumque per ora
> Volvere laxatum gemino de vertice rivum;
> Ut tenues oblita sonos audacibus alis
> 5 Surgat in officium venerandi Musa parentis.
> Hoc utcunque tibi gratum pater optime carmen
> Exiguum meditatur opus, nec novimus ipsi
> Aptius a nobis quae possunt munera donis
> Respondere tuis, quamvis nec maxima possint
> 10 Respondere tuis, nedum ut par gratia donis
> Esse queat, vacuis quae redditur arida verbis.
> Sed tamen haec nostros ostendit pagina census,
> Et quod habemus opum charta numeravimus ista,
> Quae mihi sunt nullae, nisi quas dedit aurea Clio
> 15 Quas mihi semoto somni peperere sub antro,
> Et nemoris laureta sacri Parnassides umbrae.
> Nec tu vatis opus divinum despice carmen,
> Quo nihil aethereos ortus, et semina caeli,
> Nil magis humanam commendat origine mentem,
> 20 Sancta Prometheae retinens vestigia flammae.
> Carmen amant superi, tremebundaque Tartara carmen
> Ima ciere valet, divosque ligare profundos,
> Et triplici duros Manes adamante coercet.
> Carmine sepositi retegunt arcana futuri
> 25 Phoebades, et tremulae pallentes ora Sibyllae;

¶ 44. 1. *Pierios*] on Pierus, see *Elegia IV* 29–32*n*, p. 55 above.
14. *Clio*] J. T. Shawcross, *N & Q* ccvi (1961) 178–9, thinks Clio, in this
passage 'the personification of man's individual history', but cites no
classical precedent. It seems more likely that she is named as guardian of
lustration. See *Elegia IV* 29–32*n*, p. 55 above.
20. *Prometheae . . . flammae*] Prometheus stole fire from heaven and brought
it to man, as Hesiod relates, *Theog.* 565. Conti 317–18 explains that Prome-
theus, whose name means 'the forethinker', symbolizes reason or prudence.
21–3. See *L'Allegro* 145–50*n*.
25. *Phoebades*] Priestesses of Apollo, whose temple at Delphi contained a
famous oracle.    *Sibyllae*] Prophetesses; it is the Cumaean sibyl who
escorts Aeneas to the underworld in *Aen.* vi.

Carmina sacrificus sollennes pangit ad aras
Aurea seu sternit motantem cornua taurum;
Seu cum fata sagax fumantibus abdita fibris
Consulit, et tepidis Parcam scrutatur in extis.
30  Nos etiam patrium tunc cum repetemus Olympum,
Aeternaeque morae stabunt immobilis aevi,
Ibimus auratis per caeli templa coronis,
Dulcia suaviloquo sociantes carmina plectro,
Astra quibus, geminique poli convexa sonabunt.
35  Spiritus et rapidos qui circinat igneus orbes,
Nunc quoque sydereis intercinit ipse choreis
Immortale melos, et inenarrabile carmen;
Torrida dum rutilus compescit sibila serpens,
Demissoque ferox gladio mansuescit Orion;
40  Stellarum nec sentit onus Maurusius Atlas.
Carmina regales epulas ornare solebant,
Cum nondum luxus, vastaeque immensa vorago
Nota gulae, et modico spumabat coena Lyaeo.
Tum de more sedens festa ad convivia vates
45  Aesculea intonsos redimitus ab arbore crines,
Heroumque actus, imitandaque gesta canebat,
Et chaos, et positi late fundamina mundi,
Reptantesque deos, et alentes numina glandes,
Et nondum Aetneo quaesitum fulmen ab antro.

32–3. Cp. *Rev.* iv 4: 'They had on their heads crowns of gold', and v 8 'having every one of them harps.'

35–7. M.'s spirit, released from his body by learning, sings amid the starry choir. The theory of this release is derived from Cicero's *Somnium Scipionis* and Macrobius' commentary on it, as John Carey points out, *RES* n.s. xv (1964) 180–4.

38. *serpens*] The constellation of the Serpent, between the Greater and Lesser Bear.

39. *Orion*] See *Prae E* 53–4n (p. 26).

40. *Maurusius*] in Mauritania (the modern Fez and Morocco).     *Atlas*] See *Id Plat* 24n (p. 67).

43. *Lyaeo*] Bacchus, god of wine, was also called Lyaeus ('the Relaxer').

48. Tillyard (*Seventeenth-Century Studies presented to Sir Herbert Grierson* (Oxford 1938) 219) takes this as a reference to the infancy of the Olympian gods as described by Hesiod. Hesiod, however, mentions neither crawling nor acorns. A closer parallel is Ovid's description of the creation, where the gods are said to inhabit first the 'floor' of heaven (*Met.* i 73), and where acorns (*Met.* i 106) are included in the diet of the first, golden age, when Saturn reigned.

49. Jupiter, who succeeded Saturn, was armed with thunderbolts forged in a cave under Etna by the Cyclopes, as Virgil describes (*Georg.* iv 170–5).

50  Denique quid vocis modulamen inane iuvabit,
    Verborum sensusque vacans, numerique loquacis?
    Silvestres decet iste choros, non Orphea cantus,
    Qui tenuit fluvios et quercubus addidit aures
    Carmine, non cithara, simulachraque functa canendo
55  Compulit in lacrymas; habet has a carmine laudes.
        Nec tu perge precor sacras contemnere Musas,
    Nec vanas inopesque puta, quarum ipse peritus
    Munere, mille sonos numeros componis ad aptos,
    Millibus et vocem modulis variare canoram
60  Doctus, Arionii merito sis nominis haeres.
    Nunc tibi quid mirum, si me genuisse poetam
    Contigerit, charo si tam prope sanguine iuncti
    Cognatas artes, studiumque affine sequamur:
    Ipse volens Phoebus se dispertire duobus,
65  Altera dona mihi, dedit altera dona parenti,
    Dividuumque Deum genitorque puerque tenemus.
        Tu tamen ut simules teneras odisse camoenas,
    Non odisse reor, neque enim, pater, ire iubebas
    Qua via lata patet, qua pronior area lucri,
70  Certaque condendi fulget spes aurea nummi:
    Nec rapis ad leges, male custoditaque gentis
    Iura, nec insulsis damnas clamoribus aures.
    Sed magis excultam cupiens ditescere mentem,
    Me procul urbano strepitu, secessibus altis
75  Abductum Aoniae iucunda per otia ripae
    Phoebaeo lateri comitem sinis ire beatum.
    Officium chari taceo commune parentis,
    Me poscunt maiora, tuo pater optime sumptu
    Cum mihi Romuleae patuit facundia linguae,
80  Et Latii veneres, et quae Iovis ora decebant
    Grandia magniloquis elata vocabula Graiis,

---

52–5. Orpheus makes oak trees listen to his song in Virgil (*Georg.* iv 510).
During his visit to the underworld, as described by Ovid, he walked among
ghosts (*Met.* x 14 *simulacraque functa*) and made them weep (x 41).

60. *Arionii*] Herodotus i 23–4 tells how Arion, a famous lyre-player, so
charmed a dolphin with his music that it rescued him from the waves
when he was thrown overboard. M.'s father was a musician of some repute.

64. *Phoebus*] God of poetry and music.

67. *camoenas*] See *Elegia VI* 3*n* (p. 113).

71. Ovid refers to his own unwillingness to follow the legal profession,
*Am.* I xv 5–6.

75. *Aoniae . . . ripae*] See *Elegia IV* 29–32*n* (p. 55).

79. *Romuleae . . . facundia linguae*] Echoes Ovid, *Ex Ponto* I ii 67: *Romanae
facundia . . . linguae*.

Addere suasisti quos iactat Gallia flores,
Et quam degeneri novus Italus ore loquelam
Fundit, barbaricos testatus voce tumultus,
85  Quaeque Palaestinus loquitur mysteria vates.
Denique quicquid habet caelum, subiectaque coelo
Terra parens, terraeque et coelo interfluus aer,
Quicquid et unda tegit, pontique agitabile marmor,
Per te nosse licet, per te, si nosse libebit.
90  Dimotaque venit spectanda scientia nube,
Nudaque conspicuos inclinat ad oscula vultus,
Ni fugisse velim, ni sit libasse molestum.
    I nunc, confer opes quisquis malesanus avitas
Austriaci gazas, Peruanaque regna praeoptas.
95  Quae potuit maiora pater tribuisse, vel ipse
Iupiter, excepto, donasset ut omnia, coelo?
Non potiora dedit, quamvis et tuta fuissent,
Publica qui iuveni commisit lumina nato
Atque Hyperionios currus, et fraena diei,
100  Et circum undantem radiata luce tiaram.
Ergo ego iam doctae pars quamlibet ima catervae
Victrices hederas inter, laurosque sedebo,
Iamque nec obscurus populo miscebor inerti,
Vitabuntque oculos vestigia nostra profanos.
105  Este procul vigiles curae, procul este querelae,
Invidiaeque acies transverso tortilis hirquo,
Saeva nec anguiferos extende Calumnia rictus;
In me triste nihil faedissima turba potestis,
Nec vestri sum iuris ego; securaque tutus
110  Pectora, vipereo gradiar sublimis ab ictu.
    At tibi, chare pater, postquam non aequa merenti
Posse referre datur, nec dona rependere factis,

---

85. *Palaestinus . . . vates*] A Hebrew prophet.

93. Echoing Ovid, *Her.* xii 204: *i nunc . . . confer opes.*

94. *Peruanaque regna*] Peru was conquered by Spain in the 1530s and mercilessly exploited for its gold during the sixteenth and seventeenth centuries.

97–100. See *Natur* 25n (p. 62).

98. *Publica . . . lumina*] Ovid's name for the sun in his story of Phaëthon, *Met.* ii 35.

99. *Hyperionios*] Belonging to Hyperion, father of the sun.

102. *hederas*] Horace calls the ivy 'the reward of poets' brows', *Odes* I i 29, and Virgil, *Ecl.* viii 13, envisages his poet's ivy mingling with the laurel about the brows of the victorious Pollio.

106. *transverso . . . hirquo*] Echoes Virgil, *Ecl.* iii 8: *transversa tuentibus hircis.*

107. *Calumnia*] See Q *Nov* 146n (p. 42).

Sit memorasse satis, repetitaque numera grato
Percensere animo, fidaeque reponere menti.
115 Et vos, O nostri, iuvenilia carmina, lusus,
Si modo perpetuos sperare audebitis annos,
Et domini superesse rogo, lucemque tueri,
Nec spisso rapient oblivia nigra sub Orco,
Forsitan has laudes, decantatumque parentis
120 Nomen, ad exemplum, sero servabitis aevo.

Now I should like the Pierian[1] fountains to divert their watery channels
through my heart; I should like every drop of that stream which trickles
out from the twin peak to pour between my lips, so that my Muse, forgetting
her trivial songs, may soar on fearless wings to do her duty and honour my
father. Whether you approve or not, best of fathers, she is now engaged on
this poem–this little offering–and I do not know what I may give you that
can more fittingly repay your gifts to me. In fact, though, even my greatest
gifts could never repay yours, much less could that barren thanks which is
paid in empty words make up for the things you have given me. Still, this
page shows you what I do possess: I have counted out my wealth upon this
sheet of paper, and that wealth is only what golden Clio[14] has provided–the
fruit of dreams dreamt in a cavern far away, fruit of the laurel groves in a
sacred wood, of the shady groves on Parnassus.

Do not despise divine poetry, the poet's creation. Nothing shows our
celestial beginnings, our heavenly seed, more clearly: nothing better graces
by its origin our human intellect, for poetry still retains some blessed trace
of the Promethean fire.[20] The gods love poetry: poetry has power to stir
the quivering depths of Tartarus[21] and to bind the deities of hell: it grips
the heartless ghosts in a threefold band of steel.[23] With poetry the priestesses
of Apollo and the trembling, pale-lipped sybils[25] reveal the secrets of the
distant future. The sacrificing priest who stands before the ceremonial altar
utters poetry as he strikes down the bull, its gilded horns tossing, or when,
skilled in prophecy, he reads the hidden lines of destiny in the steaming
entrails and searches for fate in the beast's hot guts. And we, when we return
to Olympus, our first home, and when the eternal ages of changeless time
stand still, shall walk through the temples of heaven crowned with gold[32]
and wedding our sweet songs to the smooth-voiced strings,[33] and the stars
and the vaults of both the hemispheres will make their music in reply. My
fiery spirit which whirls round the hurtling spheres is already singing, as it
flies among the starry choirs, a deathless melody, an indescribable song. The
glittering serpent[38] checks his scorching hisses at the sound, savage Orion[39]
grows calm and lets fall his sword, and Mauretanian Atlas[40] no longer feels
the weight of the stars.

Songs were the usual ornaments of royal banquets in the days when
luxury and the great maw of insatiable gluttony were still things of the
future, and when the table foamed with wine,[43] but only in moderation.
Then it was customary for the bard to have a place at the happy feast, his
flowing locks crowned with a garland of oak leaves, and he sang of the deeds
of heroes, of their exploits and good example, of chaos and of the wide

118. Orco] See *Elegia VII* 83*n* (p. 73).

foundations on which the earth was laid, of gods who crawled about and lived on acorns,[48] and of the thunderbolt not yet brought from its cave under Etna.[49] And after all, what use is the voice if it merely hums an inane tune, without words, meaning or the rhythm of speech? That kind of song is good enough for the woodland choristers, but not for Orpheus[52] who with his singing, not his lute, held streams spellbound and gave ears to the oak-trees and moved lifeless phantoms to tears. It is to his singing that he owes his reputation.[55]

I beg you, stop scorning the sacred Muses: don't think them worthless or unprofitable. It is their gift which has made you able to fit a thousand notes to apt rhythms and skilful in adjusting your tuneful voice to a thousand melodies – may you deservedly inherit Arion's fame.[60] No wonder, then, that you should have the good luck to beget me, a poet, or that we who are so closely related by ties of affection and blood should cultivate sister arts and have kindred interests. Phoebus,[64] wishing to share himself between the two of us, gave one lot of gifts to me and the other to my father, with the result that father and son have each one half of a god. But although you pretend to hate the dainty Muses,[67] I do not believe that you hate them really. For, father, you did not tell me to go where the road lies broad and open, where the ground is more favourable for fortune-hunters, and where the golden hope of making piles of money shines bright and clear. You do not force me to enter the legal profession[71] or study our nation's ill-preserved statutes: you do not condemn my ears to that absurd clamour. Instead you have taken me far away from the din of the city into this deep seclusion, with the intention of enriching my already cultivated mind still further, and you allow me to walk by Phoebus's side, happy to be his companion, amidst the leisurely delights of the Aonian spring.[75]

I will not mention the kindnesses which a loving father usually bestows upon his son: there are more considerable things which demand my attention. Best of fathers, when the eloquence of the Roman tongue[79] had been made accessible to me, at your expense, the beauties of Latin and the high-sounding words of the sublime Greeks, words which graced the mighty lips of Jove himself, then you persuaded me to add to my stock those flowers which are the boast of France, and that language which the modern Italian pours from his degenerate mouth (his speech makes him a living proof of the barbarian invasions), and also those mysteries which the prophet of Palestine[85] utters. Should I choose to do so, in fact, I have the chance, thanks to you, of knowing about everything that exists—in the sky, or on mother earth beneath the sky, or in the air that streams between them, or hidden beneath the waves, beneath the heaving marbly surface of the ocean. The mists clear, and science comes into view. Naked, she bends her bright face for my kisses—if I do not choose to run away, if I do not find it irksome to taste her kisses.

Go on, then, pile up your wealth,[93] all you who have an unhealthy hankering for the royal heirlooms of Austria or the realms of Peru.[94] What greater treasures could have been given by a father, or by Jove himself for that matter, even if he had given everything, unless he had included heaven as well? That father[97] who trusted his young son with the universal light[98] of the world and the chariot of Hyperion,[99] with the reins of day and the diadem which radiates waves of light, gave (even had those gifts been safe) no better gifts than my father's.[100] Therefore I, who already have a place, though a very low one, in the ranks of the learned, shall one day sit among those who wear the ivy[102] and the laurels of victory. Now I shall no longer mix with the brainless mob: my steps will shun the sight of common eyes. Away with you, sleep-destroying worries, away with you, complaints, and the squinting eye of envy with its crooked goatish look.[106] Do not stretch your snaky jaws at me, cruel calumny.[107] Your whole filthy gang can do me no harm: I am not within your power. I shall stride on in safety with an unwounded heart, lifted high above your viperous sting.

As for you, dear father, since I am powerless to repay you as you deserve, or to do anything that can requite your gifts, let it suffice that I have recorded them, that I count up your repeated favours with a feeling of gratitude, and store them safely away in my memory.

And you, my youthful poems, my pastimes, if only you are bold enough to hope for immortality, to hope that you will survive your master's funeral pyre and keep your eyes upon the light, then perhaps, if dark oblivion does not after all plunge you down beneath the dense crowds of the under-world,[118] you may preserve this eulogy and my father's name, which has been the subject of my verse, as an example for a far-off age.

# 45 Note on Ariosto

*Date.* 1632? Before the preface of his copy of Harington's translation of the *Orlando Furioso*, M. wrote an elegiac couplet, of which the first line is cut away, and this second line cancelled. Columbia xviii 605 dates the line 'about 1642', presumably because elsewhere in the Harington volume M. wrote *Questo libro due volte ho letto, Sept 21. 1642*. ('I have read this book twice'): but the substance of the line makes a date nearer to the renunciation of the legal profession in *Ad Patrem* preferable.

Tu mihi iure tuo Iustiniane vale. J.M.

Farewell, Justinian, with your law book.

# 46 Arcades

*Date.* Summer (reference to thick foliage *88–9*) 1633? There is no certainty about the date. The first item in the Trinity MS as it now survives is a draft of *Arcades* (for variant readings see notes) which, according to J. T. Shawcross, *N & Q* cciv (1959) 359–64, is a transcript made after the first performance.

¶ 45. *1. Iustiniane*] Justinian I (A.D. 483–565), Emperor, and codifier of the Roman law.
¶ 46. *Title. Arcades*] Inhabitants of Arcady (Arcadia). In *Trin. MS Arcades* is first headed 'Part of a masque'; this is cancelled and 'Arcades / Part of an Entertainment' substituted.

Alice, Dowager Countess of Derby, was about seventy-two in 1633, and died Jan. 1636. She had long been honoured by poets: Spenser dedicated his *Tears of the Muses* (1591) to her and she was the 'sweet Amaryllis' of his *Colin Clout's Come Home Again*. Marston wrote an *Entertainment* (1607) for her. In 1609 John Davies of Hereford dedicated his *Holy Rood* to her and the same year she played Zenobia in Jonson's *Masque of Queens*. She married her second husband, Sir Thomas Egerton, Lord Keeper, in 1600: a year later they bought Harefield (twelve miles north of Horton). Her second daughter married Sir Thomas's son, Sir John, who became Earl of Bridgewater in 1617. *Comus* was written for him, and probably *Arcades* as well. M.'s connection with the Egertons was through Henry Lawes, who had taught music to the Earl's children since 1626 or earlier (Evans 62). C. G. Osgood, *JEGP* iv (1902) 370–8, argues from the tone of Lawes's epistle prefixed to *Comus* that M. and the Egertons were not personally acquainted, but the Lawes connection makes it probable that the actors of *Arcades* included those of *Comus*.

French (i 226) dates *Arcades* 1631, but the great scandal of that year was the trial and execution (14 May) of the Dowager Countess's son-in-law, the Earl of Castlehaven, for unnatural practices and for causing his wife to be ravished. 1631 is thus a very unlikely date.

*Publication.* *1645* (*91.* sits]sits, *97.* banks,]banks. ) *1673* (the text followed here except in *46* where *1673* prints a full stop after 'grove' and *47* where it prints a semi-colon after 'quaint').

*Modern criticism.* J. M. Wallace, *JEGP* lviii (1959) 627–36, sees the theme of *Arcades* as a pilgrimage from profane to religious, from classical south to Christian north. The central symbol is the Countess, personifying heavenly wisdom. The Queen of Sheba's amazement at the wisdom of Solomon (*1 Kings* x 6–7) is recalled in *8–13*: the Countess is Solomon's female counterpart. She is connected with Latona (*20*) because Latona was (according to Diodorus Siculus ii 47) born on the isle of the Hyperboreans (commonly identified with Britain), and was regarded by the mythographers Conti and Sandys as a personification of that goodness and innocence which hope to arrive at celestial beauty. Cybele (*21*) was 'admired for her intelligence' (Diodorus Siculus iii 58).

*Part of an entertainment presented to the Countess Dowager of Derby at Harefield, by some noble persons of her family, who appear on the scene in pastoral habit, moving toward the seat of state, with this song.*

### I. SONG

> Look nymphs, and shepherds look,
> What sudden blaze of majesty
> Is that which we from hence descry
> Too divine to be mistook:
> 5  This this is she
> To whom our vows and wishes bend,

Here our solemn search hath end.

Fame that her high worth to raise,
Seemed erst so lavish and profuse,
10  We may justly now accuse
Of detraction from her praise,
   Less than half we find expressed,
   Envy bid conceal the rest.

Mark what radiant state she spreads,
15  In circle round her shining throne,
Shooting her beams like silver threads,
This this is she alone,
   Sitting like a goddess bright,
   In the centre of her light.

20  Might she the wise Latona be,
Or the towered Cybele,
Mother of a hundred gods;
Juno dares not give her odds;
   Who had thought this clime had held
25    A deity so unparalleled?

*As they come forward, the Genius of the Wood appears, and turning
toward them, speaks.*

      *Gen.* Stay gentle swains, for though in this disguise,
I see bright honour sparkle through your eyes,
Of famous Arcady ye are, and sprung
Of that renowned flood, so often sung,

10–11. *We may ... Of*] In *Trin. MS* inserted beside a previous version
'Now seems guilty of abuse / And . . .'

12. *we find*] In *Trin. MS* inserted beside previous version 'she hath'.

17. Perhaps a memory of Jonson, *Entertainment at Althorp* 113–7: 'This
is shee / This is shee, / In whose world of grace / Every season, person,
place, / That receive her, happy be.'

18. *Sitting*] *Trin. MS*: *seated* 'sitting'.

20. *Latona*] Mother of Apollo and Diana.

21–2. Virgil, *Aen.* vi 785–7, calls Cybele mother of a hundred gods and
describes her towered crown.

23. *Juno*] Cancelled in *Trin. MS* and 'Ceres' substituted, but 'Juno'
restored later.    *give her odds*] offer to contest with her on terms which
favour the Countess.

24. *had thought*] *Trin. MS*: *would have* 'had' thought.

26. Evans 64–5 suggests that the Genius (protecting local deity) was played
by Lawes, and that *Il Penseroso* 154 refers to him.   *gentle*] well-born.

28. *Arcady*] Arcadia, 'famous' as the home of pastoral singers in Theocritus
and Virgil, *Ecl.* x 31–6, and more recently because of Sidney's *Arcadia*

30    Divine Alpheus, who by secret sluice,
       Stole under seas to meet his Arethuse;
       And ye the breathing roses of the wood,
       Fair silver-buskined nymphs as great and good,
       I know this quest of yours, and free intent
35    Was all in honour and devotion meant
       To the great mistress of yon princely shrine,
       Whom with low reverence I adore as mine,
       And with all helpful service will comply
       To further this night's glad solemnity;
40    And lead ye where ye may more near behold
       What shallow-searching Fame hath left untold;
       Which I full oft amidst these shades alone
       Have sat to wonder at, and gaze upon:
       For know by lot from Jove I am the power
45    Of this fair wood, and live in oaken bower,
       To nurse the saplings tall, and curl the grove
       With ringlets quaint, and wanton windings wove.
       And all my plants I save from nightly ill,
       Of noisome winds, and blasting vapours chill.
50    And from the boughs brush off the evil dew,
       And heal the harms of thwarting thunder blue,
       Or what the cross dire-looking planet smites,
       Or hurtful worm with cankered venom bites.

(1590) with its 'shepheards boy piping, as though he should never be old' (I ii).    *ye*] *Trin. MS:* you.

*30–1. Alpheus*] An Arcadian river. Ovid, *Met.* v 574–641 tells how the nymph Arethusa bathed in its waters and, when pursued by the amorous river-god, was herself transformed to a river which passed under the Adriatic to Sicily, still pursued by Alpheus.    *secret*] hidden    *sluice*] channel.

*32. breathing*] emitting fragrance.

*40. ye . . . ye*] *Trin. MS:* you . . . you.

*41. What shallow-searching*] *Trin. MS: Those virtues which dull* 'What shallow-searching'.

*46. curl*] Drayton, *Polyolbion* vii 109 and Browne i 126 have groves with 'curled heads', and in Sylvester (Du Bartas 38) winds 'curl' the locks of trees.

*47. With*] *Trin. MS:* In.    *quaint*] ingeniously contrived.    *wove*] woven.

*50. boughs*] *Trin. MS: leaves* 'boughs'.    *evil dew*] mildew; cp. *Tempest* I ii 321: 'As wicked dew as e'er my mother brush'd'.

*51. thwarting*] crossing with a streak; cp. *Julius Ceasar* I iii 50: 'the cross blue lightning'.

*52. planet*] Saturn, the malign planet.

*53. worm . . . cankered*] Cankerworm was a name given to caterpillars and insect larvae which destroyed leaves and buds.

When evening grey doth rise, I fetch my round
55  Over the mount, and all this hallowed ground,
And early ere the odorous breath of morn
Awakes the slumbering leaves, or tasselled horn
Shakes the high thicket, haste I all about,
Number my ranks, and visit every sprout
60  With puissant words, and murmurs made to bless,
But else in deep of night when drowsiness
Hath locked up mortal sense, then listen I
To the celestial sirens' harmony,
That sit upon the nine enfolded spheres,
65  And sing to those that hold the vital shears,
And turn the adamantine spindle round,
On which the fate of gods and men is wound.
Such sweet compulsion doth in music lie,
To lull the daughters of Necessity,
70  And keep unsteady Nature to her law,
And the low world in measured motion draw
After the heavenly tune, which none can hear
Of human mould with gross unpurged ear;

59. *ranks*] of trees. As. C. G. Osgood, *JEGP* iv (1902) 370-8 points out there was an avenue of elms at Harefield called The Queen's Walk in memory of Queen Elizabeth's visit to the house in 1602. In *Trin. MS* the present form of the line is substituted for the earlier 'And number all my ranks, and every sprout'.

60. *puissant . . . bless*] powerful magic charms and blessings.

62. *Hath . . . sense*] *Trin. MS* : *Hath chained mortality* 'Hath locked up mortal *eyes'* 'sense'.

63-72. M. is paraphrasing Plato, *Republic* x 616-7. In Plato the spindle of Necessity has a shaft of adamant (steel) upon which are threaded the eight concentric whorls of the universe. On the rim of each whorl stands a siren who utters a single note, and the notes together produce a harmony. The end of the spindle rests on the knees of Necessity, and at equal distance round sit her daughters, the three Fates, Lachesis, Clotho and Atropos, who turn the spindle with their hands. Strictly speaking the 'vital shears' (the shears which cut the thread of life) were held by Atropos only.

64. *nine*] M. makes Plato's eight spheres nine, following Dante who relates the nine spheres to the nine orders of angels, *Paradiso* xxviii 25-78. As J. Hutton points out, *EM* ii (1951) 23-5, the same relation is found in Ficino and Gafori.

72-3. In *Prolusion II* (Columbia xii 148-57, Yale i 234-9) M. again refers to the Pythagorean doctrine that the music of the spheres is unheard only because human ears are unworthy to hear it. He perhaps recalls *Merchant of Venice* v i 64-5 'But whilst this muddy vesture of decay / Doth grossly

And yet such music worthiest were to blaze
75  The peerless height of her immortal praise,
Whose lustre leads us, and for her most fit,
If my inferior hand or voice could hit
Inimitable sounds, yet as we go,
Whate'er the skill of lesser gods can show,
80  I will assay, her worth to celebrate,
And so attend ye toward her glittering state;
Where ye may all that are of noble stem
Approach, and kiss her sacred vesture's hem.

II. SONG

O'er the smooth enamelled green
85  Where no print of step hath been,
    Follow me as I sing,
    And touch the warbled string.
Under the shady roof
Of branching elm star-proof.
90      Follow me,
I will bring you where she sits
Clad in splendour as befits
    Her deity.
Such a rural queen
95  All Arcadia hath not seen.

III. SONG

Nymphs and shepherds dance no more
By sandy Ladon's lilied banks,

close it in, we cannot hear it', and *Midsummer Night's Dream* III i 159
'I will purge thy mortal grossness so'.
74. *blaze*] proclaim.
84. *enamelled*] beautified with various colours (this meaning developed
early in the seventeenth century).
89. *elm*] See 59n.    *star-proof*] Cp. Virgil's gloomy elm at the entrance
to the underworld, *Aen.* vi. 282–3, also Statius, *Theb.* x 85: *nulli
penetrabilis astro*; and Spenser, *F.Q.* I i 7: 'Not perceable with power of
any starre.'
91. *you*] Trin. MS: ye.
97. *Ladon*] a river in Arcadia, flowing into the Alpheus; 'sandy' is from
Ovid, *Met.* i 702: *arenosi . . . Ladonis.*

On old Lycaeus or Cyllene hoar,
    Trip no more in twilight ranks,
*100*    Though Erymanth your loss deplore,
    A better soil shall give ye thanks.
From the stony Maenalus,
Bring your flocks, and live with us,
Here ye shall have greater grace,
*105*    To serve the Lady of this place.
    Though Syrinx your Pan's mistress were,
    Yet Syrinx well might wait on her.
      Such a rural queen
    All Arcadia hath not seen.

# 47 At a Solemn Music

*Date.* 1633? There is no firm evidence for dating. The Trinity MS has two heavily corrected preliminary drafts, followed by a separate draft of *17–28*, followed by a fair copy of the whole (these four drafts are referred to in the notes as (*a*), (*b*), (*c*) and (*d*) respectively). The drafts begin on the reverse of the leaf containing the end of *Arcades. Solemn Music* can therefore be dated after, probably soon after, *Arcades* (itself not precisely dateable). The drafts are followed by the first draft of the letter to a friend (see headnote to *Sonnet VII* p. 146 above) which is undated but perhaps as late as 1633 (W. R. Parker, *RES* xi (1935) 278–9). *Time* and *Circumcision* do not appear until after the second draft of this letter: they appear, however, as fair copies, so no conclusions about their date of composition relative to that of *Solemn Music* can be drawn from this position. In *1645 Time* and *Circumcision* precede *Solemn Music,* but it cannot be proved that the order of poems in *1645* is strictly chronological.
*Publication.* 1645 (6. concent,]content, ) *1673* (the text followed here).
*Modern criticism.* The history of the idea of world harmony (*musica mundana*),

*98–102. Lycaeus ... Cyllene ... Erymanth ... Maenalus*] mountains in Arcadia; Virgil, *Georg.* i 16–7, mentions the first and last as haunts of Pan. Starnes and Talbert (292–3) note that these names, along with 'Ladon' and 'Pan', are included in Stephanus *s.v. Arcadia.* 'Hoar' (snow-covered) was perhaps suggested by Virgil, *Aen.* viii 139: 'Cyllene's frozen peak'.
*106. Syrinx*] Arcadian nymph, pursued by Pan; she fled to the river Ladon and was turned into a reed. In *Trin. MS* ll. 106–7 appear as a later insertion: Todd v 181 takes them as a complimentary allusion to Jonson, *Entertainment at Althorp* 20–1: 'And the dame hath Syrinx grace! / O that Pan were now in place', where the 'dame' was Queen Anne, whom the Countess's father, Lord Spencer of Althorp, was entertaining.

with which *Solemn Music* is concerned, and of the related harmony of man (*musica humana*), is traced by L. Spitzer, *Traditio* ii (1944) 409–64 and iii (1945) 307–64. The second of these articles contains a detailed analysis of the poem, showing that it can be divided into three sections (Graeco-Roman, Jewish and Christian), according to the technical terms and concepts used. John Hollander relates the poem to contemporary ideas about music in *The Untuning of the Sky* (Princeton 1961) pp. 324–31.

*Versification in M.'s 'canzone poems'*. A. Oras, *N & Q* cxcvii (1952) 314–5, suggested that the model for the stanza form of *Circumcision* (a10b10c10b10a10c10c10d7d7c10e10f7f4e6) was Tasso's *canzone* to the Virgin of Loreto. Tasso's rhyme scheme, however, differs slightly from M.'s (his first six lines rhyme *abcabc*). As Prince 62 demonstrates, M.'s actual model was Petrarch's *canzone* to the Blessed Virgin (*Vergine bella, che di Sol vestita*). M.'s only modification to the scheme of this poem is to make two separate lines out of the two sections into which Petrarch's last line falls. Even this modification, which is merely typographical, was an afterthought (see *13–14n* and *27–28n*). Petrarch's *canzone* is 137 lines long: M. stops after 28, and does not again attempt the exact repetition of a complex stanza, which is the basis of the *canzone*. In the internal architecture of his stanza he swerves from his Petrarchan model, ignoring the syntactical break at the end of *6* which in Petrarch marks off the *fronte* from the *coda* (M.'s first stanza is a single sentence). For this, however, he had ample precedent in sixteenth-century Italian poetry.

*Time* and *Solemn Music* (which may have been written either before or after *Circumcision*) adopt the less taxing form of the madrigal–a single, unrepeated stanza of the *canzone* type. Tasso and his Italian followers had used this for epigrammatic effects. Previous to M., Drummond of Hawthornden was the only English poet to imitate their madrigals closely. Both M.'s madrigals are less intricately rhymed and make heavier use of the couplet-rhyme (over half of *Solemn Music* is decasyllabic couplets) than would be usual in Italian, but M. avoids the regularity of couplets by diversifying his syntax and its relation to the line. His closing alexandrine inserts a Spenserian flavour into each poem.

> Blest pair of sirens, pledges of heaven's joy,
> Sphere-borne harmonious sisters, Voice, and Verse,
> Wed your divine sounds, and mixed power employ

¶ 47. *1–2. sirens*] See *Arcades* 63–72*n*, p. 159 above.          *pledges*] Earthly music is a pledge or assurance of heavenly bliss because it makes us recollect the divine music. James Hutton, *EM* ii (1951) 1–63, indicates the currency of this idea among Renaissance neo-Platonists.          *Sphere-borne*] carried on spheres.          *sisters*] Cp. Marino, *Adone* vii 1: *Musica e Poesia son due sorelle.*

3. *Trin.* MS (*a*): [. . .]vine power and joint force employ. (*b*): *Mix your choice chords, and happiest sounds employ* (deleted, present version inserted).

Dead things with inbreathed sense able to pierce,
5   And to our high-raised phantasy present,
That undisturbed song of pure concent,
Ay sung before the sapphire-coloured throne
To him that sits thereon
With saintly shout, and solemn jubilee,
10   Where the bright seraphim in burning row
Their loud uplifted angel trumpets blow,
And the cherubic host in thousand choirs
Touch their immortal harps of golden wires,

4. *Dead things*] Alluding to the myth of Orpheus, whose music could attract trees, streams and rocks.

5. *high-raised phantasy*] Phantasy was thought of in the seventeenth century as intermediate between sense and reason (see *PL* v 100–13). The idea that music could produce an ecstasy, separating soul from body, was common. It can be traced to the Church Fathers, such as Basil and Chrysostom, and to the neo-Platonists and neo-Pythagoreans, Iamblichus, Porphyry and Plotinus. M. here asks for only the 'phantasy', not the soul, to be 'raised', but see *Nativity Ode* 98 and *Il Penseroso* 165–6 (pp. 105 and 146 above). For a discussion of the whole subject see G. L. Finney, *Journal of the History of Ideas* viii (1947) 153–86. Between 4 and 5 *Trin. MS* (*a*) inserts: [. . .]whilst your 'equal' raptures tempered sweet/[. . .]happy spousal meet/[. . .]th a while/[. . .]home-bred 'woes' beguile. *Trin. MS* (*b*): And *whilst* 'as' your equal raptures tempered sweet/In high mysterious *holy* 'happy' spousal meet/Snatch us from earth a while/Us of ourselves and *home-bred* 'native' woes beguile.     *high-raised phantasy present*] *Trin. MS* (*a*): [. . .]*fancies then* 'phantasy' present. *Trin. MS* (*b*): high 'up' *up-raised* 'high-raised' phantasy present.

6. *concent*] harmony, concord. Each of the *Trin. MS* drafts reads 'concent'. In a Bodleian copy of *1645* (8° M168 Art) a hand possibly M.'s has altered 'content' to 'concent'.

7. *Trin. MS* (*a*): [. . .]ounds [. . .]ay surrounds the *sovereign* 'sapphire-coloured' throne.     *sapphire-coloured*] Cp. *Ezek.* i 26: 'the likeness of a throne, as the appearance of a sapphire stone'.

9. *Trin. MS* (*a*): [. . .]vers a[. . .] and solemn cry. (Not deleted; present version inserted).

10. *Trin. MS* (*a*): [. . .]e the ser[. . .] princely row. (*b*): Where the bright seraphim in *tripled* 'burning' row.

11. *Trin. MS* (*a*): [. . .]ire loud unsa[. . .]trumpets blow 'Loud symphony of 'silver' trumpets blow'. (*b*): 'Their' *high-lifted* loud 'uplifted' *arch*-angel trumpets blow.

12. *Trin. MS* (*a*): And *the* youthf[. . .]ubim 'heaven's henchmen' sweet-winged squires.

13. *Trin. MS* (*a*): In ten thous[. . .]es.

With those just spirits that wear victorious palms,
15   Hymns devout and holy psalms
Singing everlastingly;
That we on earth with undiscording voice
May rightly answer that melodious noise;
As once we did, till disproportioned sin
20   Jarred against nature's chime, and with harsh din
Broke the fair music that all creatures made
To their great Lord, whose love their motion swayed
In perfect diapason, whilst they stood
In first obedience, and their state of good.

14. *Trin. MS (a)*: With those just[. . .] that 'bear' wear the *fresh green* 'blooming' 'victorious' palms. *(b)*: With those just spirits that wear the blooming 'blooming or victorious' palms.      palms] Cp. *Rev.* vii 9: 'a great multitude . . . clothed with white robes, and palms in their hands'.

15. *Trin. MS (a)*: *In* hymns d[. . .] and sacred psalms. *(b)* Hymns devout and sacred 'holy' psalms.

16–17. *Trin. MS (a)* and *(b)* insert two lines between 16 and 17. *Trin. MS (a)*: 'While *that* all the f[. . .]e of 'whilst the whole frame of' 'while *then* all the starry' heaven and arches blue / Resound and echo Hallelu. *(b)*: *While all the starry rounds and arches blue / Resound and echo Hallelu.*

17. *Trin. MS (a)*: That we *below may learn with* 'with undiscording' heart and voice. *(b)*: That we 'on earth' with undiscording *heart and* voice.

18. *May rightly answer*] *Trin. MS (a)*: 'May' Rightly *to* answer.

19. *Trin. MS (a)* and *(b)* omit ll. 19–25 and read instead, *(a)*: By leaving out. those harsh chromatic jars / Of sin that all our music mars / And in our lives and in our song. *(b)*: By leaving out those harsh *chromatic* 'ill-sounding' jars / Of clamorous sin that all our music mars / And in our lives and in our song. *Trin. MS (c)*: As once we could 'did' till disproportioned sin. *(d)*: As once we *could* 'did' till disproportioned sin.

19–24. Cp. Du Bartas 256, where it is explained that the 'hidden love' which still exists between 'steel and Load-stone' or '*Elm* and the *Vine*', 'Is but a spark or shadow of that Love /Which at the first in every thing did move, / When as th' Earths *Muses* with harmonious sound / To Heav'ns sweet *Musick* humbly did resound. / But *Adam*, being chief of all the strings / Of this large Lute, o're-retched, quickly brings / All out of tune.' The idea that the singing of the heavenly host was audible to human ears till the fall is found in Dante, *Purgatorio* xxix 22–30; M. refers to it again, *PL* iv 680–8 and vii 561.

20. *Trin. MS (c)*: *Drowned* 'Jarred against' nature's chime and with *tumultuous* 'harsh' din.      *nature's chime*] Echoing Jonson, *Underwoods* lxxv 26–7: 'The Month of youth, which calls all Creatures forth / To doe their Offices in Natures Chime.'

23. *diapason*] concord, harmony: literally, the concord through all the notes of the musical scale.

25   O may we soon again renew that song,
     And keep in tune with heaven, till God ere long
     To his celestial consort us unite,
     To live with him, and sing in endless morn of light.

# 48 On Time

*Date.* 1633 ? There is no certain evidence for dating. For *Time*'s position in the Trinity MS and *1645* see headnote to *Solemn Music*, p. 161 above. Fletcher ii 174, 417–23 dates *Time* 1627–8 on the grounds that its metrics reflect the influence of Pindar and its content that of M.'s study of physics, begun some time during the academic year 1626–7. These reasons are clearly insufficient in themselves, and the appearance of even a fair copy of *Time* in the Trinity MS suggests a date later than Fletcher's.

In MS the poem was originally headed '[. . .] set on a clock case'. Later this was deleted and 'On Time' substituted.

*Publication. 1645 (10.* all]all, ) *1673* (the text followed here).

     Fly envious Time, till thou run out thy race,
     Call on the lazy leaden-stepping hours,
     Whose speed is but the heavy plummet's pace;
     And glut thyself with what thy womb devours,
5   Which is no more than what is false and vain,
     And merely mortal dross,
     So little is our loss,
     So little is thy gain.
     For when as each thing bad thou hast entombed,
10  And last of all thy greedy self consumed,

*25. Trin. MS (c):* O may we soon 'again' renew that song.
*26. And keep] Trin. MS (a)* and *(b):* May keep.
*27. consort]* a company of musicians.
*28. Trin. MS (a):* To live and sing with him in ever-endless 'ever-glorious' 'uneclipsed' 'where day dwells without night' 'in endless morn 'cloudless birth' of' 'in never-parting' light. *(b), (c)* and *(d):* To live and sing with him in endless morn of light.
¶ 48. *2. leaden-stepping]* Controlled by the movement of the lead plummet and moving in regular jerks or steps as the result of the functioning of the clock's escapement.
*3. plummet]* Commonly used in the seventeenth century, as here, to mean the weight of a clock.

Then long eternity shall greet our bliss
With an individual kiss;
And joy shall overtake us as a flood,
When every thing that is sincerely good
15 And perfectly divine,
With truth, and peace, and love shall ever shine
About the supreme throne
Of him, to whose happy-making sight alone,
When once our heavenly-guided soul shall climb,
20 Then all this earthy grossness quit,
Attired with stars, we shall for ever sit,
　　Triumphing over Death, and Chance, and thee
　　O Time.

# 49 Upon the Circumcision

*Date.* 1633 ? There is no certain evidence for dating. The feast of the Circumcision is 1 Jan., which may be relevant. For position in the Trinity MS and *1645* see headnote to *Solemn Music* and *Time* (pp. 161 and 165 above). *Publication.* *1645*, *1673* (no significant variants).

Ye flaming powers and winged warriors bright,
That erst with music, and triumphant song
First heard by happy watchful shepherds' ear,

*12. individual*] Usually explained as 'inseparable', a common seventeenth-century meaning, i.e. a kiss in which the lips meet and can never again divide. But O. B. Hardinson Jr, *Texas Studies in Lit. and Lang.* iii (1961) 107–22, argues that the word means 'peculiar to a particular person', 'not collective', and that it thus represents M.'s contribution to the controversy, still active in the seventeenth century, over the Averroists' denial of personal immortality–a denial countered by St Thomas in the *De Unitate Intellectus Contra Averroistas Parisienses*. M.'s argument in *De doctrina* i 33 (Columbia xvi 352) that each man will rise from the dead with the same identity as he had in life supports Hardison's thesis.
*14. sincerely*] purely.
*18. happy-making sight*] an anglicization of the term 'beatific vision'. Bodleian MS Ashmole 36,37 f. 22r. has a version of *Time* in a seventeenth-century hand which omits ll. 18–22 and reads instead 'Of him whose happy-making sight alone / Shall heap our days with everlasting store / When death and chance and thou, O time, shall be no more'.
¶ 49. 1. *powers*] the sixth order of angels in the pseudo-Dionysian nine. M. seems, however, to use the word loosely: it was the seraphim that were 'flaming'.　　*winged warriors*] Cp. Tasso, *Ger. Lib.* IX lx 1 : *guerrieri alati*.
*2. erst*] formerly.

So sweetly sung your joy the clouds along
5      Through the soft silence of the listening night;
Now mourn, and if sad share with us to bear
Your fiery essence can distil no tear,
Burn in your sighs, and borrow
Seas wept from our deep sorrow,
10     He who with all heaven's heraldry whilere
Entered the world, now bleeds to give us ease;
Alas, how soon our sin
Sore doth begin
His infancy to seize!
15     O more exceeding love or law more just?
Just law indeed, but more exceeding love!
For we by rightful doom remediless
Were lost in death, till he that dwelt above
High-throned in secret bliss, for us frail dust
20     Emptied his glory, even to nakedness;
And that great covenant which we still transgress
Entirely satisfied,
And the full wrath beside
Of vengeful justice bore for our excess,
25     And seals obedience first with wounding smart
This day, but O ere long
Huge pangs and strong
Will pierce more near his heart.

6–9. If the angels cannot weep, M. advises them to burn and so, like the sun, draw up water (seas of tears) from the earth.

10. *heraldry*] heraldic pomp (the first recorded instance of the word in this sense).      *whilere*] some time ago.

13–14. These two lines are first written as one in *Trin. MS* and then re-written as two in the margin.

15–16. For the rhetorical pattern, cp. Virgil, *Ecl.* viii 49–50: *Crudelis mater magis, an puer improbus ille?* | *improbus ille puer: crudelis tu quoque, mater.*

17. *doom*] judgment.

19. *secret*] hidden.

20. *Emptied his glory*] Cp. *Philipp.* ii 7: 'made himself of no reputation', where the Vulgate reads *semetipsum exinanivit*, and M. in *De doctrina* I xvi gives *ipse sese inanivit* (Columbia xv 302).

21. *covenant*] the Mosaic law; cp. *Matt.* v 17: 'Think not that I am come to destroy the law ... I am not come to destroy, but to fulfil.' M. argues the point in *De doctrina* I xvi (Columbia xv 316).

27–8. These two lines were first written as one in *Trin. MS*, and then re-written as two in the margin.

28. *Will*] *Trin. MS*(margin): *Shall* Will.

# 50 A Masque presented at Ludlow Castle, 1634 [Comus]

*Date.* 1634. First acted 29 Sept. 1634. The Earl of Bridgewater had been made President of the Council of Wales 26 June 1631, and Lord Lieutenant of Wales and the counties on the Welsh border 8 Jul. 1631. His youngest daughter Alice, aged fifteen, played the Lady, and his only surviving sons John, aged eleven, and Thomas, aged nine, were the Elder and Younger Brothers. The boys had acted in Thomas Carew's *Coelum Britannicum* on 18 Feb. 1634. Portraits of the children are reproduced in Lady Alix Egerton's edition of *Comus* (1910). Henry Lawes, their music teacher, wrote the music for *Coelum Britannicum* and for *Comus*, and played the Attendant Spirit. BM Add. MS 11518 has five songs from *Comus*, with music (reproduced Fletcher[3] i 341–4), in a hand which (see French i 283) may be Lawes's. The Church MS (described by Evans 235f.) has the same songs in a hand apparently that of Lawes. The Bridgewater MS of *Comus* (referred to below as *Bridg.*), preserved at Bridgewater House, was once thought to be in Lawes's hand, but D. H. Stevens, *MP* xxiv (1927) 315–20, has demonstrated that it is the work of a professional scrivener. Facsimiles of the text of *Comus* as it appears in *Bridg.*, the Trinity MS, the anonymous first edition (*1637*), *1645* and *1673*, will be found in Fletcher[3] i 56, 193, 265, 301 and 399. C. S. Lewis's study of the surviving versions, *RES* viii (1932) 170–6, shows that the uncorrected state of the Trinity MS preceded *Bridg.* (a poor copy made without M.'s supervision), that various changes were made in the Trinity MS after *Bridg.* had been copied, that *1637* was based on the Trinity MS at an early stage of correction, and that M.'s tendency in revision was to delete technical terms and colloquialisms and increase the gnomic element at the expense of the dramatic. J. S. Diekhoff, *PMLA* lii (1937) 705–27, has demonstrated that even the uncorrected state of the Trinity MS is not the original draft of *Comus* but a later transcript. He makes a detailed examination, *PMLA* lv (1940) 748–72, of the alterations made by M. in the process of composition, which supplements the less minute study by L. E. Lockwood, *MLN* xxv (1910) 201–5. He also attempts to show, *PMLA* li (1936) 757–98, that the punctuation of *Comus* in *1645* (which differs little from that in *1673*) is frequently, though not consistently, rhetorical and prosodic. J. T. Shaw-cross, *Bibliog. Soc. of America Papers* liv (1960) 38–56 and 293–4, argues convincingly that *Bridg.* was probably not transcribed until autumn or winter 1637–8 and was derived from a copy of the Trinity MS text during its development into the version which survives; that *1637* (which may have been published early in 1638) was set from a revised intermediate copy (between the Trinity MS and *Bridg.*) with some corrections from the Trinity MS; and that the copy used for *1645* derived from a corrected *1637*.

*Publication.* *1637* is the first edition of *Comus*. It does not bear M.'s name.
The text is preceded by a letter from Henry Lawes to John, Viscount Brack-
ley (the Elder Brother), which makes it clear that Lawes is responsible for
publishing. The reason he gives is that 'the often copying of it hath tired my
pen to give my several friends satisfaction'. The title-page motto, from
Virgil, *Ecl.* ii–*Eheu quid volui misero mihi ! floribus austrum/ Perditus* ('Alas,
what harm did I mean to my wretched self when I let the south wind blow
upon my flowers?') – implies that M. (if M. chose it) had qualms about
publishing. The publisher is not named on the title-page, but was probably
John Raworth, whose widow Ruth printed *1645*. Probably not more than
fifteen copies of this edition now survive (the Bodleian has two and the
British Museum three).

*1637* is generally more lightly punctuated than *1645* or *1673*. Compared
with the text printed here it omits 181 commas, one semicolon, one full stop
and one question mark; prints comma for semicolon 10 times, for question
mark 5 times, for colon 4 times and for full stcp 4 times; semicolon for
colon twice and for full stop once. On the other hand, heavier punctuation
in *1637*, though rare, is not unexampled. It adds 29 commas, prints semicolon
for comma 5 times, full stop for comma (*918*), for semicolon (*553*), question
mark for comma (*753*), and inserts one full stop (at the end of *967*). In *20*
*1637* misprints 'my' for 'by'. Otherwise its verbal variants are: *43.* you]ye
*73.* is]in    *167–8. as 1645*    *194.* stole]stol'n    *213.* hovering]flittering
*251.* it]she    *389.* a]an    *436.* Hath]Has    *471.* Lingering]Hovering
*512.* ye]you    *537.* To]T'    *579.* further]farther    *604.* forms]bugs
*607.* to a foul death]and cleave his scalp    *608.* Cursed as his life]Down
to the hips    *780.* contemptuous]reproachful    *955.* grow]are.

*1645* was the next edition. (It has the following variants from the text
printed here: *43.* you]ye    *127.* report,]report.    *146.* ground.]ground,
*167–8.* And . . . aside]Whom thrift keeps up about his country gear, / But
here she comes, I fairly step aside / And hearken, if I may, her business here.
(*see footnote*)    *347.* yet]yet,    *354.* fears,]fears.    *473.* sensuality]
sensualty    *485.* again, again,]again again    *512.* vain]vain,    *535.*
bowers,]bowers.    *549.* dissonance]dissonance,    *553.* sleep;]sleep.
*660.* statue,]statue;    *763.* abundance]abundance,    *781.* chastity;]
chastity,    *828.* The]She    *855.* virgin]virgin,    *922.* line]line,    *970.*
truth,]truth.    *996.* mortals]mortals, ). The text followed here is *1673*,
except in *86*, *93*, *165* and *970* where *1673* prints full stops after 'song',
'fold', 'dust' and 'truth' (in the last of these instances it has the support of
*1645*, see above. I have substituted a comma because the full stop may obs-
cure the sense for a modern reader); and in *546*, *555* and *926*, where *1673*
misprints 'meditate upon' for 'meditate', 'stream' for 'steam' and 'tum-
bled' for 'tumble'.

*Genre and style.* The work which we call *Comus* was not put before the
public under that title until 1738 when John Dalton (1709–63) adapted it
for the eighteenth-century stage. In *1637*, *1645* and *1673* its title is *A*
*Masque presented at Ludlow Castle, 1634*. The seventeenth-century masque

developed in various directions (notably towards opera and towards a morality-type drama) so that generalization about it is misleading. But it is safe to say that pageantry and dancing play a smaller part in *Comus* than in most masques. Browne's *Inner Temple Masque* and Jonson's *Pleasure Reconciled to Virtue* are its closest relations in the masque form. The association of Circe with the sirens (classically unprecedented) and the anti-masque of monsters are found in Browne, and his description of Circe's power resembles Comus's speech on the reversal of natural order ('she that by charms can make / The scaled fish to leave the briny lake, / And on the seas walk as on land she were; / She that can pull the pale moon from her sphere, / And at mid-day the world's all-glorious eye / Muffle with clouds in long obscurity' 33–8). In Jonson's masque the figure of Comus first appeared on the stage. Both masques, however, are brief and frivolous compared with M.'s work. *Comus's* most important affinity with court masques is undoubtedly the personal relationship existing in it and them between actors and members of the audience, resulting in an intimate atmosphere and a minute awareness of the relationships between real and assumed characters. These finer points are now lost irrevocably.

The attempts of Welsford and Haun (see below) to ally *Comus* generically with moral entertainments like Nabbes' *Microcosmus* and Ford and Dekker's *Sun's Darling* cannot survive an impartial reading of those works. They are latterday morality plays mixing low comic relief with stereotyped encounters between an everyman figure and allegorical representations of his attributes.

The Attendant Spirit's first speech, it has often been pointed out, resembles a Euripidean prologue, and there is one passage of stichomythia (*276–90*), but the structural debt to Greek drama does not extend beyond this.

*Comus* is, then, not a masque nor a moral entertainment (in the early seventeenth-century sense) so much as a Platonic pastoral drama. It derives its ethics largely from Plato's *Phaedo* (its fanciful cosmology is also affected by this work but more extensively by Plutarch's *Moralia*, see footnotes). Its pastoral dramatics stem from Tasso's *Aminta* (see Praz, below) and Guarini's *Pastor Fido*, not directly but by way of Fletcher's *Faithful Shepherdess*. This play prefigures the Lady in its chaste heroines, Clorin and Amoret, and Comus in its lascivious enchanter, the Sullen Shepherd, who, in his encounter with the priest (V i) also uses naturalistic arguments ('Hath not our Mother Nature for her store / And great increase, said it is good and just, / And wills that every living creature must / Beget his like ?'), and who, when he meets Amoret benighted in the wood (III i) gives false news of her lost companion and is thanked by her ('Thanks, gentle shepherd') in a way which recalls *Comus 290–329*. Clorin's speech about the protective power of chastity (I i) is close to the Elder Brother's (*420–37*). Fletcher's Satyr, commissioned by Pan to patrol the wood ('Here I must stay / To see what mortals lose their way' III i) prefigures M.'s Attendant Spirit, and the God of the River who can cure the wounded Amoret only because she is a virgin (III i) is a prototype of Sabrina and talks, like her, in heptasyllables ('If thou be'st a virgin pure / I can give a present cure'). These parallels, and the constant struggle between chastity and vice in Fletcher's play, make it the most important single 'source'.

Shakespeare is M.'s stylistic master in *Comus*. Several speeches read like Shakespeare-pastiche (e.g. *325–9* and *596–8*, recalling, on the one hand, Hermione's tone in the *Winter's Tale* trial scene and, on the other, that of the lovers in *Antony and Cleopatra*), and there are thirty-two indisputable echoes, coming from fourteen of the plays and from *Lucrece*. The plays most drawn on are *Midsummer Night's Dream* (5 echoes), *Measure for Measure* and *Tempest* (4), and *Hamlet* and *Macbeth* (3). 'Votarist' (*188*), 'mountaineer' (*425*) and 'throng' (in a transitive sense) (*712*) are words first used by Shakespeare. Sylvester (10 echoes) and Jonson (7) are the other notable English influences. There are seven remarkably close echoes of Virgil and three of Horace. Surprisingly Spenser contributes only one or two phrases, but his effect on the vocabulary is considerable. Words like 'mickle' (*31*) betray an intermittent desire to give the diction Spenserian colour. 'Finny' (*115*), 'single' (in the sense 'absolute') (*203*), 'shroud' (meaning 'seek shelter') (*315*), 'shagged' (*428*) and 'surprisal' (*617*), are Spenserian in origin. 'Swinked' (*292*) is a pseudo-archaism of Spenserian type. M.'s verbal originality in *Comus* derives largely from imitation of Spenser's methods of coinage – adding prefixes ('un-', 'in-' etc.) and suffixes ('-n', '-y' etc.) to existing adjectives, nouns and, occasionally, verbs: 'unprincipled' (*366*), 'unenchanted' (*394*), 'ill-greeting' (*405*), 'unblenched' (*429*), 'imbrutes' (*467*), 'immanacled' (*664*), 'cateress' (*763*), 'azurn' (*892*), 'cedarn' (*989*), 'jocundry' and 'shroudy', both in cancelled passages in the Trinity MS; producing new participial forms: 'swilled' (*177*); coupling: 'love-lorn' (*233*) 'home-felt' (*261*), 'over-exquisite' (*358*); and giving new senses to current forms: 'blear' (in transferred use) (*155*), 'rife' (loud sounding) (*202*), 'siding' (taking side of a person) (*211*), 'mantling' (in transferred use) (*293*), 'unmuffle' (intransitive) (*330*), 'stoop' (bend neck or head) (*332*), 'rule' (shaft of light) (*339*), 'plumes' (preens) (*337*), 'unowned' (lost) (*406*), 'unharboured' (affording no shelter) (*422*), 'embodies' (takes on material character) (*467*), 'brow' (verb) (*531*), 'stabled' (put into stable) (*533*), 'budge' (adjective) (*706*), 'fence' (art of fencing) (*790*).

*Modern criticism.* In addition to the works specified above, Peele's *Old Wives' Tale* is sometimes mentioned as a 'source'. Arthos 1–15 reviews the case for it. R. H. Singleton, *PMLA* lviii (1943) 949–57, draws attention to the marked resemblances between the description and conception of Comus in M. and in the neo-Latin prose *Comus* (1608) of Erycius Puteanus (Hendrik van der Putten), Professor of Classical Literature at Louvain, which was reprinted at Oxford in 1634. There is less to be said for G. L. Finney's theory, *SP* xxxvii (1940) 482–500, that the form to which *Comus* belongs is the *dramma per musica*, and that it is to a large extent based on *La Catena d'Adone* (1626) by Tronsarelli. Mario Praz claims, on slender evidence, that Tasso's *Aminta* is the real model for *Comus* (*Seventeenth Century Studies Presented to Sir Herbert Grierson* (Oxford 1938) p. 202), and J. M. Major, *Shakespeare*

*Quarterly* x (1959) 177–83, thinks *The Tempest* influential. A large number of apparent borrowings from Shakespeare, especially *Romeo and Juliet*, are noted by E. Seaton, *E & S* xxxi (1945) 68–80. J. Arthos, *Anglia* lxxix (1961) 204–13, traces elements of the Sabrina episode to Virgil's description of the nymph Cyrene and her sisters in *Georg*. iv, and to Porphyry's neo-Platonic allegorization, in the *De antro nympharum*, of the cave of the nymphs in Homer, *Od*. xiii.

G. F. Sensabaugh, *SP* xli (1944) 238–49, views *Comus* as a reassertion of the genuine Platonic doctrine of love, in opposition to the debased court Platonism encouraged by Henrietta Maria; while for Hanford[3] 81 M.'s masque is a reply to the libertine philosophy of Randolph's *Muse's Looking Glass*.

The doctrine of chastity or virginity in *Comus* has occasioned much controversy. Tillyard 373–83 concludes that, at the time he wrote *Comus*, M. 'intended his celibacy to last his life'. In a later study, (Tillyard[3] 82–99: a revised version of *E & S* xxviii (1942) 22–37), he suggests that M.'s own ideal changed between 1634 and 1637, and that in the 1637 *Comus* it is represented neither by the Lady (who derives from Spenser's Belphoebe and Phineas Fletcher's Parthenia, and stands for virginity), nor by Comus (who stands for licence). Rather the ideal of *Comus* in its final version is marriage, and this is revealed, as Tillyard sees it, in *998–1010* (lines added some time between the first draft of the Trinity MS and *1637*). W. Haller, *JELH* xiii (1946) 79–97, also feels that virginity cannot be the ideal of *Comus*, because Puritan teaching about sex presented Christian marriage as the ideal: Haller assumes M.'s conformity with the usual Puritan religious and moral training. K. Muir, *Penguin New Writing* xxiv (1945) 141–3, rejects Tillyard's claim that M.'s ideal changed between 1634 and 1637, and holds that *1637* merely makes more explicit what had been M.'s meaning all along: that the views attributed to the Lady are one-sided and exaggerated. J. C. Maxwell, *Cambridge Journal* i (1948) 376–80, denies that there is any suggestion that the Lady's virtue is narrow or one-sided, and maintains that there is no contradiction between her speeches and the doctrine of the Attendant Spirit's last speech. It is merely that the main action displays the negative aspect of virtue, resistance to temptation, while the last speech emphasises the positive aspect, ascent. A. E. Dyson, *E & S* n.s. viii (1955) 89–114, agrees with Maxwell. Before the appearance of Tillyard's second study A. S. P. Woodhouse had argued, *UTQ* xi (1941) 46–71, that M. did set a marked value on the Christian concept of virginity at the time of writing *Comus*, but that the poem's meaning has two levels, one referring to the 'order of nature', the other to the 'order of grace', and that what virginity represents on the level of grace is represented on the level of nature by temperance and continence. C. Clarke, *Wind and Rain* vi (1949) 103–7, correctly objects that interpretations like those of Maxwell and Woodhouse ignore the Sabrina episode, in which 'the transition from a restrictive state of virtue to a positive one is worked out concretely in the poetry'. In reply Woodhouse, *UTQ* xix (1950) 218–23, reasserts his former view of *Comus*, but agrees that

Sabrina is introduced 'to transform chastity into a positive virtue, a principle of action, not in nature, but in grace'. When Sabrina sprinkles water, it represents a new infusion of divine grace, as *937* implies.

More individual judgments of *Comus* are those of D. C. Allen, *JELH* xvi (1949) 104–19, who considers that M. failed to reconcile the discordant elements of masque and drama, and of Circe myth and Sabrina story; R. H. Bowers, *SAMLA* 72–9, who believes that *Comus* is chiefly about the emotional problems of adolescence, that its moral conflict is limned in unsubtle black and white because youth regards life's choices in this way, and that the watchful guardian and the happy outcome emphasize that we are concerned with the world not merely of children but of privileged children; and D. Wilkinson, *E in C* x (1960) 32–43, who points out that, whereas on its first night *Comus* was the enactment of a family ritual, at later, public performances one might hope for something to compensate for private dramatic tensions, but in fact Comus and the Lady fail to engage: he is 'nominally' overwhelmed in an undramatic manner, and her rejection is merely 'nasty assertiveness', implying basic insecurity.

The labyrinthine and musical imagery is examined by Wilson Knight 65–7. In interpreting the rescue scene he suggests that 'mental inhibition is shadowed by the frozen paralysis during resistance imposed by Comus. The reversal of Comus's rod is needed to unbind the spell: which suggests a redirection of the same instinct. But the rod is lost; instinct sunk in repression.' A similar close attention to language and image leads Brooks and Hardy 188–237 to the conclusion that the susceptible Lady and the naïvely self-confident Elder Brother are treated ironically, and that 'haemony' (*637*) symbolizes virtue in a state of awareness of its own imperfection, as opposed to the virtue of the Elder Brother. This and other imaginative readings of *Comus* are rejected by R. M. Adams, *MP* li (1953) 18–32, who offers instead 'the simple beauties of obvious commonplaces set in musical language'. The light and dark imagery, made more complex by the fact that Circe is the Sun's daughter (*51*), is discussed by Tuve[2] 112–61, who regards the Circe myth as the 'hinge' of the masque. As she and others have pointed out (see especially M. Hughes, *Journal of the Hist. of Ideas* iv (1943) 381–99), Conti VI vi allegorizes Circe as lust (*libido*), the conflict between her and Ulysses as that between nature and reason, and moly as *divina clementia*. Tuve takes both haemony and water in *Comus* as symbols of grace, and thinks that M. kept primarily to the traditional purport of the Circe story, as recorded by Conti. This, however, does not make *Comus* 'pagan'–the Circe story had been Christianized before M. took it over. On the other hand J. Arthos, *Studies in the Renaissance* vi (1959) 261–74, sees *Comus* as an attempt to maintain the dignity of philosophy and non-Christian virtue. He explains M.'s association of 'chastity with temperance, prudence, wisdom, the power of contemplation, and the power of a special virtue over nature' by supposing that M. is using 'chastity' as a translation of Plato's σωφροσύνη in the *Charmides* and of Ficino's *temperantia* in his commentary on that work, which Arthos believes to be one of the sources of *Comus*. M. not only substitutes chastity for charity in the list of the three Christian theological virtues but also, says Arthos, secularizes faith and hope, which in the *De vita coelitus comparanda* Ficino names as the necessary prerequisites of effective magic. Another neo-Platonic interpretation is offered by S. Jane, *PMLA* lxxiv (1959) 533–43. He takes Jove (*20*) as the World Soul, and also divine providence, and Neptune (*18*) as natural providence. The action takes place in the realm of natural providence (of which both Comus and Sabrina are ministers) and represents the descent of the soul from heaven, its struggles against the demands of the flesh, and its victorious return. The human soul is represented jointly by the Lady (Reason) and Sabrina (a natural power of the soul, the *mens*, which preserves a memory of divinity). Haemony stands for Christian philosophical knowledge, the Elder Brother for idealism and the Younger Brother for patience. Chastity is one of the seven ways listed by Ficino in which the turning point in the soul's journey, the rejection of the flesh, can be accomplished before physical death.

The genre to which *Comus* belongs is discussed by E. Welsford, *The Court Masque* (Cambridge 1927) pp. 215–16, 315–16, who categorizes it as a moral entertainment like Nabbes' *Microcosmus* and Shirley's *Honoria and Mammon*. She also lists the similarities between *Comus* and Jonson's *Pleasure Reconciled to Virtue* and elaborates upon the differences between *Comus* and the normal court masque. Her conclusions are largely corroborated by E. Haun (Curry 221–39), who adds Ford and Dekker's *Sun's Darling*, Nabbes' *Spring's Glory* and Heywood's *Queen's Masque* to her examples of works in the same genre as *Comus*, and who compares *Bridg.* and the Trinity MS in order to demonstrate that *Comus* originally contained much more music than has come down to us: 'There is every reason to assume that *Comus* was continuous music from the invocation of Sabrina until the end of the masque, with only one interval of speech of nineteen lines.'

# THE PERSONS

The Attendant Spirit, afterwards in the habit of Thyrsis.
Comus, with his crew.
The Lady.
1. Brother.
2. Brother.
Sabrina the Nymph.

The chief persons which presented, were
The Lord Brackley,
Mr. Thomas Egerton his brother,
The Lady Alice Egerton.

The first scene discovers a wild wood.
*The Attendant Spirit descends or enters.*

Before the starry threshold of Jove's court
My mansion is, where those immortal shapes
Of bright aerial spirits live ensphered
In regions mild of calm and serene air,

¶ 50. *Stage direction. The Attendant . . . enters*] In *Trin. MS* this direction reads 'A guardian spirit, or daemon', and in *Bridg.* 'Then a guardian spirit or daemon descends or enters'.

*1. Bridg.* inserts before l. 1 the lines which appear in the printed texts as 975–98, but with the following variations: *975.* To the ocean]From the heavens     *978.* fields]field     *983–6. omitted*     *987.* That there]There *994–5 Bridg. inserts between these lines* Yellow, watchet, green and blue *995.* with Elysian dew]oft with manna dew     *996. omitted*     *998.* young Adonis]many a cherub.

*1–6.* As B. A. Wright remarks, *TLS* (27 Oct. 1945) 367 and 511, the Spirit's 'mansion' (dwelling-place) is what Socrates calls the true surface of the earth. Socrates explains (*Phaedo* 109–111) that the earth 'has many hollows of very various forms and sizes, into which the water and mist and air have run together'. What men call earth is actually one of these hollows, 'but the earth itself is pure, and is situated in the pure heaven in which the stars are. . . . We do not perceive that we live in the hollows, but think we live on the upper surface of the earth. . . . By reason of feebleness and sluggishness we are unable to attain to the upper surface of the air. . . . People there have no diseases, and live much longer than we, and in sight and hearing and wisdom, and all such things, are as much superior to us as air [ἀήρ, hence M.'s 'aerial' (3)] is purer than water.' Apparently combined with this in M.'s mind is what Plutarch says in the *Moralia* about 'daemons': they are the souls of those who have 'done with the contests of life, and by prowess of soul become daemons' (593D): they aid those souls on earth which strive towards virtue (593F–594A): they live on the moon, just outside the earth's shadow (591B–C, 942F): theirs is an intermediary state–they await the separation of soul and mind, when mind will finally return to the sun (944E)–this is why M.'s daemon dwells *before* the threshold of Jove's court: they can descend from the moon to the earth 'as warders against misdeeds and chastisers of them' (944D): the earth below appears to them as an 'abyss' from which are heard 'innumerable roars and groans of animals, the wailing of innumerable babes, the mingled lamentations of men and women' (590F). *3. ensphered*] placed in a celestial sphere. In Cicero's *Somnium Scipionis* the souls of the just dwell in the Milky Way, in the sphere of the fixed stars (cp. 'the pure heaven in which the stars are' in the previous note, and *Il Penseroso* 88–9 'unsphere / The spirit of Plato'). *4–5.* Between these lines *Trin. MS* inserts, and later deletes: Amidst the 'gardens' Hesperian gardens, ON WHOSE BANKS 'where the banks' / Bedewed with nectar and celestial songs / Eternal roses GROW, 'yield' 'blow' 'bloss'm' 'grow' and hyacinth / And fruits of golden rind, on whose fair tree / The scaly-harnessed *watchful* dragons 'ever' keeps / His *never charmed* 'unenchant-

5   Above the smoke and stir of this dim spot,
Which men call earth, and, with low-thoughted care
Confined, and pestered in this pinfold here,
Strive to keep up a frail, and feverish being
Unmindful of the crown that virtue gives
10  After this mortal change, to her true servants
Amongst the enthron'd gods on sainted seats.
Yet some there be that by due steps aspire
To lay their just hands on that golden key
That opes the palace of eternity:
15  To such my errand is, and but for such,
I would not soil these pure ambrosial weeds,
With the rank vapours of this sin-worn mould.

ed' eye, and round the verge / And sacred limits of this *happy* 'blissful'
'blissful' isle / The jealous Ocean that old river winds / His far-extended
arms, till with steep fall / Half his waste flood the wide Atlantic fills / And
half the slow unfathomed 'pool of Styx' Stygian pool / *I doubt me gentle
mortals these may seem* / *Strange distances to hear and unknown climes* / 'But soft
I was not sent to court your wonder / With distant worlds and strange
removed climes' / Yet thence I come and oft from thence behold.

5. *Trin. MS*: 'Above' The smoke and stir of this dim *narrow* spot.

7. *pestered*] 'crowded together' or 'with movements obstructed, like hobbled
animals'.     *pinfold*] a pound for confining stray horses and cattle (see l.
776n).

7–8. *Trin. MS*: '2.' Strive to keep up a frail and feverish being / *Beyond the
written date of mortal change* / '1.' Confined and pestered in this pinfold here.
(M.'s inserted numerals indicate that he wishes the order of the lines to be
reversed).

10. *mortal change*] Brooks and Hardy 189 comment: 'The phrase "mortal
change", for *death*, implies also that *change* is the rule of mortal existence'.

11. Cp. *Rev.* iv 4: 'And round about the throne were four and twenty seats:
and upon the seats I saw four and twenty elders sitting, clothed in white
raiment; and they had on their heads crowns of gold.'

12. *by*] *Bridg.*: with.

13. *golden key*] Cp. *Lycidas* 111 'The golden opes', and *Matt.* xvi 19:
'And I will give unto thee the keys of the kingdom of heaven'; also Jonson,
*Hymenaei* 896–8, describing Truth: 'Her right hand holds a sunne with
burning rayes, / Her left a curious bunch of golden kayes, / With which
heaven gates she locketh, and displayes.'

14. *opes*] *Trin. MS*: shews 'opes'.

16. *ambrosial*] immortal, hence, belonging to paradise, as here.    *weeds*]
clothes.

17. *vapours*] Cp. 'into which the water and mist and air have run together',
ll. 1–6n, above.    *sin-worn*] either 'worn out by sin' or, with reference
to the first sense of 'mould', 'worn, as a garment, by or among sin'.

But to my task. Neptune besides the sway
Of every salt flood, and each ebbing stream,
20 Took in by lot 'twixt high, and nether Jove,
Imperial rule of all the sea-girt isles
That like to rich, and various gems inlay
The unadorned bosom of the deep,
Which he to grace his tributary gods
25 By course commits to several government,
And gives them leave to wear their sapphire crowns,
And wield their little tridents, but this isle
The greatest, and the best of all the main
He quarters to his blue-haired deities,
30 And all this tract that fronts the falling sun
A noble peer of mickle trust, and power
Has in his charge, with tempered awe to guide

*mould*] either 'earth, as the material of the human body' or 'the world, the earth'.

*18. Trin. MS*: But to my *business now* 'task.' Neptune *whose sway* 'besides the sway'.

*20. Took in*] annexed; perhaps M. is recalling Sylvester (Du Bartas 1003): 'Both upper Joves and neathers diverse Thrones'. In Homer, *Il.* xv 187–93, Poseidon tells how he and his two brothers drew lots for territories: he drew the sea, Zeus the heavens, Hades ('nether Jove') the underworld.

*21. Trin. MS*: 'Imperial' *The* rule *and title of each* 'all the' sea-girt isles. *sea-girt isles*] Echoes Jonson, *Underwoods* lxvii 33: 'sea-girt Isle'.

*22. Trin. MS*: That like to rich *gems inlay* 'and various gems inlay'. Echoing *Rich. II* II i 46: 'This precious stone set in the silver sea'.

*24. grace*] confer honour upon.        *tributary*] paying tribute. For a catalogue of the river-gods who follow Neptune, see Spenser, *F.Q.* IV xi 11–47.

*25. By course*] duly.        *several*] assigned distributively to a number of individuals.

*28. the main*] *Trin. MS*: his empire 'the main'.

*29. quarters*] assigns.        *blue-haired deities*] Jonson, *Masque of Blackness* 32, introduces six Tritons, 'their upper parts humane, save that their haires were blue, as partaking of the sea-colour'. Jonson's marginal note refers to Ovid, *Met.* i 333 *caeruleum Tritona*. Cp. also Phineas Fletcher, *Sicelides* II vi: 'blue-beard Neptune'.

*30. this tract*] Wales and the Marches. H. Spencer, *MLN* xxiii (1908) 30, traces the line to Aeschylus, *Suppliants* 254–5: 'I rule all the region . . . on the side toward the setting sun.'

*31. peer*] the Earl of Bridgewater.        *mickle*] great. One of the words Spenser employs to give his poetry an archaic ring. He uses it twenty-seven times.

*32. tempered*] free from extremes.        *awe*] power to inspire fear or reverence.

An old, and haughty nation proud in arms:
Where his fair offspring nursed in princely lore,
35   Are coming to attend their father's state,
And new-entrusted sceptre, but their way
Lies through the perplexed paths of this drear wood,
The nodding horror of whose shady brows
Threats the forlorn and wandering passenger.
40   And here their tender age might suffer peril,
But that by quick command from sovran Jove
I was despatched for their defence, and guard;
And listen why, for I will tell you now
What never yet was heard in tale or song
45   From old, or modern bard in hall, or bower.
    Bacchus that first from out the purple grape,
Crushed the sweet poison of misused wine
After the Tuscan mariners transformed
Coasting the Tyrrhene shore, as the winds listed,
50   On Circe's island fell (who knows not Circe
The daughter of the Sun? Whose charmed cup
Whoever tasted, lost his upright shape,

33. *nation*] the Welsh.     *proud in arms*] Echoes Virgil, *Aen.* i 21: *populum
. . . belloque superbum.*
37. *perplexed*] entangled.     *wood*] A symbol for the temptations of life
in Dante, *Inferno* i 1–3 and Spenser, *F.Q.* I i 7–10. J. C. Maxwell, *N & Q*
cciv (1959) 364, traces this line to Virgil, *Aen.* ix 391–2: *perplexum iter . . . fal-
lacis silvae.*
44. *never yet was heard*] Echoing Horace, *Odes* III i 2–3: *carmina non prius
audita.*
45. *From*] *Trin. MS:* By 'From'.
46. *grape*] *Bridg.*: grapes.
47. *sweet poison*] Echoes *King John* I i 213: 'Sweet, sweet, sweet poison for the
age's tooth.'
48. *After . . . transformed*] After the Tuscan (Italian) sailors had been trans-
formed. The incident is described by Ovid, *Met.* iii 650–91: Bacchus,
kidnapped by pirates, changes them to dolphins and their ship to an arbour
of ivy.
49. *Tyrrhene*] The Tyrrhenian Sea lies between Italy and Corsica and Sar-
dinia.     *listed*] chose.
50–1. *Circe's island*] Cp. Homer, *Od.* x 135–8: 'We came to the isle of
Aeaea, where dwelt fair-tressed Circe . . . sprung from Helius, who gives
light to mortals'; also Browne, *Inner Temple Masque* 32: 'mighty Circe
daughter to the Sun'.     *who knows not Circe*] the figure is common in
Spenser; cp. *Shep. Cal.* August 141: 'Of Rosalend (who knowes not Rosa-
lend?)' and *F.Q.* VI x 16: 'Poore Colin Clout, (who knowes not Colin
Clout?)'.

And downward fell into a grovelling swine)
This nymph that gazed upon his clustering locks,
55   With ivy berries wreathed, and his blithe youth,
Had by him, ere he parted thence, a son
Much like his father, but his mother more,
Whom therefore she brought up and Comus named,
Who ripe, and frolic of his full-grown age,
60   Roving the Celtic, and Iberian fields,
At last betakes him to this ominous wood,
And in thick shelter of black shades embowered,
Excels his mother at her mighty art,
Offering to every weary traveller,
65   His orient liquor in a crystal glass,
To quench the drought of Phoebus, which as they taste
(For most do taste through fond intemperate thirst)
Soon as the potion works, their human countenance,
The express resemblance of the gods, is changed

55. *ivy berries*] See *Elegia VI* 15–6n (p. 114).
58. *Whom*] *Trin. MS*: Which 'Whom' *Bridg.*: Which.        *Comus named*]
*Trin. MS*: *named him* Comus 'named'.
    The parentage given for Comus is M.'s invention: the name corresponds
to the Gk noun κῶμος (revelry). Comus is described in Philostratus, *Ima-
gines* i 2, as a youth crowned with roses, and with a torch in his hand,
standing, but falling into a drunken sleep. He appears as 'the god of cheere,
or the belly' in Jonson's *Pleasure Reconciled to Virtue*, and, as R. C. Fox, *N
& Q* ccvii (1962) 52–3, points out, in Jonson's *Poetaster* III iv 115–6 his name
appears between those of Bacchus and Priapus. As Whiting 172 observes,
Burton III ii 3 names Comus and Hymen together as loving 'masks and
all such merriments above measure'. Massinger, *City Madam* IV ii has
'the god of pleasure . . . Comus'.
all such merriments above measure'.
59. *frolic*] gay.
60. *Celtic, and Iberian fields*] France and Spain.
62. *shelter*] *Trin. MS*: *covert* 'shelter'.        *shades*] *Trin. MS*: shade.
63. *mighty*] *Trin. MS*: *potent* 'mighty'.
65. *orient*] shining, lustrous. *Trin. MS*: orient *like* liquor.
66. *drought of Phoebus*] thirst caused by the sun.
67. *fond*] foolish. *Trin. MS*: *weak* 'fond'.
68–75. E. G. Ainsworth, *MLN* xlvi (1931) 91–2, thinks that M. is following
Ariosto's description of the rout of monsters outside Alcina's bower,
*Orlando Furioso* vi 60–6, because the disfigurement is only from the neck
upwards, and because the monsters are not aware of it: in Homer, *Od.*
x 239–40, Ulysses' men are changed to swine, but their minds remain as
before. In Browne's *Inner Temple Masque*, as in Ariosto, only the heads are
changed. *potion*] *Trin. MS*: potion*s*.
69. *express resemblance*] Cp. *Gen.* i. 27: 'So God created man in his own

70   Into some brutish form of wolf, or bear,
     Or ounce, or tiger, hog, or bearded goat,
     All other parts remaining as they were,
     And they, so perfect is their misery,
     Not once perceive their foul disfigurement,
75   But boast themselves more comely than before
     And all their friends, and native home forget
     To roll with pleasure in a sensual sty.
     Therefore when any favoured of high Jove,
     Chances to pass through this advent'rous glade,
80   Swift as the sparkle of a glancing star,
     I shoot from heaven to give him safe convoy,
     As now I do: but first I must put off
     These my sky-robes spun out of Iris' woof,
     And take the weeds and likeness of a swain,
85   That to the service of this house belongs,
     Who with his soft pipe, and smooth-dittied song,
     Well knows to still the wild winds when they roar,
     And hush the waving woods, nor of less faith,
     And in this office of his mountain watch,

image', and *Heb.* i 3: 'the express image of his person.'        *of the*] *Trin. MS*: of o'the.

71. *ounce*] lynx.

72. *they were*] *Trin. MS*: *before* 'they were'.

75–6. Cp. Homer, *Od.* ix 94–7: 'Whoever ate of the honey-sweet fruit of the lotus, had no longer any wish to bring back word or to return, but there they were fain to abide among the Lotus-eaters, feeding on the lotus, and forgetful of their homeward way.' Plutarch, *Moralia* 985D–992E has a dialogue in which Gryllus, one of Ulysses' companions transformed into a hog by Circe, converses with Ulysses and refuses to be turned back to human shape. This Gryllus appears in Spenser, *F.Q.* II xii 86–7 and Browne, *Inner Temple Masque* 193–216.

   J. S. Diekhoff, *PQ* xx (1941) 603–4, remarks that the 1645 and 1673 punctuation allows two senses to emerge: they boast that not only 'themselves' but also 'all their friends' are 'more comely', and also they 'forget' all their friends.

79. *advent'rous*] *Trin. MS*: adventu᷈'rous.

83. *sky-robes*] *Bridg.*: sky-webs      *Iris' woof*] the woven fabric of the rainbow. The Attendant Spirit, called 'daemon' in *Trin. MS* and *Bridg.*, has neo-Platonic origins. Psellus, *De operatione daemonum* xviii, says that daemons' bodies are ductile and can take any form, as can clouds, and that they are also capable, like air or like water, of taking various colours.

86–8. A compliment to Lawes as a musician, equating him with Orpheus.

88. *nor of less faith*] no less loyal (than skilful as a musician).

90   Likeliest, and nearest to the present aid
     Of this occasion. But I hear the tread
     Of hateful steps, I must be viewless now.

*Comus enters with a charming-rod in one hand, his glass in the other,*
*with him a rout of monsters, headed like sundry sorts of wild beasts,*
*but otherwise like men and women, their apparel glistering, they come*
*in making a riotous and unruly noise, with torches in their hands.*

  *Comus.* The star that bids the shepherd fold,
     Now the top of heaven doth hold,
95   And the gilded car of day,
     His glowing axle doth allay
     In the steep Atlantic stream,
     And the slope sun his upward beam
     Shoots against the dusky pole,

*90. Trin. MS*: Nearest and likeliest to *give* 'the' present *aid* 'chance' 'aid'.
*92. hateful*] *Trin. MS: virgin* 'hateful'.     *viewless*] invisible. The word is
first recorded in *Measure for Measure* III i 124.
*Stage direction. Comus enters . . . hands*] *Trin. MS: Exit* goes out. / Comus
enters 'with a charming rod and GLASS of liquor' with his rout all headed
like some wild beasts their / garments some like men's and some like wo-
men's they *begin* 'come on in' a wild and / *humorous* 'antic' fashion / in-
trant κωμάζοντες. *Bridg.* stage direction reads as *1673*, with following
variants: l. 1. his glass]and a glass of liquor   ll. 2–3. headed . . . women]like
men and women but headed like wild beasts.
*93. star*] Hesperus, the evening star; cp. *Measure for Measure* IV ii 218:
'Look, th' unfolding star calls up the shepherd', and, as P. C. Ghosh, *TLS*
(19 Feb. 1931) 135, notes, Virgil, *Ecl.* vi 85–6: 'Vesper gave the word to
fold the flocks.'
*95–6. gilded car . . . glowing axle*] M. probably recalls the description of the
sun's chariot ('car') in Ovid, *Met.* ii 107–10: 'Its axle was of gold, the pole
of gold; its wheels had golden tyres, and a ring of silver spokes', and ii
230: 'He feels the chariot growing white-hot beneath his feet'.    *allay*]
cool.
*97. steep*] flowing precipitously. The Greeks imagined the Ocean as a river
encircling the earth. As their geographical knowledge extended the name
was applied to the outer sea, especially the Atlantic. Athenaeus, *Deipnoso-*
*phistae* xi 469D–470D, cites several authorities, including Mimnermus and
Aeschylus, in support of the belief that the sun travelled back over the waves
of the Ocean in a golden bed, bowl or cauldron from the place of its setting
to that of its rising.    *Atlantic*] *Trin. MS: Tartessian* 'Atlantic'.
*98. slope*] sloping, descending.
*99. dusky*] *Trin. MS: northern* 'dusky' *Bridg.*: northern.   *pole*] sky
(Latin *polus*, the heavens).

*100*    Pacing toward the other goal
       Of his chamber in the east.
       Meanwhile, welcome joy, and feast,
       Midnight shout, and revelry,
       Tipsy dance, and jollity.
*105*    Braid your locks with rosy twine
       Dropping odours, dropping wine.
       Rigour now is gone to bed,
       And Advice with scrupulous head,
       Strict Age, and sour Severity,
*110*    With their grave saws in slumber lie.
       We that are of purer fire
       Imitate the starry quire,
       Who in their nightly watchful spheres,
       Lead in swift round the months and years.
*115*    The sounds, and seas with all their finny drove
       Now to the moon in wavering morris move,
       And on the tawny sands and shelves,
       Trip the pert fairies and the dapper elves;
       By dimpled brook, and fountain-brim,
*120*    The wood-nymphs decked with daisies trim,
       Their merry wakes and pastimes keep:
       What hath night to do with sleep?
       Night hath better sweets to prove,
       Venus now wakes, and wakens Love.

*101. chamber*] Cp. *Ps.* xix 4–5: 'the sun, which is as a bridegroom coming out of his chamber'.

*108. And Advice with*] *Trin. MS*: And *nice* [*Cus* ?]*tom* 'Advice' with *her*. Advice is personified in *Rape of Lucrece* 907.

*110. saws*] maxims.

*111–4.* The idea of the universe as a great dance had been popularized by Sir John Davies's *Orchestra* (1596). Plato, *Tim.* 40 describes the stars and planets 'circling as in a dance'.     *We . . . purer fire*] Echoes Randolph ii 609: 'But we whose souls are made of purer fire, / Have other aims.'    *watchful spheres*] See *Vacation Exercise* 40n (p. 77).     *Lead in*] *Trin. MS*: Lead *with* 'in'.

*115. sounds*] straits.     *finny drove*] As E. S. Le Comte, *N & Q* clxxxiv (1943) 17–8, points out, the phrase is taken from Spenser, *F.Q.* III viii 29, who coined the adjective 'finny'.

*116. morris*] morris (i.e. Moorish) dance.

*117. tawny*] *Trin. MS*: *yellow* 'tawny' (a change perhaps made to avoid too obvious a reminiscence of *Tempest* I ii 376, where Ariel sings of dancing on the 'yellow sands').    *shelves*] sandbanks.

*121. wakes*] revels.

*123. hath*] *Bridg.*: has.

125　Come let us our rites begin,
　　　'Tis only daylight that makes sin
　　　Which these dun shades will ne'er report,
　　　Hail goddess of nocturnal sport
　　　Dark-veiled Cotytto, to whom the secret flame
130　Of midnight torches burns; mysterious dame
　　　That ne'er art called, but when the dragon womb
　　　Of Stygian darkness spits her thickest gloom,
　　　And makes one blot of all the air,
　　　Stay thy cloudy ebon chair,
135　Wherein thou rid'st with Hecat', and befriend
　　　Us thy vowed priests, till utmost end
　　　Of all thy dues be done, and none left out,
　　　Ere the blabbing eastern scout,
　　　The nice Morn on th' Indian steep
140　From her cabined loophole peep,
　　　And to the tell-tale sun descry
　　　Our concealed solemnity.

*129. Cotytto*] A Thracian goddess whose licentious rites were held secretly at night. Stephanus (*s.v. Cotytto*) calls her *dea impudentiae* and refers to her *nocturna sacra* and the lascivious dances of her priests. Cp. Juvenal ii 91–2, which Stephanus quotes.

*130. burns*] Bridg.: burn.

*131. dragon*] See *Prae E* 56–8n, p. 26 above.

*133. Trin. MS*: *And makes a blot of nature* 'And throws a blot on' 'And makes one blot of' all the air.

*134–7. Trin. MS*: Stay thy *polished* 'cloudy' ebon chair / *And favour our close revelry* 'jocundry' 'Wherein thou rid'st with Hecate and befriend / Us thy vowed priests till utmost end' / *Till* 'Of' all thy dues be done and *nought* 'none' left out. (This is the first occurrence of 'jocundry' cited in *OED*).

*135. Hecat'*] Hecate, goddess of sorcery, invoked by witches.

*138. blabbing*] Echoes II *Henry VI* IV i 1: 'The gaudy, blabbing and remorseful day'.

*139. nice*] affectedly modest. The morn (Aurora) was not really modest, but had carried off Cephalus against his will, as Ovid describes, *Met.* vii 700–13.　　*steep*] mountain slope; cp. *Midsummer Night's Dream* II i 69: 'the furthest steep of India'.

*140. cabined loophole*] tiny window: Comus envisages a tiny part of the rising sun peeping above the horizon. 'Loophole' meant particularly 'port-hole', thus there is play on 'cabined' (cramped or confined).

*141. tell-tale*] Echoes Shakespeare, *Lucrece* 806: 'tell-tale Day'.　　*descry*] reveal.

*142. solemnity*] celebration.

Come, knit hands, and beat the ground,
In a light fantastic round.

### The Measure.

145   Break off, break off, I feel the different pace,
Of some chaste footing near about this ground.
Run to your shrouds, within these brakes and trees,
Our number may affright: some virgin sure
(For so I can distinguish by mine art)
150   Benighted in these woods. Now to my charms,
And to my wily trains, I shall ere long
Be well stocked with as fair a herd as grazed
About my mother Circe. Thus I hurl
My dazzling spells into the spongy air,
155   Of power to cheat the eye with blear illusion,
And give it false presentments, lest the place
And my quaint habits breed astonishment,
And put the damsel to suspicious flight,
Which must not be, for that's against my course;
160   I under fair pretence of friendly ends,
And well-placed words of glozing courtesy
Baited with reasons not unplausible

144. *Trin. MS: With* 'In' *a light* and frolic *fantastic round    round*] a ring-
dance: cp. the 'round' which Titania's fairies dance in the moonlight in
*Midsummer Night's Dream* II i 140.
*Stage direction. The Measure*] In the seventeenth century 'measure' could
denote either a tune or a dance. *Trin. MS* and *Bridg.* add 'in a wild rude and
wanton antic'.
145. *feel*] *Trin. MS: hear* feel.
147. *shrouds*] hiding places.
147-8. *Trin. MS: Some virgin sure benighted in these woods / For so I can
distinguish by mine art / Run to your shrouds within these brakes and trees*—
They all scatter / Our number may affright. Some virgin sure. *Bridg.* reads
as *1673* but, like *Trin. MS*, adds the direction 'they all scatter' to l. 147.
150. *charms*] *Trin. MS: trains* charms.
151. *trains*] allurements. *Trin. MS: mother's charms* wily trains.
154. *dazzling*] *Trin. MS: powdered* 'dazzling' (cp. 'magic dust' l. 165–Comus
evidently threw some kind of glittering powder into the air).    *spongy*]
absorbent (i.e. absorbing his spells).
155. *with blear illusion*] *Trin. MS:* with *sleight* 'blind' 'blear' illusion. 'Blear'
means 'dim, misty', and was originally applied only to the eyes. This is the
first recorded usage of the word in a transferred sense.
156. *presentments*] appearances.    *lest*] *Trin. MS: else* 'lest'.
157. *quaint habits*] unfamiliar dress.
161. *glozing*] flattering. *Bridg.*: glowing.

Wind me into the easy-hearted man,
And hug him into snares. When once her eye
165    Hath met the virtue of this magic dust,
I shall appear some harmless villager
And hearken, if I may her business hear.
But here she comes, I fairly step aside.

*The Lady enters.*

*Lady.* This way the noise was, if mine ear be true,
170    My best guide now, methought it was the sound
Of riot, and ill-managed merriment,
Such as the jocund flute, or gamesome pipe
Stirs up among the loose unlettered hinds,
When for their teeming flocks, and granges full,
175    In wanton dance they praise the bounteous Pan,
And thank the gods amiss. I should be loth
To meet the rudeness, and swilled insolence
Of such late wassailers; yet O where else

163. *Wind me into*] insinuate myself into the confidence of.

164. *snares*] *Trin. MS: nets* 'snares'.

165. *virtue*] power, efficacy.

166–8. As will be seen from the headnote, *1637* and *1645* have a line between ll. 166 and 167 which *1673* omits, and print ll. 167 and 168 in the reverse order. In *1673* l.167 was originally printed 'And hearken, if I may, her business here', but the *Errata* corrected the punctuation, and the spelling of 'here', to make the line read as in the present text. This attention paid to l. 167 in the *1673 Errata* makes it unlikely that the differences between *1637* and *1645* on the one hand, and *1673* on the other, can at this point be attributed merely to the printer. Perhaps the rhyme of 'gear' and 'here' in *1637* and *1645* offended M.'s ear, and made him decide to change the passage. *Trin. MS* and *Bridg.* read with *1645*, except that *Trin. MS* inserts 'thirst' as a marginal alternative to 'thrift' in the line later omitted.

168. *fairly*] softly.

169. *mine*] *Trin. MS:* my.

170. *My best guide*] *Trin. MS:* My 'best' guide.

173. *loose*] dissolute.       *hinds*] farm workers. *Hero and Leander* ii 218 has 'illit'rate hinds'.

174. *Trin. MS:* 'When 'That' 'When' for their teeming flocks, and *garners* 'granges' full'.       *teeming*] breeding offspring.

175. *they praise*] *Trin. MS:* THEY PRAISE 'adore'.       *Pan*] god of woods and shepherds.

177. *swilled*] To 'swill' is to fill with drink: *OED* records this as the only occurrence of the participial adjective.

178. *wassailers*] revellers.

Shall I inform my unacquainted feet
180   In the blind mazes of this tangled wood?
My brothers when they saw me wearied out
With this long way, resolving here to lodge
Under the spreading favour of these pines,
Stepped as they said to the next thicket-side
185   To bring me berries, or such cooling fruit
As the kind hospitable woods provide.
They left me then, when the grey-hooded Even
Like a sad votarist in palmer's weed
Rose from the hindmost wheels of Phoebus' wain.
190   But where they are, and why they came not back,
Is now the labour of my thoughts, 'tis likeliest
They had engaged their wand'ring steps too far,
And envious darkness, ere they could return,
.Had stole them from me, else O thievish Night
195   Why shouldst thou, but for some felonious end,
In thy dark lantern thus close up the stars,
That Nature hung in heaven, and filled their lamps
With everlasting oil, to give due light
To the misled and lonely traveller?
200   This is the place, as well as I may guess,
Whence even now the tumult of loud mirth
Was rife, and perfect in my listening ear,
Yet nought but single darkness do I find.

*179.* In *Trin. MS* this line is a later insertion.

*180. Trin. MS:* In the blind *alleys* 'mazes' of *these* 'this' *arched* 'tangled' wood.

*187-9. Bridg.* omits.

*188. votarist*] one who has taken a vow (of pilgrimage): the word is first used by Shakespeare, *Measure for Measure* I iv 5.    *palmer*] a pilgrim who had visited the Holy Land, and carried a branch of palm as a sign of this.

*189. wain*] *Trin. MS: chair* 'wain'.

*192. wand'ring*] *Trin. MS: youthly* 'wand'ring'.

*193. And envious*] *Trin. MS: To the soon-parting light* and envious.

*194. stole*] *Trin. MS:* stol'n.

*194-224. Else . . . grove*] *Bridg.* omits.

*196. dark lantern*] A lantern with a slide or arrangement by which the light can be concealed. M.'s use here antedates the first occurrence in *OED* (1650).

*197-8.* Cp. *Macbeth* II i 4-5: 'there's husbandry in heaven, / Their candles are all out.'

*198. due*] *Trin. MS: their* 'due'.

*202. rife*] loud-sounding (the first occurrence in this sense in *OED*).    *perfect*] heard distinctly.

*203. single*] absolute–a sense first found in Spenser, *F.Q.* II x 21.

What might this be? A thousand fantasies
205    Begin to throng into my memory
Of calling shapes, and beckoning shadows dire,
And airy tongues, that syllable men's names
On sands, and shores, and desert wildernesses.
These thoughts may startle well, but not astound
210    The virtuous mind, that ever walks attended
By a strong siding champion Conscience. . . .
O welcome pure-eyed Faith, white-handed Hope,
Thou hovering angel girt with golden wings,
And thou unblemished form of Chastity,
215    I see ye visibly, and now believe
That he, the Supreme Good, t' whom all things ill
Are but as slavish officers of vengeance,
Would send a glistering guardian if need were
To keep my life and honour unassailed.
220    Was I deceived, or did a sable cloud
Turn forth her silver lining on the night?
I did not err, there does a sable cloud
Turn forth her silver lining on the night,
And casts a gleam over this tufted grove.
225    I cannot hallo to my brothers, but
Such noise as I can make to be heard farthest
I'll venture, for my new-enlivened spirits
Prompt me; and they perhaps are not far off.

207. *airy tongues*] Echoes *Romeo and Juliet* II i 163 'airy tongue'.    *that . . .
names*] Trin. MS: *that lure night-wanderers* 'that syllable men's names'.
Perhaps M. recalls Purchas iii 75: 'They say that there [in the Desert of Lop]
dwell many spirits which cause great and mervailous Illusions to Travellers
to make them perish. For if any stay behind that he cannot see his company,
he shall be called by name, and so going out of the way is lost.'
211. *siding*] the first recorded use of the word in the sense 'taking the side of
a person'.
213. *hovering*] Trin. MS: *flittering* 'hovering'. Diekhoff 723 and Shawcross[2]
42 think 'flittering' the better reading.
214. *unblemished*] Trin. MS: *unspotted* 'unblemished'.
215. Trin. MS: I see ye visibly, *and while I see ye | This dusky hollow is a
paradise | And heaven gates o'er my head* 'and' now I believe.
216. *That he, the*] Trin. MS: That 'He' the.
218. *guardian*] Trin. MS: *cherub* 'guardian'.
220-3. Imitating Ovid, *Fasti* v 549: *Fallor, an arma sonant? non fallimur,
arma sonabant* (Am I deceived, or is that the sound of arms? I am not de-
ceived, it is the sound of arms).

SONG

Sweet Echo, sweetest nymph that liv'st unseen

230        Within thy airy shell

By slow Meander's margent green,

And in the violet-embroidered vale

Where the love-lorn nightingale

Nightly to thee her sad song mourneth well.

235    Canst thou not tell me of a gentle pair

That likest thy Narcissus are?

O if thou have

Hid them in some flowery cave,

Tell me but where

240       Sweet queen of parley, daughter of the sphere.

So mayst thou be translated to the skies,

And give resounding grace to all heaven's harmonies.

*Comus.* Can any mortal mixture of earth's mould
Breathe such divine enchanting ravishment?
245    Sure something holy lodges in that breast,
And with these raptures moves the vocal air
To testify his hidden residence;
How sweetly did they float upon the wings
Of silence, through the empty-vaulted night

---

*229–42.* The 'echo scene', in which the echo catches up and twists the ends
of the speaker's sentences, had been common in Elizabethan and Jacobean
drama (e.g. Browne, *Inner Temple Masque* 267–79, Jonson, *Cynthia's
Revels* I ii, Webster, *Duchess of Malfi* V iii). The Lady's loneliness is enhanced
because, unusually, no echo replies.

*230. airy shell*] *Trin. MS:* airy shell 'cell'. The 'shell' is the vault of the sky
(cp. 'daughter of the sphere', l. 241, where 'sphere' seems to mean 'the
apparent outward limit of space, viewed from the earth'). Starnes and Talbert
249 quote from Stephanus *Echo, Nympha, nullo oculo viso . . . Amicam . . .
Moderatoris omnium corporum coelestium, ex quibus ipsa componitur atque
temperatur.*

*231. By slow*] *Trin. MS:* By 'slow'.

*233. love-lorn*] The first recorded occurrence. In later usage it comes to mean
'forsaken by one's love', but as Philomela (the nightingale) was raped by her
brother-in-law Tereus, M. presumably uses the term to mean 'lost or
ruined through love'.

*240. parley*] speech.

*242. And . . . grace*] *Trin. MS: And hold a counterpoint* 'And give resounding
grace'. *Bridg.*: And hold a counterpoint. This is the only alexandrine in
*Comus,* mimicking the lengthening of heaven's song by echo.

*242–3. Trin. MS* inserts: Comus *enters* 'looks in and speaks'.

*247. his*] i.e. that of the 'something holy'.

250    At every fall smoothing the raven down
       Of darkness till it smiled: I have oft heard
       My mother Circe with the Sirens three,
       Amidst the flowery-kirtled Naiades
       Culling their potent herbs, and baleful drugs,
255    Who as they sung, would take the prisoned soul,
       And lap it in Elysium, Scylla wept,
       And chid her barking waves into attention,
       And fell Charybdis murmured soft applause:
       Yet they in pleasing slumber lulled the sense,
260    And in sweet madness robbed it of itself,
       But such a sacred, and home-felt delight,
       Such sober certainty of waking bliss
       I never heard till now. I'll speak to her
       And she shall be my queen. Hail foreign wonder
265    Whom certain these rough shades did never breed
       Unless the goddess that in rural shrine

*250. fall*] cadence.

*251.* For the conception of darkness as a bird, see *L'Allegro* 6.     *it*] darkness. *Trin. MS* and *Bridg.*: she.

*252-3. Circe . . . Sirens three*] In Homer, *Od.* xii 37-72, it is Circe who tells Ulysses of the Sirens, but Browne, *Inner Temple Masque* 1-96, like M., represents the Sirens as Circe's attendants. In Homer and Browne there are only two Sirens.     *Naiades*] freshwater nymphs: in Homer, *Od.* x 348-51, the maidens who wait on Circe are 'children of the springs and groves and of the sacred rivers that flow forth to the sea'.

*253-4. Trin. MS*: "*Sitting*' amidst the flowery-kirtled Naiade'e's / Culling their *potent* 'powerful' 'mighty' 'potent' herbs and baleful drugs'.

*254. potent herbs*] Echoes Virgil, *Aen.* vii 19, where it is with *potentibus herbis* that Circe transforms men.

*255. as*] *Bridg.*: when.

*256. wept*] *Trin. MS*: would weep 'wept'.

*256-8.* Apparently suggested by Silius Italicus xiv 476, where, at the pipe-playing of Daphnis 'Scylla's dogs were silent, black Charybdis stood still'. *barking waves*] Echoes Virgil, *Aen.* vii 588: *latrantibus undis*.     *fell Charybdis*] Both Sandys 248 and Sylvester (Du Bartas 273) have this phrase.

*257. And child*] *Trin. MS*: And 'And' chide'ing'.

*261. home-felt*] felt intimately. This is the first recorded occurrence of the word.

*264-6. Hail . . . . goddess*] Echoes *Tempest* I ii 22-6, where Ferdinand first meets Miranda, 'Most sure, the goddess / On whom these airs attend! . . . O you wonder!'

*265. Whom certain these*] *Trin. MS*: Whom 'certain' these.

*266. Unless . . . . goddess*] unless (you are) the goddess.

Dwell'st here with Pan, or Sylvan, by blest song
Forbidding every bleak unkindly fog
To touch the prosperous growth of this tall wood.
270 *Lady.* Nay gentle shepherd ill is lost that praise
That is addressed to unattending ears,
Not any boast of skill, but extreme shift
How to regain my severed company
Compelled me to awake the courteous Echo
275 To give me answer from her mossy couch.
*Comus.* What chance good lady hath bereft you thus?
*Lady.* Dim darkness, and this leafy labyrinth.
*Comus.* Could that divide you from near-ushering
guides?
*Lady.* They left me weary on a grassy turf.
280 *Comus.* By falsehood, or discourtesy, or why?
*Lady.* To seek i' the valley some cool friendly spring.
*Comus.* And left your fair side all unguarded lady?
*Lady.* They were but twain, and purposed quick return.
*Comus.* Perhaps forestalling night prevented them.
285 *Lady.* How easy my misfortune is to hit!
*Comus.* Imports their loss, beside the present need?
*Lady.* No less than if I should my brothers lose.
*Comus.* Were they of manly prime, or youthful bloom?
*Lady.* As smooth as Hebe's their unrazored lips.
290 *Comus.* Two such I saw, what time the laboured ox
In his loose traces from the furrow came,
And the swinked hedger at his supper sat;

267. *Dwell'st*] Trin. MS: *Liv'st* 'Dwell'st'.   *Pan ... Sylvan*] See l. 175*n*
and *Il Penseroso* 134*n* (p. 145). Virgil also mentions the two gods together,
*Ecl.* x 24–6.
269. *prosperous*] Trin. MS: *prospering* 'prosperous'. Bridg.: prospering.
272. *shift*] expedient necessitated by stress of circumstances.
276–89. An imitation of the dialogue in alternate lines of verse (sticho-
mythia) common in Greek drama.
277. *Dim darkness*] Echoes Shakespeare, *Lucrece* 118 'dim darkness'.
278. *near-ushering guides*] Trin. MS: *their* 'near' ushering *hands* 'guides'.
279. *weary*] Trin. MS: wearied.
281. *some cool*] Trin. MS: some 'cool'.
285. *hit*] guess.
286. *Imports their loss*] Is their loss of importance?
289. *Hebe's*] See *Vacation Exercise* 38*n* (p. 77).
290–1. *Two such*] Trin. MS: Such two. Homer, *Il.* xvi 779, calls evening
'the time for the unyoking of oxen', and at evening in Virgil, *Ecl.* ii 66:
'The bullocks drag home by the yoke the hanging plough.'
292. *swinked*] wearied. This is the first occurrence of the word in *OED;*

I saw them under a green mantling vine
That crawls along the side of yon small hill,
295 Plucking ripe clusters from the tender shoots,
Their port was more than human, as they stood;
I took it for a faëry vision
Of some gay creatures of the element
That in the colours of the rainbow live
300 And play i' the plighted clouds. I was awe-struck,
And as I passed, I worshipped; if those you seek
It were a journey like the path to heaven,
To help you find them.
*Lady.*                    Gentle villager
What readiest way would bring me to that place?
305 *Comus.* Due west it rises from this shrubby point.
*Lady.* To find out that, good shepherd, I suppose,
In such a scant allowance of star-light,
Would overtask the best land-pilot's art,
Without the sure guess of well-practised feet.
310 *Comus.* I know each lane, and every alley green
Dingle, or bushy dell of this wild wood,
And every bosky bourn from side to side
My daily walks and ancient neighbourhood,
And if your stray attendance be yet lodged,
315 Or shroud within these limits, I shall know

M. has coined an archaistic past-participial adjective (O.E. *swincan*, to labour).
*293. saw them*] Trin. MS and *Bridg.*: saw'em.      *mantling*] the first recorded usage of the word in the sense 'spreading and covering': previously it had been applied only to liquids, meaning 'gathering a coating of scum'.
*296. port*] bearing. An echo of Euripides, *Iphigenia in Tauris* 260–74, where the herdsman tells how one of his companions mistook Pylades and Orestes for gods.
*298. element*] sky.
*299. colours*] *Bridg.*: coolness.
*300. plighted*] folded. In the *History of England* (Columbia x 69) M. has 'she [Boadecea] wore a plighted Garment of divers colours'.
*303. them*] Trin. MS: them *out*.
*309. the sure guess*] Trin. MS: 'the' sure *steerage of* guess.
*311. Dingle*] hollow between hills.      *wild*] Trin. MS: wide 'wild'.
*Bridg.*: wide. Diekhoff 723 and Shawcross[2] 42 prefer 'wide'.
*312. bosky bourn*] bushy stream.
*314. attendance*] attendants.
*315. Or shroud within these limits*] Trin. MS: 'Or shroud'*ed*'' 'within'
*Within* these *shroudy* limits. (This is the only occurrence of 'shroudy' re-

Ere morrow wake, or the low-roosted lark
From her thatched pallet rouse, if otherwise
I can conduct you lady to a low
But loyal cottage, where you may be safe
320 Till further quest.
Lady.                    Shepherd I take thy word,
And trust thy honest-offered courtesy,
Which oft is sooner found in lowly sheds
With smoky rafters, than in tap'stry halls
And courts of princes, where it first was named,
325 And yet is most pretended: in a place
Less warranted than this, or less secure
I cannot be, that I should fear to change it,
Eye me blest Providence, and square my trial
To my proportioned strength. Shepherd lead on. . . .

*The two Brothers.*

330 *Eld. Bro.* Unmuffle ye faint stars, and thou fair moon
That wont'st to love the traveller's benison,
Stoop thy pale visage through an amber cloud,
And disinherit Chaos, that reigns here

corded in *OED*). 'Shroud', meaning 'seek shelter', is a Spenserianism, first
recorded in *Shep. Cal.* February 122.
*316. Ere . . . wake*] *Trin. MS: Ere the lark rouse* 'Ere morrow wake'.     *–roos-*
*ted*] *Bridg.*: –rooster.
*317. pallet*] bed of straw.
*320. quest*] *Trin. MS:* quest *be made.*
*321–5.* Cp. Ariosto, *Orlando Furioso* xiv 62, which Harington xiv 52 trans-
lates: 'As curtesie oft times in simple bowres / Is found as great as in the
stately towres'; also Spenser, *F.Q.* VI, which is full of types of rural courtesy
like the savage man (VI v) and Pastorella, Sir Calidore's own lady: the
graces dance around Colin Clout in a pastoral setting, and it is they who
bestow courtesy (VI x 23).
*323. With*] *Trin. MS: And* 'With'.
*324. where . . . named*] 'courtesy' derives from 'court'.
*325. yet . . . pretended*] *Trin. MS: is pretended yet* yet is most pretended.
*326. or . . . secure*] *Trin. MS: I cannot be* or less secure.
*328. square*] adjust.     *my trial*] *Trin. MS: this* 'my' trial.
*330. Unmuffle*] remove a muffling–the first recorded intransitive use of
'unmuffle'. Echoes Sylvester (Du Bartas 251): 'While nights black muffler
hoodeth up the skies', (614) 'A sable ayr so muffles-up the Sky'.
*331. wont'st*] are accustomed to.     *benison*] blessing.
*332. Stoop*] *OED* records this as the first usage in the sense 'bend the head,
face or neck'.
*333. disinherit*] dispossess.

In double night of darkness, and of shades;
335    Or if your influence be quite dammed up
With black usurping mists, some gentle taper
Though a rush-candle from the wicker hole
Of some clay habitation visit us
With thy long levelled rule of streaming light,
340    And thou shalt be our star of Arcady,
Or Tyrian Cynosure.
     *Sec. Bro.*           Or if our eyes
Be barred that happiness, might we but hear
The folded flocks penned in their wattled cotes,
Or sound of pastoral reed with oaten stops,
345    Or whistle from the lodge, or village cock
Count the night-watches to his feathery dames,
'Twould be some solace yet some little cheering
In this close dungeon of innumerous boughs.
But O that hapless virgin our lost sister
350    Where may she wander now, whither betake her
From the chill dew, amongst rude burs and thistles?
Perhaps some cold bank is her bolster now
Or 'gainst the rugged bark of some broad elm
Leans her unpillowed head fraught with sad fears,

337. *wicker hole*] window covered in wickerwork.

339. *thy*] *Trin. MS*: a 'thy'.    *rule*] the first recorded usage in the sense 'shaft or beam of light'. In Euripides, *Suppliants* 650, a ray of the sun is called a 'clear rule'.

340–1. *Cynosure*] constellation of the Lesser Bear, or the Pole Star, at the tip of its tail. 'Tyrian', because the Phoenicians steered by the Lesser Bear, the Greeks by the Greater. 'Star of Arcady', because Arcas, who was stellified as Arcturus, was the son of Callisto, daughter of Lycaon, king of Arcadia. M. may have known the story from Hyginus or, more probably, think Starnes and Talbert 244, from the summary of his version in Stephanus.

343. *in their*] *Trin. MS*: in 'their'.

344. *pastoral reed with oaten stops*] shepherd's pipe: the 'stops' were the finger-holes. Cp. Spenser, *Shep. Cal.* January 72 'oaten pype', and October 8 'Oten reedes' (glossed there *Avena* by E. K.–a word Virgil uses, *Ecl.* i 2, for the shepherd's pipe).

348. *In ... close*] *Trin. MS*: In 'this' *lone* 'sad' 'close'. *Bridg.*: In this lone. *innumerous*] innumerable.

350. *she wander*] *Trin. MS*: she 'wander'.

351. *amongst ... thistles*] *Trin. MS*: *in this dead solitude* 'surrounding wild' 'perhaps some cold hard bank' 'amongst rude burs and thistles'.

354. *Trin. MS*: She leans her *thoughtful head musing at our unkindness* 'unpillowed head fraught with sad fears'.

355  What if in wild amazement, and affright,
Or while we speak within the direful grasp
Of savage hunger, or of savage heat?
*Eld Bro.* Peace brother, be not over-exquisite
To cast the fashion of uncertain evils;
360  For grant they be so, while they rest unknown,
What need a man forestall his date of grief,
And run to meet what he would most avoid?
Or if they be but false alarms of fear,
How bitter is such self-delusion!
365  I do not think my sister so to seek,
Or so unprincipled in virtue's book,
And the sweet peace that goodness bosoms ever,
As that the single want of light and noise
(Not being in danger, as I trust she is not)
370  Could stir the constant mood of her calm thoughts,
And put them into misbecoming plight.
Virtue could see to do what Virtue would
By her own radiant light, though sun and moon
Were in the flat sea sunk. And Wisdom's self

*355. What if* ] *Trin. MS: Or else* 'What if '. *Bridg.: Or else.*

*356-64. Trin. MS* and *Bridg.* omit. *Trin. MS* has instead three deleted lines
'*So fares as did forsaken Proserpine* / *When the big* 'rolling' *wallowing flakes
of pitchy clouds* / *And darkness wound her in. 1 Bro.: Peace brother peace*', and a
marginal note '[r]ead the [pa]per over [a]gainst [i]nstead of [. . .]'–but the
paper referred to is lost. *Bridg.* has the same three lines as *Trin. MS*, but un-
deleted, and with 'wallowing' omitted from the second.

*358. over-exquisite*] A Miltonic coinage, 'too careful, too subtle'.

*359. cast*] calculate, forecast.

*360. so*] i.e. evils.

*365. so to seek*] so wanting (in a requisite quality).

*366. unprincipled*] not instructed or grounded (the first recorded occurrence
of the word).

*367. bosoms*] carries enclosed in its bosom (the first recorded use of 'bosom'
in this figurative sense is in *L'Allegro* 78).

*368. single*] mere.

*369. trust*] *Bridg.: hope.*

*370. constant*] *Trin. MS: steady constant.*

*371. misbecoming*] unbecoming.

*372.* Echoing Jonson, *Pleasure Reconciled to Virtue* 339-422: 'She, she it is,
in darkness shines, / 'Tis she that still herself refines, / By her owne light,
to everie eye, / More seene, more knowne, when Vice stands by.' Also
Spenser, *F.Q.* I i 12: 'Vertue gives her selfe light through darknesse for to
wade.'

375    Oft seeks to sweet retired solitude,
        Where with her best nurse Contemplation
        She plumes her feathers, and lets grow her wings
        That in the various bustle of resort
        Were all to-ruffled, and sometimes impaired.
380    He that has light within his own clear breast
        May sit i' the centre, and enjoy bright day,
        But he that hides a dark soul, and foul thoughts
        Benighted walks under the midday sun;
        Himself is his own dungeon.
        *Sec. Bro.*               'Tis most true
385    That musing Meditation most affects
        The pensive secrecy of desert cell,
        Far from the cheerful haunt of men, and herds,
        And sits as safe as in a senate-house,
        For who would rob a hermit of his weeds,
390    His few books, or his beads, or maple dish,
        Or do his grey hairs any violence?
        But Beauty like the fair Hesperian tree

*375. Oft seeks to*] often resorts to. *Trin. MS: Oft seeks to solitary sweet retire* Oft seeks to.

*377. plumes*] preens or dresses (*OED* does not record this sense until 1821).

*378. resort*] concourse of people.

*379. to-ruffled*] 'to-' is an intensive prefix.

*380. his own*] *Trin. MS:* his 'own'.

*381. centre*] of the earth.

*383–4. Benighted . . . dungeon*] *Trin. MS* and *Bridg.:* Walks in black vapours, though the noontide brand/Blaze in the summer solstice. (In *Trin. MS* these lines are deleted and the present version inserted.)

*385. affects*] loves.

*387. and*] *Trin. MS:* or 'and'. *Bridg.:* or.

*389. a*] *Bridg.:* an.    *weeds*] *Trin. MS: beads* 'gown' 'beads' 'weeds'.

*390. His . . . beads*] *Trin. MS:* His 'few' books, 'or' his *hairy gown* 'beads'. *beads*] rosary.

*392. Hesperian tree*] The tree which bore golden apples, given by Ge to Hera as a wedding-present, and guarded by the Hesperides (daughters of Hesperus) and by the dragon, Ladon, which Hercules had to kill as one of his labours. The Younger Brother's sentiment recalls *As You Like It* I iii 107: 'Beauty provoketh thieves sooner than gold.' M. was clearly recalling also Jonson, *Every Man in His Humour* (1601) III i 16–23: 'Who will not judge him worthy to be robd, / That sets his doores wide open to a theefe, / And shewes the felon, where his treasure lyes? / Againe, what earthy spirit but will attempt / To taste the fruite of beauties golden tree, / When leaden sleepe seales up the dragons eyes? / Oh beauty is a Project of some power, / Chiefely when oportunitie attends her.'

Laden with blooming gold, had need the guard
Of dragon-watch with unenchanted eye,
395    To save her blossoms, and defend her fruit
From the rash hand of bold Incontinence.
You may as well spread out the unsunned heaps
Of miser's treasure by an outlaw's den,
And tell me it is safe, as bid me hope
400    Danger will wink on opportunity,
And let a single helpless maiden pass
Uninjured in this wild surrounding waste.
Of night, or loneliness it recks me not,
I fear the dread events that dog them both,
405    Lest some ill-greeting touch attempt the person
Of our unowned sister.
    *Eld. Bro.*         I do not, brother,
Infer, as if I thought my sister's state
Secure without all doubt, or controversy:
Yet where an equal poise of hope and fear
410    Does arbitrate the event, my nature is
That I incline to hope, rather than fear,

*394. unenchanted*] The first recorded occurrence of the word.

*398. treasure*] *Bridg.*: treasures.

*399. hope*] *Trin. MS*: *think* hope.

*400. wink on*] *Bridg.*: wink at.

*401. And let*] *Bridg.*: And she.

*402. in . . . waste*] *Trin. MS*: *th* in this *vast and hideous wild* wide surrounding waste. (Diekhoff 723 and Shawcross² 42 prefer 'wide' to the 'wild' of the printed editions).

*403. it recks me not*] I do not mind (whether night or loneliness is in question).

*405. ill-greeting*] A Miltonic coinage.

*406. unowned*] No other occurrence of the word in the sense 'lost' is recorded: usually it meant 'not possessed as property'.

*407. Infer*] draw a conclusion or inference.

*408. or controversy*] *Trin. MS* and *Bridg.*: or question, no.

*408–9.* Between these lines *Trin. MS* inserts: *Beshrew me but I would* I could be willing though now i'th'dark to try / A tough *passado* 'encounter' with the shaggiest ruffian / That lurks by hedge or lane of this dead circuit / To have her by my side, though I were sure / She might be free from peril where she is. *Bridg.* inserts the same lines in their corrected state.

*409. Yet*] *Trin. MS* and *Bridg.*: But.    *equal poise*] Echoes *Measure for Measure* II iv 69: 'equal poise of sin and charity'.    *hope and fear*] *Trin. MS*: hopes and fears.

*410. arbitrate*] judge of (the only instance of the word in this sense recorded in *OED*).    *event*] outcome.

And gladly banish squint suspicion.
My sister is not so defenceless left
As you imagine, she has a hidden strength
415 Which you remember not.
   *Sec. Bro.*             What hidden strength,
Unless the strength of heaven, if you mean that?
*Eld. Bro.* I mean that too, but yet a hidden strength
Which if heaven gave it, may be termed her own:
'Tis chastity, my brother, chastity:
420 She that has that, is clad in complete steel,
And like a quivered nymph with arrows keen
May trace huge forests, and unharboured heaths,
Infamous hills, and sandy perilous wilds,
Where through the sacred rays of chastity,
425 No savage fierce, bandit, or mountaineer
Will dare to soil her virgin purity,
Yea there, where very desolation dwells
By grots, and caverns shagged with horrid shades,
She may pass on with unblenched majesty,
430 Be it not done in pride, or in presumption.

412. *gladly banish*] *Trin. MS* has the two words in this order, but M. has subjoined numerals to indicate that the order should be reversed.    *squint suspicion*] Cp. Spenser, *F.Q.* III xii 15, where Suspect is 'Under his eiebrowes looking still askaunce'.

414. *imagine, she*] *Trin. MS* and *Bridg.*: imagine brother she.

420. *complete steel*] Echoes *Hamlet* I iv 52: 'complete steel'.

421. *Trin. MS: And may* ('*up' on any needful accident* / *Be it not 'done' in pride or 'in' wilful tempting*) '*presumption*)' [the present version of l. 421 is inserted after deletion].

422. *May trace*] *Trin. MS: Walk through* 'May trace'. Echoes Shakespeare, *Midsummer Night's Dream* II i 25: 'trace the forests'.    *unharboured*] affording no shelter (the first recorded use of the word in this sense).

423. *Infamous hills*] Echoes Horace, *Odes* II iii 20: *infames scopulos.*

424. *rays*] *Trin. MS: awe* 'rays'.

425. *mountaineer*] mountain dweller. Shakespeare invented the word and always uses it to mean a villanous or monstrous being.

426. *Will*] *Trin. MS: Shall* 'Will'.

427. *there, where*] *Trin. MS* and *Bridg.*: even where.

428. *shagged*] A Spenserianism, first recorded *F.Q.* V ix 10.

428–9. Between these lines *Trin. MS* and *Bridg.* insert: And yawning dens where glaring monsters house [*Trin. MS* later deletes].

429. *unblenched*] undismayed (the first recorded occurrence of the word).

Some say no evil thing that walks by night
In fog, or fire, by lake, or moorish fen,
Blue meagre hag, or stubborn unlaid ghost,
That breaks his magic chains at curfew time,
435 No goblin, or swart faëry of the mine,
Hath hurtful power o'er true virginity.
Do ye believe me yet, or shall I call
Antiquity from the old schools of Greece
To testify the arms of chastity?
440 Hence had the huntress Dian her dread bow
Fair silver-shafted queen for ever chaste,
Wherewith she tamed the brinded lioness
And spotted mountain pard, but set at nought
The frivolous bolt of Cupid, gods and men
445 Feared her stern frown, and she was queen o' the
woods.
What was that snaky-headed Gorgon shield
That wise Minerva wore, unconquered virgin,
Wherewith she freezed her foes to congealed stone?
But rigid looks of chaste austerity,

---

*431–6.* M. recalls Fletcher, *Faithful Shepherdess* I i 114–20: 'Yet I have heard
(my mother told it me) / And now I do believe it, if I keep / My virgin
flower uncropt, pure, chaste, and fair, / No Goblin, Wood-god, Fairy,
Elfe, or Fiend, / Satyr or other power that haunts the Groves, / Shall hurt
my body, or by vain illusion / Draw me to wander after idle fires.'
*431. Some say*] *Trin. MS*: *Some say* 'Nay more' 'Some say'. *Bridg.*: Nay
more. Echoing *Hamlet* I i 120–3: 'Some say . . . no spirit dare stir abroad.'
*432. fire*] *ignis fatuus.* *moorish*] boggy. *Trin. MS*: moory.
*433. meagre*] *Trin. MS: wrinkled* 'meagre'. *stubborn*] refusing to be
exorcised. *unlaid ghost*] Cp. *Cymbeline* IV ii 278: 'Ghost unlaid'.
*436. Hath hurtful power o'er*] *Trin. MS*: Has 'hurtful' power ov''er. *Bridg.*:
Has hurtful power o'er.
*438. schools of Greece*] The Greek philosophers.
*441. silver-shafted*] *Bridg.*: silver shafter. (In *Trin. MS* the whole line is a
marginal insertion).
*442. brinded*] tawny, striped with darker colour.
*443. pard*] panther.
*447. That*] *Bridg.*: The. *unconquered*] *Trin. MS*: eternal 'unvanquished'
'unconquered'. In Homer, Minerva carries the Gorgon Medusa's head on
her shield, and this is explained by Conti IV v: *Gorgonis caput in pectore
gestabat, quia nemo contra solis claritatem aut contra sapientiam aciem oculorum
intendere impune potest* (She wore the Gorgon's head on her breast, because
no one can turn his eyes against the light of the sun or against wisdom
and remain unharmed).

450 And noble grace that dashed brute violence
With sudden adoration, and blank awe.
So dear to heaven is saintly chastity,
That when a soul is found sincerely so,
A thousand liveried angels lackey her,
455 Driving far off each thing of sin and guilt,
And in clear dream, and solemn vision
Tell her of things that no gross ear can hear,
Till oft converse with heavenly habitants
Begin to cast a beam on the outward shape,
460 The unpolluted temple of the mind,
And turns it by degrees to the soul's essence,
Till all be made immortal: but when lust
By unchaste looks, loose gestures, and foul talk,
But most by lewd and lavish act of sin,

451. *and blank awe*] Trin. *MS*: '*of her pureness*' '*of bright rays*' and blank awe.
453. *a . . . so*] Trin. *MS*: *it finds* a soul '*is found*' sincerely so.
455. In Trin. *MS* the whole line is a marginal insertion.
457. *gross ear*] See *Arcades* 72–3n (p. 159).
458–62. The doctrine of the transformation of flesh into spirit is developed in Raphael's speech to Adam, *PL* v 497–500. Cp. *Hermetica* x 6 'He who has apprehended the beauty of the Good can apprehend nothing else . . . he forgets all bodily sensation and all bodily movements, and is still. But the beauty of the Good bathes his mind in light, and takes all his soul up to itself, and draws it forth from the body, and changes the whole man into eternal substance'; also Fulke Greville, *Alaham* Prologue 58–69 (the speaker is a ghost from hell): 'My first charge is, the ruine of mine owne: / Hell keeping knowledge still of earthlinesse, / None coming there but spirits overgrowne, / And more embodied into wickednesse, / The bodie by the spirit living ever, / The spirit in the body joying never: / In heaven perchance no such affections be; / Those angell-soules in flesh imprisoned, / Like strangers living in mortalitie, / Still more and more themselves enspirited, / Refining nature to Eternity; / By being maids in Earths adulterous bed.'
459. *Begin*] Trin. *MS*: Begins. *Bridg.*: Begins.
460. *temple*] Cp. 1 *Cor.* iii 16: 'ye are the temple of God, and . . . the Spirit of God dwelleth in you'; and *John* ii 21: 'the temple of his body'.
464. *But*] Trin. *MS* and *Bridg.*: And.     *by . . . lavish*] Trin. *MS*: by *the lascivious* 'lewd and lavish'.
464–74. Cp. Plato, *Phaedo* 81: 'If when it [the soul] departs from the body it is defiled and impure, because it was always with the body, and cared for it and loved it . . . so that it thought nothing was true except the corporeal, which one can touch and see and drink and eat and employ in the pleasures of love . . . it will be interpenetrated with the corporeal which intercourse and communion with the body have made part of its nature . . . And such

465     Lets in defilement to the inward parts,
        The soul grows clotted by contagion,
        Embodies, and imbrutes, till she quite lose
        The divine property of her first being.
        Such are those thick and gloomy shadows damp
470     Oft seen in charnel-vaults, and sepulchres
        Lingering, and sitting by a new-made grave,
        As loth to leave the body that it loved,
        And linked itself by carnal sensuality
        To a degenerate and degraded state.

475     *Sec. Bro.* How charming is divine philosophy!
        Not harsh, and crabbed as dull fools suppose,
        But musical as is Apollo's lute,
        And a perpetual feast of nectared sweets,
        Where no crude surfeit reigns.
        *Eld. Bro.*                       List, list, I hear
480     Some far-off hallo break the silent air.
        *Sec. Bro.* Methought so too; what should it be?
        *Eld. Bro.*                       For certain
        Either some one like us night-foundered here,
        Or else some neighbour woodman, or at worst,
        Some roving robber calling to his fellows.

a soul is weighed down by this and is dragged back into the visible world,
through fear of the invisible and of the other world, and so, as they say, it
flits about the monuments and the tombs, where shadowy shapes of souls
have been seen, figures of those souls which were not set free in purity but
retain something of the visible; and this is why they are seen.'
467. *Embodies*] takes on a material character (the first recorded occurrence
of the word in this sense).        *imbrutes*] becomes bestial (the first recorded
occurrence of the word).        *quite lose*] In *Trin.MS* M. subjoins numerals to
these two words, indicating that their order should be reversed.
470. *sepulchres*] *Trin. MS: monume sepulchres.*
471. *Lingering*] *Trin. MS* and *Bridg.*: Hovering.
473. *sensuality*] *Trin. MS: sensualty.*
475. At the end of this line *Trin. MS* has deleted stage direction: *Hallo
within.*
477. Echoing *Love's Labour's Lost* IV iii 339–40: 'Sweet and musical / As
bright Apollo's lute.'
479. *crude*] indigestible.        *List ... hear*] *Trin. MS:* List bro. list, *me thought*
'I heard'.
480. At the end of this line *Trin. MS* has the stage direction: 'Hallo far off'.
482. *night-foundered*] sunk in night.
484. *Some ... robber*] *Trin. MS:* Some curled 'hedge' man of the sword
'some roving robber'.

485   *Sec. Bro.* Heaven keep my sister, again, again, and near,
Best draw, and stand upon our guard.
*Eld. Bro.*                  I'll hallo,
If he be friendly he comes well, if not,
Defence is a good cause, and heaven be for us.

*The Attendant Spirit habited like a shepherd.*

That hallo I should know, what are you? speak;
490   Come not too near, you fall on iron stakes else.
*Spir.* What voice is that, my young Lord? speak again.
*Sec. Bro.* O brother, 'tis my father shepherd sure.
*Eld. Bro.* Thyrsis? Whose artful strains have oft delayed
The huddling brook to hear his madrigal,
495   And sweetened every musk-rose of the dale,
How cam'st thou here good swain? hath any ram
Slipped from the fold, or young kid lost his dam,
Or straggling wether the pent flock forsook?
How couldst thou find this dark sequestered nook?
500   *Spir.* O my loved master's heir, and his next joy,
I came not here on such a trivial toy
As a strayed ewe, or to pursue the stealth
Of pilfering wolf, not all the fleecy wealth
That doth enrich these downs, is worth a thought
505   To this my errand, and the care it brought.
But O my virgin Lady, where is she?
How chance she is not in your company?

485. *again, again*] *Trin. MS: yet again, again.*
488. *Trin. MS: Had best look to* 'He may chance scratch' *his forehead, here be
brambles* 'a just Defence is a' 'Defence is a good cause, and Heaven be for us'.
490. *iron*] *Trin. MS: pointed* 'iron'.
492. *father*] *Trin. MS and Bridg.*: father's.
493. *Thyrsis*] the pastoral singer in Theocritus i, and the losing contestant in
the singing-match in Virgil, *Ecl.* vii.
494. *huddling*] The waters in front stop to listen, and those behind 'huddle'
up against them.
495. *dale*] *Trin. MS: valley* dale.
496. *swain*] *Trin. MS and Bridg.*: shepherd.
497. *Slipped . . . fold*] *Trin. MS: Leapt o'er the pen* 'Slipped from his fold'.
498. *wether the*] *Trin. MS*: wether *hath* the.
500. *next*] nearest.
506. J. F. Bense, *Englische Studien* xlvi (1913) 333–5, complains that the
Attendant Spirit has no reason for asking this question: as he goes on to
explain, he knows perfectly well where the Lady is (ll. 561–79). Nor is it
clear what 'fears' (l. 510) are confirmed by the brothers' words. He has
already seen the Lady's danger, and heard her speak about her brothers.

*Eld. Bro.* To tell thee sadly shepherd, without blame,
Or our neglect, we lost her as we came.
510　　*Spir.* Ay me unhappy then my fears are true.
*Eld. Bro.* What fears good Thyrsis? Prithee briefly
　　　　shew.
*Spir.* I'll tell ye, 'tis not vain or fabulous,
(Though so esteemed by shallow ignorance)
What the sage poets taught by the heavenly Muse,
515　　Storied of old in high immortal verse
Of dire chimeras and enchanted isles,
And rifted rocks whose entrance leads to hell,
For such there be, but unbelief is blind.
　　　　Within the navel of this hideous wood,
520　　Immured in cypress shades a sorcerer dwells
Of Bacchus, and of Circe born, great Comus,
Deep skilled in all his mother's witcheries,
And here to every thirsty wanderer,
By sly enticement gives his baneful cup,
525　　With many murmurs mixed, whose pleasing poison
The visage quite transforms of him that drinks,
And the inglorious likeness of a beast
Fixes instead, unmoulding reason's mintage
Charactered in the face; this have I learnt
530　　Tending my flocks hard by i' the hilly crofts,
That brow this bottom glade, whence night by night
He and his monstrous rout are heard to howl
Like stabled wolves, or tigers at their prey,

*508. sadly*] seriously.
*511. good Thyrsis*] *Trin. MS*: good *shep.* 'Thyrsis'.
*512. ye*] *Trin. MS* and *Bridg.*: you.
*512–7.* As D. C. Allen points out, *JEGP* lx (1961) 617, these lines recommend
the allegorical interpretation of pagan literature in Christian terms: this
should help to define the reader's attitude towards the Attendant Spirit's last
speech.
*516. chimeras*] monsters part lion, part goat and part dragon.
*518.* In *Trin. MS* the whole line is a marginal insertion.
*519. navel*] centre.
*522. Deep skilled*] *Trin. MS: Inured* 'Deep learnt' 'skilled'.
*530. hilly crofts*] *Trin. MS*: pastured lawns 'hilly crofts'. *OED* suggests that
M.'s use of 'crofts' (fields) here may be influenced by Dutch *knoft* (high and
dry land).
*531. brow*] form a brow to (the first recorded use of 'brow' as verb).
*533. stabled*] *OED* cites this as first usage of the word in sense 'put into a
stable'. M. may recall Virgil, *Ecl.* iii 80 *Triste lupus stabulis* (Baneful to folds

Doing abhorred rites to Hecate
535 In their obscured haunts of inmost bowers,
Yet have they many baits, and guileful spells
To inveigle and invite the unwary sense
Of them that pass unweeting by the way.
This evening late by then the chewing flocks
540 Had ta'en their supper on the savoury herb
Of knot-grass dew-besprent, and were in fold,
I sat me down to watch upon a bank
With ivy canopied, and interwove
With flaunting honeysuckle, and began
545 Wrapt in a pleasing fit of melancholy
To meditate my rural minstrelsy,
Till fancy had her fill, but ere a close
The wonted roar was up amidst the woods,
And filled the air with barbarous dissonance
550 At which I ceased, and listened them a while,
Till an unusual stop of sudden silence
Gave respite to the drowsy frighted steeds
That draw the litter of close-curtained sleep;
At last a soft and solemn-breathing sound

is the wolf). But in *PL* xi 747-8 'sea-monsters whelped / And stabled', the word seems to mean simply 'in their lairs'.

*534. Hecate*] See l. 135*n.*

*538. unweeting*] unheeding.

*541. knot-grass*] *polygonum aviculare*, a weed with numerous creeping stems and small pink flowers.

*542-4.* Echoing *Midsummer Night's Dream* II i 249-51: 'I know a bank where the wild thyme blows, / Where oxlips and the nodding violet grows; / Quite over-canopied with lush woodbine.'

*544. flaunting*] *Trin. MS: suckling* 'blowing' 'flaunting' 'blowing' 'flaunting'.

*545-6.* These lines are written in the reverse order in *Trin. MS*, but marginal numerals inserted by M. indicate that they should be read in the present order.

*546. meditate ... minstrelsy*] play my shepherd's pipe: see *Lycidas* 66*n*, p. 244 below.

*547. a close*] *Trin. MS: the* 'a' close. A 'close' is the conclusion of a musical phrase.

*551. unusual stop*] i.e. at l. 145.

*552. frighted*] *Trin. MS:* flighted.

*553. close-curtained sleep*] Echoes *Macbeth* II i 51, 'curtained sleep', and *Romeo and Juliet* III ii 5, 'Spread thy close curtain . . . night.'

*554. soft*] *Trin. MS: soft* 'still' 'sweet' 'soft'. *Bridg.*: sweet.

*554-9.* Echoing *Antony and Cleopatra* II ii 217-23: 'A strange invisible perfume hits the sense / . . . The city cast / Her people out upon her; and

555  Rose like a steam of rich distilled perfumes,
     And stole upon the air, that even Silence
     Was took ere she was ware, and wished she might
     Deny her nature, and be never more
     Still to be so displaced. I was all ear,
560  And took in strains that might create a soul
     Under the ribs of death, but O ere long
     Too well I did perceive it was the voice
     Of my most honoured Lady, your dear sister.
     Amazed I stood, harrowed with grief and fear,
565  And O poor hapless nightingale thought I,
     How sweet thou sing'st, how near the deadly snare!
     Then down the lawns I ran with headlong haste
     Through paths, and turnings often trod by day,
     Till guided by mine ear I found the place
570  Where that damned wizard hid in sly disguise
     (For so by certain signs I knew) had met
     Already, ere my best speed could prevent,
     The aidless innocent Lady his wished prey,
     Who gently asked if he had seen such two,
575  Supposing him some neighbour villager;
     Longer I durst not stay, but soon I guessed
     Ye were the two she meant, with that I sprung
     Into swift flight, till I had found you here,
     But further know I not.
     *Sec. Bro.*                 O night and shades,
580  How are ye joined with hell in triple knot
     Against the unarmed weakness of one virgin

Antony, / . . . did sit alone, / Whistling to the air; which but for vacancy, /
Had gone to gaze on Cleopatra too, / And made a gap in nature.'
555. *Trin. MS*: Rose like *the* 'a' *soft* steam of 'slow' 'rich' distill'd perfumes.
*Bridg.*: Rose like the soft steam of distill'd perfumes.
557. *took*] charmed.
559. *be so displaced*] *Trin. MS*: be 'so' displaced.
562. *did*] *Trin. MS* and *Bridg.*: might.
571. *knew*] *Bridg.*: know.
573. *aidless*] *Trin. MS*: helpless 'aidless'.
573–4. *prey, / Who gently*] *Trin. MS*: prey *who took him* / Who *gen* Who
gently.
576. J. F. Bense, *Englische Studien* xlvi (1913) 333–5, complains that the
Attendant Spirit's behaviour is unaccountable. He had the magic herb with
him, and should surely have rescued the Lady immediately, rather than
leaving her to find the brothers.
577. *with that*] *Trin. MS*: *and* with that.
580. *ye*] *Bridg.*: you.

Alone, and helpless! Is this the confidence
You gave me brother?
*Eld. Bro.*              Yes, and keep it still,
Lean on it safely, not a period
585    Shall be unsaid for me: against the threats
Of malice or of sorcery, or that power
Which erring men call chance, this I hold firm,
Virtue may be assailed, but never hurt,
Surprised by unjust force, but not enthralled,
590    Yea even that which mischief meant most harm
Shall in the happy trial prove most glory.
But evil on itself shall back recoil,
And mix no more with goodness, when at last
Gathered like scum, and settled to itself
595    It shall be in eternal restless change
Self-fed, and self-consum'd, if this fail,
The pillared firmament is rottenness,
And earth's base built on stubble. But come let's on
Against the opposing will and arm of heaven
600    May never this just sword be lifted up,
But for that damned magician, let him be girt
With all the grisly legions that troop
Under the sooty flag of Acheron,
Harpies and hydras, or all the monstrous forms
605    'Twixt Africa and Ind, I'll find him out,
And force him to restore his purchase back,
Or drag him by the curls, to a foul death,

*584. period*] sentence.
*585. for me*] as far as I am concerned.
*593. And mix*] *Trin. MS: Till all to place and mix.*
*595–6.* Cp. Sin in *PL* ii 798–800, gnawed by whelps from her own womb.
*597. pillared firmament*] Cp. *Job* xxvi 11: 'the pillars of heaven'.
*603. sooty flag*] Echoes Phineas Fletcher, *Locusts* ii 39: 'All hell run out, and sooty flags display, / A foul deformed rout.'    *Acheron*] See *Q Nov 7n* (p. 36).
*604–5. Harpies and hydras*] Echoes Sylvester (Du Bartas 261): 'Hydraes and Harpies'. Harpies were birds with women's faces, and the hydra was the nine-headed serpent killed by Hercules near the Lernean Lake.    *forms*] *Trin. MS* and *Bridg.*: bugs.    *'Twixt Africa and Ind*] Perhaps echoing Fairfax's translation of Tasso, *Jerusalem Delivered* xv 51: 'All monsters which hot Afric doth forthsend, / 'Twixt Nilus, Atlas, and the southern cape.'
*606. restore . . . back*] *Trin. MS: release his new got prey* restore his purchase back.    *purchase*] booty.
*607. curls*] In Jonson, *Pleasure Reconciled to Virtue* 8, Comus has 'his haire curld'.    *to . . . death*] *Trin. MS* and *Bridg.*: and cleave his scalp.

Cursed as his life.
*Spir.*                  Alas good venturous youth,
I love thy courage yet, and bold emprise,
610  But here thy sword can do thee little stead,
Far other arms, and other weapons must
Be those that quell the might of hellish charms,
He with his bare wand can unthread thy joints,
And crumble all thy sinews.
*Eld. Bro.*                  Why prithee shepherd
615  How durst thou then thyself approach so near
As to make this relation?
*Spir.*                  Care and utmost shifts
How to secure the Lady from surprisal,
Brought to my mind a certain shepherd lad
Of small regard to see to, yet well skilled
620  In every virtuous plant and healing herb
That spreads her verdant leaf to the morning ray,
He loved me well, and oft would beg me sing,
Which when I did, he on the tender grass
Would sit, and hearken even to ecstasy,
625  And in requital ope his leathern scrip,
And show me simples of a thousand names
Telling their strange and vigorous faculties;
Amongst the rest a small unsightly root,
But of divine effect, he culled me out;
630  The leaf was darkish, and had prickles on it,
But in another country, as he said,
Bore a bright golden flower, but not in this soil:

608. *Cursed . . . life*] Trin. MS: Down to the *hips lowest* hips. *Bridg.*: Down
to the hips.
609. *emprise*] chivalric enterprise.
610. *sword . . . stead*] Trin. MS: *swo steel* 'sword' can do thee LITTLE STEAD
*small avail.*
613. *unthread*] Trin. MS: *unquilt* 'unthread'.
614. *all thy*] Trin. MS: *every* 'all thy'.
615. *then thyself approach*] Bridg.: then approach.
617. *surprisal*] surprise, a Spenserian coinage (*Virgil's Gnat* 536).
618. *shepherd lad*] Variously identified with Diodati (Masson iii 229),
M. himself (J. H. Hanford, *TLS* (3 Nov. 1932) 815) and Nathaniel Weld
(B. G. Hall, *TLS* (12 Oct. 1933) 691).
619. *to see to*] to look at.
620. *virtuous*] See *Il Penseroso* 113*n*, p. 144 above.
625. *scrip*] bag.
626. *simples*] medicinal herbs.     *names*] Trin. MS: *hues* names.
631–6. *Bridg.* omits.

> Unknown, and like esteemed, and the dull swain
> Treads on it daily with his clouted shoon,
> 635 And yet more med'cinal is it than that moly
> That Hermes once to wise Ulysses gave;
> He called it haemony, and gave it me,

*633–4.* S. Elledge, *MLN* lviii (1943) 551–3, compares a fragment possibly by Sappho, preserved in Demetrius, *De Elocutione* (one of the rhetorics recommended by M. in *Of Education*): 'Like the hyacinth-flower, that shepherd folk 'mid the mountains tread underfoot, and low on the earth her bloom dark-splendid is shed.' Cp. Marvell, 'Appleton House', 357–60.

*634. clouted*] studded with broad-headed nails. Echoing *II Hen. VI* IV ii 182: 'clouted shoon'.

*635–6.* These lines are inserted in the margin of *Trin. MS. med'cinal . . . once*] *Trin. MS*: med'cinal 'is it' than that *ancient* moly / *That* Which *Mercury* 'Hermes once'.          *moly*] Plant with black root and white flower given to Ulysses (*Od.* x 302–6) to make him proof against the charms of Circe. According to Pliny xxv 27 some 'Greek authorities have painted its blossom yellow'. R. M. Adams, *MP* li (1953) 24, lists several authorities, including Sandys[3] 479–81, for the allegorical association of moly with prudence and temperance. In Browne, *Inner Temple Masque* 128, Circe uses moly as a charm to banish sleep from Ulysses. S. R. Watson, *N & Q* clxxvi (1939) 244, points out that Drayton (i 130 and iii 290) has two references to moly in his pastoral verse.

*637. haemony*] The name may be derived from *Haemonia* (Thessaly), the land of magic herbs (see *Elegia II* 7–8n, p. 31 above). It is used to mean 'Thessaly' by Spenser, *Astrophel* 3, and this leads S. R. Watson, *N & Q* clxxviii (1940) 260–1, to conjecture that 'haemony' in *Comus* represents pastoral, as opposed to epic poetry. Or the word may be connected with Gk. $\alpha\tilde{\iota}\mu\alpha$ (blood): Coleridge, *Letters* ed. E. L. Griggs (Oxford 1956) ii 866–7, derived it from $\alpha\tilde{\iota}\mu\alpha$–$o\tilde{\iota}\nu o\varsigma$ (blood-wine), and suggested that it represented redemption by the Cross. Similarly E. S. Le Comte, *PQ* xxi (1942) 283–98, favouring a derivation from $\alpha\tilde{\iota}\mu\omega\nu\iota o\varsigma$ (blood-red), conjectures that 'haemony' is connected with the account of moly given by Eustathius in his commentary on the *Odyssey* (namely, that moly sprung from the blood of Pikolous, struck dead by the sun when trying to ravish Circe). He interprets 'haemony' as grace, and associates it with 'rhamnus', a plant mentioned as an antidote against enchantment in Fletcher, *Faithful Shepherdess* II ii 15–8, one type of which is called Christ's Thorn and is mentioned in Gerard's *Herbal* as the material of the Crown of Thorns. R. M. Adams, *MP* li (1953) 24–5, points out rightly the tenuousness of Le Comte's reasoning, but T. P. Harrison, *PQ* xxii (1943) 251–4, takes up the 'rhamnus' suggestion, and argues that M. transferred to the fanciful 'haemony' the attributes of the real 'rhamnus' as described not in Gerard but in Lyte's *New Herbal* (1578). A further allegorical interpretation is put forward by J. H. Hanford, *TLS* (3 Nov. 1932) 815, who understands 'haemony' as

And bade me keep it as of sovran use
'Gainst all enchantments, mildew blast, or damp
640    Or ghastly Furies' apparition;
I pursed it up, but little reckoning made,
Till now that this extremity compelled,
But now I find it true; for by this means
I knew the foul enchanter though disguised,
645    Entered the very lime-twigs of his spells,
And yet came off: if you have this about you
(As I will give you when we go) you may
Boldly assault the necromancer's hall;
Where if he be, with dauntless hardihood,
650    And brandished blade rush on him, break his glass,
And shed the luscious liquor on the ground,
But seize his wand, though he and his cursed crew
Fierce sign of battle make, and menace high,
Or like the sons of Vulcan vomit smoke,
655    Yet will they soon retire, if he but shrink.
*Eld. Bro.* Thyrsis lead on apace, I'll follow thee,
And some good angel bear a shield before us.

a symbol for the Platonic doctrine of virtue, and the reference to 'another
country' as contrasting the creative mind of England and N. Europe with
that of Greece and Italy. Some similarity between M.'s description of
'haemony' and Virgil's of *amellus* (*Georg.* iv 271–8) is suggested by J.
Arthos, *N & Q* ccvi (1961) 172.

*640. ghastly Furies*] Echoes Sylvester (Du Bartas 254): 'ghastly Furies'.
*645. lime-twigs*] Twigs smeared with bird-lime for catching birds.
*647. when . . . go*] *Trin. MS: as we go* 'when on the way' 'when we go'.
*648. the necromancer's*] *Trin. MS: his* 'the' *necroman*ti*c*'cer's'.
*649. dauntless hardihood*] *Trin. MS: sudden violence* 'dauntless hardihood'.
*650. brandished blade*] Cp. *Od.* x 294–5, where Hermes advises Ulysses to
spring upon Circe with drawn sword.
*651. shed*] *Trin. MS: pour* 'shed'.    *liquor*] *Trin. MS: potion* 'liquor'.
M. recalls Spenser, *F.Q.* II xii 57, where Guyon breaks the cup of Excess
'And with the liquor stained all the lond'.
*652. But*] *Trin. MS: And* 'But'.    *cursed crew*] Echoing Sylvester (Du
Bartas 17): 'cursed crew'.
*654. sons of Vulcan*] Echoes Virgil, *Aen.* viii 252–3, where Cacus, a son of
Vulcan *fumum . . . evomit*.
*655. will they*] *Trin. MS*: they will (but M. has subjoined numerals indica-
ting that the order of the words should be reversed).
*656. I'll*] *Trin. MS* and *Bridg.*: I.
*657. And . . . us*] *Trin. MS: And good Heaven cast his best regard upon us*
'And some good angel bear a shield before us'.

*The scene changes to a stately palace, set out with all manner of delicious-*
*ness: soft music, tables spread with all dainties. Comus appears with*
*his rabble, and the Lady set in an enchanted chair, to whom he offers*
*his glass, which she puts by, and goes about to rise.*

      *Comus.* Nay lady sit; if I but wave this wand,
      Your nerves are all chained up in alabaster,
660    And you a statue, or as Daphne was
      Root-bound, that fled Apollo,
      *Lady.*                   Fool do not boast,
      Thou canst not touch the freedom of my mind
      With all thy charms, although this corporal rind
      Thou hast immanacled, while heaven sees good.
665    *Comus.* Why are you vexed Lady? why do you frown?
      Here dwell no frowns, nor anger, from these gates
      Sorrow flies far: see, here be all the pleasures
      That fancy can beget on youthful thoughts,
      When the fresh blood grows lively, and returns
670    Brisk as the April buds in primrose season.
      And first behold this cordial julep here
      That flames, and dances in his crystal bounds
      With spirits of balm, and fragrant syrups mixed.
      Not that Nepenthes which the wife of Thone,

*659.* Recalling *Tempest* I ii 484-5, where Prospero with his wand charms
Ferdinand: 'Thy nerves are in their infancy again, / And have no vigour
in them.'
*660. or as*] *Trin. MS: fixed,* 'or' as.     *Daphne*] her transformation into a
laurel is described by Ovid, *Met.* i 545-52.
*661. do not boast*] *Trin. MS: thou art over proud* 'do not boast'.
*661-5. Fool . . . Lady?*] The Lady's speech and the first five words of Comus's
reply are inserted in the margin in *Trin. MS.* Originally Comus's speech
continued uninterrupted: '. . . that fled Apollo. Why do you frown?'
See l. 754*n.*
*662-4.* Cp. Cicero, *De Finibus* III xxii (of the wise man): 'rightly will he be
called unconquerable, for though his body be thrown into fetters, no
bondage can enchain his soul.'
*664. immanacled*] The first recorded occurrence of the verb 'immanacle'.
*668. Trin. MS: That youth and fancy* fancy can BEGET 'invent' *on youthful
thoughts.
*669. fresh*] *Trin. MS: brisk* 'fresh'.
*670-704.* In *Trin. MS* these lines are inserted on a pasted leaf. Comus's
speech originally continued uninterrupted: '. . . in primrose season. / O
foolishness of men!' See l. 754*n.*
*671. julep*] sweet drink.
*674-5.* In Homer, *Od* iv 219-32, Helen puts into Menelaus' drink a drug

675　In Egypt gave to Jove-born Helena
　　　Is of such power to stir up joy as this,
　　　To life so friendly, or so cool to thirst.
　　　Why should you be so cruel to yourself,
　　　And to those dainty limbs which Nature lent
680　For gentle usage, and soft delicacy?
　　　But you invert the covenants of her trust,
　　　And harshly deal like an ill borrower
　　　With that which you received on other terms,
　　　Scorning the unexempt condition
685　By which all mortal frailty must subsist,
　　　Refreshment after toil, ease after pain,
　　　That have been tired all day without repast,
　　　And timely rest have wanted, but fair virgin
　　　This will restore all soon.
　　　*Lady*.　　　　　　　　　'Twill not false traitor,
690　'Twill not restore the truth and honesty
　　　That thou hast banished from thy tongue with lies,
　　　Was this the cottage, and the safe abode
　　　Thou told'st me of? What grim aspects are these,
　　　These ugly-headed monsters? Mercy guard me!
695　Hence with thy brewed enchantments, foul deceiver,
　　　Hast thou betrayed my credulous innocence
　　　With vizored falsehood, and base forgery,
　　　And wouldst thou seek again to trap me here
　　　With liquorish baits fit to ensnare a brute?

which dispels grief ($\nu\eta\pi\epsilon\nu\theta\acute{\epsilon}s$), which she had been given by Polydamna, an Egyptian woman, the wife of Thon. In *Trin. MS* the Greek word is written in the margin.

678–87. On the pasted sheet in *Trin. MS* l. 677 is followed by two lines: '*Poor lady thou hast need of some refreshing* / That *hast* 'have' been tried all day without repast.' After the deletion of the first of these lines, the present 678–86 are inserted in the margin. *Bridg.* omits ll. 678–86 and has instead the two original *Trin. MS* lines in their uncorrected state (i.e. reading 'hast' in the second).

687. *That have*] Refers back to 'you' (l. 681).

688. *And*] *Bridg.*: A.　　*have*] *Trin. MS*: *hast* 'have'.　　*but*] *Trin. MS*: *here* 'but'. *Bridg.*: here.

695. *brewed . . . deceiver*] *Trin. MS*: *hell-brewed opiate foul* 'brewed' brewed enchantments foul deceiver.

696–9. *Bridg.* omits.

697. *vizored*] having the face covered with visor or mask.　　*forgery*] *Trin. MS*: forgeries.

699. *liquorish*] pleasant to the taste. The word could also mean 'lustful', and it retains some of that meaning here.

700   Were it a draught for Juno when she banquets,
      I would not taste thy treasonous offer; none
      But such as are good men can give good things,
      And that which is not good, is not delicious
      To a well-governed and wise appetite.
705   *Comus.* O foolishness of men! that lend their ears
      To those budge doctors of the Stoic fur,
      And fetch their precepts from the Cynic tub,
      Praising the lean and sallow Abstinence.
      Wherefore did Nature pour her bounties forth,

*700–1.* Echoing Jonson, *Forrest* ix 7–8: 'But might I of Jove's Nectar sup, / I would not change for thine.'

*701–2.* Cp. Euripides, *Medea* 618: 'A bad man's gifts convey no benefit.'

*706. budge*] First use of word as adjective recorded in *OED*: meaning possibly 'solemn in demeanour, pompous'. There is probably some reference intended to the fur 'budge' (lamb's skin with wool dressed outwards) used in academic gowns.     *Stoic fur*] *Trin. MS*: Stoic *gown* 'fur'. The Stoic school of philosophy was founded by Zeno at the end of the fourth century B.C., taking its name from the N. Stoa of the Athenian agora. Zeno began as a Cynic, and his system grew out of that of the Cynics. Among Roman Stoics, Seneca and Epictetus are the most important. Seneca regards the body as a mere husk or prison of the soul: only with its departure does the soul's true life begin. Epictetus advises renunciation of the world: in his great maxim 'bear and forbear', the last element is a command to refrain from the external advantages of nature. C. W. Broadribb, *TLS* (8 May 1937) 364, replies to Landor's objection ('It is the first time that Cynic or Stoic ever put on fur'), with the information that there is an illustration in Erasmus, *Encomium Moriae*, showing a Stoic philosopher wearing fur.

*707. Cynic*] This school of philosophers derived their name from the Gk κυών (dog), and took a dog as their badge. The chief Cynics were Antisthenes, Crates and Diogenes: of these the first laid down the principles of the school, concentrating on the development of the individual will, and regarding the ordinary pleasures of life as harmful, because they interrupted the operation of the will. He claimed that the highest end of life was self-knowledge, and that for this disrepute and poverty were advantageous, because they drove a man back upon himself and increased his self-control. *tub*] Diogenes Laertius vi 23 recounts that when a friend failed to get a cottage for Diogenes, the philosopher 'took for his abode the tub in the Metroön'.

*708. sallow*] *Bridg.*: shallow.

*709–35.* A large number of parallels to Comus's arguments have been cited, including Seneca, *Hippolytus* 435–82, Pettie, *Petite Pallace* (ed. I. Gollancz (1908) i 82–4), Sidney, *Arcadia* (1590) iii 10, Gabriel Harvey, *Letter Book* (ed. E. J. Scott (1884) 86–7), Warner, *Albion's England* v 24 (quoted by D.

710   With such a full and unwithdrawing hand,
        Covering the earth with odours, fruits, and flocks,
        Thronging the seas with spawn innumerable,
        But all to please, and sate the curious taste?
        And set to work millions of spinning worms,
715   That in their green shops weave the smooth-haired silk
        To deck her sons, and that no corner might
        Be vacant of her plenty, in her own loins
        She hutched the all-worshipped ore, and precious gems
        To store her children with; if all the world
720   Should in a pet of temperance feed on pulse,
        Drink the clear stream, and nothing wear but frieze,
        The all-giver would be unthanked, would be
          unpraised,
        Not half his riches known, and yet despised,
        And we should serve him as a grudging master,

Bush, *PMLA* xliv (1929) 726), Marlowe, *Hero and Leander* i 199–310, Shakespeare, *Venus and Adonis* 163–74, Daniel, *Complaint of Rosamond* 246–52, 260–73, 512–32 (the Marlowe, Shakespeare and Daniel parallels are noted by H. Schaus, *UTSE* xxv (1946) 129–41), Drayton, *Heroical Epistles* 'John to Matilda' 51–8, 119–56, Spenser, *F.Q.* II vi 15–17 (an imitation of Tasso, *Jerusalem Delivered* xiv 62–4), Brandon, *The Virtuous Octavia* 891–932, Donne, *Confined Love*, Heywood, *Troia Britannica* ii 53–4 and Randolph, *Muse's Looking Glass* II iii (G. C. Moore Smith, *TLS* (19 Jan. 1922) 44, suggests this parallel, noting that, though the play was not printed till 1638, it was probably acted at Cambridge where M. and Randolph were contemporaries).

*711. fruits, and flocks*] Trin. MS: *and with* fruits, 'and flocks'.

*712. Thronging*] Trin. MS: Cramming 'Thronging'. 'Throng' in a trans. sense ('fill a place with a large number of objects') is first found in *Coriolanus* III iii 36. Cp. Lucretius's praise of Venus as a cosmic force, *quae mare ... concelebras* (who throngest the sea), *De Rerum Natura* i 3–4, and Ovid's imitation of it, *Fasti* iv 106 : *innumeris piscibus implet aquas* (she fills the waters with innumerable fish). Ovid goes on to discuss allurements to love.

*713.* Trin. MS: *The fields with cattle and the air with fowl* [the present line is inserted after deletion].

*715. shops*] workshops.

*716. To deck*] Trin. MS: To deck 'To adorn' 'deck'.

*718. hutched*] laid up as in a hutch (i.e. coffer).

*720. pulse*] Trin. MS: pulse 'vetches' 'pulse'. Cp. *Daniel* i 12–16, where Daniel and his companions at the court of Nebuchadnezzar insist on eating pulse (i.e. beans, peas, etc.) and drinking water.

*721. frieze*] coarse woollen cloth.

725 As a penurious niggard of his wealth,
    And live like Nature's bastards, not her sons,
    Who would be quite surcharged with her own weight,
    And strangled with her waste fertility;
    The earth cumbered, and the winged air darked with
        plumes,
730 The herds would over-multitude their lords,
    The sea o'erfraught would swell, and the unsought
        diamonds
    Would so emblaze the forehead of the deep,
    And so bestud with stars, that they below
    Would grow inured to light, and come at last
735 To gaze upon the sun with shameless brows.
    List Lady be not coy, and be not cozened
    With that same vaunted name virginity,
    Beauty is Nature's coin, must not be hoarded,
    But must be current, and the good thereof
740 Consists in mutual and partaken bliss,

725. In *Trin. MS* this line is a marginal insertion.
726. *And live like*] *Trin. MS*: 'And' *liv*'*e*'*ing as* 'for' 'like'.
729. In *Trin. MS* this line is a marginal insertion.
731. *Trin. MS*: *The sea o'erfraught* The *o'er* 'sea' *o'erfraught would heave her waters up* 'swell' / *Above the shore* and th'unsought diamonds.
731–5. H. F. Robins, *MLQ* xii (1951) 422–8, explains 'the deep' (l. 732) as 'the central part of the earth'. The 'forehead' or top of the deep, is that part of the inside of the earth's globe which lies nearest the surface. This is envisaged as studded with diamonds, and therefore appearing to those in the centre of the earth like a sky studded with stars. 'They below' (l. 733) are the evil, hell-dwelling spirits, demons and monsters of classical mythology (see *Comus* 601–5, and *PL* ii 624–8). The belief, found in Pliny, that precious stones reproduced themselves like animals, is relayed in later 'encyclopaedias' of science like John Maplet's *A Greene Forest* (1567), which M. is known to have read.
732–3. *Trin. MS*: *Would so bestud the centre with their starlight* / *Were they not taken thence* that they below [after deletion, the present version of the lines is inserted]. *Bridg.*: Would so emblaze with stars, that they below [732 omitted].
733. *bestud*] M. probably recalls Sylvester (Du Bartas 187), who calls stars 'the gilt studs of the Firmament'.
734. *light*] *Trin. MS*: *day* 'light'.
736. *and be*] *Trin. MS*: NOR 'and' 'nor' be.
736–43. Comus's advice owes something to the *carpe diem* tradition, stemming from Horace and Ausonius and popular with neo-Latin and vernacular poets on the continent in the sixteenth and seventeenth centuries.

Unsavoury in the enjoyment of itself
If you let slip time, like a neglected rose
It withers on the stalk with languished head.
Beauty is Nature's brag, and must be shown
745 In courts, at feasts, and high solemnities
Where most may wonder at the workmanship;
It is for homely features to keep home,
They had their name thence; coarse complexions
And cheeks of sorry grain will serve to ply
750 The sampler, and to tease the housewife's wool.
What need a vermeil-tinctured lip for that
Love-darting eyes, or tresses like the morn?
There was another meaning in these gifts,
Think what, and be advised, you are but young yet.
755 *Lady.* I had not thought to have unlocked my lips
In this unhallowed air, but that this juggler
Would think to charm my judgement, as mine eyes
Obtruding false rules pranked in reason's garb.

Some previous examples are collected by F. Bruser, *SP* xliv (1947) 625–44.
*736–54. Bridg.* omits.
*742–3.* Echoing *Midsummer Night's Dream* I i 76–8: 'Earthlier-happy is the rose distill'd / Than that ... withering on the virgin thorn.' This seems closer to M. than Spenser's famous translation from Tasso (*F.Q.* II xii 75), which he may also have had in mind.
*743. with ... head*] *Trin. MS*: *and fades away* 'with languished head'.
*744. brag*] show, display.
*745. and high*] *Trin. MS*: on high.
*748. name ... complexions*] *Trin. MS*: name '*from*' thence, coarse *beetle brows* complexions.
*749. grain*] colour.
*750. sampler, and*] *Trin. MS*: sample, or. *tease*] comb, in preparation for spinning.
*752. Love-darting eyes*] Echoes Sylvester (Du Bartas 499): 'love-darting Eyn'.
*754. Trin. MS*: Think what, *and look upon this cordial julep* 'and be advised, you are but young yet'. Between l. 754 and l. 755 *Trin. MS* inserts what are now ll. 672–7, followed by the two lines 'Poor lady ... repast' (see ll. 678–87n), followed by an early form of ll. 688–9 (l. 688. but ... virgin] *Trin. MS*: *here sweet Lady* 'fair virgin'. l. 689. 'Twill not] *Trin. MS*: Stand back), followed by ll. 662–4, followed by l. 692 and an early and much corrected form of ll. 693–6, followed by 'if thou give me it / I throw it on the ground' (a threat by the Lady nowhere included in the final version), followed by an early form of ll. 700–2. The whole passage is then heavily deleted. Clearly M. went on to insert its various parts in the places where they now appear (see notes to ll. 670–704 and 661–5).

I hate when vice can bolt her arguments,
760  And virtue has no tongue to check her pride:
Imposter do not charge most innocent Nature,
As if she would her children should be riotous
With her abundance she good cateress
Means her provision only to the good
765  That live according to her sober laws,
And holy dictate of spare temperance:
If every just man that now pines with want
Had but a moderate and beseeming share
Of that which lewdly-pampered Luxury
770  Now heaps upon some few with vast excess,
Nature's full blessings would be well-dispensed
In unsuperfluous even proportion,
And she no whit encumbered with her store,
And then the giver would be better thanked,
775  His praise due paid, for swinish gluttony
Ne'er looks to heaven amidst his gorgeous feast,
But with besotted base ingratitude
Crams, and blasphemes his feeder. Shall I go on?
Or have I said enough? To him that dares
780  Arm his profane tongue with contemptuous words
Against the sun-clad power of chastity;
Fain would I something say, yet to what end?
Thou hast nor ear, nor soul to apprehend
The sublime notion, and high mystery

759. *bolt*] sift, so as to make the thing sifted appear fine and pure.
762. *would*] *Trin. MS*: *meant* 'would'.
763. *cateress*] The first recorded instance of the word.
764. *Means*] *Trin. MS*: *Intends* 'Means'.
767–73. Cp. *King Lear* IV i 70–4: 'Let the superfluous and lust-dieted man / That slaves your ordinance, that will not see / Because he doth not feel, feel your power quickly; / So distribution should undo excess, / And each man have enough.'
771. *blessings*] *Bridg.*: blessing.
775–6. Cp. Plato, *Republic* 586A, of those who 'have no experience of wisdom and virtue': 'With eyes ever bent upon the earth and heads bowed down over the tables they feast like cattle, grazing and copulating.'
777. *besotted*] *Trin. MS*: *a* 'be'sottish'ed'.
778–805. *Shall . . . strongly*] *Trin. MS* and *Bridg.* omit.
781. *sun-clad*] Cp. *Rev.* xii 1: 'a woman clothed with the sun', and Petrarch, *Canzone* viii 1 (to the Virgin Mary): *Vergine bella, che di sol vestita . . .* (see note on *Versification in M.'s 'canzone poems'* p. 162 above).
784. *mystery*] Cp. M. in the *Apology* (Columbia iii 306, Yale i 892): 'having had the docrine of holy Scripture unfolding those chaste and high mysteries

785   That must be uttered to unfold the sage
      And serious doctrine of virginity,
      And thou art worthy that thou shouldst not know
      More happiness than this thy present lot.
      Enjoy your dear wit, and gay rhetoric
790   That hath so well been taught her dazzling fence,
      Thou art not fit to hear thyself convinced;
      Yet should I try, the uncontrolled worth
      Of this pure cause would kindle my rapt spirits
      To such a flame of sacred vehemence,
795   That dumb things would be moved to sympathize,
      And the brute Earth would lend her nerves, and
          shake,
      Till all thy magic structures reared so high,
      Were shattered into heaps o'er thy false head.
Comus. She fables not, I feel that I do fear
800   Her words set off by some superior power;
      And though not mortal, yet a cold shuddering dew
      Dips me all o'er, as when the wrath of Jove
      Speaks thunder, and the chains of Erebus
      To some of Saturn's crew. I must dissemble,
805   And try her yet more strongly. Come, no more,
      This is mere moral babble, and direct
      Against the canon laws of our foundation;

with timeliest care infus'd, that *the body is for the Lord and the Lord for the body.*'

*785–6. sage | And serious*] Cp. 'our sage and serious Poet *Spencer*' (Columbia iv 311, Yale ii 516).

*789. rhetoric*] Perhaps echoing Marlowe, *Hero and Leander* i 338: 'Who taught thee rhetoric to deceive a maid?'

*790. fence*] art of fencing (the first instance of the word in this sense cited in OED).

*792. uncontrolled*] uncontrollable.

*796. brute Earth*] Echoes Horace, *Odes* I xxxiv 9–12: *bruta tellus . . . concutitur.     nerves*] sinews.

*799. She fables not*] Echoes *I Hen. VI* IV ii 42: 'He fables not; I hear the enemy.'

*802–4.* Cronos (Saturn) was defeated in battle and deposed by his son Zeus (Jove), who used thunderbolts as weapons, and who then imprisoned the losers in Tartarus.     *Erebus*] primeval Darkness, son of Chaos, according to Hesiod.

*805. no more*] Trin. MS: *y'are too moral 'no more'.*

*806–9.* Trin. MS: *This is mere moral stuff 'Your moral stuff' the very 'tilted' lees | And settlings of a melancholy blood.* (After deletion the present ll. 806–9 are inserted in the margin.)

I must not suffer this, yet 'tis but the lees
And settlings of a melancholy blood;
810    But this will cure all straight, one sip of this
Will bathe the drooping spirits in delight
Beyond the bliss of dreams. Be wise, and taste. . . .

*The Brothers rush in with swords drawn, wrest his glass out of his*
*hand, and break it against the ground; his rout make sign of resistance*
*but are all driven in. The Attendant Spirit comes in.*

*Spir.* What, have you let the false enchanter scape?
O ye mistook, ye should have snatched his wand
815    And bound him fast; without his rod reversed,
And backward mutters of dissevering power,
We cannot free the Lady that sits here
In stony fetters fixed, and motionless;
Yet stay, be not disturbed, now I bethink me,
820    Some other means I have which may be used,
Which once of Meliboeus old I learnt
The soothest shepherd that e'er piped on plains.

*808–9. lees . . . blood*] Cp. Nashe, *Terrors of Night* (*Works* ed. R. B. McKerrow
(1904–10) i 354–7): 'The grossest part of our blood is the melancholy
humour, which . . . sinketh downe to the bottome like the lees of wine, and
that corrupteth all the blood, and is the causer of lunacie', and Sylvester
(Du Bartas 26): 'The pure red part, amid the Mass of Blood, / The Sanguine
Aire commands: the clutted mud, / Sunk down in Lees, Earths Melan-
choly showes.'     *settlings*] *Bridg.*: settling.
*812–3. Trin. MS* stage direction reads: 'The brothers rush in strike his glass
down the *monsters* shapes make as though they would resist but are all
driven in. Daemon enter with them.' *Bridg.* stage direction is the same as
the printed version except that for 'glass' *Bridg.* reads 'glass of liquor'
and for 'The Attendant Spirit comes in', 'the Demon is to come in with the
brothers'.
*813. you let*] *Bridg.*: ye left.     *scape*] *Trin. MS*: pass 'scape'.
*815. rod*] *Trin. MS*: *art* 'rod'.     *reversed*] Echoes Sandys[3] 462, where Ovid,
*Met.* xiv 300 is translated 'her rod reverst', and 481, where it is explained
'as Circe's rod, waved over their heads from the right side to the left: pre-
sents those false and sinister persuasions of pleasure, which so much de-
forms them: so the reversion thereof, by discipline, and a view of their owne
deformity, restores them to their former beauties'. Cp. also Spenser, *F.Q.*
III xii 36, where, compelled by Britomart, Busirane 'gan streight to over-
looke / Those cursed leaves, his charmes backe to reverse'.
*817. sits*] *Trin. MS*: *remains* 'sits'.
*820. Some . . . which*] *Trin. MS*: *There is another way* 'Some other means I
have' that. *Bridg.*: Some other means I have that.
*821. Meliboeus*] Tityrus and Meliboeus are the characters in Virgil, *Ecl.* i.

There is a gentle nymph not far from hence,
That with moist curb sways the smooth Severn stream,
825  Sabrina is her name, a virgin pure,
Whilom she was the daughter of Locrine,
That had the sceptre from his father Brute.
The guiltless damsel flying the mad pursuit
Of her enraged stepdame Guendolen,
830  Commended her fair innocence to the flood
That stayed her flight with his cross-flowing course,
The water-nymphs that in the bottom played,
Held up their pearled wrists and took her in,
Bearing her straight to aged Nereus' hall,
835  Who piteous of her woes, reared her lank head,
And gave her to his daughters to imbathe
In nectared lavers strewed with asphodel,
And through the porch and inlet of each sense

Tityrus is Spenser's name for Chaucer (*Shep. Cal.* February 92), and pro-
bably as J. F. Bense, *Neophilologus* i (1916) 62–4, suggests, Meliboeus is
M.'s name for Spenser, who tells the story of Sabrina *F.Q.* II x.

*825. pure*] *Trin. MS: goddess chaste pure.*

*825–30.* R. Blenner-Hasset, *MLN* lxiv (1949) 315–8, notes that, in Geoffrey
of Monmouth, Guendolen is not Sabrina's 'stepdame': she is the first wife
of Locrine (son of Brutus, the Trojan founder of Britain), and Locrine leaves
her for Astrild, by whom he became Sabrina's father. Guendolen defeats
Locrine and has both Astrild and her daughter drowned: M.'s implication
that Sabrina threw herself into the river finds no support in Geoffrey.
M.'s account of the story in his *History of Britain* (Columbia x 15–6) does not,
however, deviate from Geoffrey's, nor does Spenser's (*F.Q.* II x 17–9),
except that in Spenser Astrild (Estrild) is killed outright and only Sabrina
thrown into the river. Drayton, *Polyolbion* vi 130–78, also follows Geoffrey.

*827. That*] *Bridg.*: Who.

*830. flood*] *Trin. MS: flood* 'stream' 'flood'.

*833. pearled . . . took*] *Trin. MS: white* 'pearled' wrists *to receive* 'and carry'
'take' 'took'. The nymphs in Jonson, *Masque of Blackness* 76–8 wear 'on
front, eare, neck, and wrists . . . ornament . . . of the most choise and orient
pearle', and Drayton, *Polyolbion* v 16–7, personifying the Severn as Sabrina,
says 'And where she meant to goe / The path was strew'd with Pearle.'

*834. Bearing . . . straight*] *Trin. MS: And bore* 'Bearing' her 'straight'.

*836. daughters*] Cp. the nymphs who dress Marinell's wound, Spenser, *F.Q.*
III iv 40: 'They pourd in soveraine balme and Nectar good.'

*837. lavers*] basins.    *asphodel*] the immortal flower which covers the
meadows of the Elysian fields in Homer, *Od.* xi 539.

*838. porch*] Echoes *Hamlet* I v 63–4: 'And in the porches of mine ears did
pour / The leperous distilment.'

Dropped in ambrosial oils till she revived,
840 And underwent a quick immortal change
Made goddess of the river; still she retains
Her maiden gentleness, and oft at eve
Visits the herds along the twilight meadows,
Helping all urchin blasts, and ill-luck signs
845 That the shrewd meddling elf delights to make,
Which she with precious vialed liquors heals.
For which the shepherds at their festivals
Carol her goodness loud in rustic lays,
And throw sweet garland wreaths into her stream
850 Of pansies, pinks, and gaudy daffodils.
And, as the old swain said, she can unlock
The clasping charm, and thaw the numbing spell,
If she be right invoked in warbled song,
For maidenhood she loves, and will be swift
855 To aid a virgin such as was herself
In hard-besetting need, this will I try,
And add the power of some adjuring verse.

*839. ambrosial oils*] Cp. Homer, *Il.* xxiii 186–7, where Aphrodite anoints
Hector's body with 'oil, rose-sweet, ambrosial', to protect it.
*840–1.* L. Bradner, *Musae Anglicanae* (New York 1940) pp. 38–9, thinks
that Sabrina's metamorphosis into a goddess was suggested to M. by Giles
Fletcher, *De literis antiquae Britanniae* (1633).
*844. urchin blasts*] A 'blast' is a sudden infection, and since 'urchin' can mean
'a roguish or mischievous youngster', the meaning here may be 'mis-
chievous': but Scot, *Discovery of Witchcraft* vii 15, gives 'urchins' in a cata-
logue with 'spirits, witches . . . elves, hags, fairies' and other 'bugs'. Cp.
*Tempest* II ii 3–5: 'spirits . . . urchin-shows.'
*845. make*] *Trin. MS*: *leave* `makes'.
*845–6. Trin. MS* inserts between these lines: 'And often takes our cattle with
strange pinches'.
*846. Bridg.* omits.
*848. rustic*] *Trin. MS*: *lovely* `rustic'.
*850. Trin. MS*: Of pansies *and of* `pinks and' *bonny* `gaudy' daffodils.
*851. old swain*] Meliboeus.
*852. Trin. MS*: *Each* `The' clasping charm and *secret holding spell* `melt
each' `thaw the' numbing spell.
*856. In . . . need*] *Trin. MS*: *In honoured virtue's cause* `In hard distressed
need'.
*857. power . . . adjuring*] *Trin. MS*: *power* `call' `power' of some *strong*
`adjuring'.

### SONG

Sabrina fair
Listen where thou art sitting
860      Under the glassy, cool, translucent wave,
In twisted braids of lilies knitting
The loose train of thy amber-dropping hair,
Listen for dear honour's sake,
Goddess of the silver lake,
865             Listen and save.

Listen and appear to us
In name of great Oceanus,
By the earth-shaking Neptune's mace,
And Tethys' grave majestic pace,
870    By hoary Nereus' wrinkled look,
And the Carpathian wizard's hook,
By scaly Triton's winding shell,
And old soothsaying Glaucus' spell,
By Leucothea's lovely hands,

---

*859. where . . . sitting*] *Trin. MS*: *virgin* where thou *sitt'st* 'art sitting'.

*862. amber-dropping*] dropping ambergris: cp. Sylvester (Du Bartas[2] 1204): 'Locks like streames of liquid Amber.' E. M. Clark *SP* lvi (1959) 626–42 notes Sabrina's 'lockes of amber' in Wither, *Epithalamia*. verse to sing or not'.

*867. Oceanus*] See l. 97n.

*868. earth-shaking*] Homer, *Il.* ix 183 describes Poseidon as 'the god that holds the earth and shakes it'.

*868–73.* In *Trin. MS* these lines are a marginal insertion.

*869. Tethys*] wife of Oceanus: Hesiod, *Theog.* 368, calls her πότνια (queenly, reverend).

*870. Nereus*] father of Nereids (sea nymphs): Virgil, *Georg.* iv 392 calls him *grandaevus*. *Bridg.* gives 'El. bro.' (Elder Brother) as speaker at beginning of l. 870, '2. bro.' (Second Brother) at l. 872, 'El. bro.' at l. 874, '2. bro.' at l. 876, 'El. bro.' at l. 878 and 'De.' (Daemon) at l. 882.

*871. Carpathian wizard*] Proteus: according to Virgil, *Georg.* iv 387 he lives in the Carpathian sea, and is a *vates* (seer). He has a 'hook' (shepherd's crook) because he is the shepherd of Poseidon's seals in *Od.* iv 411–3: he could change his shape and was 'skilled in wizard arts', *Od.* iv 460.

*872. Triton*] Ovid, *Met.* i. 330–8, depicts him as Neptune's herald, blowing through a huge conch-shell.

*873. soothsaying Glaucus*] Echoes Spenser, *F.Q.* IV xi 13: 'Glaucus, that wise southsayes understood.' Glaucus tells Scylla of his metamorphosis from mortal to sea god and of his reception by Oceanus and Tethys in Ovid, *Met.* xiii 917–65.

*874. Leucothea*] 'The bright goddess', rises 'from the deep like a sea-mew on

875 And her son that rules the strands,
By Thetis' tinsel-slippered feet,
And the songs of Sirens sweet,
By dead Parthenope's dear tomb,
And fair Ligea's golden comb,
880 Wherewith she sits on diamond rocks
Sleeking her soft alluring locks,
By all the nymphs that nightly dance
Upon thy streams with wily glance,
Rise, rise, and heave thy rosy head
885 From thy coral-paven bed,
And bridle in thy headlong wave,
Till thou our summons answered have.

Listen and save.

*Sabrina rises, attended by water-nymphs, and sings.*

By the rushy-fringed bank,
890 Where grows the willow and the osier dank,
My sliding chariot stays,
Thick set with agate, and the azurn sheen
Of turkis blue, and emerald green
That in the channel strays,

the wing' and gives Odysseus a veil which saves him when 'earth-shaking' Poseidon shatters his raft. When he gets ashore he throws the veil back into the water, and Leucothea receives it in her hands, *Od.* v 333–462.

*875. her son*] Melicertes. Sailors, safe in port, 'pay their vows on the shore' to him in Virgil, *Georg.* i 436–7.

*876. Thetis*] One of the Nereids: wife of Peleus and mother of Achilles. Homer, *Il.* xviii 127, calls her 'silver-footed'.

*878. Parthenope*] One of the sirens. Strabo I ii 13 refers to her monument near Naples.

*878–81.* In *Trin. MS* these lines are deleted.

*879. Ligea*] The other siren: her name means 'shrill-voiced'. Her 'shining tresses float over her snowy neck' in Virgil, *Georg.* iv 336.

*882. that*] *Bridg.*: of.

*882–3.* In *Trin. MS* these lines are a marginal insertion.

*885. coral-paven*] *Trin. MS*: coral-paved 'n'.

*891.* 'As an immortal she is, of course, fragile to the point of weightlessness. Thus her "sliding chariot" is simply the water, and "stays", waits for her, beside the bank, only in the paradoxical sense that there is always the flowing water there. The jewels that adorn it are only the names of gems applied to the colours of the water' (Brooks and Hardy 225).

*892. azurn*] azure: a Miltonic coinage (*OED* records no other example). *Bridg.*: azur'd.

*894. Trin. MS*: *That my rich wheels inlays.* [After deletion, present version substituted].

895    Whilst from off the waters fleet
        Thus I set my printless feet
        O'er the cowslip's velvet head,
           That bends not as I tread,
        Gentle swain at thy request
900           I am here.
        *Spir.* Goddess dear
        We implore thy powerful hand
        To undo the charmed band
        Of true virgin here distressed,
905    Through the force, and through the wile
        Of unblessed enchanter vile.
        *Sabr.* Shepherd 'tis my office best
        To help ensnared chastity;
        Brightest Lady look on me,
910    Thus I sprinkle on thy breast
        Drops that from my fountain pure,
        I have kept of precious cure,
        Thrice upon thy finger's tip,
        Thrice upon thy rubied lip,
915    Next this marble venomed seat
        Smeared with gums of glutinous heat
        I touch with chaste palms moist and cold,
        Now the spell hath lost his hold;
        And I must haste ere morning hour
920    To wait in Amphitrite's bower.

    *Sabrina descends, and the Lady rises out of her seat.*

    *Spir.* Virgin, daughter of Locrine,
    Sprung of old Anchises' line

896. *set*] *Bridg.*: rest.    *printless feet*] Echoes *Tempest* V i 34: 'printless foot'.

897. *velvet*] *Bridg.* omits.

898. *bends not*] *Trin. MS*: bends 'not'. M. recalls Virgil's Camilla, *Aen.* vii 808–11: 'She might have sped over the topmost blades of unmown corn, nor in her course bruised the tender ears.'

899. *request*] *Trin. MS*: behe request.

903. *charmed*] *Trin. MS*: *mag* charmed.

906. *enchanter*] *Bridg.*: enchanters.

909. *Brightest*] *Trin. MS*: *Virtuous* 'Brightest'.

910. *thy*] *Bridg.*: this.

916. *glutinous*] sticky, gluey.

920. *Trin. MS*: To wait o'i'n Amphitrite''s' *in her* bower. Amphitrite was wife to Neptune.

922. *Anchises' line*] The legendary Trojan kings of Britain descended from

      May thy brimmed waves for this
      Their full tribute never miss
925  From a thousand petty rills,
      That tumble down the snowy hills;
      Summer drouth, or singed air
      Never scorch thy tresses fair,
      Nor wet October's torrent flood
930  Thy molten crystal fill with mud,
      May thy billows roll ashore
      The beryl, and the golden ore,
      May thy lofty head be crowned
      With many a tower and terrace round,
935  And here and there thy banks upon
      With groves of myrrh, and cinnamon.
      Come Lady while heaven lends us grace,
      Let us fly this cursed place,
      Lest the sorcerer us entice
940  With some other new device.
      Not a waste or needless sound
      Till we come to holier ground,
      I shall be your faithful guide
      Through this gloomy covert wide,
945  And not many furlongs thence
      Is your father's residence,
      Where this night are met in state
      Many a friend to gratulate
      His wish'd presence, and beside
950  All the swains that there abide,
      With jigs, and rural dance resort,
      We shall catch them at their sport,
      And our sudden coming there
      Will double all their mirth and cheer;

Anchises, father of Aeneas (Anchises–Aeneas–Ascanius–Silvius –Brutus–Locrine).

923. *brimmed*] *Trin. MS: crystal* 'brimmed'.

926. *the*] *Trin. MS: from* 'the'.

936. *Trin. MS* and *Bridg.* insert stage-direction: 'Song ends'.

937. *Come Lady*] *Bridg.*: El. bro.: Come *Lady* 'sister'.

943. *Bridg.* inserts speaker at beginning of line: 'De.' (Daemon).

947. *met*] *Trin. MS: come* 'met'.

950. *there*] *Trin. MS* and *Bridg.*: near.

952. *their*] *Bridg.*: this.

955   Come let us haste, the stars grow high,
      But night sits monarch yet in the mid sky.

*The scene changes, presenting Ludlow Town and the President's Castle; then come in Country Dancers, after them the Attendant Spirit, with the two Brothers and the Lady.*

### SONG

*Spir.* Back, shepherds, back, enough your play,
      Till next sunshine holiday,
      Here be without duck or nod
960   Other trippings to be trod
      Of lighter toes, and such court guise
      As Mercury did first devise
      With the mincing Dryades
      On the lawns, and on the leas.

*This second song presents them to their father and mother.*

965   Noble Lord, and Lady bright,
      I have brought ye new delight,
      Here behold so goodly grown
      Three fair branches of your own,
      Heaven hath timely tried their youth,
970   Their faith, their patience, and their truth,

955. *Bridg.* inserts speaker at beginning of line: 'El. bro.'      *grow*] *Trin. MS: are* 'grow'. *Bridg.*: are.
956. *sits*] *Trin. MS*: reigns sits.
956-7. In *Trin. MS* stage direction reads: 'Exeunt / The scene changes and then is presented Ludlow town / and the president's castle then enter country dances and such / like gambols etc. / *After* 'At' those sports the Daemon with the 2. bro. and the Lady enter / the Daemon sings'. In *Bridg.* 'The scene changes then is presented Ludlow town / and the President's Castle, then come in Country / dances, and the like etc., towards the end of these / sports the demon with the 2 brothers and the / lady come in. The spirit sings.'
958. *sunshine holiday*] Cp. *L'Allegro* 98.
961. *Trin. MS*: Of *speedier* 'nimbler' 'of lighter' toeing's', and *courtly* 'such neat' guise Of lighter toes, and such court guise.
962. *Trin. MS*: *Such as Hermes* 'Mercury' did 'first' devise. Cp. Jonson *Pan's Anniversary* 176-8: 'The best of Leaders, Pan, / That leads the Naiads, and the Dryads forth; / And to their daunces more then Hermes can.'
963. *Dryades*] wood nymphs.
969. *timely*] early.
970. *patience*] *Trin. MS: patience* 'temperance' patience.

And sent them here through hard assays
With a crown of deathless praise,
To triumph in victorious dance
O'er sensual folly, and intemperance.

*The dances ended, the Spirit epiloguizes.*

975    *Spir.* To the ocean now I fly,
      And those happy climes that lie
      Where day never shuts his eye,
      Up in the broad fields of the sky:
      There I suck the liquid air
980    All amidst the gardens fair

972. *With*] *Trin. MS: To* 'With'.    *praise*] *Trin. MS: bays* 'praise'.

974-5. In *Trin. MS* the stage direction reads: 'They dance. The dances all ended / the Daemon sings. or says'. The last two words seem to be a later insertion. *Bridg.* has the same stage direction, but with no point after 'sings'.

975-8. See ll. 1-6n, and l. 97n. The daemon flies to the 'moon' (l. 1016)– his dwelling place, according to Plutarch–where day does not 'shut his eye' because, except at times of eclipse, it is 'beyond the range of the earth's shadow' (*Moralia* 942F). The 'ocean' is not only that of the old cosmology (see ll. 980-1n) but also that which in Timarchus' vision 'drifts round smoothly and evenly in a circle' with 'islands illuminated by one another with soft fire' (590C-D)–this ocean is the celestial sphere; the islands, stars and planets.

975-1010. *Bridg.* omits (but see l. 1n).

975-1022. *Trin. MS* has two versions of these lines. The first, referred to in the following notes as *Trin. MS (a)*, is crossed through and the second, referred to as *Trin. MS (b)*, is substituted on a separate sheet.

978. Cp. Virgil, *Aen.* vi 887 *aeris in campis latis.*    *broad*] *Trin. MS (a)*: *plain* 'broad'.

978-9. *Trin. MS (a)* inserts: *Far beyond the earth's end / Where the welkin clear* 'low' *doth bend*.

979. *liquid*] clear, bright: cp. ll. 1-6n.

980-1. According to Plutarch, *Moralia* 944C, 'the Elysian plain is the part of the moon which is turned towards Heaven', and as D. T. Starnes points out, *UTSE* xxxi (1952) 44, the identification of Elysium with the Gardens of Hesperus, though not made in antiquity, is suggested in Stephanus and Conti (cp. 'Elysian dew' 995). J. Arthos, *MLN* lxxvi (1961) 321-4, adds that Ficino, *In decimum dialogum de Iusto*, distinguishes between two Elysian fields: one corresponding to Plato's 'true earth' (see ll. 1-6n), the other to the eighth sphere.

Hesiod, *Theog.* 215, says that the Hesperides 'tend the fair golden apples beyond glorious Okeanos'. R. Eisler, *TLS* (14 Sep. 1945) 451, notes that the *Scholia Basiliensia* (1542, reprinted in the Heinsius edition of Hesiod, 1603) explain these golden apples as the stars which Herakles, the rising sun,

> Of Hesperus, and his daughters three
> That sing about the golden tree:
> Along the crisped shades and bowers
> Revels the spruce and jocund Spring,
> 985    The Graces, and the rosy-bosomed Hours,
> Thither all their bounties bring,
> That there eternal summer dwells,
> And west winds, with musky wing
> About the cedarn alleys fling
> 990    Nard, and cassia's balmy smells.
> Iris there with humid bow,
> Waters the odorous banks that blow
> Flowers of more mingled hue
> Than her purfled scarf can shew,
> 995    And drenches with Elysian dew
> (List mortals if your ears be true)

plucks in that he makes them disappear. Perhaps it was this idea which suggested to M. the fusion of the Gardens of Hesperus, which were according to Pliny islands surrounded by ocean, with the less earthbound Elysian plain of Plutarch: Stephanus and Conti would then provide corroboration. Starnes and Talbert 312–13 have demonstrated that many of M.'s details–the 'liquid air', the fragrant west wind, the flowers, especially hyacinths and roses, and the presence of Venus–strongly suggest his recollection of Conti's chapter on the Elysian fields.

*981. Trin.* MS (*a*): Of *Atlas* 'Hesperus' and his DAUGHTERS 'nieces' three.

*982. Trin.* MS (*b*): *Where grows the right-born gold upon his native tree* [after deletion the present version, already present in *Trin.* MS (*a*), is substitued].

*983. crisped*] curled.

*983–7. Along . . . That*] *Trin.* MS (*a*) omits.

*985. Hours*] See *Prae E* 39–40n (p. 25).

*988. musky*] smelling of musk.

*989. cedarn*] *Trin.* MS (*a*): *myrtle* 'cedarn' (no previous occurrence of 'cedarn' is recorded in *OED*).

*990. Trin.MS* (*a*): *Balm* 'Nard', and cassia's *fragrant* 'balmy' smells.    *Nard*] spikenard, an aromatic plant.    *cassia*] a bark resembling cinnamon, but less aromatic.

*991. Iris*] the rainbow.    *humid*] *Trin.* MS (*a*): *garnished* 'garish' 'humid'.

*994. purfled*] *Trin.* MS (*a*): *watchet* 'purfled'. By the seventeenth century 'purfled', which meant originally 'having a decorated border', could mean 'variegated'.

*994–5*. Between these lines *Trin.* MS (*a*) and (*b*) insert: Yellow, watchet, green and blue [in (*b*) this is later deleted].

*995. with . . . dew*] *Trin.* MS (*a*): oft with manna dew. *Trin.* MS (*b*): with *Sabaean* 'Elysian' dew.    *Elysian*] See ll. 980–1n.

*996*. This warning that the following lines are not to be taken as mere

Beds of hyacinth, and roses,
Where young Adonis oft reposes,
Waxing well of his deep wound
*1000*    In slumber soft, and on the ground
Sadly sits the Assyrian queen;
But far above in spangled sheen

mythological decoration is a marginal insertion in *Trin. MS (b)*, omitted
from *Trin. MS (a)*.

*998. young . . . oft*] *Trin. MS (a)*: many a cherub soft.

*998–1001.* Venus and Adonis are types of natural love. Conti v 16 identifies
Adonis (the author and nourisher of all seeds) with the sun (as does the Or-
phic *Hymn to Adonis*, from which Conti quotes), and the boar with winter.
Sandys 209 repeats these identifications, and identifies Venus with the earth
which mourns for the sun's absence and is 'recreated againe by his approach,
and procreative vertue'. Spenser's Garden of Adonis, where the wounded
Adonis lies, is on earth (*F.Q.* III vi 29), and is 'the first seminarie / Of all
things that are borne to live and die' (III vi 30). But M.'s Venus and Adonis
lie in the Elysian fields of the moon (see ll. 980–1*n*): there, as daemons, they
are in a transitional state (see ll. 1–6*n*.): they await the separation of soul and
mind, when mind will finally return to its source, the sun 'through which
shines forth manifest the desirable and fair and divine', Plutach, *Moralia*
943E. This sun is to be distinguished from that of mere earthly fruitfulness,
which Adonis represents. Plutarch 945A points out that the separation of
mind and soul, and final release of the mind, is quickly achieved by 'tem-
perate' and philosophical souls, but those which have been very attached to
earthly pursuits have to wait on the moon for a long time before release
is attained. Their state is not 'blessed or divine' until this 'second death'
(942F). Thus Adonis, as a type of earthly love, takes time to recover from
his 'wound'.

*999–1011. Waxing . . . But*] *Trin. MS (a)* omits.

*1001. Assyrian queen*] Venus: Pausanias I xiv 6 says she was first worshipped
by the Assyrians.

*1002. spangled sheen*] Echoes *Midsummer Night's Dream*, II i 29: 'spangled
starlight sheen'.

*1002–4.* Spenser's Cupid and Psyche play in the Garden of Adonis (on
earth), and have a daughter, Pleasure (*F.Q.* III vi 50). In Apuleius, *Met.*
vi 23–4, however, Jove has Psyche brought up to heaven by Mercury,
makes her immortal with a draught of ambrosia, and holds a great wedding
feast for her and Cupid, at which the Hours deck the place with roses and
the Graces throw balm around (cp. ll. 985, 990). In due time Psyche has a
child, *Voluptas*. Boccaccio, *Gen. Deor.* v 22, paraphrases Apuleius and
develops the allegory: Psyche, he explains, represents the soul, and joined
to her is that which preserves the rational element (pure Love). She passes
through trials and 'at length she regains the enjoyment of divine bliss and
contemplation and is joined to her lover for ever . . . from this love is born

Celestial Cupid her famed son advanced,
Holds his dear Psyche sweet entranced
1005 After her wandering labours long,
Till free consent the gods among
Make her his eternal bride,
And from her fair unspotted side
Two blissful twins are to be born,
1010 Youth and Joy; so Jove hath sworn.
  But now my task is smoothly done,
I can fly, or I can run
Quickly to the green earth's end,
Where the bowed welkin slow doth bend,
1015 And from thence can soar as soon
To the corners of the moon.
  Mortals that would follow me,
Love Virtue, she alone is free,
She can teach ye how to climb

Pleasure, which is eternal bliss and joy'. M.'s allegory is near to Boccac-
cio's: Psyche has attained that release which Venus and Adonis still await.
1003. *Celestial Cupid*] Cp. *Dam* 191*n*, p. 277 below. In so far as he
represents Christ he is the 'son' of Venus (earth) in that he is Son of Man.
*advanced*] raised, elevated.
1007. *eternal bride*] Cp. *Rev*. xxi 9: 'I will shew thee the bride, the Lamb's
wife.'
1010. *Youth and Joy*] not Pleasure (see ll. 1002–4*n*); perhaps there is a refer-
ence to *Rev*. xxi 1: 'a new Heaven and a new Earth'; and xxi 4: 'God shall
wipe away all tears from their eyes; and there shall be no more death,
neither sorrow, nor crying.' Thus Youth (newness) and Joy will be pro-
duced. M. concludes the first book of his *De doctrina* (Columbia xvi 379)
with a citation of these texts and the comment: 'Our glorification will be
accompanied by the renovation of heaven and earth, and of all things
therein adapted to our service or delight.'
1011. *But now*] *Trin. MS* (*a*) and *Bridg.*: Now.    *task . . . done*] *Trin. MS*
(*a*): *message well 'business' 'task' is 'smoothly' done.*
1012–3. Cp. *Midsummer Night's Dream* IV i 102–3: 'We the globe can com-
pass soon, / Swifter than the wandering moon.'
1013. *green earth's*] *Trin. MS* (*a*): *earth's* green 'earth's' *Bridg.*: earth's
green.
1014. *bowed welkin*] the curved vault of the sky.
1016. *corners of the moon*] Echoes *Macbeth* III v 24: 'Upon the corner of the
moon.' 'Corner' means 'horn' (Latin *cornu*).
1017–8. Cp. Plutarch, *Moralia* 942F: 'To this point [the moon] rises no
one who is evil or unclean.'
1019. *ye*] *Bridg.*: you.
1019–20. *sphery chime*] the music of the spheres: see *Ad Pat* 35–7*n* (p. 150).

*1020*   Higher than the sphery chime;
        Or if Virtue feeble were,
        Heaven itself would stoop to her.

# 51 Psalm cxiv

*Date.* Nov. 1634. In a Latin letter to Alexander Gill dated 4 Dec. 1634,
M. says that he is sending in return for some verses of Gill's 'what is not
really mine, but belongs just as much to the truly divine poet. Last week
I adapted this song (*hanc Oden*) of his to the rule of Greek heroic verse. I did
so with no deliberate intention certainly, but acted upon some sudden
impulse. I wrote it before daybreak, while I was still practically in bed'
(Columbia xii 14–17, Yale i 321–2). If, as seems likely, this 'song' is *Psalm
cxiv* it must have been written at the end of Nov. 1634. In the letter to Gill
M., apologising for any shortcomings, explains 'this is the first and only
thing I have composed in Greek since I left your school'.
*Publication.* 1645 and 1673 (no significant variants: 1673 misprints in the
following    instances:   2. Αἰγύπτιον]Αἰγυπτον    15. σκαρθμοῖσιν]
σκαφμοῖσιν   16. σφριγόωντες]σφριγόωντης   18. μητέρι]μητήρι).
Sometimes in 1645, and often in 1673, accents and breathings are misplaced
or missing. The present text silently supplies and corrects these. Columbia
i 590 conjectures that 'the confusion of 1673 resulted when it was attempted
to move the breathings and accents to the beginnings of some of the capital
letters, which had been after those letters in 1645, and to correct the other-
wise badly printed Greek text of 1645. The printer was evidently worse
confused than ever by the corrections, and the result an even worse version
than the uncorrected copy'.

> Ἰσραὴλ ὅτε παῖδες, ὅτ' ἀγλαὰ φῦλ' Ἰακώβου
> Αἰγύπτιον λίπε δῆμον, ἀπεχθέα, βαρβαρόφωνον,
> Δὴ τότε μοῦνον ἔην ὅσιον γένος υἱες Ἰούδα·
> Ἐν δὲ θεὸς λαοῖσι μέγα κρείων βασίλευεν.

*1021–2.* Perhaps echoing Marlowe, *Hero and Leander* i 365–6: 'hands so
pure, so innocent ... might have made Heaven stoop'; cp. Plutarch,
*Moralia* 593F–594A: 'But when in the course of countless births a soul has
stoutly and resolutely sustained a long series of struggles, and as her cycle
draws to a close, she approaches the upper world, bathed in sweat, in immi-
nent peril and straining every nerve to reach the shore, God holds it no sin
for her daemon to go to her rescue, but lets whoever will lend aid.' M.
wrote these two lines in Camillo Cardoyn's album when he was at Geneva
10 Jun. 1639 (French i 419).
*1022. stoop*] *Trin. MS (a):* bow 'stoop'.

5 Εἶδε καὶ ἐντροπάδην φύγαδ' ἐρρώησε θάλασσα
Κύματι εἰλυμένη ῥοθίῳ, ὁ δ' ἄρ' ἐστυφελίχθη
Ἱρὸς Ἰορδάνης ποτὶ ἀργυροειδέα πηγήν.
Ἐκ δ' ὄρεα σκαρθμοῖσιν ἀπειρέσια κλονέοντο,
Ὡς κριοὶ σφριγόωντες ἐϋτραφερῷ ἐν ἀλωῇ.
10 Βαιότεραι δ' ἅμα πᾶσαι ἀνασκίρτησαν ἐρίπναι,
Οἷα παραὶ σύριγγι φίλῃ ὑπὸ μητέρι ἄρνες.
Τίπτε σύγ' αἰνὰ θάλασσα πέλωρ φύγαδ' ἐρρώησας;
Κύματι εἰλυμένη ῥοθίῳ; τί δ' ἄρ' ἐστυφελίχθης
Ἱρὸς Ἰορδάνη ποτὶ ἀργυροειδέα πηγήν;
15 Τίπτ' ὄρεα σκαρθμοῖσιν ἀπειρέσια κλονέεσθε
Ὡς κριοὶ σφριγόωντες ἐϋτραφερῷ ἐν ἀλωῇ;
Βαιότεραι τί δ' ἄρ' ὔμμες ἀνασκιρτήσατ' ἐρίπναι,
Οἷα παραὶ σύριγγι φίλῃ ὑπὸ μητέρι ἄρνες,
Σείεο γαῖα τρέουσα θεὸν μεγάλ' ἐκτυπέοντα
20 Γαῖα θεὸν τρείουσ' ὕπατον σέβας Ἰσσακίδαο
Ὅς τε καὶ ἐκ σπιλάδων ποταμοὺς χέε μορμύροντας,
Κρήνην τ' ἀέναον πέτρης ἀπὸ δακρυοέσσης.

When the children of Israel, when the glorious tribes of Jacob left the land of Egypt, hateful, barbarous in speech, then indeed were the sons of Judah the one devout race; and God ruled in great might among the peoples. The sea saw, and rushed in headlong flight, wrapped in surging waves; and holy Jordan was thrust back towards its silvery source. The topless mountains came forth and tumbled together, leaping like lusty rams in a rich pasture. And all the smaller crags skipped with them, like lambs beneath their dear mother at the sound of the pipe. Why, O huge sea, did you rush terribly in flight, wrapped in surging waves? And why, holy Jordan, were you thrust back towards your silvery source? Why, topless mountains, did you tumble together leaping, like lusty rams in a rich pasture? And why, you smaller

¶ 51. 5. ἐντροπάδην] not found in surviving Gk literature. M. was probably thinking of προτροπάδην ('headlong'). ἐρρώησε] there is no such form: M. presumably confused ἠρώησε and ἐρρώσατο (both = 'rushed').

9. ἐϋτραφερῷ ἐν ἀλωῇ] M. evidently means 'in rich pasture'; but ἀλωή should be cultivated ground (vineyard, orchard, garden), or a threshing-floor, and there is no such word as ἐϋτραφερός. Apparently a half-memory of Hesiod's ἐϋτροχάλῳ ἐν ἀλωῇ ('on a rounded threshing-floor') confused with εὐτραφής ('thriving, nourishing') and perhaps with τραφερός (used by Theocritus as 'well-fed, fat').

12. πέλωρ] A noun ('monster'), used by M. as if it were the adjective πελώριος, πέλωρος ('monstrous, huge').

19. μεγάλ' ἐκτυπέοντα] An error for μεγάλα κτυπέοντα. The participle has κτ- not ἐκτ-; M. wrote ἐκτ- under the influence of the indicative form μεγάλ' ἔκτυπε ('thundered loudly'), three times in Homer.

crags, did you skip like lambs beneath their dear mother at the sound of the
pipe? Shake, earth, in fear of God who thunders loud; shake, earth, in fear
of the high majesty revered of the son of Isaac; who pours forth sounding
torrents from the crags, and an everflowing spring from a weeping rock.


## 52 *Haec ego mente . . .*

### [A postscript to his love poems]

*Date.* 1635? These verses were appended to *Elegia VII* in *1645* (see headnote
to that poem, p. 69 above). They must therefore be post-1628. There is no
other evidence for dating. It is possible that they were composed as early as
*Elegia VI*. Bateson 161 argues that the force of *olim* (*1*) puts them at least as
late as 1635: he views them as 'perhaps the most repellent product of that
social vacuum to which M. consigned himself in the reaction against
Cambridge'. Or it may be that M. did not write this retraction until he was
preparing to publish *1645* (entered on *Stationers' Register* 6 Oct. 1645):
the present tenses of the closing lines would come oddly from a married
man, however.
*Publication. 1645, 1673* (no significant variants: in *10 1673* misprints *ipse*
for *ipsa*).

> Haec ego mente olim laeva, studioque supino
>   Nequitiae posui vana trophaea meae.
> Scilicet abreptum sic me malus impulit error,
>   Indocilisque aetas prava magistra fuit.
> 5 Donec Socraticos umbrosa Academia rivos
>   Praebuit, admissum dedocuitque iugum.
> Protinus extinctis ex illo tempore flammis,
>   Cincta rigent multo pectora nostra gelu.
> Unde suis frigus metuit puer ipse sagittis,
> *10*  Et Diomedeam vim timet ipsa Venus.

These lines are the trifling memorials of my levity which, with a warped
mind and a base spirit, I once raised. This, in fact, is how mischievous error
seduced me and drove me on: my ignorant youth was a vicious teacher, until
the shady Academy offered me its Socratic streams,[5] and taught me to

¶ 52. *5.* Cp. *Apology* (1642): 'Thus from the Laureat fraternity of Poets,
riper yeares, and the ceaselesse round of study and reading led me to
the shady spaces of philosophy, but chiefly to the divine volumes of *Plato*'
(Columbia iii 305, Yale i 891).
*10.* In Homer, *Il.* v 330–51 Diomedes chases Venus, who is trying to protect
Aeneas, and wounds her in the wrist.

unloose the yoke to which I had submitted. From that moment onward the
flames were quenched. My heart is frozen solid, packed around with thick
ice; so that even the boy himself is afraid to let the frost get at his arrows,
and Venus fears the strength of a Diomedes.[10]

# 53 Lycidas

*Date.* Nov. 1637. Edward King, a Fellow of Christ's, was drowned 10 Aug.
1637. In the Trinity MS *Lycidas* is headed 'Novemb: 1637'. A volume of
memorial verses by King's Cambridge acquaintances appeared in 1638, of
which the first part is entitled *Justa Eduardo King naufrago, ab Amicis moeren-
tibus amoris & μνείας χάριν* (Obsequies for Edward King, lost at sea, writ-
ten by his sorrowful friends in love and remembrance) and contains
twenty-three pieces of Greek and Latin verse: the second part, *Obsequies
to the memory of Mr Edward King,* contains thirteen English poems, of which
M.'s (signed J.M.) is the last and longest. The motto for the volume, from
Petronius, reads *Si recte calculum ponas, ubique naufragium est* (If you reckon
rightly, shipwreck is everywhere). The Latin preface explains that King's
ship struck a rock not far from the British coast and that, while other
passengers endeavoured to save their lives, King knelt in prayer on the
deck and went down with the ship. According to Edward Phillips 'a
particular friendship and intimacy' existed between M. and King (Dar-
bishire 54).
*Publication.* In *Obsequies to the memory of Mr Edward King* (1638). This text
differs from *1645* and *1673* chiefly in its placing of commas. It omits commas
after 'rude' (*4*), 'dear' (*6*), 'wind' (*13*), 'well' (*15*), 'turn' (*21*), 'mute'
(*32*), 'heel' (*34*), 'caves' (*39*), 'willows' (*42*), 'green' (*42*), 'seen' (*43*),
'flowers' (*47*), 'bards' (*53*), 'Druids' (*53*) (as *1645*, see below), 'roar' (*61*),
'eyes' (*81*), 'brine' (*98*), 'sake' (*114*), 'intrude' (*115*), 'list' (*123*), 'past'

¶ 53. *Title.* The name Lycidas appears in Theocritus vii (where he is 'best
of pipers') and xxvii, Bion ii and vi and Virgil, *Ecl.* vii and ix. E. A. Strath-
mann, *MLN* lii (1937) 398–400 points out that in Bathurst's translation of the
*Shepheardes Calender* Piers, the Protestant pastor of the May eclogue, is
called Lycidas. E. E. Duncan-Jones, *N & Q* cci (1956) 249, suggests that in
choosing the name M. was influenced by Lucan, *Pharsalia* iii 638–9, *Mersus
foret ille profundo / sed prohibent socii* (He would sink in the sea, but his
friends prevent it) which refers to a character called Lycidas. There is another
Lycidas, significantly described as not widely known (*vix urbe sua, vix colle
propinquo / cognitus*: known hardly by his own city, hardly by the neigh-
bouring hill) among the shepherds who bring gifts to Mary and her child
in Sannazaro, *De Partu Virginis* iii 185–93.

(*132*), 'use' (*136*), 'winds' (*137*), 'shores' (*154*), 'ore' (*170*), 'high' (*172*),
'above' (*178*), 'troops' (*179*), 'shore' (*183*) and 'woods' (*193*); and inserts
commas after 'more' (*1*), 'passes' (*21*), 'herself' (*59*) (as *1645*, see below),
'raise' (*70*), 'lives' (*81*), 'wings' (*93*), 'bark' (*100*), 'Return' (*132*), 'return'
(*133*), 'low' (*136*), 'violet' (*145*), 'Hebrides' (*156*) (as *1645*, see below),
'shepherds' (*165*), 'societies' (*179*), 'Now' (*181*) and 'Lycidas' (*181*).
The only other regular punctuation-variant is the printing of a semi-colon
where the later editions have a comma: after 'spring' (*16*), 'lies' (*80*),
'reeds' (*86*), 'story' (*95*), 'strayed' (*97*), 'more' (*165*), 'song' (*176*)
and 'grey' (*187*). The other variants from the present text are: *no
headnote* 9. Young Lycidas,](Young Lycidas!)    peer:]peer.    15. *no indentation in one surviving state of 1638, represented by British Museum copy 1077 d.*
51    17. string.]string:    18. excuse,]excuse.    24. flock;]flock,    rill.]
rill;    25. *no indentation*    26. opening]glimmering    30. star that
rose, at evening, bright]ev'n star bright    31. westering]burnisht    33.
flute,]flute:    36. Damaetas]Dametas    39. shepherd]shepherds    50.
*no indentation*    51. loved]lord (*corrected to* lov'd *in the Cambridge University Library copy* (*CUL*) *and British Museum copy C. 21. c. 42*(*BM*) *in a hand probably M.'s*)    53. your]the (*corrected to* your *in CUL and BM*)    59.
son]son?    64. *no indentation*    66. strictly]stridly    muse,]muse?
67. use]do (*corrected to* use *in CUL and BM*)    69. Or with]Hid in    Neaera's]Neera's    73. when]where    76. life.]life;    77. ears;]ears.    82.
Jove;]Jove:    85. *no indentation*    87. mood:]mood.    90. plea,]plea.
94. promontory;]promontory:    99. played.]played:    103. *no indentation*
Camus, reverend sire,]Chamus (reverend sire)    107. Ah;]Ah!    114.
Enow]Enough    118. guest;]guest.    129. nothing]little    said,]said.
131. smite no] smites no    153. surmise.]surmise;    157. whelming]
humming (*corrected to* whelming *in CUL and BM*)    163. ruth.]ruth,
167. floor,]floor:    177. *omitted, but written in the margin of CUL and BM*
192. blue:]blue, .Next printed *1645* (8. prime,]prime    30. bright,]bright
36. Damaetas]Damoetas    53. Druids,]Druids    59. herself]herself,
107. Ah;]Ah!    113. thee,]thee    swain,]swain.    118. guest;]guest.
142. dies,]dies.    156. Hebrides]Hebrides, ) and *1673* (the text followed here
except in *65* where *1673* misprints 'end' for 'tend', and in *142* and *173* where
*1673* prints a full stop after 'dies' and omits the semi-colon after 'waves').
*Versification and style. Lycidas* is made up of eleven verse paragraphs of
varying length and differing rhyme pattern. It includes ten unrhymed
lines (*1, 13, 15, 22, 39, 51, 82, 91, 118, 161*) and has fourteen six-syllable lines
mingled with its decasyllables, each usually rhyming with the decasyllable
immediately before it. The paragraph-lengths run: 14, 10, 12, 13, 14, 21,
18, 29, 33, 21, 8. It will be seen that only twice does a paragraph exceed
its predecessor by more than three or four lines. In the first instance the
reply of Phoebus (*76–84*) and in the second the denunciation of the clergy
by St Peter (*113–31*) is responsible for the elongation. These two preliminary resolutions are thus thrown into relief.
Though the structure of *Lycidas* cannot be exactly paralleled in Italian

literature, it is clearly an extension of M.'s experimentation with Italian verse forms in *Time* and *Solemn Music* (see p. 162 above). Prince 71–81 has drawn attention to the similarities with the *canzone*: the mixture of long and short lines, the conclusion of each paragraph with a couplet (as recommended by Dante in the *De Vulgari Eloquentia*), and the *ottava rima* of the final paragraph corresponding to the *commiato* of the *canzone*. He considers that M.'s adaptation of *canzone* features was influenced by the irregularly rhymed passages of lyric and dialogue in Tasso's *Aminta* and Guarini's *Pastor Fido;* also that *Lycidas* shares the technical aims of sixteenth-century Italian pastoral verse (as represented by the eclogues of Sannazaro and Berardino Rota), in attempting to evolve a poetic diction equivalent to that of Virgil, and to combine the tradition of the *canzone* with that of the classical eclogue. *Lycidas* has ten echoes of Virgil's *Eclogues*, ranging from scraps of phrasing to major associations of ideas (see footnotes). Though the *Lycidas* verse paragraph does not, like the *canzone* stanza, have a key line (*chiave*) which links the stanza's two halves by both introducing a new set of rhymes and rhyming with the last line of the first half, M. does use the *chiave* principle at several points (e.g. *17, 108, 136*) where a line which looks backwards for its rhyme looks forward, from the viewpoint of meaning, to a new set of ideas.

M.'s Spenserian pastoralism in *Lycidas* contrasts markedly with the 'metaphysical' diction and imagery of the other contributors to the 1638 volume. All but one of the poem's seven or eight echoes of Spenser are from the *Shepheardes Calender*. M. gives pastoral colour by dialect words like 'rathe' (used twice in the *Calender*) and 'scrannel' (not recorded in literature before), and by the colloquial, rustic-sounding 'daffadillies' (akin to the *Calender*'s 'daffadowndillies'). The 'quills' and the 'oaten' shepherd's pipe are both *Calender* properties. 'Guerdon'–a word found nowhere else in M.'s poetry–is used twenty-three times by Spenser, who was also the first to use 'pledge' (*10*) in the sense 'child'. M.'s own coinages are 'inwrought' (*105*) and 'freaked' (*144*).

*Modern criticism.* M. Lloyd, *N & Q* n.s. v (1958) 432–4, has suggested that the *Justa Eduardo King* volume was intended as a unified work within a flexible, comprehensive design, and that M.'s poem is a summary and interpretation of themes already stated in the volume.

Tillyard 80–5 claims that King is only the nominal 'subject' of *Lycidas*: fundamentally the poem concerns M. himself. Mindful of the similarity between King's career and his own, he writes in fear of premature death. The 'real subject' is the resolving of that fear (and of his bitter scorn of the clergy) into an exalted state of mental calm. Similarly Tuve[2] 73–111 views *Lycidas* as 'the most poignant and controlled statement in English poetry of the acceptance of that in the human condition which seems to man unacceptable'. To Daiches 73–92 the subject is neither King nor M. but 'man in his creative capacity, as Christian humanist poet-priest'.

John Crowe Ransom, in an important seminal article, *AR* i (1933) 179–203, regards Renaissance poetry as ideally anonymous, form and content being both traditional. Because M. was young and 'insubordinate' the 'anonymity' of *Lycidas* is disturbed (*a*) metrically, in that although M. derived his form from the Italian *canzone* he did not keep each verse paragraph the same in structure and length, and introduced ten unrhymed lines 'as a gesture of his rebellion against the formalism of his art': (*b*) stylistically, in that M. departs from the Virgilian grand style in the St Peter passage, where he shows a M. 'who is angry, violent, and perhaps a little bit obscene'; and (*c*) from the viewpoint of 'the logic of composition', in that M. starts his elegy as monologue but then breaks into narrative (*76*), and 'the narrative breaks the monologue several times more, presenting action sometimes in the present tense, sometimes in the past'. M. C. Battestin, *College English* xvii (1956) 223–8, disposes of Ransom's metrical argument by referring to Prince's demonstration that M.'s technical liberties were not unprecedented but modelled upon the efforts which Tasso and Guarini had made to liberate lyric poetry from strict *canzone* patterns: also that authoritative precedent for M.'s rhymeless lines may be found as early as Dante (Prince 71–88). Less satisfactory is Battestin's explanation of M.'s shifts of tense in terms of the Latin practice of alternating between narrative past and historic present. The contradictory tenses are an important part of *Lycidas* as Nelson 64–76 and 138–52 maintains: they strengthen the impression of the poem as performance and ceremony, and dramaticality is further enhanced by the rhetorical situation, so that *Lycidas* may be viewed as 'one of the most nearly complete fulfilments of peculiarly baroque tendencies in style'.

J. E. Hardy, *KR* vii (1945) 99–113, sees *Lycidas* as concerning itself with the expression of the problem of the relationship between two world-views, pagan and Christian, as exemplified in the dual connotational meanings of the word 'shepherd'. The resolution of this problem, Hardy considers, depends on the expression of the conviction that the double meaning of the word represents a bond of necessary kinship between the poetic and the religious experiences, just as poet and preacher are combined in King. Brett 39–50 argues, however, that *Lycidas* represents not a mingling of pagan and sacred, but a conflict between them. M. is torn between the rival claims of Renaissance humanism and deepening Protestant conviction: the former shows itself in the poem's pastoralism, the latter in the three passages (*56–7*, *76–84* and *108–31*) where M. breaks from the pastoral mood. In *193* M. bids farewell to the pastoral tradition and all that it symbolizes. The division which M. Lloyd, *EC* xi (1961) 390–402, considers basic to *Lycidas* is not that between pagan and sacred, however, but that between the self-absorbed world and the world of the good shepherd. The theme is the duty, judgment and salvation of the religious teacher, and poetry, as well as preaching, is elevated to be the shepherd's medium. The self-absorbed world has 'blind' shepherds (*119*) and is ruled by a 'blind' fury (*75*) with 'shears' like those at the 'shearers' feast' where the rapacious shepherds 'scramble' (*117*). But from the viewpoint of the poem's other world, Lloyd argues, the shearers' feast is, as in *1 Sam.* xxv, an occasion for rejoicing:

it may command a 'worthy bidden guest' (*118*)–the words echo Matthew's
account of the nuptial feast that represents man's admission to the kingdom
of heaven. A view nearer to Brett's is developed by A. S. P. Woodhouse
(Norwood 261–78) who takes the pattern of *Lycidas* to be dependent on the
contrast between the unreal Arcadian world of the pastoral and the concerns
of the real 'extra-aesthetic' life which break in upon it. Similarly J. S. Lawry,
*PMLA* lxxvii (1962) 27–32, approaching *Lycidas* as dialectic, draws attention
to the opposition beween the initial 'ideal' pastoral world (thesis) and the
'actual' world, represented by the two 'digressions' (antithesis). From their
encounter there arises a third statement, one of mystic certainty (synthesis).

    The earliest studies seriously to explore the structure of *Lycidas* by con-
centration upon myth and image were those of C. W. Mayerson, *PMLA*
lxiv (1949) 189–207, and R. P. Adams, *PMLA* lxiv (1949) 183–88. Miss
Mayerson emphasizes the importance of the Orpheus image (*56–63*). For
M.'s readers Orpheus was a type of the poet-prophet, a harmonizing and
civilizing influence: the mythographers interpreted the legend of his
death as an allegory of the destruction of human wisdom and art by barbar-
ism, and their reappearance in succeeding cycles of culture. He was also
associated with Christ. The Renaissance view of Orpheus is further inspected
by D. P. Walker, *Journal of the Warburg and Courtauld Institutes* xvi (1953)
100–20, who points out that to the neo-Platonists Orpheus was the source
of all Greek theology, through whom Pythagoras and hence Plato had
learned that the structure of all things is based on numerical proportions.
It was believed that the Jewish revelation, made to Moses, had filtered
through to the Egyptians: Orpheus had read the Pentateuch in Egypt, and
thus a line could be traced from Moses, through Hermes Trismegistus and
the *Orphica* to Plato: Platonism and Christianity could thus be reconciled,
since they originated in the same revelation, and M.'s readers might well
regard Orpheus as no more pagan than Moses or the Old Testament. R. P.
Adams' study concerns itself with the death-and-rebirth pattern more
widely than Miss Mayerson's: this pattern is inherent in the imagery of
hyacinth (*106*), rose (*45*) and violet (*145*)–flowers which sprung from the
blood of Hyacinthus, Adonis and Attjs–and particularly in the images of
water, the prime source of fertility in all ancient cults as M. knew from
Selden's *De Dis Syris*, Lucian's *De Dea Syrea* and Plutarch's *Of Osiris*.
Fifty of *Lycidas*'s 193 lines are concerned with water, often treating it as a
fertility symbol (*24, 29, 137, 140*) or as a symbol of death and rebirth, as in
the references to Alpheus and Arethusa (*132–3*) and to Orpheus (*58*).
M. goes to some lengths to show that water, the principle of life, was not
responsible for the death of Lycidas (*89–99*): the blame is put on the man-
made ship, built in defiance of the powers of nature (*101*). Commenting on
Adams' article E. R. Marks, *Explicator* ix (1951) 44, distinguishes between the
poem's treatment of salt water, which is destructive, and fresh water, which
nourishes life. The same distinction is made in Brooks and Hardy 169–86:
'The streams and fountains which run throughout the poem flow with
life-giving water . . . whereas the seas flow chaotically, without pattern . . .

It is ironical, of course, that the streams all have for their destination the sea ... the lives of men, too, with their purposes and meanings, spill themselves finally into the sea of oblivion.' The water imagery is further inspected by W. Shumaker, *PMLA* lxvi (1951) 485–94, along with that of vegetation. Shumaker notes that the catalogue of flowers which 'sad embroidery' wear picks up and utilizes many preceding references to a blight that has been placed on vegetative nature by King's death: with 'remarkable consistency' M. makes 'every mention of vegetation in the first 132 lines of the elegy suggest a sympathetic frustration in nature to balance the human frustrations about which the poem is built.' The connection of the flower passage with what precedes it is rather differently viewed by Allen 41–70, who illustrates the poem's movement from death to life by pointing out that whereas in the first half the flowers are colourless and the waters becalmed or almost motionless, in the second the waters race and thunder and the flowers flash into brightness. The most whole-hearted discussion of *Lycidas* as a reworking of literary archetypes is that by Northrop Frye (Patrides 200–11), who takes the Adonis myth as the shaping principle: like Adonis, Lycidas is associated with the cyclical rhythms of nature, particularly the daily cycle of the sun across the sky, the yearly cycle of the seasons, and the cycle of water flowing from wells and fountains through rivers to the sea.

The interpretations of Tillyard, Ransom, Hardy, Adams and Frye are viewed sceptically by M. H. Abrams (Patrides 212–31), in a study which reasserts the importance of the poem's surface meaning, laying particular emphasis on the persona, the pastoral elegist who speaks the poem: 'that the rise, evolution and resolution of the troubled thought of the elegist is the key to the structure of *Lycidas*, M. made as emphatic as he could. He forced it on our attention by the startling device of ending the elegy, in a passage set off as a stanza in *ottava rima*, not with Lycidas, but with the elegist himself.'

The best of the source studies is still J. H. Hanford's, *PMLA* xxv (1910) 403–47, which examines as forerunners of *Lycidas* Theocritus i, the *Lament for Bion*, Virgil's *Ecl.* x, Petrarch's *Ecl.* vi and vii, which introduce ecclesiastical satire into pastoral, Castiglione's *Alcon* and Sannazaro's first piscatory eclogue where, as in *Lycidas*, the subject meets death by drowning, and where the lament is spoken by a character named Lycidas. In English Hanford selects as likely influences Spenser's *Shepheardes Calender* and *Astrophel*. Hanford sees M. as original in introducing into the pastoral lament ecclesiastical satire and references to his own poetic career. Sir J. E. Sandys, *TRSL* xxxii (1914) 233–64, repeats several of Hanford's suggestions and adds Amalteo's first eclogue (entitled *Lycidas*) to the possible sources. F. R. B. Godolphin, *MLN* xlix (1934) 162–6, adds Propertius' elegy on the drowning of Paetus (III vii), and W. B. Austin, *SP* xliv (1947) 41–55, discovers general similarities between several passages in *Lycidas* and two Latin elegies by Giles Fletcher on Clere and Walter Haddon. Details like Panope (*101*) and the dolphins (*164*) lead T. B. Stroup (*SAMLA* 100–13) to associate

*Lycidas* with the Marinell-Florimell story as told by Spenser (*F.Q.* III iv, viii, IV xi–xii). G. Finney, *HLQ* xv (1952) 325–50, argues that the early seventeenth-century Italian musical drama, particularly Striggio's libretto *La favola d'Orfeo*, set by Monteverdi, should be placed among the influences that went to form *Lycidas*.

The vocabulary of M.'s elegy is examined by G. C. Taylor, *N & Q* clxxviii (1940) 56–7, who estimates that only forty-six of its 1,500 words entered the language after 1500, and that eighty per cent of the total are Anglo-Saxon in derivation; also by Josephine Miles (Patrides 95–100), who analyses *Lycidas* in terms of its repeated use of certain words, commenting on the high proportion of these that refer to the natural world, and concluding that the poem's essential motion is from low to high and past to future, with 'fresh', 'high', 'new', 'pure' and 'sacred' as the especial value terms.

The rhyme schemes of the verse paragraphs are scrutinized by Ants Oras, *MP* lii (1954) 12–22, who demonstrates that within each paragraph the complexity of rhyme arrangement first increases and then decreases, so that the design of each paragraph mirrors the broader architectonics of the whole poem. On the evidence of the Trinity MS Oras reconstructs the process by which M. added complexity to the rhyme structure of paragraph nine – in its final form the highest point in rhyme organization reached in *Lycidas*. He shows that the poem's rhyme structure has been largely influenced by the Italian madrigal, especially the madrigals of Bembo, and those which go to make up Tasso's *Il Rogo di Corinna*.

The nature of the 'engine' (*130–1*) has been much disputed. As the *OED* shows 'engine' could mean 'a machine or instrument used in warfare', and in *Pilgrim's Progress* one of the 'engines' Christian sees at the Palace Beautiful is the sword of God. M.'s 'engine' has thus been identified with the two-edged sword which issues from God's mouth in *Rev.* i 16 and xix 15. This interpretation is favoured by L. Howard, *HLQ* xv (1952) 173–84, who points out that the sword of *Rev.* was habitually taken to refer to the word of God; M. presumably identifies this with the power of the Protestant Reformation, substituting the authority of the Bible for that of the church. Supporting Howard J. M. Steadman, *N & Q* cci (1956) 249–50, notes that a two-handed broadsword was used to symbolize the word of God as active in the Reformation in the device of the Geneva printer, John Gerard; T. B. Stroup points to the same symbolic use of the sword device in Phineas Fletcher's *Locusts* (1627). Whiting[2] 29–58 also seconds Howard's suggestion, and thinks that the 'keys' (l. *110*) and the 'engine' are aspects of the same thing. E. S. Le Comte, *SP* xlvii (1950) 589–606, likewise insists that the 'engine' is the biblical sword of God, but identifies it with that manifestation of God's sword which Savonarola saw in his vision and which is referred to in his sermon denouncing the corrupt clergy. E. L. Marilla, *PMLA* lxvii (1952) 1181–4, agrees with Le Comte and suggests that in *131*, as in *Animadversions* (Columbia iii 148, Yale 707) there is evidence that M. shared the conviction that the Protestant movement was rapidly ushering in the Kingdom of Christ on earth. M. Kelley, *N & Q* clxxxi (1941) 273, argues that it is the sword of Michael which is referred to (as in *PL* vi 250–3): M. C. Treip, *N & Q* cciv (1959) 364–6, agrees. R. E. Hughes, *N & Q* cc (1955) 58–9, favours the 'two-edged sword' of *Ps.* cxlix 6. Others have thought that M.'s 'engine' is the axe that is laid to the root of the tree in *Matt.* iii 10, which M. in *Of Reformation* (Columbia iii 47, Yale i 582) identifies with the Protestant movement; or the sheep-hook (l. *120*) which had an iron spud at one end and could be used as a weapon: C. W. Brodribb, *TLS* (June 5 1943) 271, favours this interpretation, supported by L. W. Coolidge, *PQ* xxix (1950) 444–5, who refers to the bishop striking down hardened transgressors with his sheep-hook in *Piers Plowman* viii 94–7. J. M. French, *MLN* lxviii (1953) 229–31, identifies the 'engine' with the 'keys' (l. *110*) (reading 'smite' in a figurative sense): W. A. Turner, *JEGP* xlix (1950) 562–565, prefers to think of it as the lock on St Peter's door. D. A. Stauffer, *MLR* xxxi (1936) 57–60, reads it as the two nations, England and Scotland, recently united. Less likely suggested 'engines' are the executioner's axe, which was to behead Laud, the two houses of Parliament, the 'abhorred shears' (l. *75*), and the iron flail of Spenser's Talus in *F.Q.* v (C. G. Osgood, *RES* i (1925) 339–41). H. F. Robbins, *RES* n. s. v (1954) 25–36, interprets 'engine' as 'agent', and thinks the agent in question is the Son of God, as depicted in *Matt.* xxv 31–46: the phrase 'at the doors' occurs in *Matt.* xxiv 33 meaning 'in the immediate future'. M.'s 'But' (l. *130*) has sometimes been taken as adversative only to the preceding words 'and nothing said': this reading makes the 'engine' a further item in the list of evils under prelacy–perhaps Spain and France, the double threat of Catholicism. W. J. Grace, *SP* lii (1955) 583–9, strongly urges this interpretation: he associates M.'s 'engine' with a passage from Burton and concludes that the twin superstitious appeals of the devil and the Roman Catholic church–hope and fear–are referred to. The *1645* and *1673* headnote ('And by occasion . . . height'), which must refer to the 'engine' couplet, is a serious obstacle to this theory.

In this monody the author bewails a learned friend, unfortunately drowned in his passage from Chester on the Irish Seas, 1637. And by occasion foretells the ruin of our corrupted clergy then in their height.

> Yet once more, O ye laurels, and once more
> Ye myrtles brown, with ivy never sere,

*Headnote. Trin. MS* omits 'And by occasion . . . height'.
*1–2. Yet once more*] D. S. Berkeley, *N & Q* ccvi (1961) 178, thinks that these words are meant to echo *Heb.* xii 26–7 where they are used as a formula signifying God's separation of things transitory from things eternal. *laurels . . . myrtles . . . ivy*] The conjunction is discussed by J. B. Trapp *Journal of the Warburg and Courtauld Institutes* xxi (1958) 227–55; who suggests that it derives from a conflation of Virgil, *Ecl.* viii 12–3 and ii 54. He points out that the crown which Albertino Mussato received from his fellow-citizens at Padua in 1315 mingled the three foliages, and M. may have known

> I come to pluck your berries harsh and crude,
> And with forced fingers rude,
> 5   Shatter your leaves before the mellowing year.
> Bitter constraint, and sad occasion dear,
> Compels me to disturb your season due:
> For Lycidas is dead, dead ere his prime,
> Young Lycidas, and hath not left his peer:
> 10  Who would not sing for Lycidas? he knew
> Himself to sing, and build the lofty rhyme.
> He must not float upon his watery bier
> Unwept, and welter to the parching wind,

of this ceremony from Mussato's own works. He almost certainly knew Petrarch's *Oration* delivered at his crowning (with ivy, bay and myrtle) in 1341, and of the account of this coronation ascribed to Senuccio dei Bene in which the reasons for the foliages are given (ivy, because Bacchus crowned the first poet with it; bay, the tree of victory; and myrtle, Venus' tree, because poets are abnormally amorous). The crown of three foliages appears in later editions of Ripa's *Iconologia* (after 1630), in the image of *Accademia*. In Horace, *Odes* I i 29 the ivy-crown, usually associated with Bacchus, is mentioned as the reward of learning.   *brown*] Horace, *Odes* I xxv 18 calls myrtle 'brown'.   *never sere*] evergreen – the adjective applies to all three plants.

*1–14.* K. Rinehart, *N & Q* cxcviii (1953) 103, refers to the rhyme scheme of these lines as that of a 'broken sonnet' and suggests that M. adopts this form to show that he is 'forcing' himself poetically.

*4–5. Trin. MS* has two drafts of ll. 1–14, of which one is on a separate sheet, and reads here: *Before the mellowing year* 'And with forced fingers rude' / *And crop your young* 'Shatter your leaves before the mellowing year'.

*6. dear*] heartfelt. The word can also mean 'dire' and Brooks and Hardy 170 think the effect of the ambiguity is to emphasize the inescapable, fatal character of the poet's obligation to Lycidas.

*8. ere his prime*] King was twenty-five.

*10. Who would not sing*] Cp. Virgil, *Ecl.* x 3: *neget quis carmina Gallo?*   *he knew*] *Trin. MS* has 'he well knew', and 'well' is inserted in a hand probably M.'s in the Cambridge University Library copy of *1638*. J. S. Diekhoff, *PQ* xvi (1937) 408–10, argues against and Shawcross (330) for the inclusion of 'well'.

*10–11. he . . . sing*] Masson[2] i 648–9 lists ten extant sets of Latin verses by King, nine of them contributed to volumes of encomiastic occasional poetry dedicated to various members of the Royal family by scholars of the University, and one prefixed to Peter Hausted's *Senile Odium* (1633).

*11. build*] Imitates the Latin use of *condo* as in Horace, *Epist.* I iii 24: *condis amabile carmen* (you build charming poetry). R. Y. Tyrrell, *CR* ix (1895) 11–12 compares Pindar's use of τέκτονες (*Pyth.* iii 113).

*13. welter*] be tossed or tumbled about. In the seventeenth century the

Without the meed of some melodious tear.
15      Begin then, sisters of the sacred well,
That from beneath the seat of Jove doth spring,
Begin, and somewhat loudly sweep the string.
Hence with denial vain, and coy excuse,
So may some gentle muse
20  With lucky words favour my destined urn,
And as he passes turn,
And bid fair peace be to my sable shroud.
For we were nursed upon the self-same hill,
Fed the same flock; by fountain, shade, and rill.
25      Together both, ere the high lawns appeared
Under the opening eye-lids of the morn,
We drove a-field, and both together heard

word retained its sense 'writhe, wriggle', thus the idea of King suffering a terrible death comes into the line.      *parching*] drying.

*14. tear*] Collections of elegiac verse were often entitled *Lacrymae* (Tears): thus 'tear' means 'elegy'.

*15. sisters*] The muses.      *well*] Aganippe, on Mount Helicon, where there was an altar to Jove. At the beginning of Hesiod's *Theogony* the muses 'haunt the high and holy mount of Helicon and dance with soft feet around the violet spring and the altar of the mighty son of Kronos'.

*19-22. muse*] G. M. Gathorne-Hardy, *TLS* (18 Jan. 1934) 44, suggests that this is one of the nine sisters, not a future poet; that 'my destined urn' means 'the memorial (this poem) I am now preparing for Lycidas'; and that 'he' means Lycidas himself, who 'passes' in the funeral procession. This rather strained reading was produced in reply to J. A. S. Barrett, *TLS* (11 Jan. 1934) 28, who pointed out that 'urn' and 'shroud' were incompatible, the one implying cremation, the other burial.      *sable*] black. M. is the first to apply this epithet to a shroud: shrouds are normally white or grey. It is true that Sylvester (Du Bartas² 991) has the conjunction 'sable Shrowd', but there the 'Shrowd' is being worn by a living woman, and means not 'winding-sheet' but 'clothing'.

*20. lucky*] G. O. Marshall, *Explicator* xvii (1959) 66, takes this to mean not 'well-omened' (the *OED* explanation) but 'having an unstudied or unsought felicity' (a literary sense not recorded by the *OED* until 1700). The muse, Marshall explains, is to favour M.'s urn in the pastoral strain in which the 'uncouth swain' is favouring the urn of Lycidas.

*22. And*] Substituted in *Trin. MS* for 'to'.

*25. lawns*] Open spaces between woods, glades. 'Lawn' does not mean 'a piece of closely-mown grass' until the 1730s. The countryside round Cambridge is more realistically described in *Elegia I* 11-14.

*26. opening*] In *Trin. MS* substituted for 'glimmering'. Cp. *Job* xli 18, and Middleton, *Game at Chess* I: 79 'the opening eyelids of the morn'.

*27. a-field*] *1645* and *1673* omit hyphen. *1638* has it, and in a scrap of proof

What time the grey-fly winds her sultry horn,
Battening our flocks with the fresh dews of night,
30   Oft till the star that rose, at evening, bright,
Toward heaven's descent had sloped his westering
     wheel.
Meanwhile the rural ditties were not mute,
Tempered to the oaten flute,
Rough satyrs danced, and fauns with cloven heel,
35   From the glad sound would not be absent long,
And old Damaetas loved to hear our song.

from an earlier state of *1638* (23–35) now in Cambridge University Library,
the hyphen is inserted in a hand possibly M.'s. *Trin. MS*: afield. In the same
scrap of proof the correcting hand hyphenates 'eye-lids' (l. 26) and places a
full-stop after 'wheel' (l. 31). *1638*, *1645* and *1673* have both these correc-
tions.

*28. grey-fly*] The name seems to have been used to designate various kinds
of insect, including the dung-beetle and the may-fly.      *sultry*] presu-
mably indicates that 'What time' (Latin *quo tempore*) is midday.

*29. Battening*] fattening.

*30. star*] Hesperus, the evening star. *Trin. MS* has 'Oft till the ev'n star
bright' (the 1638 reading) corrected to 'Oft till the star that rose in evening
bright'. Shawcross 330 argues that 'in' should be retained instead of 'at'.

*31. westering*] In *Trin. MS* substituted for 'burnished'.

*33. oaten*] Cp. 'Oten reeds' in Spenser, *Shep. Cal.* October 8, which E. K.
glosses *Avena*, referring to Virgil, *Ecl.* i 2, *tenui . . . avena* ('on slender reed',
i.e. on the shepherd's pipe).

*34. fauns*] There are dancing fauns in Virgil, *Ecl.* vi 27–8.

*36. Damaetas*] *Trin. MS* has 'Damoetas'. There is a Dametas in Sidney's
*Arcadia* who is a loutish clown. This fact led Jerram (56) to suggest that the
name was adopted by M. as an insulting reference to his tutor Chappell.
F. Pyle, *Hermathena* lxxi (1948) 83–92, makes the same suggestion and,
taking the 'fauns' and 'satyrs' to be Cambridge undergraduates, thinks that
the 'song' must be *Vacation Exercise*. E. S. De Beer, *N & Q* cxciv (1949)
336–7, agreeing that there is an allusion to the Dametas of the *Arcadia*,
interprets it as meaning simply that M. and King could please even an
unlearned audience. M. H. Nicolson, *MLN* xli (1926) 293–300, does not
think the reference derogatory: she argues that M.'s Damaetas is not
Chappell but Joseph Mead, another and popular fellow of Christ's. The
whole question is reviewed by H. Fletcher, *JEGP* lx (1961) 250–7. He
associates the name Δαμόιτας with the verb δαμάζω (to tame) and con-
cludes that a tutor is meant. The Damoetas of Theocritus vi is clearly
young: so, too, in Virgil, *Ecl.* iii and v. Only in *Ecl.* ii 37 do we have an old,
indeed dying Damoetas. It seems that Mead did not like poetry, so he will
not do as a candidate. Fletcher favours Chappell, who was interested in
poetry, especially neo-Latin poetry: he suggests also, as possibilities,

But O the heavy change, now thou art gone,
Now thou art gone, and never must return!
Thee shepherd, thee the woods, and desert caves,
40   With wild thyme and the gadding vine o'ergrown,
And all their echoes mourn.
The willows, and the hazel copses green,
Shall now no more be seen,
Fanning their joyous leaves to thy soft lays.
45   As killing as the canker to the rose,
Or taint-worm to the weanling herds that graze,
Or frost to flowers, that their gay wardrobe wear,
When first the white-thorn blows;
Such, Lycidas, thy loss to shepherd's ear.
50      Where were ye nymphs when the remorseless deep
Closed o'er the head of your loved Lycidas?
For neither were ye playing on the steep,
Where your old bards, the famous Druids, lie,

Michael Honeywood, a fellow of Christ's since 1618, and Abraham
Wheelock (1593–1653), first Professor of Arabic. Both have verses which
appear in collections along with King's, and Honeywood contributed to
the *Justa Eduardo King.*
*39–44.* Cp. *Lament for Bion* 1–7, 27–35 where the orchards and groves wail
for Bion, the trees cast their fruit on the ground and the flowers wither,
and Echo mourns among her rocks. Similarly in Ovid, *Met.* xi 44–8 the
birds, beasts, rocks, trees and rivers weep for Orpheus.
*40. gadding*] wandering, straggling.
*45. canker*] See *Arcades* 53n (p. 158).
*46. taint-worm*] Bateson 159 identifies this as 'the intestinal worm that the
modern farmer calls "husk", which is normally only fatal, as M. correctly
says, to newly weaned calves when they start grazing'.
*47. wardrobe wear*] Trin. *MS*: *buttons* 'wardrobe' *wear* 'bear' 'wear'.
*48–9.* Echoing Shakespeare, *Midsummer Night's Dream* I i 184–5: 'More
tuneable than lark to shepherd's ear, / When wheat is green, when hawthorn
buds appear.'
*50–5.* Similarly in Theocritus i 66–9 Thyrsis asks the nymphs where they
were when Daphnis was dying, for they were not by Anapus or on Etna.
Virgil imitates this passage in *Ecl.* x 9–12.
*51. loved*] In Trin. *MS* substituted for 'youn[g]'.
*52–4. steep*] The slope of a mountain: M. distinguishes between the slopes
and the 'top' of Mona (Anglesey): the nymphs were in neither place.
Mona and Anglesey are identified and named as the home of the Druids by
Drayton, *Polyolbion* ix 415–29, 436: Selden's note to 417 helps to explain
M.'s 'shaggy', since it describes Anglesey as 'well stored with thicke Woods,
and religious Groves, in so much that it was called Inis-Dowil [the Dark
Isle]'.

Nor on the shaggy top of Mona high,
55  Nor yet where Deva spreads her wizard stream:
Ay me, I fondly dream!
Had ye been there . . . for what could that have done?
What could the muse herself that Orpheus bore,
The muse herself for her enchanting son
60  Whom universal nature did lament,
When by the rout that made the hideous roar,
His gory visage down the stream was sent,
Down the swift Hebrus to the Lesbian shore.
Alas! What boots it with uncessant care
65  To tend the homely slighted shepherd's trade,
And strictly meditate the thankless muse,
Were it not better done as others use,

55. *Deva*] The Dee. See *Vacation Exercise* 98n (p. 80).

57. In *Trin. MS* 'Had ye' and 'for' are deleted.

58–63. *muse*] Calliope. The first version of the lines in *Trin. MS* reads:
'What could the golden-haired Calliope / For her enchanting son / When
she beheld (the gods far-sighted be) / His gory scalp roll down the Thracian
lea'. The last two lines are cancelled and 'Whom universal nature might
lament / And heaven and hell deplore / When his divine head down the
stream was sent / Down the swift Hebrus to the Lesbian shore' inserted.
The present version is then substituted on a separate leaf, but with 'might
lament' (corrected to 'did lament') and 'divine visage' (corrected to 'gory
visage'). D. S. Berkeley, *N & Q* cciii (1958) 335–6, suggests reasons for the
successive changes, pointing out that the epithet 'golden-haired' belonged
also to Dionysus, and hence might be associated with the Bacchantes,
enemies to Calliope: also that '(the gods far-sighted be)', a parenthesis
reminiscent of Spenser's pastoral speech, runs counter to meaning: if gods
are 'far-sighted' why are the nymphs, Hippotades and even Neptune
ignorant of the causes of Lycidas's death? Cp. *Greek Anthol.* vii 8, on the
death of Orpheus: 'Thy mother Calliope . . . bewailed thee. Why sigh we
for our dead sons, when not even the gods have power to protect their
children from death?'

61–3. Ovid. *Met.* xi 1–55, relates how Orpheus was torn to pieces by the
Thracian women and how his severed head floated down the Hebrus and was
carried across to the island of Lesbos. The story is also in Virgil, *Georg.*
iv 454–527.     *swift*] Echoes Virgil, *Aen.* i 317: *volucrem . . . Hebrum.*

64–84. L. S. Friedland, *MLN* xxvii (1912) 246–50, finds similarities between
this question and Phoebus' reply and passages in Spenser's *Ruins of Time.*

64. *boots*] profits, avails.

66. *meditate*] M.'s use of the word imitates Virgil's *musam meditaris* (*Ecl.*
i 2) and *meditabor . . . musam* (*Ecl.* vi 8).

67–8. Cp. Virgil, *Ecl.* ii 14–15: *Nonne fuit satius tristis Amaryllidis iras / atque
superba pati fastidia* (Was it not better to put up with Amaryllis' sullen rage

To sport with Amaryllis in the shade,
Or with the tangles of Neaera's hair?
70　Fame is the spur that the clear spirit doth raise
(That last infirmity of noble mind)
To scorn delights, and live laborious days;
But the fair guerdon when we hope to find,
And think to burst out into sudden blaze,
75　Comes the blind Fury with th' abhorred shears,
And slits the thin-spun life. But not the praise,
Phoebus replied, and touched my trembling ears;
Fame is no plant that grows on mortal soil,
Nor in the glistering foil
80　Set off to the world, nor in broad rumour lies,
But lives and spreads aloft by those pure eyes,
And perfect witness of all-judging Jove;

and scornful disdain?) In *Ecl*. i Tityrus, reclining 'in the shade', makes the
woods echo with the name of Amaryllis: she appears again in *Ecl*. iii and ix.
Virgil borrowed her from Theocritus iii and iv.

*69. Or with*] P. Maas, *RES* xix (1943) 397–8, prefers the reading of
*Trin. MS* (before correction) and of *1638*, 'Hid in'.　　*Neaera's*] Neaera
appears in Virgil, *Ecl*. iii 3, and among the elegies of Tibullus are six addressed
to her by Lygdamus of which III ii 11–12 refers to her tangled hair. Horace
writes of her in *Epode* xv and in *Odes* III xiv 21 her hair is about to be fastened
in a knot. Joannes Secundus addresses his *Basia* to Neaera, as R. J. Schoeck
points out, *N & Q* cci (1956) 190–1, and *Basium* viii develops the image of
tangled hair. Buchanan also uses the name in his Latin poetry: in the last of
his elegies and in *Epigram* 44 he refers to the chains of her hair.

*70.* Cp. Spenser, *Tears of the Muses* 404: 'Due praise that is the spur of
dooing well.'

*71.* H. MacL. Currie, *N & Q* cciii (1958) 106–7 suggests that Silius Italicus,
*Punica* vi 332–3 *fax mentis honestae | gloria* (fame, the torch of a noble mind),
may have contributed to this line, but a nearer parallel is Tacitus, *Hist*. iv 6:
*Etiam sapientibus cupido gloriae novissima exuitur* (even with wise men the
desire for glory is the last to be abandoned).

*75. Fury*] Atropos was one of the Fates, not a Fury. See *Winchester Epitaph*
28*n* and *Arcades* 63–72*n*, pp. 128 and 159 above.

*77.* Echoing Virgil, *Ecl*. vi 3–4: *Cynthius aurem | vellit et admonuit* (the
Cynthian plucked my ear and warned me).

*78–84.* Phoebus' reply is paralleled by a passage in M.'s seventh Prolusion,
as Allen 66 points out, (Columbia xii 278–81, Yale i 302). Daiches 84 com-
ments: 'The pat aphoristic nature of that final couplet could not possibly
be a solution to such a complex poem as *Lycidas*. There is almost a note of
irony in the copy-book lesson. It is a deliberately false climax.'

*79. foil*] The thin leaf of gold or silver placed under a precious stone to
increase its brilliancy.

As he pronounces lastly on each deed,
Of so much fame in heaven expect thy meed.
85      O fountain Arethuse, and thou honoured flood,
Smooth-sliding Mincius, crowned with vocal reeds,
That strain I heard was of a higher mood:
But now my oat proceeds,
And listens to the herald of the sea
90      That came in Neptune's plea,
He asked the waves, and asked the felon winds,
What hard mishap hath doomed this gentle swain?
And questioned every gust of rugged wings
That blows from off each beaked promontory;
95      They knew not of his story,
And sage Hippotades their answer brings,
That not a blast was from his dungeon strayed,
The air was calm, and on the level brine,
Sleek Panope with all her sisters played.
100     It was that fatal and perfidious bark

*85–6.* The invocation signals the return to pastoral after the 'higher mood' of Phoebus' speech. The Arethuse (see *Arcades* 30–1n, p. 158 above) represents Sicilian, and the Mincius (Virgil's native river) Roman pastoral. Virgil refers to the sedges and reeds of Mincius in *Ecl.* vii 12–3, *Georg.* iii 14–5, and *Aen.* x 205–6, and in the second of these passages describes its course 'wandering in slow windings'. D. C. Allen, *MLN* lxxi (1956) 172–3, points out that Fulgentius in the *Mitologiae* allegorizes the Alpheus-Arethuse myth, interpreting Arethuse as the nobility of justice (*nobilitas Aequitatis*) and Alpheus as the light of truth (*vertitatis lux*). The unpolluted passage of Alpheus' waters through the ocean illustrates the incorruptibility of truth. Sandys repeats this interpretation in his commentary on the *Metamorphoses.*      *honoured*] *Trin. MS: smooth* '*famed*' '*honoured*'.
*Smooth-sliding*] In *Trin. MS* substituted for 'soft-sliding'. Sylvester has 'smooth-sliding floods' (Du Bartas 218).
*89 herald*] Triton.
*90. in Neptune's plea*] to defend Neptune against the charge of responsibility for King's death.
*91. felon*] savage, wild. T. P. Harrison, *UTSE* xv (1935) 22, points out that de Baïf, in *Eclogue* xv, has *de vents felons* in close association with Neptune and his waves.
*96. Hippotades*] A Homeric and Ovidian name for Aeolus, god of winds, son of Hippotes. Virgil represents him as imprisoning the winds in a vast cavern, *Aen.* i 52–63. As D. T. Starnes remarks (Taylor² 42–3) Aeolus is called *vir sapiens* in Conti (hence, perhaps, M.'s 'sage').
*99. Panope*] One of the fifty Nereids (sea nymphs), mentioned by Virgil, *Aen.* v 240.
*100. bark*] M. Lloyd, *MLN* lxxv (1960) 103–8, suggests that the 'bark'

Built in the eclipse, and rigged with curses dark,
That sunk so low that sacred head of thine.
   Next Camus, reverend sire, went footing slow,
His mantle hairy, and his bonnet sedge,
*105*   Inwrought with figures dim, and on the edge
Like to that sanguine flower inscribed with woe.
Ah; who hath reft (quoth he) my dearest pledge?
Last came, and last did go,
The pilot of the Galilean lake,
*110*   Two massy keys he bore of metals twain,

is the human body, subject to death ('fatal'), and built in the eclipse man has endured since Adam's fall; also that the 'mount' (161) is not only St Michael's Mount but also the mount of Paradise from which Michael drove man 'without remorse' (*PL* xi 105)–now he is asked to 'melt with ruth'.

*101. eclipse*] Eclipses were considered evil omens; the witches' cauldron in *Macbeth* IV i 27–8 contains 'slips of yew / Sliver'd in the moon's eclipse'.

*103. Camus*] The river Cam, representing Cambridge University. J. M. Morse, *N & Q* cciii (1958) 211, suggests that M. is slyly aware of the derivation of 'pedant' from Italian *pedare* 'to foot it', in Florio's *World of Words*.

*104. hairy*] Refers to the fur of the academic gown.     *sedge*] A name applied to various rush-like or flag-like plants, growing near water. It is a common adornment of river-gods in masques, as in Jonson, *King's Entertainment* 101–7, where Tamesis wears bracelets of willow and sedge and a crown of sedge and reed. Jonson cites Virgil, *Aen.* viii 31–4, which M. probably recalled here.

*105. Inwrought*] The first recorded appearance of the word; in *Trin. MS* substituted for 'scrawled o'er'. The leaf of the flag has dusky streaks in the middle and is serrated at the edge.

*106. flower*] The hyacinth. Theocritus x 28 speaks of the 'lettered' hyacinth, and *Lament for Bion* 6 mentions its 'writing'. Its letters were *AI* ('Alas'), marked on its leaves because it sprung from the blood of Apollo's beloved Hyacinthus. Ovid retells the story, *Met.* x 214–6: 'Phoebus . . . inscribed his grieving words upon the leaves, and the flower bore the marks AI AI, letters of lamentation.'

*107. pledge*] child (in that a child is a token of its parents' love); the word is first used in this sense by Spenser, *F.Q.* I x 4.

*109. pilot*] R. E. Hone, *SP* lvi (1959) 55–61, argues that this figure is not St Peter, but Christ, who is described as a bishop in *1 Pet.* ii 25, and by M. in *Animadversions* (Columbia iii 157, Yale i 715–6), who carries keys, *Rev.* i 18, and who saves the disciples' boat from shipwreck, *John* vi 15–21. The keys which Christ gives to St Peter (*Matt.* xvi 19) seem to fit the description here, however, better than those in *Rev.* i 18. Peter denounces false teachers in *2 Pet.* ii.

(The golden opes, the iron shuts amain)
He shook his mitred locks, and stern bespake,
How well could I have spared for thee, young swain,
Enow of such as for their bellies' sake,
115  Creep and intrude, and climb into the fold?
Of other care they little reckoning make,
Than how to scramble at the shearers' feast,
And shove away the worthy bidden guest;
Blind mouths! that scarce themselves know how to hold
120  A sheep-hook, or have learned aught else the least
That to the faithful herdman's art belongs!
What recks it them? What need they? They are sped;
And when they list, their lean and flashy songs
Grate on their scrannel pipes of wretched straw,

*111. amain*] with force, vehemently.

*113–31.* G. R. Coffman, *JELH* iii (1936) 101–13, finds some resemblances between M.'s handling of the parable from *John* x 1–28 and that in Bernard of Morlais's *De Contemptu Mundi*, available in four editions by 1637. E. L. Brooks, *N & Q* cci (1956) 67–8, indicates similarities between the 'pilot's' speech and Ezek. xxxiv, and K. McKenzie, *Italica* xx (1943) 121–6, compares Beatrice's denunciation of presumptuous preachers in *Paradiso* xxix 70–126. J. M. Steadman, *N & Q* (1958) 141–2, considers that M. may also have been familiar with a scene which takes place between St Peter and the condemned clergy in *La rappresentazione del dì del giudizio*.

*114. Enow*] enough.

*115. Creep*] Echoes the discussion of false shepherds in Spenser, *Shep. Cal.* May 126: 'There crept in Wolves.'    *climb*] Cp. *John* x 1: 'He that entereth not by the door into the sheepfold, but climbeth up some other way.'

*119. Blind mouths*] Ruskin, *Sesame and Lilies* i 22 comments: 'A "Bishop" means "a person who sees". A "Pastor" means "a person who feeds". The most unbishoply character a man can have is therefore to be blind. The most unpastoral is, instead of feeding, to want to be fed–to be a Mouth.' J. A. Himes, *MLN* xxxv (1920) 441, suggests rather that M. is translating the term τυφλόστομος which the geographer Strabo (IV i 8) applies to the mouth of a river choked with mud and sand. Thus M.'s term would imply shallowness and impeded utterance. R. J. Kane, *MLN* lxviii (1953) 239–40, also gives the Strabo reference.

*121. herdman's*] Shawcross 330 argues for the retention of the *Trin. MS* reading 'herdsman's'.

*122. What . . . them?*] What business is it of theirs?    *sped*] satisfied.

*123. list*] choose, please. The construction seems to be 'When they choose to grate out their songs the sheep [attracted by the sound] look up'. The *1638* omission of the comma after 'list' makes the connection of 'list' and 'grate' clearer.    *flashy*] watery, insipid.

*124. scrannel*] The first recorded appearance of the word; *OED* suggests

125    The hungry sheep look up, and are not fed,
       But swoll'n with wind, and the rank mist they draw,
       Rot inwardly, and foul contagion spread:
       Besides what the grim wolf with privy paw
       Daily devours apace, and nothing said,
130    But that two-handed engine at the door,
       Stands ready to smite once, and smite no more.
           Return Alpheus, the dread voice is past,
       That shrunk thy streams; return Sicilian muse,
       And call the vales, and bid them hither cast
135    Their bells, and flowrets of a thousand hues.
       Ye valleys low where the mild whispers use,
       Of shades and wanton winds, and gushing brooks,
       On whose fresh lap the swart star sparely looks,

connection with a dialect word meaning 'thin'. Cp. Virgil, *Ecl.* iii 27
*stridenti miserum stipula disperdere carmen* (to murder a rotten tune on a harsh-
sounding straw).
*125-7.* E. S. Le Comte, *MLN* lxix (1954) 403-4, shows that M.'s description
of sheep-rot is closely modelled on one in Petrarch, *Eclogue* ix, where Pet-
rarch is recalling the Black Death; he suggests M. has the plague in mind.
Cp. also Dante, *Paradiso* xxix 106-7: *Si che le pecorelle, che non sanno, | Tornan
dal pasco pasciute di vento* (So that the sh ep, without knowledge, come back
from pasture fed on wind). Northrop Frye considers M.'s description of the
sheep as 'picking up' the image of Lycidas' body weltering to the parching
wind in l. 13.
*128. wolf*] The Roman Catholic Church, particularly, as E. S. Le Comte, *SP*
xlvii (1950) 606, points out, the Jesuits; the arms of their founder, St Ig-
natius Loyola, included two grey wolves. Webster describes a Jesuit as 'a
gray Woolfe' (*Overburian Characters*, ed. W. J. Paylor (Oxford 1936)
p. 75). M. is referring to the proselytism carried on by the Catholic party
in England.
*129. nothing said*] *Trin. MS* corrects to 'little said': Shawcross 330 argues for
the retention of this reading.
*130-1.* See headnote.
*132.* On this transition Tuve[2] 103 comments: 'Pastoral has its way of re-
asserting a fundamental and harmonious sympathy, and of proclaiming
that not decay and death but life and creativity and love is the universal
principle.' And Brooks and Hardy 182: 'The dread voice has been endowed
with something of the effect of blazing light–a hot sun inimical to the cool
shadows of mythology and the flowers of pastoral poetry.'
*136. use*] go frequently, haunt.
*137. gushing*] In *Trin. MS* substituted for 'goshing'.
*138. fresh lap*] Echoes Shakespeare, *Midsummer Night's Dream* II i 108:
'the fresh lap of the crimson rose'.      *swart star*] The Dog-star, Sirius:
the Dog-days (the days around the heliacal rising of Sirius) are notorious

> Throw hither all your quaint enamelled eyes,
> 140   That on the green turf suck the honied showers,
> And purple all the ground with vernal flowers.
> Bring the rathe primrose that forsaken dies,
> The tufted crow-toe, and pale jessamine,
> The white pink, and the pansy freaked with jet,
> 145   The glowing violet

for heat: 'swart' (darkened by heat) is transferred from effect to cause. *sparely*] *Trin. MS: sparely 'faintly' 'sparely'.*

*139. Throw*] In *Trin. MS* substituted for 'Bring'.    *enamelled*] See *Arcades* 84*n* p. 160 above.

*139–40.* Brooks and Hardy 181 suggest that these sucking eyes balance the 'blind mouths' (l. 119). Even the flowers, by contrast with the worthless shepherds, have the kind of spiritual life and awareness we attribute to the seeing eye.

*142. rathe*] early, a dialect word with pastoral colour for M. because used by Spenser in *Shep. Cal.* July 78 and December 98.

*142–50.* This flower passage is an afterthought. In the *Trin. MS* draft l. 141 is followed immediately by l. 151, but on a separate sheet there are inserted two versions of ll. 142–50, of which the earlier reads: 'Bring the rathe primrose that unwedded dies / Colouring the pale cheek of unenjoyed love / And that sad flower that strove / To write his own woes on the vermeil grain / Next add Narcissus that still weeps in vain / The woodbine and the pansy freaked with jet / The glowing violet / The cowslip wan that hangs his pensive head / And every bud that sorrow's livery wears / Let daffadillies fill their cups with tears / Bid amaranthus all his beauty shed / To strew the laureate hearse etc.' The second version is, in its corrected state, the same as *1645* and *1673*, except for 'beauties' (l. 149): in its uncorrected state l. 146 read 'The musk-rose and the garish columbine' and l. 148 'And every flower that sad escutcheon bears', and ll. 149–50 were inverted. H. H. Adams, *MLN* lxv (1950) 468–72, thinks that the changes M. made in his draft of the flower-passage were intended partly to conceal his debt to *Winter's Tale* IV iv 113–132, and partly to remove erotic elements which would be out of place in a funeral elegy. W. L. Thompson, *N & Q* cxcvii (1952) 97–9, suggests that M.'s passage is more indebted to Jonson, *Pan's Anniversary* 11–38 than to *Winter's Tale*. Spenser, *Shep. Cal.* April 136–44 is also frequently compared.

*143. crow-toe*] A popular name for the wild hyacinth.    *jessamine*] jasmine, a climbing shrub with fragrant white flowers.

*144. freaked*] A coinage. There was a noun 'freak' meaning 'capricious humour, whim, vagary', but M. was the first to use the word as a verb. J. F. Killeen, *N & Q* ccvii (1962) 70–3, thinks that M. had in mind the use of the past participle passive of Latin *ludere* (i.e. *lusus*), in the sense 'adorned'. The 'jet' is a sign of mourning.

The musk-rose, and the well-attired woodbine,
With cowslips wan that hang the pensive head,
And every flower that sad embroidery wears:
Bid amaranthus all his beauty shed,

150   And daffadillies fill their cups with tears,
To strew the laureate hearse where Lycid lies.
For so to interpose a little ease,
Let our frail thoughts dally with false surmise.
Ay me! Whilst thee the shores, and sounding seas

155   Wash far away, where'er thy bones are hurled,
Whether beyond the stormy Hebrides
Where thou perhaps under the whelming tide
Visit'st the bottom of the monstrous world;
Or whether thou to our moist vows denied,

*146. woodbine*] The herbals identify this with the honeysuckle, but in Shakespeare, *Midsummer Night's Dream* IV i 47 it is distinguished from the honeysuckle and seems to be equated with convolvulus or bindweed.

*147. wan*] pale.

*149. amaranthus*] The immortal flower of Paradise (see *PL* iii 353–7), linked with a poet's death by Spenser, *F.Q.* III vi 45.    *beauty*] In *Trin. MS* the cancelled version of the flower-passage reads 'beauty' but the final version reads 'beauties': Shawcross 330 argues for the retention of this reading.

*150. daffadillies*] Cp. Spenser, *Shep. Cal.* April 140 'Daffadowndillies'. G. S. Fraser comments (Kermode³ 35) 'Spenser's "daffadowndillies" is matched by M.'s "daffadillies", where Shakespeare, Ben Jonson and Herrick all write of "daffodils".'

*153. frail*] In *Trin. MS* substituted for cancelled 'sad'.    *false surmise*] The surmise is false because King's body is missing, so there is no chance of strewing his hearse. But also, as Brooks and Hardy 183 point out, because the flowers are not really wearing 'sad embroidery' for Lycidas: the cups of the daffodils are not filled with tears for him. Nature is neutral: it does not participate in grief for the dead man. From this viewpoint the function of the flower passage 'in the full context of the poem, is ironic'.

*154. shores*] In *Trin. MS* M. first wrote 'floods' (a more logical subject for 'wash'), then altered to 'shores', which gives an impression of land and sea in league, the land rejecting the body, the sea tossing it.

*157. whelming*] *Trin. MS* has 'humming', the 1638 reading, and in the BM and Cambridge University copies of *Justa Eduardo King* 'humming' is starred and 'whelming' written in the margin in a hand probably M.'s. 'Humming' recalls *Pericles* III i 64, 'humming water must o'erwhelm thy corpse', of which the 'o'erwhelm' perhaps suggested 'whelming'.

*158. Visit'st*] Tuve² 96 comments: 'the irony of the intimate communication in "visit'st" is less grim than piteous'.    *monstrous world*] The world of sea-monsters.

*159. moist vows*] tearful prayers.

*160*    Sleep'st by the fable of Bellerus old,
        Where the great vision of the guarded mount
        Looks toward Namancos and Bayona's hold;
        Look homeward angel now, and melt with ruth.
        And, O ye dolphins, waft the hapless youth.
*165*        Weep no more, woeful shepherds weep no more,
        For Lycidas your sorrow is not dead,
        Sunk though he be beneath the watery floor,

*160. Bellerus*] In *Trin. MS* M. first wrote 'Corineus' (one of the legendary
warriors who, as M. notes in the *History of Britain*, came to Britain with
Brutus, Aeneas' great-grandson, and ruled over Cornwall). 'Bellerus'
seems to be an eponymous hero invented by M. to explain the name
*Bellerium* (the Latin name for Land's End), found on Ortelius's map of
Britain.

*161. vision of the guarded mount*] The chapter on Cornwall in Camden's
*Britannia* relates that the monks who had cells on St Michael's Mount said
that St Michael himself had appeared there.

*162. Namancos*] Nemancos is an ancient name for a district in N.W. Spain,
one of the subdivisions of the archbishopric of Santiago de Compostella.
The name, as A. S. Cook points out, *MLR* ii (1907) 124–8, was misspelt
'Namancos' on Ojea's map of Galicia, first published in the 1606 Ortelius,
and subsequent maps, including those in the editions of *Mercator's Atlas*
in and after 1613, perpetuated this error.     *Bayona*] A fortress town about
fifty miles south of Cape Finisterre. The two names represent the threat of
Spanish Catholicism, against which St Michael guards England.

*163. angel*] Michael. As L. H. Kendall Jr points out, *N & Q* cxcviii (1953)
145, 'melt with ruth' is found in Chaucer, *Troilus* i 84 and Spenser, *F.Q.*
III vii 9.

*164. waft*] convey safely by water. T. O. Mabbott, *Explicator* v (1947) 26,
argues that the usual interpretation of this line as a reference to Arion who,
unlike Lycidas, was not drowned but saved, is unsatisfactory. He proposes
Palaemon (the 'son' of *Comus* 876) who according to Pausanias II i 3, was
drowned and buried at Corinth and whose body was brought to land by a
dolphin: he became a patron of mariners, like Lycidas. Tuve[2] 96 insists,
however, that the reference should include 'the love and rescuing pity which
had long been thought of as the beauty of Arion's story' and which 'are
like in character to the saving heavenly Love that walked the waves'.
M. Lloyd, *MLN* lxxv (1960) 106–7, also maintains that the Arion reference
should be kept, because the Arion myth emphasizes the dolphin's love of
music, and so this allusion looks back to and completes the Orpheus allusion.
Lloyd adds that in the myth of Icadius, preserved in a note by Servius to
*Aen.* iii 332, Apollo appears in the form of a dolphin to save Icadius from
shipwreck and waft him to Parnassus.

So sinks the day-star in the ocean bed,
And yet anon repairs his drooping head,
*170*    And tricks his beams, and with new spangled ore,
Flames in the forehead of the morning sky:
So Lycidas sunk low, but mounted high,
Through the dear might of him that walked the waves;
Where other groves, and other streams along,
*175*    With nectar pure his oozy locks he laves,
And hears the unexpressive nuptial song,
In the blest kingdoms meek of joy and love.
There entertain him all the saints above,
In solemn troops, and sweet societies
*180*    That sing, and singing in their glory move,
And wipe the tears for ever from his eyes.
Now Lycidas the shepherds weep no more;
Henceforth thou art the genius of the shore,
In thy large recompense, and shalt be good
*185*    To all that wander in that perilous flood.
     Thus sang the uncouth swain to the oaks and rills,
While the still morn went out with sandals grey,

*168. day-star*] The sun. R. Y. Tyrrell, *CR* ix (1895) 11–2, compares Pindar, *Isth.* iv 40–1 (of Fame): 'She was fallen on sleep; but now she is roused again with beaming form, like the star of morning, a sight to see amid the other stars.'

*170. tricks*] trims.    *ore*] Presumably meaning 'gold'. *OED* gives 1639 for the first use of 'ore' in the sense 'precious metal'. M. is probably influenced by *Hamlet* IV i 25–7: 'like some ore / Among a mineral of metals base, / Shows itself pure.'

*173. him*] Christ, who walks on the sea in *Matt.* xiv 25–6.

*174. groves . . . streams*] Cp. *Rev.* xxii 2: 'the tree of life, which bare twelve manner of fruits'; and *Rev.* vii 17: 'living fountains of waters'.

*175. nectar*] The brooks in Eden run with nectar, *PL* iv 240.    *oozy*] slimy from contact with the sea. Cp. *Nativity Ode* 124 'the welt'ring waves their oozy channel keep', the only other place M. uses the word in his poetry.

*176. And hears*] In *Trin. MS* substituted for 'Listening'.    *unexpressive*] See *Nativity Ode* 116n p. 106 above.    *nuptial*] Pertaining to the 'marriage of the Lamb', *Rev.* xix 7.

*181.* Cp. *Rev.* vii 17: 'God shall wipe away all tears from their eyes', also *Rev.* xxi 4.

*183. genius*] Local protective deity. In Virgil, *Ecl.* v 64–5, the dead Daphnis is imagined as a god, being good to his worshippers.

*186. uncouth*] unknown. The meaning 'uncomely, awkward' was, however, developing during the seventeenth century.

He touched the tender stops of various quills,
With eager thought warbling his Doric lay:
190    And now the sun had stretched out all the hills,
And now was dropped into the western bay;
At last he rose, and twitched his mantle blue:
Tomorrow to fresh woods, and pastures new.

## 54 Fix here . . .

*Date.* Apr. 1638? These two lines are jotted down in M.'s hand on the back of a letter to him from Lawes which enclosed his passport, and which was written probably in Apr. 1638, just before M. went abroad. (For text of letter see Columbia xii 325–6, Yale i 339).

*Publication.* First printed in Horwood xvi, with *overdaled* for *overdated* in l. *1*. *Overdated* (antiquated, out of date) is not recorded in *OED* until 1641, when M. himself uses it in *Of Reformation.*

Fix here ye overdated spheres
That wing the restless foot of time.

## 55 *Ad Leonoram Romae canentem*
### [To Leonora singing at Rome]

*Date.* Oct.–Nov. 1638 or Jan.–Feb. 1639. It is not certain on which of M.'s two visits to Rome he heard Leonora Baroni sing. Her mother, Adriana

*188. stops*] The finger-holes in the pipes.      *quills*] The hollow reeds of the shepherd's pipe, for which Spenser uses the same word, *Shep. Cal.* June 67: 'homely shepheards quill'.

*189. Doric*] Theocritus, Moschus and Bion wrote in the Doric dialect. In *Lament for Bion* 18, Bion is called the Doric Orpheus.

*190.* The meaning is presumably that the setting sun had stretched out or elongated the shadows of the hills. Cp. Virgil, *Ecl.* i 83 *maioresque cadunt altis de montibus umbrae* (and longer shadows fall from the mountain heights).

*191.* Brooks and Hardy 186 comment that, when contrasted with the two lines on the rising sun (ll. 170–1) the effect of this line is not to deny the radiant vision of promise, but only to place it in a realistic perspective; 'we are simply reminded that the vision is one of hope, not yet fulfilled, that the elegy has been composed and delivered in a real world in which suns rise and set'.

*192. blue*] R. C. Fox, *Explicator* ix (1951) 54, notes that though shepherds usually wear grey in the pastoral, blue is the traditional symbol of hope. In Spenser, *F.Q.* I x 14, Speranza (Hope) wears blue.

*193.* S. R. Watson, *N & Q* clxxx (1941) 258, compares Phineas Fletcher,

Baroni, had also been a famous musician (contemporary poets celebrated her in the *Teatro della gloria d'Adriana* of 1623): Leonora was born in Mantua *c.* 1610, and was a fine singer and theorbo-player. A volume of *Applausi Poetici alle Glorie della Signora Leonora Baroni* (Rome 1639) was collected by Costazuti. It used to be assumed that M. heard Leonora at the entertainment in the palace of Cardinal Barberini, described in his letter to Lukas Holste of 30 Mar. 1639 (Columbia xii 40). But J. S. Smart, *MLR* viii (1913) 91–2, and G. L. Finney, *PMLA* lviii (1943) 658, point out that the Barberini entertainment was not a concert but an opera, Rospigliosi's *Chi sofre, speri*, presented in Feb. 1639, and that women were not allowed to sing in the performances at the Palazzo Barberini. Wherever M. heard Leonora, it was not here.

*Publication. 1645* and *1673* (no significant variants).

> Angelus unicuique suus (sic credite gentes)
>   Obtigit aethereis ales ab ordinibus.
> Quid mirum? Leonora tibi si gloria maior,
>   Nam tua praesentem vox sonat ipsa Deum.
> 5 Aut Deus, aut vacui certe mens tertia coeli
>   Per tua secreto guttura serpit agens;
> Serpit agens, facilisque docet mortalia corda
>   Sensim immortali assuescere posse sono.
> Quod si cuncta quidem Deus est, per cunctaque fusus,
> 10  In te una loquitur, caetera mutus habet.

A winged angel from the heavenly ranks—believe me, you nations—has been allotted to each particular individual. It is no wonder if you have a greater privilege, Leonora. And in fact the sound of your voice makes it clear that God is present, or, if not God, at any rate a third mind[5] which has left heaven and creeps warbling along, hidden within your throat. Warbling he creeps and graciously teaches mortal hearts how to grow accustomed, little by little, to immortal sound. If God is all things, and omnipresent, nevertheless he speaks in you alone, and possesses all other creatures in silence.

*Purple Island* vi 77: 'Tomorrow shall ye feast in pastures new', and Mantuan, *Eclogue* ix: *Candide, coge pecus melioraque pascere quaere* (Candidus, drive the herd and seek better pasture).

¶. 55. *5. mens tertia*] Perhaps a reference to the mysterious and variously interpreted passage in the (almost certainly spurious) second *Epistle* of Plato (312E): 'Related to the King of All are all things, and for his sake they are, and of all things fair he is the cause. And related to the Second are the second things; and related to the Third, the third.' Ficino (*Commentary on the Symposium* II iv) and others explain the 'Third' as the World-Soul.

# 56 *Ad eandem*
## [To the same]

*Date.* See headnote to previous poem.
*Publication.* *1645* and *1673* (no significant variants).

Altera Torquatum cepit Leonora poetam,
    Cuius ab insano cessit amore furens.
Ah miser ille tuo quanto felicius aevo
    Perditus, et propter te Leonora foret!
5   Et te Pieria sensisset voce canentem
    Aurea maternae fila movere lyrae,
Quamvis Dircaeo torsisset lumina Pentheo
    Saevior, aut totus desipuisset iners,
Tu tamen errantes caeca vertigine sensus
10      Voce eadem poteras composuisse tua;
Et poteras aegro spirans sub corde quietem
    Flexanimo cantu restituisse sibi.

The poet Torquato[1] fell in love with another Leonora, and his mad love
for her drove him out of his mind. Ah, poor man, how much more fortunate
for him had he been your contemporary and lost his reason on your account,
Leonora! How much more fortunate had he heard you singing with your
Pierian[5] voice, and heard the golden strings of your mother's harp vibrating.
Even if he had rolled his eyes more savagely than Dircaean Pentheus,[7] or
even if he had been utterly dull and witless, you could have calmed his
reeling senses with your voice; you could have made him himself again,
breathing peace into his sick heart with your soul-soothing song.

# 57 *Ad eandem*
## [To the same]

*Date.* See headnote to *Leon* (p. 254).
*Publication.* *1645* and *1673* (no significant variants).

¶ 56. *1. Torquatum*] Tasso, whose madness and consequent imprisonment
(1579–86) in the Ospedale d'Sant'Anna by his patron, Alphonso, Duke of
Ferrara, was sometimes connected with his alleged love for Alphonso's
sister, Leonora d'Este, to whom he wrote poems. He was also supposed
to have been in love with Leonora Santivale, Countess of Scandiano.
*5. Pieria*] See *Elegia IV* 29–32*n* (p. 55).
*7. Dircaeo ... Pentheo*] Dirce was a fountain near Thebes, thus 'Dircaean'
means 'Theban'. Pentheus, King of Thebes, scorned the Bacchic orgies
and was therefore torn to pieces by the Bacchantes. His rage, and the effect
it had on his eyes, is described by Ovid, *Met.* iii 577–8.

Credula quid liquidam sirena Neapoli iactas,
  Claraque Parthenopes fana Achelöiados,
Littoreamque tua defunctam naiada ripa
  Corpora Chalcidico sacra dedisse rogo?
5 Illa quidem vivitque, et amoena Tibridis unda
  Mutavit rauci murmura Pausilipi.
Illic Romulidum studiis ornata secundis,
  Atque homines cantu detinet atque deos.

Why, credulous Naples, do you boast of your clear-voiced siren and of the
famous shrine of Acheloüs' daughter Parthenope?[2] Why do you boast that
when she died upon your shore you placed her, a Naiad of the sands, on a
Neapolitan[4] pyre? The fact is, she is still alive, and has changed the booming
of hoarse Posillipo[6] for the gentle waters of the Tiber. There, enthusiastically
applauded by Roman audiences, her singing holds both men and gods
spellbound.

## 58 *Ad Salsillum poetam Romanum aegrotantem. Scazontes.*

[Scazons addressed to Salzilli, a Roman poet, when he was ill.]

*Date.* Late 1638 or 1639. M. visited Rome Oct.–Nov. 1638 and Jan.–Feb.
1639. It is implied (*10*) that *Salsill* was written not long after his arrival in
Italy. Giovanni Salzilli wrote four flattering lines of Latin verse preferring
M. to Homer, Virgil and Tasso: these, along with other commendatory
verses, M. later printed before his Latin poems in *1645*. Masson (i 309)
discovered a volume called *Poesie de' Signori Accademici Fantastici* (Rome
1637) to which Salzilli is one of the 51 contributors. Nothing more is known
of him.

*Publication.* *1645* (5. lectum,]lectum. ) *1673*.

¶ 57. *2. Parthenopes ... Achelöiados*] See *Comus* 879n (p. 221). The sirens
were daughters of the river-god Acheloüs and Terpsichore.

*4. Chalcidico*] Neapolitan, because Greek colonists from the island of Eu-
boea, of which the chief town is Chalcis, settled at Naples. Virgil, *Aen.*
vi 17, applies the adjective to Naples.

*6. Pausilipi*] Mount Posillipo, N.W. of Naples, is pierced by a tunnel
through which the newer Via Antiniana, dating from the time of Agrippa,
passes: *murmura* presumably refers to the rumble of traffic in the tunnel.

¶ 58. *Title. Scazontes*] Iambic trimeters with spondees or trochees taking
the place of the final iambs, (from Gk σκάζειν, to limp). C. Symmons,
*CJ* ix (1814) 342, notes that M.'s scazons admit spondees and even anapaests
in the fifth foot. The Greeks sometimes used a spondee in this position,
but the Latins always an iamb.

O musa gressum quae volens trahis claudum,
Vulcanioque tarda gaudes incessu,
Nec sentis illud in loco minus gratum,
Quam cum decentes flava Dëiope suras
5   Alternat aureum ante Iunonis lectum,
Adesdum et haec s'is verba pauca Salsillo
Refer, camoena nostra cui tantum est cordi,
Quamque ille magnis praetulit immerito divis.
Haec ergo alumnus ille Londini Milto,
10   Diebus hisce qui suum linquens nidum
Polique tractum, (pessimus ubi ventorum,
Insanientis impotensque pulmonis
Pernix anhela sub Iove exercet flabra)
Venit feraces Itali soli ad glebas,
15   Visum superba cognitas urbes fama
Virosque doctaeque indolem iuventutis,
Tibi optat idem hic fausta multa Salsille,
Habitumque fesso corpori penitus sanum;
Cui nunc profunda bilis infestat renes,
20   Praecordiisque fixa damnosum spirat.
Nec id pepercit impia quod tu Romano
Tam cultus ore Lesbium condis melos.
O dulce divum munus, O salus Hebes
Germana! Tuque Phoebe morborum terror
25   Pythone caeso, sive tu magis Paean
Libenter audis, hic tuus sacerdos est.
Querceta Fauni, vosque rore vinoso
Colles benigni, mitis Evandri sedes,
Siquid salubre vallibus frondet vestris,

2. *Vulcanioque . . . incessu*] For the cause of Vulcan's lameness see *Elegia VII* 81–2*n*, p. 73 above.

4. *Dëiope*] Deiopea, in Juno's opinion the loveliest of the nymphs, is promised by her to Aeolus as a reward for destroying Aeneas' fleet (Virgil, *Aen.* i 71–5).

22. *Lesbium . . . melos*] Alcaeus and Sappho were natives of Lesbos. This regularly iambic line, among scanzons, may be M.'s compliment to Salzilli's smoothness, or an error (M. again makes *melos* a spondee on p. 325, l.8).

23. *Hebes*] See *Vacation Exercise* 38*n* (p. 77).

25. *Pythone caeso*] See *Elegia VII* 31–4*n* (p. 71).    *Paean*] an appellation of Apollo, as god of healing. For the construction cp. Horace, *Sat.* II vi 20: *seu Iane libentius audis.*

27. *Fauni*] Faunus, as Virgil relates (*Aen.* vii 45–8), was father of Latinus. It is in a grove 'black with the shade of holm-oaks' that, according to Ovid, *Fast.* iii 295, Numa speaks with him.

28. *Colles*] The hills of Rome.    *Evandri sedes*] In Roman legend Evander

30   Levamen aegro ferte certatim vati.
Sic ille charis redditus rursum musis
Vicina dulci prata mulcebit cantu.
Ipse inter atros emirabitur lucos
Numa, ubi beatum degit otium aeternum,
35   Suam reclivis semper Aegeriam spectans.
Tumidusque et ipse Tibris hinc delinitus
Spei favebit annuae colonorum:
Nec in sepulchris ibit obsessum reges
Nimium sinistro laxus irruens loro:
40   Sed fraena melius temperabit undarum,
Adusque curvi salsa regna Portumni.

My muse, you trail a lame foot deliberately: you enjoy imitating Vulcan's walk as you hobble along. This seems to you just as delightful, in its right place, as blonde Deiopea[4] with her trim ankles skipping before Juno's golden couch. Come along now, if you please, and take these few words to Salzilli. My poetry is so dear to him that he prefers it, quite undeservedly, to that of mighty and godlike poets. Young Milton, London-born-and-bred, sends this message, then: Milton, who recently left his nest and his own little bit of sky (where the worst of winds, powerless to control its madly heaving lungs, puffs its panting gusts helter-skelter beneath the heavens), and came to see Italy's fertile soil, its cities—the theme of vaunting fame—its peoples, and the genius of its young intellectuals. This same Milton wishes you every good fortune, Salzilli, and a complete return to health for your tired body. At present an overflow of bile is upsetting your liver and, lodged in your stomach, exhales disease. The disrespectful stuff has shown you no mercy, even though you are such a cultured man, and even though your Roman lips can frame original Greek lyrics![22]

is an Arcadian, son of Carmentis, who founded a colony of his countrymen on the banks of the Tiber at the place where Rome was later to stand.

*33–5.* Numa Pompilius, second of the legendary kings of Rome, forsook city life and, according to Plutarch, *Numa* iv, 'determined to live for the most part in country places, and to wander alone, passing his days in the groves of the gods'. It was in these groves, Plutarch adds, that he was said to consort with his goddess-love, Egeria. Ovid, *Met.* xv 487–8, tells how at Numa's death Egeria ' fled from the city and hid herself away in the dense forests of the Arician vale'.

*38–9.* Horace, *Odes* I ii 13–20, recalls how the Tiber overflowed its left bank and flooded the *monumenta regis* (i.e. the Regia, the official residence of the Pontifex Maximus). The building to which M. is probably referring, and to which he may have thought Horace was, is the Mausoleum of Augustus in the Campus Martius, where Augustus and many of the emperors were interred.

*41. Portumni*] Portumnus was properly god of harbours but, as Harding (56) points out, he was commonly referred to in the Renaissance as god of the sea; *curvus* is used of the sea by Ovid, *Met.* xi 505.

Sweet gift of the gods, health, sister of Hebe,[23] and you, Phoebus (or Paean, if you would rather be called by that name), the terror of all diseases since your slaying of Python,[25] this man Salzilli is your priest. You oak-groves of Faunus,[27] you hills[28] generously hung with juicy grapes, Evander's mellow home, if any health-giving plant sprouts in your valleys, bring it eagerly to cure your sick poet. Then, restored to his dear muses once more, he will soothe the meadows all around with his sweet song. Numa[33] himself will be filled with wonder as he lies at ease among those dark groves where he spends his blessed eternity of rest gazing for ever upon his dear Egeria.[35] Even the flood-swollen Tiber, charmed by the song, will be kind to the farmers' yearly hopes. He will not go rushing along with his left rein held too loosely, to besiege kings in their tombs,[38] but will keep a better grip on the reins of his waters till they come to the salt kingdom of hump-backed Portumnus.[41]

# 59 *Mansus*
## [Manso]

*Date.* Jan. 1639? After his first stay in Rome M. travelled to Naples Nov.– Dec. 1638. 'Here', he writes (Columbia viii 123–5) 'I was introduced . . . to John Baptista Manso, Marquis of Villa, a man of the first rank and authority, to whom the illustrious Italian poet, Torquato Tasso, addressed his book on friendship. By him I was treated, while I stayed there, with all the warmth of friendship: for he conducted me himself over the city and the viceregent's court, and more than once came to visit me at my own lodgings. On my leaving Naples he gravely apologized for showing me no more attention, alleging that although it was what he wished above all things, it was not in his power in that city, because I had not thought proper to be more guarded on the point of religion.' Manso (1560?–1645) founded the Accademia degli Oziosi, which met at his villa, and befriended Tasso, who seems to have stayed with him in 1588, 1592 and 1594, on the last occasion completing his *Gerusalemme Conquistata*: their friendship must have begun before 1586 when Tasso's *Il Manso*, to which M.'s headnote refers, was published. After Tasso's death (1595) Manso befriended Giambattista Marino. Manso's own works include two sets of dialogues on love and beauty (1608 and 1618), a volume of poems (1635) and a *Life of Tasso* (1619): M. prints a Latin couplet by him as part of the prefatory material of the 1645 *Poemata*: *Ut mens, forma, decor, facies, mos, si pietas sic / Non Anglus, verum hercle Angelus ipse fores* (If your religious persuasions were equal to your mind, your handsome figure, your fame, your face and your manners, then–good heavens!–you would be an angel, not an Englishman).

*Publication.* 1645, 1673 (no significant variants: in 27 1673 misprints *longinguam* for *longinquam*).

*Joannes Baptista Mansus Marchio Villensis vir ingenii laude, tum literarum studio, nec non et bellica virtute apud Italos clarus in primis est. Ad quem Torquati Tassi dialogus extat de Amicitia scriptus; erat enim Tassi amicissimus; ab quo etiam inter Campaniae principes celebratur, in illo poemate cui titulus* Gerusalemme conquistata, lib 20.

Fra cavalier magnanimi, e cortesi
Risplende il Manso———

*Is authorem Neapoli commorantem summa benevolentia prosecutus est, multaque ei detulit humanitatis officia. Ad hunc itaque hospes ille antequam ab ea urbe discederet, ut ne ingratum se ostenderet, hoc carmen misit.*

Haec quoque Manse tuae meditantur carmina laudi
Pierides, tibi Manse choro notissime Phoebi,
Quandoquidem ille alium haud aequo est dignatus
    honore,
Post Galli cineres, et Mecaenatis Hetrusci.
5  Tu quoque si nostrae tantum valet aura Camoenae,
Victrices hederas inter, laurosque sedebis.
Te pridem magno felix concordia Tasso
Iunxit, et aeternis inscripsit nomina chartis.
Mox tibi dulciloquum non inscia Musa Marinum
10  Tradidit, ille tuum dici se gaudet alumnum,
Dum canit Assyrios divum prolixus amores;
Mollis et Ausonias stupefecit carmine nymphas.
Ille itidem moriens tibi soli debita vates
Ossa tibi soli, supremaque vota reliquit.
15  Nec manes pietas tua chara fefellit amici,
Vidimus arridentem operoso ex aere poetam.
Nec satis hoc visum est in utrumque, et nec pia cessant
Officia in tumulo, cupis integros rapere Orco,
Qua potes, atque avidas Parcarum eludere leges:
20  Amborum genus, et varia sub sorte peractam
Describis vitam, moresque, et dona Minervae;
Aemulus illius Mycalen qui natus ad altam
Rettulit Aeolii vitam facundus Homeri.

¶ 59. *2. Pierides*] The Muses: see *Elegia IV* 29–32n (p. 55).

*4. Galli*] Cornelius Gallus, the elegiac poet (d. 27 B.C.), admired by Ovid and friend of Virgil, who commemorates him, *Ecl.* vi 64–73.   *Mecaenatis*] Maecenas (d. 8 B.C.) was the most famous of the Roman patrons of letters.

*11.* Marino's long poem *L'Adone* (1623) is a version of the Venus and Adonis story.   *Assyrios*] See *Nativity Ode* 200 and 204nn (p. 110).

*18. Orco*] See *Elegia VII* 83n (p. 73).

*19. Parcarum*] See *Proc Med* 2n (p. 27).

*20. Amborum*] Manso's life of Marino is not extant.

*21. Minervae*] Minerva was goddess of wisdom.

*22–3. illius*] Herodotus, born at Halicarnassus.   *Mycalen*] The promontory of Mycale in Ionia is on the coast not far north of Halicarnassus.   *Aeolii*] Aeolis was a country in Asia Minor, north of Ionia. The first chapter of the *Life of Homer* which used to be attributed to Herodotus tells how Homer was

Ergo ego te Clius et magni nomine Phoebi
25   Manse pater, iubeo longum salvere per aevum
Missus Hyperboreo iuvenis peregrinus ab axe.
Nec tu longinquam bonus aspernabere musam,
Quae nuper gelida vix enutrita sub Arcto
Imprudens Italas ausa est volitare per urbes.
30   Nos etiam in nostro modulantes flumine cygnos
Credimus obscuras noctis sensisse per umbras,
Qua Thamesis late puris argenteus urnis
Oceani glaucos perfundit gurgite crines.
Quin et in has quondam pervenit Tityrus oras.
35   Sed neque nos genus incultum, nec inutile Phoebo,
Quo plaga septeno mundi sulcata Trione
Brumalem patitur longa sub nocte Booten.
Nos etiam colimus Phoebum, nos munera Phoebo
Flaventes spicas, et lutea mala canistris,

conceived in the town of Cyme in Aeolis, but born near Smyrna on the bank
of the river Meles.

24. *Clius*] See *Ad Pat* 14n (p. 149). Phoebus is invoked because Manso has
befriended poets, Clio, because he has written accounts of their lives.

26. *Hyperboreo . . . ab axe*] Diodorus Siculus II xlvii 1 places the island of the
Hyperboreans in the northern ocean, beyond the land of the Celts.

30–4. *cygnos*] swans (i.e. poets), cp. Jonson viii 392 (of Shakespeare): 'Sweet
Swan of *Avon*! what a sight it were / To see thee in our waters yet appeare,/
And make those flights upon the bankes of *Thames*, / That did so take *Eliza*,
and our *James*!' Spenser was born in London and uses the Thames-swan
symbol in *Prothalamion*. That M. had him in mind is confirmed by the name
Tityrus (for Chaucer), used in *Shep. Cal.* February 102. Chaucer visited Italy
1372 and 1378.

36–7. *septeno . . . Trione*] The constellation of Ursa Major was compared to
a waggon with oxen yoked to it: it has seven prominent stars.    *Booten*]
See *Elegia V* 35–6n (p. 82).

38. *Nos . . . Phoebum*] Diodorus Siculus II xlvii 2–3 tells of the legend that
Leto was born on the island of the Hyperboreans, 'and for that reason Apollo
is honoured among them above all other gods; and the inhabitants are looked
upon as priests of Apollo'. In his notes to *Polyolbion* viii and ix (Drayton iv
156, 194–5), Selden sets out his reasons for thinking that the ancient British
god Belin, the Druids' god of healing, is to be identified with Apollo.

38–48. Herodotus iv 33–5 records how the Hyperboreans brought offerings
wrapped in wheat-straw to Apollo and Artemis at Delos: the first Hyper-
boreans to arrive were the maidens Arge and Opis, who 'came with the
gods themselves, and received honours of their own from the Delians. For
the women collected gifts for them, calling them by their names in the hymn
made for them by Olen, a man of Lycia; it was from Delos that the islanders
and Ionians learnt to sing hymns to Opis and Arge.' In Callimachus, *Hymn*

40   Halantemque crocum (perhibet nisi vana vetustas)
     Misimus, et lectas Druidum de gente choreas.
     (Gens Druides antiqua sacris operata deorum
     Heroum laudes imitandaque gesta canebant)
     Hinc quoties festo cingunt altaria cantu
45   Delo in herbosa Graiae de more puellae
     Carminibus laetis memorant Corineida Loxo,
     Fatidicamque Upin, cum flavicoma Hecaerge
     Nuda Caledonio variatas pectora fuco.
     Fortunate senex, ergo quacunque per orbem
50   Torquati decus, et nomen celebrabitur ingens,
     Claraque perpetui succrescet fama Marini,
     Tu quoque in ora frequens venies plausumque virorum,
     Et parili carpes iter immortale volatu.
     Dicetur tum sponte tuos habitasse penates
55   Cynthius, et famulas venisse ad limina musas:
     At non sponte domum tamen idem, et regis adivit
     Rura Pheretiadae coelo fugitivus Apollo;
     Ille licet magnum Alciden susceperat hospes;
     Tantum ubi clamosos placuit vitare bubulcos,
60   Nobile mansueti cessit Chironis in antrum,
     Irriguos inter saltus frondosaque tecta

iv 283–99, the Hyperborean maidens Upis, Loxo and Hecaerge, 'and those who were then the best of the young men', bring 'cornstalks and holy sheaves of corn-ears' to Delos. M. stains the maidens with woad because Caesar, *Bell. Gall.* v 14 says all Britons dye themselves in this way. He makes one of them daughter to Corineus who, according to Drayton iv 13–4, came to Britain with Brutus and defeated the giant Gogmagog at wrestling so that Brutus gave him Cornwall ('of *Corin, Cornwall* call'd').

*42–3.* Druidical rites are described by Selden (Drayton iv 193–4). Caesar, *Bell. Gall.* vi 14 says Druids are concerned with divine worship and all ritual matters, and refers to their strict poetic training.

*55. Cynthius*] Apollo, so called from his birthplace, Mount Cynthus on Delos.

*56–7.* Apollo, banished from heaven for killing the Cyclopes, served as herdsman to Admetus, king of the Pherae in Thessaly and son of Pheres (hence *Pheretiades*). Euripides in a beautiful chorus, *Alcestis* 568–86, describes the music Apollo made while Admetus' guest.

*58.* Apollo granted Admetus that he should not die, when the time came for his death, if a substitute could be found. His wife Alcestis offered herself and died in his stead. In accordance with the laws of hospitality Admetus concealed her death from his guest, Hercules, but the latter discovered the truth, set upon Thanatos (Death) and rescued Alcestis.

*60–6. Chironis*] See *Proc Med* 25–6n (p. 29). Homer, *Il.* xi 832 calls him 'the most righteous of the Centaurs'. Apollo's visits are M.'s invention, but as

Peneium prope rivum: ibi saepe sub ilice nigra
Ad citharae strepitum blanda prece victus amici
Exilii duros lenibat voce labores.
65   Tum neque ripa suo, barathro nec fixa sub imo,
Saxa stetere loco, nutat Trachinia rupes,
Nec sentit solitas, immania pondera, silvas,
Emotaeque suis properant de collibus orni,
Mulcenturque novo maculosi carmine lynces.
70   Diis dilecte senex, te Iupiter aequus oportet
Nascentem, et miti lustrarit lumine Phoebus,
Atlantisque nepos; neque enim nisi charus ab ortu
Diis superis poterit magno favisse poetae.
Hinc longaeva tibi lento sub flore senectus
75   Vernat, et Aesonios lucratur vivida fusos,
Nondum deciduos servans tibi frontis honores,
Ingeniumque vigens, et adultum mentis acumen.
O mihi si mea sors talem concedat amicum
Phoebaeos decorasse viros qui tam bene norit,
80   Si quando indigenas revocabo in carmina reges,
Arturumque etiam sub terris bella moventem;
Aut dicam invictae sociali foedere mensae,

Apollodorus II v 4 relates, Chiron's home was Mount Pelion (until he was
driven from it by the Lapiths) and this is about ten miles from Pherae. The
Peneus, though a Thessalian river, is not near Pelion, however, and Oeta
('the Trachinian cliff'—so called because the town of Trachis stood on its
slopes) is sixty miles south-west of Pelion.

72. *nepos*] Mercury, son of Maia, god of eloquence.

75. *Aesonios*] See *Elegia II* 7–8n (p. 31).        *fusos*] spindles, see *Arcades* 63–72n
(p. 159).

78–93. W. R. Parker, *MLN* lxxii (1957) 488, suggests that these lines imply
that M. already knew of Diodati's death when he wrote *Mansus*.

80–4. See *Dam* 162–71 (p. 275). Arthur was not among the twenty-eight sub-
jects from British history set down by M. in *Trin. MS* as possible epic sub-
jects. P. F. Jones, *PMLA* xlii (1927) 901–9, argues that M. dropped the idea
of an Arthuriad partly because of doubts about the truth of the Arthurian
story: cp. *History of Britain* (Columbia x 127–8): 'But who *Arthur* was, and
whether ever any such reign'd in *Britain*, hath bin doubted heertofore, and
may again with good reason.'

81. *etiam sub terris bella moventem*] The descent to the underworld seems to be
one of the earliest components of the Arthurian cycle. It is recorded in the
Welsh *Spoils of Annwfn* (*Book of Taliesin* xxx), which describes the expedition
undertaken by Arthur and his men to a fortress representing the Celtic
Hades, which is conceived of as a twilit underworld, with the purpose of
carrying off the magic cauldron of the Otherworld.

Magnanimos heroas, et (O modo spiritus ad sit)
Frangam Saxonicas Britonum sub Marte phalanges.
85 Tandem ubi non tacitae permensus tempora vitae,
Annorumque satur cineri sua iura relinquam,
Ille mihi lecto madidis astaret ocellis,
Astanti sat erit si dicam sim tibi curae;
Ille meos artus liventi morte solutos
90 Curaret parva componi molliter urna.
Forsitan et nostros ducat de marmore vultus,
Nectens aut Paphia myrti aut Parnasside lauri
Fronde comas, at ego secura pace quiescam.
Tum quoque, si qua fides, si praemia certa bonorum,
95 Ipse ego caelicolum semotus in aethera divum,
Quo labor et mens pura vehunt, atque ignea virtus
Secreti haec aliqua mundi de parte videbo
(Quantum fata sinunt) et tota mente serenum
Ridens purpureo suffundar lumine vultus
100 Et simul aethereo plaudam mihi laetus Olympo.

Giovanni Battista Manso, Marquis of Villa, is one of the most famous
gentlemen of Italy, not only because of his reputation for intellectual ability
but also because of his devotion to literature and his courage in war. The
dialogue *On Friendship* which Torquato Tasso dedicated to him is still extant.
He was a close friend of Tasso, and is given honourable mention among the
princes of Italy in the *Jerusalem Conquered* xx:
> Among magnanimous and courteous knights
> Shines Manso . . .
While the author was staying in Naples the Marquis looked after him in an
extremely thoughtful way and did him many kind services. Accordingly he
sent the Marquis this poem, before his visit to the city came to an end, in
order not to appear ungrateful.

Manso, the Muses[2] are singing this song, too, in your praise, yes, yours,
Manso, Phoebus' choir knows all about you, because since Gallus[4] and
Etruscan Maecenas died Phoebus has thought hardly anyone so worthy of
honour as you. If my Muses have breath enough for you, like Gallus and
Maecenas, will get a seat among the victorious wreaths of laurel and ivy.

Great Tasso and you were once joined by a happy friendship which has
written your names on the pages of eternity. Not long afterwards the Muse—
who knew what she was doing—entrusted her sweet-voiced Marino to your
care. He was glad to be called your foster-child while he was writing his long
poem about the love of the Assyrian god and goddess[11]—smooth versifier,
his song struck the girls of Italy dumb with admiration. So when he died

---

*83. ad sit*] for *adsit*.
*84.* The various defeats of the invading Saxons by Arthur and his British
army are described at length in Geoffrey of Monmouth's *History*.
*92. Paphia*] Paphos, a city in Cyprus, had a famous temple of Venus, to whom
the myrtle was sacred (cp. Ovid, *Ars Am.* iii 181 *Paphias myrtos*).    *Parnasside lauri*] See *Elegia IV* 29–32n and *Elegia V* 13n (pp. 55 and 81).

he left his body, as was right, to you alone, and to you alone confided his last wishes. And your loving devotion did not fail your friend's spirit: I have seen the poet's features smiling at me from an exquisite bronze. But it did not seem to you that you had done enough for either poet: your devotion and generosity did not end at the grave. You are eager to snatch them unharmed from the jaws of death,[18] if it lies in your power, and to cheat the laws of the devouring Fates.[19] So you are writing an account of their[20] lineage, of the various ups and downs of their lives, of the personalities and of their intellectual gifts.[21] Thus you rival that eloquent biographer[22] of Aeolian Homer who was born near high Mycale.[23] Therefore, father Manso, I, a young stranger sent from Hyperborean skies,[26] wish you a long and healthy life in the name of Clio[24] and of great Phoebus. You, in your goodness, will not be scornful of a Muse from a far-off land who, though poorly nourished beneath the frozen Bear, has recently been rash enough to venture a flight through the cities of Italy. I think that I, too, have heard swans[30] on my native river singing among the night's dark shadows, where the silver Thames pours her green tresses from shining urns and spreads them wide among the swirling currents of the ocean. Why, our Tityrus, too, once visited your land.[34]

But we who have to put up with wintry Boötes for long nights on end, in that region of the world which is furrowed by his seven-starred wagon,[36] are neither an uncultured race, nor useless to Phoebus.[38] We worship Phoebus too: we have sent him gifts—golden ears of grain, and flame-coloured apples in baskets, and the fragrant crocus (if ancient tradition is not a mere fairy-tale) and choirs chosen from the Druid race. The Druids,[42] an ancient race, were well practised in the rituals of the gods and used to sing the praises of heroes and their exemplary exploits.[43] So now whenever Grecian girls stand and sing round the altars on grassy Delos, as they usually do on holidays, their happy songs commemorate Corineus' daughter Loxo, and prophetic Upis, and golden-haired Hecaerge—girls whose bare breasts were stained with woad.[48]

Lucky old man! Wherever in the world the glory and great name of Torquato are honoured, wherever the fame of deathless Marino shines and flourishes, your name and your praises, too, will be on everyone's lips, and you will fly on your way to immortality side by side with them. Men will say that, of his own free will, Apollo[55] dwelt in your house, and that the Muses came like servants to your doors. Yet[56] that same Apollo, when he was a fugitive from heaven, came unwillingly to King Admetus' farm,[57] although Admetus had been host to mighty Hercules.[58] When he wanted to get away from the bawling ploughmen Apollo could, at any rate, retreat to gentle Chiron's[60] famous cave, among the moist woodland pastures and leafy shades beside the river Peneus. There often, beneath a dark oak tree, he would yield to his friend's flattering persuasion and, singing to the music of his lute, would soothe the hardships of exile. Then neither the river banks, nor the boulders lodged in the quarry's depths stayed in their places: the Trachinian cliff[66] nodded to the tune, and no longer felt its huge and familiar burden of forest trees; the mountain ashes were moved and came hurrying down their slopes, and spotted lynxes grew tame as they listened to the strange music.

Old man, dear to the gods, Jupiter must have been favourable when you were born, and Phoebus and the grandson[72] of Atlas must have looked at you with kindly eyes: for unless he is dear to the heavenly gods from his birth, a man does not have the chance to befriend a great poet. That is why your old age is green and spring-like, with lingering flowers; that is why it is vigorous and has a thread of life as long as Aeson's,[75] keeping your handsome features still intact, your intellect active and your wit keen and mature. O may it be my good luck to find such a friend,[78] who knows so well how to honour Phoebus's followers, if ever I bring back to life in my songs the kings of my native land[80] and Arthur, who set wars raging even under the earth,[81] or tell of the great-hearted heroes of the round table, which their fellowship made invincible, and–if only the inspiration would come[83]–smash the Saxon phalanxes beneath the impact of the British charge.[84] Then at last, when I had lived out a life in which poetry was not dumb, when I had reached a ripe old age and paid my last debt to the grave, then that friend would stand by my bed with tears in his eyes, and it would be enough for me to say to him as he stood there, 'Look after me'. He would see to it that when my limbs were blue and heavy with death they were laid gently in a little urn. Perhaps he might have my features carved in marble, binding my hair with a wreath of Paphian myrtle[92] or of Parnassian laurel: and I shall rest safe and at peace.[93] Then, too, if one can be sure of anything, and if rewards do really lie in store for the righteous, I myself, far away in the ethereal home of the heavenly gods, the region to which perseverance and a pure mind and ardent virtue carry a man, shall watch this earth and its affairs–as much, that is, as the Fates permit–from some corner of that far-off world, and, with all my soul calmly smiling, a bright red blush will spread over my face, and I shall joyfully applaud myself on ethereal Olympus.

# 60 *Epitaphium Damonis*
## [Damon's Epitaph]

*Date.* Autumn 1639. M.'s headnote and *15–17* imply composition shortly after his return to England. J. T. Shawcross, *MLN* lxxi (1956) 322–4, suggests Oct.–Nov. on grounds that *58–61* sound like the English weather of these months. Diodati died in London and was buried 27 Aug. 1638: there is some doubt about when M. heard of his death. Shawcross argues that it was in Apr. 1639, while M. was in Florence: he believes that *9–13* refer to Italian crops (in the Arno valley each year there are two wheat harvests–Mar. and Aug.–thus by Apr. 1639 two harvests would have passed since Diodati's death). However W. R. Parker, *MLN* lxxii (1957) 486–8, points out that *9–13* say nothing of M.'s ignorance of Diodati's death: they mean only that

¶ 60. *Title*] A. S. P. Woodhouse (Norwood 265–6) suggests that the choice of the name Damon may be intended to recall the friendship of Damon and Pythias who were, significantly, votaries of the discipline of Pythagoras which M., in *Elegia VI* adopts as a symbol of the virtue and purity essential to the poet of heroic themes.

M. was in Florence in Apr. 1639. Parker maintains that M. heard the news in Naples in Dec. 1638 or Jan. 1639, and that it caused him to cancel his intended journey to Sicily and Greece.

*Publication.* An apparently unique copy of a previously unknown anonymous undated edition of *Dam* was discovered by L. Bradner, *TLS* (18 Aug. 1932) 581, in the British Museum (C. 57. d. 48). Bradner dates this 'probably 1640'. It has no verbal variants but is much more lightly punctuated than 1645 or 1673. Compared with the present text it omits commas after 'querelis' (5), 'Fluminaque' (6), 'recessus' (6), 'umbras' (11), 'aurea' (23), 'agmen' (24), 'comes' (38), 'umbra' (52), 'risus' (55), 'oberro' (58), 'umbrae' (59), 'astrum' (78), 'severi' (84), 'verba' (91), 'iuvenci' (94), 'volitet' (102), 'discors' (107), 'sodale' (118), 'eram' (129), 'myrtos' (131), 'retardat' (147), 'Inogeniae' (163), 'arma' (167), 'lauri' (180), 'Mansus' (181), 'dedit' (183), 'silvae' (186), 'Amor' (191), 'pharetrae' (191), 'perennes' (205) and 'beatis' (218); full stops after 'ulmo' (49), 'magistrum' (67), 'plumbo' (80), 'silvae' (160), 'agni' (161) and 'undis' (178); semi-colons after 'pyropo' (192), 'arcum' (204), and 'hymenaeos' (217); the colon after 'carmen' (3); the exclamation-mark after 'mihi' (19) and the question-mark after 'herbis' (40). Its other variants are: 12. Thyrsis;]Thyrsis,    19. coelo,]coelo?    20. Damon;]Damon!    30. illi]illi,    42. lupos]lupos,    53. nymphae.] nymphae,    66. iuvant;]iuvant,    90. fluenti;]fluenti,    98. onagri;]onagri,    107. Gens homines]Gens, homines,    132. Menalcam.]Menalcam,    135. Fiscellae;]Fiscellae,    (as 1645, see below) 153. Ah](Ah    154. magistro.]magistro.)    214. honores;]honores,    . Next printed 1645 (127. Damon.]Damon,    135. Fiscellae;]Fiscellae, ) and 1673 (the text followed here except in 8 where 1673 misprints 'perrerans' and in 57 where it omits the usual comma after 'vacat').

*Modern criticism.* T. P. Harrison, *PMLA* l (1935) 480–93, cites a number of parallels between *Dam* and Castiglione's *Alcon*, and W. A. Montgomery (Read 207–20) compares *Dam* with the pastoral laments of Theocritus, Bion, Moschus and Virgil. Ralph W. Condee, *SP* lxii (1965) 577–94, defends the poem's structure against Tillyard 99–100 who suspects it stretches to 219 lines only because M. felt it ought to be longer than *Lycidas*. Condee reads *Dam* as a progressive and deliberate abandonment of pastoralism: the refrain reflects 'the restlessness of a deeply emotional poem within its pastoral garments'. Eventually (210) Diodati's pastoral disguise is cast aside and 'the ecstatic hymn which the poem has at last become soars beyond the conventional pastoralism'.

## Argumentum

*Thyrsis et Damon eiusdem viciniae pastores, eadem studia sequuti a pueritia amici erant, ut qui plurimum. Thyrsis animi causa profectus peregre de obitu Damonis nuncium accepit. Domum postea reversus et rem ita esse comperto, se, suamque solitudinem hoc carmine deplorat. Damonis autem sub persona hic intelligitur Carolus Deodatus ex urbe Hetruriae Luca paterno genere oriundus, caetera Anglus; ingenio, doctrina, clarissimisque caeteris virtutibus, dum viveret, iuvenis egregius.*

Himerides nymphae (nam vos et Daphnin et Hylan,
Et plorata diu meministis fata Bionis)
Dicite Sicelicum Thamesina per oppida carmen:
Quas miser effudit voces, quae murmura Thyrsis,
5   Et quibus assiduis exercuit antra querelis,
Fluminaque, fontesque vagos, nemorumque recessus,
Dum sibi praereptum queritur Damona, neque altam
Luctibus exemit noctem loca sola pererrans.
Et iam bis viridi surgebat culmus arista,
10  Et totidem flavas numerabant horrea messes,
Ex quo summa dies tulerat Damona sub umbras,
Nec dum aderat Thyrsis; pastorem scilicet illum
Dulcis amor musae Thusca retinebat in urbe.
Ast ubi mens expleta domum, pecorisque relicti
15  Cura vocat, simul assueta seditque sub ulmo,
Tum vero amissum tum denique sentit amicum,
Coepit et immensum sic exonerare dolorem.
    Ite domum impasti, domino iam non vacat, agni.
Hei mihi! quae terris, quae dicam numina coelo,
20  Postquam te immiti rapuerunt funere Damon;
Siccine nos linquis, tua sic sine nomine virtus
Ibit, et obscuris numero sociabitur umbris?
At non ille, animas virga qui dividit aurea,
Ista velit, dignumque tui te ducat in agmen,

1. *Himerides*] The Himera is a Sicilian river, mentioned by Theocritus, v 124
and vii 75: the nymphs of Himera represent the 'Sicilian muses' of pastoral
poetry who inspired Theocritus and Moschus (see *Lycidas* 133).
*Daphnin*] Daphnis was a shepherd-boy of Ida, changed to stone by a
jealous nymph, and mourned in Theocritus i.      *Hylan*] See *Elegia VII*
24n; here a false quantity–the first syllable of *Hylas* is short.
2. *Bionis*] Moschus iii is a lament for the pastoral poet Bion.
3. Echoing Virgil, *Georg.* ii 176: *Ascraeumque cano Romana per oppida carmen.*
4. *Thyrsis*] The name of Theocritus' shepherd in the lament for Daphnis, ta-
ken over by Virgil in *Ecl.* vii, here represents M.
13. *Thusca . . . in urbe*] In Florence. M. was there Aug.–Sep. 1638 and
Mar.–Apr. 1639.
18. M.'s refrain is a modification of the last line of Virgil's last eclogue: *Ite
domum saturae, venit Hesperus, ite capellae* (Go home, my full-fed goats, the
evening-star comes, go home). It occurs seventeen times: in Theocritus i the
refrain occurs nineteen times, and in Moschus iii, thirteen. Brett 48–9 argues
that M.'s refrain, like the last line of *Lycidas*, represents a farewell to the
pastoral tradition and all that it symbolizes: he is now to turn to epic
(ll. 168–71).
23. *ille*] Mercury. Virgil, *Aen.* iv 242–3, refers to his *virga* 'with which he
calls pale ghosts from Orcus, and sends others down to gloomy Tartarus'.

25    Ignavumque procul pecus arceat omne silentum.
        Ite domum impasti, domino iam non vacat, agni.
        Quicquid erit, certe nisi me lupus ante videbit,
        Indeplorato non comminuere sepulchro,
        Constabitque tuus tibi honos, longumque vigebit
30    Inter pastores: illi tibi vota secundo
        Solvere post Daphnin, post Daphnin dicere laudes
        Gaudebunt, dum rura Pales, dum Faunus amabit:
        Si quid id est, priscamque fidem coluisse, piumque,
        Palladiasque artes, sociumque habuisse canorum.
35    Ite domum impasti, domino iam non vacat, agni.
        Haec tibi certa manent, tibi erunt haec praemia
            Damon,
        At mihi quid tandem fiet modo? quis mihi fidus
        Haerebit lateri comes, ut tu saepe solebas
        Frigoribus duris, et per loca foeta pruinis,
40    Aut rapido sub sole, siti morientibus herbis?
        Sive opus in magnos fuit eminus ire leones
        Aut avidos terrere lupos praesepibus altis;
        Quis fando sopire diem, cantuque solebit?
        Ite domum impasti, domino iam non vacat, agni.
45    Pectora cui credam? quis me lenire docebit
        Mordaces curas, quis longam fallere noctem
        Dulcibus alloquiis, grato cum sibilat igni
        Molle pyrum, et nucibus strepitat focus, at malus auster
        Miscet cuncta foris, et desuper intonat ulmo.
50    Ite domum impasti, domino iam non vacat, agni.
        Aut aestate, dies medio dum vertitur axe,

27. There was a superstition that if a man was seen by a wolf before he saw it, he was struck dumb: cp. Virgil, *Ecl.* ix 53–4: 'Even voice itself now fails Moeris; wolves have seen Moeris first.'

31. *Daphnin*] See l. 1n.

32. *Pales*] Roman goddess, protectress of flocks.     *Faunus*] See *Elegia V* 127n p. 85 above.     The form of M.'s line mimics Virgil, *Ecl.* v 76–80 'long as the boar loves the mountain ridges, as the fish the streams; long as the bees feed on thyme and the cicalas on dew, so long shall thy honour and name and glories abide'.

34. *Palladiasque artes*] See *Proc Med* 33n (p. 29).

46. *Mordaces curas*] See *L'Allegro* 135n (p. 138); Lucan ii 681 has *curis . . . mordacibus*.

47. *Dulcibus alloquiis*] Horace uses the same phrase, *Epod.* xiii 18, when telling his friends to pass the winter merrily.

48. *pyrum*] R. W. Condee (see headnote) replies to Keightley's objection that one roasts crab-apples, not pears, by producing a mention of roast pears in Gervase Markham, *The English House-Wife* (1631) 136.

Cum Pan aesculea somnum capit abditus umbra,
Et repetunt sub aquis sibi nota sedilia nymphae.
Pastoresque latent, stertit sub sepe colonus,
55  Quis mihi blanditiasque tuas, quis tum mihi risus,
Cecropiosque sales referet, cultosque lepores?
    Ite domum impasti, domino iam non vacat, agni.
At iam solus agros, iam pascua solus oberro,
Sicubi ramosae densantur vallibus umbrae,
60  Hic serum expecto, supra caput imber et Eurus
Triste sonant, fractaeque agitata crepuscula silvae.
    Ite domum impasti, domino iam non vacat, agni.
Heu quam culta mihi prius arva procacibus herbis
Involvuntur, et ipsa situ seges alta fatiscit!
65  Innuba neglecto marcescit et uva racemo,
Nec myrteta iuvant; ovium quoque taedet, at illae
Moerent, inque suum convertunt ora magistrum.
    Ite domum impasti, domino iam non vacat, agni.
Tityrus ad corylos vocat, Alphesiboeus ad ornos,
70  Ad salices Aegon, ad flumina pulcher Amyntas,
Hic gelidi fontes, hic illita gramina musco,
Hic Zephyri, hic placidas interstrepit arbutus undas;
Ista canunt surdo, frutices ego nactus abibam.
    Ite domum impasti, domino iam non vacat, agni.
75  Mopsus ad haec, nam me redeuntem forte notarat
(Et callebat avium linguas, et sydera Mopsus)
Thyrsi quid hoc? dixit, quae te coquit improba bilis?

52. In Theocritus i 15–7 the goatherd refuses to pipe at noon for fear of waking Pan from his midday sleep.

56. *Cecropiosque sales*] Cecrops was first king of Attica and founder of the citadel of Athens; Attic wit was renowned.

65. *Innuba*] The Latin poets speak of the vine as 'wedded' to elm or poplar. Horace calls trees without vines 'celibate' or 'widowed', *Odes* II xv 4, IV v 30.

69–70. *Tityrus*] One of the shepherds in Virgil, *Ecl.* i: used as a general name for 'shepherd' in *Ecl.* viii 55.    *Alphesiboeus*] The name means, in Greek, 'bringer-in of oxen': one of the rival singers in *Ecl.* viii.    *Aegon*] The owner of a flock in *Ecl.* iii 2.    *Amyntas*] The beloved of the shepherd Menalcas in *Ecl.* iii.

71. In Virgil, *Ecl.* x 42–3, Gallus sings to the loved one who has deserted him 'Here are cool springs, Lycoris, here soft meadows, here woodland'. Virgil is imitating Theocritus v 33–4: 'There's cool water falling yonder, and here's grass and a greenbed, and the locusts at their prattling.'

75. *Mopsus*] A *Mopso* is mentioned in Tasso's *Aminta* I ii 459, *ch'intende il parlar de gli augelli* (who understands the language of birds).

76. *avium*] M. contracts the word, incorrectly, into a disyllable.

Aut te perdit amor, aut te male fascinat astrum,
Saturni grave saepe fuit pastoribus astrum,
80  Intimaque obliquo figit praecordia plumbo.
Ite domum impasti, domino iam non vacat, agni.
Mirantur nymphae, et quid te Thyrsi futurum est?
Quid tibi vis? aiunt, non haec solet esse iuventae
Nubila frons, oculique truces, vultusque severi,
85  Illa choros, lususque leves, et semper amorem
Iure petit, bis ille miser qui serus amavit.
Ite domum impasti, domino iam non vacat, agni.
Venit Hyas, Dryopeque, et filia Baucidis Aegle
Docta modos, citharaeque sciens, sed perdita fastu,
90  Venit Idumanii Chloris vicina fluenti;
Nil me blanditiae, nil me solantia verba,
Nil me, si quid adest, movet, aut spes ulla futuri.
Ite domum impasti, domino iam non vacat, agni.
Hei mihi quam similes ludunt per prata iuvenci,
95  Omnes unanimi secum sibi lege sodales,
Nec magis hunc alio quisquam secernit amicum
De grege, sic densi veniunt ad pabula thoes,
Inque vicem hirsuti paribus iunguntur onagri;
Lex eadem pelagi, deserto in littore Proteus
100  Agmina phocarum numerat, vilisque volucrum

79–80. *Saturni . . . astrum*] In astrology those born under Saturn were of melancholy temperament.    *obliquo . . . plumbo*] Cp. Spenser, *F.Q.* II ix 52: 'oblique Saturne'; the metal associated with Saturn in alchemy was lead. Horace, *Odes* II xvii 22–3, talks of 'baleful Saturn', and Propertius IV i 84 of 'Saturn that brings woe to one and all'.

86. Echoing Guarini, *Pastor Fido* I i 132–6: *Che se t'assale alla canuta etate | Amorosa talento, | Avrai doppio tormento, | E di quel che, potendo, non volesti, | E di quel che, volendo, non potrai* (For if amorous desire assails you when you are greyhaired, you will suffer the double torment of him who, when he can, does not want to, and of him who, when he wants to, can't).

88–9, *Hyas*] Ovid, *Fast.* v 169–82, tells how Hyas, a beautiful young hunter, son of Atlas and Aethra, was killed by a lioness.    *Dryopeque*] 'The most beautiful of all the Oechalian maids', changed, as Ovid describes, *Met.* ix 330–93, into a lotus-tree. She was mother of Amphissos by Apollo.    *Baucidis*] In Ovid, *Met.* viii 631–724 'pious old Baucis' and her husband Philemon, entertain Jupiter and Mercury. Ovid gives her no daughters.    *Aegle*] 'Loveliest of the Naiads' in Virgil, *Ecl.* vi 21. Horace's Chloe, *Odes* III ix 10, is *docta modos et citharae sciens*.    Presumably M.'s classical names here stand for real people, mutual acquaintances of himself and Diodati.

90. *Idumanii . . . fluenti*] In the chapter on Essex in his *Britannia* Camden identifies Ptolemy's *Idumanum aestuarium* as Blackwater Bay.

99. *Proteus*] See *Elegia III* 26n (p. 50).

Passer habet semper quicum sit, et omnia circum
Farra libens volitet, sero sua tecta revisens,
Quem si fors letho obiecit, seu milvus adunco
Fata tulit rostro, seu stravit arundine fossor,
105 Protinus ille alium socio petit inde volatu.
Nos durum genus, et diris exercita fatis
Gens homines aliena animis, et pectore discors,
Vix sibi quisque parem de millibus invenit unum,
Aut si sors dederit tandem non aspera votis,
110 Illum inopina dies qua non speraveris hora
Surripit, aeternum linquens in saecula damnum.
    Ite domum impasti, domino iam non vacat, agni.
Heu quis me ignotas traxit vagus error in oras
Ire per aereas rupes, Alpemque nivosam!
115 Ecquid erat tanti Romam vidisse sepultam?
Quamvis illa foret, qualem dum viseret olim,
Tityrus ipse suas et oves et rura reliquit;
Ut te tam dulci possem caruisse sodale,
Possem tot maria alta, tot interponere montes,
120 Tot sylvas, tot saxa tibi, fluviosque sonantes.
Ah certe extremum licuisset tangere dextram,
Et bene compositos placide morientis ocellos,
Et dixisse vale, nostri memor ibis ad astra.
    Ite domum impasti, domino iam non vacat, agni.
125 Quamquam etiam vestri nunquam meminisse pigebit
Pastores Thusci, musis operata iuventus,
Hic charis, atque lepos; et Thuscus tu quoque Damon.
Antiqua genus unde petis Lucumonis ab urbe.
O ego quantus eram, gelidi cum stratus ad Arni
130 Murmura, populeumque nemus, qua mollior herba,
Carpere nunc violas, nunc summas carpere myrtos,
Et potui Lycidae certantem audire Menalcam.

117. *Tityrus*] In Virgil, *Ecl.* i 26, Meliboeus asks Tityrus (i.e. Virgil, who went
to Rome and appealed successfully to Octavian against the confiscation of
his farm), *Et quae tanta fuit Romam tibi causa videndi* (And what was the great
occasion of your seeing Rome?)
127–8. 'In the sixteenth century, the Diodatis were already honoured as one
of the oldest patrician families in the flourishing little north-Italian republic
of Lucca. Their earlier history has been traced to Coreglia, a small town about
twenty miles north of Lucca' (Dorian 5). M. made an excursion to Lucca on
his second visit to Florence.
128. *Lucumonis*] *lucumo* (inspired person) was an appellation of the Etruscan
princes and priests.
129. *Arni*] Florence stands on the Arno.
132–7. *Lycidae ... Menalcam*] In Theocritus vii Lycidas and Simichidas

Ipse etiam tentare ausus sum, nec puto multum
Displicui, nam sunt et apud me munera vestra
*135*   Fiscellae; calathique et cerea vincla cicutae,
Quin et nostra suas docuerunt nomina fagos
Et Datis, et Francinus, erant et vocibus ambo
Et studiis noti, Lydorum sanguinis ambo.
    Ite domum impasti, domino iam non vacat, agni
*140*   Haec mihi tum laeto dictabat roscida luna,
Dum solus teneros claudebam cratibus hoedos.
Ah quoties dixi, cum te cinis ater habebat,
Nunc canit, aut lepori nunc tendit retia Damon,
Vimina nunc texit, varios sibi quod sit in usus;
*145*   Et quae tum facili sperabam mente futura
Arripui voto levis, et praesentia finxi,
Heus bone numquid agis? nisi te quid forte retardat,
Imus? et arguta paulum recubamus in umbra,
Aut ad aquas Colni, aut ubi iugera Cassibelauni?

engage in a singing match, and in viii Daphnis the neatherd and Menalcas the
shepherd do the same. M. is referring to the poetical contests at the academies
in Florence where, as he relates, 'the manner is that every one must give some
proof of his wit and reading' (Columbia iii 235, Yale i 809). Friends in
Florence mentioned by M. include Jacopo Gaddi, Carlo Dati, Pietro Fres-
cobaldi, Agostino Coltellini, Benedetto Bonmattei, Valerio Chimentelli
and Antonio Francini (Columbia viii 122). Gaddi had founded an academy
of his own, the *Svogliati* ('Disgusted'), and Coltellini had founded the *Apa-
tisti* ('Apathetics'). On 16 Sep. 1638 M. read 'a very learned Latin poem in
hexameters' to the *Svogliati* (French i 389), and on 17 Mar. 1639 he read
'some noble Latin verses' and on 24 Mar. 'various Latin poems' to the same
academy (French i 408–9). He attended again on 31 Mar. (French i 414). M.
recalls that the poems hē read 'met with acceptance above what was lookt
for' and that some of them 'were receiv'd with written encomiums'
(Columbia iii 236, Yale i 809–10). Dati–born 1619: best known for his *Lives
of the Old Painters* (1667)–and Francini both wrote encomia which were later
printed in the 1645 *Poemata*: these are probably the *munera* of 134, given
pastoral disguise in 135. One of M.'s letters to Dati, and two of Dati's to M.
survive (Columbia xii 296–314, Yale ii 762–75).

*138. Lydorum*] Herodotus i 94 tells how the Lydians migrated from Asia
Minor to N. Italy.

*140. roscida luna*] The phrase is Virgil's, *Georg.* iii 337.

*142. cinis ater habebat*] The phrase is Virgil's, *Aen.* iv 633.

*149. Colni*] The Colne, a tributary of the Thames, flows near Horton.
*iugera Cassibelauni*] Caesar, *Bell. Gall.* v 11, mentions a British chief Cas-
sivellaunus and says that his territory 'is divided from the maritime states by
the river called Thames, about eighty miles from the sea'. M. repeats this
information in the *History of Britain* (Columbia x 44). The Thames forms the

150 Tu mihi percurres medicos, tua gramina, succos,
   Helleborumque, humilesque crocos, foliumque
      hyacinthi,
   Quasque habet ista palus herbas, artesque medentum,
   Ah pereant herbae, pereant artesque medentum
   Gramina, postquam ipsi nil profecere magistro.
155 Ipse etiam, nam nescio quid mihi grande sonabat
   Fistula, ab undecima iam lux est altera nocte,
   Et tum forte novis admoram labra cicutis,
   Dissiluere tamen rupta compage, nec ultra
   Ferre graves potuere sonos, dubito quoque ne sim
160 Turgidulus, tamen et referam, vos cedite silvae.
      Ite domum impasti, domino iam non vacat, agni.
   Ipse ego Dardanias Rutupina per aequora puppes
   Dicam, et Pandrasidos regnum vetus Inogeniae,
   Brennumque Arviragumque duces, priscumque
      Belinum,

southern boundary of Buckinghamshire, thus Cassivellaunus' territory would include Horton.

*153–60.* Dorian 180–1 comments: 'These lines, with what one critic [i.e. Visiak 91] has aptly called "the effect of an emotional breaking-point", just achieve that almost impossible concord between a genuine outcry of grief and coherent artistic expression.'

*160. vos cedite silvae*] In Virgil, *Ecl.* x 63, Gallus bids farewell to pastoral life with the words *concedite silvae.*

*162.* On M.'s projected British epic see *Mansus* 80–4*n* p. 264 above. On the Trojans in Britain see *Elegia I* 73*n* (p. 22).     *Rutupina*] In his chapter on Kent in the *Britannia* Camden identifies Ptolemy's *Rhutupiae* at the mouth of the Wantsum as Richborow.

*163. Inogeniae*] According to Geoffrey of Monmouth I ix–xi, Ignoge (Imogen) was given to the Trojan Brutus as wife by her father Pandrasus after Brutus had defeated him. Spenser calls her 'fayre Inogene of Italy' (*F.Q.* II x 13). M. tells the story in the *History of Britain* (Columbia x 7–11).

*164. Brennumque . . . Belinum*] Geoffrey of Monmouth III i–ix and Spenser, *F.Q.* II x 40, tell how Brennus and Belinus, sons of Dunwallo Molmutius, king of Britain, marched victorious through Gaul and finally captured Rome. M. relates that 'by these two all *Gallia* was overrun, the story tells; and what they did in *Italy*, and at *Rome*, if these be they, and not the *Gauls*, who took that City, the Roman Authors can best relate' (Columbia x 25). The reference is to the sack of Rome in 390 B.C.     *Arviragumque*] Geoffrey IV xiii–xvi and Spenser, *F.Q.* II x 52, make Arviragus son to King Cymbeline and brother of Guiderius, who was killed in battle after refusing to pay tribute to the Romans. Arviragus submitted to the Roman general Claudius and married his daughter Genuissa, but later revolted against Rome. In the *History of Britain* M. names Cymbeline's sons Togodumnus and Caractacus,

165 Et tandem Armoricos Britonum sub lege colonos;
Tum gravidam Arturo fatali fraude Iogernen
Mendaces vultus, assumptaque Gorlois arma,
Merlini dolus. O mihi tum si vita supersit,
Tu procul annosa pendebis fistula pinu
170 Multum oblita mihi, aut patriis mutata camoenis
Brittonicum strides, quid enim? omnia non licet uni
Non sperasse uni licet omnia, mi satis ampla
Merces, et mihi grande decus (sim ignotus in aevum
Tum licet, externo penitusque inglorius orbi)
175 Si me flava comas legat Usa, et potor Alauni,
Vorticibusque frequens Abra, et nemus omne Treantae,
Et Thamesis meus ante omnes, et fusca metallis

and adds: 'The Monmouth Writer names these two Sones of *Cunobeline*, *Guiderius*, and *Arviragus*; that *Guiderius* beeing slaine in fight, *Arviragus* to conceale it, put on his Brothers Habillements, and in his person held up the Battel to a Victorie; the rest, as of *Hamo* the *Roman Captaine*, *Genuissa* the Emperors Daughter, and such like stuff, is too palpably untrue to be worth rehersing in the midst of Truth' (Columbia x 56).

165. According to William of Malmsbury I i, Constantine founded a colony on the W. coast of Gaul with a force of veteran British soldiers. In the *History of Britain* (Columbia x 118–9) M. tells how some of the inhabitants of Kent, fleeing from Picts, Scots and Saxons, reached '*Armorica*, peopl'd, as som think, with *Britans* long before; either by guift of *Constantine* the *Great*, or else of *Maximus* to those *British* Forces which had serv'd them in Forein Wars . . . But the antient Chronicles of those Provinces attest thir coming thether to be then first when they fled the *Saxons*, and indeed the name of *Britain* in *France* is not read till after that time. Yet how a sort of fugitives who had quitted without stroke thir own Country, should so soon win another, appears not; unless joyn'd to som party of thir own settl'd there before.'

166–8. Geoffrey of Monmouth VIII xix tells how Uther Pendragon, through Merlin's magic, appeared to Igraine (*Igerna*) in the form of her dead husband, Gorlois, King of Cornwall, and had by her a son, Arthur.

169. *fistula*] The shepherd's pipe; M. is renouncing pastoral verse and echoing Virgil, *Ecl.* vii 24 *pendebit fistula pinu*.

175. *Usa*] The Ouse.　　*potor Alauni*] Camden, in the *Britannia*, mentions a river 'Alaun' in Hampshire, near Christ Church, where Stour and Avon join and enter the sea, and a river 'Alne' (Ptolemy's *Alaunus*) in Northumberland.

176. *Vorticibusque frequens Abra*] In his chapter on the East Riding Camden says that the Ouse 'being very broad, swift and noisy, pours out his stream into the frith of salt water Abus–for that is what Ptolemy calls that arm of the sea which we name Humber. . . . It rises as high as the ocean at every flood tide, and when the same tide ebbs it brings its own stream and the current of the sea together most forcibly and with a mighty noise.'

Tamara, et extremis me discant Orcades undis.
Ite domum impasti, domino iam non vacat, agni.
*180* Haec tibi servabam lenta sub cortice lauri,
Haec, et plura simul, tum quae mihi pocula Mansus,
Mansus Chalcidicae non ultima gloria ripae
Bina dedit, mirum artis opus, mirandus et ipse,
Et circum gemino caelaverat argumento:
*185* In medio rubri maris unda, et odoriferum ver
Littora longa Arabum, et sudantes balsama silvae,
Has inter Phoenix divina avis, unica terris
Caeruleum fulgens diversicoloribus alis
Auroram vitreis surgentem respicit undis.
*190* Parte alia polus omnipatens, et magnus Olympus,
Quis putet? hic quoque Amor, pictaeque in nube
pharetrae,

*178. Tamara*] The Tamar flows between Cornwall and Devonshire: the tin and other metals of Cornwall explain *fusca metallis*.     *Orcades*] the Orkneys.

*181–97. Mansus*] See *Mansus* headnote (p. 260). M. De Filippis, *PMLA* li (1936) 745–56, takes these 'cups' to be two of Manso's books, the *Erocallia* (twelve Platonic dialogues about love and beauty), and the *Poesie Nomiche*, which include an Italian translation of Claudian's *Phoenix*. D. C. Dorian, *PMLA* liv (1939) 612–3, supports this suggestion, pointing out that Pindar, *Olymp.* vii 1–10, refers to a poem as a cup, thus affording M. classical precedent. For the inclusion of an elaborate description of a cup in a pastoral lament M. had to look only to Theocritus i 29–56 (a passage imitated by Virgil, *Ecl.* iii 36–48). A. S. P. Woodhouse (Norwood 270) explains that whereas the figures on Theocritus' bowl represent the life and loves of earth, those on M.'s bowls represent the life and love of heaven, and a promise of resurrection. The fragrant spring betokens the symbolic promise of renewal; the waters of the Red Sea suggest divine protection; Arabia, with trees dropping balm, stands for divine healing (the heavenly completion of Diodati's fallible earthly art); the phoenix and the rising dawn beyond the waters symbolize resurrection.

*182. Chalcidicae*] See *Leon III 4n* (p. 257).

*185–9.* Hartwell 123–32 suggests that these lines show the influence of a Latin poem *De Ave Phoenice* ascribed to Lactantius. R. Gottfried, *SP* xxx (1933) 497–503, thinks, however, that M.'s source was Tasso's *La Fenice* which combines details from pseudo-Lactantius with others from Claudian's *Phoenix*.

*191. Amor*] Cp. the 'Celestial Cupid' of *Comus* 1004, and Plato's distinction in the *Symposium* 180–5 between the common and heavenly Aphrodite. Those who are inspired by the offspring of the heavenly Aphrodite turn in love to the male, and are interested rather in mind than body: 'This is the Love that belongs to the Heavenly Goddess, heavenly itself and precious to

Arma corusca faces, et spicula tincta pyropo;
Nec tenues animas, pectusque ignobile vulgi
Hinc ferit, at circum flammantia lumina torquens
195 Semper in erectum spargit sua tela per orbes
Impiger, et pronos nunquam collimat ad ictus,
Hinc mentes ardere sacrae, formaeque deorum.
     Tu quoque in his, nec me fallit spes lubrica Damon,
Tu quoque in his certe es, nam quo tua dulcis abiret
200 Sanctaque simplicitas, nam quo tua candida virtus?
Nec te Lethaeo fas quaesivisse sub Orco,
Nec tibi conveniunt lacrymae, nec flebimus ultra,
Ite procul lacrymae, purum colit aethera Damon,
Aethera purus habet, pluvium pede reppulit arcum;
205 Heroumque animas inter, divosque perennes,
Aethereos haurit latices et gaudia potat
Ore sacro. Quin tu coeli post iura recepta
Dexter ades, placidusque fave quicunque vocaris,
Seu tu noster eris Damon, sive aequior audis
210 Diodotus, quo te divino nomine cuncti
Coelicolae norint, sylvisque vocabere Damon.
Quod tibi purpureus pudor, et sine labe iuventus
Grata fuit, quod nulla tori libata voluptas,
En etiam tibi virginei servantur honores;
215 Ipse caput nitidum cinctus rutilante corona,
Letaque frondentis gestans umbracula palmae

both public and private life: for this compels lover and beloved alike to feel a zealous concern for their own virtue.' Ficino in his *Commentary on the Symposium* II vii says that the Love which is paired with the heavenly Aphrodite 'is stimulated to know the beauty of God', and (VI vii) is 'an imitation of the angelic contemplation'. M.'s description also recalls Spenser, *Hymn of Heavenly Love* 1–4: 'Love, lift me up upon thy golden wings, / From this base world unto thy heaven's hight / Where I may see those admirable things / Which there thou workest by thy soveraine might.'

*193. ignobile vulgi*] The phrase is Virgil's, *Aen.* i 149.

*194. flammantia lumina torquens*] The phrase is taken from Virgil's description of the water-snake, *Georg.* iii 433.

*201. Lethaeo . . . Orco*] See *Q Nov* 132*n* and *Elegia VII* 83*n* (pp. 41 and 73).

*210. divino nomine*] Diodati means 'God-given'.

*212–3. purpureus pudor*] The phrase is Ovid's, *Am.* I iii 14.   *quod . . . voluptas*] Cp. *Rev.* xiv 4: 'These are they which were not defiled with women.'

*215. corona*] Cp. *1 Pet.* v 4: 'And when the chief Shepherd shall appear, ye shall receive a crown of glory that fadeth not away.'

*216. palmae*] Cp. *Rev.* vii 9: 'A great multitude . . . stood before the throne, and before the Lamb, clothed with white robes, and palms in their hands.'

Aeternum perages immortales hymenaeos;
Cantus ubi, choreisque furit lyra mista beatis,
Festa Sionaeo bacchantur et orgia thyrso.

*Thyrsis and Damon, shepherds of the same neighbourhood, had cultivated the same interests and been the closest possible friends from childhood on. Thyrsis, while travelling abroad for pleasure, received news of Damon's death. Later, when he had returned home and found that this news was true, he bewailed his lot and his loneliness in this poem. 'Damon' here represents Charles Diodati, who was descended on his father's side from the Tuscan city of Lucca, but who was, in every other respect, English. He was, while he lived, a young man extraordinarily endowed with talents, learning and other gifts of a most exemplary kind.*

Nymphs of Himera,[1] you keep fresh the memory of Daphnis and Hylas and of Bion's[2] sad fate, long lamented. Now sing your Sicilian air through Thames-side towns.[3] Sing of the cries and moans which poor Thyrsis[4] uttered; his ceaseless laments, which shattered the peace of the caves and the streams, of the wandering rills and the woodland dells, when he wept for Damon, who was snatched from him before his time. Through lonely fields he wandered, filling even the depths of the night with his cries of grief. Already the stalk had twice thrust upwards with its green beard of grain, and the granaries had counted in two yellow harvests, since Damon's last day had swept him down among the shades—yet still Thyrsis was missing: the sweet love of the muse detained him in a Tuscan city.[13] But when he had seen enough abroad, and anxiety for the flock he had left behind called him home, he sat down beneath the old familiar elm tree and then, then at last, he felt the loss of his friend and began to ease his huge burden of pain with these words: 'Go home unfed, lambs, your shepherd has no time for you now.'[18] Ah, what powers in earth or heaven can I call divine, Damon, now that they have clutched you with rigid death? Is this the way you leave me? Must your virtue vanish without trace and mingle with the nameless dead? But no! I pray that he[23] who divides the ghostly ranks with his golden wand may not let that happen: may he guide you to companions who are worthy of you, and keep back the worthless mob whose names are heard no more. 'Go home unfed, lambs, your shepherd has no time for you now.' Whatever happens, one thing is certain: unless a wolf sees me first[27] you will not crumble to dust in the grave unlamented. Your fame will outlive you: it will live on the lips of shepherds for long years to come. It will be their delight to make their vows to you, as second only to Daphnis,[31] and to sing your praises, as second only to the praises of Daphnis, as long as Pales[32] or Faunus continue to love the countryside—this shall be so, unless it is of no avail that a man should have kept the faith of his fathers, observed justice, cultivated the arts of Pallas,[34] and had a poet for his friend. 'Go home unfed, lambs, your shepherd has no time for you now.' You can count on these things, Damon, these will be your reward. But what is to become of me? What loyal comrade will stay by my side, as you often used to do, through

217. *hymenaeos*] Cp. *Rev.* xix 7: 'Let us be glad and rejoice . . . for the marriage of the Lamb is come.'
219. *thyrso*] The *thyrsus* was a staff entwined with ivy and vines carried by Bacchus and the Bacchantes.

the hard winter weather, in fields stiff with frost, or under the fierce sun when plants were dying of thirst, whether our job was to stalk the fully grown lions, or to scare the hungry wolves away from our high sheepfolds? Who now will soothe the daylight hours with talk and with song? 'Go home unfed, lambs, your shepherd has no time for you now.' To whom shall I open my heart? Who will teach me to calm eating cares[46] or to beguile the long night with pleasant chatter[47] while soft pears hiss before the cheery blaze and the hearth crackles with nuts, and while the cruel south wind throws everything into confusion out of doors and thunders through the tops of the elms. 'Go home unfed, lambs, your shepherd has no time for you now.' Or in summertime, at high noon, when Pan is asleep,[52] hidden away in the shade of an oak tree, and the nymphs dive down again to their haunts beneath the water, and the shepherds shelter from the sun, and the farm labourer snores under the hedge, who will bring back again for me the charms of your talk, who will bring back your laughter, your flashes of Attic wit[56] and your cultured jokes? 'Go home unfed, lambs, your shepherd has no time for you now.' But now I wander all alone through fields and pastures. I wait for evening in valleys where the shadows of branches are thick and black: over my head the rain and the southeast wind make mournful sounds in the restless twilight of the windswept wood. 'Go home unfed, lambs, your shepherd has no time for you now.' Alas how choked with gadding weeds are my once trim fields! Even the tall grain is spongy with mildew; the unpropped vine rots,[65] its clusters of grapes neglected, and the myrtle groves are joyless. I am even tired of my sheep, and they turn to their shepherd with reproachful eyes. 'Go home unfed, lambs, your shepherd has no time for you now.' Tityrus[69] is calling me to the hazels, Alphesiboeus to the ash-trees, Aegon to the willows, lovely Amyntas[70] to the streams: 'Here are cool fountains! Here is turf covered with moss! Here are soft breezes! Here the wild strawberry tree mingles its murmurs with the mild streams.'[71] They sing to deaf ears. I managed to reach the thickets and escape from them. 'Go home unfed, lambs, your shepherd has no time for you now.' Mopsus,[75] too—Mopsus who knows about the stars and the language of birds[76]—called out, when he happened to see me running away: 'What's the matter, Thyrsis? What melancholy fit is tormenting you? Either love is making you pine away or some malign star has bewitched you. Saturn's star[79] has often been a bane to shepherds: he pierces their heart of hearts with his slanting leaden shaft.'[80] 'Go home unfed, lambs, your shepherd has no time for you now.' The nymphs are amazed and cry 'What will become of you, Thyrsis? What do you mean by all this? Young brows are not usually clouded like yours; young eyes are not usually grim, nor young features so stern. By rights youth should wish for dances and gaiety and games and love, always love. Twice wretched is the man who loves when he is old.'[86] 'Go home unfed, lambs, your shepherd has no time for you now.' Along comes Hyas[88] and Dryope and Baucis's daughter Aegle (a clever musician, good on the lute, but her conceit lets her down),[89] along comes Chloris, who lives by the Idumanean river.[90] No charms, no comforting words, nothing which they can do, no hopes of the future mean anything to me. 'Go home unfed, lambs, your shepherd has no time for you now.' Ah, how like one another are the young bulls which gambol through the meadows! They are all friends together, all of one mind. Not one of them singles out another from the herd as his particular friend. It's the same with wolves, they hunt their food in packs; and the shaggy wild asses mate together by turn. The law of the sea is the same: on the deserted shore Proteus[99] counts his seals in packs. The sparrow, the humblest of birds, always has a companion with whom he flits gaily round every stack of corn, and returns late to his own nest. And if by chance death carries off his mate, if a hook-billed kite cuts short its days or a peasant brings it to earth with his arrow, he goes off and looks for another, there and then, to keep him company as he flies about. But we men are a hard race: a race harassed by cruel fates. Our minds are unfriendly, our hearts discordant. It is hard for a man to find one kindred spirit among thousands of his fellows; and if at last, softened by our prayers, fate grants one, there comes the unexpected day, the unlooked-for hour, which snatches him away, leaving an eternal emptiness. 'Go home unfed, lambs, your shepherd has no time for you now.' Alas, what wanderlust drove me to foreign shores, across the skyey summits of the snow-clad Alps? Was it so very important for me to see buried Rome? Would it have been, even if the city had looked as it once did when Tityrus[117] himself left his flocks and fields to see it? Was it important enough to justify my leaving so sweet a companion and setting between us so many mountains and forests, so many rocks and roaring rivers? Ah, I could at least have held your dying hand and gently closed your lids in peaceful death, and said 'Goodbye! Remember me as you fly up to the stars.' 'Go home unfed, lambs, your shepherd has no time for you now.' And yet I shall never be regretful when I remember you, shepherds of Tuscany, young men formed by the muses: grace and charm dwell with you. You too, Damon, were a Tuscan,[127] descended from the ancient city of Lucca.[128] O how grand I felt, lying by the cool, murmuring Arno,[129] in the shade of a poplar grove, on the soft turf, where I was able to pluck violets and myrtle-tips, and listen to Menalcas and Lycidas[132] having a singing match. I was even bold enough to compete myself, and I don't think I can have been too unpopular, for I still have your gifts, rush baskets and wicker baskets and pipes fastened together with wax. What is more, Dati and Francini,[137] famous poets and scholars both, and both of Lydian[138] blood, made their native beech trees resound with my name. 'Go home unfed, lambs, your shepherd has no time for you now.' These were the sounds which the dewy moon[140] would repeat to me while, happy and solitary, I penned my tender kids in the wattled folds. Ah, how often I used to say (when in reality the black ashes of death had claimed you),[142] 'Now Damon is singing, or laying nets to catch a hare, or making baskets of osiers to serve his various needs.' All unsuspecting, I was quick to seize upon the scenes which I hoped for so longingly in the future, and to imagine them as present: 'Hallo there! What are you up to? If there's nothing else you have to do let's go and lie down a bit in the chequered shade beside the streams of Colne[149] or among the acres of Cassivellaunus. Then, as I listen, you can run through your list of healing potions and herbs–hellebore, humble crocus, hyacinth leaf–all the plants of the fenland, and all the skills of medicine.' O confound herbs and plants and medical skills:[153] they were not able to save their master! And I–for my pipe was sounding some lofty strain, I know not what, eleven nights and a day ago, and I had by chance set my lips to a new set of pipes, when their fastening broke and they fell apart: they could bear the grave notes no longer–I am afraid that I am being swollen-headed, but still, I will tell of that strain. Give place, woods.[160]

'Go home unfed, lambs, your shepherd has no time for you now.' I shall tell of Trojan keels ploughing the sea off the Kentish coast,[162] and of the ancient kingdom of Inogene,[163] daughter of Pandrasus, of the chieftains Brenus and Arviragus and of old Belinus,[164] and of the settlers in Brittany, subject at last to British law.[165] Then I shall tell of Igraine,[166] pregnant with Arthur as a result of fatal deception: I shall tell of the lying features which misled her, and of the borrowing of Gorlois's armour, Merlin's trick.[168] O, if I have any time left to live, you, my pastoral pipe,[169] will hang far away on the branch of some old pine tree, utterly forgotten by me, or else, transformed by my native muses, you will whistle a British tune. But after all, one man cannot do everything, or even hope to do everything. I shall have ample reward, and shall think it great glory, although I be for ever unknown and utterly without fame in the world outside, if only yellow-haired Usa[175] reads my poems, and he who drinks from the Alan, and Humber, full of whirling eddies,[176] and every grove of Trent, and above all my native Thames and the Tamar,[178] stained with metals, and if the Orkneys among their distant waves will learn my song. 'Go home unfed, lambs, your shepherd has no time for you now.' I was keeping these things for you, wrapped in tough laurel bark, these, and more as well. And I was keeping also the two cups[181] which Manso gave me—Manso, not the least glory of the Neapolitan[182] shore. They are a marvellous work of art, and he a marvellous man. Around them he had placed an engraving with a double subject. In the middle are the waves of the Red Sea,[185] and the spicy-smelling spring, the long shores of Arabia, and forests dripping with balsam. Among these the phoenix, the divine bird, the only one on earth, gleams green and blue with parti-coloured wings, and watches Aurora rising from the glassy waves.[189] Another part of the design shows the boundless sky and great Olympus, and here—who would have thought it?—is Cupid[191] with his brightly coloured quivers ringed by a cloud, his glittering arms, his torches and his bronze-coloured arrows. From that height he does not hit trivial spirits or the base hearts of the rabble[193] but, peering all round him with flaming eyes[194] he always releases his darts upwards among the heavenly spheres with tireless aim, and never aims downwards. These shafts kindle holy minds and the forms of the gods themselves.[197] You, too, are among the gods—no deceitful hope beguiles me, Damon—you are among them without doubt, for where else could your sweet and holy simplicity and your snow-white virtue have gone? It would be wrong to look for you in Lethean Orcus.[201] Nothing is here for tears. I shall weep no more. Away with you, tears. Damon dwells now in the pure ether: pure himself, his home is the ether. He spurns the rainbow with his foot, and among the souls of heroes, among the eternal gods, he drinks the draughts of heaven and drains its joys with his holy lips.

Now that you have received your dues in heaven, be present at my side and gently favour me, whatever name you may now bear, whether you are Damon—the name I have given you—or whether you prefer Diodati, the divine name[210] by which all the hosts of heaven will know you, though the woods still call you Damon.

Because the blush of modesty[212] and a youth without stain were your choice, and because you never tasted the delight of the marriage bed,[213] see—virginal honours are reserved for you! Your radiant head circled with a gleaming crown,[215] the joyful, shady branches of leafy palm[216] in your hands, you will take part for ever in the immortal marriage-rite,[217] where singing is heard and the lyre rages in the midst of the ecstatic dances, and where the festal orgies rave in Bacchic frenzy under the thyrsus[219] of Zion.

# 61 Translations from 'Of Reformation'

Date. Jan.–May 1641. Of Reformation was written during the early months of 1641, and published before the end of May.

(i) From Dante, Inf. xix 115–7: Ahi, Costantin, di quanto mal fu matre, / Non la tua conversion, ma quella dote / Che da te prese il primo ricco patre!

(ii) From Petrarch cxxxix 9–13: Fondata in casta et umil povertate, / contr'a'tuoi fondatori alzi le corna, / putta sfacciata: e dove hai poste spene? / Ne gli adùlteri tuoi? ne le mal nate / richezze tante? Or Constantin non torna.

(iii) From Ariosto, Orlando Furioso XXXIV lxxiii: Non stette il duca a ricercare il tutto: / che là non era asceso a quello effetto. / Da l' apostolo santo fu condutto / in un vallon fra due montagne istretto, / ove mirabilmente era ridutto / ciò che si perde o per nostro difetto, / o per colpa di tempo o di Fortuna: / ciò che si perde qui, là si raguna. The translation M. quotes is Harington's. Though he owned a copy of the 1591 edition of this, he is here apparently quoting from memory, since he makes two minor changes (And for Harington's But 1, and Into for Unto 2).

(iv) From Ariosto, Orlando Furioso XXXIV lxxx: Di varii fiori ad un gran monte passa / ch'ebbe già buno odore, or putia forte. / Questo era il dono (se però dir lece) / che Constantino al buon Silvestro fece. Here M. owes little to Harington, who translates: 'Then by a fayre green mountain he did passe, / That once smelt sweet, but now it stinks perdye. / This was the gift (be't said without offence) / That Constantin gave Silvester long since.'

(i)   Ah Constantine, of how much ill was cause
      Not thy conversion, but those rich domains
      That the first wealthy Pope received of thee.

(ii)  Founded in chaste and humble poverty,
      'Gainst them that raised thee dost thou lift thy horn,
      Impudent whore, where hast thou placed thy hope?
      In thy adulterers, or thy ill-got wealth?
5     Another Constantine comes not in haste.

(iii) And to be short, at last his guide him brings
      Into a goodly valley, where he sees
      A mighty mass of things strangely confused,
      Things that on earth were lost, or were abused.

(iv)  Then passed he to a flowery mountain green,
      Which once smelt sweet, now stinks as odiously;
      This was that gift (if you the truth will have)
      That Constantine to good Sylvestro gave.

## 62 Translation from 'Reason of Church-Government'

*Date.* 4 Aug. 1641 to 1 Jan. 1642 (the dates of composition of *Reason of Church-Government*).

The Greek line Ἐμοῦ θανόντος γαῖα μιχθήτω πυρί, probably from a lost play of Euripides (*Bellerophon*), was a favourite saying of Tiberius according to Dio, *Roman History* lviii 23: when someone quoted it to Nero, Suetonius relates, he corrected it to Ἐμοῦ ζῶντος ('When I live . . .') (*Nero* 38). Cicero alludes to the line (*De Finibus* III xix 64) as if it were too familiar to quote. Jonson has it, and the Dio reference, in *Sejanus* II 330.

When I die, let the earth be rolled in flames.

## 63 Translations from 'Apology for Smectymnuus'

*Date.* Apr. 1642.
(i) From Horace, *Sat.* I i 24–6: *Quamquam ridentem dicere verum / quid vetat? ut pueris olim dant crustula blandi / doctores, elementa velint ut discere prima.*
(ii) *Ibid.* I x 14–5: *Ridiculum acri / fortius et melius magnas plerumque secat res.*
(iii) From Sophocles, *Electra* 624–5 (Electra talking to Clytemnestra): σύ τοι λέγεις νιν, οὐκ ἐγώ. σὺ γὰρ ποιεῖς / τοὔργον· τὰ δ᾽ἔργα τοὺς λόγους εὑρίσκεται.

(i)       Laughing to teach the truth
What hinders? as some teachers give to boys
Junkets and knacks, that they may learn apace.

(ii)       Jesting decides great things
Stronglier, and better oft than earnest can.

(iii) 'Tis you that say it, not I, you do the deeds,
And your ungodly deeds find me the words.

## 64 Sonnet VIII. When the assault was intended to the City

*Date.* Nov.? 1642. In the Trinity MS there is a fair copy in the hand of an amanuensis headed 'On his door when the City expected an assault'. This is crossed through, and 'When ˈtheˈ assault was intended to the City' substi-

tuted in M.'s hand, with the date '1642', later deleted. In the printed editions
the heading is merely VIII.

After Edgehill (23 Oct. 1642) Essex withdrew to Warwick, leaving the
road to London undefended. The advance of the Royalist army caused panic
in the capital; on 12 Nov. a Parliamentary force was defeated at Brentford.
The city was hastily defended with earthworks and the trained bands were
called out and reinforced with the remainder of Essex's army. Thus on 13
Nov. an army of 24,000 was drawn up on Turnham Green to face the
Royalists: Charles, however, ordered a retreat. At the time M. was living
in Aldersgate Street, educating his two young nephews: his wife had left
him.

*Publication.* 1645 (3. If deed of honour did thee ever] If ever deed of honour
did thee ), 1673 (the text followed here).

> Captain or colonel, or knight in arms,
>   Whose chance on these defenceless doors may seize,
>   If deed of honour did thee ever please,
>   Guard them, and him within protect from harms,
> 5 He can requite thee, for he knows the charms
>   That call fame on such gentle acts as these,
>   And he can spread thy name o'er lands and seas,
>   Whatever clime the sun's bright circle warms.
> Lift not thy spear against the muses' bower,
> 10  The great Emathian conqueror bid spare
>   The house of Pindarus, when temple and tower
> Went to the ground: and the repeated air
>   Of sad Electra's poet had the power
>   To save the Athenian walls from ruin bare.

¶ 64. *1. colonel*] Trisyllabic, as often in the seventeenth century.

*3. If . . . ever*] *Trin. MS*: If ever deed of honour did thee.

*10. Emathian conqueror*] Alexander; Emathia was a district of Macedon, of
which his father was king (Ovid calls him *dux Emathius, Tristia* III v 39).
Plutarch, *Alexander* 11 and Pliny vii 29 recount that when his army sacked
Thebes (335 B.C.) he spared the house once occupied by Pindar, and showed
mercy to the poet's descendants.

*10–14.* Finley 38 compares Horace's frequent practice of ending an ode
with two or three examples (e.g. IV vii and viii).

*12–13.* Plutarch, *Lysander* 15, describes how, when the Spartans with their
allies the Thebans and Corinthians had defeated Athens (404 B.C.), Erianthus,
a Theban, proposed that Athens should be razed to the ground; but a man
from Phocis was heard singing the first chorus from Euripides' *Electra*,
'Electra, Agamemnon's child, I come / Unto thy desert home . . .'), upon
which all the hearers were melted with compassion and refused to destroy a
city which had produced such great men.

# 65 Sonnet X. To the Lady Margaret Ley

*Date.* 1642 ? There is no certain evidence for dating. According to Edward Phillips (Darbishire 64): 'Our Author, now as it were a single man again [i.e. after his wife's return home in or around July 1642], made it his chief diversion now and then in an Evening to visit the Lady Margaret Lee ... This Lady being a Woman of great Wit and Ingenuity, had a particular Honour for him, and took much delight in his Company, as likewise her Husband Captain Hobson ... ; and what esteem he at the same time had for Her, appears by a Sonnet he made in praise of her.' She and her husband, who fought on the Parliamentarian side in the Civil War, lived in Aldersgate Street, and were thus near neighbours of M.

*Sonnet X* is printed as the last of the ten sonnets in *1645*, so presumably it was written before 6 Oct. 1645, when *1645* was entered in the Stationers' Register. No evidence for dating can be drawn from its position in the Trinity MS, since it is there in fair copy. It is headed 'To the Lady Margaret Ley'.

*Publication. 1645 (3.* fee.]fee,     *10.* you,]you ) *1673* (the text followed here).

> Daughter to that good Earl, once President
> Of England's Council, and her Treasury,
> Who lived in both, unstained with gold or fee.
> And left them both, more in himself content,
> 5   Till the sad breaking of that Parliament

¶ 65. *1–2. Earl ... Treasury*] James Ley (1550–1629), who became Lord Chief Justice in 1622 and was created Earl of Marlborough in 1626 by Charles I. He retired from the Bench in Dec. 1624 to become Lord High Treasurer. Resigning this post in 1628, he was made President of the Council. Finley 53 calls this opening Horatian in that it achieves its poetic effect out of the description of a man's official life: he compares Horace, *Odes* II i 13–6.

*3.* Sir James Whitelocke, *Liber Famelicus* (Camden Society, 1858) p. 108 says that Ley was crafty, deceitful, underhand and 'an old dissembler ... wont to be called Vulpone, and I think he as well deserveth it now as ever'. He borrowed money from certain judges when Lord Chief Justice and then, when Lord High Treasurer, attempted to pay these judges their salaries but to withold those of others. The attempt was 'verye honestly' thwarted, says Whitelocke, by Sir Robert Pye.

*4. left them*] Ley retired from the Presidentship of the Council 14 Dec. 1628.

*5–6.* Ley died 14 Mar. 1629. On 2 Mar. Charles had directed that Parliament should be adjourned, but the speaker was held down in his chair while Sir John Eliot read out three resolutions calling the country's attention to the

Broke him, as that dishonest victory
At Chaeronea, fatal to liberty
Killed with report that old man eloquent,
Though later born, than to have known the days
10    Wherein your father flourished, yet by you,
Madam, methinks I see him living yet;
So well your words his noble virtues praise,
That all both judge you to relate them true,
And to possess them, honoured Margaret.

# 66 Sonnet IX

*Date.* 1643? In the Trinity MS a working copy of this sonnet follows a fair copy of *Sonnet VIII* (Nov.? 1642). There is no other evidence for dating it, except the presence of the poem in *1645*. The identity of the 'Lady' is not known: some have been tempted to identify her with the 'Lady' of *Comus* (who did not marry until 1652, and who was twenty-four in 1643) but there is no evidence that M. saw her after 1634.
*Publication.* *1645* (5. Mary and with Ruth,]Mary, and the Ruth, 9. fixed]fixed, ) *1673* (the text followed here).

Lady, that in the prime of earliest youth,
Wisely hath shunned the broad way and the green,
And with those few art eminently seen,
That labour up the hill of heavenly truth,

King's misdemeanours. Two days later Eliot and eight other members were sent to the Tower; Parliament was dissolved on 10 Mar.. M. implies that this open breach between Charles and the Parliamentary leaders hastened Ley's end.
*6. dishonest*] shameful.
*7. Chaeronea*] Here in 338 B.C. Philip of Macedon defeated the Athenians and Thebans, thus gaining control of the Greek city states.
*8. old man*] Isocrates. Dionysius of Halicarnassus, in a short biography included in his *Commentaries on the Ancient Orators*, says that Isocrates lived ninety-eight years and died a few days after Chaeronea, for he had vowed that he would not survive the good of Athens. Stephanus repeats this information (*s.v.* Isocrates).
¶ *66. 2. hath*] Trin. *MS*: hast. *broad way*] Cp. *Matt.* vii 13: 'Broad is the way, that leadeth to destruction.'
*4. hill . . . truth*] Cp. Donne, *Sat.* iii 79–81: 'On a huge hill, / Cragged, and steep, Truth stands, and hee that will / Reach her, about must, and about must goe.' But the hill of truth was a commonplace.

5   The better part with Mary and with Ruth,
    Chosen thou hast, and they that overween,
    And at thy growing virtues fret their spleen,
    No anger find in thee, but pity and ruth.
    Thy care is fixed and zealously attends
10      To fill thy odorous lamp with deeds of light,
    And hope that reaps not shame. Therefore be sure
Thou, when the bridegroom with his feastful friends
    Passes to bliss at the mid-hour of night,
    Hast gained thy entrance, virgin wise and pure.

# 67 Translation from title-page of 'Areopagitica'

*Date.* Nov. 1644.

The translation is of Euripides, *Supplices* 438–41 τοὐλεύθερον δ' ἐκεῖνο·
τίς θέλει πόλει/χρηστόν τι βούλευμ' εἰς μέσον φέρειν ἔχων;/καὶ ταῦθ'
ὁ χρῄζων λαμπρός ἐσθ', ὁ μὴ θέλων / σιγᾷ. τί τούτων ἔστ' ἰσαίτερον
πόλει;

    This is true liberty when freeborn men
    Having to advise the public may speak free,
    Which he who can, and will, deserves high praise,
    Who neither can nor will, may hold his peace;
5   What can be juster in a state than this?

# 68 Translation from 'Tetrachordon'

*Date.* Feb. 1645. *Tetrachordon* was published 4 Mar.

The translation is of Horace, *Epist.* I xvi 40–5: *Vir bonus est quis? |* '*qui
consulta patrum, qui leges iuraque servat, | quo multae magnaeque secantur iudice*

5. *Mary . . . Ruth*] Mary sat at Jesus' feet, while Martha was 'cumbered about
much serving'. Christ's reply, when Martha complained, was 'one thing
is needful: and Mary hath chosen that good part', *Luke* x 39–42. Ruth, un-
like Orpah, refused to go off and find a husband, and did not follow 'young
men', *Ruth* i 14–7, iii 10.
7. *growing virtues*] Trin. *MS: blooming 'prospering' virtues 'growing virtues'.*
11–14. Cp. *Rom.* v 5, 'hope maketh not ashamed', and the parable of the
ten virgins, *Matt.* xxv 1–13.
13. *Trin. MS: Opens the door of bliss, that hour of night 'Passes to bliss at the
mid-watch  hour' [of] night'.*

*lites, | quo res sponsore et quo causae teste tenentur.' | sed videt hunc omnis*
*domus et vicinia tota | introrsum turpem, speciosum pelle decora.*

Whom do we count a good man, whom but he
Who keeps the laws and statutes of the senate,
Who judges in great suits and controversies,
Whose witness and opinion wins the cause;
5  But his own house, and the whole neighbourhood
Sees his foul inside through his whited skin.

## 69 *In Effigiei eius Sculptor*
[On the Engraver of his Portrait]

*Date.* 1645. The portrait which prefaced *1645* was an engraving by William
Marshall. These lines were engraved under it, and it seems likely that M.
played a practical joke on Marshall in causing him to engrave a condem-
nation of his own skill in language of which he was ignorant. The portrait of
M. is labelled *Anno Aetatis Vigess: Pri:* (At the age of twenty-one), and it has
therefore been assumed that Marshall was working from the so-called Onslow
portrait of M. at twenty-one, now in the National Portrait Gallery. The
two portraits are, though, quite dissimilar: Marshall's is plainly of an older
man, in spite of its label. Referring to the Marshall portrait M. later claimed
that he 'consented, at the instance and from the importunity of the book-
seller [Humphrey Moseley], to employ an unskilful engraver, because at that
period of the war there was no other to be found in the city' (Columbia ix
125). Masson[2] iii 457 thinks that M. may have had a grudge against
Marshall because he was the engraver of the caricatures of Anabaptists and
other sectarians in Daniel Featley's *Dippers Dipt* (1645)–in *Tetrachordon* M.
says he does not commend Featley's 'marshalling' (Columbia iv 69, Yale ii
583).

Marshall, who limited himself entirely to book illustration, was the most
prolific of the early English engravers. Two of his best known works are the
portrait of Donne at the age of eighteen (printed in Donne's *Poems* 1635)
and the emblematical frontispiece to the *Eikon Basilike* (1648).

*Publication.* 1645, 1673 (no significant variants. The portrait was omitted
from *1673*, and the epigram on Marshall printed with the other Greek
poems).

> Ἀμαθεῖ γεγράφθαι χειρὶ τήνδε μὲν εἰκόνα
> Φαίης τάχ' ἄν, πρὸς εἶδος αὐτοφυὲς βλέπων·
> Τὸν δ' ἐκτυπωτὸν οὐκ ἐπιγνόντες φίλοι
> Γελᾶτε φαύλου δυσμίμημα ζωγράφου.

¶ 69. *4.* δυσμίμημα] The word involves a false quantity, and is also an im-
proper formation (though paralleled by δυσχείρωμα in Sophocles, *Ant.*

You would say, perhaps, that this picture was drawn by an ignorant hand, when you looked at the form that nature made. Since you do not recognize the man portrayed, my friends, laugh at this rotten picture of a rotten artist.

# 70 Sonnet XIII. To Mr H. Lawes, on his Airs

*Date.* 9 Feb. 1646. The Trinity MS has three drafts: (*a*), headed '13 / To my friend Mr Hen. Lawes Feb. 9 1645', heavily corrected (see notes) and later crossed through, and (*b*), headed '13 / To Mr Hen. Lawes on the publishing of his Airs', are in M.'s hand. Draft (*c*), headed '13 / To Mr Hen. Law'e's on *the publishing of* his Airs', is a fair copy in another hand.

On M's friendship with Lawes see Evans. Lawes had been a member of the King's Music, and his sympathies were Royalist. His brother William fell fighting for the King at Chester (1645). The 1648 *Choice Psalmes*, which Lawes published to commemorate William, and which contained examples of the latter's work, was dedicated to Charles I, then a prisoner. *Sonnet XIII* was first printed in this volume (headed 'To my Friend Mr Henry Lawes').

The heading of Trinity MS (*b*) looks like a later insertion, since the first of Lawes's three volumes of *Airs and Dialogues* did not appear until 1653. *Publication. Choice Psalmes* 1648 (*4.* long;]long, *6.* wan;]wan: *7.* man,] man *10.* choir]choir, *11.* hymn,]hymn *13.* sing]sing, ) *1673* (the text followed here, except in *9* where *1673* misprints 'send' for 'lend' )

> Harry whose tuneful and well-measured song
>    First taught our English music how to span
>    Words with just note and accent, not to scan
> With Midas' ears, committing short and long;
> 5  Thy worth and skill exempts thee from the throng,

126). T. O. Mabbott, *Explicator* viii (1950) 58, points out that δυσμίμημα ζωγράφου may mean a bad picture by or of an artist: he thinks this ambiguity intentional, the idea being that the picture represents the man who made it, not the supposed subject.

¶ 70. *3. Trin.* MS (*a*): *Words with just notes, which till then used* 'when most were wont' to scan 'when most were wont to scan' 'words with just note and accent, not to scan' 'words with just note and accent, not to scan'.

*4. Midas*] As a punishment for preferring the music of Pan to that of Apollo he was, as Ovid relates, *Met.* xi 146–79, given ass's ears. *committing*] *Trin.* MS (*a*): *committing* 'misjoining'. The verb 'commit' meaning 'engage (parties) as opponents' is here, according to *OED*, used figuratively for the first time. Waller (*Poems* ed. G. Thorn Drury (1893) i 19–20) also praises Lawes's music for not obscuring the meaning of the verse he is setting.

*5. worth*] *Trin.* MS (*a*): *worth* 'wit' 'worth'. *exempts . . . throng*] Horace is similarly exempted, *Odes* I i 32.

With praise enough for envy to look wan;
To after age thou shalt be writ the man,
That with smooth air couldst humour best our
    tongue.
Thou honour'st verse, and verse must lend her wing

*10*    To honour thee, the priest of Phoebus' choir
That tun'st their happiest lines in hymn, or story.
Dante shall give fame leave to set thee higher
Than his Casella, whom he wooed to sing
Met in the milder shades of Purgatory.

# 71 Sonnet XII. On the Detraction which followed upon my Writing Certain Treatises

*Date.* 1646. There are two versions of this sonnet in the Trinity MS (referred to as *Trin. MS* (*a*) and (*b*) below). *Trin. MS* (*a*) is not a fair copy (it contains two alterations: see notes) and it appears after and on the same page as a rough draft and a fair copy of *Sonnet XIII*, of which the rough draft is dated 9 Feb.

*6. Trin. MS* (*a*): *And gives thee praise above* the pipe of Pan.

*7. the*] *Trin. MS* (*a*): a.

*8. Trin. MS* (*a*): That didst reform thy art, the chief among (*b*): That with smooth air*s couldst* cou'dst humour best our tongue.

*11. story*] *Choice Psalmes* has a marginal note: 'The story of Ariadne set by him in music.' William Cartwright's *Complaint of Ariadne* was set by Lawes and printed in his first book of *Airs*.

*12. Trin. MS* (*a*): 'Dante shall give' Fame *by the Tuscan's leave shall* 'to' set thee higher.

*12–14.* In *Purgatorio* ii 76–119 Dante meets the shade of Casella, a Florentine musician who had been his friend, on the threshold of Purgatory. In life Casella had set some of Dante's canzoni to music, and when Dante now asks the shade to sing it complies with the canzone *Amor che nella mente mi ragiona.*

*13. Trin. MS* (*a*): Than *old* 'his' *Casell'* 'Casella' whom *Dante* 'he' won 'oed' to sing.

*14. milder*] *Trin. MS* (*a*): *mildest* 'milder'. Masson iii 289 takes this to mean that the shades of Purgatory are 'milder' than those of Hell, but J. S. Diekhoff, *MLN* lii (1937) 409–10, draws attention to the first reading in *Trin. MS* (*a*)—what is referred to is the mildness of the threshold of Purgatory, where the meeting occurs, by comparison with other parts of Purgatory.

1645 [i.e. 1646]. Therefore *Sonnet XII* must be dated after 9 Feb. 1646. Both versions are headed with the figure 11 [altered later to 12 in *Trin. MS (b)*], and with the title given above [later deleted in *Trin. MS (a)*]. *Trin. MS (b)* is followed by a version of *Sonnet XI* (headed 12), but this order is reversed in *1673* where *XI* precedes *XII*.

The position of *Trin. MS (a)* relative to *Sonnet XIII* was used, as above, to date *Sonnet XII* by J. H. Hanford, *MP* xviii (1921) 144–5. Previously D. H. Stevens, *MP* xvii (1919) 27–8 had suggested a date in the autumn of 1644, and more recently J. T. Shawcross, *N & Q* viii (1961) 179–80 has favoured Sep. 1645.

The *Treatises* referred to in the title are the divorce tracts, which appeared as follows: (i) *The Doctrine and Discipline of Divorce* (anonymous) 1 Aug. 1643. Second edition (bearing M.'s name) 2 Feb. 1644. Third and fourth editions 1645. (ii) *The Judgment of Martin Bucer* (entered 15 Jul. 1644: M.'s name appears at end of address to Parliament, in which he asserts that, on the appearance of *Doctrine and Discipline*, 'some of the clergie began to inveigh and exclaim on what I was credibly inform'd they had not read' (Columbia iv 12, Yale ii 434). On 24 Aug. 1644 (French ii 106–8) the Stationers presented a petition to Parliament in which complaint was made against 'the Pamphlet . . . concerning Divorce', and in Sep. 1644 William Prynne's *Twelve Considerable Serious Questions* hoped for the suppression of the same pamphlet. In Dec. M. was summoned to the House of Lords for examination (French ii 116) but, according to John Phillips (Darbishire 24) 'soon dismiss'd'). (iii) *Tetrachordon* (4 Mar. 1645: bears M.'s name: not licensed or registered. In the address to Parliament M. vindicates himself from the attacks of two ministers, Herbert Palmer, who called for the suppresssion of *Doctrine and Discipline* in a sermon preached before Parliament 13 Aug. 1644 (French ii 106) and Dr Daniel Featley who attacked the same work in *The Dippers Dipt*, 1645) (iv) *Colasterion* (4 Mar. 1645: bears M.'s initials: unlicensed and unregistered. The title means, in Greek, 'instrument of correction'. A reply to the anonymous *Answer to The Doctrine and Discipline of Divorce*, Nov. 1644 (reprinted in Parker 170–216). In Nov. 1645 (French ii 132–3) Robert Baillie attacked M.'s divorce views in *A Dissuasive from the Errors of the Time*, and in Feb. 1646 (French ii 143) Thomas Edwards did the same in *Gangraena*. Other and later attacks than those mentioned here are listed by Parker 73–84).

*Publication. 1673.*

*Modern criticism.* N. H. Henry, *MLN* lxvi (1951) 509–13, thinks that *Sonnet XII* is directed not so much against the Presbyterians who rejected M.'s divorce proposals as against the 'lunatic fringe' of the Independents who embraced them in an embarrassing way (e.g. the Mrs Attaway, mentioned in Edwards's *Gangraena*, who left her husband after reading M. on divorce and became 'the mistress of all the she-preachers of Coleman Street').

> I did but prompt the age to quit their clogs
> By the known rules of ancient liberty,

When straight a barbarous noise environs me
Of owls and cuckoos, asses, apes and dogs.
5   As when those hinds that were transformed to frogs
Railed at Latona's twin-born progeny
Which after held the sun and moon in fee.
But this is got by casting pearl to hogs;
That bawl for freedom in their senseless mood,
10   And still revolt when truth would set them free.
Licence they mean when they cry liberty;
For who loves that, must first be wise and good;
But from that mark how far they rove we see
For all this waste of wealth, and loss of blood.

# 72 On the New Forcers of Conscience under the Long Parliament

*Date.* Aug. 1646? By an ordinance of Jan. 1645 Parliament adopted the Directory for Public Worship in place of the Book of Common Prayer (the 'liturgy' of *2*), but not until 28 Aug. 1646 did Parliament draw up the rules of ordination by the Classical Presbyteries. D. H. Stevens, *MP* xvii (1919) 30, thinks that the poem must be dated after this, but before 4 Jun. 1647, when Charles was captured by the army. J. H. Hanford, *MP* xviii (1921) 145, agrees, but feels that a date just before the final realization of the 'just fears' of M. and the Independents on 28 Aug. is also possible.

*Trin. MS* has a corrected draft in the hand of an amanuensis with a note requiring that the poem should be inserted after *Sonnet XI* (1647?) and before *Fairfax* (Aug. 1648?).

¶ 71. *4. cuckoos*] *Trin MS* (*a*): buzzards.
*5–7.* Ovid. *Met.* vi 317–81, narrates how when Latona, with her baby twins Apollo and Diana, later deities of sun and moon, wanted to drink at a pool, some Lycian peasants stirred up the water to make it muddy, whereupon Jove turned them to frogs. W. R. Parker, *Explicator* viii (1949) 3, thinks that M. introduced the fable of the 'twin-born progeny' because he had in mind the reception given to his own 'twins', *Tetrachordon* and *Colasterion*, which were published on the same day, 4 Mar. 1645.
*10. still . . . free*] *Trin. MS* (*a*): *hate the truth whereby they should be free* 'still revolt when truth would set them free' (*b*): still revolt when truth would *make* 'set' them free. Cp. *John* viii 32: 'And the truth shall make you free.'
*11.* Smart 68–9 points out that the distinction between licence and liberty was common in Roman authors. Finley cites Plato, *Rep.* viii 560E. M. has the distinction in his letter to Parliament prefaced to the *Doctrine and Discipline* (Columbia iii 370, Yale ii 225) and in the *History of Britain* (Columbia x 104).
*13. rove*] To shoot an arrow away from the 'mark' (target).

*Publication. 1673.*
*Modern criticism.* Smart 127 points out that this is an example of the *sonetto caudato* ('tailed sonnet')–a form popular with Italian satirists, particularly those of the school of Berni. M.'s sonnet has two 'tails', each of a half-line and a couplet.

> Because you have thrown off your prelate lord,
>    And with stiff vows renounced his liturgy
>    To seize the widowed whore plurality
>    From them whose sin ye envied, not abhorred,
> 5 Dare ye for this adjure the civil sword
>    To force our consciences that Christ set free,
>    And ride us with a classic hierarchy
>    Taught ye by mere A. S. and Rutherford?

¶ 72. *1. thrown . . . lord*] Episcopacy was formally abolished in England by a decree of the Long Parliament, Sep. 1646, but Parliament's ordinance of June 1643 summoning the Assembly of Divines made it quite clear that episcopacy was condemned since one purpose of the Assembly was to decide what should replace it.

*3. widowed*] Trin. MS: *vacant* 'widowed'.    *plurality*] The practice of holding more than one living. In his *History of Britain* (Columbia x 322), M. complains that members of the Westminster Assembly were quick 'to seise into thir hands or not unwillinglie to accept (besides one sometimes two or more of the best Livings) collegiat master-ships in the universities, rich lectures in the cittie. . . . By which meanes those great rebukers of nonresidence among so many distant cures were not asham'd to be seen so quicklie pluralists and nonresidents themselves.'

*5. adjure*] charge, entreat. M., always opposed to the interference of the civil power in religious matters, complains of the Westminster Assembly's attempt to impose Presbyterianism by force, 'while they taught compulsion without convincement (which not long before they so much complain'd of as executed unchristianlie against themselves) thir intents were cleere to be no other then to have set up a spiritual tyrannie by a secular power' (Columbia x 322).

*6. our*] Trin. MS: *the* 'our'.

*7. classic*] Parliament resolved that the English parishes or congregations were to be grouped in Presbyteries or 'Classes' after the Scottish pattern.

*8. A.S.*] Dr Adam Stewart, Scottish Presbyterian controversialist and Professor of Philosophy at Leyden. When the five leading Independents in the Assembly (Goodwin, Simpson, Nye, Burroughs and Bridge) put their case in the *Apologetical Narration* 1644, Stewart's *Some Observations* (signed A. S.) was one of several replies.    *Rutherford*] Samuel Rutherford (1600–61), one of the four Scottish divines on the Assembly and Professor of Divinity at St Andrew's. His pamphlets included *A Plea for Presbytery* 1642 and *The Due Right of Presbyteries* 1645.

Men whose life, learning, faith and pure intent
10     Would have been held in high esteem with Paul
Must now be named and printed heretics
By shallow Edwards and Scotch What-d'ye-call:
But we do hope to find out all your tricks,
Your plots and packing worse than those of Trent,
15         That so the Parliament
May with their wholesome and preventive shears
Clip your phylacteries, though baulk your ears,
And succour our just fears

9. *Men*] Smart 129 thinks these are the five authors of the *Apologetical Narration*.

12. *shallow*] *Trin. MS: hare-brained* 'shallow'.     *Edwards*] Thomas Edwards. His *Antapologia*, advocating strict Presbyterianism, was a reply to the *Apologetical Narration*, and his *Gangraena: or a Catalogue of many . . . Heresies . . . of this Time* 1646 included a denunciation of M.'s views on divorce (quoted Parker 76–7).     *What-d'ye-call*] probably Robert Baillie, Professor of Divinity at Glasgow. His *Dissuasive from the Errors of the Time* 1645 attacked M.'s divorce-writings: 'I doe not know certainly whither this man professeth Independency (albeit all the Hereticks here, whereof ever I heard, avow themselves Independents)' (quoted Parker 75).

14. *packing*] *Trin. MS*: packings. *OED* defines the word as 'the corrupt constitution or manipulation of a deliberative body', but gives no example before 1653. M. is referring to the overwhelming Presbyterian predominance in the Assembly.     *Trent*] the Council of Trent (1545–63) reformulated the doctrines of the Roman Catholic church after the Reformation.

17. *Trin. MS: Crop ye as close as marginal P----'s ears* 'Clip your phylacteries, though baulk your ears'. The first version alludes to the cropping of William Prynne's ears in 1634 because passages in his attack on the stage, *Histriomastix*, were taken to refer to the King and Queen. In 1637 he was sentenced to lose the rest of his ears and to be branded for an attack on Wren, Bishop of Norwich. He wrote several pamphlets against Independency and attacked M.'s divorce-views in *Twelve Considerable Serious Questions* 1644. *phylacteries*] a phylactery is a small leather box containing four scriptural texts (*Deut.* vi 4–9; xi 13–21; *Exod.* xiii 1–10, 11–16), worn by Jews during morning prayer as a mark of obedience to their literal interpretation. Christ in *Matt.* xxiii 5 uses the phrase 'make broad their phylacteries' in the sense 'vaunt their own righteousness'; thus 'phylactery' in English comes to mean 'an ostentatious or hypocritical display of piety'–first used by M. thus in 1641 (Yale i 897) antedating *OED*'s citing of *Tetrachordon* (Yale ii 582).     *baulk*] miss. D. C. Dorian, *MLN* lvi (1941) 62–4, detects the implication that the Presbyterians will be lucky if they escape a far severer punishment than ear-clipping–their own exclusion from the clergy, because the Mosaic qualifications for the priesthood excluded any man with a physical blemish (*Lev.* xxi 17–23).

> When they shall read this clearly in your charge
> 20    New *Presbyter* is but old *Priest* writ large.

# 73 Sonnet XIV

*Date.* Dec. 1646. The Trinity MS has three drafts: (*a*) a working copy later struck through, headed 'On the religious memory of Mrs Catharine Thom'a'son my Christian friend deceased *16* Decem. 1646' (it was Smart 81 who first noticed the inserted 'a' and thus identified the subject of the sonnet. The deleted *16* are the first two numerals of the year [1646], which M. crossed through in order to insert, first, the month. Mrs Thomason was buried 12 Dec. 1646); (*b*), a second draft, also in M.'s hand, headed '14'; and (*c*) a fair copy made by an amanuensis. Mrs Thomason was the wife of George Thomason, a bookseller whose magnificent collection of civil war pamphlets is now in the British Museum. Several of M.'s treatises contained in it are marked *Ex dono authoris*. Smart 79 suggests that Thomason is the intimate friend (*mihi familiarissimo*) to whom M. entrusted his letter to Carlo Dati in Florence (Columbia xii 52, Yale ii 765) in Apr. 1647. Very little is known of Mrs Thomason. She had nine children, and the mention of her library in her husband's will (Smart 81) indicates scholarly leanings.
*Publication. 1673.*
*Modern criticism.* R. L. Ramsay, *SP* xv (1918) 123–58, claims that this sonnet, in its first Trinity MS draft, reads like a condensed version of *Everyman* and is the most detailed example of M.'s use of the medieval allegory.

> When faith and love which parted from thee never,
>     Had ripened thy just soul to dwell with God,
>     Meekly thou didst resign this earthy load
>     Of death, called life; which us from life doth sever.
> 5   Thy works and alms and all thy good endeavour
>     Stayed not behind, nor in the grave were trod;

19. *they*] *Trin. MS: you* 'they'.
20. 'Priest' is etymologically a contracted form of Latin *presbyter* (an elder); thus 'priest' 'writ large' (expanded) would be 'presbyter'. 'Priest' is found in Old English, but 'presbyter' is a late sixteenth century word.          *writ large*] *Trin. MS:* writ *at* large.
¶ 73. 1. *which*] *Trin. MS (a):* that.
3. *load*] *Trin. MS (a):* clod 'load'.
4. *death . . . doth*] *Trin. MS (a): flesh and sin* 'death, called life' *which man* 'us' *from heav'n* 'life' *doth.*
5. *and all*] *Trin. MS (a):* 'and' all. Cp. *Acts* x 4: 'Thy prayers and thine alms are come up for a memorial before God.'
6. *Trin. MS (a): Straight followed thee the path that saints have trod* 'Stayed not behind, nor in the grave were trod'.

But as faith pointed with her golden rod,
Followed thee up to joy and bliss for ever.
Love led them on, and faith who knew them best
10    Thy handmaids, clad them o'er with purple beams
And azure wings, that up they flew so dressed,
And speak the truth of thee on glorious themes
Before the judge, who thenceforth bid thee rest
And drink thy fill of pure immortal streams.

## 74 Ad Joannem Rousium Oxoniensis Academiae Bibliothecarium

*De libro Poematum amisso, quem ille sibi denuo mitti postulabat, ut cum aliis nostris in Bibliotheca publica reponeret, Ode*

[To John Rouse, Librarian of Oxford University. An Ode on a lost Book of Poems. He requested that a second copy of it should be sent, so that he could place it in the public library with my other books]

*Date.* 23 Jan. 1647. This date is given in the *1673* heading. Bodleian MS Lat. Misc. f15 is a fair copy of this ode, possibly in M.'s hand, but if so 'in a most formal, set hand, unlike anything we possess today known to have been written by M.' (Fletcher³ i 458). The Bodleian MS is pasted to the verso of the Latin title-page of a copy of *1645* which may be the substitute copy sent to Rouse by M. There is no evidence that Rouse (1574–1652), who became Bodley's librarian in 1620, was a personal friend of M.'s. M. sent him copies of the eleven prose pamphlets of 1641–44, and these are now bound in one volume in Bodley (4°F.56) bearing, in M.'s hand, a list of the books sent and a presentation inscription which says that Rouse had requested the pamphlets should be sent. On 30 Dec. 1645 Rouse caused something of a stir by

7. *Trin. MS (a)*: *Still as 'when' they journeyed from this dark abode* 'But as Faith pointed with her golden rod'.
8. *Trin. MS (a)*: *Up to the realm of peace and joy for ever* 'Followed thee up to joy and bliss for ever'. Cp. *Rev.* xiv 13: 'Blessed are the dead which die in the Lord . . . their works do follow them.'
9. *Trin. MS (a)*: Faith *who led on* 'showed' the way, and *knew* 'she who saw' them best (b): Faith 'Love' *showed* 'Love led' the'm' *way* 'on', and *she* 'Faith' who *saw* 'knew' them best.
11. *that*] *Trin. MS (a)*: *thence* 'that'.
12. *speak . . . on*] *Trin. MS (a)* and (b): spake the truth of thee in   (c): spake the truth of 'thee' on. H. J. C. Grierson, *TLS* (15 Jan. 1925) 40, prefers 'in glorious' (*Trin. MS (a)* and (b) reading) to 'on glorious', and suggests that 'themes' is being used in a musical sense (meaning 'strains').

refusing to allow Charles I to borrow the *Histoire Universelle du Sieur d'Aubigné* from the Bodleian (which is not a lending library) although the request was countersigned by Fell, the Vice-Chancellor. In 1643 Rouse contributed £50 to a loan to Charles, but he was a lukewarm Royalist: see E. Craster, *Bodleian Library Record* v (1954–6) 130–46. *Publication. 1673.*

*Modern criticism.* From the viewpoint of versification the ode is a daring experiment, and was sharply censured by nineteenth-century critics like Landor (*Imaginary Conversations* (1883) iv 105–6)–'on no occasion has any Latin poet so jumbled together the old metres'–and Symmons (*Life of M.* (1806) 230), who called it 'a wild chaos of verses and no verses heaped together confusedly and licentiously'. W. R. Parker, *PQ* xxviii (1949) 145–66, points out that it is only paralleled by the choruses of *Samson Agonistes* and notes that M. uses the same terms to describe each (see p. 345 below).

### *Strophe 1.*

Gemelle cultu simplici gaudens liber,
Fronde licet gemina,
Munditieque nitens non operosa,
Quam manus attulit
5  Iuvenilis olim,
Sedula tamen haud nimii poetae;
Dum vagus Ausonias nunc per umbras
Nunc Britannica per vireta lusit
Insons populi, barbitoque devius
10  Indulsit patrio, mox itidem pectine Daunio
Longinquum intonuit melos
Vicinis, et humum vix tetigit pede;

### *Antistrophe.*

Quis, te, parve liber, quis te fratribus
Subduxit reliquis dolo?
15  Cum tu missus ab urbe,
Docto iugiter obsecrante amico,
Illustre tendebas iter
Thamesis ad incunabula
Caerulei patris,
20  Fontes ubi limpidi

¶ 74. *1. Gemelle . . . liber*] *1645* formed a 'twin' volume since it contained the English poems and then the Latin, each with separate pagination and title-page (*Fronde . . . gemina*).
*10. Daunio*] Daunia was the name given in classical times to a part of Apulia: M. presumably means merely 'Italian,' referring to the Latin poems.

> Aonidum, thyasusque sacer
> Orbi notus per immensos
> Temporum lapsus redeunte coelo,
> Celeberque futurus in aevum;

*Strophe 2.*

25  Modo quis deus, aut editus deo
    Pristinam gentis miseratus indolem
    (Si satis noxas luimus priores
    Mollique luxu degener otium)
    Tollat nefandos civium tumultus,
30  Almaque revocet studia sanctus
    Et relegatas sine sede musas
    Iam pene totis finibus Angligenum;
    Immundasque volucres
    Unguibus imminentes
35  Figat Apollinea pharetra,
    Phineamque abigat pestem procul amne Pegaseo.

*Antistrophe.*

> Quin tu, libelle, nuntii licet mala
> Fide, vel oscitantia
> Semel erraveris agmine fratrum,
40  Seu quis te teneat specus,
    Seu qua te latebra, forsan unde vili
    Callo tereris institoris insulsi,
    Laetare felix, en iterum tibi
    Spes nova fulget posse profundam
45  Fugere Lethen, vehique superam
    In Iovis aulam remige penna;

*21. Aonidum*] See *Elegia IV* 29–32*n* (p. 55).

*25–36.* Cp. Horace's similar appeal to an unnamed god or hero, *Odes* I ii 25–52, and castigation of civil war, 21–4.

*29–31.* The Civil War had broken out in 1642; Oxford was the Royalist headquarters.

*33–6.* The *volucres* are the harpies, called *Phineam . . . pestem* because Apollonius of Rhodes, *Argon.* ii 187–93, tells how they were sent by Zeus to punish the prophet-king Phineus by defiling him and snatching away his food. The Argonauts, not Apollo, delivered Phineus from the harpies, but M. looks to Apollo because he is a monster-slayer (see *Elegia VII* 31–4*n*, p. 71) and god of poetry. The 'river of Pegasus' is the Thames, on which Oxford stands: Pegasus, the winged horse of the Muses, caused the fountain Hippocrene to flow from Mount Helicon with a blow of his hoof.

*45. Lethen*] See *Q Nov* 132*n* (p. 41).

*Strophe 3.*

Nam te Roüsius sui
Optat peculi, numeroque iusto
Sibi pollicitum queritur abesse,
50 Rogatque venias ille cuius inclyta
Sunt data virum monumenta curae:
Teque adytis etiam sacris
Voluit reponi quibus et ipse praesidet

Aeternorum operum custos fidelis,
55 Quaestorque gazae nobilioris,
Quam cui praefuit Iön
Clarus Erechtheides
Opulenta dei per templa parentis
Fulvosque tripodas, donaque Delphica
60 Iön Actaea genitus Creusa.

*Antistrophe.*

Ergo tu visere lucos
Musarum ibis amoenos,
Diamque Phoebi rursus ibis in domum
Oxonia quam valle colit
65 Delo posthabita,
Bifidoque Parnassi iugo:
Ibis honestus,
Postquam egregiam tu quoque sortem
Nactus abis, dextri prece sollicitatus amici.
70 Illic legeris inter alta nomina
Authorum, Graiae simul et Latinae
Antiqua gentis lumina, et verum decus.

*Epodos.*

Vos tandem haud vacui mei labores,
Quicquid hoc sterile fudit ingenium,

---

56–60. Ion was son of Apollo by Creusa, daughter of Erechtheus, king of
Athens. His early history is told by Euripides, *Ion* 1–81: he was exposed in a
cave by his mother, but carried to Delphi by Hermes and later made guardian
of the treasuries of the sanctuary of Apollo there. The treasuries at Delphi
border the sacred way which winds up the hillside to the temple of Apollo.
Famous among the thank-offerings there was a golden tripod erected, out of
the booty of Plataea, on a bronze column formed of three serpents inter-
twined.　　*Actaea*] Actaean (from *Acte*, the old name for Attica) means
Attic or Athenian.
65–6. Delos is an island shrine in the Cyclades, the birthplace of Apollo and
Diana.　　*Parnassi*] See *Elegia IV* 29–32n (p. 55).

75 Iam sero placidam sperare iubeo
Perfunctam invidia requiem, sedesque beatas
Quas bonus Hermes
Et tutela dabit solers Roüsi,
Quo neque lingua procax vulgi penetrabit,
atque longe
80 Turba legentum prava facesset;
At ultimi nepotes,
Et cordatior aetas
Iudicia rebus aequiora forsitan
Adhibebit integro sinu.
85 Tum livore sepulto,
Si quid meremur sana posteritas sciet
Roüsio favente.

Ode tribus constat Strophis, totidemque Antistrophis una demum
epodo clausis, quas, tametsi omnes nec versuum numero, nec certis
90 ubique colis exacte respondeant, ita tamen secuimus, commode
legendi potius, quam ad antiquos concinendi modos rationem
spectantes. Alioquin hoc genus rectius fortasse dici monostrophicum
debuerat. Metra partim sunt κατὰ σχέσιν, partim ἀπολελυμένα.
Phaleucia quae sunt, spondaeum tertio loco bis admittunt, quod
95 idem in secundo loco Catullus ad libitum fecit.

*Strophe* 1 Twin-born book,[1] rejoicing in a single cover but with a double
title-page, bright with that unlaboured neatness which a boyish hand once
gave you—an earnest, but not too poetic hand—while he wandered in play
through the shades of Italy or the green fields of England, roaming about,
untainted by the crowd, in unfrequented places, giving himself up to the
music of his native lute; or, presently, thundering out to the bystanders a
song from far away, strumming a Daunian[10] string, his feet hardly touching
the ground;
*Antistrophe* Who was it, little book, who was it that craftily took you from
your brothers when, in reply to my learned friend's ceaseless entreaties, you
had been sent from the city and were making that lovely journey to the
birthplace of deep-blue Father Thames, where the clear springs of the
Aonides[21] are found and the sacred Bacchic dance, known to all the world
through the vast tracts of the vanished years and revolving seasons, and
famous for all time?
*Strophe* 2 But what god[25] or god-begotten man will be moved to pity by the
native talents which our race has displayed throughout history and—if
we have done enough penance for our past evils, and for the degenerate
idleness of our womanish luxury—will put an end to this damnable civil
war and its skirmishes,[29] restore with his holy power our life-giving pursuits,
recall the homeless Muses[31]—banished now from almost every corner of
England, transfix with arrows from Apollo's quiver the foul birds[33] who

94. *Phaleucia*] The regular Phaleucian line consists of a spondee, a dactyl and
three trochees.

hover over us with threatening claws, and drive Phineus' bane far from the river of Pegasus?[36]

*Antistrophe* But, little book, though through the messenger's dishonesty or negligence you have wandered on this one occasion from the company of your brothers; though now you lie in some ditch or on some hidden shelf from which, perhaps, you are taken and thumbed over by a block-headed bookseller with calloused, grimy hands–cheer up, lucky little book! See, here is a gleam of hope for you–hope that you will be able to escape from the depths of Lethe[45] and, beating your wings, soar to the high courts of Jove.

*Strophe* 3 For Rouse wants you to be a part of his collection. He complains that, though you were promised to him, you are missing from the list, and he asks that you should come to him–Rouse, to whose care are entrusted the glorious monuments of illustrious men–he wants you to have a place in those holy sanctuaries over which he presides in person, faithful guardian of immortal works, custodian of a treasure richer than that which far-famed Ion[56] watched over–Ion of Erechtheus's line, Actaean Creusa's son–in the sumptuous temple of his father, Apollo, with its golden tripods and its Delphic treasuries.[60]

*Antistrophe* So you will go and feast your eyes on the lovely glades of the Muses, you will go again to that divine home of Phoebus in the Vale of Oxford–that home which he prefers to Delos[65] or forked Parnassus.[66] You will go in honour, when you leave my side, for you have been remarkably lucky: you have received a pressing invitation from a friend who wishes you well. There you will be read among authors whose great names were of old the guiding lights and are now the true glory of the Greek and Latin race.

*Epode.* So, my labours, you have not been in vain, as it turns out: not in vain, the tricklings of my sluggish genius. Now at last I can tell you to look forward to peace and rest, all envy past, and to the happy home which kind Hermes and Rouse with his expert guardianship will provide: a home to which the insolent clamourings of the rabble will never penetrate, far away from the vulgar mob of readers. But perhaps the children of the future, in some distant and wiser age, will see things in a fairer light and with unprejudiced hearts. Then, when spite and malice are buried in the past, posterity with its balanced judgment will know–thanks to Rouse–what, if anything, I have deserved.

This ode consists of three strophes and three antistrophes with a concluding epode. Though the strophes and antistrophes do not exactly correspond either in the number of their lines or in the distribution of their particular metrical units, nevertheless I have cut the poem up in this way in order to make it easier to read, rather than with a view to imitating any ancient method of versification. It would perhaps be more correct, in other respects, to call this kind of composition monostrophic. The metres are partly determined by correlation, partly free. In the Phaleucian[93] lines I have twice admitted a spondee in the third foot: Catullus does so quite freely in the second foot.

# 75 Sonnet XI

*Date.* 1647? J. H. Hanford, *MP* xviii (1921) 144–5, argues for a date in 1647 or later on the evidence of the position of *Sonnet XI* in the Trinity MS. This, he claims, would fit the meaning of ll. *3–4* better than an earlier date.

The Trinity MS has two versions: a working draft (*a*) and a fair copy (*b*). The latter follows the fair copy of *Sonnet XII.* but in *1673* this order is reversed (see headnote to *Sonnet XII* p. 291 above).

*Publication.* 1673.

> A book was writ of late called *Tetrachordon*;
> And woven close, both matter, form and style;
> The subject new: it walked the town awhile,
> Numbering good intellects; now seldom pored on.
> 5 Cries the stall-reader, Bless us! what a word on
> A title-page is this! And some in file
> Stand spelling false, while one might walk to Mile-
> End Green. Why is it harder sirs than Gordon,
> Colkitto, or Macdonnel, or Galasp?

¶75. *1. A . . . writ*] *Trin. MS* (*a*): *I writ a book* 'A book was writ'. For details of *Tetrachordon*'s publication, see headnote to *Sonnet XII* (p. 291). The name means 'four-stringed', and is a reference, as M.'s title-page explains, to 'The four chief places in Scripture, which treat of Marriage, or nullities in Marriage' (i.e. *Gen.* i 27–8 compared with ii 18, 23–4; *Deut.* xxiv 1–2; *Matt.* v 31–2 compared with *Matt.* xix 3–11; *1 Cor.* vii 10–6).

*2. woven*] *Trin. MS* (*a*): *weav'd it* 'wov'n'.

*3. The . . . walked*] *Trin. MS* (*a*): *It went off well about* 'The subject new; it walked'. Finley 71–2 compares Horace, *Epist.* I xx, where Horace addresses his book as if it were a prostitute gadding about.

*4. Numbering*] *OED* gives this as the first instance of the vb *number* in the sense 'to have (so many things or persons)'.    *intellects; now*] *Trin. MS* (*a*): *wits; but* 'intellects' now *is*.

*7. spelling false*] misinterpreting.

*7–8. Mile-End Green*] Mile-End was at the first mile stone on the Roman road which left the city at Aldgate: to 'walk to Mile-End Green' is to walk to the outskirts of the city.

*8. Gordon*] There were several Gordons among Montrose's men: the most famous was George, Lord Gordon, eldest son of the Marquis of Huntly.

*9. Colkitto, or Macdonnel*] Montrose's lieutenant was called Alexander Macdonald. His father was Coll Keitache (a name abbreviated to Colkitto in the lowlands, and sometimes applied to the son).    *Galasp*] George Gillespie, one of the leaders of the Scottish Covenant, and a member of the Westminster Assembly.

10      Those rugged names to our like mouths grow sleek
        That would have made Quintilian stare and gasp.
    Thy age, like ours, O soul of Sir John Cheke,
        Hated not learning worse than toad or asp;
    When thou taught'st Cambridge, and King
        Edward Greek.

# 76 Psalms lxxx-lxxxviii

*Date.* Apr. 1648. This date heads M.'s translations in *1673*.
*Publication. 1673.*
*Modern criticism.* Masson i 243 believed that M. was prompted to translate
these psalms in 1648 by the current controversy over the metrical psalter –
the Commons preferred the version of Francis Rous (1641, revised 1646) and
the Lords that of William Barton (1644). M.'s metre, accordingly, is Com-
mon Measure, like Rous's except that Rous rhymes second and fourth lines,
M. first and third.

E. C. Baldwin, *MP* xvii (1919) 457–63, criticising the translations from
the viewpoint of the original Hebrew, concluded that M.'s heading implied

*10. rugged*] Trin. *MS* (*a*): *barbarous* 'rough-hewn' 'rugged'.        *like*] 'rugged'
also.        W. F. Smith, *N & Q* ii (1916) 7, connects this line with the English
proverb 'Like lips like lettuce' and its Latin equivalent *similes habent labra
latuces* which Jerome interprets (*Ad Chromatium*) in the light of the anecdote
about M. Crassus (Cicero, *De Finibus* v 92) – that he laughed only once in
his life, and that was when he saw an ass eating thistles instead of lettuces
because they matched his mouth better.
*11. Quintilian*] In his discussion of 'barbarisms' Quintilian I v 8 includes the
use of foreign words, and cites examples.
*12. Sir John Cheke*] Cheke (1514–57) was the first Professor of Greek at
Cambridge, and one of the most famous English humanists: tutor to Edward
VI.        Masson iii 283 took 'like ours' to mean 'your age did not hate learn-
ing *as ours does*'. Smart 73–4, however, paraphrases 'Many men in that age
(which has been thought so propitious to such studies), *hated not learning
worse than toad or asp*–but as much as they hated either'. In support of this
interpretation he quotes from Cheke's *De Pronuntiatione Graecae* (1555) some
remarks about general opposition to the growth of Greek studies. H. Schultz,
*MLN* lxix (1954) 495–7, agrees with Smart, adding that in 1641 Langbaine's
reissue of Cheke's *The True Subject* set the latter's learning off against a back-
ground of contemporary obscurantism. J. M. French, *MLN* lxx (1955)
404–5, favours Masson's reading, calling attention to *Tetrachordon* itself,
where M. refers to the reign of Edward VI as 'on record for the purest and
sincerest that ever shon yet on the reformation of this Iland' (Columbia iv
231, Yale ii 716).

a more literal rendering than he had attained, and that his knowledge of Hebrew was deficient. Baldwin found M.'s versions overlong, and pointed to the frequent use of synonyms, the tendency to substitute the vaguely generic for the concrete (e.g. lxxxi *43-4* means literally 'Open thy mouth wide and I will fill it'), and the weak conventionality of many of the words— especially the adjectives – M. italicizes as insertions (e.g. lxxx *5, 36, 53* etc.). Moreover there are more insertions than the italics would suggest (e.g. lxxxvii *21-4* contain nine words with no equivalent in the Hebrew, and in lxxxv *14* 'and us restore' is not in the original). Baldwin thought the Vulgate responsible for some of M.'s errors (e.g. lxxxiii *49* 'wheel' should be 'that which is blown along by the wind' (i.e. dust or chaff), but the Vulgate has *rotam*).

M. H. Studley, *PQ* iv (1925) 364-72, attempting a defence against Baldwin, suggests that M. was following the traditional phraseology of English metrical translations (which were very numerous) rather than the Hebrew: this might explain his tendency to expansion and generalization of the concrete (e.g. at lxxxi *43-4*, which Baldwin specifies, George Wither's translation (1632) reads 'And will thy largest asking give'). M. chose lxxx-lxxxviii, thinks Studley, because these psalms express the need of the church for God's guidance: his translations thus parallel his controversial pamphlets.

H. F. Fletcher, *M.'s Semitic Studies* (Chicago 1926) pp. 97-110, agrees that M. often depended upon previous metrical renderings – not, however, because his Hebrew was deficient, but because of his difficulty in writing strict Common Measure. Fletcher demonstrates his point by a detailed comparison of lxxxii with the Hebrew original: e.g. at lxxxii *2* the Hebrew has 'assembly of God': M. realizes his 'kings and lordly states' are not there, and so italicizes: but Tremellius had *magistratus*, the Great Bible (1539) 'prynces', the A.V. 'the mighty', Buchanan's Latin metrical version (1566) 'reges', and Sternhold and Hopkins 'men of might'. M. is following a tradition of translation.

Comparison of M.'s versions with earlier ones has been taken furthest by W. B. Hunter Jr, *PQ* xxviii (1949) 125-44 and xl (1961) 485-93, who finds that about half the lines in these nine psalms can be matched from other psalters: quatrains in which no parallels can be found are rare (e.g. lxxx 10-11; lxxxi 4-5, 7, 9, 15; lxxxii 1-2, 4). Psalters which most frequently parallel M. are: Sternhold and Hopkins (1562), Ainsworth (1612), Dod (1620), the so-called 'King James' version' (1636), the *Bay Psalm Book* (1640), Barton (1644), Westminster (i.e. Rous) (1646), and Boyd (1648). Because of his expansions M.'s versions are usually much longer than those in other psalters, except Sternhold and Hopkins.

Developing Masson's point (above) Hunter observes that the Westminster Assembly appointed a committee to revise Rous's version in Jul. 1647, that this committee was reconstituted in Apr. 1648 (the month of M.'s translations), and that for the purposes of committee-work the psalms were divided into four sections, of which the third began at lxxx (M.'s starting-point).

M.'s notes (included in the footnotes below) supply the original Heb., or a literal translation of it, at points where his own translation expands or paraphrases.

*Nine of the Psalms done into metre, wherein all but what is in a different character, are the very words of the text, translated from the original.*

## PSALM lxxx

1    Thou shepherd that dost Israel *keep*
      Give ear *in time of need*,
   Who leadest like a flock of sheep
      *Thy loved* Joseph's seed,
5    That sitt'st between the Cherubs *bright*
      *Between their wings outspread*
   Shine forth, *and from thy cloud give light*,
      *And on our foes thy dread*

2 In Ephraim's view and Benjamin's,
10       And in Manasseh's sight
   Awake thy strength, come, and *be seen*
      *To* save us *by thy might*.

3 Turn us again, *thy grace divine*
      *To us* O God *vouchsafe*;
15    Cause thou thy face on us to shine
      And then we shall be safe.

4 Lord God of Hosts, how long wilt thou,
      How long wilt thou declare
   Thy smoking wrath, *and angry brow*
20       Against thy people's prayer.

5 Thou feed'st them with the bread of tears,
      Their bread with tears they eat,
   And mak'st them largely drink the tears
      *Wherewith their cheeks are wet*.

25 6 A strife thou mak'st us *and a prey*
      To every neighbour foe,
   Among themselves they laugh, they play,
      And flouts at us they throw

7 Return us, *and thy grace divine*,
30       O God of Hosts *vouchsafe*

---

¶ 76. lxxx 6. M.'s insertion alludes to the ark of the covenant, which had two golden cherubs kneeling, with their wings meeting above (*Exod.* xxv 18–22).

lxxx *11. Awake*] 'Gnorera' (M.): lit. 'arouse'.

lxxx *18–19. declare / Thy smoking wrath*] 'Gnashanta' (M.): lit. 'smoke'.

lxxx *23. largely*] 'Shalish' (M.): lit. 'third of a measure'.

lxxx *27–8. laugh . . . play . . . flouts . . . throw*] 'Jilnagu' (M.): lit. 'mock'.

Cause thou thy face on us to shine,
And then we shall be safe.

8 A vine from Egypt thou hast brought,
*Thy free love made it thine,*
35 And drov'st out nations *proud and haught*
To plant this *lovely* vine.

9 Thou didst prepare for it a place
And root it deep and fast
That it *began to grow apace,*
40 *And* filled the land *at last.*

10 With her *green* shade *that* covered *all,*
The hills were *overspread*
Her boughs as *high as* cedars tall
*Advanced their lofty head.*

45 11 Her branches *on the western side*
Down to the sea she sent,
And *upward* to that river *wide*
Her other branches *went.*

12 Why hast thou laid her hedges low
50 And broken down her fence,
That all may pluck her, as they go,
*With rudest violence?*

13 The *tusked* boar out of the wood
Upturns it by the roots,
55 Wild beasts there browse, and make their food
*Her grapes and tender shoots.*

14 Return now, God of Hosts, look down
From heaven, thy seat divine,
Behold *us, but without a frown,*
60 And visit this *thy* vine.

15 Visit this vine, which thy right hand
Hath set, and planted *long,*
And the young branch, that for thyself
Thou hast made firm and strong.

65 16 But now it is consumed with fire,
And cut *with axes* down,
They perish at thy dreadful ire,
At thy rebuke and frown.

17 Upon the man of thy right hand
70 Let thy *good* hand be *laid,*
Upon the Son of Man, whom thou
Strong for thyself hast made.

18 So shall we not go back from thee
*To ways of sin and shame,*

lxxx 35. proud and haught] Echoing *Rich. III* II iii 28: 'haught and proud'.

75      Quicken us thou, then *gladly* we
            Shall call upon thy name.
        Return us, *and thy grace divine*
            Lord God of Hosts *vouchsafe,*
        Cause thou thy face on us to shine,
80          And then we shall be safe.

## PSALM lxxxi

1   To God our strength sing loud, *and clear*
        Sing loud to God *our King,*
    To Jacob's God, *that all may hear*
        Loud acclamations ring.
5   2 Prepare a hymn, prepare a song
        The timbrel hither bring
    The *cheerful* psaltery bring along
        And harp *with* pleasant *string,*
    3 Blow, *as is wont,* in the new moon
10      With trumpets' *lofty sound,*
    The appointed time, the day whereon
        Our solemn feast *comes round.*
    4 This was a statute *given of old*
        For Israel *to observe*
15  A law of Jacob's God, *to hold*
        *From whence they might not swerve.*
    5 This he a testimony ordained
        In Joseph, *not to change,*
    When as he passed through Egypt land;
20      The tongue I heard, was strange.
    6 From burden, *and from slavish toil*
        I set his shoulder free;
    His hands from pots, *and miry soil*
        Delivered were *by me.*
25  7 When trouble did thee sore assail,
        *On me then* didst thou call,
    And I to free thee *did not fail,*
        *And led thee out of thrall.*
    I answered thee in thunder deep
30      With clouds encompassed round:
    I tried thee at the water *steep*
        Of Meriba *renowned.*
    8 Hear O my people, *hearken well,*
        I testify to thee
35      *Thou ancient flock of* Israel,
        If thou wilt list to me,

lxxxi *29. in thunder deep*] 'Besether ragnam' (M.): lit. 'in the secret of thunder'.

9 Throughout the land of thy abode
   No alien god shall be
   Nor shalt thou to a foreign god
40    In honour bend thy knee.

10 I am the Lord thy God which brought
   Thee out of Egypt land
   Ask large enough, and I, *besought,*
   Will grant thy full demand.

45 11 And yet my people would not *hear,*
   *Nor* hearken to my voice;
   And Israel *whom I loved so dear*
   Misliked me for his choice.

12 Then did I leave them to their will
50    And to their wandering mind;
   Their own conceits they followed still
   Their own devices blind.

13 O that my people would *be wise*
   *To* serve me *all their days,*
55 And O that Israel would *advise*
   *To* walk my *righteous* ways.

14 Then would I soon bring down their foes
   *That now so proudly rise,*
   And turn my hand against *all those*
60    *That are* their enemies.

15 Who hate the Lord should *then be fain*
   *To* bow to him and bend,
   But *they, his people, should remain,*
   Their time should have no end.

65 16 And we would feed them *from the shock*
   With flour of finest wheat,
   And satisfy them from the rock
   With honey *for their meat.*

## PSALM lxxxii

1 God in the great assembly stands
   *Of kings and lordly states,*
   Among the gods on both his hands
   He judges and debates.

5 2 How long will ye pervert the right
   With judgment false and wrong

lxxxii *1. great assembly*] 'Bagnadath-el' (M.): lit. 'assembly of God'.
lxxxii *3. Among . . . on both his hands*] 'Bekerev' (M.): lit. 'in the midst of'.
lxxxii *5–6. pervert the right | With judgment false and wrong*] 'Tishphetu gnavel'
(M.): lit. 'judge falsely'.

Favouring the wicked *by your might*
*Who thence grow bold and strong.*

3 Regard the weak and fatherless
10    Despatch the poor man's cause,
And raise the man in deep distress
By just and equal laws.

4 Defend the poor and desolate,
And rescue from the hands
15    Of wicked men the low estate
Of him *that help demands.*

5 They know not nor will understand,
In darkness they walk on
The earth's foundations all are moved
20    And out of order gone.

6 I said that ye were gods, yea all
The sons of God most high

7 But ye shall die like men, and fall
As other princes *die.*

25 8 Rise God, judge thou the earth *in might,*
This *wicked* earth redress,
For thou art he who shalt by right
The nations all possess.

## PSALM lxxxiii

1 Be not thou silent *now at length*
O God hold not thy peace,
Sit not thou still O God of *strength*
*We cry and do not cease.*

5 2 For lo thy *furious* foes *now* swell
And storm outrageously,

---

lxxxii *9–10. Regard the weak . . . / Despatch the poor man's cause*] 'Shiphtu-dal'
(M.): lit. 'judge the poor'.
lxxxii *11–12. raise . . . / By just and equal laws*] 'Hatzdiku' (M.): lit. 'justify'.
lxxxii *19–20. are moved / And out of order gone*] 'Jimmotu' (M.): lit. 'slip'.
lxxxii *24. As other*] E. C. Baldwin, *MP* xvii (1919) 101, points out that M.
has here mistaken the Hebrew word meaning 'one' for the closely similar
word meaning 'other'. But H. F. Fletcher (see headnote) produces several
previous translations which make a similar mistake (e.g. Tremellius: *sicut
unus aliorum principum*; Geneva Bible: 'like others'; Bishops' Bible: 'as
others do'; Diodati's Italian version–to which M. refers in *Tetrachordon*:
*come qualunque altro de' principi*).
lxxxii. *25–6. judge . . . redress*] 'Shophta' (M.): lit. 'judge'.
lxxxiii *5–6. swell . . . storm outrageously*] 'Jehemajun' (M.): lit. 'are in
tumult'.

And they that hate thee *proud and fell*
Exalt their heads full high.

3 Against thy people they contrive
    *10*    Their plots and counsels deep,
Them to ensnare they chiefly strive
Whom thou dost hide and keep.

4 Come let us cut them off say they,
Till they no nation be
    *15*    That Israel's name for ever may
Be lost in memory.

5 For they consult with all their might,
And all as one in mind
Themselves against thee they unite
    *20*    And in firm union bind.

6 The tents of Edom, and the brood
Of *scornful* Ishmael,
Moab, with them of Hagar's blood
*That in the desert dwell,*

    *25*    7 Gebal and Ammon *there conspire,*
And *hateful* Amalek,
The Philistims, and they of Tyre
*Whose bounds the sea doth check.*

8 With them *great* Ashur also bands
    *30*    *And doth confirm the knot*
*All these have lent their armed hands*
To aid the sons of Lot.

9 Do to them as to Midian *bold*
*That wasted all the coast*
    *35*    To Sisera, and as *is told*
*Thou didst* to Jabin's *host,*
*When* at the brook of Kishon *old*
*They were repulsed and slain,*

10 At Endor quite cut off, and rolled
    *40*    As dung upon the plain.

lxxxiii *9–10. contrive / Their plots and counsels deep*] '*Jagnarimu Sod*' (M.): lit. 'devise cunning counsel'.

xxxiii *11. to ensnare . . . chiefly strive*] '*Jithjagnatsu gnal*' (M.): lit. 'conspire against'.

lxxxiii *11–12. Them . . . / Whom thou dost hide and keep*] '*Tsephuneca*' (M.): lit. 'stored-up things'.

lxxxiii *17. with all their might*] '*Lev jachdau*' (M.): lit. 'with heart together'.

lxxxiii *22. scornful*] Cp. *Gen.* xxi 9: 'mocking'.

lxxxiii *24.* Cp. *Gen.* xxi 20: 'He grew, and dwelt in the wilderness'.

lxxxiii *26. hateful*] Cp. *Deut.* xxv 17–19.

lxxxiii *28.* Cp. *Ezek.* xxvii 4: 'Thy borders are in the midst of the seas'.

lxxxiii *37. old*] Cp. *Judges* v 21: 'that ancient river, the river Kishon'.

11  As Zeb and Oreb evil sped
      So let their princes speed
    As Zeba, and Zalmunna *bled*
      So let their princes *bleed*.

45  12  *For they amidst their pride* have said
      By right now shall we seize
    God's houses, and *will now invade*
      Their stately palaces.

    13  My God, O make them as a wheel
50        *No quiet let them find*,
      Giddy and *restless* let *them reel*
        Like stubble from the wind.

    14  As *when* an *aged* wood takes fire
          *Which on a sudden strays*,
55        The *greedy* flame runs higher and higher
            Till all the mountains blaze,
    15  So with thy whirlwind them pursue,
          And with thy tempest chase;
    16  And till they yield thee honour due;
60        Lord fill with shame their face.

    17  Ashamed and troubled let them be,
          Troubled and shamed for ever,
      Ever confounded, and so die
        With shame, *and 'scape it never*.

65  18  Then shall they know that thou whose name
          Jehovah is alone,
      Art the Most High, *and thou the same*
        O'er all the earth *art One*.


                        PSALM lxxxiv

    1  How lovely are thy dwellings fair!
        O Lord of Hosts, how dear
      The *pleasant* tabernacles are!
        *Where thou dost dwell so near*.
5   2  My soul doth long and almost die
          Thy courts O Lord to see,
      My heart and flesh aloud do cry,
        O living God, for thee.
    3  There even the sparrow *freed from wrong*
10        Hath found a house of *rest*,

lxxxiii *47–48. God's houses . . . / Their stately palaces*] '*Neoth Elohim bears both*'
(M.): meaning that the single Heb. expression can be translated by either of
these English phrases. *Neoth* strictly means 'pastures', hence 'dwellings'.
lxxxiii *59. they yield thee honour*] '*They seek thy Name* Heb.'(M.).

The swallow there, to lay her young
  Hath built her *brooding* nest,
Even *by* thy altars Lord of Hosts
  *They find their safe abode,*
15   *And home they fly from round the coasts*
  *Toward thee*, my King, my God.

4 Happy, who in thy house reside
  Where thee they ever praise,
5 Happy, whose strength in thee doth bide,
20   And in their hearts thy ways.

6 They pass through Baca's *thirsty* vale,
  *That dry and barren ground*
As through a fruitful wat'ry dale
  Where springs and showers abound.

25 7 They journey on from strength to strength
  *With joy and gladsome cheer*
*Till* all before *our* God *at length*
  In Sion do appear.

8 Lord God of Hosts hear *now* my prayer
30   O Jacob's God give ear,
9 Thou God our shield look on the face
  Of thy anointed *dear*.

10 For one day in thy courts *to be*
  Is better, *and more blest*
35 Than *in the joys of vanity*,
  A thousand days *at best*.
I in the temple of my God
  Had rather keep a door,
Than dwell in tents, *and rich abode*
40   With sin *for evermore*.

11 For God the Lord both sun and shield
  Gives grace and glory *bright*,
No good from them shall be withheld
  Whose ways are just and right.

45 12 Lord *God* of Hosts *that reign'st on high*,
  That man is *truly* blest,
Who *only* on thee doth rely,
  And in thee only rest.

## PSALM lxxxv

1 Thy land to favour graciously
  Thou hast not Lord been slack,
Thou hast from *hard* captivity
  Returned Jacob back.

5 2 The iniquity thou didst forgive
  *That wrought* thy people woe,

And all their sin, *that did thee grieve*
Hast hid *where none shall know.*
3 Thine anger all thou hadst removed,
10        And *calmly* didst return
From thy fierce wrath which we had proved
Far worse than fire to burn.
4 God of our saving health and peace,
Turn us, and us restore,
15   Thine indignation cause to cease
Toward us, *and chide no more.*
5 Wilt thou be angry without end,
For ever angry thus
Wilt thou thy frowning ire extend
20        From age to age on us?
6 Wilt thou not turn, and *hear our voice*
And us again revive,
That so thy people may rejoice
By thee preserved alive.
25 7 Cause us to see thy goodness Lord,
To us thy mercy shew
Thy saving health to us afford
*And life in us renew.*
8 *And now* what God the Lord will speak
30        I will *go straight and* hear,
For to his people he speaks peace
And to his saints *full dear,*
To his dear saints he will speak peace,
But let them never more
35   Return to folly, *but surcease*
*To trespass as before.*
9 Surely to such as do him fear
Salvation is at hand
And glory shall *ere long appear*
40        *To* dwell within our land.
10 Mercy and Truth *that long were missed*
Now *joyfully* are met
*Sweet* Peace and Righteousness have kissed
*And hand in hand are set.*
45 11 Truth from the earth *like to a flower*
Shall bud and blossom *then,*
And Justice from her heavenly bower
Look down *on mortal men.*

lxxxv 11. *thy fierce wrath*] 'Heb. *The burning heat of thy wrath*' (M.).
lxxxv 21–2. *turn, and . . . us again revive*] 'Heb. *Turn to quicken us*' (M.).

12 The Lord will also then bestow
50          Whatever thing is good
        Our land shall forth in plenty throw
          Her fruits *to be our food*.
13 Before him Righteousness shall go
          *His royal harbinger*,
55      Then will he come, and not be slow
          His footsteps cannot err.


## PSALM lxxxvi

1 Thy *gracious* ear, O Lord, incline,
      O hear me *I thee pray*,
  For I am poor, and almost pine
      With need, *and sad decay*.
5 2 Preserve my soul, for I have trod
      Thy ways, and love the just,
  Save thou thy servant O my God
      Who *still* in thee doth trust.
3 Pity me Lord for daily thee
10      I call; 4 O make rejoice
  Thy servant's soul; for Lord to thee
      I lift my soul *and voice*,
5 For thou art good, thou Lord art prone
      To pardon, thou to all
15    Art full of mercy, thou *alone*
      To them that on thee call.
6 Unto my supplication Lord
      Give ear, and to the cry
  Of my *incessant* prayers afford
20      Thy hearing graciously.
7 I in the day of my distress
      Will call on thee *for aid*;
  For thou wilt *grant* me *free access*
      And answer, *what I prayed*.

lxxxv 54–5. E. C. Baldwin, MP xvii (1919) 101, comments that M. has not realized that 'Righteousness', a masculine noun, is the subject of the verb in the second half of the parallelism as well as in the first.

lxxxv 55–6. *Then will he come, and not be slow | His footsteps cannot err.*] 'Heb. *He will set his steps to the way*' (M.).

lxxxvi 5–6. *I have trod | Thy ways, and love the just*] 'Heb. *I am good, loving, a doer of good and holy things*' (M.). The Heb. term, which M. expands, can be literally translated in any one of the three ways he suggests in his note.

25    8 Like thee among the gods is none
          O Lord, nor any works
          *Of all that other gods have done*
          Like to thy *glorious* works.
      9 The nations all whom thou hast made
30          Shall come, *and all shall frame*
          To bow them low before thee Lord,
          And glorify thy name.
     10 For great thou art, and wonders great
          By thy strong hand are done,
35        Thou *in thy everlasting seat*
          Remainest God alone.
     11 Teach me O Lord thy way *most right*,
          I in thy truth will bide,
          To fear thy name my heart unite
40          *So shall it never slide*
     12 Thee will I praise O Lord my God
          *Thee honour, and adore*
          With my whole heart, and blaze abroad
          Thy name for evermore.
45   13 For great thy mercy is toward me,
          And thou hast freed my soul
          Even from the lowest hell set free
          *From deepest darkness foul.*
     14 O God the proud against me rise
50          And violent men are met
          To seek my life, and in their eyes
          No fear of thee have set.
     15 But thou Lord art the God most mild
          Readiest thy grace to shew,
55        Slow to be angry, and *art styled*
          Most merciful, most true.
     16 O turn to me *thy face at length*,
          And me have mercy on,
          Unto thy servant give thy strength,
60          And save thy handmaid's son.
     17 Some sign of good to me afford,
          And let my foes *then* see
          And be ashamed, because thou Lord
          Dost help and comfort me.

## PSALM lxxxvii

      1 Among the holy mountains *high*
          Is his foundation fast,
          *There seated in his sanctuary,*
          *His temple there is placed.*

5   2 Sion's *fair* gates the Lord loves more
        Than all the dwellings *fair*
     Of Jacob's *land, though there be store,*
        *And all within his care.*
    3 City of God, most glorious things
10        Of thee *abroad* are spoke;
    4 I mention Egypt, *where proud kings*
        *Did our forefathers yoke,*
     I mention Babel to my friends,
        Philistia *full of scorn,*
15     And Tyre with Ethiop's *utmost ends,*
        Lo this man there was born:
    5 But *twice that praise shall in our ear*
        Be said of Sion *last*
     This and this man was born in her,
20        High God shall fix her fast.
    6 The Lord shall write it in a scroll
        That ne'er shall be out-worn
     When he the nations doth enrol
        That this man there was born.
25  7 Both they who sing, and they who dance
        *With sacred songs are there,*
     In thee *fresh brooks, and soft streams glance*
        *And* all my fountains *clear.*

## PSALM lxxxviii

    1 Lord God that dost me save and keep,
        All day to thee I cry;
     And all night long, before thee *weep*
        Before thee *prostrate lie.*
5   2 Into thy presence let my prayer
        *With sighs devout ascend*
     And to my cries, that *ceaseless are,*
        Thine ear with favour bend.
    3 For cloyed with woes and trouble store
10        Surcharged my soul doth lie,
     My life *at death's uncheerful door*
        Unto the grave draws nigh.
    4 Reckoned I am with them that pass
        Down to the *dismal* pit
15     I am a man, but weak alas
        And for that name unfit.
    5 From life discharged and parted quite
        Among the dead *to sleep,*

lxxxviii 15. *a man, but weak . . . And for that name unfit*] 'Heb. *A man without manly strength*' (M.).

And like the slain *in bloody fight*
20          That in the grave lie *deep.*
Whom thou rememberest no more,
Dost never more regard,
Them from thy hand delivered o'er
*Death's hideous house hath barred.*
25      6 Thou in the lowest pit *profound*
Hast set me *all forlorn,*
Where thickest darkness *hovers round,*
In horrid deeps *to mourn.*
7 Thy wrath *from which no shelter saves*
30          Full sore doth press on me;
Thou break'st upon me all thy waves,
And all thy waves break me.
8 Thou dost my friends from me estrange,
And mak'st me odious,
35          Me to them odious, *for they change,*
And I here pent up thus.
9 Through sorrow, and affliction great
Mine eye grows dim and dead,
Lord all the day I thee entreat,
40          My hands to thee I spread.
10 Wilt thou do wonders on the dead,
Shall the deceased arise
And praise thee *from their loathsome bed*
*With pale and hollow eyes?*
45    11 Shall they thy loving-kindness tell
On whom the grave *hath hold,*
Or they *who* in perdition *dwell*
Thy faithfulness *unfold?*
12 In darkness can thy mighty *hand*
50          *Or* wondrous acts be known,
Thy justice in the *gloomy* land
Of *dark* oblivion?
13 But I to thee O Lord do cry
*Ere yet my life be spent,*
55          And *up to thee* my prayer *doth hie*
Each morn, and thee prevent.
14 Why wilt thou Lord my soul forsake,
And hide thy face from me,
15 That am already bruised, and shake

lxxxviii *31–2. Thou break'st upon me all thy waves, | And all thy waves break me*]
'*The* Heb. *bears both*' (M.). M.'s note suggests that either line would be a
correct translation of the Heb. In fact, only the first would.
lxxxviii *59. shake*] 'Heb. *Prae Concussione*' (M.). The meaning of the Heb.

60       With terror sent from thee;
         Bruised, and afflicted and *so low*
         As ready to expire,
         While I thy terrors undergo
         Astonished with thine ire.
65  16 Thy fierce wrath over me doth flow
         Thy threat'nings cut me through.
   17 All day they round about me go,
         Like waves they me pursue.
   18 Lover and friend thou hast removed
70       And severed from me far.
         They *fly me now* whom I have loved,
         And as in darkness are.

# 77 On the Lord General Fairfax at the siege of Colchester

*Date.* Aug. 1648. After defeating the Kentish Royalists at Maidstone (2 Jun. 1648) Fairfax laid siege to Colchester (13 Jun.). The town fell on 27 Aug. Of the Royalist leaders Sir Charles Lucas and Sir George Lisle were immediately shot after trial by court-martial, and the Earl of Norwich and Lord Capel were left to the mercy of Parliament; Capel was subsequently executed. The military career of Sir Thomas Fairfax up to 1648 had been a brilliant one. In Jan. 1643 he recaptured Leeds, and in May took Wakefield. With Cromwell he was victorious at Winceby in Oct., and in Jan. 1644 he defeated Lord Byron at Nantwich. In Mar. he returned to Yorkshire and was victorious at Selby: at Marston Moor (Jul.) he commanded the Parliamentarian right wing. In Jan. 1645 he was made Commander-in-chief of the New Model Army, and on 14 Jun. inflicted a crippling defeat on the King at Naseby, where he behaved with reckless courage and captured a Royalist standard with his own hands. He went on to recapture Leicester, defeat Goring at Langport (10 Jul.), and take Bridgwater (24 Jul.) and Bristol (10 Sep.). In the campaign of 1646 he defeated Hopton at Torrington and took Exeter (9 Apr.) and Oxford (20 Jun.). M.'s hope that Fairfax might take over the management of peacetime affairs was not realised: after the execution of the King, of which he disapproved, he resigned his Commandership (25 Jun. 1650) and retired to his seat, Nun Appleton, Yorkshire. M. includes a long eulogy of him in the *Defensio Secunda* (Columbia viii 216–19).
*Publication. Fairfax* was never printed by M. It first appeared in the *Letters of State* edited by Edward Phillips in 1694. Phillips' text (Fletcher[3] i 372)

is disputed. M. brings out one of the meanings of the Heb. root, 'shaking' (Lat. *concussio*). Another meaning is 'boyhood', hence the A.V. translation 'from my youth up'.

differs in several respects from the fair copy in M.'s hand in the *Trin. MS* (which the present text follows): *1694* verbal variants are indicated in the notes. *Modern criticism.* Finley considers this and M.'s other sonnets of the period, particularly *Cromwell* and *Vane*, eminently Horatian in tone and spirit. He compares ll. *3–4* with Horace's repeated enumerations of foreign peoples (e.g. *Odes* I xxxv 9–12, II xx 13–20), and l. *7* with Horace's hydra reference (IV iv 61–2).

> Fairfax, whose name in arms through Europe rings
>     Filling each mouth with envy, or with praise,
>     And all her jealous monarchs with amaze,
>     And rumours loud, that daunt remotest kings,
> 5   Thy firm unshaken virtue ever brings
>     Victory home, though new rebellions raise
>     Their hydra heads, and the false North displays
>     Her broken league, to imp their serpent wings,
>   O yet a nobler task awaits thy hand;
> 10    For what can war, but endless war still breed,

¶ 77. *2. Filling each mouth*] *1694*: And fills all mouths.

*4. that*] *1694*: which.

*5. virtue*] *1694*: valour. M. is using 'virtue' in the Latin sense, meaning 'courage'.

*6. though*] *1694*: while.

*6–7. new rebellions . . . heads*] The hydra had nine heads: it was one of Hercules' labours to destroy it, and he did so with the aid of Iolaus who held a lighted torch to the stump when Hercules cut a head off, to stop it growing again. The rebellions are hydra-headed in that they break out in several regions: there were Royalist risings in S. Wales and Kent, and the Scots invaded from the north.

*7. false North*] The Scots, having come to an understanding with Charles, invaded England in violation of the Solemn League and Covenant. They were defeated by Cromwell at Preston (17 Aug. 1648). Smart 84 takes the present tense ('displays') as an indication that *Fairfax* was written before this date.

*8. imp*] When a falcon had broken wing-feathers its flight was impaired, and new feathers were therefore fixed to the stumps of the old to remedy the loss: this process was called 'imping'.    *their*] *1694*: her. J. T. Shawcross, *N & Q* cc (1955) 195–6, wishes to read 'her', claiming that in *Trin. MS* 'her' has been altered to 'their' by some hand other than M.'s. The 'e' and the 'r' of the word, however, seem too far apart to allow this theory.

*10. war, but endless*] *1694*: war, but acts of. Shawcross (see note to l. 8) claims that the reading should be 'wars but endless'. What appears to be a comma after 'war' in *Trin. MS* is in fact, he says, the bottom part of an 's', of which the top part is still visible on the end of the 'r'. He is unable, however, to

Till truth, and right from violence be freed,
And public faith cleared from the shameful brand
Of public fraud. In vain doth valour bleed
While avarice, and rapine share the land.

# 78 Translation from 'Tenure of Kings and Magistrates'

Date. Feb. 1649. The pamphlet appeared 13 Feb., a fortnight after Charles' execution, which it defended. The translation is from Seneca, *Hercules Furens* 922–4 *victima haud ulla amplior | potest magisque opima mactari Iovi | quam rex iniquus.*

There can be slain
No sacrifice to God more acceptable
Than an unjust and wicked king.

# 79 Translations from 'The History of Britain'

Date. Feb.–Mar. 1649. M. says in *Defensio Secunda* (Columbia viii 136–8) that before he was appointed Secretary for Foreign Tongues (13 Mar. 1649) he had finished four books of his *History*. He seems to imply, in the same place, that he began the *History* only after writing *Tenure of Kings and Magistrates* (published 13 Feb. 1649). He had, of course, been collecting material

produce another example of 'r' and 's' joined in M.'s hand where the top of the 's' resembles the mark at the end of the 'r' in 'war' to which he refers.
11. *truth, and right*] *1694*: injured truth.
12. *cleared . . . shameful*] *1694*: be rescued from the.
13–4. The financial chaos under the Long Parliament (with Royalist estates changing hands at bargain prices) is denounced by M. in *History of Britain* (Columbia x 319–20): 'Straite every one betooke himself, setting the commonwealth behinde and his private ends before, to doe as his own profit

for some time. French ii 214 quotes from Samuel Hartlib's notebook for 1648: 'Milton is . . . writing a Univ. History of Engl.'
*Publication. 1670.*
(i) and (ii) are from Geoffrey of Monmouth, *History* I xi [Brutus' prayer to Diana] *Diva potens nemorum, terror silvestribus apris: | Cui licet amfractus ire per aethereos, | Infernasque domos: terrestria iura resolve, | Et dic quas terras nos habitare velis? | Dic certam sedem qua te venerabor in aevum, | Qua tibi virgineis templa dicabo choris?* [and Diana's reply] *Brute sub occasum solis trans Gallica regna | Insula in Oceano est undique clausa mari: | Insula in Oceano est habitata gigantibus olim, | Nunc deserta quidem: gentibus apta tuis. | Hanc pete, namque tibi sedes erit illa perennis: | Sic fiet natis altera Troia tuis: | Sic de prole tua reges nascentur: et ipsis | Totius terrae subditus orbis erit.*
(iii) In the *Flores Historiarum*, under A.D. 821, the story is told of the murder of young Kenelm. The location of his body, it is said, was announced miraculously by a dove which appeared over the altar of St Peter's in Rome carrying a message *In clenc cu beche Kenelm cunebearn lith under thorne haudes bereafed.* This the *Flores* translates into Latin as *In pastura vaccarum Kenelmus regis filius iacet sub spina, capite privatus,* and a couplet version is added (which M. here translates) attributed in the margin to Abbot John de Cella *In clenc sub spina iacet in convalle bovina, | Vertice privatus, Kenelmus rege creatus.*

   (i)  Goddess of shades, and huntress, who at will
       Walk'st on the rolling sphere, and through the deep,
       On thy third reign the earth look now, and tell
       What land, what seat of rest thou bidd'st me seek,
5     What certain seat, where I may worship thee
       For ay, with temples vowed, and virgin choirs.

   (ii) Brutus far to the west, in the ocean wide
       Beyond the realm of Gaul, a land there lies,
       Sea-girt it lies, where giants dwelt of old,
       Now void, it fits thy people; thither bend
5     Thy course, there shalt thou find a lasting seat,
       There to thy sons another Troy shall rise,
       And kings be born of thee, whose dreaded might
       Shall awe the world, and conquer nations bold.

   (iii) Low in a mead of kine under a thorn,
       Of head bereft li'th poor Kenelm king-born.

or ambition led him. Then was justice delai'd & soone after deny'd, spite and favour determin'd all . . . ev'ry where wrong & oppression, foule and dishonest things commited daylie . . . Some who had bin call'd from shops & warehouses without other merit to sit in supreme councels & committies, as thir breeding was, fell to hucster the common-wealth.'

# 80 Epigram from *Defensio Pro Populo Anglicano*

*Date.* 1650. M.'s *Defensio* was entered in the Stationers' Register 31 Dec.
1650. It was a reply to the *Defensio Regia Pro Carolo I*, published in Holland
(1649), which the English Royalists had employed Claude de Saumaise
(1588–1653), one of the greatest classical scholars of the seventeenth century,
to write. In his *Defensio* (Columbia vii 428–9) M. mocks at Saumaise's
misuse of English terms in the *Defensio Regia*, and adds this epigram (an
adaptation of Persius, *Prologue* 8–14 'Who was it that made the parrot so
glib with his "Good morning"? . . .'), with the words and phrases which are
copied exactly from Persius italicized.
*Publication.* 24 Feb. 1651.

> *Quis expedivit* Salmasio suam Hundredam,
> Picamque *docuit verba nostra conari?*
> *Magister artis venter*, et Iacobei
> Centum, exulantis viscera marsupii regis.
> 5 *Quod si dolosi spes refulserit nummi,*
> Ipse Antichristi qui modo primatum Papae
> Minatus uno est dissipare sufflatu,
> *Cantabit* ultro Cardinalitium *melos.*

Who was it made Saumaise so gl¹b with his 'hundreda',¹ and taught that
magpie to try our words? His stomach was his schoolmaster–that, and the
hundred Jacobuses³ which were the vitals of the exiled king's purse. If hope
of turning a dishonest penny so much as glimmers he–who⁶ recently threat-
ened to shatter the supremacy of the Pope, the Antichrist, with a single
puff⁷–will willingly sing the Cardinals' tune.

# 81 To the Lord General Cromwell

*Date.* May 1652. The sonnet appears in the Trinity MS in the hand of an
amanuensis, headed 'To the Lord General Cromwell, May 1652. / On the

¶ 80 *1. Hundredam*] In *Defensio Regia* 204, Saumaise (*Salmasius*) gives the
plural of 'Hundred' as 'Hundreda', a mistake not corrected in the *Errata.*
*3–4. Iacobei / Centum*] Charles II met the expenses of printing the *Defensio
Regia*, and paid Saumaise £100. 'Jacobus' was a slang name for a coin first
struck in 1603 and called officially the sovereign (worth 20s. originally and
about 24s. by mid-seventeenth century).
*6–7.* Saumaise was a Protestant. His first publication (1608) was an edition
of a work by a fourteenth-century bishop of Thessalonica, Nilus Cabasilas,

proposals of certain ministers 'at the Committee' for Propagation of the Gospel'. This committee, of which Cromwell was a member, had been appointed 10 Feb. 1652, to consider questions like the payment of ministers and limits of toleration. On 18 Feb. 1652 John Owen (formerly Cromwell's chaplain) and other Independent ministers laid certain proposals before it. They advocated an established church with clergy paid for by the state: dissenters were to be allowed freedom of worship so long as they did not promulgate doctrines contrary to fifteen fundamental tenets. Cromwell, however, was in favour of unlimited liberty of dissent. M. urges him away from establishment altogether: this would entail the union of civil and religious power ('secular chains'), which he always opposed, and a stipendiary clergy ('hireling wolves'). On 29 Apr. Parliament had resolved that the tithe system should be continued until the committee had evolved some other means of providing for the clergy: this resolve seemed to take it for granted that the clergy should be stipendiary, hence M.'s alarm. The text printed here follows the Trinity MS.

*Publication.* First printed in Phillips's *Letters of State* (1694) in a mangled form (see notes for *1694* readings, and headnote to *Fairfax*, p. 319).

> Cromwell, our chief of men, who through a cloud
> Not of war only, but detractions rude,
> Guided by faith and matchless fortitude
> To peace and truth thy glorious way hast ploughed,
> 5 And on the neck of crowned fortune proud
> Hast reared God's trophies and his work pursued,
> While Darwen stream with blood of Scots imbrued,
> And Dunbar field resounds thy praises loud,

against the primacy of the Pope. This was republished in 1645 with an accompanying treatise by Saumaise himself, *De Primatu Papae.*

¶ 81. *1. who ... cloud*] *1694*: that ... crowd. M.'s 'cloud' echoes Virgil, *Aen.* x 809 *nubem belli.* Finley 48–9 compares this opening with Horace's addresses to Augustus (*Odes* IV v 1, 5; xiv 6).

*2. detractions*] *1694*: distractions.

*5. crowned fortune*] Refers to Charles I and to his successor whose army Cromwell defeated at Worcester after he had been crowned king in Scotland, 1 Jan. 1651.

*5–6. And ... pursued*] *1694*: And fought God's battles, and his work pursued.

*7. Darwen stream*] *1694*: Darwent streams. The Darwen, in Lancashire, joins the Ribble near Preston where, 17–19 Aug. 1648, Cromwell, joining Lambert, routed the invading Scottish army under the Duke of Hamilton, destroying almost half of it.

*7–9.* Finley 60–1 comments on the Horatian quality of this list of victories, and compares *Odes* II ix 19–24.

*8. Dunbar field*] *Trin. MS: Dunbar field* 'Worcester's laureate wreath' [this

And Worcester's laureate wreath; yet much remains
10     To conquer still; peace hath her victories
No less renowned than war, new foes arise
Threatening to bind our souls with secular chains:
Help us to save free conscience from the paw
Of hireling wolves whose gospel is their maw.

# 82 To Sir Henry Vane the Younger

*Date.* Jun.–Jul. 1652. In George Sikes's *Life and Death of Sir Henry Vane* (1662) 93–4, M.'s sonnet is printed (reproduced Fletcher[3] i 368) together with the information that it was sent to Vane by M. 3 Jul. 1652.

In the Trinity MS the sonnet appears in the hand of an amanuensis, headed 'To Sir Henry Vane the Younger' (this title is crossed through and the figure '17' inserted above). Vane (1613–62), called 'the younger' because his father did not die until 1655, emigrated to New England in 1635 and became Governor of Massachusetts. Returning to England (1637) he became Treasurer of the Navy (1639): the successful issue of the Dutch war was largely due to his efficient administration. Elected a member of the Council of State (Feb. 1649), he was appointed (13 Mar.) to the committee to consider relations with other European powers; M., as secretary to this committee, learnt to respect his skill as a statesman. Vane, like M., was utterly opposed to an established church. He broke with Cromwell (1653) over the dissolution

correction is obviously erroneous: see next line]. At Dunbar, 3 Sep. 1650, Cromwell, after being virtually surrounded, routed the Scottish army under Leslie: 3,000 Scots fell and 10,000 were taken.     *resounds*] *1694*: resound.
9. *Worcester's . . . wreath*] *Trin. MS*: *twenty battles more* 'Worcester's laureate wreath' [this is obviously the correction for which that in 8 was an error]. At Worcester, 3 Sep. 1651, Cromwell virtually annihilated Charles II's Royalist Scottish army.
10–11. *peace . . . war*] Cp. Cicero, *De Officiis* I xxii 74: *Cum plerique arbitrentur res bellicas maiores esse quam urbanas vere autem si volumus iudicare, multae res extiterunt urbanae maiores clarioresque quam bellicae* (Most people think that the achievements of war are more important than those of peace . . . but there have been many instances of achievement in peace more important and no less renowned than in war), and M. in *Defensio Secunda*, addressing his countrymen (Columbia viii 240–1): 'If, after putting an end to war, you neglect the arts of peace; if war be your peace and liberty, war alone your virtue, your highest glory, you will find, believe me, that your greatest enemy is peace itself; peace itself will be by far your hardest warfare.'
11. *renowned than*] *1694*: than those of.

of the Long Parliament. Although he did not approve of the King's exe-
cution he was excluded from the Act of Indemnity and executed 14 Jan.
1662.

*Publication.* 1662 in Sikes's *Life* (see above): this is the text followed here.
1694 in Phillips's *Letters of State* (see headnote to *Fairfax*, p. 319); the Phillips
text is very poor.

> Vane, young in years, but in sage counsel old,
>    Than whom a better senator ne'er held
>    The helm of Rome, when gowns not arms repelled
>    The fierce Epirot and the African bold.
> 5  Whether to settle peace or to unfold
>    The drift of hollow states, hard to be spelled,
>    Then to advise how war may best, upheld,
>    Move by her two main nerves, iron and gold
>    In all her equipage: besides to know
> 10    Both spiritual power and civil, what each means,

¶ 82. *1. young in years*] Echoes Sylvester (Du Bartas 424): 'Isaac, in yeers
yong, but in wisdom growen.'    *counsel*] *Trin. MS*: counsels.
*3–4. gowns not arms*] Cicero, *De Officiis* I xxii 77, quotes the dictum *cedant
arma togae* when arguing in favour of civic rather than military virtues. The
firmness of the senators in the face of constant defeat, and their refusal to
allow the Romans captured by Hannibal at Cannae to be ransomed is de-
scribed by Livy XXII lx–lxi 4–5.    *Epirot*] Pyrrhus, King of Epirus.
*African*] Hannibal.
*6. drift*] *Trin. MS*: drifts.    *hollow*] a punning reference to Holland, 'hol-
low' because much of it is below sea-level, but also, implies M., 'hollow'
in a moral sense. Ill-feeling between Holland and England was brought to a
head 19 May 1652, when shots were exchanged between the English fleet
under Blake and the Dutch fleet under Tromp in the Downs. The Dutch
ambassadors remained in London, ostensibly to continue friendly relations
but actually, it was believed in some quarters, for purposes of espionage.
Vane was appointed (4 Jun.) to the committee to prepare an answer to the
Dutch ambassadors. This answer, though not ruling out further negotia-
tions, accused the Dutch of attempting to destroy the English fleet by sur-
prise. The Dutch ambassadors withdrew, and war became inevitable.
*8. by*] *Trin. MS*: on 'on' 'by'.    *nerves . . . gold*] Machiavelli, *Discourses*
ii 10, argues that money is not the sinew of war (*Dico pertanto, non l'oro, come
grida la comune opinione, essere il nervo della guerra*), but that iron is (*la guerra si
faceva col ferro e non con l'oro*). M. notes this twice in his Commonplace Book
(Columbia xviii 160, 212, Yale i 414–5, 498): Maurice Kelley, *Studies in
Bibliography* iv (1951–2) 123–7, dates these Machiavelli notes between Nov.
1651 and Feb. 1652.
*10. Trin. MS*: *What power the Church and what the civil means* 'Both spiritual
power and civil, what *it means* each means'.
*10–11.* Refers to Vane's support of disestablishment (see headnote).

What severs each, thou hast learned, which few
    have done.
The bounds of either sword to thee we owe;
    Therefore on thy firm hand Religion leans
    In peace, and reckons thee her eldest son.

# 83 Sonnet XVI

*Date.* 1652? There is some doubt about the exact date. French iii 201 thinks 1652 likely, shortly after M. became totally blind (i.e. about 28 Feb., according to French). L. Kemp's theory, *Hopkins Review* vi (1952) 80–3, that the poem's subject is not blindness but loss of inspiration, and that it should be dated 1642, is ably countered by M. Kelley, *XVIIth-Century News* xi (1953) 29. Kelley himself, *MP* liv (1956) 20–5, favours mid or late 1655, on the evidence of the order of the later sonnets in *1673*, which he takes as chronological. W. R. Parker, *PMLA* lxxiii (1958) 196–200, questions this assumption. He argues that M. considered himself blind for all practical purposes in Nov. 1651, when he was forty-two years old. Since his father lived to be at least eighty-four (when, according to Aubrey, he could read without spectacles), 'Ere half my days' (2) may be a reference to M.'s age as compared with his father's. Parker thus dates the sonnet late 1651. Another explanation of 'Ere half my days' is offered by D. C. Dorian, *Explicator* x (1951) 16, who interprets 'days' as 'working days'–at forty-two M. was perhaps less than halfway through a working life. J. T. Shawcross, *N & Q* iv (1957) 442–6, dates Oct.–Nov. 1655, on the grounds that 'half my days is estimated with reference to *Isa.* lxv 20 ('an hundred years old'): this verse, however, is taken from a prophecy about the new Jerusalem, and relates to a future, not an actual state of affairs.

*Publication.* 1673

*Modern criticism.* J. L. Potter, *N & Q* iv (1957) 447, refers to Barnabe Barnes, *Divine Century of Spiritual Sonnets* (1595) xxvi and xxxviii to show that M. was not the first sonnetteer to use the parable of the talents (*Matt.* xxv 14–30) as a conceit.

*11. Trin. MS:* Thou *teachest best, which few have ever done* 'hast learnt well, a praise which few have won' 'What severs each thou' hast learnt, which few have do[ne]'.

*12. either sword]* i.e. civil and spiritual sword. In *Observations on the Articles of Peace* (Columbia vi 262) M. remarks that to extirpate 'Heresy, Schism, and prophaness' 'can be no work of the Civil sword, but of the spirituall, which is the Word of God'.

*13. firm]* Trin. *MS: right* 'firm'.

When I consider how my light is spent,
 Ere half my days, in this dark world and wide,
 And that one talent which is death to hide,
 Lodged with me useless, though my soul more bent
5 To serve therewith my maker, and present
 My true account, lest he returning chide,
 Doth God exact day-labour, light denied,
 I fondly ask; but Patience to prevent
That murmur, soon replies, God doth not need
10  Either man's work or his own gifts, who best
 Bear his mild yoke, they serve him best, his state
Is kingly. Thousands at his bidding speed
 And post o'er land and ocean without rest:
 They also serve who only stand and wait.

# 84 Samson Agonistes

*Date.* 1647–53? Forceful reasons for abandoning the traditional dating (1666–70) are advanced by W. R. Parker, *PQ* xxviii (1949) 145–66 and *N & Q* v (1958) 201–2. Edward Phillips, who was in close contact with M.

*9–10.* M. repeats this sentiment in *De Doctrina* (Columbia xvii 20–2) quoting *Job* xxii 2.

*11. mild yoke*] Cp. *Matt.* xi 30: 'My yoke is easy.'

*12–3.* Cp. *Ps.* lxviii 17: 'The chariots of God are twenty thousand, even thousands of angels', and *Zech.* i 10: 'These are they whom the Lord hath sent to walk to and fro through the earth.'

*14.* H. F. Robins, *RES* n. s. vii (1956) 360–6, reiterates the conclusion of Sir Herbert Grierson, *Poems of John Donne* (Oxford 1912) ii 5, that 'They' are the four highest orders of angels who, according to pseudo-Dionysius and Aquinas do not act as messengers like the inferior orders ('thousands' l. 12), but stand about God's throne, waiting on him and passing on to the inferior orders the secrets of the divine mysteries. F. Pyle, *RES* n.s. ix (1958) 376–87, notes however that in *De doctrina* M. does not regard any angels as reserved for exclusive service in heaven, and in *PL* Cherub and Seraph are not confined to God's presence. Pyle agrees with Smart 109–10, that 'They' are devout men on earth, who obey such frequent biblical injunctions as *Ps.* xxxvii 14, 'Wait on the Lord' (cp. the parable in *Luke* xii 35–40 about 'men that wait for their Lord'). J. L. Jackson and W. E. Weese, *MLN* lxxii (1957) 91–3, associate the use of 'stand' with that in *Ephes.* vi 14, where the word means 'take up a position against the enemy'. R. A. Haug, *N & Q* clxxxiii (1942) 224–5, thinks the source for the idea *1 Sam.* xxx 24, where David allots an equal share of booty to those who pursue and to those who wait behind.

¶ 84. *Title. Samson*] In both Blount's *Glossographia* (1656) and Edward Phillips's *New World of Words* (1658) the name is said to mean 'there the

during the last years of his life, affirms that *PR* was written entirely between
1667 and 1670, which he considers 'a wonderful short space considering the
sublimeness of it' (Darbishire 75). If he believed *SA* had also been written
in that period, it is highly unlikely that Phillips would not have fhought it
worth comment. He says, however, that when *SA* was written 'cannot
certainly be concluded' (Darbishire 75).

M.'s note added to late issues of the first edition of *PL* in 1668 attacks
rhyme as 'the invention of a barbarous age, to set off wretched matter and
lame metre' rejected 'long since' by 'our best English tragedies'. Yet about
one-eleventh of *SA* is rhymed. M. could not, when writing it, have felt
about rhyme as he did in 1668.

Parker thinks that *SA* was begun 1646–7 (Phillips was resident in M.'s
house until about 1646, so ought to have known about the composition of
*SA* if it was going on then), and taken up again 1652–3. The Trinity MS
contains clear evidence of amanuenses preparing M.'s poems for publica-
tion, and these preparations seem to belong to 1653. In 1653, *1645* was still
in print, so the only reason for a new edition could be the addition of a
new work of some size, and *SA* seems the only possibility. The audacious
metrical experiments of *SA*'s choruses are matched only by those of the
Latin ode to Rouse (1647), and M. uses precisely the same terms to explain
the versification of the two works (see pp. 301 and 343). Further, the ex-
perience of approaching and of new blindness reflects in the psalm transla-
tions of Apr. 1648 and Aug. 1653 and, in similar tones, in *SA*. Samson's great
speeches on blindness do not seem to be those of a man resigned to a long-
lived-with disability. This last point, however, is less telling than Parker's
others, since it smacks of that autobiographical interpretation which he
elsewhere distrusts. Fanciful identifications (M. is Samson; Salmasius,
Harapha; Mary Powell, Dalila etc.) have often been undertaken by critics
attempting to date *SA*, but there is little to be said for them. By depicting
himself as a character punished with blindness for loss of virtue, M. would be
taking the side of the Royalist satirists and pamphleteers. Early biographers
and critics seem unaware of any autobiographical or topical elements.

second time'. If M. believed in this (incorrect) etymology it would be a pos-
sible starting-point for his idea of a second encounter with Dalila. No such
encounter occurs in *Judges*, where he resists her three times by lying, then falls
(xvi 6–17).        *Agonistes*] In Greek the word can mean a contestant in the
games (Samson is a contestant at the Philistines' games, though unopposed,
*SA* 1628) or a champion. Phillips's *New World of Words* (1658 and 1663)
defines 'agonize' as 'play the champion' (cp. *SA* 705, 1152, 1751). Krouse
110–16 connects the term *agonistes* with the exertion of mind and spirit
called for in the Platonic ethic (ἀγών came to mean 'spiritual struggle', and
ἀγωνιστής, 'a fully educated person, ready to take his place in the ἀγών
of life'), and in the Christian tradition (Theodoret uses ἀγωνιστής to
mean 'saint' or 'martyr'; Christ's atonement was looked upon as an ἀγών–
Augustine wrote a treatise called *De Agone Christiano*).

E. Sirluck's attempt, *JEGP* lx (1961) 749–85, to counter Parker's theory leaves it in the main unimpaired: so does A. S. P. Woodhouse's ill-supported plea for a date between the Restoration (May 1660) and the spring of 1661, *Trans. of the Royal Soc. of Canada* xliii (1949) 157–75. Ants Oras's statistical analysis of the blank verse of *Comus, PL, PR* and *SA* (*SAMLA* 128–197) is designed to support the traditional chronology, but much of his evidence goes against it (e.g. the relative percentages of terminal and medial strong pauses are exactly the same in *Comus* and *SA;* the percentage of run-on lines in *SA* is nearer to that in *Comus* than to that in *PL* or *PR;* the relative percentages of feminine and masculine pauses in *SA* are nearer to those in *Comus* than to those in *PL* or *PR;* the frequency of feminine line-endings in *SA* is nearer to that in *Comus* than to that in *PL* or *PR*).

*Publication.* The volume containing *PR* and *SA* (*1671*) was licensed 2 Jul. 1670 by Thomas Tomkyns, and entered in the Stationers' Register 10 Sep. 1670. The volume was advertised in the 1670 Michaelmas Term catalogue. All known title-pages, however, have the date 1671. Parker suggests that the delay in appearance was due to the time taken by the blind M. supervising proof-reading. There are two slightly different states of some pages in *1671*; see notes to *306, 548, 1033, 1078, 1086, 1093, 1337* and *1340*.

*Modern criticism.* Criticism of *SA* has centred round two major questions: its structure and its spirit. The second of these, leading to discussions about whether the play is 'Hellenic', 'Hebraic' or 'Christian', has also motivated examination of its sources, its claims to 'tragic' stature, its differences from or similarities to previous Samson literature, and its 'meaning'.

Argument over the structure of *SA* began with Johnson's declaration (*Rambler* 139) that 'the poem . . . has a beginning and an end . . . but it must be allowed to want a middle, since nothing passes between the first act and the last, that either hastens or delays the death of Samson'. J. W. Tupper, *PMLA* xxxv (1920) 375–89, sides with Johnson: the Dalila and Harapha episodes are 'mere padding'. P. F. Baum, *PMLA* xxxvi (1921) 354–71, in reply, makes the obvious point that 'dramatic action includes not only visible acts but also the invisible mental changes which underlie and mould actual events'. From this viewpoint the central episodes of *SA* are necessary to the action, though they do not follow one another, as Aristotle required, in probable or necessary sequence. It is this last fact which mars the play for E. C. Knowlton, *MLN* xxxvii (1922) 333–9: as he sees it, tragic action 'depends for its value structurally and spiritually upon the principle of causality': not only are the Dalila and Harapha episodes themselves without proper cause, but they do not cause the death of Samson. The catastrophe, however, is not the death of Samson but his victory-through-death, as W. C. Curry insists, *Sewanee Review* xxxii (1924) 336–52, and the spiritual development necessary for this is a direct result of the central episodes. Dalila is still attractive to Samson (*952–3, 1003–7*), thus her appearance gives him a chance to redeem himself by resisting precisely that temptation to which he formerly succumbed. After this it is necessary that he should be roused from lethargy, and the behaviour of Harapha is calculated to have that effect. An alternative reply to Johnson is framed by M. E. Grenander, *UTQ* xxiv (1955) 377–89, who points out that the play's action begins long before the play itself, with Samson's initial victory over the Philistines: viewed thus the action has a beginning, middle and end, as Aristotle required. Another aspect of *SA*'s structure–its symmetry–is studied by W. R. Parker, *MLN* l (1935) 355–60, who draws attention to the similarity in length between successive speeches and episodes, and between *prologos* and *kommos*.

The argument about whether *SA* is 'Hellenic' or 'Hebraic' in spirit was begun by R. C. Jebb, *Proc. of the Brit. Acad.* iii (1907–8) 341–8. In spite of its Greek form, and in spite of the fact that, as a drama of inward action, it can find a parallel in the *Prometheus Bound* of Aeschylus, *SA* seems to Jebb to have the spirit of the Hebrew prophets. Samson is a tribal champion: Jehovah and Dagon, tribal Gods. The issue of the drama is that Jehovah has prevailed over Dagon, Israel over Philistia. It is Hebraism which thus contrasts God and his servants with idols and their servants: Hellenism contrasts man with fate. Jebb's case is strongly attacked by W. R. Parker *E & S* xx (1934) 21–44. Greek tragedy, Parker argues, is serious, thoughtful, didactic, religious and sublime: so is *SA*. It is dominated by fate: so is *SA*, where Samson's fate is decreed before his birth (*38–9*), and where dramatic irony (which implies a fatalistic philosophy of life) runs through the entire action. *SA* is Sophoclean rather than Aeschylean in that it displays unmerited suffering: Parker feels that Samson suffers more than he deserves: despite the final chorus, human passions and wrongs are seen to be more real than the divine scheme into which they are supposed to fit. Parker's reply to Jebb later became the basis for his book (Parker[2]) which also reprints and expands previous articles on the play's tragic irony, *Études Anglaises* i (1937) 314–20; its *kommos* (which, Parker considers, extends from *1660* to the end of the play, and resembles that in Aeschylus' *Suppliants*), *SP* xxxii (1935) 240–4; and its alleged misogyny, which Parker denies, *PQ* xvi (1937) 139–44. He includes two chapters (168–85) on *SA*'s debt to the *Oedipus at Colonus* and the *Prometheus Bound*, maintaining that W. Brewer, *PMLA* xlii (1927) 910–20, was mistaken in asserting that M. took his plot 'almost entirely' from these two plays: the debt, Parker believes, is more miscellaneous. Comparison with the *Oedipus at Colonus* had been made before Brewer by P. H. Epps, *SP* xiii (1916) 190–6, and Sir Maurice Bowra has returned to it in his study of *SA*, *Inspiration and Poetry* (1955) 112–29. The extent of M.'s knowledge of Aeschylus has been questioned by J. C. Maxwell, *RES* n.s. iii (1952) 366–71: though the structure of the *Prometheus Bound* almost certainly influenced that of *SA*, there are no convincing verbal parallels between M. and Aeschylus at all. The influence of the third Greek tragic dramatist, Euripides, has been studied by P. W. Timberlake (Parrott 315–40): the litigious element, the sententiousness, and the treatment of the messenger, making for suspense, all smack of Euripides, quite apart from verbal similarities (e.g. *SA 1–2*, *Phoenician Maidens* 834–5; *SA 115–6*, *Orestes* 140; *SA 1034f.*, *Hippolytus* 616f. and *Orestes* 604–5).

Claims that *SA* is neither 'Hellenic' nor 'Hebraic' but Christian have been made by several critics. T. S. K. Scott-Craig, *Renaissance News* v (1952) 45–53, sees it as 'a poem on the spiritual agony of Christ': 'the celebration of the agony of Samson is a surrogate for the unbloody sacrifice of the Mass', and the catastrophe, with Samson's prayer and destruction of the theatre, is a typological version of Christ's passion, with the prayer in Gethsemane followed by physical accompaniments of the crucifixion like the rending of the temple veil and the earthquake. In support of Scott-Craig it can be said that, as Krouse has made clear (41, 51, 69), the conception of Samson as a figure of Christ was the main current in the Samson tradition of the Middle Ages and the Renaissance. It originated, apparently, in Ambrose, and received its fullest treatment in Augustine's *Sermo de Samsone*: the most ingenious of the scholastic writers in finding parallels between Samson and Christ was Rupert of St Heribert (d. 1135). As late as 1640, Thomas Hayne in his *General View of the Holy Scriptures* prints an elaborate tabular analysis of the parallels between the two figures. However it must be stressed that, in view of this tradition, it is all the more striking that M. should refrain from making any explicit comparison between his protagonist and Christ. Krouse's insistence that the temptations of M.'s Samson are equivalent to the temptations of Christ in the wilderness as schematized by Protestant theologians (Manoa representing temptation by necessity; Dalila, temptation by fraud; Harapha, temptation by violence), cannot be said to convince. Scott-Craig's view is shared by M. M. Ross, *Poetry and Dogma* (New Brunswick 1954) pp. 12–3. A less extreme Christianization is offered by Allen 82–94, who reads the play as an 'analysis of the problem of Christian despair': the episode with Manoa shows Samson resisting the enticement to sloth, while that with Harapha, which to Allen is the hinge of the tragedy, enables him to subdue his apathy.

If *SA* is Christian, can it also be 'tragic'? P. F. Baum, *PMLA* xxxvi (1921) 354–71, thinks not: tragic force is diminished by the play's insistence on a beneficent divine providence–'with this belief there can be no properly tragic catastrophe'. Bowra (see above) agrees–'since all is best, there is nothing to regret'–and so does Miss Ellis-Fermor, *Frontiers of Drama* (1945) 17–33–'by justifying the ways of God to man he leaves no room for tragic ecstasy and substitutes an ecstasy of another kind'. W. C. Curry, *Sewanee Review* (1924) xxxii 336–52, on the other hand, thinks that a belief in beneficent divine providence is not incompatible with tragedy but only with Greek tragedy, and J. H. Hanford, *Studies in Shakespeare, Milton and Donne* (New York 1925) pp. 167–89, maintains that 'all is best' does not represent our feeling at the end of the drama: in spite of M.'s Christianity, a keen sense of the reality of suffering, and a habitual stoicism remain. A. S. P. Woodhouse, *UTQ* xxviii (1959) 205–22, finds the drama, though Christian, also 'tragic' in that M. makes 'the way of repentance and restoration, the way back to God, also the way that leads inevitably to the catastrophe, and has thus achieved at a stroke the only kind of irony that is at once compatible with a Christian outlook and as potent as any to be found in tragedy anywhere'.

One objection to the view of *SA* as a Christian work is that it condones and centres upon an act of vengeance (Kenneth Burke, *Hudson Review* i (1948) 151–67, calls it 'a wonder-working spell by a cantankerous old fighter-priest who would slay the enemy in effigy'). This difficulty is examined by K. Fell, *English Studies* xxxiv (1953) 145–55, who finds that, in spite of its mature concentration on purgation and dedication, the play fails to transcend the limitations inherent in its vengeful ending – an integral part of its primitive story, which is an ancient solar myth of Syrian origin. That the ending is indeed morally disgusting does not seem to be realised by E. L. Marilla, *Studia Neophilologica* xxix (1957) 67–76; to him the moral of *SA* – a moral of which he approves – is that man must 'unreservedly commit himself, without regard for possible costs in personal sacrifice, to upholding the ideals that are entrusted to him as a spiritual being'. A hardly less objectionable moral (from the viewpoint of the slaughtered Philistines) is drawn by J. D. Ebbs, *MLQ* xxii (1961) 377–89: M. teaches that 'a just and glorious end awaits those who are repentant, have patience under trials, and show faith in the ultimate manifestation of God's will'.

One interpretation which falls outside the Hellenic-Hebraic-Christian question is the political. E. M. Clark, *UTSE* vii (1927) 144–54, reads the play as a political allegory of the temporary downfall and ultimate triumph of the Puritan state, and draws attention to M.'s previous allegorization of the Samson story in *Reason of Church Government* (Columbia iii 276–7, Yale i 858–9).

In determining the spirit of *SA* it is clear that its divergence from or agreement with previous handlings of the Samson story will be significant. W. Kirkconnell's mainly irrelevant study of six sixteenth-century treatments of the story, *Trans. of the Royal Soc. of Canada* xliii (1949) 73–85, is far too narrow in scope, but Krouse allows the play to be seen in its full cultural context. The elevated nature of M.'s Samson, when compared with the Samson of *Judges*, which E. M. Clark, *UTSE* viii (1928) 88–99, had previously commented on, Krouse proves to be not so much the achievement of M. as of the historical tradition in which he wrote. The history of the Christian conception of Samson helps to explain why M. saw a tragic hero in the biblical figure who seems an often undignified tribal hero. Tradition had drawn attention away from the earlier, less dignified part of his life: Josephus had seen his fall as the result of *hubris*, and to Gregory the Great he had exemplified *hamartia*. The Renaissance minimized the physical aspects of his fall and magnified the spiritual: the idea of his repentance and mental anguish (not recorded in the Bible) was so prevalent by the late-sixteenth century that Nashe coined the verb 'sampsown' meaning 'to cast down in dejection and anguished thought'. Similarly the supernatural nature of Samson's strength and his status as God's champion are ideas which M. takes over from tradition rather than from *Judges*, where the state of affairs is more doubtful.

Search for possible sources outside Greek tragedy has produced very little. R. Galland, *Revue Anglo-Américaine* xiii (1936) 326–33, finds some dubious 'parallels' between *SA* and the anonymous English translation (1642) of Buchanan's *Baptistes*, and A. Gossman, *Renaissance News* xiii (1960) 11–15, suggests two classical analogues for Manoa's ransom attempt–that of Crito in Plato's *Crito* and that of Priam in *Il.* xxiv 484–502. Prince 145–68, analysing the verse of the choruses, finds no precise parallels in Italian verse, but some similar features in the choruses and lyrical passages of Tasso's *Aminta*, Guarini's *Pastor Fido* and Andreini's *L'Adamo*. Frank Kermode on the other hand, *Durham Univ. Journal* xiv (1952) 59–63, suggests that in the lyric portions of *SA* M. is following up his rejection of the Greek ode in *PR*, and imitating Hebrew lyric measures and rhymes as he understood them.

The source and nature of M.'s Harapha figure has been the topic of some debate. D. C. Boughner, *JELH* xi (1944) 297–306, finds him a comic figure: his ancestors, Boughner believes, are the mock-chivalric cowardly braggarts with their farcical employment of the code of honour, of the sixteenth- and early seventeenth-century Italian stage, who pass into English drama in such characters as Jonson's Bobadill and Shakespeare's Don Armado. J. M. Steadman, *JEGP* lx (1961) 786–95, is dubious: to him, the primary source of M.'s giant is not Renaissance comedy but the description of his son, Goliath, in *1 Sam.* xvii. G. R. Waggoner, *PQ* xxxix (1960) 82–92, suggests that the Harapha episode is primarily chivalric rather than comic: like the entries in M.'s Commonplace Book under the heading 'Of Duels', it displays an interest in single combat and in the conventions of the duel perhaps stimulated by M.'s reading of his friend John Selden's *Duello* (1610). E. Wright, *N & Q* vii (1960) 222–4, finds a similar chivalric flavour elsewhere in *SA* (e.g. in the details of armour, *131–4*, as well as *1119–21*, and in the mention of lists, *462–3*).

*Style and imagery.* The Elizabethan influences so marked in M.'s other attempt at drama, *Comus*, are severely excised from *SA*, which has only half-a-dozen echoes of Shakespeare, one of Sylvester and none of Spenser. More in evidence are Euripides and Sophocles, who are repeatedly recalled both by M.'s phrasing and by his situations (see footnotes).

Most of M.'s stylistic mannerisms in *SA* can be illustrated from Samson's first speech (*1–114*). Modern readers are likely to be struck first by the insistent disturbances of English word order, (e.g. ' Who this high gift of strength committed to me, / In what part lodged, how easily bereft me, / Under the seal of silence could not keep' (*47–9*), where the imitation of the Latin initial copulative relative is followed by an inverted construction in which the object and the indirect questions connected with it precede the verb which, as often in Latin, occupies the final position). A common displacement of normal word order in *SA* is the promotion of adverbs or adverbial phrases or clauses to the start of a clause, sentence or, sometimes, speech: e.g. 'A little onward lend' (*1*), 'Daily in the common prison else enjoined' (*6*), 'Scarce half I seem to live' (*79*). Notable instances from later in the drama are 'With cause this hope relieves thee' (*472*), 'All otherwise to me my thoughts portend' (*590*, also *594*), Dalila's first words (*732–3*), and Samson's first reasoned reply to her (*819*). This adverbial promotion can become elaborate, e.g. 'Wherever fountain or fresh current flowed / Against the eastern ray, translucent, pure / With touch ethereal of heaven's fiery rod / I drank' (*547–50*).

The objects of verbs are similarly up-graded to leading positions: e.g. 'Immeasurable strength they might behold' (*206*), 'The first I saw at Timna' (*219*), 'That fault I take not on me' (*241*), 'His pardon I impore' (*521*). Sometimes both adverb and object take precedence: e.g. 'unwillingly this rest / Their superstition yields me' (*14–15*), 'Me easily indeed mine may neglect' (*291*), and Samson's last words, reported by the messenger, 'Hitherto, Lords, what your commands imposed / I have performed' (*1640–1*).

*SA* is full of questions: all the characters ask them, so does the chorus. There are six in Samson's first speech; seven in Manoa's first speech after his entrance (*340–71*). The catastrophe is signalled through Manoa's two questions 'What noise or shout was that? It tore the sky' (*1472*), and 'O what noise?' (*1508*). Speakers frequently answer their own questions and meet their own objections (a figure known as *anthypophora*): e.g. in Samson's first speech, 'Yet stay, let me not...' (*43*) and 'But peace, I must not...' (*60*). Besides the interrogative, the imperative mood is prominent: 'lend' (*1*), 'leave' (*11*), 'ask' (*40*), 'stay' (*43*) etc. There are twenty-seven speeches with an imperative in the opening line.

M.'s habit of using a word in its original Latin rather than its developed English sense is fairly widely exemplified: Samson's first speech has 'popular noise' (*16*) ('popular' already had its modern sense at the beginning of the seventeenth century), 'Annulled' meaning 'reduced to nothing' (*72*), and 'obvious' meaning 'exposed' (*95*) (the modern senses, 'cancelled, declared invalid' and 'palpable', were already current when M. wrote).

The speeches gain internal vigour not only from their knotty and unaccustomed syntax but also from the persistent use of rhetorical figures involving repetition. Immediate repetition of a word (*epizeuxis*) is rare, e.g. 'dark, dark, dark' (*80*), 'No, no, of my condition take no care' (*928*), but repetition with intervening words (*ploce*) constantly occurs, e.g. in Samson's first speech, 'strength ... strength' (*36*), 'the vilest ... the vilest' (*73–4*), 'dark ... dark' (*80–1*), 'life ... life' (*90–1*). Moments of tension, introspective or argumentative, are screwed tighter by heightening the density of this, as of other figures. When Samson engages in dispute with Dalila he uses 'weakness' and 'love' four times each in ten lines (*829–38*), matching Dalila's four uses of each word in the previous speech (*766–818*). A closer patterning is supplied when this figure approaches *antimetabole* (repetition with inversion), as in *423–5* 'occasion ... foes / foes ... occasion', *462–3*, *686* etc.; *anaphora* (repetition of initial words or phrases), as in *361*, *394–5*, *445–6*, *449*, *487*, *493*, *890*, etc.; and *anadiplosis* (starting a line with the last word of the line before), as in *17–18*, *247–8*, *376–7*, *878–9* etc. *Traductio* (the repetition of a word in a different grammatical form) starts in the first speech, 'deliver ... deliverer' (*39–40*), 'affliction ... afflict' (*113–4*), and is heavily used right through to the conclusion when, with *ploce*, it welds together the brief speeches of Manoa and the chorus (*1508–22*), bridges the two semi-choruses, 'blindness . . . blind' (1686–7), and lends an air of finality to Manoa's summing-up, 'heroically hath finished / A life heroic' (1709–10). Figures which depend upon the juxtaposition of two elements are called upon to emphasise contrasts like that between Samson's past and present, his blindness and the light which surrounds him, and the uncertain relationship between Dalila's inner and outer selves: e.g. *antithesis*, 'In power of others, never in my own' (78), also 195, 234, 270–1, 305, 338–9, 689 etc.; *oxymoron*, 'dark in light' (75), also 100, 307 etc.; *zeugma*, 'O'ercome with importunity and tears' (51), 'With doubtful feet and wavering resolution' (732). Bitter or sardonic word-play sharpens Samson's own speeches even when he is at his most dejected: e.g. 'a *moving* grave' (102), 'my *accomplished* snare' (230), 'My *capital* secret '(394), 'food / *Consume* me' (574–5) etc.

A way of building up swift climax of sound or stress which *SA* constantly avails itself of is the listing of adjectives or nouns, or even verbs and adverbs, either with conjunctions (*polysyndeton*) or without (*asyndeton*). Samson's first speech, for example, has 'Betrayed, captived, and both my eyes put out' (33), 'vast, unwieldly, burdensome, / Proudly secure, yet liable to fall' (54–5), 'chains, / Dungeon, or beggary, or decrepit age!' (68–9), 'fraud, contempt, abuse and wrong' (76). There are fifteen examples in the first 500 lines, and the figure is regularly repeated until the conclusion. After the entrance of the officer (1308) his asyndeton, 'With sacrifices, triumph, pomp, and games' (1312), is capped by Samson's 'gymnic artists, wrestlers, riders, runners, / Jugglers and dancers, antics, mummers, mimics' (1324–5), and Samson's subsequent asyndetic self-justification, 'how vile, contemptible, ridiculous, / What act more execrably unclean, profane?' (1361–2), is parried by the chorus's deployment of the same figure, 'Yet with this strength thou serv'st the Philistines, / Idolatrous, uncircumcised, unclean' (1363–4).

A remarkable verbal feature of *SA* is the amount of activity delegated to abstract nouns. They carry the weight of the action, either as the subjects or as the objects of the verbs. In Samson's first speech '*chance* / Relieves' (4–5), '*superstition* yields' (14–15), '*strength*' is 'put to the *labour*' (36–7), '*wisdom* bears command' (57), '*miseries* . . . ask' (64–6); Samson fears to 'call in doubt / Divine *prediction*' (43–4), bewails his '*impotence* of mind' (52), hesitates to 'quarrel with the *will* / of highest *dispensation*' (60–1), hears 'the *tread* of many feet' (111) and takes it to be sightseers coming to 'stare / At my *affliction*' (112–3). This abstraction might be thought a way of conveying Samson's blindness, if it were not prominent in the speeches of the other characters also, and of the chorus. When the chorus recall, for example, Samson's previous exploits, where solidity might be expected, we find it was 'the *forgery* / Of brazen shield and spear' (131–2) that he made useless. Manoa counsels that '*self-preservation* bids' Samson to avoid punishment or leave 'the *execution* . . . to high *disposal*' (504–6). Of M.'s dozen or so coinages in *SA* two, 'ramp' (139) and '*obstriction*' (312) are abstract nouns.

If the internal nature of Samson's drama is unobtrusively clarified by the abstract character of many grammatical agents and objects, another result is that the play's sparse imagery is thrown into bolder relief. Ricks 49–56 is disappointed with the metaphors of *SA* because they do not 'live along the line': they are not enlivened by and do not extend tendrils into their immediate context. He instances the counterfeit 'coin' of *189* which suddenly becomes a 'swarm' two lines later. But the base coin is not, from the perspective of the whole work, as lonely as he would have us suppose. Dalila as Danae in the shower of Philistian gold (*388–91, 831*) keeps it company in Samson's tormented mind. It is only isolated if viewed in isolation from the rest of the work. The rarity of *SA*'s imagery allows it to make connections across areas too large for Ricks's focus. The connections seem at first merely to reinforce the explicit meanings of the play: to add definition to the curve which takes the protagonist from zenith to nadir and back again. But, if allowed, they prove ready to contribute meanings of their own which run counter to the drama's apparent values and threaten to pull the curve out of shape.

The marine imagery–which provides, at Dalila's entrance, the play's one moment of flamboyance, is introduced in the opening speech, where Samson characterizes the Philistines' god, Dagon, as 'their sea-idol' (*13*). The suggestion that the power of the sea is on the side of Samson's enemies becomes more pronounced when he views his present anguish in marine terms–'suffers not / Mine eye to harbour sleep' (*458–9*)–and his past ruin as a shipwreck: he was and is unable to combat the sea's force:'Who like a foolish pilot have shipwrecked, / My vessel trusted to me from above, / Gloriously rigged; and for a word, a tear' (*198–200*). It is bitterly ironic that a 'tear' of Dalila's–so small a quantity of salt water–should have been enough to wreck Samson's glorious vessel, and the irony lends her later tears, to which both she and the chorus draw Samson's attention (*729, 735*), a dangerous potency. The temptation which she presents is enhanced, just as the subtler temptation to despair which the chorus, for all their intended 'counsel and consolation', bring, is delicately underlined when Samson hears them 'steering' (*111*) towards him. ('Steer', originally an exclusively nautical word, was still alive with marine associations for the seventeenth century, and M. in *PL* ix 513–5, 'As when a ship ... steers, and shifts her sail', was the first to use it with ship rather than helmsman as agent.) The famous ship-simile which announces Dalila (*714–9*) is, however, the major indication of her power. She is able to control the sea, that element which had overcome Samson, with effortless ease: 'stately', 'trim', decked with streamers and 'courted' by the winds, she moves upon its surface. The simile also connects her with the Philistines, worshippers of the 'sea-idol', and she is, in fact, a Philistine in M., though not in *Judges*. One question, at her entrance, is whether she is still in league with them, or whether love and pity for Samson are behind her return. It is posed, in terms of the predominant image, by the chorus: 'But who is this, what thing of sea or land?' (*710*). The other question is whether Samson will be able to withstand her. That he is still in love with her is clear. He dare not even let her touch him: 'Not for thy life, lest fierce remembrance wake / My sudden rage to tear thee joint by joint'. If he hated her he would hardly warn her against risking her life. Blindness protects him from her physical attractions to some extent, (though as the chorus notice (720), she has artfully perfumed herself with ambergris – another link with the sea), but he knows he will not be able to resist the feel of her body: 'other senses', as Dalila is aware, 'want not their delights'. The chorus, too, guess what 'secret sting of amorous remorse' (1007) Samson feels. Only if Dalila is still an enticement to Samson will his temptation be the same as that which caused his fall – and it must be so if her reappearance is to be a genuine second chance for him. (To seventeenth-century etymologists his name meant 'There-the-second-time': this may be at the back of his unscriptural second encounter with Dalila in SA). It is self-esteem, as the perceptive Manoa tells him, that he has lost – he is 'self-displeased / For self-offence' (514–5) – and he is able to regain it by standing firm where before he succumbed. Dalila's entrance is therefore the hinge of the drama. The fanfare of imagery which heralds her is a structural pointer.

Because Samson resists this cardinal temptation, he takes upon himself the power of the sea. Dalila finds him more unappeasable than the sea itself. The 'stately ship of Tarsus' which was 'courted' by the winds, cannot calm the tempest into which Samson is now transformed: 'I see thou art implacable, more deaf / To prayers than winds and seas, yet winds to seas / Are reconciled at length, and sea to shore: / Thy anger, unappeasable, still rages, / Eternal tempest never to be calmed' (960–4). In the chorus's opinion, Samson's chances of successful navigation, now that Dalila has been rejected, are improved: 'What pilot so expert but needs must wreck / Embarked with such a steers-mate at the helm?' (1044–5) is their comment on her departure: the blame for what has happened is tactfully shifted from the 'foolish pilot' to his mate. But Dalila has seen Samson, in his anger, as a 'tempest', and just as the images of his 'gloriously rigged' vessel and of her ship with its 'tackle trim' and 'streamers waving' tend to draw the two of them into an implied, and disturbing, parallelism, so this tempest image aligns him, unexpectedly, with Harapha, whose blustering entrance as a 'tempest' (1063) is next announced. Harapha's tempestuous lack of self-control is less of a threat than Dalila's dangerous mastery. The difference between them is implied in terms of shipping: 'What wind hath blown him hither / I less conjecture than when first I saw / The sumptuous Dalila floating this way' (1070–2). Samson is still a tempest when he destroys the Philistines. Just before the noise of the calamity is heard Manoa speaks of his son's locks 'waving' down (1493) – a word which clarifies the sea echoes of the earlier 'redundant locks' (568) – and, as the messenger relates, it is 'with the force of winds and waters' and 'with burst of thunder' (1647–51) that the pillars are tugged down. The destructive and amoral power of the sea which, at the opening of the drama, was specifically associated with the Philistines, has now been transferred to Samson. His last bloody act of vengeance, which the surface voice of the drama invites us to applaud, is condemned, at a deeper level, by the progression of imagery.

Snakes and serpents are not so obtrusively present in the language of *SA* as the sea is. Samson is afraid that, if he pardons Dalila, he will be 'entangled with a poisonous bosom snake' (*763*). At her spiteful leave-taking the chorus recognize her as 'a manifest serpent by her sting / Discovered in the end', and Samson agrees that she is a 'viper' (*997–1001*). The revelation of Dalila as a stinging creature sets her among Samson's torments and disappointments: the 'deadly swarm of hornets' (*19–20*), the 'scorpion's tail' (*360*) and the thoughts 'armed with deadly stings' that 'Mangle my apprehensive tenderest parts' (*623*) – the physical reference stabs excruciatingly at the area of sexual betrayal, as does the 'thorn intestine' (*1037–8*) which is also Dalila. Samson's physical prowess, his tearing of the lion (*128*), draws to itself, like the lion's swarming carcass, both honey and sting: Dalila, the stinging creature, with her 'honied words' (*1066*), and a 'swarm' (*192*) of deceitful friends. But as Samson assumed the power of the sea, so he tells Dalila in his crucial interview with her that he has learned 'adder's wisdom' (*936*), and when he destroys the Philistines he uses snake-like cunning, creeping in below the 'roosts' of their amphitheatre to divert their attention downwards, while striking them from above: 'And as an evening dragon came, / Assailant on the perched roosts, / And nests in order ranged / Of tame villatic fowl; but as an eagle / His cloudless thunder bolted on their heads' (*1692–6*). 'Dragon', especially when coupled with 'fiery' (*1690*), throws a specious glamour over the snake which, when the blind Samson first learned to envy it, was a mere 'worm' (*74*). 'Dragon' sounds better with 'eagle', and the eagle, like the Phoenix (*1699*) belongs to and completes the explicit elevation of Samson which is engineered through the imagery of birds and animals. (Samson, a 'lion' before his fall (*128, 139*), is caught in Dalila's 'snares' (*230, 409, 532, 931*), 'gins' and 'toils' (*933*), becomes a farmyard animal, 'a tame wether' (*538*), in his subjection to her, and is 'Put to the labour of a beast' (*37*) among the 'asses' (*1162*) at the mill. But the first words he speaks to Dalila – 'Out, out hyaena' (*748*) – transfer his animal baseness to her, and in the Harapha episode the 'chafed wild boars' and 'ruffled porcupines' (*1138*) – wild and heraldic creatures – show him rapidly regaining his animal nobility. His insistence that the Philistines 'shall not trail me through their streets / Like a wild beast' (*1402–3*) acquires irony from the sequence). But 'dragon' means 'snake' nevertheless (*OED* defines it as 'huge serpent or snake; python'): the eagle and the Phoenix are undercut by the snake in the henroost, which looks much more like the 'serpent' Dalila than they do, but which is Samson.

If Dalila is ship and snake, she is also flower. The chorus describe her, weeping, 'with head declined / Like a fair flower surcharged with dew' (*727–8*). There is a sense in which this image, like that of the ship, emphasizes Dalila's dangerous potentiality, and it does this not only through the attractiveness implied by 'flower' but also through the coolness implied by 'dew'. From the outset Samson's torment is presented as an 'inflammation' (*626*); his griefs are 'sores', 'tumours', 'festered wounds' (*184–6*) which 'ferment and rage', 'Rankle, and fester, and gangrene' (*619–21*). The sug-

gested lenitives are all evocations of coolness–'cooling herb', 'breath of
vernal air from snowy alp' (626–8), 'Salve', 'balm' (184–6), 'The breath
of heaven fresh-blowing' (10)–and they connect, naturally enough, with
Samson's earlier mode of life before his fall and anguish, when he drank
'the cool crystalline stream' from 'fountain or fresh current' (546–7).
This healing coolness is felt for the last time, pathetically, in the 'lavers pure
and cleansing herbs' and the 'shade / Of laurel ever green and branching
palm' (1727–35) of Manoa's funeral preparations, but it is twice utilized, in
the course of the drama, to accentuate the pressure of a particular tempta-
tion: once when Samson describes death as the 'balm' (651) of all his miser-
ies, and the second time when Dalila stands like a flower 'surcharged with
dew'. But the flower image does not only provide this kind of emphasis.
Like other images, it narrows the apparent disparity between Dalila and the
Philistines on the one hand and Samson on the other. Dalila, 'with head
declined', is a flower, perhaps one of the 'flower' (1654) of the Philistine
nobility upon whose 'heads' (1652), declined as they watch him in the arena
below, Samson tugs down the roof. In his early exploits, also, it was the
'flower of Palestine' (144) that he cut down. But he, too, was in the 'flower'
(938) of his youth and strength when Dalila destroyed him, and at his death
Manoa grieves that the 'first-born bloom of spring' has been 'Nipped with
the lagging rear of winter's frost' (1576–7). Dalila imagines that her 'tomb'
will be 'visited' with 'annual flowers' (986–7), and Manoa, mourning his
son, prophesies that the virgins will 'Visit his tomb with flowers' (1742).
A flower is recognizably an apt emblem for Dalila. Its beauty, like hers, is
external: her behaviour makes the chorus wonder whether it was because
'outward ornament /Was lavished' on women 'that inward gifts / Were
left for haste unfinished' (1025–7). What might escape notice, without the
flower symbol, is the similarity between this and the externality confessed
by Samson (58–9, 206–8). This aspect of Milton's Samson, his weak-minded-
ness, is not emphasized either in Judges or in the Christian tradition of
Samson literature. It is revealing, in this context, that both Dalila and Samson
tend to externalize intellectual or moral debate–internal conflict–through
the use of military terminology. To Dalila the persuasive arguments of the
Philistine magistrates are 'assaults' and 'sieges' (845–6), and Samson appre-
hends Dalila's enticements as a 'peal' of artillery (235), as 'feminine assaults'
and 'Tongue-batteries' which 'storm' (403–5) the undefended 'gate' (560)
of his 'fort of silence' (236).

The flames among which the Phoenix dies into life (1699–1707) mark the
termination of a line of fires which have flared all along the course of Sam-
son's career. His birth was foretold by an angel which ascended 'in flames'
(25, 1433), 'As in a fiery column' (27); ropes to him were 'threads / Touched
with the flame' (262); 'heaven's fiery rod' (549) pointed out a fountain for
his thirst; his fall is marked by his inability to share the 'blaze' of noon (80);
as he leaves the stage the chorus call down 'a shield, / Of fire' (1434–5) for
him. The elevatory force of this fire imagery is, however, sharply questioned
when, shortly before the apparently 'extinguished' Samson rouses his own

'fiery virtue' into 'sudden flame' (*1688–92*), he is warned not to add fuel to the 'flame' (*1351*) of the Philistine lords, and himself speaks of the priests and worshippers of Dagon 'fired' with zeal and 'unquenchable' (*1419–22*). An equivalence between the religious fervour of the Philistines and that of the protagonist is momentarily revealed.

In *SA*, then, the imagery does not merely reinforce the drama's triumphant upward arc. On the contrary, it contributes meanings which threaten to invert this arc and bring the weak-minded, vengeful hero to the level of Dalila and the Philistines. In this way it makes a major contribution to the moral maturity of the work.

## OF THAT SORT OF DRAMATIC POEM WHICH IS CALLED TRAGEDY

TRAGEDY, as it was anciently composed, hath been ever held the gravest, moralest, and most profitable of all other poems: therefore said by Aristotle to be of power by raising pity and fear, or terror, to purge the mind of those and such-like passions, that is to temper
5  and reduce them to just measure with a kind of delight, stirred up by reading or seeing those passions well imitated. Nor is nature wanting in her own effects to make good his assertion: for so in physic things of melancholic hue and quality are used against melancholy, sour against sour, salt to remove salt humours. Hence philosophers and
10  other gravest writers, as Cicero, Plutarch and others, frequently cite out of tragic poets, both to adorn and illustrate their discourse. The Apostle Paul himself thought it not unworthy to insert a verse of Euripides into the text of Holy Scripture, 1 Cor. xv. 33, and Paraeus

*Introduction 1–9. Tragedy . . . humours*] P. R. Sellin, *JEGP* lx (1961) 712–30, notes that, although M.'s version of Aristotelian catharsis, with its homoeopathic analogy, has been traced to Minturno, *De Poeta* (1563) and Guarini, *Il Compendio della Poesia Tragicomica* (1601), Minturno conceives of catharsis as the driving out of undesirable passions rather than the reduction of all passions to a norm, as in M.'s account, and Guarini takes Aristotle's τοιούτων παθημάτων, which M. translates 'of those and such-like passions', to refer to pity and fear alone, and goes on to make a distinction, not in M., between good fear and pity and bad. A theory of catharsis nearer to M.'s, though not identical is advanced by Daniel Heinsius, *De Tragoediae Constitutione* (1611), which Sellin thinks M.'s source. However, in Heinsius' theory, as in Guarini's, pity and fear seem the only emotions involved in the tragic catharsis. *Introduction 12–13 verse of Euripides*] J. J. Lynch, *N & Q* iii (1956) 477, says that the maxim referred to ('Evil communications corrupt good manners') is from Menander's *Thais*, not Euripides. But in fact the fragment in which it survives is found in editions of both Euripides and Menander. *Introduction 13. Paraeus*] David Paraeus (1548–1622), a German Calvinist whose *Commentary on Romans* (1609) was publicly burned by the universities of Oxford and Cambridge. His work *On the Divine Apocalypse* (1618), to which M. here refers, was translated into English by Elias Arnold, 1644. A. C.

commenting on the *Revelation*, divides the whole book as a tragedy,
15   into acts distinguished each by a chorus of heavenly harpings and
song between. Heretofore men in highest dignity have laboured not a
little to be thought able to compose a tragedy. Of that honour
Dionysius the elder was no less ambitious, than before of his attaining
to the tyranny. Augustus Caesar also had begun his *Ajax*, but unable to
20   please his own judgement with what he had begun, left it unfinished.
Seneca the philosopher is by some thought the author of those
tragedies (at least the best of them) that go under that name. Gregory
Nazianzen a Father of the Church, thought it not unbeseeming the
sanctity of his person to write a tragedy, which he entitled, *Christ*
25   *Suffering*. This is mentioned to vindicate tragedy from the small
esteem, or rather infamy, which in the account of many it undergoes
at this day with other common interludes; happening through the
poet's error of intermixing comic stuff with tragic sadness and gravity;
or introducing trivial and vulgar persons, which by all judicious hath
30   been counted absurd; and brought in without discretion, corruptly
to gratify the people. And though ancient tragedy use no prologue,
yet using sometimes in case of self-defence, or explanation, that
which Martial calls an epistle; in behalf of this tragedy coming forth
after the ancient manner, much different from what among us passes
35   for best, thus much beforehand may be *epistled*; that chorus is here
introduced after the Greek manner, not ancient only but modern,
and still in use among the Italians. In the modelling therefore of this

Cook, *Archiv für das Studium der Neueren Sprachen* cxxix (1912) 74–80, quotes
the relevant passages from Paraeus.

*Introduction 18. Dionysius*] Tyrant of Syracuse (431–367 B.C.). Diodorus
Siculus xiv 109 tells how his poems were ridiculed at the Olympic games,
and, xv 74, how he died from a debauch following the news that his play had
won the prize at the Lenaea at Athens.

*Introduction 19. Augustus Caesar ... Ajax*] Suetonius ii 85 says Augustus,
dissatisfied with what he had written of the *Ajax*, erased it.

*Introduction 21. Seneca*] Lucius Annaeus Seneca (3 B.C.–65 A.D.). There are
ten tragedies which bear his name (the *Octavia*, also ascribed to him, is
certainly later). The doubt as to his authorship of the tragedies is due to a
mistake of Sidonius Apollinaris, *Carmen* ix 230–8, who clearly distinguishes
between Seneca the philosopher and Seneca the tragedian.

*Introduction 22–3. Gregory Nazianzen*] Bishop of Constantinople (AD 325 ?–
390 ?); his *Christus Patiens*, a piece of Byzantine Euripidean pastiche, has also
been ascribed to Apollinarius the elder.

*Introduction 28. sadness*] seriousness.

*Introduction 31. prologue*] M. uses the term in its modern sense (a preliminary
address to the audience), not in Aristotle's sense (the part of a tragedy which
precedes the entrance of the chorus).

*Introduction 33*. Martial (epistle to *Epig.* ii) notes that tragedies and
comedies may need epistles since 'they cannot speak for themselves'.

*Introduction 37. Italians*] Tasso's *Aminta* and Guarini's *Pastor Fido*, for example,

poem, with good reason, the ancients and Italians are rather followed, as of much more authority and fame. The measure of verse used in
40 the chorus is of all sorts, called by the Greeks monostrophic, or rather apolelymenon, without regard had to strophe, antistrophe or epode, which were a kind of stanzas framed only for the music, then used with the chorus that sung; not essential to the poem, and therefore not material; or being divided into stanzas or pauses, they may be called
45 alloeostropha. Division into act and scene referring chiefly to the stage (to which this work never was intended) is here omitted.

It suffices if the whole drama be found not produced beyond the fifth act. Of the style and uniformity, and that commonly called the plot, whether intricate or explicit, which is nothing indeed but such
50 economy, or disposition of the fable as may stand best with verisimilitude and decorum; they only will best judge who are not unacquainted with Aeschylus, Sophocles, and Euripides, the three tragic poets unequalled yet by any, and the best rule to all who endeavour to write tragedy. The circumscription of time wherein
55 the whole drama begins and ends, is according to ancient rule, and best example, within the space of twenty-four hours.

## THE ARGUMENT

Samson made captive, blind, and now in the prison at Gaza, there to labour as in a common workhouse, on a festival day, in the general

both have a chorus, as did sixteenth-century Italian tragic drama frequently. M. cites 'the Italian Commentaries of Castelvetro, Tasso, Mazzoni, and others', along with Aristotle and Horace, as authorities in *Of Education* (Columbia iv 286, Yale ii 404).
*Introduction 40-1. monostrophic*] of one stanza only. *apolelymenon*] Greek 'freed' (i.e. from the restraint of any firm stanza pattern). In Gk drama the strophe was a stanza sung by the chorus as it moved from right to left, the antistrophe, corresponding exactly to the strophe in structure, as it moved in the opposite direction. The concluding epode was sung standing still. M. says that if his choruses do seem at times to divide into stanzas, then they should be called alloeostropha (Greek 'of irregular strophes').
*Introduction 49. intricate ... explicit*] Aristotle, *Poetics* 6, divides plots into two classes, simple ($\dot{\alpha}\pi\lambda o\hat{\imath}$) and complex ($\pi\epsilon\pi\lambda\epsilon\gamma\mu\acute{\epsilon}\nu o\iota$). *which is nothing indeed*] i.e. the plot is merely the management ('economy') of the events: the 'putting together of the incidents', as Aristotle calls it.
*Introduction 52. Aeschylus*] J. C. Maxwell, *RES* n.s. iii (1952) 366–71, points out that Aeschylus was not popular, even among scholars, in the seventeenth century, and that M. is unusual in ranking him with Sophocles and Euripides here.
*Introduction 55-6. ancient rule*] Aristotle, *Poetics* 5, gives no 'rule'. It was Renaissance criticism that hardened his general statement into the 'unity of time'. *best example*] there are five exceptions among surviving Greek tragedies: Aeschylus' *Persians*, *Agamemnon* and *Eumenides*, Sophocles' *Trachiniae* and Euripides' *Suppliants*.

cessation from labour, comes forth into the open air, to a place nigh,
60  somewhat retired there to sit a while and bemoan his condition. Where
he happens at length to be visited by certain friends and equals of
his tribe, which make the Chorus, who seek to comfort him what they
can; then by his old father Manoa, who endeavours the like, and
withal tells him his purpose to procure his liberty by ransom; lastly,
65  that this feast was proclaimed by the Philistines as a day of thanks-
giving for their deliverance from the hands of Samson, which yet
more troubles him. Manoa then departs to prosecute his endeavour
with the Philistian lords for Samson's redemption; who in the mean-
while is visited by other persons; and lastly by a public officer to
70  require his coming to the feast before the lords and people, to play
or show his strength in their presence; he at first refuses, dismissing
the public officer with absolute denial to come; at length persuaded
inwardly that this was from God, he yields to go along with him,
who came now the second time with great threatenings to fetch him;
75  the Chorus yet remaining on the place, Manoa returns full of joyful
hope, to procure ere long his son's deliverance: in the midst of which dis-
course an Hebrew comes in haste confusedly at first; and afterwards
more distinctly relating the catastrophe, what Samson had done to the
Philistines, and by accident to himself; wherewith the tragedy ends.

## THE PERSONS

Samson
Manoa, the father of Samson
Dalila his wife
Harapha of Gath
Public Officer
Messenger
Chorus of Danites

### The Scene before the Prison in Gaza

*Sam.* A little onward lend thy guiding hand
To these dark steps, a little further on;
For yonder bank hath choice of sun or shade,
There I am wont to sit, when any chance
5   Relieves me from my task of servile toil,
Daily in the common prison else enjoined me,

---

*1–2.* This opening has been compared to the first scene of the *Oedipus at
Colonus*, where Oedipus is led forward by Antigone, and to Euripides,
*Phoenician Maidens* 834–5, where Tiresias asks his daughter to lead him on,
and says she is as eyes to his 'blind feet'. In Sidney, *Arcadia* II x 3, the blinded
king of Paphlagonia complains that there is no one to 'lende me a hande to
guide my darke steppes'.
*3. choice of sun or shade*] 'The opening lines, describing mere physical sensa-
tion, also suggest the internal drama to come' (Stein[2] 139).

     Where I a prisoner chained, scarce freely draw
     The air imprisoned also, close and damp,
     Unwholesome draught: but here I feel amends,
*10*  The breath of heaven fresh blowing, pure and sweet,
     With day-spring born; here leave me to respire.
     This day a solemn feast the people hold
     To Dagon their sea-idol, and forbid
     Laborious works, unwillingly this rest
*15*  Their superstition yields me; hence with leave
     Retiring from the popular noise, I seek
     This unfrequented place to find some ease,
     Ease to the body some, none to the mind
     From restless thoughts, that like a deadly swarm
*20*  Of hornets armed, no sooner found alone,
     But rush upon me thronging, and present
     Times past, what once I was, and what am now.
     O wherefore was my birth from heaven foretold
     Twice by an angel, who at last in sight
*25*  Of both my parents all in flames ascended
     From off the altar, where an offering burned,
     As in a fiery column charioting
     His godlike presence, and from some great act
     Or benefit revealed to Abraham's race?
*30*  Why was my breeding ordered and prescribed
     As of a person separate to God,
     Designed for great exploits; if I must die
     Betrayed, captived, and both my eyes put out,
     Made of my enemies the scorn and gaze;
*35*  To grind in brazen fetters under task

*[handwritten margin note: Rails Against God's justice]*

10. Stein² 139 takes this line as an early note of the regeneration theme.

11. *day-spring*] daybreak; cp. *Luke* i 78: 'The day-spring from on high hath visited us.'

13. *Dagon*] National deity of the Philistines, presented in *PL* i 462–3 as half-man, half-fish (the name is possibly derived from Heb. *Dag*, 'fish'). His chief temples were at Gaza(*Judges* xvi 23) and Ashdod (*1 Sam.* v 1–2).

24. *Twice*] First to his mother alone, *Judges* xiii 3–5, and later to both parents, xiii 10–20.

27. *charioting*] Cp. the fiery chariot of Elijah, *2 Kings* i 11, and Josephus, *Antiquities* v 8, who says that the angel ascended from the rock on which Manoa's sacrifice burned 'by means of the smoke, as by a vehicle'.

28. *from*] The angel ascended 'From off the altar' and 'from' revealing 'some great act / Or benefit'.

31. *separate*] 'Nazarite' is derived from Heb. *nazar*, 'to separate oneself', and the angel says to Samson's mother, *Judges* xiii 7: 'The child shall be a Nazarite unto God.'

With this heaven-gifted strength? O glorious strength
Put to the labour of a beast, debased
Lower than bond-slave! Promise was that I
Should Israel from Philistian yoke deliver;
40    Ask for this great deliverer now, and find him
Eyeless in Gaza at the mill with slaves,
Himself in bonds under Philistian yoke;
Yet stay, let me not rashly call in doubt
Divine prediction; what if all foretold
45    Had been fulfilled but through mine own default,
Whom have I to complain of but myself?
Who this high gift of strength committed to me,
In what part lodged, how easily bereft me,
Under the seal of silence could not keep,
50    But weakly to a woman must reveal it,
O'ercome with importunity and tears.
O impotence of mind, in body strong!
But what is strength without a double share
Of wisdom, vast, unwieldly, burdensome,
55    Proudly secure, yet liable to fall
By weakest subtleties, not made to rule,
But to subserve where wisdom bears command.
God, when he gave me strength, to show withal
How slight the gift was, hung it in my hair.
60    But peace, I must not quarrel with the will
Of highest dispensation, which herein
Haply had ends above my reach to know:
Suffices that to me strength is my bane,
And proves the source of all my miseries;
65    So many, and so huge, that each apart
Would ask a life to wail, but chief of all,
O loss of sight, of thee I most complain!
Blind among enemies, O worse than chains,
Dungeon, or beggary, or decrepit age!
70    Light the prime work of God to me is extinct,
And all her various objects of delight
Annulled, which might in part my grief have eased,

38. *Promise was*] Cp. *Judges* xiii 5: 'He shall begin to deliver Israel out of the hand of the Philistines.'

52. This aspect of M.'s Samson, his weak-mindedness, is not emphasised either in *Judges* or in the Christian tradition of Samson literature (Krouse 100).

53–4. Cp. Horace, *Odes* III iv 65: 'Brute force bereft of wisdom falls to ruin by its own weight.'

66–7. Contrast l. 195.

Inferior to the vilest now become
Of man or worm; the vilest here excel me,
75    They creep, yet see, I dark in light exposed
To daily fraud, contempt, abuse and wrong,
Within doors, or without, still as a fool,
In power of others, never in my own;
Scarce half I seem to live, dead more than half.
80    O dark, dark, dark, amid the blaze of noon,
Irrecoverably dark, total eclipse
Without all hope of day!
O first-created beam, and thou great word,
Let there be light, and light was over all;
85    Why am I thus bereaved thy prime decree?
The sun to me is dark
And silent as the moon,
When she deserts the night
Hid in her vacant interlunar cave.
90    Since light so necessary is to life,
And almost life itself, if it be true
That light is in the soul,
She all in every part; why was the sight
To such a tender ball as the eye confined?

77. *still*] always.

79–109. For a rhetorical analysis of this passage see J. B. Broadbent, *MP* lvi (1959) 226–7.

83–4. Cp. *Gen.* i 3.

87–9. *silent*] The time when the moon is in conjunction with the sun is called, says Pliny xvi 74, either the day of the silent moon (*silentis lunae*) or the interlunar day (*interlunii*). *OED* first records the word 'silent' meaning 'not shining', as applied to the moon, in 1646. Pathetically Samson translates a visual fact, the moon's absence, into the terms of the sense he still retains, hearing.    *vacant*] M. thinks of the moon at leisure (Latin *vacare*) resting in a cave.

92–3. A. Williams, *MLN* lxiii (1948) 537–8, refers to the theory that the soul is whole in the whole body and whole in every part of the body – a commonplace deriving from the Fathers. He compares Augustine, *De Trinitate* vi 6: *anima . . . in unoquoque corpore, et in toto tota est, et in qualibet eius parte tota est* (The soul . . . in any body, is both all in the whole, and all in every part).

93–7. T. Spencer and J. Willis, *N & Q* cxcvi (1951) 387, quote a parallel from Arnobius, *Adversus Gentes* ii 59–a writer to whom M. refers twice elsewhere – *Cur cum esset utilius oculis nos illuminare compluribus ad periculum caecitatis, duorum sumus angustiis applicati?* (Why, since it would be an advantage considering the danger of blindness for us to be enlightened with many eyes, are we tied to the inconvenience of two?)

95　　So obvious and so easy to be quenched,
　　　And not as feeling through all parts diffused,
　　　That she might look at will through every pore?
　　　Then had I not been thus exiled from light;
　　　As in the land of darkness yet in light,
100　　To live a life half dead, a living death,
　　　And buried; but O yet more miserable!
　　　Myself, my sepulchre, a moving grave,
　　　Buried, yet not exempt
　　　By privilege of death and burial
105　　From worst of other evils, pains and wrongs,
　　　But made hereby obnoxious more
　　　To all the miseries of life,
　　　Life in captivity
　　　Among inhuman foes.
110　　But who are these? for with joint pace I hear
　　　The tread of many feet steering this way;
　　　Perhaps my enemies who come to stare
　　　At my affliction, and perhaps to insult,
　　　Their daily practice to afflict me more.
115　　*Chor.* This, this is he; softly a while,
　　　Let us not break in upon him;
　　　O change beyond report, thought, or belief!
　　　See how he lies at random, carelessly diffused,
　　　With languished head unpropped,
120　　As one past hope, abandoned,
　　　And by himself given over;
　　　In slavish habit, ill-fitted weeds
　　　O'er-worn and soiled;
　　　Or do my eyes misrepresent? Can this be he,
125　　That heroic, that renowned,
　　　Irresistible Samson? whom unarmed
　　　No strength of man, or fiercest wild beast could
　　　　　　　withstand;
　　　Who tore the lion, as the lion tears the kid,
　　　Ran on embattled armies clad in iron,
130　　And weaponless himself,

---

95. *obvious*] exposed.

106. *obnoxious*] liable to.

118–9. *diffused . . . languished*] Echoes Ovid, *Ex Ponto* III iii 8: *fusaque erant
toto languida membra toro* (languid limbs diffused over the bed).

128. Cp. *Judges* xiv 6: 'And he rent him [the young lion] as he would have
rent a kid.'

> Made arms ridiculous, useless the forgery
> Of brazen shield and spear, the hammered cuirass,
> Chalybean-tempered steel, and frock of mail
> Adamantean proof;
> *135* But safest he who stood aloof,
> When insupportably his foot advanced,
> In scorn of their proud arms and warlike tools,
> Spurned them to death by troops. The bold Ascalonite
> Fled from his lion ramp, old warriors turned
> *140* Their plated backs under his heel;
> Or grovelling soiled their crested helmets in the dust.
> Then with what trivial weapon came to hand,
> The jaw of a dead ass, his sword of bone,
> A thousand foreskins fell, the flower of Palestine
> *145* In Ramath-lechi famous to this day:
> Then by main force pulled up, and on his shoulders
>        bore
> The gates of Azza, post, and massy bar
> Up to the hill by Hebron, seat of giants old,

*131. forgery*] The craft of forging metal.

*133. Chalybean*] Cp. Virgil, *Georg.* i 58: 'the naked Chalybes give us iron'—they were famous metal-workers. Starnes and Talbert 246 quote from Stephanus *Chalybs, fluvius in Hispania, in quo ferrum optime temperatur.*

*134. Adamantean*] the only recorded instance of the adjective in *OED*; 'adamant' (*adamas*) was the name applied by Latin writers to the hardest known substance—at first steel, later diamond.    *proof*] a noun (= 'proof armour', armour which was considered impenetrable), in apposition to 'frock of mail'.

*136. insupportably*] irresistibly.

*138. Ascalonite*] Ascalon is mentioned in *1 Sam.* vi 17 as one of the five main cities of the Philistines. In *Judges* xiv 19, Samson goes down to Ascalon and kills thirty men there.

*139. lion*] lion-like.    *ramp*] act of ramping (the first occurrence of the noun in this sense recorded in *OED*); to 'ramp' is to raise the forepaws in the air.

*140. plated*] wearing armour.

*143.* In *Judges* xv 15–6 Samson finds the jawbone of an ass, and kills a thousand men with it.

*144. foreskins*] uncircumcised Philistines.

*145. Ramath-lechi*] The marginal note to A.V. *Judges* xv 17 translates 'Ramath-lehi' as meaning 'The lifting up' or 'casting away of the jawbone'.

*146–8.* This exploit is narrated in *Judges* xvi 3. 'Azza' is a variant form of Gaza.

*148. seat of giants*] Hebron was the city of Arba, *Josh.* xiv 15, father of Anak, xv 13–4, whose children, the Anakim, were giants, *Num.* xiii 33.

No journey of a sabbath-day, and loaded so;
*150*     Like whom the Gentiles feign to bear up heaven.
          Which shall I first bewail,
          Thy bondage or lost sight,
          Prison within prison
          Inseparably dark?
*155*     Thou art become (O worst imprisonment!)
          The dungeon of thyself; thy soul
          (Which men enjoying sight oft without cause complain)
          Imprisoned now indeed,
          In real darkness of the body dwells,
*160*     Shut up from outward light
          To incorporate with gloomy night;
          For inward light alas
          Puts forth no visual beam.
          O mirror of our fickle state,
*165*     Since man on earth unparalleled!
          The rarer thy example stands,
          By how much from the top of wondrous glory,
          Strongest of mortal men,
          To lowest pitch of abject fortune thou art fallen.
*170*     For him I reckon not in high estate
          Whom long descent of birth
          Or the sphere of fortune raises;
          But thee whose strength, while virtue was her mate,
          Might have subdued the earth,
*175*     Universally crowned with highest praises.
          *Sam.* I hear the sound of words, their sense the air
          Dissolves unjointed ere it reach my ear.
          *Chor.* He speaks, let us draw night. Matchless in might,
          The glory late of Israel, now the grief;

150. *whom*] Atlas.
157. (*Which ... complain*)] i.e. men often complain that the soul is imprisoned in the body. *1671* prints 'complain'd', but the *Errata* corrects to 'complain'.
161. *incorporate with*] combine with.
163. *visual beam*] beam of eyesight.
165. *Since ... unparalleled!*] i.e. O mirror, unparalleled since man was on earth!
166–7. *The rarer ... By how much*] The spectacular nature of Samson's fall makes his example proportionately more noteworthy. M.'s construction is based on the Latin use of *eo ... quo* with a comparative.
170–5. Parker[2] 112 takes these lines as M.'s justification of his disobedience to Aristotle (*Poetics* 13) who said the tragic hero should be 'a personage like Oedipus, Thyestes, or other illustrious men of such families'.

*180*  We come thy friends and neighbours not unknown
       From Eshtaol and Zora's fruitful vale
       To visit or bewail thee, or if better,
       Counsel or consolation we may bring,
       Salve to thy sores, apt words have power to 'suage
*185*  The tumours of a troubled mind,
       And are as balm to festered wounds.
       *Sam.* Your coming, friends, revives me, for I learn
       Now of my own experience, not by talk,
       How counterfeit a coin they are who friends
*190*  Bear in their superscription (of the most
       I would be understood) in prosperous days
       They swarm, but in adverse withdraw their head
       Not to be found, though sought. Ye see, O friends,
       How many evils have enclosed me round;
*195*  Yet that which was the worst now least afflicts me,
       Blindness, for had I sight, confused with shame,
       How could I once look up, or heave the head,
       Who like a foolish pilot have shipwrecked,
       My vessel trusted to me from above,
*200*  Gloriously rigged; and for a word, a tear,
       Fool, have divulged the secret gift of God
       To a deceitful woman: tell me friends,
       Am I not sung and proverbed for a fool
       In every street, do they not say, how well
*205*  Are come upon him his deserts? yet why?
       Immeasurable strength they might behold
       In me, of wisdom nothing more than mean;
       This with the other should, at least, have paired,
       These two proportioned ill drove me transverse.
*210*  *Chor.* Tax not divine disposal, wisest men
       Have erred, and by bad women been deceived;
       And shall again, pretend they ne'er so wise.
       Deject not then so overmuch thyself,
       Who hast of sorrow thy full load besides;

*181.* Samson was born at Zora, *judges* xiii 2, and buried between Zora and
Eshtaol, xvi 31. These towns lay 'in the valley' and are ascribed to both
Judah and Dan (*Josh.* xv 33 and xix 41).
*190. superscription*] The stamp on a coin.
*203. proverbed*] Cp. *Ps.* lxix 11: 'I became a proverb to them', and Job xxx
9: 'And now am I their song, yea, I am their byword' (Vulg. *proverbium*).
*207. mean*] average.
*209. transverse*] sideways, off-course, a nautical term, continuing the ship
image of 198–200.

215    Yet truth to say, I oft have heard men wonder
       Why thou shouldst wed Philistian women rather
       Than of thine own tribe fairer, or as fair,
       At least of thy own nation, and as noble.
       *Sam.* The first I saw at Timna, and she pleased
220    Me, not my parents, that I sought to wed,
       The daughter of an infidel: they knew not
       That what I motioned was of God; I knew
       From intimate impulse, and therefore urged
       The marriage on; that by occasion hence
225    I might begin Israel's deliverance,
       The work to which I was divinely called;
       She proving false, the next I took to wife
       (O that I never had! fond wish too late.)
       Was in the vale of Sorec, Dalila,
230    That specious monster, my accomplished snare.
       I thought it lawful from my former act,
       And the same end; still watching to oppress
       Israel's oppressors: of what now I suffer
       She was not the prime cause, but I myself,

*215–8.* This is the reply to Samson's question, ll. 203–5.

*216.* In assuming that Dalila was a Philistine M. follows one stream of exegetical tradition and rejects another, deriving from Cajetan, which suggested that she might have been an Israelite (Krouse 102).

*219–26.* M. follows the account in *Judges* xiv 1–4 exactly, except in the detail of Samson's 'intimate impulse', which is not in *Judges*–the reason Samson gives there for the match is 'she pleaseth me well'. Krouse 96 points out that Christian tradition had argued from Theodoret onwards that all Samson's apparent waywardness–like his marrying the woman of Timna–was at the instigation of God. In M.'s own age Calvin, Brenz, Bullinger, Paraeus and others had defended Samson on these grounds.

*222. motioned*] 1671 prints 'mention'd' but the *Errata* corrects to 'motioned'.

*227. proving false*] In *Judges* xiv 5–20 she extracts from Samson the answer to the riddle he has set the young men of Timna, and tells it to them. Her father then gives her to Samson's 'companion, whom he had used as his friend'.    *to wife*] The Samson of *Judges* was not married to Dalila. Krouse 76 comments that the question most discussed in the Renaissance was whether she had been his wife or his concubine: many commentators followed Chrysostom in maintaining that she was his wife. M.'s Samson calls her a 'concubine' (l. 537), but M. makes her Samson's wife from the outset (see list of 'Persons' p. 346 above).

*229.* Cp. *Judges* xvi 4: 'He loved a woman in the valley of Sorek.' Stein[2] 146 comments: 'The first feeling for Dalila . . . is to be heard in the softened beauty of the line that announces her.'

*230. specious*] having a deceptively attractive appearance.    *accomplished*]

235 Who vanquished with a peal of words (O weakness!)
    Gave up my fort of silence to a woman.
    *Chor.* In seeking just occasion to provoke
    The Philistine, thy country's enemy,
    Thou never wast remiss, I bear thee witness:
240 Yet Israel still serves with all his sons.
    *Sam.* That fault I take not on me, but transfer
    On Israel's governors, and heads of tribes,
    Who seeing those great acts which God had done
    Singly by me against their conquerors
245 Acknowledged not, or not at all considered
    Deliverance offered: I on the other side
    Used no ambition to commend my deeds,
    The deeds themselves, though mute, spoke loud the
        doer;
    But they persisted deaf, and would not seem
250 To count them things worth notice, till at length
    Their lords the Philistines with gathered powers
    Entered Judea seeking me, who then
    Safe to the rock of Etham was retired,
    Not flying, but forecasting in what place
255 To set upon them, what advantaged best;
    Meanwhile the men of Judah to prevent
    The harass of their land, beset me round;
    I willingly on some conditions came
    Into their hands, and they as gladly yield me

The snare is accomplished in that it has fulfilled its function and caught Samson, and Dalila is accomplished because she has various accomplishments, persuasiveness, for example.

*235. peal*] The military imagery ('fort') suggests that 'peal' is here an artillery term. A peal of guns was used as a salute or sign of rejoicing: the guns were not weapons of attack when pealing. Samson's disgrace is all the more bitter: he gave up his fort at the mere sound of guns.

*242.* In *Judges* xv 20, xvi 32 Samson himself rules Israel for twenty years: this does not suit M.'s conception of an unsupported leader.

*247. ambition*] in the sense of Latin *ambitio*, 'walking about to solicit votes or applause'.

*251–5.* In *Judges* xv Samson burns the Philistines' standing corn. They, in revenge, burn his wife and her father, 5–6; he smites them 'hip and thigh with a great slaughter' and goes to dwell 'in the top of the rock Etam', 8. 'Then the Philistines went up, and pitched in Judah', 9.

*256–7.* Cp. *Judges* xv 11–2.

*258. on some conditions*] *Judges* xv 12: 'Swear unto me, that ye will not fall upon me yourselves.'

*259–64.* Cp. *Judges* xv 13–6, where the men of Judah bind Samson 'with

260    To the uncircumcised a welcome prey,
       Bound with two cords; but cords to me were threads
       Touched with the flame: on their whole host I flew
       Unarmed, and with a trivial weapon felled
       Their choicest youth; they only lived who fled.
265    Had Judah that day joined, or one whole tribe,
       They had by this possessed the towers of Gath,
       And lorded over them whom now they serve;
       But what more oft in nations grown corrupt,
       And by their vices brought to servitude,
270    Than to love bondage more than liberty,
       Bondage with ease than strenuous liberty;
       And to despise, or envy, or suspect
       Whom God hath of his special favour raised
       As their deliverer; if he aught begin,
275    How frequent to desert him, and at last
       To heap ingratitude on worthiest deeds?
       *Chor.* Thy words to my remembrance bring
       How Succoth and the fort of Penuel
       Their great deliverer contemned,
280    The matchless Gideon in pursuit
       Of Madian and her vanquished kings;
       And how ingrateful Ephraim

two new cords' and hand him over to the Philistines, but 'the cords that
were upon his arms became as flax that was burnt with fire, and his bands
loosed from off his hands'. He then kills a thousand men with the ass's
jawbone.

*266. by this*] by this time.        *Gath*] one of the five great cities of Philistia.
*271.* Cp. *PL* ii 255–7n.

*275. frequent*] accustomed; a fairly common seventeenth-century sense.

*277–89. Gideon*] Cp. *Judges* viii 5–9 where Gideon, pursuing 'Zebah and
Zalmunna, kings of Midian', asks for bread for his three hundred followers
from Succoth and Penuel, but is refused. 'Madian' is the Vulgate form
and Sylvester's (Du Bartas 468 'Madian Kings').        *Jephtha*] Cp. *Judges*
xi 12–33 and xii 1–6 where the Ephraimites refuse to help Jephtha against
the Ammonites, whom he nevertheless first refutes in argument and then
defeats in battle. Later the Ephraimites pick a quarrel with Jephtha and his
Gileadites, but he takes the passages of the Jordan, and anyone wishing to
go over is asked 'Art thou now an Ephraimite?' If any Ephraimite denied
his nationality: 'Then said they unto him, Say now Shibboleth: and he
said Sibboleth; for he could not frame to pronounce it right. Then they
took him, and slew him.' Forty-two thousand Ephraimites were thus
killed. The Heb. *shibboleth* means either 'ear of corn' or 'stream in flood'.
Krouse 98 comments that Gideon and Jephtha were considered saints like
Samson, and for the same reason: they had been mentioned by Paul, *Heb.*
xi 32.

Had dealt with Jephtha, who by argument,
Not worse than by his shield and spear
285    Defended Israel from the Ammonite,
Had not his prowess quelled their pride
In that sore battle when so many died
Without reprieve adjudged to death,
For want of well pronouncing *Shibboleth*.
290    *Sam.* Of such examples add me to the roll,
Me easily indeed mine may neglect,
But God's proposed deliverance not so.
*Chor.* Just are the ways of God,
And justifiable to men;
295    Unless there be who think not God at all,
If any be, they walk obscure;
For of such doctrine never was there school,
But the heart of the fool,
And no man therein doctor but himself.
300       Yet more there be who doubt his ways not just,
As to his own edicts, found contradicting,
Then give the reins to wandering thought,
Regardless of his glory's diminution;
Till by their own perplexities involved
305    They ravel more, still less resolved,
But never find self-satisfying solution.
      As if they would confine the interminable,
And tie him to his own prescript,
Who made our laws to bind us, not himself,
310    And hath full right to exempt
Whom so it pleases him by choice
From national obstriction, without taint
Of sin, or legal debt;
For with his own laws he can best dispense.
315       He would not else who never wanted means,
Nor in respect of the enemy just cause
To set his people free,
Have prompted this heroic Nazarite,

291. *mine*] my people.
298. Cp. *Ps.* xiv 1: 'The fool hath said in his heart, There is no God.'
305. *ravel*] become entangled.
306. There are two different *1671* states of this line. In the first it, as well as l. 307, is indented.
312. *obstriction*] M.'s coinage. The obligation referred to is *Deuk.* vii 3, but seemingly no O.T. prohibition bars marriage with Philistives.
313. *legal debt*] duty owed to the (Mosaic) law. Like 'national obstriction' 'legal debt' is the object of 'exempt from'.

Against his vow of strictest purity,
320　To seek in marriage that fallacious bride,
Unclean, unchaste.
　　　Down Reason then, at least vain reasonings down,
Though Reason here aver
That moral verdict quits her of unclean:
325　Unchaste was subsequent, her stain not his.
　　　But see here comes thy reverend sire
With careful step, locks white as down,
Old Manoa: advise
Forthwith how thou ought'st to receive him.
330　*Sam.* Ay me, another inward grief awaked,
With mention of that name renews the assault.
*Man.* Brethren and men of Dan, for such ye seem,
Though in this uncouth place; if old respect,
As I suppose, towards your once gloried friend,
335　My son now captive, hither hath informed
Your younger feet, while mine cast back with age
Came lagging after; say if he be here.
*Chor.* As signal now in low dejected state,
As erst in highest, behold him where he lies.
340　*Man.* O miserable change! is this the man,
That invincible Samson, far renowned,
The dread of Israel's foes, who with a strength
Equivalent to angel's walked their streets,
None offering fight; who single combatant
345　Duelled their armies ranked in proud array,

---

*319.* Celibacy was not in the Nazarite vow (*Num.* vi 1–21), and marriage
with Gentiles was not impurity until after the reformation of Ezra.

*322–5.* The chorus first (l. 322) dispose of those who attempt to reason about
God's ways (ll. 300–6), and call their 'reasoning' vain. What is more, they
go on, even reason must confess that the woman (of Timna) whom God
prompted Samson to marry was, at the time, neither morally unclean nor
unchaste. She was unclean only in a legal sense, as a Gentile, and her un-
chastity took place afterwards ('was subsequent'); cp. *Judges* xiv 20: 'Sam-
son's wife was given to his companion.' Thus ll. 323–5 justify Samson's
first marriage from a 'reasonable' point of view.

*324. quits]* acquits.

*333. uncouth]* unknown.

*334. once gloried]* The phrase may mean 'friend once boasted of' or 'friend
once honoured': *OED* records this as the only instance of the past participle
of the verb 'glory'.

*338. signal]* remarkable.

*340. miserable change]* The phrase is Shakespeare's, *Antony and Cleopatra*
IV xv 51.

Himself an army, now unequal match
To save himself against a coward armed
At one spear's length. O ever-failing trust
In mortal strength! and O what not in man
350 Deceivable and vain! Nay what thing good
Prayed for, but often proves our woe, our bane?
I prayed for children, and thought barrenness
In wedlock a reproach; I gained a son,
And such a son as all men hailed me happy;
355 Who would be now a father in my stead?
O wherefore did God grant me my request,
And as a blessing with such pomp adorned?
Why are his gifts desirable, to tempt
Our earnest prayers, then given with solemn hand
360 As graces, draw a scorpion's tail behind?
For this did the angel twice descend? for this
Ordained thy nurture holy, as of a plant;
Select, and sacred, glorious for a while,
The miracle of men: then in an hour
365 Ensnared, assaulted, overcome, led bound,
Thy foes' derision, captive, poor, and blind
Into a dungeon thrust, to work with slaves?
Alas methinks whom God hath chosen once
To worthiest deeds, if he through frailty err,
370 He should not so o'erwhelm, and as a thrall
Subject him to so foul indignities,
Be it but for honour's sake of former deeds.
*Sam.* Appoint not heavenly disposition, father,
Nothing of all these evils hath befall'n me
375 But justly; I myself have brought them on,
Sole author I, sole cause: if aught seem vile,
As vile hath been my folly, who have profaned
The mystery of God given me under pledge
Of vow, and have betrayed it to a woman,
380 A Canaanite, my faithless enemy.
This well I knew, nor was at all surprised,

*354. And such*] *1671* prints 'Such,' but the *Errata* supplies 'And'.
*373. Appoint*] *OED* gives meaning as 'arraign'. G. C. Moore Smith, *MLR*
iii (1907–8) 74, disagrees, preferring the more common meaning 'prescribe
or determine the course of', but E. Weekley, *MLR* iii (1907–8) 373–4,
supports *OED*, noting that Fr. *appointer* can mean 'arraign' in legal contexts.
*377. profaned*] published (Latin *profanus*, 'outside the temple', hence 'public').
*380. Canaanite*] The Philistines were actually immigrants into Canaan from
'Caphtor' (i.e. Crete? Phoenicia?), *Amos* ix 7.

But warned by oft experience: did not she
Of Timna first betray me, and reveal
The secret wrested from me in her height
385    Of nuptial love professed, carrying it straight
To them who had corrupted her, my spies,
And rivals? In this other was there found
More faith? who also in her prime of love,
Spousal embraces, vitiated with gold,
390    Though offered only, by the scent conceived
Her spurious first-born; treason against me?
Thrice she assayed with flattering prayers and sighs,
And amorous reproaches to win from me
My capital secret, in what part my strength
395    Lay stored, in what part summed, that she might know:
Thrice I deluded her, and turned to sport
Her importunity, each time perceiving
How openly and with what impudence
She purposed to betray me, and (which was worse
400    Than undissembled hate) with what contempt
She sought to make me traitor to myself;
Yet the fourth time, when mustering all her wiles,
With blandished parleys, feminine assaults,
Tongue-batteries, she surceased not day nor night
405    To storm me over-watched, and wearied out.
At times when men seek most repose and rest,
I yielded, and unlocked her all my heart,
Who with a grain of manhood well resolved
Might easily have shook off all her snares:
410    But foul effeminacy held me yoked
Her bond-slave; O indignity, O blot
To honour and religion! servile mind
Rewarded well with servile punishment!

*382–7.* See l. 227*n*.

*388–9. Spousal embraces*] In apposition to 'prime of love'; 'vitiated' (corrupted) qualifies 'who'.

*390. Though offered only*] Qualifying 'gold'. Cp. *Judges* xvi 5: 'And we will give thee every one of us eleven hundred pieces of silver.'

*392. Thrice*] Cp. *Judges* xvi 6–15.

*393. amorous reproaches*] Cp. *Judges* xvi 15: 'How canst thou say, I love thee, when thine heart is not with me?'

*394. capital*] A pun: 'most important', and also 'pertaining to the head' (Latin *caput*).

*403. blandished*] invested with flattery or blandishment (the only occurrence of the word recorded in *OED*).

*405. over-watched*] kept awake too long.

The base degree to which I now am fall'n,
415  These rags, this grinding, is not yet so base
As was my former servitude, ignoble,
Unmanly, ignominious, infamous,
True slavery, and that blindness worse than this,
That saw not how degenerately I served.
420  *Man.* I cannot praise thy marriage-choices, son,
Rather approved them not; but thou didst plead
Divine impulsion prompting how thou might'st
Find some occasion to infest our foes.
I state not that; this I am sure; our foes
425  Found soon occasion thereby to make thee
Their captive, and their triumph; thou the sooner
Temptation found'st, or over-potent charms
To violate the sacred trust of silence
Deposited within thee; which to have kept
430  Tacit, was in thy power; true; and thou bear'st
Enough, and more the burden of that fault;
Bitterly hast thou paid, and still art paying
That rigid score. A worse thing yet remains,
This day the Philistines a popular feast
435  Here celebrate in Gaza; and proclaim
Great pomp, and sacrifice, and praises loud
To Dagon, as their god who hath delivered
Thee Samson bound and blind into their hands,
Them out of thine, who slew'st them many a slain.
440  So Dagon shall be magnified, and God,
Besides whom is no god, compared with idols,
Disglorified, blasphemed, and had in scorn
By the idolatrous rout amidst their wine;
Which to have come to pass by means of thee,
445  Samson, of all thy sufferings think the heaviest,
Of all reproach the most with shame that ever
Could have befall'n thee and thy father's house.
*Sam.* Father, I do acknowledge and confess
That I this honour, I this pomp have brought
450  To Dagon, and advanced his praises high
Among the heathen round; to God have brought
Dishonour, obloquy, and oped the mouths

423. *infest*] harass.
424. *state*] OED records this as the only instance of the verb in the sense 'assign a value to, have an opinion upon'.
433. *score*] account of a debt.
439. *them*] An imitation of a Latin dative: 'to their loss'.
442. *Disglorified*] deprived of glory.

℞.          Of idolists, and atheists; have brought scandal
            To Israel, diffidence of God, and doubt
      455   In feeble hearts, propense enough before
            To waver, or fall off and join with idols;
            Which is my chief affliction, shame and sorrow,
            The anguish of my soul, that suffers not
            Mine eye to harbour sleep, or thoughts to rest.
      460   This only hope relieves me, that the strife
            With me hath end; all the contest is now
            'Twixt God and Dagon; Dagon hath presumed,
            Me overthrown, to enter lists with God,
            His deity comparing and preferring
      465   Before the God of Abraham. He, be sure,
            Will not connive, or linger, thus provoked,
            But will arise and his great name assert:
            Dagon must stoop, and shall ere long receive
            Such a discomfit, as shall quite despoil him
      470   Of all these boasted trophies won on me,
            And with confusion blank his worshippers.
            *Man.* With cause this hope relieves thee, and these
                words
            I as a prophecy receive: for God,
            Nothing more certain, will not long defer
      475   To vindicate the glory of his name
            Against all competition, nor will long
            Endure it, doubtful whether God be Lord,
            Or Dagon. But for thee what shall be done?
            Thou must not in the meanwhile here forgot
      480   Lie in this miserable loathsome plight
            Neglected. I already have made way
            To some Philistian lords, with whom to treat
            About thy ransom: well they may by this
            Have satisfied their utmost of revenge
      485   By pains and slaveries, worse than death inflicted
            On thee, who now no more canst do them harm.

---

*453. idolists*] idolators.

*455. propense*] inclined, disposed.

*466. connive*] remain dormant. *OED* gives this and *PL* x 624 as the only two
instances of the word in this sense.

*469. discomfit*] defeat.

*471. blank*] nonplus.

*481.* In having Manoa sue with the Philistines for the release of his son, M.
made an innovation in the story for which there is no warrant either in
Scripture or in the Samson tradition (Krouse 99).

*Sam.* Spare that proposal, father, spare the trouble
Of that solicitation; let me here,
As I deserve, pay on my punishment;
490   And expiate, if possible, my crime,
Shameful garrulity. To have revealed
Secrets of men, the secrets of a friend,
How heinous had the fact been, how deserving
Contempt, and scorn of all, to be excluded
495   All friendship, and avoided as blab,
The mark of fool set on his front!
But I God's counsel have not kept, his holy secret
Presumptuously have published, impiously,
Weakly at least, and shamefully: a sin
500   That Gentiles in their parables condemn
To their abyss and horrid pains confined.
*Man.* Be penitent and for thy fault contrite,
But act not in thy own affliction, son,
Repent the sin, but if the punishment
505   Thou canst avoid, self-preservation bids;
Or the execution leave to high disposal,
And let another hand, not thine, exact
Thy penal forfeit from thyself; perhaps
God will relent, and quit thee all his debt;
510   Who evermore approves and more accepts
(Best pleased with humble and filial submission)
Him who imploring mercy sues for life,
Than who self-rigorous chooses death as due;
Which argues over-just, and self-displeased
515   For self-offence, more than for God offended.
Reject not then what offered means, who knows
But God hath set before us, to return thee
Home to thy country and his sacred house,
Where thou may'st bring thy off'rings, to avert
520   His further ire, with prayers and vows renewed.
*Sam.* His pardon I implore; but as for life,
To what end should I seek it? when in strength

*493. fact*] deed.

*499–501.* Alluding to the myth of Tantalus who was placed in Hades for revealing the secrets of the gods.

*503–8.* Cp. *De doctrina* ii 8 (Columbia xvii 200–1): 'The love of man towards himself consists in loving himself next to God . . . Opposed to this is, first, a perverse hatred of self . . . In this class are to be reckoned those who lay violent hands on themselves.'

*509. quit . . . debt*] remit all your debt to him ('thee' is a dative).

*514. argues over-just*] proves a man just to excess.

*515. self-offence*] offence against oneself.

All mortals I excelled, and great in hopes
With youthful courage and magnanimous thoughts
525 Of birth from heaven foretold and high exploits,
Full of divine instinct, after some proof
Of acts indeed heroic, far beyond
The sons of Anak, famous now and blazed,
Fearless of danger, like a petty god
530 I walked about admired of all and dreaded
On hostile ground, none daring my affront.
Then swoll'n with pride into the snare I fell
Of fair fallacious looks, venereal trains,
Softened with pleasure and voluptuous life;
535 At length to lay my head and hallowed pledge
Of all my strength in the lascivious lap
Of a deceitful concubine who shore me
Like a tame wether, all my precious fleece,
Then turned me out ridiculous, despoiled,
540 Shaven, and disarmed among my enemies.
*Chor.* Desire of wine and all delicious drinks,
Which many a famous warrior overturns,
Thou couldst repress, nor did the dancing ruby
Sparkling, out-poured, the flavour, or the smell,
545 Or taste that cheers the heart of gods and men,
Allure thee from the cool crystalline stream.
*Sam.* Wherever fountain or fresh current flowed
Against the eastern ray, translucent, pure
With touch ethereal of heaven's fiery rod
550 I drank, from the clear milky juice allaying

*526. instinct*] impulse.

*528. sons of Anak*] See 148n. *famous . . . blazed*] Qualifies 'I': 'blazed' means 'published, made famous'.

*533. venereal trains*] snares of sexual desire.

*536. lap*] Cp. *Judges* xvi 19: 'She made him sleep upon her knees.'

*537. shore*] In *Judges* xvi 19 Dalila calls for a man to shave Samson's head: here she apparently does it herself.

*541–6.* As a Nazarite Samson vowed to abstain from strong drink, *Num.* vi 3.

*545. cheers . . . men*] Cp. *Judges* ix 13: 'wine, which cheereth God and man'.

*548. Against*] in the direction of. In *Ezek.* xlvii 8–9 the waters which flow eastward are attributed life-giving powers; cp. Burton, *Anatomy* II ii 1 i: 'Rain water is purest . . . Next to it fountain water that riseth in the east, and runneth eastward.' *pure*] The first state of *1671* has a full stop after this word.

*549. fiery rod*] Cp. Euripides, *Suppliants* 650, where the sunbeam is called κανὼν σαφής.

*550. milky*] The same adjective for fresh water is used *PL* v 306. The concept

Thirst, and refreshed; nor envied them the grape
Whose heads that turbulent liquor fills with fumes.
*Chor.* O madness, to think use of strongest wines
And strongest drinks our chief support of health,
555 When God with these forbidden made choice to rear
His mighty champion, strong above compare,
Whose drink was only from the liquid brook.
*Sam.* But what availed this temperance, not complete
Against another object more enticing?
560 What boots it at one gate to make defence,
And at another to let in the foe
Effeminately vanquished? by which means,
Now blind, disheartened, shamed, dishonoured,
         quelled,
To what can I be useful, wherein serve
565 My nation, and the work from heaven imposed,
But to sit idle on the household hearth,
A burdenous drone; to visitants a gaze,
Or pitied object, these redundant locks
Robustious to no purpose clustering down,
570 Vain monument of strength; till length of years
And sedentary numbness craze my limbs
To a contemptible old age obscure.
Here rather let me drudge and earn my bread,
Till vermin or the draff of servile food
575 Consume me, and oft-invocated death
Hasten the welcome end of all my pains.
*Man.* Wilt thou then serve the Philistines with that gift
Which was expressly given thee to annoy them?
Better at home lie bed-rid, not only idle,
580 Inglorious, unemployed, with age outworn.

is of earth as mother: cp. Sir John Davies, *Orchestra* lii, where hills are called
'The Earth's great duggs: for every wight is fed / With sweet fresh moisture
from them issuing'. Possibly M. recalls *Song of Solomon* v 12: 'doves by the
rivers of water, washed with milk', where the last phrase can be translated
'Splashed by the milky water'.
557. *liquid*] transparent (Latin *liquidus*).
560. *What boots it*] of what use is it?
567. *gaze*] object gazed at.
568. *redundant*] abounding to excess (the first instance of the word in this
sense recorded in *OED*).
569. *Robustious*] robust, strong (a common seventeenth-century word).
571. *craze*] render decrepit.
574. *draff*] refuse, pig-swill.
578. *annoy*] molest, harm.

But God who caused a fountain at thy prayer
From the dry ground to spring, thy thirst to allay
After the brunt of battle, can as easy
Cause light again within thy eyes to spring,
585　Wherewith to serve him better than thou hast;
And I persuade me so; why else this strength
Miraculous yet remaining in those locks?
His might continues in thee not for naught,
Nor shall his wondrous gifts be frustrate thus.
590　*Sam.* All otherwise to me my thoughts portend,
That these dark orbs no more shall treat with light,
Nor the other light of life continue long,
But yield to double darkness nigh at hand:
So much I feel my genial spirits droop,
595　My hopes all flat, nature within me seems
In all her functions weary of herself;
My race of glory run, and race of shame,
And I shall shortly be with them that rest.
*Man.* Believe not these suggestions, which proceed
600　From anguish of the mind and humours black,
That mingle with thy fancy. I however
Must not omit a father's timely care
To prosecute the means of thy deliverance
By ransom or how else: meanwhile be calm,
605　And healing words from these thy friends admit.

*581–98.* M. seems to have remembered the exchange between Jason and Phineus in Apollonius Rhodius, *Argonautica* ii 438–48 'Assuredly there was then, Phineus, some god who cared for thy bitter woe ... and if too he should bring sight to thine eyes, verily I should rejoice. ... Thus he spake, but Phineus replied to him with downcast look: "Son of Aeson, that is past recall, nor is there any remedy hereafter, for blasted are my sightless eyes. But instead of that may the god grant me death at once, and after death I shall take my share in perfect bliss".'

*581–3.* Cp. *Judges* xv 19: 'But God clave an hollow place that was in the jaw [or 'in Lehi'], and there came water thereout.' Some translators take the verse to mean that the water came from the jawbone itself, some that it came from the rock which takes its name from the jawbone. M. accepts the latter explanation, as did Josephus, *Antiquities* v 8: 'God ... raised him up a plentiful fountain of sweet water at a certain rock.'

*594. genial*] pertaining to genius or natural disposition.

*595. flat*] overthrown (*OED* gives this as the first figurative application of the word in this sense).

*600. humours black*] The black humour was melancholy (black bile).

*601. fancy*] imagination.

*603. prosecute*] persist in.

*605. healing words*] Cp. Euripides, *Hippolytus* 478: λόγοι θελκτήριοι.

*Sam.* O that torment should not be confined
   To the body's wounds and sores
   With maladies innumerable
   In heart, head, breast, and reins;
610 But must secret passage find
   To the inmost mind,
   There exercise all his fierce accidents,
   And on her purest spirits prey,
   As on entrails, joints, and limbs,
615 With answerable pains, but more intense,
   Though void of corporal sense.
      My griefs not only pain me
   As a lingering disease,
   But finding no redress, ferment and rage,
620 Nor less than wounds immedicable
   Rankle, and fester, and gangrene,
   To black mortification.
   Thoughts my tormentors armed with deadly stings
   Mangle my apprehensive tenderest parts,
625 Exasperate, exulcerate, and raise
   Dire inflammation which no cooling herb
   Or med'cinal liquor can assuage,
   Nor breath of vernal air from snowy alp.
   Sleep hath forsook and given me o'er
630 To death's benumbing opium as my only cure.
   Thence faintings, swoonings of despair,
   And sense of heaven's desertion.
      I was his nursling once and choice delight,
   His destined from the womb,
635 Promised by heavenly message twice descending.
   Under his special eye
   Abstemious I grew up and thrived amain;
   He led me on to mightiest deeds
   Above the nerve of mortal arm
640 Against the uncircumcised, our enemies.

609. *reins*] kidneys.
612. *accidents*] In medical terminology, 'symptoms'.
615. *answerable*] corresponding.
620. *wounds immedicable*] Cp. Ovid, *Met.* x 189: *immedicabile vulnus.*
622. *mortification*] gangrene.
624. *apprehensive*] sensitive.
625. *Exasperate*] increase the fierceness of a disease.     *exulcerate*] cause ulcers.
628. *alp*] Used from late sixteenth century to mean any high, snow-capped mountain.
639. *nerve*] muscle.

But now hath cast me off as never known,
And to those cruel enemies,
Whom I by his appointment had provoked,
Left me all helpless with the irreparable loss
645    Of sight, reserved alive to be repeated
The subject of their cruelty, or scorn.
Nor am I in the list of them that hope;
Hopeless are all my evils, all remediless;
This one prayer yet remains, might I be heard,
650    No long petition, speedy death,
The close of all my miseries, and the balm.
*Chor.* Many are the sayings of the wise
In ancient and in modern books enrolled;
Extolling patience as the truest fortitude;
655    And to the bearing well of all calamities,
All chances incident to man's frail life
Consolatories writ
With studied argument, and much persuasion sought
Lenient of grief and anxious thought,
660    But with the afflicted in his pangs their sound
Little prevails, or rather seems a tune,
Harsh, and of dissonant mood from his complaint,
Unless he feel within
Some source of consolation from above;
665    Secret refreshings, that repair his strength,
And fainting spirits uphold.
God of our fathers, what is man!

*643. appointment*] command.

*645. repeated*] spoken of as.

*656.* Echoing *Timon* V i 203–5: 'With other incident throes / That nature's fragile vessel doth sustain / In life's uncertain voyage.' *1671* prints a full stop after 'life', but the *Errata* deletes it.

*657. Consolatories*] writings containing topics of comfort (the noun is first recorded in *OED* in 1654).

*658. persuasion sought*] persuasion painstakingly constructed.

*659. Lenient of*] tending to soothe (*OED* first records 'lenient' in this sense in 1652, and gives the present instance as the first example of its construction with 'of'). Cp. Horace, *Epist.* I i 34: *sunt verba et voces quibus hunc lenire dolorem / possis* (There are words and sayings with which you may soothe the pain).

*660. with*] *1671* prints 'to' but the *Errata* corrects to 'with'.

*667.* Cp. *Ps.* viii 4: 'What is man, that thou art mindful of him ?'

That thou towards him with hand so various,
Or might I say contrarious,
670 Temper'st thy providence through his short course,
Not evenly, as thou rul'st
The angelic orders and inferior creatures mute,
Irrational and brute.
Nor do I name of men the common rout,
675 That wandering loose about
Grow up and perish, as the summer fly,
Heads without name no more remembered,
But such as thou hast solemnly elected,
With gifts and graces eminently adorned
680 To some great work, thy glory,
And people's safety, which in part they effect:
Yet toward these thus dignified, thou oft
Amidst their height of noon,
Changest thy countenance, and thy hand with no
regard
685 Of highest favours past
From thee on them, or them to thee of service.
    Nor only dost degrade them, or remit
To life obscured, which were a fair dismission,
But throw'st them lower than thou didst exalt them
high,
690 Unseemly falls in human eye,
Too grievous for the trespass or omission,
Oft leav'st them to the hostile sword
Of heathen and profane, their carcases
To dogs and fowls a prey, or else captived:
695 Or to the unjust tribunals, under change of times,
And condemnation of the ingrateful multitude.
If these they scape, perhaps in poverty
With sickness and disease thou bow'st them down,
Painful diseases and deformed,
700 In crude old age;
Though not disordinate, yet causeless suffering
The punishment of dissolute days, in fine,

688. *dismission*] dismissal.
693-4. Echoing Homer, *Il.* i 4-5 (of the dead in the Trojan war) 'made a spoil for dogs and all manner of birds'.
700. *crude*] premature.
701-2. *Though ... days*] i.e. though they are not themselves immoderate they suffer, without cause, the punishment (illness) which usually follows an intemperate life.

Just or unjust, alike seem miserable,
For oft alike, both come to evil end.
705    So deal not with this once thy glorious champion,
The image of thy strength, and mighty minister.
What do I beg? how hast thou dealt already?
Behold him in this state calamitous, and turn
His labours, for thou canst, to peaceful end.
710    But who is this, what thing of sea or land?
Female of sex it seems,
That so bedecked, ornate, and gay,
Comes this way sailing
Like a stately ship
715    Of Tarsus, bound for th' isles
Of Javan or Gadire
With all her bravery on, and tackle trim,
Sails filled, and streamers waving,
Courted by all the winds that hold them play,
720    An amber scent of odorous perfume
Her harbinger, a damsel train behind;
Some rich Philistian matron she may seem,
And now at nearer view, no other certain
Than Dalila thy wife.
725    *Sam.* My wife, my traitress, let her not come near me.
*Chor.* Yet on she moves, now stands and eyes thee fixed,
About t' have spoke, but now, with head declined
Like a fair flower surcharged with dew, she weeps
And words addressed seem into tears dissolved,
730    Wetting the borders of her silken veil:

*714.* Various 'sources' for the Dalila/ship simile have been suggested.
G. M. Young, *TLS* (9 Jan. 1937) 28, traces it to a passage in Harrington's
*A Word Concerning a House of Peers* (1659), and R. C. Fox, *N & Q* vi (1959)
370–2, to Vida, *Christiad* 304–34. More sensibly J. G. McManaway, *TLS*
(20 Feb. 1937) 131, comments that the comparison of woman and ship is a
commonplace of Tudor and Stuart literature. One striking parallel he cites
is from Robert Wilkinson, *Merchant Royal* (1607)–a sermon on *Prov.* xxxi
14. Barbara K. Lewalski, *N & Q* vi (1959) 372–3, relates the ship image here
to a larger pattern of ship and tempest imagery in the play (see ll. 197–200,
960–64, 1044–5, 1070, 1061–3, 1647–51).
*715. Tarsus*] The biblical phrase 'ships of Tarshish' (i.e. probably, Tartessus
in S. Spain) is found *Isa.* xxiii 1, 14 and *Ps.* xlviii 7.
*715–6. isles / Of Javan*] Ionian isles. Javan, son of Japhet (*Gen.* x 2) and grand-
son of Noah was the supposed ancestor of the Ionians.      *Gadire*] Cadiz,
on the S. coast of Spain.
*719. hold them play*] keep them moving.
*720. amber scent*] scent as of ambergris.

But now again she makes address to speak.
*Dal.* With doubtful feet and wavering resolution
I came, still dreading thy displeasure, Samson,
Which to have merited, without excuse,
735  I cannot but acknowledge; yet if tears
May expiate (though the fact more evil drew
In the perverse event than I foresaw)
My penance hath not slackened, though my pardon
No way assured. But conjugal affection
740  Prevailing over fear, and timorous doubt
Hath led me on desirous to behold
Once more thy face, and know of thy estate.
If aught in my ability may serve
To lighten what thou suffer'st, and appease
745  Thy mind with what amends is in my power,
Though late, yet in some part to recompense
My rash but more unfortunate misdeed.
*Sam.* Out, out hyaena; these are thy wonted arts,
And arts of every woman false like thee,
750  To break all faith, all vows, deceive, betray,
Then as repentant to submit, beseech,
And reconcilement move with feigned remorse,
Confess, and promise wonders in her change,
Not truly penitent, but chief to try
755  Her husband, how far urged his patience bears,
His virtue or weakness which way to assail:
Then with more cautious and instructed skill
Again transgresses, and again submits;
That wisest and best men full oft beguiled
760  With goodness principled not to reject
The penitent, but ever to forgive,

*731. makes address*] prepares.

*732.* Parker[2] 126 compares the following episode with that between Helen and Menelaus in Euripides, *Troades* 895–1059.

*736. fact*] deed (i.e. her betrayal).

*737. perverse event*] unpropitious outcome.

*748. hyaena*] According to Pliny viii 44, the hyaena is believed to contain within itself both sexes, to imitate the human voice and thus lure men out to devour them, and to be the only animal that digs up graves to get at the bodies of the dead. Magicians, he says (xxviii 27), believe it has magical powers and can deprive human beings of their senses. All these attributes help to give point to Samson's abuse. Cp. also Jonson, *Volpone* IV vi 3 'now, thine eies / Vie teares with the hyaena'. M. abuses More with this term in the *Pro Se Defensio* (Columbia ix 124–5) 'Hyaena! or if there be any other

Are drawn to wear out miserable days,
Entangled with a poisonous bosom snake,
If not by quick destruction soon cut off
765   As I by thee, to ages an example.
        *Dal.* Yet hear me Samson; not that I endeavour
To lessen or extenuate my offence,
But that on the other side, if it be weighed
By itself, with aggravations not surcharged,
770   Or else with just allowance counterpoised,
I may, if possible, thy pardon find
The easier towards me, or thy hatred less.
First granting, as I do, it was a weakness
In me, but incident to all our sex,
775   Curiosity, inquisitive, importune
Of secrets, then with like infirmity
To publish them, both common female faults:
Was it not weakness also to make known
For importunity, that is for naught,
780   Wherein consisted all thy strength and safety?
To what I did thou show'dst me first the way.
But I to enemies revealed, and should not.
Nor shouldst thou have trusted that to woman's frailty
Ere I to thee, thou to thyself wast cruel.
785   Let weakness then with weakness come to parle
So near related, or the same of kind,
Thine forgive mine; that men may censure thine
The gentler, if severely thou exact not
More strength from me, than in thyself was found.
790   And what if love, which thou interpret'st hate,
The jealousy of love, powerful of sway
In human hearts, nor less in mine towards thee,
Caused what I did? I saw thee mutable
Of fancy, feared lest one day thou wouldst leave me
795   As her at Timna, sought by all means therefore
How to endear, and hold thee to me firmest:
No better way I saw than by importuning

brute equally destructive, and equally infamous for the blackness of its
guile'.
763. *bosom snake*] Cp. the proverb 'to nourish a snake (viper) in one's bosom'
(Tilley V68).
769. *aggravations*] exaggerations.
775. *importune / Of secrets*] irksomely persistent in discovering secrets (the
construction with 'of' is not recorded in *OED*).
784. *thou . . . cruel*] Cp. Shakespeare, *Sonnet* i: 'to thy sweet self too cruel'.
785. *parle*] parley.

To learn thy secrets, get into my power
Thy key of strength and safety: thou wilt say,
800  Why then revealed? I was assured by those
Who tempted me, that nothing was designed
Against thee but safe custody, and hold:
That made for me, I knew that liberty
Would draw thee forth to perilous enterprises,
805  While I at home sat full of cares and fears,
Wailing thy absence in my widowed bed;
Here I should still enjoy thee day and night
Mine and love's prisoner, not the Philistines',
Whole to myself, unhazarded abroad,
810  Fearless at home of partners in my love.
These reasons in love's law have passed for good,
Though fond and reasonless to some perhaps;
And love hath oft, well meaning, wrought much woe,
Yet always pity or pardon hath obtained.
815  Be not unlike all others, not austere
As thou art strong, inflexible as steel.
If thou in strength all mortals dost exceed,
In uncompassionate anger do not so.
*Sam.* How cunningly the sorceress displays
820  Her own transgressions, to upbraid me mine!
That malice not repentance brought thee hither,
By this appears: I gave, thou say'st, the example,
I led the way; bitter reproach, but true,
I to myself was false ere thou to me,
825  Such pardon therefore as I give my folly,
Take to thy wicked deed: which when thou seest
Impartial, self-severe, inexorable,
Thou wilt renounce thy seeking, and much rather
Confess it feigned, weakness is thy excuse,
830  And I believe it, weakness to resist
Philistian gold: if weakness may excuse,
What murderer, what traitor, parricide,
Incestuous, sacrilegious, but may plead it?
All wickedness is weakness: that plea therefore
835  With God or man will gain thee no remission.
But love constrained thee; call it furious rage
To satisfy thy lust: love seeks to have love;
My love how couldst thou hope, who took'st the way

800–3. In *Judges* xvi 5, the Lords of the Philistines say to Dalila: 'Entice
him . . . that we may bind him to afflict [marginal note: 'or *humble*'] him'
(A.V.) The Vulgate has *affligere*.
803. *made for me*] was to my advantage.

To raise in me inexpiable hate,
*840* Knowing, as needs I must, by thee betrayed?
In vain thou striv'st to cover shame with shame,
Or by evasions thy crime uncover'st more.
*Dal.* Since thou determin'st weakness for no plea
In man or woman, though to thy own condemning,
*845* Hear what assaults I had, what snares besides,
What sieges girt me round, ere I consented;
Which might have awed the best-resolved of men,
The constantest to have yielded without blame.
It was not gold, as to my charge thou lay'st,
*850* That wrought with me: thou know'st the magistrates
And princes of my country came in person,
Solicited, commanded, threatened, urged,
Adjured by all the bonds of civil duty
And of religion, pressed how just it was,
*855* How honourable, how glorious to entrap
A common enemy, who had destroyed
Such numbers of our nation: and the priest
Was not behind, but ever at my ear,
Preaching how meritorious with the gods
*860* It would be to ensnare an irreligious
Dishonourer of Dagon: what had I
To oppose against such powerful arguments?
Only my love of thee held long debate;
And combated in silence all these reasons
*865* With hard contest: at length that grounded maxim
So rife and celebrated in the mouths
Of wisest men; that to the public good
Private respects must yield; with grave authority
Took full possession of me and prevailed;
*870* Virtue, as I thought, truth, duty so enjoining.
*Sam.* I thought where all thy circling wiles would end;
In feigned religion, smooth hypocrisy.
But had thy love, still odiously pretended,
Been, as it ought, sincere, it would have taught thee
*875* Far other reasonings, brought forth other deeds.
I before all the daughters of my tribe
And of my nation chose thee from among
My enemies, loved thee, as too well thou knew'st,

---

840. *Knowing . . . betrayed*] knowing myself to be betrayed.
857. *priest*] No priest is mentioned in the biblical account.
865. *grounded*] firmly established.
878–81. *loved thee . . . Too well . . . could deny thee nothing*] Echoes *Othello*
III iii 83: 'I will deny thee nothing'; V ii 345: 'lov'd not wisely, but too
well'.

Too well, unbosomed all my secrets to thee,
880  Not out of levity, but overpowered
By thy request, who could deny thee nothing;
Yet now am judged an enemy. Why then
Didst thou at first receive me for thy husband?
Then, as since then, thy country's foe professed:
885  Being once a wife, for me thou wast to leave
Parents and country; nor was I their subject,
Nor under their protection but my own,
Thou mine, not theirs: if aught against my life
Thy country sought of thee, it sought unjustly,
890  Against the law of nature, law of nations,
No more thy country, but an impious crew
Of men conspiring to uphold their state
By worse than hostile deeds, violating the ends
For which our country is a name so dear;
895  Not therefore to be obeyed. But zeal moved thee;
To please thy gods thou didst it; gods unable
To acquit themselves and prosecute their foes
But by ungodly deeds, the contradiction
Of their own deity, Gods cannot be:
900  Less therefore to be pleased, obeyed, or feared,
These false pretexts and varnished colours failing,
Bare in thy guilt how foul must thou appear!
*Dal.* In argument with men a woman ever
Goes by the worse, whatever be her cause.
905  *Sam.* For want of words no doubt, or lack of breath,
Witness when I was worried with thy peals.
*Dal.* I was a fool, too rash, and quite mistaken
In what I thought would have succeeded best.
Let me obtain forgiveness of thee, Samson,
910  Afford me place to show what recompense
Towards thee I intend for what I have misdone,
Misguided; only what remains past cure
Bear not too sensibly, nor still insist
To afflict thyself in vain: though sight be lost,
915  Life yet hath many solaces, enjoyed
Where other senses want not their delights

890. Echoes *Troilus and Cressida* II ii 184–5: 'these moral laws / Of nature
and of nations'.
897. *acquit themselves*] discharge the duties of their position.
901. *varnished colours*] speciously tricked-out excuses.
906. *peals*] See l. 235n.
913. *Bear ... sensibly*] do not feel too acutely.
916. Dalila slyly reminds Samson of the pleasures of her bed (cp. ll. 806–8).

*Dalila*

At home in leisure and domestic ease,
Exempt from many a care and chance to which
Eyesight exposes daily men abroad.
920 I to the lords will intercede, not doubting
Their favourable ear, that I may fetch thee
From forth this loathsome prison-house, to abide
With me, where my redoubled love and care
With nursing diligence, to me glad office,
925 May ever tend about thee to old age
With all things grateful cheered, and so supplied,
That what by me thou hast lost thou least shalt miss.
*Sam.* No, no, of my condition take no care;
It fits not; thou and I long since are twain;
930 Nor think me so unwary or accursed
To bring my feet again into the snare
Where once I have been caught; I know thy trains
Though dearly to my cost, thy gins, and toils;

*represented*
*Circe's*
*cousin*

Thy fair enchanted cup, and warbling charms
935 No more on me have power, their force is nulled,
So much of adder's wisdom I have learnt
To fence my ear against thy sorceries.
If in my flower of youth and strength, when all men
Loved, honoured, feared me, thou alone could hate me,
940 Thy husband, slight me, sell me, and forgo me;
How wouldst thou use me now, blind, and thereby
Deceivable, in most things as a child
Helpless, thence easily contemned, and scorned,
And last neglected? How wouldst thou insult
945 When I must live uxorious to thy will
In perfect thraldom, how again betray me,
Bearing my words and doings to the lords
To gloss upon, and censuring, frown or smile?
This jail I count the house of liberty
950 To thine whose doors my feet shall never enter.
*Dal.* Let me approach at least, and touch thy hand.
*Sam.* Not for thy life, lest fierce remembrance wake
My sudden rage to tear thee joint by joint.
At distance I forgive thee, go with that;

---

926. *grateful*] pleasing.
932. *trains*] snares.
934. *cup . . . charms*] Alludes to the Circe story.
936–7. The proverb 'As deaf as an adder' (Tilley A32) originated in *Ps.*
lviii 4: 'They are like the deaf adder that stoppeth her ears.'
948. *gloss upon*] comment on.

955 Bewail thy falsehood, and the pious works
It hath brought forth to make thee memorable
Among illustrious women, faithful wives:
Cherish thy hastened widowhood with the gold
Of matrimonial treason: so farewell.
960 *Dal.* I see thou art implacable, more deaf
To prayers than winds and seas, yet winds to seas
Are reconciled at length, and sea to shore:
Thy anger, unappeasable, still rages,
Eternal tempest never to be calmed.
965 Why do I humble thus myself, and suing
For peace, reap nothing but repulse and hate?
Bid go with evil omen and the brand
Of infamy upon my name denounced?
To mix with thy concernments I desist
970 Henceforth, nor too much disapprove my own.
Fame if not double-faced is double-mouthed,
And with contrary blast proclaims most deeds,
On both his wings, one black, the other white,
Bears greatest names in his wild aery flight.
975 My name perhaps among the circumcised
In Dan, in Judah, and the bordering tribes,
To all posterity may stand defamed,
With malediction mentioned, and the blot
Of falsehood most unconjugal traduced.
980 But in my country where I most desire,
In Ecron, Gaza, Asdod, and in Gath
I shall be named among the famousest
Of women, sung at solemn festivals,
Living and dead recorded, who to save
985 Her country from a fierce destroyer, chose
Above the faith of wedlock-bands, my tomb
With odours visited and annual flowers.

967. *omen*] prophetic sign. Dalila is referring to Samson's sarcastic remark about her future reputation, ll. 956–7.
971–4. No source has been found for M.'s representation of Fame as male, double-mouthed and with one wing black, one white. In Silius Italicus, *Punica* xv 6–9 *Infamia* flies with black wings (*atris . . . pennis*) and *Victoria* with white (*niveis . . . alis*). In Chaucer's *House of Fame* 1571–82, 1637, Fame employs Aeolus, god of winds, as trumpeter and he has two trumpets, one 'Clere Laude' the other, coloured black, 'Sklaundre'.
976. *Dan*] Samson's tribe.
981. Four of the five chief Philistine cities.
987. *odours*] from burnt spices: cp. *Jerem.* xxxiv 5: 'So shall they burn odours for thee.'

Not less renowned than in Mount Ephraim
Jael, who with inhospitable guile
990    Smote Sisera sleeping through the temples nailed.
Nor shall I count it heinous to enjoy
The public marks of honour and reward
Conferred upon me for the piety
Which to my country I was judged to have shown.
995    At this whoever envies or repines,
I leave him to his lot, and like my own.
*Chor.* She's gone, a manifest serpent by her sting
Discovered in the end, till now concealed.
*Sam.* So let her go, God sent her to debase me,
1000   And aggravate my folly who committed
To such a viper his most sacred trust
Of secrecy, my safety, and my life.
*Chor.* Yet beauty, though injurious, hath strange power,
After offence returning, to regain
1005   Love once possessed, nor can be easily
Repulsed, without much inward passion felt
And secret sting of amorous remorse.
*Sam.* Love-quarrels oft in pleasing concord end,
Not wedlock-treachery endangering life.
1010   *Chor.* It is not virtue, wisdom, valour, wit,
Strength, comeliness of shape, or amplest merit
That woman's love can win or long inherit;
But what it is, hard is to say,
Harder to hit,
1015   (Which way soever men refer it)
Much like thy riddle, Samson, in one day
Or seven, though one should musing sit;

988–90. In *Judges* iv 21 Jael, Heber's wife, kills Sisera the Canaanite general
by driving a nail into his temples as he sleeps after taking refuge in her tent
from Barak and the Israelites. Jael's praises are sung (v 24) by Barak and by the
prophetess Deborah, who lived (iv 5) in Mount Ephraim.

995–6. Cp. Sophocles, *Ajax* 1038–9: 'If there be any in whose mind this
wins no favour, let him hold to his own thoughts, as I hold to mine.'

1000. *aggravate*] add to the gravity of.

1008. Cp. the tag quoted by Chremes in Terence, *Andria* iii: *amantium irae
amoris integratio est.*

1012. *inherit*] hold.

1016–7. *riddle*] Cp. *Judges* xiv 8–14: Samson, finding that bees have made
honey in the carcase of the lion he killed, sets the thirty companions a riddle
'Out of the eater came forth meat, and out of the strong came forth sweet-
ness', and gives them seven days to solve it.

> If any of these or all, the Timnian bride
> Had not so soon preferred
>
> 1020 Thy paranymph, worthless to thee compared,
> Successor in thy bed,
> Nor both so loosely disallied
> Their nuptials, nor this last so treacherously
> Had shorn the fatal harvest of thy head.
>
> 1025 Is it for that such outward ornament
> Was lavished on their sex, that inward gifts
> Were left for haste unfinished, judgement scant,
> Capacity not raised to apprehend
> Or value what is best
>
> 1030 In choice, but oftest to affect the wrong?
> Or was too much of self-love mixed,
> Of constancy no root infixed,
> That either they love nothing, or not long?
> Whate'er it be, to wisest men and best
>
> 1035 Seeming at first all heavenly under virgin veil,
> Soft, modest, meek, demure,
> Once joined, the contrary she proves, a thorn
> Intestine, far within defensive arms
> A cleaving mischief, in his way to virtue
>
> 1040 Adverse and turbulent, or by her charms
> Draws him awry enslaved
> With dotage, and his sense depraved
> To folly and shameful deeds which ruin ends.
> What pilot so expert but needs must wreck
>
> 1045 Embarked with such a steers-mate at the helm?

*1020. paranymph*] groomsman. In *Judges* xiv 20 Samson's wife is 'given to his companion, whom he had used as his friend'. M. takes 'friend' in the technical sense (groomsman), following the Vulgate *pronubus*.

*1022. both*] both first and second wives.     *disallied*] M. seems to have coined the verb 'disally' (cancel by separation) for this line.

*1025. for that*] because.

*1033. nothing,*] In its first state *1671* has no comma.

*1034–7.* Cp. *Doctrine and Discipline of Divorce* (Columbia iii 394, Yale ii 294): 'The sobrest and best govern'd men are least practiz'd in these affairs; and who knowes not that the bashful mutenes of a virgin may oft-times hide all the unlivelines and naturall sloth which is really unfit for conversation.'

*1037. thorn*] Cp. *2 Cor.* xii 7: 'a thorn in the flesh'.

*1038. Intestine*] domestic.

*1039–40. cleaving*] Perhaps a reference to the poisoned shirt sent to Hercules by Deianira. Cp. Euripides, *Orestes* 605–6: 'Women were born to mar the lives of men / Ever, unto their surer overthrow.'

Favoured of heaven who finds
One virtuous rarely found,
That in domestic good combines:
Happy that house! his way to peace is smooth:
1050  But virtue which breaks through all opposition,
And all temptation can remove,
Most shines and most is acceptable above.
  Therefore God's universal law
Gave to the man despotic power
1055  Over his female in due awe,
Nor from that right to part an hour,
Smile she or lour:
So shall he least confusion draw
On his whole life, not swayed
1060  By female usurpation, nor dismayed.
  But had we best retire, I see a storm?
*Sam.* Fair days have oft contracted wind and rain.
*Chor.* But this another kind of tempest brings.
*Sam.* Be less abstruse, my riddling days are past.
1065  *Chor.* Look now for no enchanting voice, nor fear
The bait of honeyed words; a rougher tongue
Draws hitherward, I know him by his stride,
The giant Harapha of Gath, his look
Haughty as is his pile high-built and proud.
1070  Comes he in peace? what wind hath blown him hither
I less conjecture than when first I saw
The sumptuous Dalila floating this way:
His habit carries peace, his brow defiance.

1046–9. Cp. *Prov.* xxxi 10–28.
1062. *contracted*] brought together.
1064. *riddling days*] See ll. 1016–7n.
1068. *Harapha*] W. R. Parker, *TLS* (2 Jan. 1937) 12, notes that the 1671 edition of Edward Phillips's *New World of Words* is the first to mention 'Harapha', glossing the name as 'a medicine' (a meaning which arises, as J. Leveen, *TLS* (23 Jan. 1937) 60, points out, from Phillips's quite mistaken association of the name with Hebrew *rephu'ah*, 'medicine'), and as 'a Philistim whose sons being gyants were slain by David and his servants' (an allusion to 2 *Sam.* xxi, where A. V. translates merely 'the giant' but some commentators take *harapha* as a proper name). H. Loewe, *TLS* (23 Jan. 1937) 60, adds that Hebrew *Rephaim*, 'giants' is a euphemism (from *rapha*, 'to be weak') meaning 'the flabby, powerless ones'–a pointer to the real nature of M.'s Harapha?
1069. *pile*] can mean 'a mole or pier in the sea' or 'a lofty mass of buildings'; *OED* gives the present instance as the first figurative application of the word in the latter sense.

*Sam.* Or peace or not, alike to me he comes.
1075    *Chor.* His fraught we soon shall know, he now arrives.
     *Har.* I come not Samson, to condole thy chance,
     As these perhaps, yet wish it had not been,
     Though for no friendly intent. I am of Gath,
     Men call me Harapha, of stock renowned
1080    As Og or Anak and the Emims old
     That Kiriathaim held, thou know'st me now
     If thou at all art known. Much I have heard
     Of thy prodigious might and feats performed
     Incredible to me, in this displeased,
1085    That I was never present on the place
     Of those encounters, where we might have tried
     Each other's force in camp or listed field:
     And now am come to see of whom such noise
     Hath walked about, and each limb to survey,
1090    If thy appearance answer loud report.
     *Sam.* The way to know were not to see but taste.
     *Har.* Dost thou already single me; I thought
     Gyves and the mill had tamed thee? O that fortune
     Had brought me to the field where thou art famed
1095    To have wrought such wonders with an ass's jaw;
     I should have forced thee soon wish other arms,

*1075. fraught*] the cargo of a ship.

*1078. Gath,*] The first state of *1671* omits the comma.

*1080–1. Og*] Cp. *Deut.* iii 11: 'Only Og king of Bashan remained of the remnant of the giants.'     *Anak*] Cp. *Numb.* xiii 33: 'And there we saw the giants, the sons of Anak . . . and we were in our own sight as grasshoppers.' *Emims . . . Kiriathaim*] Cp. *Deut.* ii 10–11: 'The Emims dwelt therein . . . Which also were accounted giants', and *Gen.* xiv 5: 'the Emims in Shaveh [margin 'the plain of'] Kiriathaim'.

*1082. known*] possessed of knowledge.

*1086. encounters,*] The first state of *1671* omits the comma.

*1087. camp*] open field (Latin *campus*).     *listed*] provided with lists for tournament (*OED* gives this instance as the first example of this sense).

*1089.* The use of the verb 'walk' with subjects like 'report' or 'fame' is common from fourteenth century onwards, though obsolete by end of seventeenth.

*1092. single*] single out. *OED* gives this as first recorded example of verb 'single' in sense 'separate person from others'.

*1093. thee?*] The first state of *1671* has semicolon for second state's question mark.

*1096. wish*] A. H. Gilbert, *MLN* xxix (1914) 161–2, claims that the *1671* reading is 'with', and argues that the line means 'I should have forced you (i.e. taken you prisoner) with my arms (cp. 1119, 1130) which are more

Or left thy carcase where the ass lay thrown:
So had the glory of prowess been recovered
To Palestine, won by a Philistine
1100 From the unforeskinned race, of whom thou bear'st
The highest name for valiant acts, that honour
Certain to have won by mortal duel from thee,
I lose, prevented by thy eyes put out.
*Sam.* Boast not of what thou wouldst have done, but do
1105 What then thou wouldst, thou seest it in thy hand.
*Har.* To combat with a blind man I disdain,
And thou hast need much washing to be touched.
*Sam.* Such usage as your honourable lords
Afford me assassinated and betrayed,
1110 Who durst not with their whole united powers
In fight withstand me single and unarmed,
Nor in the house with chamber ambushes
Close-banded durst attack me, no not sleeping,
Till they had hired a woman with their gold
1115 Breaking her marriage faith to circumvent me.
Therefore without feigned shifts, let be assigned
Some narrow place enclosed, where sight may give
          thee,
Or rather flight, no great advantage on me;
Then put on all thy gorgeous arms, thy helmet
1120 And brigandine of brass, thy broad habergeon,
Vantbrace and greaves, and gauntlet, add thy spear
A weaver's beam, and seven-times-folded shield,
I only with an oaken staff will meet thee,
And raise such outcries on thy clattered iron,
1125 Which long shall not withhold me from thy head,

effective than a jawbone'. However Fletcher[3] iv 253 gives the *1671* reading
as 'wish' in all sixty copies examined (including, incidentally, a copy num-
bered 30 supplied by Gilbert himself). R. I. McDavid, *PQ* xxxiii (1954)
86–9, has checked all the copies used by Fletcher and finds that all read
'wish'. The first edition to read 'with' is the Tonson edition of 1720: the
reading, therefore, has no authority.

*1109. assassinated*] wounded by treachery.

*1113. Close-banded*] secretly banded together.

*1120–2. brigandine*] body armour of metal rings or plates sewn on canvas or
leather.     *habergeon*] sleeveless coat of mail.     *Vantbrace*] armour for the
fore-arm.     *weaver's beam*] the wooden roller in a loom on which the warp
is wound before weaving, and the similar roller on which the cloth is wound
as it is woven; cp. *1 Sam.* xvii 7 (of Goliath) 'the staff of his spear was like a
weaver's beam'.     *shield*] Cp. the shield of Ajax, *Il.* vii 220, made of seven
layers of bull's hide.

That in a little time while breath remains thee,
Thou oft shalt wish thyself at Gath to boast
Again in safety what thou wouldst have done
To Samson, but shalt never see Gath more.

*1130*    *Har.* Thou durst not thus disparage glorious arms
Which greatest heroes have in battle worn,
Their ornament and safety, had not spells
And black enchantments, some magician's art,
Armed thee or charmed thee strong, which thou from heaven

*1135* Feign'dst at thy birth was given thee in thy hair,
Where strength can least abide, though all thy hairs
Were bristles ranged like those that ridge the back
Of chafed wild boars or ruffled porcupines.
   *Sam.* I know no spells, use no forbidden arts;

*1140* My trust is in the living God who gave me
At my nativity this strength, diffused
No less through all my sinews, joints and bones,
Than thine, while I preserved these locks unshorn,
The pledge of my unviolated vow.

*1145* For proof hereof, if Dagon be thy god,
Go to his temple, invocate his aid
With solemnest devotion, spread before him
How highly it concerns his glory now
To frustrate and dissolve these magic spells,

*1150* Which I to be the power of Israel's God
Avow, and challenge Dagon to the test,
Offering to combat thee his champion bold,
With the utmost of his godhead seconded:
Then thou shalt see, or rather to thy sorrow

*1155* Soon feel, whose God is strongest, thine or mine.
   *Har.* Presume not on thy God, whate'er he be,
Thee he regards not, owns not, hath cut off
Quite from his people, and delivered up

---

1132-4. As Krouse 130 notes, Rupert of St Heribert, the only commentator who ever called Samson's sainthood into question, suggested that perhaps he wrought his wondrous feats by magic and by alliance with Satan.
1138. *chafed*] angered.    *ruffled*] with quills sticking out irregularly.
1139. Cp. the oath taken by the parties in a single combat to the effect that they were not aided by magic: Selden, *Duello* (1610) 34: 'that hee was free from all use of Art Magique, that he did not carry with him any hearbe, stone or other kinde of experiment of Witchcraft', and *Antiduello* (1632) 52: 'Sweare . . . that you have . . . no stone no hearbe of vertue; no charme, experiment, or any other inchantment, by whose power you beleeve you may the easier overcome your adversary.'

Into thy enemies' hand, permitted them
1160  To put out both thine eyes, and fettered send thee
Into the common prison, there to grind
Among the slaves and asses thy comrades,
As good for nothing else, no better service
With those thy boisterous locks, no worthy match
1165  For valour to assail, nor by the sword
Of noble warrior, so to stain his honour,
But by the barber's razor best subdued.
_Sam._ All these indignities, for such they are
From thine, these evils I deserve and more,
1170  Acknowledge them from God inflicted on me
Justly, yet despair not of his final pardon
Whose ear is ever open; and his eye
Gracious to readmit the suppliant;
In confidence whereof I once again
1175  Defy thee to the trial of mortal fight,
By combat to decide whose god is God,
Thine or whom I with Israel's sons adore.
_Har._ Fair honour that thou dost thy God, in trusting
He will accept thee to defend his cause,
1180  A murderer, a revolter, and a robber.
_Sam._ Tongue-doughty giant, how dost thou prove me
these?
_Har._ Is not thy nation subject to our lords?
Their magistrates confessed it, when they took thee
As a league-breaker and delivered bound
1185  Into our hands: for hadst thou not committed
Notorious murder on those thirty men
At Ascalon, who never did thee harm,
Then like a robber stripp'dst them of their robes?
The Philistines, when thou hadst broke the league,
1190  Went up with armed powers thee only seeking,
To others did no violence nor spoil.

1169. _thine_] thy people.
1180. Samson's challenge to single combat is justified by this accusation;
cp. Selden, _Duello_ (1610) 24: 'Treason . . . Murder, Robery, or such like,
have from ancient time . . . beene tryable at the Defendant's pleasure by the
Duell.'
1182-5. See ll. 259-64n.
1185-8. Cp. _Judges_ xiv 19. Samson had wagered 'thirty change of garments'
that his 'companions' would not be able to solve his riddle: they extracted
the answer from his wife, so he killed thirty men at Ascalon and took their
clothes in order to be able to pay the wager.

*Sam.* Among the daughters of the Philistines
    I chose a wife, which argued me no foe;
    And in your city held my nuptial feast:
*1195*  But your ill-meaning politician lords,
    Under pretence of bridal friends and guests,
    Appointed to await me thirty spies,
    Who threatening cruel death constrained the bride
    To wring from me and tell to them my secret,
*1200*  That solved the riddle which I had proposed.
    When I perceived all set on enmity,
    As on my enemies, wherever chanced,
    I used hostility, and took their spoil
    To pay my underminers in their coin.
*1205*  My nation was subjected to your lords.
    It was the force of conquest; force with force
    Is well ejected when the conquered can.
    But I a private person, whom my country
    As a league-breaker gave up bound, presumed
*1210*  Single rebellion and did hostile acts.
    I was no private but a person raised
    With strength sufficient and command from heaven
    To free my country; if their servile minds
    Me their deliverer sent would not receive,
*1215*  But to their masters gave me up for nought,
    The unworthier they; whence to this day they serve.
    I was to do my part from heaven assigned,
    And had performed it if my known offence
    Had not disabled me, not all your force:
*1220*  These shifts refuted, answer thy appellant
    Though by his blindness maimed for high attempts,

*1195. politician*] politic, in a bad sense.

*1197. spies*] There is nothing in *Judges* to support this claim that the thirty
'companions' were spies. Josephus v 8, however, says: 'now the people of
Timnath, out of dread of the young man's strength, gave him during the
time of the wedding feast . . . thirty of the most stout of their youth, in pre-
tence to be his companions, but in reality to be a guard upon him, that he
might not attempt to give them any disturbance.'

*1201–3.* Seeing himself surrounded by enemies, he treated them as enemies
(with hostility) wherever he came upon them.

*1204. pay . . . in their coin*] They threatened to kill in order to win a wager:
he killed in order to pay it. For the proverb, see Tilley C507.    *underminers*]
secret assailants.

*1208.* See l. 242*n.*

*1220. appellant*] one who challenges another to single combat.

Who now defies thee thrice to single fight,
As a petty enterprise of small enforce.
*Har.* With thee a man condemned, a slave enrolled,
1225    Due by the law to capital punishment?
To fight with thee no man of arms will deign.
*Sam.* Cam'st thou for this, vain boaster, to survey me,
To descant on my strength, and give thy verdict?
Come nearer, part not hence so slight informed;
1230    But take good heed my hand survey not thee.
*Har.* O Baal-zebub! can my ears unused
Hear these dishonours, and not render death?
*Sam.* No man withholds thee, nothing from thy hand
Fear I incurable; bring up thy van,
1235    My heels are fettered, but my fist is free.
*Har.* This insolence other kind of answer fits.
*Sam.* Go baffled coward, lest I run upon thee,
Though in these chains, bulk without spirit vast,
And with one buffet lay thy structure low,
1240    Or swing thee in the air, then dash thee down
To the hazard of thy brains and shattered sides.
*Har.* By Astaroth ere long thou shalt lament
These braveries in irons loaden on thee.
*Chor.* His giantship is gone somewhat crestfall'n,
1245    Stalking with less unconscionable strides,
And lower looks, but in a sultry chafe.

1222. *thrice*] Previously at ll. 1151 and 1175: cp. Selden, *Duello* (1610) 33:
'At the third proclamation, the Esquire appeares mounted.'
1223. *enforce*] effort.
1224–6. Cp. Vincentio Saviolo, *Practice* (1595) ii ('Of Honour and Honour-
able Quarrels') sig. Cc3v (under the heading 'Who is not to be admitted to
the proof of Arms'): 'They are not to be admitted proofe by armes, who
have committed any treason against their Prince or Countrie . . . Likewise,
all theeves, robbers, ruffians, taverne hunters, excommunicate persons,
hereticks, usurers, and all other persons, not living as a Gentleman or a
Souldier.'
1231. *Baal-zebub*] god of the flies; a Philistine idol, with temple at Ekron,
2 *Kings* i 2.      *unused*] not used to hearing 'dishonours'.
1234. *van*] foremost division of a military force; Samson is mockingly
grandiloquent.
1237. *baffled*] Another of the episode's chivalric terms; from the mid-
sixteenth century 'baffle' means primarily 'subject to public disgrace' and
particularly 'disgrace a perjured knight with infamy'.
1242. *Astaroth*] See *Nativity Ode* 200n (p. 110).
1244. *giantship*] Not previously recorded in *OED*.
1245. *unconscionable*] unreasonably excessive.

*Sam.* I dread him not, nor all his giant-brood,
Though fame divulge him father of five sons
All of gigantic size, Goliah chief.
1250 *Chor.* He will directly to the lords, I fear,
And with malicious counsel stir them up
Some way or other yet further to afflict thee.
*Sam.* He must allege some cause, and offered fight
Will not dare mention, lest a question rise
1255 Whether he durst accept the offer or not,
And that he durst not plain enough appeared.
Much more affliction than already felt
They cannot well impose, nor I sustain;
If they intend advantage of my labours
1260 The work of many hands, which earns my keeping
With no small profit daily to my owners.
But come what will, my deadliest foe will prove
My speediest friend, by death to rid me hence,
The worst that he can give, to me the best.
1265 Yet so it may fall out, because their end
Is hate, not help to me, it may with mine
Draw their own ruin who attempt the deed.
*Chor.* O how comely it is and how reviving
To the spirits of just men long oppressed!
1270 When God into the hands of their deliverer
Puts invincible might
To quell the mighty of the earth, the oppressor,
The brute and boisterous force of violent men
Hardy and industrious to support
1275 Tyrannic power, but raging to pursue
The righteous and all such as honour truth;
He all their ammunition
And feats of war defeats
With plain heroic magnitude of mind
1280 And celestial vigour armed,
Their armouries and magazines contemns,
Renders them useless, while
With winged expedition
Swift as the lightning glance he executes

1248. *divulge*] *1671* prints 'divulg'd' but the *Errata* corrects to 'divulge'.
1248-9. Cp 2 *Sam.* xxi 16-22 (also l. 1068*n*).
1268. *O how comely*] Cp. *Ecclesiasticus* xxv 4-5: 'O how comely a thing is judgment . . . O how comely is the wisdom of old men!'
1277. *ammunition*] military stores and supplies; a more general term in the seventeenth century than now.

*1285* His errand on the wicked, who surprised
Lose their defence distracted and amazed.
But patience is more oft the exercise
Of saints, the trial of their fortitude,
Making them each his own deliverer,
*1290* And victor over all
That tyranny or fortune can inflict,
Either of these is in thy lot,
Samson, with might endued
Above the sons of men; but sight bereaved
*1295* May chance to number thee with those
Whom patience finally must crown.
This idol's day hath been to thee no day of rest,
    Labouring thy mind
More than the working day thy hands,
*1300* And yet perhaps more trouble is behind.
For I descry this way
Some other tending, in his hand
A sceptre or quaint staff he bears,
Comes on amain, speed in his look.
*1305* By his habit I discern him now
A public officer, and now at hand.
His message will be short and voluble.
*Off.* Hebrews, the prisoner Samson here I seek.
*Chor.* His manacles remark him, there he sits.
*1310* *Off.* Samson, to thee our lords thus bid me say;
This day to Dagon is a solemn feast,
With sacrifices, triumph, pomp, and games;
Thy strength they know surpassing human rate,
And now some public proof thereof require
*1315* To honour this great feast, and great assembly;
Rise therefore with all speed and come along,
Where I will see thee heartened and fresh clad
To appear as fits before the illustrious lords.
*Sam.* Thou know'st I am an Hebrew, therefore tell
    them,
*1320* Our law forbids at their religious rites
My presence; for that cause I cannot come.
*Off.* This answer, be assured, will not content them.

---

1303. *quaint*] ingeniously contrived.
1307. *voluble*] characterized by readiness of utterance; straight forward.
1309. *remark*] distinguish; a meaning found only in the seventeenth century.
1313. *rate*] 1671 prints 'race' but the *Errata* corrects to 'rate'.
1320. *law forbids*] Cp. *Exod.* xx 4–5, xxiii 24.

  *Sam.* Have they not sword-players, and every sort
  Of gymnic artists, wrestlers, riders, runners,
*1325* Jugglers and dancers, antics, mummers, mimics,
  But they must pick me out with shackles tired,
  And over-laboured at their public mill,
  To make them sport with blind activity?
  Do they not seek occasion of new quarrels
*1330* On my refusal to distress me more,
  Or make a game of my calamities?
  Return the way thou cam'st, I will not come.
  *Off.* Regard thyself, this will offend them highly.
  *Sam.* Myself? my conscience and internal peace.
*1335* Can they think me so broken, so debased
  With corporal servitude, that my mind ever
  Will condescend to such absurd commands?
  Although their drudge, to be their fool or jester,
  And in my midst of sorrow and heart-grief
*1340* To show them feats, and play before their god,
  The worst of all indignities, yet on me
  Joined with extreme contempt? I will not come.
  *Off.* My message was imposed on me with speed,
  Brooks no delay: is this thy resolution?
*1345* *Sam.* So take it with what speed thy message needs.
  *Off.* I am sorry what this stoutness will produce.
  *Sam.* Perhaps thou shalt have cause to sorrow indeed.
  *Chor.* Consider, Samson; matters now are strained
  Up to the height, whether to hold or break;
*1350* He's gone, and who knows how he may report
  Thy words by adding fuel to the flame?
  Expect another message more imperious,
  More lordly thundering than thou well wilt bear.
  *Sam.* Shall I abuse this consecrated gift
*1355* Of strength, again returning with my hair
  After my great transgression, so requite
  Favour renewed, and add a greater sin

1324. *gymnic*] A more usual form in the seventeenth century than 'gymnas-
tic'.

1325. *antics*] clowns.

1333. *Regard thyself*]have a care for your own interests.

1337. *commands?*] In its first state *1671* has a full stop instead of a question
mark.

1340. *feats,*] The first state of *1671* omits the comma.

1342. *Joined*] enjoined. *OED* records no example of this sense after the mid-
sixteenth century.

1346. *stoutness*] pride.

By prostituting holy things to idols;
A Nazarite in place abominable
1360    Vaunting my strength in honour to their Dagon?
Besides, how vile, contemptible, ridiculous,
What act more execrably unclean, profane?
*Chor.* Yet with this strength thou serv'st the Philistines,
Idolatrous, uncircumcised, unclean.
1365    *Sam.* Not in their idol-worship, but by labour
Honest and lawful to deserve my food
Of those who have me in their civil power.
*Chor.* Where the heart joins not, outward acts defile
not.
*Sam.* Where outward force constrains, the sentence
holds
1370    But who constrains me to the temple of Dagon,
Not dragging? the Philistian lords command.
Commands are no constraints. If I obey them,
I do it freely; venturing to displease
God for the fear of man, and man prefer,
1375    Set God behind: which in his jealousy
Shall never, unrepented, find forgiveness.
Yet that he may dispense with me or thee
Present in temples at idolatrous rites
For some important cause, thou need'st not doubt.
1380    *Chor.* How thou wilt here come off surmounts my
reach.
*Sam.* Be of good courage, I begin to feel
Some rousing motions in me which dispose
To something extraordinary my thoughts.
I with this messenger will go along,
1385    Nothing to do, be sure, that may dishonour
Our Law, or stain my vow of Nazarite.
If there be aught of presage in the mind,

1368. Cp. Aristotle, *Ethics* III i 1: 'It is only voluntary actions for which
praise and blame are given; those that are involuntary are condoned, and
sometimes even pitied.'
1369. *sentence*] maxim.
1375. *jealousy*] Cp. *Exod.* xx 5: 'I the Lord thy God am a jealous God.'
1377. *dispense with*] 'arrange administratively with (a person) so as to grant
him relaxation or remission of a penalty incurred by breach of the law'
(*OED*).
1380. *come off*] escape (a sense first recorded by *OED* in *Comus* 646).
1387-9. J. C. Maxwell, *PQ* xxxiii (1954) 90-1, comments that Samson sees
his destiny dimly at this point. He does not realize that the day will be both
his 'last' and 'remarkable'. M. is perhaps indebted to Sophocles, *Trachiniae*

This day will be remarkable in my life
By some great act, or of my days the last.
*1390*  *Chor.* In time thou hast resolved, the man returns.
*Off.* Samson, this second message from our lords
To thee I am bid say. Art thou our slave,
Our captive, at the public mill our drudge,
And dar'st thou at our sending and command
*1395*  Dispute thy coming? come without delay;
Or we shall find such engines to assail
And hamper thee, as thou shalt come of force,
Though thou wert firmlier fastened than a rock.
*Sam.* I could be well content to try their art,
*1400*  Which to no few of them would prove pernicious.
Yet knowing their advantages too many,
Because they shall not trail me through their streets
Like a wild beast, I am content to go.
Masters' commands come with a power resistless
*1405*  To such as owe them absolute subjection;
And for a life who will not change his purpose?
(So mutable are all the ways of men)
Yet this be sure, in nothing to comply
Scandalous or forbidden in our Law.
*1410*  *Off.* I praise thy resolution, doff these links:
By this compliance thou wilt win the lords
To favour, and perhaps to set thee free.
*Sam.* Brethren farewell, your company along
I will not wish, lest it perhaps offend them
*1415*  To see me girt with friends; and how the sight
Of me as of a common enemy,
So dreaded once, may now exasperate them
I know not. Lords are lordliest in their wine;
And the well-feasted priest then soonest fired
*1420*  With zeal, if aught religion seem concerned:
No less the people on their holy-days
Impetuous, insolent, unquenchable;
Happen what may, of me expect to hear

1169–73, where Heracles realizes that the oracle which foretold release from his labours meant death to him, not final prosperity. M., says Maxwell, 'has transposed the riddling oracle into Christian (or Hebraic) terms by means of the notion of divine inscrutability'.

*1404–5.* Samson here 'sums up the whole history of his drama by pretending to deny it . . . In the grimly untrue we hear the true' (Stein[2] 190).

*1421–2.* Cp. Horace, *Ars Poetica* 224: 'The spectator, after the rites had been observed, was drunk and in a lawless mood.'

*1423–6.* R. F. Flatter, *TLS* (7 Aug. 1948) 443, puts forward the theory that

Nothing dishonourable, impure, unworthy
1425 Our God, our Law, my nation, or myself,
The last of me or no I cannot warrant.
*Chor.* Go, and the Holy One
Of Israel be thy guide
To what may serve his glory best, and spread his name
1430 Great among the heathen round:
Send thee the angel of thy birth, to stand
Fast by thy side, who from thy father's field
Rode up in flames after his message told
Of thy conception, and be now a shield
1435 Of fire; that spirit that first rushed on thee
In the camp of Dan
Be efficacious in thee now at need.
For never was from heaven imparted
Measure of strength so great to mortal seed,
1440 As in thy wondrous actions hath been seen.
But wherefore comes old Manoa in such haste
With youthful steps? much livelier than erewhile
He seems: supposing here to find his son,
Or of him bringing to us some glad news?
1445 *Man.* Peace with you brethren; my inducement hither
Was not at present here to find my son,
By order of the lords new parted hence
To come and play before them at their feast.
I heard all as I came, the city rings
1450 And numbers thither flock, I had no will,
Lest I should see him forced to things unseemly.
But that which moved my coming now, was chiefly
To give ye part with me what hope I have
With good success to work his liberty.
1455 *Chor.* That hope would much rejoice us to partake
With thee; say reverend sire, we thirst to hear.
*Man.* I have attempted one by one the lords,
Either at home, or through the high street passing,

these lines refer to M.'s intention to have his heterodox *De doctrina* published after his death, and are thus a personal message to his readers. This unlikely view is questioned by F. F. Farnham-Flower and M. Kelley, *TLS* (21 Aug. 1948) 471.

*1431–3.* See l. 24n and l. 27n.

*1435–6.* Cp. *Judges* xiii 25: also xiv 6 'the Spirit of the Lord came mightily upon him' (Vulg. *irruit*, rushed on).

*1454. success*] outcome.

*1457. attempted*] sought to influence.

With supplication prone and father's tears
*1460* To accept of ransom for my son their prisoner,
Some much averse I found and wondrous harsh,
Contemptuous, proud, set on revenge and spite;
That part most reverenced Dagon and his priests,
Others more moderate seeming, but their aim
*1465* Private reward, for which both god and state
They easily would set to sale, a third
More generous far and civil, who confessed
They had enough revenged, having reduced
Their foe to misery beneath their fears,
*1470* The rest was magnanimity to remit,
If some convenient ransom were proposed.
What noise or shout was that? It tore the sky.
*Chor.* Doubtless the people shouting to behold
Their once great dread, captive, and blind before them,
*1475* Or at some proof of strength before them shown.
*Man.* His ransom, if my whole inheritance
May compass it, shall willingly be paid
And numbered down: much rather I shall choose
To live the poorest in my tribe, than richest,
*1480* And he in that calamitous prison left.
No, I am fixed not to part hence without him.
For his redemption all my patrimony,
If need be, I am ready to forgo
And quit: not wanting him, I shall want nothing.
*1485* *Chor.* Fathers are wont to lay up for their sons,
Thou for thy son art bent to lay out all;
Sons wont to nurse their parents in old age,
Thou in old age car'st how to nurse thy son,
Made older than thy age through eyesight lost.
*1490* *Man.* It shall be my delight to tend his eyes,
And view him sitting in the house, ennobled
With all those high exploits by him achieved,
And on his shoulders waving down those locks,
That of a nation armed the strength contained:
*1495* And I persuade me God had not permitted
His strength again to grow up with his hair
Garrisoned round about him like a camp
Of faithful soldiery, were not his purpose
To use him further yet in some great service,

1459. *prone*] Manoa implies that he prostrated himself before the lords.
1470. It would, they said, be a magnanimous act to remit the rest of their revenge.
1472. *shout*] Cp. l. 1620.

1500    Not to sit idle with so great a gift
        Useless, and thence ridiculous about him.
        And since his strength with eyesight was not lost,
        God will restore him eyesight to his strength.
        *Chor.* Thy hopes are not ill founded nor seem vain
1505    Of his delivery, and thy joy thereon
        Conceived, agreeable to a father's love,
        In both which we, as next participate.
        *Man.* I know your friendly minds and—O what noise?
        Mercy of heaven what hideous noise was that?
1510    Horribly loud unlike the former shout.
        *Chor.* Noise call you it or universal groan
        As if the whole inhabitation perished,
        Blood, death, and deathful deeds are in that noise,
        Ruin, destruction at the utmost point.
1515    *Man.* Of ruin indeed methought I heard the noise,
        O it continues, they have slain my son.
        *Chor.* Thy son is rather slaying them, that outcry
        From slaughter of one foe could not ascend.
        *Man.* Some dismal accident it needs must be;
1520    What shall we do, stay here or run and see?
        *Chor.* Best keep together here, lest running thither
        We unawares run into danger's mouth.
        This evil on the Philistines is fall'n,
        From whom could else a general cry be heard?
1525    The sufferers then will scarce molest us here,
        From other hands we need not much to fear.
        What if his eyesight (for to Israel's God
        Nothing is hard) by miracle restored,
        He now be dealing dole among his foes,
1530    And over heaps of slaughtered walk his way?
        *Man.* That were a joy presumptuous to be thought.
        *Chor.* Yet God hath wrought things as incredible
        For his people of old; what hinders now?
        *Man.* He can I know, but doubt to think he will;
1535    Yet hope would fain subscribe, and tempts belief.
        A little stay will bring some notice hither.

1507. *next*] In interest and kinship, since, like Samson, they are Danites.
1512. *inhabitation*] population.
1521–2. Cp. a similarly hesitant chorus in Euripides, *Hippolytus* 782–5.
1529. *dealing dole*] A pun; 'dole' means 'that which is dealt' and also 'grief, pain'.
1536–7. In 1671 ll. 1527–35 and 1537 were omitted, but supplied in the *Omissa*. Thus in the uncorrected state of 1671 l. 1536 was given to the chorus, not Manoa. In the corrected state the chorus take up and finish what Manoa

*Chor.* Of good or bad so great, of bad the sooner;
For evil news rides post, while good news baits.
And to our wish I see one hither speeding,
*1540*     A Hebrew, as I guess, and of our tribe.
*Messenger.* O whither shall I run, or which way fly
The sight of this so horrid spectacle
Which erst my eyes beheld and yet behold;
For dire imagination still pursues me.
*1545*     But providence or instinct of nature seems,
Or reason though disturbed, and scarce consulted
To have guided me aright, I know not how,
To thee first reverend Manoa, and to these
My countrymen, whom here I knew remaining,
*1550*     As at some distance from the place of horror,
So in the sad event too much concerned.
*Man.* The accident was loud, and here before thee
With rueful cry, yet what it was we hear not,
No preface needs, thou seest we long to know.
*1555*     *Mess.* It would burst forth, but I recover breath,
And sense distract, to know well what I utter.
*Man.* Tell us the sum, the circumstance defer.
*Mess.* Gaza yet stands, but all her sons are fall'n,
All in a moment overwhelmed and fall'n.
*1560*     *Man.* Sad, but thou know'st to Israelites not saddest
The desolation of a hostile city.
*Mess.* Feed on that first, there may in grief be surfeit.
*Man.* Relate by whom.
*Mess.*                    By Samson.
*Man.*                                     That still lessens
The sorrow, and converts it nigh to joy.
*1565*     *Mess.* Ah Manoa I refrain, too suddenly
To utter what will come at last too soon;
Lest evil tidings with too rude irruption
Hitting thy aged ear should pierce too deep.
*Man.* Suspense in news is torture, speak them out.

is saying, thus: '(*Manoa*) a little wait will bring some information (*Chorus*)
about such a great good or evil as—judging from the noise—has just occurred:
and that information will come all the quicker if the occurrence is evil.'
*1538. baits*] travels slowly (for the proverb see Tilley N147).
*1552. here*] *1671* prints 'heard' but the *Errata* corrects to 'here'.
*1562.* Echoes *Two Gentlemen of Verona* III i 220–1 'O, I have fed upon this
woe already, / And now excess of it will make me surfeit.'
*1567. irruption*] bursting in.

*1570*  *Mess.* Then take the worst in brief, Samson is dead.
        *Man.* The worst indeed, O all my hope's defeated
        To free him hence! but death who sets all free
        Hath paid his ransom now and full discharge.
        What windy joy this day had I conceived
*1575*  Hopeful of his delivery, which now proves
        Abortive as the first-born bloom of spring
        Nipped with the lagging rear of winter's frost.
        Yet ere I give the reins to grief, say first,
        How died he? death to life is crown or shame.
*1580*  All by him fell thou say'st, by whom fell he,
        What glorious hand gave Samson his death's wound?
        —*Mess.* Unwounded of his enemies he fell.
        *Man.* Wearied with slaughter then or how? explain.
        *Mess.* By his own hands.
        *Man.*                            Self-violence? what cause
*1585*  Brought him so soon at variance with himself
        Among his foes?
        *Mess.*              Inevitable cause
        At once both to destroy and be destroyed;
        The edifice where all were met to see him
        Upon their heads and on his own he pulled.
*1590*  *Man.* O lastly over-strong against thyself!
        A dreadful way thou took'st to thy revenge.
        More than enough we know; but while things yet
        Are in confusion, give us if thou canst,
        Eye-witness of what first or last was done,
*1595*  Relation more particular and distinct.
        *Mess.* Occasions drew me early to this city,
        And as the gates I entered with sun-rise,
        The morning trumpets festival proclaimed
        Through each high street: little I had dispatched
*1600*  When all abroad was rumoured that this day
        Samson should be brought forth to show the people
        Proof of his mighty strength in feats and games;
        I sorrowed at his captive state, but minded
        Not to be absent at that spectacle.

*1570*. Cp. the announcement of Orestes's death in Sophocles, *Electra* 673
'In short, Orestes is dead.'
*1574. windy*] apparent pregnancy turns out to be flatulence.
*1576–7*. Echoing *Love's Labour's Lost* I i 100–1: 'An envious-sneaping frost, /
That bites the first-born infants of the spring.'
*1596. Occasions*] business.
*1599. little . . . dispatched*] i.e. I had not done much business.
*1605–10*. Cp. *Judges* xvi 27, where the building is called a 'house', and has

*1605*    The building was a spacious theatre,
        Half round on two main pillars vaulted high,
        With seats where all the lords and each degree
        Of sort, might sit in order to behold,
        The other side was open, where the throng
*1610*    On banks and scaffolds under sky might stand;
        I among these aloof obscurely stood.
        The feast and noon grew high, and sacrifice
        Had filled their hearts with mirth, high cheer, and
            wine,
        When to their sports they turned. Immediately
*1615*    Was Samson as a public servant brought,
        In their state livery clad; before him pipes
        And timbrels, on each side went armed guards,
        Both horse and foot before him and behind
        Archers, and slingers, cataphracts and spears.
*1620*    At sight of him the people with a shout
        Rifted the air clamouring their god with praise,
        Who had made their dreadful enemy their thrall.
        He patient but undaunted where they led him,
        Came to the place, and what was set before him
*1625*    Which without help of eye might be assayed,
        To heave, pull, draw, or break, he still performed
        All with incredible, stupendious force,
        None daring to appear antagonist.
        At length for intermission sake they led him
*1630*    Between the pillars; he his guide requested
        (For so from such as nearer stood we heard)

3,000 men and women on the roof. Also Sandys 149: 'On the North-east corner, and summite of the hill [at Gaza], are the ruines of huge arches sunke low in the earth, and other foundations of a stately building. From whence the last Sanziack conveyed marble pillars of an incredible bignesse; enforced to saw them asunder ere they could be removed ... The Jewes do fable this place to have bin the theater of Sampson, pulled down on the head of the Philistims.' Krouse 90 explains that behind M.'s determination to be specific about the details of the building lies a long tradition of rationalistic exegesis which had produced such things as the floor-plan of the temple of Dagon, provided in Arias Montanus, *De Varia Republica* (Antwerp 1592).
*1610. banks*] benches.
*1619. cataphracts*] From the Greek word for a 'coat of mail'; *OED* cites this as the first usage of 'cataphract' in the sense 'soldier in full armour'.   *spears*] spearsmen.
*1627. stupendious*] the common form of modern 'stupendous' until the late-seventeenth century.
*1630–4.* Cp. *Judges* xvi 26: 'And Samson said unto the lad that held him by

As over-tired to let him lean a while
With both his arms on those two massy pillars
That to the arched roof gave main support.
1635 He unsuspicious led him; which when Samson
Felt in his arms, with head a while inclined,
And eyes fast fixed he stood, as one who prayed,
Or some great matter in his mind revolved.
At last with head erect thus cried aloud,
1640 Hitherto, lords, what your commands imposed
I have performed, as reason was, obeying,
Not without wonder or delight beheld.
Now of my own accord such other trial
I mean to show you of my strength, yet greater;
1645 As with amaze shall strike all who behold.
This uttered, straining all his nerves he bowed,
As with the force of winds and waters pent,
When mountains tremble, those two massy pillars
With horrible convulsion to and fro
1650 He tugged, he shook, till down they came and drew
The whole roof after them, with burst of thunder
Upon the heads of all who sat beneath,
Lords, ladies, captains, counsellors, or priests,
Their choice nobility and flower, not only
1655 Of this but each Philistian city round
Met from all parts to solemnize this feast.
Samson with these immixed, inevitably
Pulled down the same destruction on himself;
The vulgar only scaped who stood without.
1660 *Chor.* O dearly-bought revenge, yet glorious!
Living or dying thou hast fulfilled

the hand, Suffer me that I may feel the pillars whereupon the house standeth, that I may lean upon them.'
*1637.* In Judges xvi 30 Samson prays: 'Let me [Heb. 'my soul'] die with the Philistines.' This speech, as Krouse 51 makes clear, with its suicidal implications, was one of the major obstacles to those who wished to regard Samson as a saint: in the Scholastic period his suicide was excused as the prompting of the Holy Ghost. Sir Herbert Grierson, *Essays and Addresses* (1940) 55–63, refers to a passage in Augustine (*De Civitate Dei* I xxi) which makes this excuse, and remarks that the Dutch dramatist Joost van den Vondel in his *Samson of Heilige Wraeck* (1660), which has sometimes been compared with *SA*, concerns himself neither with the suicide question, which M handles so carefully (cp. ll. 307–14, 1637–9, 1664–5), nor with Samson's inner conflict.
*1647–8. winds . . . pent*] The theory that the earth is full of pent-up winds which occasionally burst forth is referred to by Ovid, *Met.* xv 296–306, 346.
*1659.* Not found in the scriptural account (*Judges* xvi 30).

The work for which thou wast foretold
To Israel, and now li'st victorious
Among thy slain self-killed
*1665*    Not willingly, but tangled in the fold,
Of dire necessity, whose law in death conjoined
Thee with thy slaughtered foes in number more
Than all thy life had slain before.
*Semichor.* While their hearts were jocund and sublime,
*1670*    Drunk with idolatry, drunk with wine
And fat regorged of bulls and goats,
Chanting their idol, and preferring
Before our living dread who dwells
In Silo his bright sanctuary:
*1675*    Among them he a spirit of frenzy sent,
Who hurt their minds,
And urged them on with mad desire
To call in haste for their destroyer;
They only set on sport and play
*1680*    Unweetingly importuned
Their own destruction to come speedy upon them.
So fond are mortal men
Fallen into wrath divine,
As their own ruin on themselves to invite,
*1685*    Insensate left, or to sense reprobate,
And with blindness internal struck.
*Semichor.* But he though blind of sight,
Despised and thought extinguished quite,
With inward eyes illuminated
*1690*    His fiery virtue roused
From under ashes into sudden flame,

*1665–6. fold . . . necessity*] A. S. Cook, *MLN* xxi (1906) 78, thinks that, since 'dire necessity' is from Horace, *Odes* III xxiv 6 *dira necessitas*, the *laqueis* of III xxiv 8 may have suggested 'fold'–or possibly Orestes' characterization of the robe in which his father was wound and killed (Aeschylus, *Libation Bearers* 998–1000, Euripides, *Orestes* 25–6). F. Tupper, *MLN* xxii (1907) 46, however, doubts the influence of these Greek phrases on M.
*1667–8.* Cp. *Judges* xvi 30: 'The dead which he slew at his death were more than they which he slew in his life.'
*1669. sublime*] exalted in feeling, elated (a sense, says *OED*, found only in M.).
*1671. regorged*] re-swallowed (a sense not in *OED* before 1700) by ruminants.
*1674. Silo*] Where the ark remained from the time of Joshua until, *1 Sam.* iv 4, 'the people sent to Shiloh, that they might bring from thence the ark of the covenant.'
*1685.* Either left senseless, or left to a reprobate sense (cp. *Rom.* i 28: 'God gave them over to a reprobate mind').

And as an evening dragon came,
Assailant on the perched roosts,
And nests in order ranged
1695   Of tame villatic fowl; but as an eagle
His cloudless thunder bolted on their heads.
So virtue given for lost,
Depressed, and overthrown, as seemed,
Like that self-begotten bird
1700   In the Arabian woods embossed,
That no second knows nor third,
And lay erewhile a holocaust,
From out her ashy womb now teemed,
Revives, reflourishes, then vigorous most
1705   When most unactive deemed,
And though her body die, her fame survives,
A secular bird ages of lives.
*Man.* Come, come, no time for lamentation now,
Nor much more cause, Samson hath quit himself
1710   Like Samson, and heroicly hath finished
A life heroic, on his enemies
Fully revenged, hath left them years of mourning,
And lamentation to the sons of Caphtor
Through all Philistian bounds. To Israel
1715   Honour hath left, and freedom, let but them
Find courage to lay hold on this occasion,
To himself and father's house eternal fame;
And which is best and happiest yet, all this
With God not parted from him, as was feared,
1720   But favouring and assisting to the end.
Nothing is here for tears, nothing to wail
Or knock the breast, no weakness, no contempt,
Dispraise, or blame, nothing but well and fair,
And what may quiet us in a death so noble.

1692. *dragon*] huge snake or python (a common meaning from thirteenth century onwards).
1695. *villatic*] farmyard (adj.). M. has coined the word for this line.
1699. *bird*] The Phoenix; see *Dam* 185–9n (p. 277).
1700. *embossed*] A term used of a hunted animal when it takes shelter in wood or thicket.
1702. *holocaust*] a thing wholly consumed by fire (*OED* cites this as the first use of the word with reference to anything but a burnt sacrifice).
1707. *secular*] lasting for ages (a sense which developed at the start of the seventeenth century).
1713. *Caphtor*] See l. 380n.

1725  Let us go find the body where it lies
        Soaked in his enemies' blood, and from the stream
        With lavers pure, and cleansing herbs wash off
        The clotted gore. I with what speed the while
        (Gaza is not in plight to say us nay)
1730  Will send for all my kindred, all my friends
        To fetch him hence and solemnly attend
        With silent obsequy and funeral train
        Home to his father's house: there will I build him
        A monument, and plant it round with shade
1735  Of laurel ever green, and branching palm,
        With all his trophies hung, and acts enrolled
        In copious legend, or sweet lyric song,
        Thither shall all the valiant youth resort,
        And from his memory inflame their breasts
1740  To matchless valour, and adventures high:
        The virgins also shall on feastful days
        Visit his tomb with flowers, only bewailing
        His lot unfortunate in nuptial choice,
        From whence captivity and loss of eyes.
1745  *Chor.* All is best, though we oft doubt,
        What the unsearchable dispose
        Of highest wisdom brings about,
        And ever best found in the close.
        Oft he seems to hide his face,
1750  But unexpectedly returns
        And to his faithful champion hath in place
        Bore witness gloriously; whence Gaza mourns
        And all that band them to resist
        His uncontrollable intent,
1755  His servants he with new acquist

---

*1727. lavers*] wash-basins.

*1728. what speed*] i.e. what speed I can.

*1730–3.* Cp. *Judges* xvi 31: 'Then his brethren and all the house of his father came down, and took him, and brought him up, and buried him.'

*1745–8.* Cp. the closing chorus of Euripides, *Alcestis* 1160–4: 'Manifold things unhoped-for the Gods to accomplishment bring ... So fell this marvellous thing'. The same chorus is used at the end of *Andromache, Bacchae, Helen* and (with a different first line: 'All dooms be of Zeus in Olympus; 'tis his to reveal them') *Medea*.

*1749.* Cp. *Ps.* civ 29: 'Thou hidest thy face, they are troubled' (also xxx 7 and xxvii 9).

*1751. in place*] at hand.

*1755. acquist*] acquisition.

Of true experience from this great event
With peace and consolation hath dismissed,
And calm of mind all passion spent.

# 85 Psalms i-viii

*Date.* 1653. M. gives the day and month of each translation (except i) in
his heading to it.

*Publication. 1673.*

*Modern criticism.* M. H. Studley, *PQ* iv (1925) 364–72, remarks that this group
of translations reveals M.'s struggle and suffering in the early days of his
blindness. In vi *14* he alone of all versifiers of this psalm uses the word
'dark'. Similarly 'mark' (vi *15*) is not found in the other paraphrases, or in
the original: M. seems aware of his enemies, on the alert to watch his suffer-
ing – the same thing is shown by his inserting 'those / That do observe if I
transgress' (v *22–3*). W. B. Hunter Jr, *PQ* xxviii (1949) 125–44, comments on
the metrical range of these versions (each is in a different metre, and only the
couplets of *Psalm i* had been employed in previous metrical psalters). It is
in these translations, thinks Hunter, that we first see M. attaining his mature
prosody.

## PSALM i
### *Done into verse,* 1653

Bless'd is the man who hath not walked astray
In counsel of the wicked, and i' the way
Of sinners hath not stood, and in the seat
Of scorners hath not sat. But in the great
5    Jehovah's law is ever his delight,
And in his law he studies day and night.
He shall be as a tree which planted grows
By wat'ry streams, and in his season knows
To yield his fruit, and his leaf shall not fall,
10   And what he takes in hand shall prosper all.
Not so the wicked, but as chaff which fanned
The wind drives, so the wicked shall not stand
In judgment, or abide their trial then,
Nor sinners in the assembly of just men.
15   For the Lord knows the upright way of the just,
And the way of bad men to ruin must.

## PSALM ii
### *Done August 8,* 1653.—*Terzetti*

Why do the Gentiles tumult, and the nations
Muse a vain thing, the kings of the earth upstand
With power, and princes in their congregations
Lay deep their plots together through each land,

5    Against the Lord and his Messiah dear
       Let us break off, say they, by strength of hand
Their bonds, and cast from us, no more to wear,
       Their twisted cords: he who in heaven doth dwell
       Shall laugh, the Lord shall scoff them, then severe
10  Speak to them in his wrath, and in his fell
       And fierce ire trouble them; but I saith he
       Anointed have my king (though ye rebel)
On Sion my holy hill. A firm decree
       I will declare; the Lord to me hath said
15     Thou art my Son I have begotten thee
This day; ask of me, and the grant is made;
       As thy possession I on thee bestow
       The heathen, and as thy conquest to be swayed
Earth's utmost bounds: them shalt thou bring full low
20     With iron sceptre bruised, and them disperse
       Like to a potter's vessel shivered so.
And now be wise at length ye kings averse
       Be taught ye judges of the earth; with fear
       Jehovah serve, and let your joy converse
25  With trembling; kiss the Son lest he appear
       In anger and ye perish in the way
       If once his wrath take fire like fuel sere.
Happy all those who have in him their stay.

## PSALM iii

*August 9, 1653*

*When he fled from Absalom*

Lord how many are my foes
    How many those
    That in arms against me rise
    Many are they
5     That of my life distrustfully thus say,
No help for him in God there lies.
But thou Lord art my shield my glory,
    Thee through my story
    The exalter of my head I count
10     Aloud I cried
    Unto Jehovah, he full soon replied
And heard me from his holy mount.
I lay and slept, I waked again,
    For my sustain
15     Was the Lord. Of many millions
    The populous rout
    I fear not though encamping round about
They pitch against me their pavilions.

Rise Lord, save me my God for thou
20     Hast smote ere now
    On the cheek-bone all my foes,
    Of men abhorred
    Hast broke the teeth. This help was from
      the Lord
Thy blessing on thy people flows.

## PSALM iv
### *August* 10, 1653

Answer me when I call
God of my righteousness
In straits and in distress
Thou didst me disenthrall
5     And set at large; now spare,
Now pity me, and hear my earnest **prayer.**
    Great ones how long will ye
    My glory have in scorn
    How long be thus forborne
10     Still to love vanity,
    To love, to seek, to prize
Things false and vain and nothing else but lies?
    Yet know the Lord hath chose
    Chose to himself apart
15     The good and meek of heart
    (For whom to choose he knows)
    Jehovah from on high
Will hear my voice what time to him I cry.
    Be awed, and do not sin,
20     Speak to your hearts alone,
    Upon your beds, each one,
    And be at peace within.
    Offer the offerings just
Of righteousness and in Jehovah trust.
25     Many there be that say
    Who yet will show us good?
    Talking like this world's brood;
    But Lord, thus let me pray,
    On us lift up the light
30 Lift up the favour of thy countenance bright.
    Into my heart more joy
    And gladness thou hast put
    Than when a year of glut
    Their stores doth over-cloy
35     And from their plenteous grounds
With vast increase their corn and wine abounds.

In peace at once will I
Both lay me down and sleep
For thou alone dost keep
40     Me safe where'er I lie
As in a rocky cell
Thou Lord alone in safety mak'st me dwell.


## PSALM v

*August* 12, 1653

Jehovah to my words give ear
  My meditation weigh
  The voice of my complaining hear
My King and God for unto thee I pray.
5    Jehovah thou my early voice
    Shalt in the morning hear
    I' the morning I to thee with choice
Will rank my prayers, and watch till thou appear.
    For thou art not a God that takes
10     In wickedness delight
    Evil with thee no biding makes
Fools or mad men stand not within thy sight.
    All workers of iniquity
    Thou hat'st; and them unblest
15    Thou wilt destroy that speak a lie
The bloody and guileful man God doth detest.
    But I will in thy mercies dear
    Thy numerous mercies go
    Into thy house; I in thy fear
20  Will towards thy holy temple worship low.
    Lord lead me in thy righteousness
    Lead me because of those
    That do observe if I transgress
Set thy ways right before, where my step goes.
25    For in his faltering mouth unstable
    No word is firm or sooth
    Their inside, troubles miserable;
An open grave their throat, their tongue they smooth.
    God, find them guilty, let them fall
30    By their own counsels quelled;
    Push them in their rebellions all
Still on; for against thee they have rebelled;
    Then all who trust in thee shall bring
    Their joy, while thou from blame
35    Defend'st them, they shall ever sing,
And shall triumph in thee, who love thy name.

For thou Jehovah wilt be found
   To bless the just man still,
As with a shield thou wilt surround
40   Him with thy lasting favour and goodwill.


## PSALM vi
### *August 13, 1653*

Lord in thine anger do not reprehend me
   Nor in thy hot displeasure me correct;
   Pity me Lord for I am much deject
Am very weak and faint; heal and amend me,
5   For all my bones, that even with anguish ache,
   Are troubled, yea my soul is troubled sore
   And thou O Lord how long? Turn Lord, restore
My soul, O save me for thy goodness' sake
For in death no remembrance is of thee;
10   Who in the grave can celebrate thy praise?
   Wearied I am with sighing out my days,
Nightly my couch I make a kind of sea;
My bed I water with my tears; mine eye
   Through grief consumes, is waxen old and dark
15   I' the midst of all mine enemies that mark.
Depart all ye that work iniquity.
Depart from me, for the voice of my weeping
   The Lord hath heard, the Lord hath heard my
         prayer
   My supplication with acceptance fair
20   The Lord will own, and have me in his keeping.
Mine enemies shall all be blank and dashed
   With much confusion; then grow red with shame,
   They shall return in haste the way they came
And in a moment shall be quite abashed.


## PSALM vii
### *August 14, 1653*
*Upon the words of Chush the Benjamite against him*
       Lord my God to thee I fly
       Save me and secure me under
          Thy protection while I cry,
       Lest as a lion (and no wonder)
5     He haste to tear my soul asunder
          Tearing and no rescue nigh.

Lord my God if I have thought
Or done this, if wickedness
Be in my hands, if I have wrought
10   Ill to him that meant me peace,
Or to him have rendered less,
And not freed my foe for naught;

Let the enemy pursue my soul
And overtake it, let him tread
15   My life down to the earth and roll
In the dust my glory dead,
In the dust and there outspread
Lodge it with dishonour foul.

Rise Jehovah in thine ire
20   Rouse thyself amidst the rage
Of my foes that urge like fire;
And wake for me, their fury assuage;
Judgment here thou didst engage
And command which I desire.

25   So the assemblies of each nation
Will surround thee, seeking right,
Thence to thy glorious habitation
Return on high and in their sight.
Jehovah judgeth most upright
30   All people from the world's foundation.

Judge me Lord, be judge in this
According to my righteousness
And the innocence which is
Upon me: cause at length to cease
35   Of evil men the wickedness
And their power that do amiss.

But the just establish fast,
Since thou art the just God that tries
Hearts and reins. On God is cast
40   My defence, and in him lies
In him who both just and wise
Saves the upright of heart at last.

God is a just judge and severe,
And God is every day offended;
45   If the unjust will not forbear,
His sword he whets, his bow hath bended
Already, and for him intended
The tools of death, that waits him near.

(His arrows purposely made he
50  For them that persecute.) Behold
He travails big with vanity,
Trouble he hath conceived of old
As in a womb, and from that mould
Hath at length brought forth a lie.

55  He digg'd a pit, and delved it deep,
And fell into the pit he made,
His mischief that due course doth keep,
Turns on his head, and his ill trade
Of violence will undelayed
60  Fall on his crown with ruin steep.

Then will I Jehovah's praise
According to his justice raise
And sing the Name and Deity
Of Jehovah the Most High.

## PSALM viii
### *August* 14, 1653

O Jehovah our Lord how wondrous great
  And glorious is thy name through all the earth!
So as above the heavens thy praise to set
  Out of the tender mouths of latest birth,

5  Out of the mouths of babes and sucklings thou
    Hast founded strength because of all thy foes
To stint the enemy, and slack the avenger's brow
    That bends his rage thy providence to oppose.

When I behold thy heavens, thy fingers' art,
10  The moon and stars which thou so bright hast set,
In the pure firmament, then saith my heart,
  O what is man that thou rememberest yet,

And think'st upon him; or of man begot
  That him thou visit'st and of him art found?
15  Scarce to be less than gods, thou mad'st his lot,
  With honour and with state thou hast him crowned.

O'er the works of thy hand thou mad'st him lord,
  Thou hast put all under his lordly feet,
All flocks and herds, by thy commanding word,
20  All beasts that in the field or forest meet,

Fowl of the heavens, and fish that through the wet
  Sea-paths in shoals do slide. And know no dearth.
O Jehovah our Lord how wondrous great
  And glorious is thy name through all the earth.

# 86 Verses from *Defensio Secunda*

*Date.* 1653. Saumaise (Salmasius) died in 1653. M. says (Columbia viii 57) that he wrote *Gaudete scombri* . . . in expectation of the reply Saumaise was said to be preparing to the *Defensio Pro Populo Anglicano* (see headnote to the epigram from this work, p. 323). Saumaise's reply was eventually published by his son in 1660, *Ad Iohannem Miltonum Responsio, Opus Posthumum*.

(ii) These lines against Alexander More (1616–70) are an adaptation of Juvenal ii 20–1. The sexual misbehaviour referred to is More's seduction of Saumaise's maid, Bontia, which M. relates at length in the *Defensio Secunda* (Columbia viii 34–8). More, a distinguished Protestant divine, was, in 1652, Professor of Ecclesiastical History at Amsterdam. The *Regii Sanguinis Clamor* (1652) was generally ascribed to him, (its actual author was Pierre du Moulin). Hence he is violently attacked in the *Defensio Secunda*.
*Publication.* 30 May 1654.

    (i)   Gaudete scombri, et quicquid est piscium salo,
           Qui frigida hieme incolitis algentes freta,
           Vestrum misertus ille Salmasius eques
           Bonus amicire nuditatem cogitat;
5        Chartaeque largus apparat papyrinos
           Vobis cucullos praeferentes Claudii
           Insignia nomenque et decus Salmasii,
           Gestetis ut per omne cetarium forum
           Equitis clientes, scriniis mungentium
10       Cubito virorum, et capsulis gratissimos.

    (ii)      de virtute loquutus
           Clunem agitas: ego te ceventem, More, verebor?

(i) Mackerels, rejoice, and briny fish-folk all who spend your winters freezing in the ocean! The good knight Saumaise pities your estate, and plans to clothe your nakedness. Unsparing of paper he is designing overcoats for you, each one blazoned with the insignia, name and honours[7] of Claude Saumaise, so that you may wear them proudly through the length and breadth of the fish-market, true pages of the knight, and be heartily welcome to the chests and coffers of the gentlemen who wipe their noses on their sleeves.

(ii) Having spoken of virtue, you go a-whoring yourself. Shall I stand in awe of you, More, when you yourself are depraved?

# 87 Sonnet XVII

*Date.* Winter (see 2–5) 1653? The sonnet could have been written during any winter from 1651–2 to 1656–7. M. moved from Scotland Yard 17 Dec.

¶ 86. i 7. *nomenque et decus*] Echoes Virgil, *Aen.* ii 89: *nomenque decusque*.

1651 to 'a pretty Garden-house . . . opening into St James's Park' where, says Edward Phillips, he lived for eight years and was frequently visited by 'young Laurence (the Son of him that was President of Oliver's Council) to whom there is a Sonnet among the rest, in his Printed Poems' (Darbishire 71–4). Edward Lawrence (b. 1633) became an M.P. Nov. 1656 and died the following year, aged 24. Smart 166–72 discovered four letters from Henry Oldenburg to Edward Lawrence (one dated Apr. 1654, the others undated), and Oldenburg's letters to M. of 28 Dec. 1656 and 27 Jun. 1657 send best wishes to Lawrence (French iv 129–31, 155–7).

*Publication.* 1673.

*Modern criticism.* Finley 51–2, 64–5, reviews the sonnet's Horatian echoes and concludes that it loses 'nothing of Horace's charm, while yet conveying perfectly M.'s more puritan and austere temper'. To have omitted the reference to Christian literature (*8*) would, Finley argues, 'have shown that the classicism was superficial and could not bear the expression of M.'s complete mind'.

> Lawrence of virtuous father virtuous son,
>     Now that the fields are dank, and ways are mire,
>     Where shall we sometimes meet, and by the fire
>     Help waste a sullen day; what may be won
> 5 From the hard season gaining: time will run
>     On smoother, till Favonius reinspire
>     The frozen earth; and clothe in fresh attire
>     The lily and rose, that neither sowed nor spun.
> What neat repast shall feast us, light and choice,
> 10   Of Attic taste, with wine, whence we may rise
>     To hear the lute well touched, or artful voice
> Warble immortal notes and Tuscan air?
>     He who of those delights can judge, and spare
>     To interpose them oft, is not unwise.

¶ 87. *1. father*] Henry Lawrence (1600–64) travelled abroad during the civil war but was appointed one of the Council of State 14 Jul. 1653, and Cromwell made him permanent chairman of the Council 16 Jan. 1654. His works include a treatise *Of Baptism* (1646) and *Of Our Communion and War with Angels* (1646). There is an encomium of him by M. in *Defensio Secunda* (Columbia viii 234). The form of the line imitates Horace, *Odes* I xvi 1: *O matre pulchra filia pulchrior.*

*6. Favonius*] the west wind: M. probably recalls Horace, *Odes* I iv i: *Solvitur acris hiems grata vice veris et Favoni* (Keen winter is melting at the welcome change to spring and Favonius).

*8.* Cp. *Matt.* vi 28.

*9–12.* Horace, like M., considers song a fitting accompaniment to simple fare and wine, *Odes* I xvii 17–22, IV xi 1–2, 34–6.

*10. Attic taste*] marked by simple and refined elegance.

*13. spare*] The word is ambiguous. Masson iii 294, Smart 115 and L. Aber-

# 88 Sonnet XV. On the late Massacre in Piedmont

*Date.* May? 1655. The Vaudois, founded by Peter Valdes in the twelfth century, were looked upon as the first of the Protestant churches. The sect was formally excommunicated in 1215: in the seventeenth century its strongholds were in the Alpine villages on the borders of France and Italy. A treaty with the Duke of Savoy in 1561 granted them the right to reside within certain territorial limits, from which the lower villages, including Torre Pellice and San Giovanni, were excluded. The Vaudois continued to live in these villages until 1655 when an army under the Marquis of Pianezza was sent by Charles Emmanuel II, Duke of Savoy, to expel them. They fled to the hills; Pianezza pursued, and massacred the inhabitants of the upper villages (24 Apr.). Many who tried to escape into France by the pass of St Julian died in the snow, others were butchered. The prisoners taken were hanged at Torre Pellice bridge. The Vaudois themselves estimated their dead at 1,712. Cromwell took up their cause, and M., as Secretary, wrote letters of protest to various European heads-of-state (May 25) and an address to be delivered to the Duke of Savoy by Sir Samuel Morland, a special ambassador (French iv 24–30). Meanwhile the tide turned and the Vaudois won several victories against the Piedmontese troops, and a decisive battle on 12 Jul. A peace treaty, restoring their ancient rights, was signed 18 Aug.
*Publication.* 1673.

Avenge O Lord thy slaughtered saints, whose bones
    Lie scattered on the Alpine mountains cold,
    Even them who kept thy truth so pure of old
When all our fathers worshipped stocks and stones,

crombie, *TLS* (11 Apr. 1936) 316, take it to mean 'refrain, forbear': Keightley, *Poems of M.* (1859) i 160, F. Neiman, *PMLA* lxiv (1949) 480–3 and E. Jackson, lxv (1950) 328–9 favour the opposite meaning, 'spare time to, afford'.

¶ 88. *1–2.* Cp. *Luke* xviii 7: 'shall not God avenge his own elect', and *Rev.* vi 9–10: 'the souls of them that were slain for the word of God . . . cried with a loud voice, saying, How long, O Lord, holy and true, dost thou not judge and avenge our blood', and *Ps.* cxli 7: 'Our bones are scattered at the grave's mouth.'

*2. Alpine mountains cold*] J. Willock, *N & Q* ix (1914) 147, finds this phrase in Fairfax's translation of Tasso (xiii 60).

*4. stocks and stones*] D. S. Berkeley, *Explicator* xv (1957) 58, suggests a reminiscence of Jeremiah's condemnation (ii 27) of the idolatrous leaders of his people. M. thus links the image worship of pre-Reformation England to the adoration of Baal, Ashtoreth and other idols.

5    Forget not: in thy book record their groans
      Who were thy sheep and in their ancient fold
      Slain by the bloody Piedmontese that rolled
      Mother with infant down the rocks. Their moans
      The vales redoubled to the hills, and they
10        To heaven. Their martyred blood and ashes sow
      O'er all the Italian fields where still doth sway
      The triple Tyrant: that from these may grow
      A hundredfold, who having learnt thy way
      Early may fly the Babylonian woe.

# 89 Sonnet XVIII

*Date.* 1655? Cyriack Skinner (b. 1627) was, according to Aubrey and Wood, at one time M.'s pupil (French iv 275). He is mentioned by Edward Phillips (Darbishire 74) as a frequent visitor at the Petty France house to which M. moved Dec. 1651. Andrew Marvell, in a letter to M. of 2 Jun. 1654, says he is 'exceeding glad to thinke that Mr Skyner is got near to you', and a letter of M.'s to Henry Oldenburg of 25 Jun. 1656 sends greetings from Skinner (French iii 385–7, iv 102–4). He did not die until 1700. W. R. Parker, *TLS* (13 Sep. 1957) 547, thinks him the author of the biography of M. which Darbishire 17–34 ascribes to John Phillips, (this view, previously suggested by M. Kelley, *MP* liv (1956) 20–5, is questioned by R. W. Hunt, *TLS* (11 Oct. 1957) 609). What is now page 49 of the Trinity MS contains 5–14 of this sonnet in a hand which Parker believes to be Skinner's own. It is fairly clear that the sheet now numbered 45 and that now numbered 49, both of which are smaller in size than the other sheets in the MS, were once

5. *book*] Cp. *Rev.* v 1: 'I saw in the right hand of him that sat on the throne a book.'

8. *Mother with infant*] Cromwell's agent, Sir Samuel Morland, in his account of the massacre (*History of the Evangelical Churches of the Valleys of Piedmont* (1658) 333–84) records that the wife of Giovanni, son of Pol Parise, was hurled down a precipice with her baby in her arms–the baby survived (363); that Jacopo Pecols's wife and son were thrown down the rocks at Tagliaretto (368); and that a woman and her baby were hurled down a precipice in the mountains of Villaro (374).

10–13. As K. Svendsen remarks, *Shakespeare Assoc. Bulletin* xx (1945) 147–55, these lines blend the parable of the sower with the legend of the dragon's teeth.

12. *triple Tyrant*] the Pope with his three-tiered crown.

14. *Babylonian*] The Puritans frequently identified Rome with the Babylon of *Revelation*.

the front and back pages respectively of a separate MS booklet which probably contained only sonnets. The first of the two sheets still bears a number I in its left margin, and the second of them a number 7. Presumably it was the missing sheet 6 which had the first four lines of this sonnet.
*Publication. 1673.*

> Cyriack, whose grandsire on the royal bench
> Of British Themis, with no mean applause
> Pronounced and in his volumes taught our laws,
> Which others at their bar so often wrench;
> 5 Today deep thoughts resolve with me to drench
> In mirth, that after no repenting draws;
> Let Euclid rest and Archimedes pause,
> And what the Swede intend, and what the French.

¶ 89. *1. grandsire*] Skinner's mother was Bridget, daughter of Sir Edward Coke (1552–1634), the most celebrated lawyer of the Elizabethan and Jacobean period, who became Chief Justice of the King's Bench in 1613. He conducted the prosecution in the trials of Essex and Southampton (1600), Raleigh (1603) and the gunpowder plotters (1605). Throughout the early years of the seventeenth century he appeared as a champion of the law, opposing both the King and successive Archbishops of Canterbury in their attempts to gain judicial independence for the ecclesiastical courts. He constantly resisted James's exaggerations of the royal prerogative, and was, as a result, removed from the Chief Justiceship in 1616. After the Parliament of 1620–1 James had Coke and other members of the 'turbulent' party imprisoned. He continued his opposition to the royal prerogative in Charles's Parliaments of 1625 and 1628.

*2. Themis*] Roman goddess of justice.

*3. volumes*] Coke's major legal works are the *Reports* and *Institutes*.

*5.* 'resolve' is an imperative, and 'deep thoughts' the object of 'drench'.

*7. Let . . . pause*] discontinue, for the time being, your study of mathematics and physics. Cp. Horace, *Odes* III viii 17: *mitte civiles super urbe curas.*

*8. Swede*] Charles X of Sweden came to the throne in Jun. 1654. After a meeting of a secret committee of the Swedish Parliament (Mar. 1655) he began his Polish adventure (10 Jul.) and won brilliant initial victories but lost two thirds of his army in the winter of 1655–6.        *intend, and*] Trin. MS: intends and.        *French*] Throughout the 1650s the war between France and Spain dragged on. Cardinal Mazarin, who was in charge of French policy, approached Cromwell several times, and finally the Treaty of Westminster (24 Oct. 1655) established friendly relations between England and France and led to the expulsion of the future Charles II and the Duke of York from French dominions. M.'s line echoes Horace, *Odes* II xi 1–4: 'What the warlike Cantabrian is plotting, Quinctius Hirpinus, and the Scythian, divided from us by the intervening Adriatic, cease to enquire'.

> To measure life, learn thou betimes, and know
> 10    Toward solid good what leads the nearest way;
> For other things mild heaven a time ordains,
> And disapproves that care, though wise in show,
> That with superfluous burden loads the day,
> And when God sends a cheerful hour, refrains.

# 90 To Mr Cyriack Skinner Upon his Blindness

*Date.* 1655? A clue is provided by 'this three years' day' (*1*) but it is not clear precisely when M. came to consider himself totally blind. French iii 197–8 thinks that this was 28 Feb. 1652, Parker, *PMLA* lxxiii (1958) 196–200, suggests autumn 1651.

In the Trinity MS this sonnet appears on the sheet now numbered 49, in a hand probably Skinner's (see headnote to *Sonnet XVIII*, p. 410): this is the text followed here.

*Publication.* First printed 1694 in Edward Phillips's edition of the *Letters of State*: for *1694* verbal variants, see notes.

> Cyriack, this three years' day these eyes, though clear
> To outward view, of blemish or of spot;
> Bereft of light their seeing have forgot,
> Nor to their idle orbs doth sight appear
> 5    Of sun or moon or star throughout the year,
> Or man or woman. Yet I argue not
> Against heaven's hand or will, nor bate a jot
> Of heart or hope; but still bear up and steer
> Right onward. What supports me dost thou ask?
> 10    The conscience, friend, to have lost them overplied
> In liberty's defence, my noble task,
> Of which all Europe talks from side to side.
> This thought might lead me through the world's
>     vain mask
> Content though blind, had I no better guide.

¶ 90. 3. *light*] *1694*: sight.
4. *sight*] *1694*: day.
5. *Of*] *1694*: Or.
7. *heaven's*] *Trin. MS*: *God's* 'Heaven's'.    *a jot*] *1694*: one jot.
8. *bear up and*] *Trin. MS*: *attend to* 'bear up and'.
9. *Right onward*] *Trin. MS*: *Uphillward* 'Right onward'.
12. *talks*] *1694*: rings.
13. *the*] *1694*: this.
  . *better*] *1694*: other.

# 91 Sonnet XIX

*Date*. 1658? It is disputed whether the sonnet is about M.'s second wife, Katherine Woodcock, whom he married 12 Nov. 1656 and who died 3 Feb. 1658 having borne him a daughter, 19 Oct. 1657, or about his first wife, Mary Powell, who died May 1652, three days after giving birth to a daughter. Mary's candidature was first proposed by W. R. Parker, *RES* xxi (1945) 235–8. Mary died before the end of the period of purification laid down in *Lev*. xii 5: Katherine after it. In the sonnet the wife appears 'as' (like) one 'washed from spot of childbed taint' (5). The description fits Katherine in fact, but if the point of the line is dream-reversal of fact, then it fits Mary and not Katherine. R. M. Frye misses this distinction in his reply to Parker, *N & Q* clxxxix (1945) 239. F. Pyle, *RES* n.s. ii (1951) 152–4, thinks 'whom' (5) is the Blessed Virgin, who survived 'the days of her purification according to the Law of Moses', *Luke* ii 22. Katherine died the day after the Feast of the Purification of the Blessed Virgin. However, even if Pyle is right about 'whom', it might be argued that Mary's name associates her with the Blessed Virgin more surely than Katherine. He is on firmer ground in insisting, *RES* xxv (1949) 57–60, that the figure's 'veiled' (10) face fits Katherine, whom M. married after he was blind, better than Mary ('it is typical of M.'s habitual rectitude of mind that even in the dream state he will not endow his visionary figure with a face supplied by guesswork'). Parker, *RES* n.s. ii (1951) 147–52, admits that the veil gains in appropriateness if Katherine is the subject. Another argument for Katherine is advanced by E. S. Le Comte, *N & Q* i (1954) 245–6, who notices the poem's insistence on purity ('washed' 5, 'Purification' 6, 'white, pure' 9) and connects it with the name Katherine (from Greek *katharos*, pure): M., an inveterate etymologist, is perhaps doing what Dante had done with 'Beatrice' and Petrarch with 'Laura'. This carries more conviction than J. T. Shawcross's theory, *N & Q* iii (1956) 202–4, that the purity of the wife's mind (9) is only mentioned to contrast with the impurity of her (i.e. Mary's) body, uncleansed from childbirth.

Both C. R. Dahlberg, *N & Q* cxciv (1949) 321, and M. Kelley, *MP* liv (1956) 20–5, remark that the sonnet is written in the Trinity MS in the hand of Jeremy Picard, who also entered the deaths of Katherine and her daughter in M.'s Bible, and that there is no evidence that Picard was M.'s amanuensis earlier than Jan. 1658. Strictly, however, this helps to date only the fair-copy in the Trinity MS, not the poem's composition.

*Publication*. *1673*.

> Methought I saw my late espoused saint
> Brought to me like Alcestis from the grave,

¶ 91. 2. *Alcestis*] In Euripides' *Alcestis* she gives her life for her husband Admetus, but Hercules ('Jove's great son') wrestles with death and brings her back from the grave.

Whom Jove's great son to her glad husband gave,
Rescued from death by force though pale and faint.
5    Mine as whom washed from spot of childbed taint,
Purification in the old Law did save,
And such, as yet once more I trust to have
Full sight of her in heaven without restraint,
Came vested all in white, pure as her mind:
10    Her face was veiled, yet to my fancied sight,
Love, sweetness, goodness in her person shined
So clear, as in no face with more delight.
But O as to embrace me she inclined
I waked, she fled, and day brought back my night.

# 92 From the title-page of the second edition of 'The Ready and Easy Way'

*Date*. Mar.–Apr. 1660. The first edition of *The Ready and Easy Way* was published Mar. 3 1660.

The verse is an adaptation of Juvenal i 15–6: *Et nos / consilium dedimus Sullae, privatus ut altum / dormiret* [I too have given advice to Sulla to sleep soundly in a private station]. Juvenal uses Sulla as a type of ambition. Smart 92 thinks that M.'s Sylla is Cromwell.

*Publication*. The second edition, of which there is only one extant copy, was probably published Apr. 1660 (French iv 309–10).

et nos
Consilium dedimus Syllae, demus populo nunc.

I too have given advice to Sylla, now let me give it to the people.

6. *old Law*] Cp. *Lev.* xii 4–8, where it is laid down that, after bearing a female child a woman shall be unclean 'two weeks, as in her separation: and she shall continue in the blood of her purifying threescore and six days' (i.e. during this period 'she shall touch no hallowed thing, nor come into the sanctuary').

13–4. Cp. Odysseus' attempt to clasp his mother's shade, *Od.* xi 204–9, imitated by Virgil, *Aen.* vi 700–2, and Dante, *Purg.* ii 80–1: in each of these, however, there are three attempts; in M. only one. T. B. Stroup, *PQ* xxxix (1960) 125–6, compares *Aen.* ii 789–95, which is also an imitation of the Homeric passage.

# Paradise Regained

# 94 Paradise Regained

*Date.* 1667–70. Edward Phillips records that *PR* 'was begun and finisht and Printed after the other [*PL*] was publisht [i.e. 1667], and that in a wonderful short space considering the sublimeness of it; however it is generally censur'd to be much inferiour to the other, though he [M.] could not hear with patience any such thing when related to him' (Darbishire 75–6). *PR* was licensed 2 Jul. 1670, and entered on the Stationers' Register 10 Sep. (French v 17). Thomas Ellwood, rightly or wrongly, considered himself in some part responsible for the engendering of *PR*: he relates that, on returning to M. an MS of *PL* which M. had lent him, he said 'Thou hast said much here of *Paradise lost*; but what hast thou to say of *Paradise found*? He made me no answer, but sate some time in a Muse'. This incident is not datable, but may have occurred about Aug. 1665. 'And when afterwards I went to wait on him there[in London] . . . he shewed me his Second Poem, called *Paradise Regained*; and in a pleasant tone said to me, *This is owing to you; for you put it into my head by the question you put to me at Chalfont; which before I had not thought of*' (*History of the Life of Thomas Ellwood* (1714) 233–4).

*Publication.* 1671 (for details of this volume see headnote to *SA*, p. 330 above).
*Modern criticism.* The most thorough studies of *PR* are Pope and Lewalski. Pope undertakes an examination of the temptation tradition from the gospel onwards, noting the similarities and the differences between M.'s and previous treatments.

In the order of the three temptations M., unlike most medieval and Renaissance theologians and artists, follows *Luke* iv 1–13, rather than *Matt.* iv 1–11, which reverses the second and third. However, he follows *Matt.* in placing the three temptations after Christ's forty-day fast. In *Luke* Christ is 'forty days tempted of the devil'. Many biblical commentators assumed that there were other temptations, not mentioned by the evangelists: M. introduces two–the banqueting scene and the storm–not found in previous accounts.

In adopting the view that Christ underwent temptation only as a man, and hence did not use divine power to drive the devil away, M. was in agreement with a long line of theologians from Ambrose on (see the emphasis on Christ's manhood in *PR* i *4*, *36–7*, *122*, *150–67*, etc.). He stops short, however, of the extreme form of this theory, which was that Christ was tempted inwardly 'by his own corruption' (as the theologian Diodati put it, in opposing this interpretation): M.'s temptations are orthodox in their externality. Where M. does deviate from the majority of exegetes is in refusing Christ both foreknowledge of the temptation (in this, however, Paraeus had preceded him), and power over his own appetite (see *PR* i *290–3*, ii *245–59*).

The equation between the fall of man and the temptation of Christ is another of M.'s traditional properties. From patristic times it had been common to argue that the three sins Christ refused to commit were the three Adam had committed (gluttony, vainglory, avarice), and contained within themselves all other sins (see i *154-5*, *161-2*, ii *132-43*). M. innovates by making the temptations to all these sins occur on the second day of the temptation (see ii *337-65n*, and iii *25-30n*), and for the sake, Pope thinks, of drama and surprise, he turns the pinnacle scene from a temptation to vainglory into a murderous identity test. The storm, which he introduces beforehand, can be regarded as a temptation by violence which, as Satan points out (iv *477-83*), prefigures the passion (see, however, iv *464-83n*).

During the Middle Ages and the Renaissance it was widely assumed that Satan's chief object in attempting to seduce Christ was to find out if he really was the Son of God or, if he was, whether by nature or merely by grace. The first and the last temptations were seen as attempts to elicit from Christ an acknowledgement of his divinity, and some theologians argued also that Satan's impudent assertion that he owned the world (in the temptation of the kingdoms) was intended to provoke a counter-claim from Christ. A number of Protestant theologians (including Calvin, Knox and Taylor) rejected this whole hypothesis, however, and argued that Satan had no doubt that the Christ he was tempting was the promised Messiah. Modern critics disagree about M.'s view. Pope and Lewalski consider that M.'s Satan really is confused by the term 'Son of God' (iv *517-20*). Pope also thinks that Christ deliberately withholds evidence of his identity from Satan, but Lewalski argues that Christ is almost as much in the dark as Satan most of the time: to see Christ undergoing temptation with full consciousness of his divinity would be to destroy the dramatic conflict of *PR*. Allen (*110-21*) regards Satan's uncertainty about Christ's identity as a pretence, citing i *356* (but see note to this line), *475-7* (an admission which may, however, be a mere stratagem of Satan's) and iv *525* (but compare iv *535-6*). For diplomatic reasons, says Allen, Satan maintains the illusory doubt. The real doubt that lurks in his mind, though, is about his own failing powers as a corrupter. What motivates him is fear (see i *66*, *94-5*, iv *195*). His claim that he is beyond fear (iii *206*) is quickly contradicted (iii *220*), and his fear, turning to panic, drives him, as Allen sees it, to the violence of the storm and of the pinnacle, though he had assured his followers that he would not use force (i *97*). What uncertainty there is in the poem, Allen insists, is not in Satan but in the disciples (ii *11-12*), in Mary (ii *70*) and in Christ who, in his divine nature knows his identity and foresees his course, but in his human nature is often uncertain of both. During the poem he crosses and recrosses the boundary between the two natures: by himself he is uncertain (i *287-93*), but confronted by Satan he flares into divine certainty (ii *383-4*, iv *151*, *178-81*, *190-1*).

Stein[2], like Allen, stresses Satan's limitations: compared with the Satan of *PL* he is a severely diminished antagonist. His understanding is weakened (see ii *337-65n*): Christ's speech, ii *473-80*, would otherwise be enough to make clear to him the futility of offering the kingdoms-of-the-world temptation: but Satan is blinded by his obsession with power—all his temptations, even that of learning, are offered in terms of power. Stein, however, agrees with Pope that one of Satan's objectives is to discover Christ's identity.

Lewalski's main thesis is that *PR* is an example of 'that Epick form whereof . . . the book of Job [is] a brief model', as M. put it in *Reason of Church Government* (Columbia iii 237, Yale i 183). She firmly opposes Tillyard (316) who claims that *PR* 'is not an epic . . does not try to be an epic, and . . . must not be judged by any kind of epic standard'. She first surveys the history of the idea of the *Book of Job* as epic from patristic times to the seventeenth century, discovering that the dominant tradition emphasized *Job* i and ii and scanted the dialogues that follow, so that the two councils in heaven and the trials inflicted on Job by Satan came to be regarded as the main elements in the story. These, she claims, are the basis of *PR*'s structure: M. writes his brief epic on the Jobean model. Lewalski also undertakes an extended survey of the genre of the biblical brief epic, enlarging upon B.O. Kurth's attempt in *M. and Christian Heroism* (Berkeley 1959) to relate M.'s heroic ideals in *PR* to contemporary English biblical poems. She finds that the heavenly and hellish councils, the geographical catalogue of worldly kingdoms, the detailed descriptions of particular cities, the account of the hero's reading and education, the choice of a 'peaceful' New Testament subject (along with the intimation that it is vastly superior to the old heroic themes), and the four-book division, were common features of the genre during the humanist period. M., unlike most of the humanist writers in the genre, does not take over and Christianize the pagan supernatural nomenclature (Olympus, Avernus etc.), and he manages to give Christ's character much of the psychological interest previously found only in Old Testament heroes subject to human doubts and frailties, like Du Bartas's Judith and Robert Aylett's David. The only previous example Lewalski finds of a brief biblical epic which uses the *Book of Job* as its structural model but does not take Job as its subject is Robert Aylett's *Joseph* (1623). The only previous example she finds of a brief epic which takes the temptation as its subject is Jacobus Strasburgus's *Oratio Prima* (1565).

The two issues central to *PR*'s dramatic action, in Lewalski's view, are Christ's identity and his mission. Christ and Satan begin more or less in ignorance of both. Neither understands that Christ is the 'first-begot' who drove Satan from heaven and Christ has only partial knowledge of his future roles (i 221–3, 254, 264–7). To clarify the first issue Lewalski peruses the christology of the *De doctrina* and concludes that there, and presumably in *PR*, M. conceives of an incarnate Christ who has really emptied himself of divine understanding and will (Columbia xiv 275, 343) and who can therefore be educated and illuminated by the Father (Columbia xv 275, *PR* i 291–3). Christ, she argues, withstands each of the temptations with his limited, human understanding, and then merits a special illumination after each (e.g. *PR* i 355–6, 460–4, ii 381–4, iv 146–53, 561) bringing him to perfect and divine understanding of the aspect of himself that has been under attack in the previous temptation. Protestant commentators, and M. himself in the *De doctrina*, saw Christ's mission as threefold: he was to be prophet (or teacher, a role for which the Old Testament types were Moses and Elijah), king (over his church and his heavenly kingdom: the types were David and

Solomon) and priest (by his sacrificial death and intercession for man: the types were Job and Melchisedec). A number of commentaries, including those of William Perkins and Thomas Taylor, linked the three temptations with these three aspects of the mediatorial office. Lewalski argues that *PR* deals with each aspect in turn, and that they are basic to its structure. So is the typology, since Christ defines himself in relation to the earlier types, both Old Testament and classical (Socrates, Hercules etc.) and Satan's strategy is to get Christ to identify himself with inferior types (e.g. the oracles, i *393–6*, and Balaam, i *490–2*, inferior types of the prophetic office, and Alexander, Caesar, Pompey, Scipio, iii *31–42*, David, iii *152–3, 370–5*, iv *106–8*, and Judas Maccabaeus, iii *165*, inferior types of the kingly office). By reading all *PR*'s Old Testament and classical allusions in a typological perspective Lewalski brings added point and force to many of Christ's and Satan's speeches. At times she overstates her case, as when she insists that Hercules, who is not explicitly mentioned during the banquet–wealth temptation at all, is present by inference since aspects of the temptation resemble features of the story of Hercules' choice in Xenophon's *Memorabilia* II i 21–33. Also her interpretation of *PR*'s structure as dependent on Christ's three roles imports an imbalance into the poem since the roles of prophet and king are discussed and exemplified in detail but the priestly role is hardly introduced except in the brief storm-tower sequence: commentators, laying particular emphasis on the Temple setting, had often seen Christ's temptation on the pinnacle as foreshadowing his defeat of Sin and Death at the crucifixion (see iv *549n*).

Stein[2] is concerned to show that *PR* attempts a dramatic definition of 'heroic knowledge'. The poem juxtaposes what he considers to be the two competing theories of knowledge in the seventeenth century: Satan, the empiric, advocates knowledge derived externally from sense impression and used for power: Christ, the Platonic, represents pure thought, inaccessible to the senses. His contest with Satan is a preparation for acting transcendence in the world by uniting intuitive knowledge with proved intellectual and moral discipline. In reply J. M. Steadman, *UTQ* xxxi (1962) 416–30, claims that Stein emphasises Christ's knowledge at the expense of his rejection. The method of systematic rejection, an important structural feature of the second temptation, and its 'ethical ladder' of the voluptuous, ethical and contemplative lives, should he considers be traced not to Plato but to Aristotle's *Nicomachean Ethics*.

Merritt Hughes, *SP* xxxv (1938) 254–77, had previously drawn attention to the Aristotelian element in *PR*. Reacting against the view of the Christ of *PR* as the self-portrait of a defeated old man who had come to regret that he had tried 'to influence men's deeds instead of enlightening their minds' (Tillyard 309), Hughes insists upon the positive element in M.'s Christ. Christ's character is the result of the effort of Renaissance critics and poets to create a purely exemplary hero in heroic poetry by Christianizing the Aristotelian ideal of the magnanimous man, an effort which came to a head in the Arthur of Spenser's *F.Q.*, and which can be traced in such critical works as Tasso's *Del Poema Eroico* and *Della Virtù Eroica*. This effort produced a contemplative as opposed to an active hero, who renounces the world and masters his passions by reason. Kermode[4] agrees, but points out that the heroic ideal of M.'s Christ is in no sense derived from Tasso: M. had been working it out from the time of *Passion*, where Christ is 'Most perfect hero'. Christ's long contemplative withdrawal in *PR* is like that M. underwent at Horton and praised in Cromwell (Columbia viii 212–15); his patient endurance of suffering is of the kind exemplified in M.'s sonnet on his blindness and praised by the chorus in *SA* 1287–96; his renunciation of ambition and glory is what M. commended in Fairfax (Columbia viii 217–19) and what Phoebus preached in *Lycidas* 76–84. The renunciation of glory is of particular importance, and from this viewpoint Scipio (see *PR* ii *199–200*, iii *34–5*, *101–3*) is M.'s model. Lewalski (242–9) rather than identifying the Christ of *PR* with one particular classical ideal, argues that he assimilates principles common to the Stoics, the Academics, and the Peripatetics, especially in his definition of the ideal kingship over self (*PR* ii *457–83*), and that certainly some of his attitudes are quite un-Aristotelian. She agrees with Samuel (69–95) that ultimately Christ relates himself most closely to the Socratic-Platonic philosopher. M. M. Mahood, *Poetry and Humanism* (1950) pp. 225–37, reading the poem in the light of M.'s 'almost obsessive' longing for fame in the past, also places great weight on Christ's renunciation: 'This reorientation of "that last infirmity of noble mind" is the central theme of *PR*.'

In a later study Tillyard[3] agrees with Hughes's modification of his autobiographical approach to *PR*. The most thoroughgoing autobiographical reading is that of W. Menzies, *E & S* xxix (1948) 80–113, who explains that M. is both Christ and Satan in *PR*, and that the poem's debate 'is connected directly with the poet's own experience, his past life, and his actual circumstances'. (The theory is naively applied: e.g. the repudiation of classical learning is accounted for by the fact that 'M. was finding it more and more difficult to remember Greek'.)

Examinations of the structure of *PR* have been neither very numerous nor apart from Lewalski's (see above) very fruitful. Dick Taylor, *Tulane Studies in English* iv (1954) 57–90, advances the notion that all M.'s major poems share a structural pattern: the trial and proof of the protagonist, followed by an extension of grace accompanied by a miraculous event. A. H. Sackton, *UTSE* xxxiii (1954) 33–45, draws attention to the frequency of parallelism and contrast in *PR*: the baptismal scene, for example, is presented in three contrasting accounts (i *18–32*, *70–85*, *273–86*), and the repeated assaults and rebuttals of the second day's temptations form a structure of contrasts, in that Christ's replies are not merely negative but combine a positive with a negative theme, opposing true values to false (e.g. ii *466–7*, iii *60–2*, *400–2*, iv *143–5*, *288–92*). A. S. P. Woodhouse, *UTQ* xxv (1956) 167–82, finds symmetry in the framing of the major temptation between the two minor ones, and suggests, not very convincingly, that the way the division into books cuts across the scheme of the three temptations is a device for preventing this symmetry from becoming too mechanical. Roy Daniells, M., *Mannerism and Baroque* (Toronto 1963) pp. 194–208, likens this architecture of a threefold design dominated by a central element to that of a baroque church. L. E. Orange, *Southern Quarterly* ii (1964) 190–201, maintains that Satan's strategy of temptation is based on the seven deadly sins and that these, therefore, underlie *PR*'s structure: his demonstration of this theory wears very thin, however, as does L. S. Cox's argument, *ELH* xxviii (1961) 225–43, that the poem's structure is largely dependent on the development of recurrent imagery of food and of words. Samuel 70–1 concludes that the sequence of temptations follows, in reverse order, Socrates' scale of the five kinds of men and governments outlined in Plato's *Republic·*

At any rate the gradual advance through growing climaxes to the climax of the tower can be viewed as a counterpoint to the basic tripartite structure. Lewalski 330–1 suggests that since the kingdoms temptation deals first with private, then with public themes (the shift coming at iii *152*), one might distinguish four rather than three basic structural divisions. Still another structural counterpoint within the kingdoms temptation, overlaying this two-part division, is its organisation according to the traditional tripartite scale of ethical goods, *Voluptaria* (the banquet), *Activa* (wealth, glory, Parthia, Rome), and *Contemplativa* (learning).

A small but shrewd structural point is made by H. H. Petit, *Papers of the Michigan Academy* xliv (1958) 365–9: as Christ is second Adam, so Mary is 'second Eve' (*PL* v 387, x 183), hence the emphasis upon her humility, faith and obedience in *PR* ii, contrasting with Eve's rash pride, doubts and disobedience in *PL* ix. The last line of *PL* leaves Adam and Eve together, and the last line of *PR* does the same for second Adam and second Eve.

Christ's stance, and the style of his speeches, have come in for some adverse comment. Northrop Frye, *MP* liii (1956) 227–38, puts the case most strongly, remarking on the similarity between *PR* and *Comus* in that dramatically Christ, like the Lady, is an increasingly unsympathetic figure–'a pusillanimous quietist in the temptation of Parthia, an inhuman snob in the temptation of Rome, a peevish obscurantist in the temptation of Athens'. 'Comus and Satan get our dramatic attention because they show such energy and resourcefulness; the tempted figures are either motionless or unmoved and have only the ungracious dramatic function of saying No. Yet, of course, the real relation is the opposite of the apparent one: the real source of life and freedom and energy is in the frigid figure at the centre.' W. W. Robson (Kermode[3] 124–37) comments on Christ's plain and unpoetical vocabulary, and on the greater degree of 'presence' which Satan's speeches have by contrast. The difference was part of M.'s intention, Robson assumes: Christ was meant to be the paragon of surly virtue, hence his condemnation of the multitude (iii *50*) and of Greek philosophy (iv *291–318*). These speeches, however, and others of Christ's, amount to errors of feeling and taste, and, coupled with the tonelessness and desiccation of the verse Christ speaks, lead to a failure of incarnation. Robson concludes that M. did not succeed in combining the sacred figure and the epic hero. In reply

F. W. Bateson (Kermode[3] 138–40) defends the bare and ascetic style of much of *PR*, particularly the 'condensed and laconic art' of i *497–502*: the stylistic brilliance of such lines 'arises from, is indeed a function of, their context'. G. A. Wilkes, *English Studies* xliv (1963) 35–8, suspects that Christ's speeches have seemed so unpalatable to critics because they are delivered from set moral positions: the 'oration from a given moral standpoint' was one of the conventions of the minor sacred epic of the Renaissance, and is found in Du Bartas, *La Judith* and Drayton, *Noah's Flood*. Even if M. was influenced by this 'convention', however, the question of whether the style of the resultant speeches can be defended still remains. Louis Martz's contention, in *The Paradise Within* (New Haven 1964) pp. 171–211, that the style of the major part of *PR* is that of Virgil's *Georgics*, converted by M. from a didactic mode to a channel for religious meditation, can hardly be taken seriously in the absence of corroboratory analysis and comparison. As Lewalski 38 remarks, the expository form of the *Georgics* and their explicit abnegation of heroic subject and tone (iii 1–48) contrast sharply with the narrative / dramatic form and heroic claims of *PR*.

A determined attempt to interpret *PR* as an ecclesiastical parable is made by Howard Schultz, *M. and Forbidden Knowledge* (New York 1955). He reads Christ's condemnation of heathen philosophy as a contribution to the learned ministry controversy, similar to that made by M. in his tract *The Likeliest Means to Remove Hirelings out of the Church* (1659), where it is argued that learning, beyond knowledge of languages and of Scripture, is inessential to a minister. Schultz takes the banquet temptation to represent the lure of Popish idolatry; and the offer of earthly monarchy, the junction of civil and ecclesiastical power which M. detested. This narrowing, or sharpening, of the poem's significance is contested by E. L. Marilla, *Studia Neophilologica* xxvii (1955) 179–91, who insists that *PR* is 'inspired primarily by dynamic interest in the "practical" problems of the temporal world', and that it recommends an acute and unrelaxing awareness of the spiritual significance of man as a way through those problems. Marilla's view is essentially a reaffirmation of J. H. Hanford's, *SP* xv (1918) 176–84. Another attempt, beside Schultz's, to place *PR* in a context of seventeenth-century religious controversy, is that of M. Fixler, *M. and the Kingdoms of God* (1964). Fixler regards *PR* as M.'s reaction to the worst excesses of Puritan apocalyptic materialism: Satan treats the messianic prophecies in what was considered to be the spirit of Jewish messianism as opposed to the orthodox Christian interpretation of spiritual typology: this can be taken as M.'s comment upon the seventeenth-century revival of Jewish (i.e. temporal) messianism, and upon its intrusion into contemporary English life (e.g. in the expectations of the Fifth Monarchists).

Finally two critics, R. D. Miller, *MLN* xv (1900) 403–9, and D. Daube, *RES* xix (1943) 204–9, emphasise the historical aspect of the temptations: they represent things that were real problems to the historical Jesus. Modern biblical scholars, Daube remarks, are inclined to believe that the question of whether Jesus ought to assume political leadership and fight Rome, or whether he ought to choose strength in weakness, did play a tremendous part in his life. The temptations were subjective, internal: the scriptural narrative, with its real devil, is merely a symbolical version. M., in accepting this version at its face value, has, Miller thinks, misunderstood the temptations. They are presented, in *PR*, not as a psychological series but as the expedients of a resourceful devil: thus 'the various attempts of Satan are seemingly without connection, the transitions are lame, and the unity of the poem is lost'.

*Style and rhetoric.* That the style of *PR* is flatter and drier than that of *PL* is a common complaint, but it is also terser and tenser and, though less involved, often as delicately managed. The sentence length is abbreviated: the average in *PR* i, for example, is 7 lines. Satan's opening period in the hellish debate (i *44–69*) and Christ's musings on his youth (i *201–26*) are joint longest in this book. Satan's panoramas also extend the normal sense-unit. Rome has a sentence of 19 lines (iv *61–79*) and Athens, the climax of the temptations, reaches a peak with consecutive sentences of 25 and 24 lines (iv *236–84*). Brevity of sense-unit is a frequent mark of Christ's retorts (e.g. i *421–41* has 8 sentences: the most fragmented set of 21 lines in *PR*). Laconism features prominently in his speeches (e.g. i *335–6*; 'the same I now' i *354*; 'thou canst not more' i *496*; ii *317–8, 321–2*; 'I never liked thy talk, thy offers less' iv *171*; 'the Son of God went on / And stayed not, but in brief him answered thus. / Me worse than wet thou find'st not' iv *485–6*). It seems an inherited characteristic (see the Father's 'This is my son beloved, in him am pleased' i *85*), and Satan quickly picks it up (see his sharp rejoinder 'By miracle he may' i *337*). Monosyllabic lines, rare in *PL*, are relatively plentiful in *PR*: *PR* i has 28 (an average of 1 in 18 lines); ii has 15, iii, 14 and iv, 34. Satan as the simple rustic has 4 in 23 lines (i *321–45*), the disciples ('Plain fishermen') 2 in 28 (ii *30–57*). Satan also uses them for the sake of insistence (ii *368, 377*; iv *517, 518, 520*), and Christ for his steely parries (iii *396, 398, 407*; iv *152, 153* and, the culmination of the action, iv *561*). When Satan makes his appeal to Christ's compassion, the monosyllabic lines cluster more thickly than anywhere else in the poem (iii *204, 206, 209, 220, 223, 224*).

Satan, Christ and the narrator all use word-play: e.g. Satan's 'Pretends' (i *73*), 'deserted' (ii *316*); Christ's 'arm . . . arms' (iii *387–8*); and the narrator's 'consistory' (i *42*), 'ravens . . . ravenous' (ii *267–9*) and 'crude' (ii *349*). Satan's sardonic jocularity turns to other kinds of verbal sleight as well, e.g. his definition of 'eternal' (iv *391–2*) and his sneering 'highest is best' as he sets Christ on the highest pinnacle of the Temple (iv *553*). His professional interest in ambiguity (see i *434–5*) comes out, crucially, in his questioning of the title 'Son of God' (iv *517–21*); and the poem culminates in Christ's ambiguous 'Tempt not the Lord thy God' (iv *561*, see footnote), which Satan at any rate, since he falls not only 'smitten with amazement' (iv *562*) at Christ's balancing-feat but also 'struck with dread' (iv *576*), seems to interpret as a revelation of Christ's own godhead, whether Christ meant it like that or not. The poem's style often accommodates less obvious verbal intricacies. When God reminds Gabriel how he foretold the virgin birth to Mary 'doubting how these things could be' (i *137*) the doubt seems momentarily Gabriel's, not Mary's–an impression prearranged by God's announcement that he is about to offer Gabriel verification (i *130–3*). When we are told that Christ, entering the wilderness, had not 'marked' (observed) the way he came, so that 'return / Was difficult, by human steps untrod' (i *297–8*), the last phrase, at first sight merely conveying an unexciting attribute of deserts, becomes, when a measure of emphasis is allowed to 'human', suggestive of the twofold nature of the figure who has trodden *this* desert, and the idea of non-human steps, once present, allows a shade of the meaning 'left footprints upon' to get into 'marked'. The ordering of i *303–7* persuades the reader that he is being given an account of Christ's various habitat, only to reveal, in the last three words, that no such account is available: thus M. is able to fill in the gaps in his source and leave them scrupulously open at the same time. Verbs are fairly often connectable with more than one object (direct or indirect) and adjectives with more than one noun, so that undertones of meaning emerge. For example, iii *86–7* 'Rolling in brutish vices, and deformed, / Violent or shameful death their due reward' permits 'deformed' to adhere to 'vices', suggesting perversion (particularly in the Tiberius context), or to 'death', suggesting physical misshapenness; and 'Rolling in' can extend from 'vices' to 'death', bringing a glimpse of agonized contortions. The apparent grammatical slip in iv *583* ('him' should strictly refer to the last figure named, Satan, but obviously refers to the Son of God) is actually a splendid dismissal of Satan, now fallen, from the poem. He ceases to count even as a grammatical referent, and 'him' jumps slightingly back across his name to that of the victor. Lewalski's detection of ironic *double-entendre* in i *383* is surely valid (see footnote), and Christ's comment on the relationship between God and man, 'of whom what could he less expect / Than glory and benediction' (iii *126–7*), gives 'less' a similar duplicity: God, foreseeing all, knows how little 'glory and benediction' he is to receive from ungrateful mankind. Words which alter or complete meanings in one line are quite commonly placed at the beginning of the next line, with gains in delay and emphasis. Satan is fond of this expedient: 'single none / Durst ever, who returned, and dropped not here / His carcase' (i *323–5*) gathers a more horrible surprise from the intrusion of 'His carcase' upon what seemed the completed meaning of 'dropped' (fell exhausted); and 'whom I know / Declared the Son of God' (i *384–5*) throws a dubious weight upon declaration, as opposed to proof. Verbal echoes sound across the poem to encourage particular comparisons: the 'full frequence' of devils imitates the 'full frequence' of angels (i *128* and ii *130*), and Satan's scornful use of 'rudiments' (iii *245*) harks back to God's plans for Christ (i *157*).

Movement within *PR* is scarce. The flights to mountain-top and pinnacle are exceptional. For the most part the adversaries are locked in cerebral combat, and Christ's immobility is repeatedly stressed (e.g. iv *18–20*). Stylistically this stillness is reflected in the preference for participles rather than other parts of the verb. The past participle freezes action into posture: e.g. 'on him *baptized*' (i 29), 'by the head / *Broken*' (i 60–1), 'whom he suspected *raised*' (i 124–5), 'wet *returned* from field at eve' (i 318), 'our Saviour answered thus *unmoved*' (iii 386), 'sturdiest oaks / Bowed their stiff necks, *loaden* with stormy blasts, / Or *torn* up sheer' (iv 417–9). It is introduced in contexts where its only function seems to be to withdraw the action from the immediate and the present: e.g. 'with words *thus uttered* spake' (i 320), 'Among daughters of men the fairest *found*' (ii 154), 'With sound of harpies' wings, and talons *heard*' (ii 403). It also defines characters by reference to their past and stable rather than their present and uncertain roles: e.g. 'His first-begot' (i 89), 'this new-declared' (i 121), 'King of Israel born' (i 254), 'composed of lies' (i 407), 'the new-baptized' (ii 1). Often it gives a clipped quality to the style, particularly where one would expect some expansion, as at the annunciation, 'Hail highly favoured, among women blest' (ii 68), and in Mary's ponderings, 'From Egypt home returned . . . Full grown to man, acknowledged . . . in public shown, / Son owned' (ii 79–85). The present participle, though less stationary, reduces the swift or sudden to the continuous or gradual: e.g. 'With dread *attending*' (i 53), 'on him *rising* / Out of the water' (i 80), 'the spirit *leading*' (i 189), 'Now *missing* him' (ii 9), 'So spake the old serpent *doubting*' (ii 147), '*Suffering, abstaining,* quietly *expecting*' (iii 192), '*Appearing,* and *beginning* noble deeds' (iv 99), '*Spreading* and *overshadowing* all the earth' (iv 148). It, too, helps to sleek the style: e.g. 'a star . . . in heaven *appearing* / Guided' (i 249–50), 'they found the place, / *Affirming* it thy star' (i 252–3) (Mary, again, is the speaker). Sometimes it is hedged by past participles to reduce what activity it has, as in the description of Roman games: 'by their sports to blood *inured* / Of *fighting* beasts, and men to beasts *exposed*' (iv 139–40), where what one would expect to be action-filled is almost motionless. At other times it is coupled with the past participle so that its active force is counter-balanced by passivity: e.g. 'Hated of all, and hating' (iv 97), 'men divinely taught, and better teaching' (iv 357)–Christ's correction of Satan's 'teaching not taught' (iv 220). The present participle 'unconniving' (i 363) seems to be M.'s only coinage in *PR*.

Another mannerism which establishes balance and stasis is the pairing of adjectives, nouns and verbs with 'and' or 'or'. This is extremely popular in *PR* i but very common in the later books too, especially in Satan's speeches. It is particularly noticeable when, as often, it edges on pleonasm: e.g. 'defeated and repulsed' (i 6), 'aghast and sad' (i 43), 'Distracted and surprized' (i 108), 'care / And management' (i 111–2), 'pre-ordained and fixed' (i 127), 'path or road' (i 322), 'town or village' (i 332) etc. The triple grouping of adjectives, nouns, or verbs, though less in evidence than pairing, is still a very distinct feature of all four books: e.g. 'obscure, / Unmarked, unknown' (i 24–5), 'good, or fair, / Or virtuous' (i 381–2), 'holy wise and pure' (i 486), 'found him, viewed him, tasted him' (ii 131), 'cottage, herd or sheep-cote' (ii 288), 'virtue, valour, wisdom' (ii 431) 'Passions, desires, and fears' (ii 467) etc. Both devices imply leisure and expansiveness and thus counteract any suggestion of haste which the abbreviated participial syntax might introduce.

In spite of M.'s comment upon Satan's 'persuasive rhetoric' (iv 4), his speeches are no more marked by rhetorical figures than Christ's, or the narrator's, and no one in PR uses the various repetitive figures as freely as they are employed in PL or SA. The narrator's opening paragraph (i 1–7) is bound together by traductio, anaphora, agnomination and ploce ('sung ... By one man's disobedience ... sing ... mankind ... By one man's obedience ... temptation ... tempter'), and he is later responsible for some of the most closely schematized moments in the poem: e.g. ii 9–12 (which includes one of the few examples of anadiplosis), ii 287–8, iv 13 (epanalepsis), iv 565–71 ('foiled ... fall ... fell ... foil ... fell ... fall'). Ploce, the most common figure, is used by everyone, including Mary (i 233, 238–9). She, like the disciples, is more fond of rhetoric than Belial, a plain speaker who limits himself to a modest anaphora (ii 170–1). Traductio comes next in frequency to ploce and is, with it, the habitual weapon in the Christ / Satan exchanges: e.g. iii 44–107, where Christ, picking up Satan's five uses of 'glory' and 'inglorious' in the previous speech, replies with 'glory' or 'glorious' eleven times, and Satan follows (iii 109–20) with 'glory' or 'glorified' eight times; and iv 182–7, where Christ's four uses of 'given' or 'giver' parry Satan's 'give ... given ... give ... gift' (iv 163–9). Traductio is so natural to Christ that he uses it even in meditation (e.g. ii 249–51 'need ... needing', ii 258 'fed ... feed'), and so does his mother (ii 71–2 'birth ... bore ... born'). Satan attempts to rouse Christ by climax, 'Thy actions to *thy words* accord, *thy words* / To thy large *heart* give utterance due, thy *heart* / Contains of good, wise, just, the perfect shape' (iii 9–11), and Christ mimics the figure in reply, 'Thou neither dost persuade me to seek wealth / For *empire's* sake, nor *empire* to affect / For *glory's* sake ... For what is *glory* but the blaze of fame, / The *people's* praise, if always *praise* unmixed? / And what the *people* ...' (iii 44–9). Satan employs anadiplosis once or twice in his arguments (i 404–5, iv 90–1, iv 382–3); Christ, only once, and then in his joyful meditation upon the revelation which accompanied his baptism, 'me his, / Me his beloved Son' (i 284–5; cp. his anaphora eight lines earlier, 'Me him ... Me him'). More usually the distinction between Christ's rhetoric and Satan's, where any distinction can be made, is that Christ turns to rigorously intellectual and argumentative ends figures which Satan introduces to incite or to move. Compare Satan's emotional epistrophe (i 377–9) or the ploce, traductio and epizeuxis which make iii 203–24 one of the most elaborately patterned passages in the poem, with what is probably PR's most tightly figured section, the opening of Christ's reply to the learning-temptation (iv 286–92), with its two epanalepses within four lines (unparalleled elsewhere in the poem).

By the time the rhetorical figuring wears thinnest, in Satan's panoramas, the poem has started to take on a richness of which its opening movements are bare. It derives this partly from the exotic name catalogues which cluster round each of the later temptations (ii 347, 360–1; iii 270–93, 316–21; iv

*70–9, 257, 259, 271*: M. uses the unusual and grandiose 'Melesigenes' (see iv *259n*) to help Athens vie with the splendid nomenclature of Rome). The first of these catalogues is at ii *20–4*: another enlivens the hellish consistory (ii *186–8*). Christ's replies, as usual, show their command of the Satanic armoury by exploiting this device for their own ends (ii *446*, iv *117–8*) so as to prove that width of knowledge and a generous imagination are not the tempter's prerogatives. Similes also grow less rare as the poem proceeds (though never plentiful). Christ's 'like a fawning parasite' (i *452*) is apparently the only example in the first book. Belial's wistful memory of women 'passing fair / As the noon sky' (ii *155–6*) is almost alone in the second, if we exclude a number of typological parallels, as is Satan's 'shading cool / Interposition, as a summer's cloud' (iii *221–2*) in the third. By comparison the fourth book is richly illustrated. Besides the epic similes which colour its opening (iv *10–20*) and its climax (iv *563–75*), and Christ's employment of the biblical tree and stone (iv *147–50*), it has Christ's beautifully aloof dismissal of the erudite, 'collecting toys, . . . As children gathering pebbles on the shore' (iv *328–30*), his scorn for a style less spare than his own, 'swelling epithets thick-laid / As varnish on a harlot's cheek' (iv *343–4*), Satan's admission that Christ has stood 'as a rock / Of adamant, and as a centre, firm' (iv *533–4*: an image which looks back to Christ as rock in iv *18*), the fairytale Temple, 'like a mount / Of alabaster, topped with golden spires' (iv *547–8*) and the angelic prophecy of Satan's fall from heaven, 'like an autumnal star / Or lightning' (iv *619–20*). Asyndeton and polysyndeton, grudgingly admitted into the first book (e.g. i *117, 178–9, 413–4*) help the progressive enrichment by a more liberal appearance in the second (ii *81, 131, 422, 460, 464*), and grow to their most spacious proportions in the last (e.g. iv *36–8, 386–8*).

The spectacular visual aids with which Satan drives home his points— the banquet, the Parthian army, Rome, Athens—grow successively more actual. Contrasted with the first bleak stones-into-bread temptation, the banquet (ii *340–367*) might seem resplendently solid, but M.'s description of it is carefully remote, and its instantaneous disappearance (ii *402–3*) as well as the suspiciously supernatural setting, 'the haunt of wood-gods or wood-nymphs', help to shift it, in the reader's mind, to the realm of mirage and illusion, in spite of M.'s insistence that it is 'no dream' (ii *337*). It is in part the generous concessiveness of the description which dissipates its actuality: 'beasts of chase, *or* fowl of game, / In pastry built, *or* from the spit *or* boiled', 'And all the while harmonious airs were heard / Of chiming strings, *or* charming pipes'. The repetition, or . . . or, leaves us to make up our own minds, so that instead of forming a defined image we remain in doubt about what was actually seen and heard. Similarly total inclusiveness lands us back at the generality of the generic: '*all* fish from sea or shore, / Freshet, or purling brook, of shell or fin', cannot be grasped like 'cod' or 'oyster', but retain the mistiness of mere 'fish', like the later 'fruits and flowers'. The concentration upon the names of the fish, 'exquisitest named', which at the same time witholds those names, and the switching of the reader's attention from the table to his atlas, 'Pontus and Lucrine bay, and Afric coast', and then to myth and finally to romance, are other ruses of M.'s to prevent the banquet hardening into anything eatable, while 'more distant', 'feigned' and 'fabled' conspire to smudge what outline the scene had, some time before it finally vanishes. Even the smells, often thought blind M.'s strong point, contradict and confuse: early spring scents ('Flora's earliest smells') would be swamped by the spicier 'Arabian odours'. To reply that epic decorum demands that this whole description should be remote and general is to ignore the kitchen-worthy 'pastry', the one bit of the banquet Christ could have got his teeth into. Besides, low terms ('waggons') and technical terms ('Cuirassiers') are not expelled from the Parthian-army description (iii *303–45*). This description, with its detailed observation of 'steel bows', 'coats of mail' and 'elephants endorsed with towers / Of archers', provides more palpable ingredients than the banquet, but keeps itself just beyond the range of exact vision by some of the same subterfuges. Confusion, as with the banquet's odours, is introduced by the contradiction of 'All horsemen' and 'Nor wanted clouds of foot'; the same unsettling concessiveness appears in the repetition of 'or' and 'nor' in *327–34*, and first the atlas (*316–21*) then the romances (*337–43*) deflect the eye from the army, while giving a vague impression of pomp and splendour. The few details of dress and armour are counteracted by sweeping strokes which seem to block in the general shapes of the formations, 'rhombs and wedges, and half-moons and wings' and 'clouds', but which actually, by the words used, turn the attention to a variety of non-military contexts. 'Coats of mail' is blurred by zeugma which merges it into an abstraction, 'In coats of mail and military pride'. 'Numbers numberless' designedly thwarts the numerical imagination, and 'The field all iron cast a gleaming brown' applies a wash into which any previously-grasped details vanish. And the reader's understanding is dimmed by what seem to be incompatible military operations going on at the same time. What is happening to the Parthian army? According to Satan it is just leaving its quarters in Ctesiphon to march the 1,200-odd miles to the border province of Sogdiana where the Scythians are proving troublesome: 'they issued forth' and 'The city gates outpoured' back up this impression. But a moment later the army is not in march formation but in 'forms of battle ranged' with 'each horn' extended, and engaging in battle with some unspecified 'pursuers'. When the reader entered the geographical catalogue at *316* he was with an army just marching out of a friendly city. When he leaves it six lines later he is with an army deployed for battle and engaged. Later he is returned to the pioneers and the baggage train, still apparently strung out on the column of march.

The Roman panorama (iv *27–85*) is, by contrast, situated in almost painstakingly specific surroundings, 'Another plain, long but in breadth not wide; / Washed by the southern sea, and on the north / To equal length backed with a ridge of hills . . . in the midst / Divided by a river'. The pace swiftly changes to a pelting generality, however, with 'Porches and theatres, baths, aqueducts, / Statues and trophies, and triumphal arcs, / Gardens and groves', which leaves the eye behind in despair after the pictorially precise opening. From this welter Satan's pointing finger rescues two particulars, 'there the Capitol thou seest' and 'there Mount Palatine', though the first is deprived of architectural immediacy by personification, and the second quickly slides back into the muddled splendour, 'Turrets and terraces, and glittering spires'. After this the uncertain picture breaks up into suggestions of myth, 'Houses of gods', and of illusion, 'my airy microscope', and into its raw materials, 'cedar, marble, ivory or gold', to be lost at length in the usual geographical fanfare, with one last glimpse of 'Dusk faces with white silken turbans wreathed' on the roads out of Rome.

The last vision, Athens (iv 238–80), though the least gorgeous, is the most defined. Specification is constant throughout it: 'Look ... Westward much nearer by south-west, behold / Where on the Aegean shore a city stands', 'See there the olive-grove of Academe', 'There flowery hill Hymettus', 'there Ilissus rolls', 'Lyceum there, and painted Stoa next', 'Socrates, see there his tenement'. Unlike the contradictory scents of the first vision, the three sounds of Athens blend into a lulling but insistent accompaniment to the sight-seeing: the murmur of bees on Hymettus, the whispering river, and the nightingale which 'Trills her thick-warbled notes the summer long'.

The progress from remoteness to definition in the four visions, making the poem gradually more alive for eye and ear, is in part matched by the flowering of the wilderness between the first book and the last. Starting as a place of 'dark shades and rocks' (i 194) and 'stones' (i 343), a 'barren waste' (i 354), it ends up 'fresh and green', its plants and trees dripping with water, and birds singing 'in bush and spray' (iv 433–8); Eden is 'raised in the waste wilderness'. However the delineation of the wilderness is less neat than this implies. Christ calls it 'barren' (i 354), and the seventeenth-century sense of this, applied to land, is given by the OED as 'producing little or no vegetation; not fertile, sterile, unproductive, bare'. The only other occurrence of the word in the poem is at iii 264 where it is applied to the Persian desert, 'barren desert fountainless and dry'. Travellers in the wilderness are said to die of 'hunger' and 'drouth' (i 325), and in it Christ says he suffers 'thirst / And hunger' (iv 120–1). Yet the wilderness is also, richly wooded, (i 305–6, 502, ii 246, 263, iv 416–7) and damp (i 306, 318, iv 406, 411–12), supporting an abundance of wildlife (i 310–13, 501–2), grassy (ii 282) and, to all appearances, suitable for raising sheep (i 315, ii 287). It most resembles the wood in which the Lady of Comus wanders: both represent spiritual pilgrimage, each has its false shepherd, each is called a maze (PR ii 246 'this woody maze', Comus 180 'the blind mazes of this tangled wood'), the Lady rests on 'a grassy turf' (Comus 279), Christ on a 'grassy couch' (PR ii 282). It seems possible that M.'s attempt to amalgamate the allegorical 'woody maze' and the bare, rocky desert which later grows green has obscured both elements of the combination.

The echoes of other writers are not very frequent in PR. Scraps of Virgilian phraseology are turned to account on seven or eight occasions, and there are half a dozen recollections each of Giles Fletcher and Shakespeare (see footnotes). Spenserian diction lends colour to passages of chivalric comparison (e.g. 'prowest' and 'paynim' iii *342–3*) or nationalistic eloquence 'fulmined' iv *270*), and the disciples are made into a fishy pastoral by fusing the first line of Spenser's *Shepheardes Calender* with Phineas Fletcher's imitation of it in his *Piscatory Eclogues* (see ii *27n*).

## THE FIRST BOOK

I who erewhile the happy garden sung,
By one man's disobedience lost, now sing
Recovered Paradise to all mankind,
By one man's firm obedience fully tried
5  Through all temptation, and the tempter foiled
In all his wiles, defeated and repulsed,
And Eden raised in the waste wilderness.
    Thou spirit who led'st this glorious eremite

¶ i *1. I who erewhile*] Echoes *Aen.* i 1–4 (lines probably by Virgil, but later excised, in which he takes his farewell of pastoral and rural poetry): *Ille ego, qui quondam gracili modulatus avena / carmen. . . .*, and Spenser's imitation, *F.Q.* I introd. 1–4: 'Lo! I, the man whose Muse whylome did maske, / As time her taught, in lowly Shephards weeds, / Am now enforst, a farre unfitter taske, / For trumpets sterne to chaunge mine Oaten reeds.' Lewalski 6 comments: 'by the allusion to *PL* as a poem about a "happy garden", M. seems to imply that he has now graduated from pastoral apprentice work to the true epic subject.' She quotes (116–7) openings of other biblical epics which imitate these Virgilian lines.

i *2–4*. Cp. *Rom.* v 19: 'For as by one man's disobedience many were made sinners, so by the obedience of one shall many be made righteous.'

i *7*. Cp. *Isa.* li 3: 'He will comfort all her waste places; and he will make her wilderness like Eden, and her desert like the garden of the Lord', and Spenser, *Virgil's Gnat* 369–70: 'I carried am into waste wildernesse, / Waste wildernes, amongst Cymerian shades.'

i *8. spirit*] Pope 27–9 considers that M. here follows the orthodox line in interpreting the unspecified 'spirit' of *Luke* iv 1 as the Holy Ghost. As M. Kelley, *SP* xxxii (1935) 221–34, remarks, however, the fact that M. here invokes the 'spirit' means that it is unlikely it is to be taken as the Holy Ghost, since M. in *De doctrina* insists that the Holy Ghost should not be invoked. Robins 173 suggests that what is here referred to is Christ's own spirit, given to him at the time of his baptism, when the power and virtue of the Father were bestowed upon the Son and symbolized by the descending dove.

i *8–9. eremite . . . desert*] Greek ἐρημίτης (hermit) means, literally, 'desert-dweller'.

Into the desert, his victorious field
10   Against the spiritual foe, and brought'st him thence
By proof the undoubted Son of God, inspire,
As thou art wont, my prompted song else mute,
And bear through highth or depth of nature's bounds
With prosperous wing full summed to tell of deeds
15   Above heroic, though in secret done,
And unrecorded left through many an age,
Worthy t' have not remained so long unsung.
     Now had the great proclaimer with a voice
More awful than the sound of trumpet, cried
20   Repentance, and heaven's kingdom nigh at hand
To all baptized: to his great baptism flocked
With awe the regions round, and with them came
From Nazareth the son of Joseph deemed
To the flood Jordan, came as then obscure,
25   Unmarked, unknown; but him the Baptist soon
Descried, divinely warned, and witness bore

i *9. victorious field*] The concept of the temptation as a martial combat was, as Pope 115–20 demonstrates, a well-established aspect of the tradition, and though Michael cautions Adam against it, *PL* xii 386–95, it is employed throughout *PR* (see i 158, 174; iv 562–70 etc.). The final anthem, iv 604–9, draws the parallel between this duel on earth and the previous one in heaven.
i *12. As thou art wont*] Robins 168 takes these words to mean that the Muse of *PR* is the same as that of *PL*, and he identifies this Muse (Urania), in spite of the sex being female, with the Logos. Newton, in the 'Life' prefixed to his 1778 edn of *PL*, reports that M.'s third wife said that 'her husband used to compose his poetry chiefly in winter, and on his waking in a morning would make her write down sometimes twenty or thirty verses; and being asked whether he did not often read Homer and Virgil, she understood it as an imputation upon him for stealing from these authors, and answered with eagerness that he stole from nobody but the Muse who inspired him, and being asked by a lady present who the Muse was, replied it was God's grace and the Holy Spirit that visited him nightly'. Cp. *PL* i 6–22.
i *14. full summed*] wanting none of its feathers; a term from falconry.
i *16. unrecorded*] not in the modern sense, since they were recorded in the gospels, but 'unsung'. 'Record' was particularly used of birdsong in the seventeenth century.
i *18. great proclaimer*] John the Baptist.
i *20.* Cp. *Matt.* iii 2: 'Repent ye: for the kingdom of heaven is at hand.'
i *23. son of Joseph deemed*] Cp. *Luke* iii 23: 'being (as was supposed) the son of Joseph'.
i *26. divinely warned*] Cp. *John* i 33: 'And I knew him not; but he that sent me to baptize with water, the same said unto me, Upon whom thou shalt

As to his worthier, and would have resigned
To him his heavenly office, nor was long
His witness unconfirmed: on him baptized
*30*   Heaven opened, and in likeness of a dove
The Spirit descended, while the Father's voice
From heaven pronounced him his beloved Son.
That heard the adversary, who roving still
About the world, at that assembly famed
*35*   Would not be last, and with the voice divine
Nigh thunder-struck, the exalted man, to whom
Such high attest was given, a while surveyed
With wonder, then with envy fraught and rage
Flies to his place, nor rests, but in mid air
*40*   To council summons all his mighty peers,
Within thick clouds and dark tenfold involved,
A gloomy consistory; and them amidst
With looks aghast and sad he thus bespake.
    O ancient powers of air and this wide world,
*45*   For much more willingly I mention air,
This our old conquest, than remember hell
Our hated habitation; well ye know
How many ages, as the years of men,
This universe we have possessed, and ruled
*50*   In manner at our will the affairs of earth,

see the Spirit descending, and remaining on him, the same is he which baptizeth with the Holy Ghost.'

i *30–2.* Cp. *Matt.* iii 16–7: 'He saw the Spirit of God descending like a dove: And lo a voice from heaven, saying, This is my beloved Son, in whom I am well pleased.'

i *33. adversary*] Satan (which means 'adversary' in Hebrew).    *still*] continually.

i *33–4.* Cp. *Job* i 7: 'And the Lord said unto Satan, Whence comest thou? Then Satan answered the Lord and said, From going to and fro in the earth, and from walking up and down in it.'

i *37. attest*] attestation.

i *39. place*] home; cp. *Job* vii 10: 'He shall return no more to his house, neither shall his place know him any more.'    *mid air*] Cp. *Eph.* ii 2, the origin of the belief that the devils inhabit and rule over the air, where Satan is called 'Prince of the power of the air'.

i *42. consistory*] An ironic reference to the ecclesiastical senate in which the Pope presides over the body of Cardinals, and to the bishop's court for ecclesiastical cases in the Anglican church. Each of these bodies had the title 'consistory'.

i *48. as the years of men*] By human computation.

Since Adam and his facile consort Eve
Lost Paradise deceived by me, though since
With dread attending when that fatal wound
Shall be inflicted by the seed of Eve
55  Upon my head, long the decrees of heaven
Delay, for longest time to him is short;
And now too soon for us the circling hours
This dreaded time have compassed, wherein we
Must bide the stroke of that long-threatened wound,
60  At least if so we can, and by the head
Broken be not intended all our power
To be infringed, our freedom and our being
In this fair empire won of earth and air;
For this ill news I bring, the woman's seed
65  Destined to this, is late of woman born,
His birth to our just fear gave no small cause,
But his growth now to youth's full flower, displaying
All virtue, grace and wisdom to achieve
Things highest, greatest, multiplies my fear.
70  Before him a great prophet, to proclaim
His coming, is sent harbinger, who all
Invites, and in the consecrated stream
Pretends to wash off sin, and fit them so
Purified to receive him pure, or rather
75  To do him honour as their king; all come,
And he himself among them was baptized,
Not thence to be more pure, but to receive
The testimony of heaven, that who he is
Thenceforth the nations may not doubt; I saw
80  The prophet do him reverence; on him rising
Out of the water, heaven above the clouds

i *51. facile*] easily led.
i *53. attending*] waiting (qualifies 'me'). *when*] until. *wound*] Cp. *Gen.*
iii 15: 'And I will put enmity between thee and the woman, and between
thy seed and her seed; it shall bruise thy head, and thou shalt bruise his heel.'
i 56. Cp. *Ps.* xc 4: 'A thousand years in thy sight are but as yesterday.'
i 57. *circling hours*] Cp. *PL* vi 3; echoing *Aen.* i 234: *volventibus annis.*
i *60-1. by the head | Broken*] by the prophecy about my head being broken.
i 62. *infringed*] broken (Latin *infrangere*).
i 73. *pretends*] claims. Satan, in his sarcasm, gives the word something also
of its modern sense (already current in the seventeenth century).
i 74. Cp. *1 John* iii 3: 'Every man that hath this hope in him purifieth him-
self, even as he is pure.'
i *80. on him rising*] when he rose.

Unfold her crystal doors, thence on his head
A perfect dove descend, whate'er it meant,
And out of heaven the sovran voice I heard,
85   This is my son beloved, in him am pleased.
His mother then is mortal, but his sire
He who obtains the monarchy of heaven,
And what will he not do to advance his son?
His first-begot we know, and sore have felt,
90   When his fierce thunder drove us to the deep;
Who this is we must learn, for man he seems
In all his lineaments, though in his face
The glimpses of his father's glory shine.
Ye see our danger on the utmost edge
95   Of hazard, which admits no long debate,
But must with something sudden be opposed,
Not force, but well-couched fraud, well-woven snares,
Ere in the head of nations he appear
Their king, their leader, and supreme on earth.
100   I, when no other durst, sole undertook
The dismal expedition to find out
And ruin Adam, and the exploit performed
Successfully; a calmer voyage now
Will waft me; and the way found prosperous once
105   Induces best to hope of like success.

i *82. doors*] Cp. *Ps.* lxxviii 23: 'Though he had commanded the clouds from above, and opened the doors of heaven.'

i *83. dove*] Cp. *Matt.* iii 16: 'And he saw the Spirit of God descending like a dove.'     *whate'er it meant*] M. in *De doctrina* I vi (Columbia xiv 367) is similarly doubtful: 'The descent therefore and appearance of the Holy Spirit in the likeness of a dove, seems to have been nothing more than a representation of the ineffable affection of the Father for the Son, communicated by the Holy Spirit under the appropriate image of a dove, and accompanied by a voice from heaven declaratory of that affection.'

i *87. obtains*] holds (Latin *obtinere*) a sense common from the fifteenth-century.

i *89–91.* As W. G. Rice, *Papers of the Michigan Academy* xxii (1936) 495–6 notes, these lines lend support to the theory that Satan's attempt to discover Christ's real nature is an element of the poem's action. A possible reply is that Satan is here speaking in public, so his words cannot be taken at their face value.

i *94–5. the utmost edge / Of hazard*] Echoes *All's Well* III iii 6: 'to th'extreme edge of hazard'.

i *97. couched*] concealed.

i *100.* Cp. *PL* ii 430–66, where Satan volunteers to undertake the journey to earth.

He ended, and his words impression left
Of much amazement to the infernal crew,
Distracted and surprised with deep dismay
At these sad tidings; but no time was then
110    For long indulgence to their fears or grief:
Unanimous they all commit the care
And management of this main enterprise
To him their great dictator, whose attempt
At first against mankind so well had thrived
115    In Adam's overthrow, and led their march
From hell's deep-vaulted den to dwell in light,
Regents and potentates, and kings, yea gods
Of many a pleasant realm and province wide.
So to the coast of Jordan he directs
120    His easy steps; girded with snaky wiles,
Where he might likeliest find this new-declared,
This man of men, attested Son of God,
Temptation and all guile on him to try;
So to subvert whom he suspected raised
125    To end his reign on earth so long enjoyed:
But contrary unweeting he fulfilled
The purposed counsel pre-ordained and fixed
Of the Most High, who in full frequence bright
Of angels, thus to Gabriel smiling spake.
130        Gabriel this day by proof thou shalt behold,
Thou and all angels conversant on earth
With man or men's affairs, how I begin
To verify that solemn message late,
On which I sent thee to the virgin pure
135    In Galilee, that she should bear a son
Great in renown, and called the Son of God;
Then told'st her doubting how these things could be

i *113. dictator*] Z. S. Fink, *JEGP* xl (1941) 482–8, takes this title in its seven-
teenth-century political sense of a person or council granted unlimited
but temporary power in a time of national emergency. Harrington in
*Oceana* included a dictator as a necessary part of a commonwealth, but M.,
in his *Ready and Easy Way*, did not. Satan's ineffectiveness as a dictator in
*PR* amounts, in Fink's estimation, to a comment about political theory.
i *117. gods*] As in *PL* M. identifies the pagan gods with the fallen angels.
i *120. girded with snaky wiles*] In contrast to *Isa.* xi 5: 'righteousness shall be
the girdle of his loins', and *Eph.* vi 14: 'having your loins girt about with
truth'.
i *128. frequence*] attendance.
i *129. Gabriel*] guardian of Eden in *PL* iv, and the angel of the Annunciation.
i *134–40.* Cp. *Luke* i 26–38.

To her a virgin, that on her should come
The Holy Ghost, and the power of the Highest
*140* O'ershadow her: this man born and now upgrown,
To show him worthy of his birth divine
And high prediction, henceforth I expose
To Satan; let him tempt and now assay
His utmost subtlety, because he boasts
*145* And vaunts of his great cunning to the throng
Of his apostasy; he might have learnt
Less overweening, since he failed in Job,
Whose constant perseverance overcame
Whate'er his cruel malice could invent.
*150* He now shall know I can produce a man
Of female seed, far abler to resist
All his solicitations, and at length
All his vast force, and drive him back to hell,
Winning by conquest what the first man lost
*155* By fallacy surprised. But first I mean
To exercise him in the wilderness,

i *146. apostasy*] the apostate angels.

i *147. overweening*] arrogance.       *Job*] the first of five references to him in
*PR* (see i 369, 425; iii 64–7, 95). The *Book of Job* was the model M. suggested
for the 'brief' epic (Columbia iii 237, Yale i 813). Hughes[2] 264 considers
that M. may have been indebted to it in *PR* conceptually as well as structu-
rally: 'Job had come to be recognized as the greatest exemplar of the
Christian version of Aristotle's high-mindedness or magnanimity.' Pos-
sibly, too, M. thought that the *Book of Job* was epic in its verse form: C.W.
Jones, *SP* xliv (1947) 209–27 draws attention to the belief held by Jerome,
Origen and others of the Fathers that Hebrew poetry was metrical in a
Greek sense: Jerome, in the introduction to his translation of *Job*, says that
the verse part is mainly in hexameters.

Lewalski 112 quotes from Gregory *Moralia in Job* as a precedent for re-
lating Job and Christ as heroes exhibited by God: 'God's saying to Satan in
figure, *Hast thou considered my servant Job*, is His exhibiting in his despite the
Only-Begotten Son as an object of wonder in the form of a servant.'

i *152–3*. The distinction between 'solicitations' and 'force' foreshadows
that between the earlier trials and those of the storm and the pinnacle, which
entail violence.

i *156. exercise*] Cp. *De doctrina* i 8 (Columbia xv 86–7): 'A good temptation
is that whereby God tempts even the righteous for the purpose of proving
them, not as though he were ignorant of the disposition of their hearts,
but for the purpose of exercising (*exercendam*) or manifesting their faith or
patience.'

There he shall first lay down the rudiments
Of his great warfare, ere I send him forth
To conquer Sin and Death the two grand foes,
*160*    By humiliation and strong sufferance:
His weakness shall o'ercome Satanic strength
And all the world, and mass of sinful flesh;
That all the angels and ethereal powers,
They now, and men hereafter may discern,
*165*    From what consummate virtue I have chose
This perfect man, by merit called my Son,
To earn salvation for the sons of men.
    So spake the eternal Father, and all heaven
Admiring stood a space; then into hymns
*170*    Burst forth, and in celestial measures moved,
Circling the throne and singing, while the hand
Sung with the voice, and this the argument.
    Victory and triumph to the Son of God
Now ent'ring his great duel, not of arms,
*175*    But to vanquish by wisdom hellish wiles.
The Father knows the Son; therefore secure
Ventures his filial virtue, though untried,
Against whate'er may tempt, whate'er seduce,
Allure, or terrify, or undermine.
*180*    Be frustrate all ye stratagems of hell,
And devilish machinations come to nought.
    So they in heaven their odes and vigils tuned:
Meanwhile the Son of God, who yet some days

---

i *157–8. the rudiments / Of his great warfare*] Echoes Virgil, *Aen.* xi 156–7
*bellique . . . rudimenta.*

i *159. Sin and Death*] Cp. *PL* ii 648–73 and x 585–609.

i *161.* Cp. *1 Cor.* i 27: 'God hath chosen the weak things of the world to
confound the things which are mighty.'

i *165–7.* A. P. Fiore, *Franciscan Studies* xv (1955) 48–59, 257–82, in his study
of M.'s soteriology, relates these lines to the definition of redemption in the
*De doctrina* (Columbia xv 252–3). This definition, however, does *not* raise
the question of Christ's 'merit'. Cp. *PL* iii 308–9 and vi 43.

i *171. hand*] the hand which played upon a stringed instrument.

i *172. argument*] subject, theme.

i *176. The Father knows the Son*] Cp. *John* x 15: 'As the Father knoweth me,
even so know I the Father.'    *secure*] without anxiety.

i *180. frustrate*] frustrated; a common form from the fifteenth century to
the seventeenth.

i *182. vigils*] night hymns.

Lodged in Bethabara where John baptized,
185    Musing and much revolving in his breast,
How best the mighty work he might begin
Of saviour to mankind, and which way first
Publish his godlike office now mature,
One day forth walked alone, the spirit leading
190    And his deep thoughts, the better to converse
With solitude, till far from track of men,
Thought following thought, and step by step led on,
He entered now the bordering desert wild,
And with dark shades and rocks environed round,
195    His holy meditations thus pursued.
        O what a multitude of thoughts at once
Awakened in me swarm, while I consider
What from within I feel myself, and hear
What from without comes often to my ears,
200    Ill sorting with my present state compared.
When I was yet a child, no childish play
To me was pleasing, all my mind was set
Serious to learn and know, and thence to do
What might be public good; myself I thought
205    Born to that end, born to promote all truth,
All righteous things: therefore above my years,
The Law of God I read, and found it sweet,
Made it my whole delight, and in it grew

i *184. Bethabara*] Cp. *John* i 28: 'These things were done in Bethabara beyond Jordan, where John was baptizing.'
i *189. spirit*] See i 8*n*. *1671* has a semicolon at the end of the line which is probably an error, though not corrected in the *Errata*. The sense seems to require no stop.
i *193. desert*] Though this is clearly the desert near Bethabara, i 350–4 and ii 306–14 appear to identify it with the wilderness of Beersheba where Hagar wandered and into which Elijah retreated, and with the wilderness of Sin where the Israelites were fed with manna. M. seems to have regarded the whole desert area of the near East as a single wilderness (see i 350–4*n*).
i *200. sorting*] corresponding.
i *204. What might be public good*] Schultz 80 reviews the traditional application of utility as a criterion of learning, which Christ's qualification here implies, and points to a similar emphasis in *Of Education*.
i *204–5*. Cp. *John* xviii 37: 'To this end was I born, and for this cause came I into the world, that I should bear witness unto the truth.'
i *206–7. above my years*] Perhaps echoing *Aen.* ix 311: *Ante annos animumque gerens curamque virilem* (with a man's mind and a spirit beyond his years).
i *208. delight*] Cp. *Ps.* i 2: 'But his delight is in the law of the Lord.'

To such perfection, that ere yet my age
210  Had measured twice six years, at our great feast
I went into the Temple, there to hear
The teachers of our Law, and to propose
What might improve my knowledge or their own;
And was admired by all, yet this not all
215  To which my spirit aspired, victorious deeds
Flamed in my heart, heroic acts, one while
To rescue Israel from the Roman yoke,
Thence to subdue and quell o'er all the earth
Brute violence and proud tyrannic power,
220  Till truth were freed, and equity restored:
Yet held it more humane, more heavenly first
By winning words to conquer willing hearts,
—And make persuasion do the work of fear; ——
At least to try, and teach the erring soul
225  Not wilfully misdoing, but unware
Misled; the stubborn only to subdue.
These growing thoughts my mother soon perceiving
By words at times cast forth inly rejoiced,
And said to me apart, High are thy thoughts
230  O son, but nourish them and let them soar
To what highth sacred virtue and true worth
Can raise them, though above example high;
By matchless deeds express thy matchless sire.
For know, thou art no son of mortal man,
235  Though men esteem thee low of parentage,
Thy father is the eternal King, who rules
All heaven and earth, angels and sons of men,
A messenger from God foretold thy birth
Conceived in me a virgin, he foretold
240  Thou shouldst be great and sit on David's throne,
And of thy kingdom there should be no end.
At thy nativity a glorious choir
Of angels in the fields of Bethlehem sung

i *209–14.* Cp. *Luke* ii 46–50, where Christ, at Passover time, astonishes the
doctors of the Law with his 'understanding and answers'.
i *214. admired*] wondered at.
i *226. subdue*] *1671* has 'destroy', corrected to 'subdue' in the *Errata.* Cp.
*Luke* ix 56: 'For the Son of man is not come to destroy men's lives.'
i *233. express*] make apparent.
i *238–54.* The details are taken from *Matt.* i–ii and *Luke* i–ii.
i *239–41.* Cp. *Luke* i 32–3: 'He shall be great . . . and the Lord God shall give
unto him the throne of his father David . . . and of his kingdom there shall
be no end.'

To shepherds watching at their folds by night,
245 And told them the Messiah now was born,
Where they might see him, and to thee they came,
Directed to the manger where thou lay'st,
For in the inn was left no better room:
A star, not seen before in heaven appearing
250 Guided the wise men thither from the east,
To honour thee with incense, myrrh, and gold,
By whose bright course led on they found the place,
Affirming it thy star new-graven in heaven,
By which they knew thee King of Israel born.
255 Just Simeon and prophetic Anna, warned
By vision, found thee in the Temple, and spake
Before the altar and the vested priest,
Like things of thee to all that present stood.
This having heard, straight I again revolved
260 The Law and prophets, searching what was writ
Concerning the Messiah, to our scribes
Known partly, and soon found of whom they spake
I am; this chiefly, that my way must lie
Through many a hard assay even to the death,
265 Ere I the promised kingdom can attain,
Or work redemption for mankind, whose sins'
Full weight must be transferred upon my head.
Yet neither thus disheartened or dismayed,
The time prefixed I waited, when behold
270 The Baptist, (of whose birth I oft had heard,
Not knew by sight) now come, who was to come
Before Messiah and his way prepare.
I as all others to his baptism came,
Which I believed was from above; but he
275 Straight knew me, and with loudest voice proclaimed
Me him (for it was shown him so from heaven)
Me him whose harbinger he was; and first
Refused on me his baptism to confer,
As much his greater, and was hardly won;

i 255. *Just*] Cp. *Luke* ii 25: 'And the same man was just.'      *prophetic*] Cp.
*Luke* ii 36: 'And there was one Anna, a prophetess.'
i 258. This is the last line of Mary's speech.
i 264. *Through many a hard assay*] Echoes *F.Q.* II i 35: 'Through many hard
assayes'.
i 266-7. Cp. *Isa.* liii 6: 'The Lord hath laid on him the iniquity of us all.'
i 270-89. M. follows the accounts in *Matt.* iii, *Luke* iii and *Mark* i.
i 279. *hardly won*] persuaded with difficulty.

280    But as I rose out of the laving stream,
       Heaven opened her eternal doors, from whence
       The Spirit descended on me like a dove,
       And last the sum of all, my Father's voice,
       Audibly heard from heaven, pronounced me his,
285    Me his beloved Son, in whom alone
       He was well pleased; by which I knew the time
       Now full, that I no more should live obscure,
       But openly begin, as best becomes
       The authority which I derived from heaven.
290    And now by some strong motion I am led
       Into this wilderness, to what intent
       I learn not yet, perhaps I need not know;
       For what concerns my knowledge God reveals.
         So spake our morning star, then in his rise,
295    And looking round on every side beheld
       A pathless desert, dusk with horrid shades;
       The way he came not having marked, return
       Was difficult, by human steps untrod;
       And he still on was led, but with such thoughts
300    Accompanied of things past and to come
       Lodged in his breast, as well might recommend
       Such solitude before choicest society.
       Full forty days he passed, whether on hill
       Sometimes, anon in shady vale, each night
305    Under the covert of some ancient oak,
       Or cedar, to defend him from the dew,
       Or harboured in one cave, is not revealed;
       Nor tasted human food, nor hunger felt
       Till those days ended, hungered then at last
310    Among wild beasts: they at his sight grew mild,

i *281. eternal doors*] Cp. *Ps.* xxiv 7: 'everlasting doors'.
i *286–7. the time / Now full*] Cp. *Gal.* iv 4: 'When the fulness of time was come, God sent forth his Son.'
i *291–3.* Cp. *De doctrina* i 5 (Columbia xiv 316–7): 'Even the Son, however, knows not all things absolutely', and *Mark* xiii 32: 'But of that day and that hour knoweth no man, no, not the Son, but the Father.'
i *294. morning star*] Cp. *Rev.* xxii 16, where Jesus says 'I am . . . the bright and morning star'.
i *296. horrid*] bristling (Latin *horridus*).
i *310–13.* Pope 108–10 explains that it was part of the doctrinal tradition of the temptation story that the wild beasts did not molest Christ because he was perfect man. Cp. *Mark* i 3, the only mention of the wild beasts in the gospel accounts, also Giles Fletcher, *Christ's Victory and Triumph* i 40–1, where the animals frolic round Christ, the lion licking his feet and the lamb

Nor sleeping him nor waking harmed, his walk
The fiery serpent fled, and noxious worm,
The lion and fierce tiger glared aloof.
But now an aged man in rural weeds,
315  Following, as seemed, the quest of some stray ewe,
Or withered sticks to gather; which might serve
Against a winter's day when winds blow keen,
To warm him wet returned from field at eve,
He saw approach, who first with curious eye
320  Perused him, then with words thus uttered spake.
          Sir, what ill chance hath brought thee to this place
So far from path or road of men, who pass
In troop or caravan, for single none
Durst ever, who returned, and dropped not here
325  His carcase, pined with hunger and with drouth?
I ask the rather, and the more admire,
For that to me thou seem'st the man, whom late
Our new baptizing prophet at the ford
Of Jordan honoured so, and called thee Son
330  Of God; I saw and heard, for we sometimes
Who dwell this wild, constrained by want, come forth

and tiger standing side by side. Fletcher, like M., is here influenced by various Old Testament prophecies, e.g. *Ezek.* xxxiv 25, *Isa.* xi 6–9 and lxv 25.

i *312. noxious*] harmful. The line is based on *Micah* vii 17.

i *314. an aged man in rural weeds*] Hughes[2] 256 compares Satan's disguise with that of the fiend who 'in likeness of a man of religion' tries to bring Sir Bors into 'error and wanhope' in Malory, *Morte d'Arthur* xvi 13. Sources more usually suggested are Spenser, *F.Q.* I i 29, where Archimago appears as 'An aged Sire, in long blacke weedes yclad, / His feete all bare, his beard all hoarie gray', and Giles Fletcher, *Christ's Victory and Triumph* ii 15, where Satan comes to tempt Christ disguised as 'an aged Syre . . . slowely footing'. Pope 42–7 notes that from the fourteenth-century to the eighteenth writers and artists frequently assume that Satan comes into the wilderness in disguise: there was no general agreement about the disguise adopted. The most common was that of a benevolent old hermit, but he also appears as an old man of mean appearance, an old man richly dressed, and a handsome young man. Some artists and writers gave him three different disguises, one for each temptation (as M. seems to: see ii 298–300 and iv 449).

i *315–6*. Satan's apparent occupations relate to his usual occupation, looking for lost souls (strayed sheep) to burn. Cp. *John* xv 6: 'If a man abide not in me he is cast forth as a branch, and is withered; and men gather them, and cast them into the fire, and they are burned.'

i *324–5. dropped . . . carcase*] Cp. *Num.* xiv 29: 'Your carcases shall fall in this wilderness.'       *pined*] wasted away.

i *326. admire*] wonder.

To town or village nigh (nighest is far)
Where aught we hear, and curious are to hear,
What happens new; fame also finds us out.
335   To whom the Son of God. Who brought me hither
Will bring me hence, no other guide I seek.
      By miracle he may, replied the swain,
What other way I see not, for we here
Live on tough roots and stubs, to thirst inured
340   More than the camel, and to drink go far,
Men to much misery and hardship born;
But if thou be the Son of God, command
That out of these hard stones be made thee bread;
So shalt thou save thyself and us relieve
345   With food, whereof we wretched seldom taste.
      He ended, and the Son of God replied.
Think'st thou such force in bread? Is it not written
(For I discern thee other than thou seem'st)
Man lives not by bread only, but each word
350   Proceeding from the mouth of God; who fed
Our fathers here with manna; in the mount
Moses was forty days, nor eat nor drank,
And forty days Elijah without food
Wandered this barren waste, the same I now:
355   Why dost thou then suggest to me distrust,

i 332. nighest] the nearest town or village.

i 334. fame . . . out] rumour (Latin fama) reaches us too.

i 339. stubs] stumps of plants, shrubs or trees.

i 342–50. The original of this dialogue is Luke iv 3–4.

i 344. save thyself] See ii 245–59n.

i 349–50. Cp. Deut. viii 3: 'He . . . fed thee with manna . . . that he might make thee know that man doth not live by bread only, but by every word that proceedeth out of the mouth of the Lord.'

i 350–4. Cp. Exod. xxiv 18: 'Moses was in the mount forty days', when he received the commandments on Mt Sinai. It was, as Pope 110–12 shows, a well-documented branch of the tradition that identified the wilderness of the temptation with the desert in which the Jews wandered for forty years, and Moses and Elijah fasted for forty days. The typological appropriateness of this identification leads M. to adopt it. Other commentators, with more realistic geography, made the temptation-wilderness that between Jerusalem and Jericho.

i 353. In 1 Kings xix 8 Elijah travels to Mt Horeb for forty days and nights without food.

i 355. distrust] Pope 56–64 notes that M., in making the first temptation not one of gluttony but of distrust in God, follows Calvin and the Protestant theologians, (see iv 110–20n). He presents Eve's temptation (PL ix 703–5)

Knowing who I am, as I know who thou art?
    Whom thus answered the Arch-fiend now undis-
       guised.
'Tis true, I am that spirit unfortunate,
Who leagued with millions more in rash revolt
360 Kept not my happy station, but was driven
With them from bliss to the bottomless deep,
Yet to that hideous place not so confined
By rigour unconniving, but that oft
Leaving my dolorous prison I enjoy
365 Large liberty to round this globe of earth,
Or range in the air, nor from the heaven of heavens
Hath he excluded my resort sometimes.
I came among the sons of God, when he
Gave up into my hands Uzzean Job
370 To prove him, and illustrate his high worth;
And when to all his angels he proposed

as one of the same kind, thus preserving the traditional equation between those temptations Christ withstood and those to which Adam and Eve succumbed.

i *356. Knowing who I am*] Woodhouse 171–2 takes these words as proof that Satan's alleged doubt about Christ's identity is not real but 'assiduously fostered': 'He will not let himself acknowledge the truth'. E. L. Marilla, *Studia Neophilologica* xxvii (1955) 184, also assumes that this line destroys the theory that the temptations are Satan's attempt to establish Christ's identity. However, 'Knowing who I am' can merely mean 'Knowing that I am the Son of God': in this sense Satan knows who Christ is: what worries him is the meaning of that title.

i *363. unconniving*] unwinking, ever-vigilant; this is the only recorded example of the word; Cp. Lat. *inconivus*.

i *368–76.* Cp. *Job* i 6: 'The sons of God came to present themselves before the Lord, and Satan came also among them', and *1 Kings* xxii 20–2: 'And the Lord said, Who shall persuade Ahab, that he may go up and fall at Ramoth-gilead? And one said on this manner, and another said on that manner. And there came forth a spirit, and stood before the Lord, and said, I will persuade him. And the Lord said unto him, Wherewith? And he said, I will go forth, and I will be a lying spirit in the mouth of all his prophets.' The same encounter is related in *2 Chron.* xviii 19–22. The identification of this 'lying spirit' with Satan, and the coupling of the cases of Ahab and Job, may have been suggested by the margin of the A.V. which, at *2 Chron.* xviii 20, refers to *Job* i 6, or, as A. I. Carlisle, *RES* n.s. v (1954) 249–55, thinks, by Ludwig Lavater, *In Libros Chronicorum*, to which M. refers in *Trin. MS* when discussing *1 Kings* xxii.

i *369. Uzzean*] Cp. *Job* i 1: 'There was a man in the land of Uz whose name was Job.'

To draw the proud king Ahab into fraud
That he might fall in Ramoth, they demurring,
I undertook that office, and the tongues
375  Of all his flattering prophets glibbed with lies
To his destruction, as I had in charge.
For what he bids I do; though I have lost
Much lustre of my native brightness, lost
To be beloved of God, I have not lost
380  To love, at least contemplate and admire
What I see excellent in good, or fair,
Or virtuous, I should so have lost all sense.
What can be then less in me than desire
To see thee and approach thee, whom I know
385  Declared the Son of God, to hear attent
Thy wisdom, and behold thy godlike deeds?
Men generally think me much a foe
To all mankind: why should I? they to me
Never did wrong or violence, by them
390  I lost not what I lost, rather by them
I gained what I have gained, and with them dwell
Copartner in these regions of the world,
If not disposer; lend them oft my aid,
Oft my advice by presages and signs,
395  And answers, oracles, portents and dreams,

i 372. *fraud*] the state of being defrauded or deluded (Latin *fraus*); this sense of the word is not found outside M.

i 373. *they demurring*] while they hesitated.

i 375. *glibbed*] made smooth.

i 378. *brightness*] Cp. *PL* i 591–2, vii 132–3.

i 379–80. Cp. *PL* ii 482–3.

i 383. *What can be then less in me than desire*] This line has caused some difficulty. C. L. Barnes, *N & Q* clvi (1929) 440 and clvii (1929) 251, thought 'less' an error for 'more'; but E. Bensly, *N & Q* clvii (1929) 177–8, explains the meaning as 'How can I feel anything less than a desire too . . .'. Lewalski 351 agrees with Bensly, but praises the ironic *double-entendre*: the word-arrangement suggests the opposite and truer meaning, that there can be nothing Satan desires less than thus to confront and listen to Christ.

i 385. *attent*] attentive; a common seventeenth-century form.

i 393–6. Cp. ll. 430–3, 446–51, 455–64. The orthodox patristic view, put forward by Lactantius, *Divine Institutes* ii 16 and Eusebius, *Praeparatio Evangelica* ii, was that the fallen angels inhabited the shrines of the pagan oracles and made pronouncements in the names of the classical deities. In this they were aided by an ability to travel in spirit to any point on the earth's surface in a moment of time, and also by a foreknowledge of certain events retained from prelapsarian days.

Whereby they may direct their future life.
Envy they say excites me, thus to gain
Companions of my misery and woe.
At first it may be; but long since with woe
400 Nearer acquainted, now I feel by proof,
That fellowship in pain divides not smart,
Nor lightens aught each man's peculiar load.
Small consolation then, were man adjoined:
This wounds me most (what can it less) that man,
405 Man fall'n shall be restored, I never more.
    To whom our Saviour sternly thus replied.
Deservedly thou griev'st, composed of lies
From the beginning, and in lies wilt end;
Who boast'st release from hell, and leave to come
410 Into the heaven of heavens; thou com'st indeed,
As a poor miserable captive thrall,
Comes to the place where he before had sat
Among the prime in splendour, now deposed,
Ejected, emptied, gazed, unpitied, shunned,
415 A spectacle of ruin or of scorn
To all the host of heaven; the happy place
Imparts to thee no happiness, no joy,
Rather inflames thy torment, representing
Lost bliss, to thee no more communicable,
420 So never more in hell than when in heaven.
But thou art serviceable to heaven's King.
Wilt thou impute to obedience what thy fear
Extorts, or pleasure to do ill excites?
What but thy malice moved thee to misdeem
425 Of righteous Job, then cruelly to afflict him

i 401. *That fellowship . . . smart*] Cp. the Latin tag *solamen miseris socios habuisse doloris*, Englished in *Lucrece* 790 as 'fellowship in woe doth woe assuage'. Seneca, *De Consolatione* xii 5, considers that the solace that comes from having company in misery smacks of ill-will.

i 407. *composed of lies*] In *John* viii 44 Satan is called 'a liar, and the father of it'.

i 410–20. Though up to this point in the poem Christ has apparently no recollection of his heavenly existence before the incarnation, these lines seem to imply that memory is returning, or that God has granted illumination (see i 293). Lewalski 212, however, calls Christ's speech 'an imaginative recreation of the scene based upon traditional (Christian) exegesis of the Job story', and believes that Christ does not recollect his encounters with Satan in heaven until the tower temptation.

i 413. *prime*] foremost.

i 420. Cp. *PL* ix 467–70.

i 423. Cp. *PL* i 160.

With all inflictions, but his patience won?
The other service was thy chosen task,
To be a liar in four hundred mouths;
For lying is thy sustenance, thy food.
430    Yet thou pretend'st to truth; all oracles
By thee are given, and what confessed more true
Among the nations? that hath been thy craft,
By mixing somewhat true to vent more lies.
But what have been thy answers, what but dark
435    Ambiguous and with double sense deluding,
Which they who asked have seldom understood,
And not well understood as good not known?
Who ever by consulting at thy shrine
Returned the wiser, or the more instruct
440    To fly or follow what concerned him most,
And run not sooner to his fatal snare?
For God hath justly given the nations up
To thy delusions; justly, since they fell
Idolatrous, but when his purpose is
445    Among them to declare his providence
To thee not known, whence hast thou then thy truth,
But from him or his angels president
In every province, who themselves disdaining

i *428*. Cp. i 368–76*n*, and *1 Kings* xxii 6: 'Then the king of Israel gathered
the prophets together, about four hundred men, and said unto them, Shall
I go against Ramoth-gilead to battle, or shall I forbear? And they said, Go
up.'

i *433. vent*] utter.

i *434–5*. Cp. Cicero, *Of Divination* ii 56, of the oracle of Apollo: 'Chrysippus
filled a whole volume with your oracles; of these some, as I think, were false;
some came true by chance, as happens very often even in ordinary speech;
some were so intricate and obscure that their interpreter needs an interpreter
and the oracles themselves must be referred back to the oracle; and some so
equivocal that they require a dialectician to construe them.'

i *446–7. whence . . . But from him*] Aquinas, *Summa* II ii 172 (6) says, citing
Balaam as an example, that the pagan prophets were not always inspired
by devils but sometimes by God, and so spoke truth: thus, he explains, the
Sibyl foretold Christ's coming. Even when they were inspired by devils,
he adds, they sometimes told the truth, either through the intervention of
good spirits, or by virtue of the devils' own nature which was created by the
Holy Spirit, or because God used the devils to make the truth known and
revealed divine mysteries to them through the agency of angels.

i *447–8. angels president / In every province*] Cp. *De doctrina* I ix (Columbia
xv 102–3): 'It appears also probable that there are certain angels appointed
to preside over nations, kingdoms and particular districts.'

To approach thy temples, give thee in command
450  What to the smallest tittle thou shalt say
To thy adorers; thou with trembling fear,
Or like a fawning parasite obey'st;
Then to thyself ascrib'st the truth foretold.
But this thy glory shall be soon retrenched;
455  No more shalt thou by oracling abuse
The Gentiles; henceforth oracles are ceased,
And thou no more with pomp and sacrifice
Shalt be inquired at Delphos or elsewhere,
At least in vain, for they shall find thee mute.
460  God hath now sent his living oracle
Into the world, to teach his final will,
And sends his spirit of truth henceforth to dwell
In pious hearts, an inward oracle
To all truth requisite for men to know.
465     So spake our Saviour; but the subtle Fiend,
Though inly stung with anger and disdain,
Dissembled, and this answer smooth returned.
Sharply thou hast insisted on rebuke,
And urged me hard with doings, which not will
470  But misery hath wrested from me; where
Easily canst thou find one miserable,
And not enforced oft-times to part from truth;
If it may stand him more in stead to lie,
Say and unsay, feign, flatter, or abjure?
475  But thou art placed above me, thou art Lord;
From thee I can and must submiss endure
Check or reproof, and glad to scape so quit.
Hard are the ways of truth, and rough to walk,
Smooth on the tongue discoursed, pleasing to the ear,
480  And tunable as sylvan pipe or song;
What wonder then if I delight to hear
Her dictates from thy mouth? Most men admire
Virtue, who follow not her lore: permit me
To hear thee when I come (since no man comes)
485  And talk at least, though I despair to attain.

i 454. *retrenched*] done away with.
i 455. *oracling*] A rare word but not M.'s coinage; first recorded 1656.
i 456. *oracles are ceased*] Cp. *Nativity Ode* 173, and *Micah* v 12.
i 458. *Delphos*] Cp. *Nativity Ode* 178.
i 462. *spirit of truth*] Cp. *John* xvi 13: 'Howbeit, when he, the Spirit of truth, is come, he will guide you into all truth.'
i 466. *disdain*] anger, vexation.
i 477. *scape so quit*] escape with so light a quittance as a reproof.

Thy father, who is holy, wise and pure,
Suffers the hypocrite or atheous priest
To tread his sacred courts, and minister
About his altar, handling holy things,
490 Praying or vowing, and vouchsafed his voice
To Balaam reprobate, a prophet yet
Inspired; disdain not such access to me.
To whom our Saviour with unaltered brow.
Thy coming hither, though I know thy scope,
495 I bid not or forbid; do as thou find'st
Permission from above; thou canst not more.
He added not; and Satan bowing low
His grey dissimulation, disappeared
Into thin air diffused: for now began
500 Night with her sullen wing to double-shade
The desert, fowls in their clay nests were couched;
And now wild beasts came forth the woods to roam.


## THE SECOND BOOK

Meanwhile the new-baptized, who yet remained
At Jordan with the Baptist, and had seen
Him whom they heard so late expressly called
Jesus Messiah Son of God declared,
5 And on that high authority had believed,

i 490–2¹ When Balak, King of Moab, urged Balaam to curse the Israelites,
he replied, *Num.* xxiii 20: 'Behold, I have received commandment to bless:
and he hath blessed; and I cannot reverse it.' Fixler 254 notes that, while
Christian writers maintained an attitude of unrelieved blackness towards
Balaam, Jewish tradition was mixed, regarding him at times as a prophet
on a level with Moses.
i *494. scope*] drift, purpose.
i *495–6*. Cp. *PL* iv 1006–9.
i *498. grey dissimulation*] Perhaps an echo of Ford, *Broken Heart* IV ii 101:
'Lay by thy whining grey dissimulation.'
i *499. Into thin air diffused*] Echoes Virgil's account of the disappearance of
Mercury, *Aen.* iv 278: *procul in tenuem ex oculis evanuit auram* (vanished into
thin air, far from the eyes of men).
i *500. sullen*] dark in colour. The 'sullen wing' probably echoes *Aen.* viii
369: *Nox ruit et fuscis tellurem amplectitur alis* (night rushes down and clasps
the earth with dusky wings).     *double-shade*] Cp. *Comus* 335 and Ovid,
*Met.* xi 549–50: 'The shadows of the pitchy clouds hide all the sky and double
the darkness of the night.'

And with him talked, and with him lodged, I mean
Andrew and Simon, famous after known
With others though in Holy Writ not named,
Now missing him their joy so lately found,
*10*    So lately found, and so abruptly gone,
Began to doubt, and doubted many days,
And as the days increased, increased their doubt:
Sometimes they thought he might be only shown,
And for a time caught up to God, as once
*15*    Moses was in the mount, and missing long;
And the great Thisbite who on fiery wheels
Rode up to heaven, yet once again to come.
Therefore as those young prophets then with care
Sought lost Elijah, so in each place these
*20*    Nigh to Bethabara, in Jericho
.The city of palms, Aenon, and Salem old,
Machaerus and each town or city walled
On this side the broad lake Genezaret,
Or in Perea, but returned in vain.
*25*    Then on the bank of Jordan, by a creek:
Where winds with reeds, and osiers whisp'ring play

ii *6. lodged*] Cp. *John* i 39: 'They came and saw where he dwelt, and abode with him that day.'

ii *15. Moses . . . missing long*] Cp. *Exod.* xxxii 1: 'And when the people saw that Moses delayed to come down out of the mount, the people gathered themselves together unto Aaron and said . . . as for this Moses . . . we wot not what is become of him.'

ii *16. Thisbite*] Elijah, called 'the Tishbite' in *1 Kings* xvii 1. The city of Thisbe, or Thesbon, was east of Jordan, in Gilead.    *on fiery wheels*] Cp. *2 Kings* ii 11: 'Behold, there appeared a chariot of fire, and horses of fire, and parted them both asunder; and Elijah went up by a whirlwind into heaven.'

ii *17. yet . . . to come*] Cp. *Mal.* iv 5: 'Behold, I will send you Elijah the prophet before the coming of the great and dreadful day of the Lord.'

ii *18–19.* Cp. *2 Kings* ii 15–17; after Elijah's translation 'fifty strong men' of the 'sons of the Prophets' searched for him 'three days, but found him not'.

ii *20–21. Jericho . . . palms*] Cp. *Deut.* xxxiv 3: 'Jericho, the city of palm trees'.

ii *21. Aenon . . . Salem old*] Cp. *John* iii 23: 'And John was also baptizing in Aenon near to Salim, because there was much water there': 'old' probably means that M. identifies this 'Salim' with the Salem of *Gen.* xiv 18, of which Melchizedek was king.

ii *22. Machaerus*] A fortress in Peraea, in the desert east of the Dead Sea, the traditional scene of John the Baptist's execution.

ii *23. lake Genezaret*] the Sea of Galilee.

Plain fishermen, no greater men them call,
Close in a cottage low together got
Their unexpected loss and plaints outbreathed.
30    Alas, from what high hope to what relapse
Unlooked for are we fallen, our eyes beheld
Messiah certainly now come, so long
Expected of our fathers; we have heard
His words, his wisdom full of grace and truth,
35    Now, now, for sure, deliverance is at hand,
The kingdom shall to Israel be restored:
Thus we rejoiced, but soon our joy is turned
Into perplexity and new amaze:
For whither is he gone, what accident
40    Hath rapt him from us? will he now retire
After appearance, and again prolong
Our expectation? God of Israel,
Send thy Messiah forth, the time is come;
Behold the kings of the earth how they oppress
45    Thy chosen, to what highth their power unjust
They have exalted, and behind them cast
All fear of thee, arise and vindicate
Thy glory, free thy people from their yoke,
But let us wait; thus far he hath performed,
50    Sent his anointed, and to us revealed him,
By his great prophet, pointed at and shown,
In public, and with him we have conversed;
Let us be glad of this, and all our fears
Lay on his providence; he will not fail
55    Nor will withdraw him now, nor will recall,
Mock us with his blest sight, then snatch him hence,
Soon we shall see our hope, our joy return.
Thus they out of their plaints new hope resume
To find whom at the first they found unsought:
60    But to his mother Mary, when she saw

ii 27. Cp. Spenser, *Shep. Cal.* January 1: 'A shepeheards boye, (no better
doe him call,)', and Phineas Fletcher's imitation, which M. is imitating,
*Piscatory Eclogues* iii 1 'A fisher-lad (no higher dares he look)'.

ii 34. *full . . . truth*] Cp. *John* i 14: 'And the Word was made flesh, and dwelt
among us, . . . full of grace and truth.'

ii 36. *The kingdom . . . restored*] In *Acts* i 6 the disciples ask the resurrected
Jesus: 'Wilt thou at this time restore again the kingdom to Israel?'

ii 40. *rapt*] snatched.

ii 44. *the kings of the earth . . . oppress*] Cp. *Ps.* ii 2: 'The kings of the earth
set themselves . . . against the Lord.'

Others returned from baptism, not her son,
Nor left at Jordan, tidings of him none;
Within her breast, though calm; her breast though
    pure,
Motherly cares and fears got head, and raised
65  Some troubled thoughts, which she in sighs thus clad.
    O what avails me now that honour high
To have conceived of God, or that salute
Hail highly favoured, among women blest;
While I to sorrows am no less advanced,
70  And fears as eminent, above the lot
Of other women, by the birth I bore,
In such a season born when scarce a shed
Could be obtained to shelter him or me
From the bleak air; a stable was our warmth,
75  A manger his; yet soon enforced to fly
Thence into Egypt, till the murderous king
Were dead, who sought his life, and missing filled
With infant blood the streets of Bethlehem;
From Egypt home returned, in Nazareth
80  Hath been our dwelling many years, his life
Private, unactive, calm, contemplative,
Little suspicious to any king; but now
Full grown to man, acknowledged, as I hear,
By John the Baptist, and in public shown,
85  Son owned from heaven by his Father's voice;
I looked for some great change; to honour? no,
But trouble, as old Simeon plain foretold,
That to the fall and rising he should be
Of many in Israel, and to a sign
90  Spoken against, that through my very soul
A sword shall pierce, this is my favoured lot,

ii *61–2. not her son . . . none*] He did not return from baptism, he had not remained at Jordan, and there was no news of him.
ii *67. salute*] greeting; i.e. *Luke* i 28: 'Hail, thou that art highly favoured, the Lord is with thee: blessed art thou among women.'
ii *76. king*] Herod.
ii *82. suspicious*] worthy of suspicion.
ii *87–91.* Cp. i 255–6, and *Luke* ii 34–5: 'And Simeon blessed them, and said unto Mary his mother, Behold, this child is set for the fall and rising again of many in Israel; and for a sign which shall be spoken against; (Yea, a sword shall pierce through thy own soul also,) that the thoughts of many hearts may be revealed.'
ii *90. Spoken against*] decried.

My exaltation to afflictions high;
Afflicted I may be, it seems, and blest;
I will not argue that, nor will repine.
95    But where delays he now? some great intent
Conceals him: when twelve years he scarce had seen,
I lost him, but so found, as well I saw
He could not lose himself; but went about
His Father's business; what he meant I mused,
100   Since understand; much more his absence now
Thus long to some great purpose he obscures.
But I to wait with patience am inured;
My heart hath been a storehouse long of things
And sayings laid up, portending strange events.
105       Thus Mary pondering oft, and oft to mind
Recalling what remarkably had passed
Since first her salutation heard, with thoughts
Meekly composed awaited the fulfilling:
The while her son tracing the desert wild,
110   Sole but with holiest meditations fed,
Into himself descended, and at once
All his great work to come before him set;
How to begin, how to accomplish best
His end of being on earth, and mission high:
115   For Satan with sly preface to return
Had left him vacant, and with speed was gone
Up to the middle region of thick air,
Where all his potentates in council sat;

ii *92. exaltation*] Donne, *Sermons* ed. E. M. Simpson and G. R. Potter (Berkeley 1958) ix 193, points out that 'in pure, and Originall Hebrew, the word [Mary] signifies *Exaltation*, and whatsoever is best in the kinde thereof'.

ii *94. argue*] dispute (that she may be both afflicted and blessed).

ii *96–100.* See i 209–15.

ii *97–8. so found . . . himself*] I found him in such circumstances that I realized he was able to take care of himself.

ii *99. His Father's business*] Cp. *Luke* ii 49, 51: 'Wist ye not that I must be about my Father's business? . . . but his mother kept all these sayings in her heart.'   *mused*] wondered.

ii *101. obscures*] hides the reason for.

ii *103–4.* Cp. *Luke* ii 19: 'Mary kept all these things, and pondered them in her heart.'

ii *106. what . . . passed*] what had passed that was worthy of notice.

ii *115. preface*] Used in the literal sense of the Latin *praefatio* ('a saying before'); the only recorded example of the word in this sense. M. means that before Satan left he said he would return.

ii *116. vacant*] at leisure.

There without sign of boast, or sign of joy,
*120*   Solicitous and blank he thus began.
        Princes, heaven's ancient sons, ethereal thrones,
        Demonian spirits now, from the element
        Each of his reign allotted, rightlier called,
        Powers of fire, air, water, and earth beneath,
*125*   So may we hold our place and these mild seats
        Without new trouble; such an enemy
        Is risen to invade us, who no less
        Threatens than our expulsion down to hell;
        I, as I undertook, and with the vote
*130*   Consenting in full frequence was empowered,
        Have found him, viewed him, tasted him, but find
        Far other labour to be undergone
        Than when I dealt with Adam first of men,
        Though Adam by his wife's allurement fell,
*135*   However to this man inferior far,
        If he be man by mother's side at least,
        With more than human gifts from heaven adorned,
        Perfections absolute, graces divine,
        And amplitude of mind to greatest deeds,
*140*   Therefore I am returned, lest confidence
        Of my success with Eve in Paradise
        Deceive ye to persuasion over-sure
        Of like succeeding here; I summon all
        Rather to be in readiness, with hand
*145*   Or counsel to assist; lest I who erst
        Thought none my equal, now be overmatched.
          So spake the old serpent doubting, and from all
        With clamour was assured their utmost aid
        At his command; when from amidst them rose

ii *120 blank*] resourceless, nonplussed.

ii *122–4.* See *Il Penseroso* 93–6.

ii *130. frequence*] assembly.

ii *131. tasted*] examined, tried out; a frequent seventeenth-century sense.

ii *138. absolute*] finished, complete.

ii *139. amplitude of mind*] The critics who read the Christ of *PR* as an Aristotelian ideal treat this phrase as synonymous with Aristotle's 'magnanimity'. Cp. Cicero, *Tusculan Disputations* ii 26: 'Make this your aim: consider that largeness of soul (*amplitudinem animi*) . . . which best shows itself in scorn and contempt for pain, is the one fairest thing in the world, and all the fairer should it be independent of popular approval.'

ii *147. old serpent*] Cp. *Rev.* xii 9 and xx 2: 'That old serpent, called the Devil, and Satan.'

*150*    Belial the dissolutest spirit that fell,
        The sensualest, and after Asmodai
        The fleshliest incubus, and thus advised.
          Set women in his eye and in his walk,
        Among daughters of men the fairest found;
*155*    Many are in each region passing fair
        As the noon sky; more like to goddesses
        Than mortal creatures, graceful and discreet,
        Expert in amorous arts, enchanting tongues
        Persuasive, virgin majesty with mild
*160*    And sweet allayed, yet terrible to approach,
        Skilled to retire, and in retiring draw
        Hearts after them tangled in amorous nets.
        Such object hath the power to soften and tame
        Severest temper, smooth the rugged'st brow,
*165*    Enerve, and with voluptuous hope dissolve,
        Draw out with credulous desire, and lead
        At will the manliest, resolutest breast,
        As the magnetic hardest iron draws.
        Women, when nothing else, beguiled the heart
*170*    Of wisest Solomon, and made him build,
        And made him bow to the gods of his wives.

ii *150. Belial*] See *PL* i 490–3 and ii 109–17.

ii *151. Asmodai*] This and the form used in *PL* vi 365 'Asmadai' are closer to Hebrew *Aschemedai* ('the destroyer') than the more usual form 'Asmodeus' in *PL* iv 168 and *Tobit* iii 8. In *Tobit* Asmodeus is an evil spirit who loves Sarah and slaughters her seven husbands in turn: he is thus regarded as the personification of lust.

ii *152. incubus*] a demon specialising in the seduction of women. Augustine, *De Civitate Dei* xv 23 admits their existence.

ii *160.* See *PL* ix 490–1.

ii *161–2.* See *PL* viii 504–5.

ii *163. object*] This word seems to retain some of its older meaning, 'something put in the way so as to interrupt or obstruct a person's course', which is not recorded after the mid-sixteenth century.

ii *164. temper*] temperament.    *smooth . . . brow*] See *Il Penseroso* 58.

ii *166. credulous desire*] Perhaps echoing Horace, *Odes* IV i 30, where the ageing lover speaks of his *spes animi credula mutui* (credulous hope of mutual love).

ii *168. magnetic*] magnet; a form confined to the seventeenth century.

ii *169–71.* Cp. *1 Kings* xi 4–8: 'For it came to pass, when Solomon was old, that his wives turned away his heart after other gods . . . Then did Solomon build an high place for Chemosh, the abomination of Moab . . . And likewise did he for all his strange wives, which burnt incense and sacrificed unto their gods.'

To whom quick answer Satan thus returned.
Belial, in much uneven scale thou weigh'st
All others by thyself; because of old
*175* Thou thyself dot'st on womankind, admiring
Their shape, their colour, and attractive grace,
None are, thou think'st, but taken with such toys.
Before the flood thou with thy lusty crew,
False titled Sons of God, roaming the earth
*180* Cast wanton eyes on the daughters of men,
And coupled with them, and begot a race.
Have we not seen, or by relation heard,
In courts and regal chambers how thou lurk'st,
In wood or grove by mossy fountain-side,
*185* In valley or green meadow to waylay
Some beauty rare, Calisto, Clymene,
Daphne, or Semele, Antiopa,
Or Amymone, Syrinx, many more
Too long, then lay'st thy scapes on names adored,
*190* Apollo, Neptune, Jupiter, or Pan,
Satyr, or Faun, or Sylvan? But these haunts
Delight not all; among the sons of men
How many have with a smile made small account
Of beauty and her lures, easily scorned
*195* All her assaults, on worthier things intent!
Remember that Pellean conqueror,
A youth, how all the beauties of the East

ii *178–81.* It seems probable that Satan is not referring to the incident recorded in *Gen.* vi 2, since the orthodox interpretation of that verse, as R. H. West, *MLN* lxv (1950) 187–91, remarks, identified the 'Sons of God' who coupled with the 'daughters of men' as the descendants of Seth, and M. accepts this interpretation in *PL* xi 573–87.

ii *186–8.* These nymphs seduced or pursued by pagan gods are all from Ovid: Calisto was one of Diana's nymphs, seduced by Jove, *Met.* ii 409; Clymene, a oceanid, mother of Phaethon, *Met.* i 757; Daphne, a nymph changed into a laurel when pursued by Apollo, *Met.* i 452; Semele, mother of Bacchus by Jove, *Met.* iii 253; Antiopa, seduced by Jove disguised as a satyr, *Met.* vi 110; Syrinx, a nymph pursued by Pan and turned into a reed, *Met.* i 690; Amymone, a nymph loved by Neptune, *Am.* I x 5. Justin Martyr, *Apologia Prima* 9 and 25, explains that the lustful classical gods were really fallen angels.

ii *189. Too long*] too many to mention.

ii *191. haunts*] habits.

ii *196. Pellean conqueror*] Alexander the Great, born at Pella, capital of Macedonia. After the battle of the Issus and the capture of Darius' wife and daughters, Alexander, according to Plutarch, *Life* 21, treated the women

He slightly viewed, and slightly overpassed;
How he surnamed of Africa dismissed
200    In his prime youth the fair Iberian maid.
For Solomon he lived at ease, and full
Of honour, wealth, high fare, aimed not beyond
Higher design than to enjoy his state;
Thence to the bait of women lay exposed;
205    But he whom we attempt is wiser far
Than Solomon, of more exalted mind,
Made and set wholly on the accomplishment
Of greatest things; what woman will you find,
Though of this age the wonder and the fame,
210    On whom his leisure will vouchsafe an eye
Of fond desire? Or should she confident,
As sitting queen adored on beauty's throne,
Descend with all her winning charms begirt
To enamour, as the zone of Venus once
215    Wrought that effect on Jove, so fables tell;
How would one look from his majestic brow
Seated as on the top of virtue's hill,
Discount'nance her despised, and put to rout
All her array; her female pride deject,
220    Or turn to reverent awe! For beauty stands
In the admiration only of weak minds
Led captive; cease to admire, and all her plumes
Fall flat and shrink into a trivial toy,
At every sudden slighting quite abashed:
225    Therefore with manlier objects we must try
His constancy, with such as have more show

with honour and respect, so that they lived 'as though in sacred and inviol-
able virgins' chambers instead of in an enemy's camp'. Alexander con-
sidered 'the mastery of himself a more kingly thing than the conquest of his
enemies': seeing the other captive Persian beauties 'he merely said jestingly
that Persian women were torments to the eyes' and 'passed them by as
though they were lifeless images for display'.

ii *199. he surnamed of Africa*] Scipio Africanus: Livy xxvi 50 relates that after
the fall of New Carthage, 210 B.C., Scipio gave back a beautiful Spanish
captive to the young man to whom she was betrothed, Allucius of the Celti-
berians.

ii *205–6. wiser far | Than Solomon*] Cp. *Matt.* xii 42: 'Behold, a greater than
Solomon is here.'

ii *214–5*. In *Iliad* xiv 214–351 Jove surrenders to Juno when she comes
wearing the girdle ('zone') of Venus.

ii *222–3*. The image is based on Ovid's peacock, *Ars Amatoria* i 627, which
displays its plumes only when praised.

Of worth, of honour, glory, and popular praise;
Rocks whereon greatest men have oftest wrecked;
Or that which only seems to satisfy
230  Lawful desires of nature, not beyond;
And now I know he hungers where no food
Is to be found, in the wide wilderness;
The rest commit to me, I shall let pass
No advantage, and his strength as oft assay.

235      He ceased, and heard their grant in loud acclaim;
Then forthwith to him takes a chosen band
Of spirits likest to himself in guile
To be at hand, and at his beck appear,
If cause were to unfold some active scene
240  Of various persons each to know his part;
Then to the desert takes with these his flight;
Where still from shade to shade the Son of God
After forty days' fasting had remained,
Now hung'ring first, and to himself thus said.

245      Where will this end? Four times ten days I have passed
Wandering this woody maze, and human food
Nor tasted, nor had appetite: that fast
To virtue I impute not, or count part
Of what I suffer here; if nature need not,
250  Or God support nature without repast
Though needing, what praise is it to endure?
But now I feel I hunger, which declares,
Nature hath need of what she asks; yet God
Can satisfy that need some other way,
255  Though hunger still remain: so it remain
Without this body's wasting, I content me,
And from the sting of famine fear no harm,
Nor mind it, fed with better thoughts that feed
Me hung'ring more to do my Father's will.

ii 235. grant] assent.
ii 242. shade to shade] one night to the next.
ii 245–59. This speech makes it clear that Christ's fast was not a miracle performed by him as man, but by God, with him as object. Christ, as man, was not in control of his appetite. The miraculous nature of the fast cannot, therefore, be used, as G. W. Whiting, MLN lxvi (1951) 12–16, attempts to use it, as proof that the hero of PR is Christ in his divine nature, rather than in his human nature. Lewalski 202–3 makes the point that, since Christ first feels hunger at this juncture, he was not hungry during the stones-into-bread temptation (i 342–4).
ii 255. so] provided that.
ii 259. Cp. John iv 34: 'My meat is to do the will of him that sent me.'

260     It was the hour of night, when thus the Son
        Communed in silent walk, then laid him down
        Under the hospitable covert nigh
        Of trees thick interwoven; there he slept,
        And dreamed, as appetite is wont to dream,
265     Of meats and drinks, nature's refreshment sweet;
        Him thought, he by the brook of Cherith stood
        And saw the ravens with their horny beaks
        Food to Elijah bringing even and morn,
        Though ravenous, taught to abstain from what they
             brought;
270     He saw the prophet also how he fled
        Into the desert, and how there he slept
        Under a juniper; then how awaked,
        He found his supper on the coals prepared,
        And by the angel was bid rise and eat,
275     And eat the second time after repose,
        The strength whereof sufficed him forty days;
        Sometimes that with Elijah he partook,
        Or as a guest with Daniel at his pulse.
        Thus wore out night, and now the herald lark
280     Left his ground-nest, high towering to descry
        The Morn's approach, and greet her with his song:
        As lightly from his grassy couch uprose
        Our Saviour, and found all was but a dream,
        Fasting he went to sleep, and fasting waked.
285     Up to a hill anon his steps he reared,
        From whose high top to ken the prospect round,

ii *262–3. hospitable covert . . . trees thick interwoven*] Cp. Horace, *Odes* II
iii 9–11, where pine and poplar interweave their branches to provide
*umbram hospitalem*.
ii *266–9*. Cp. *1 Kings* xvii 5–6: 'For he went and dwelt by the brook Cherith,
that is before Jordan. And the ravens brought him bread and flesh in the
morning, and bread and flesh in the evening; and he drank of the brook.'
ii *270–6*. Cp. *1 Kings* xix 4–8. Elijah, threatened by Jezebel, flees into the
wilderness. As he sleeps under a juniper tree: 'An angel touched him, and
said unto him, Arise and eat. And he looked, and behold, there was a cake
baken on the coals, and a cruse of water at his head.' Elijah eats, sleeps again,
is again woken by the angel, eats a second time 'and went in the strength of
that meat forty days and forty nights unto Horeb the mount of God.'
ii *278*. Cp. *Dan.* i 3–21, where Daniel refuses to eat the food provided for the
children of the Hebrew nobility by order of King Nebuchadnezzar, pre-
ferring instead his simple diet of 'pulse' (lentils, beans, etc.).
ii *279. herald lark*] Cp. *Romeo and Juliet* III v 6: 'the lark, the herald of the
morn'.

If cottage were in view, sheep-cote or herd;
But cottage, herd or sheep-cote none he saw,
Only in a bottom saw a pleasant grove,
290  With chant of tuneful birds resounding loud;
Thither he bent his way, determined there
To rest at noon, and entered soon the shade
High-roofed and walks beneath, and alleys brown
That opened in the midst a woody scene,
295  Nature's own work it seemed (Nature taught Art)
And to a superstitious eye the haunt
Of wood-gods and wood-nymphs; he viewed it round,
When suddenly a man before him stood,
Not rustic as before, but seemlier clad,
300  As one in city, or court, or palace bred,
And with fair speech these words to him addressed.
       With granted leave officious I return,
But much more wonder that the Son of God
In this wild solitude so long should bide
305  Of all things destitute, and well I know,
Not without hunger. Others of some note,
As story tells, have trod this wilderness;
The fugitive bond-woman with her son
Outcast Nebaioth, yet found he relief
310  By a providing angel; all the race
Of Israel here had famished, had not God
Rained from heaven manna, and that prophet bold

ii 289. bottom] dell.
ii 295. This line raises a difficulty, as Woodhouse 179–82 points out. If the 'pleasant grove' (l. 289) was only the work of Satan's 'art', why does Christ succumb to the temptation it offers and decide to rest in its shade? A possible answer is that it was not the 'grove' but the 'woody scene' in its 'midst'–Satan's setting for his banquet–which was created by 'art'. This could not be seen from outside the wood.
ii 302. officious] eager to please (Latin officiosus).
ii 308–10. Hagar and her son Ishmael were cast out by Sarah, Gen. xxi 9–21. Ishmael would have died had not an angel shown Hagar a well. M. here calls Ishmael by the name of his eldest son, Nebaioth.
ii 309. he] Most editors print 'here', the second edn reading.
ii 310–12. Cp. Exod. xvi 35: 'And the children of Israel did eat manna forty years, until they came to a land inhabited.'
ii 312–4. See ii 270–6n. M. apparently confuses Thebez (Tubas, north-east of Mt Ephraim) where Abimelech was slain (Judges ix 50–5), with Thisbe or Thesbon in Gilead, Elijah's birthplace.

Native of Thebez wandering here was fed
Twice by a voice inviting him to eat.
315 Of thee these forty days none hath regard,
Forty and more deserted here indeed.
  To whom thus Jesus; What conclud'st thou hence?
They all had need, I as thou seest have none.
  How hast thou hunger then? Satan replied,
320 Tell me if food were now before thee set,
Wouldst thou not eat? Thereafter as I like
The giver, answered Jesus. Why should that
Cause thy refusal, said the subtle Fiend.
Hast thou not right to all created things,
325 Owe not all creatures by just right to thee
Duty and service, nor to stay till bid,
But tender all their power? Nor mention I
Meats by the law unclean, or offered first
To idols, those young Daniel could refuse;
330 Nor proffered by an enemy, though who
Would scruple that, with want oppressed? behold
Nature ashamed, or better to express,
Troubled that thou shouldst hunger, hath purveyed
From all the elements her choicest store
335 To treat thee as beseems, and as her Lord
With honour, only deign to sit and eat.

ii *313. Thebez*] This spelling is supplied by the *1671 Errata*; *1671* has
'Thebes'; the change is presumably to ensure a disyllabic pronunciation.
ii *318–9.* Lewalski 203 notices that Satan's response ironically echoes
Christ's own conclusion (ii 252–3) that the hunger is itself evidence of need.
ii *324.* Cp. *Heb.* i 2: 'His Son, whom he hath appointed heir of all things.'
Satan had similarly reminded Eve that she was mistress of creation (*PL*
ix 532–40).
ii *327–8. Nor . . . unclean*] M. Fixler, *MLN* lxx (1955) 573–7, notes that the
banquet (ii 342–7), since it includes shell-fish, would be forbidden by the
Mosaic dietary laws. Satan's assurance that it is not unclean, repeated ii 369,
may be viewed as an attempt to make Jesus reject these laws (as M. rejects
them in the *De doctrina*)–such a rejection would give Satan a lead as to
Christ's real identity. Alternatively, if Christ refuses the banquet because it
contains forbidden foods, he seems to subject himself (and his church) to the
dietary prohibitions of the law which he has come to supersede. 'Christ's
way out of the dilemma is to refuse the banquet simply on the basis of the
giver', (Lewalski 217).
ii *329.* Cp. *Dan.* i 8: 'But Daniel purposed in his heart that he would not
defile himself with the portion of the king's meat, nor with the wine which
he drank.'

He spake no dream, for as his words had end,
Our Saviour lifting up his eyes, beheld
In ample space under the broadest shade
340 A table richly spread, in regal mode,
With dishes piled, and meats of noblest sort
And savour, beasts of chase, or fowl of game,
In pastry built, or from the spit, or boiled,

ii 337–65. M.'s introduction of this banqueting scene finds no support
either in Scripture or in the tradition. Pope 70–9 regards it as an attempt to
preserve the equation between the temptations of Adam and Eve and those
of Christ (cp. ll. 348–9). Eve was guilty of greed (wanting the apple to
satisfy her appetite) and covetousness (wanting it as a beautiful object):
see PL ix 739–43 and 735–6. The second of these is paralleled in PR during
the temptation of the kingdoms (see iv 110–21n), where the primary appeal
is made to a desire for glory and opulence. The first is not paralleled by the
temptation to turn stones into bread (see i 355n), so M. inserts the banquet
scene to parallel it: here the primary appeal is made to the desire for food.
In order to complete the coincidence, it is made evident (ll. 245–59) that
Christ has not been feeling the effects of hunger for forty days, and that the
power which has sustained him is still sustaining him to the extent of
miraculously satisfying the essential demands of the flesh. Thus, like
Eve, he longs for food but does not actually require it (see ll. 252–4).
Kermode[4] 323–5 suggests that another reason for the introduction of this
non-canonical temptation may be the contrast it makes with Christ's final
reward (iv 588–90) where the food is 'celestial', 'divine' and 'ambrosial':
here the attractions are sensual, and the sensual impact proceeds from the eye,
the highest (ii 338), through smell (350–1) and ear (362–3), to the lowest,
touch and taste (369–71). Stein[2] 60 sees the banquet as Satan going back on
his announced intention not to tempt appetite with what exceeds the
natural and apparently lawful (ii 229–30). What the attempt reveals, then,
is Satan's loss of understanding: he is compulsively evil. 'What he says
and does reflects an essential loss, which is the more marked because of his
brilliant surface competence and awareness.' Lewalski (203–4) referring to
Christ's role as second Israel (a commonplace among the typologists) sees the
lush banquet as a visible embodiment of the presumptous demand of the
Israelites, 'Can the Lord furnish a table in the wilderness?' (Ps. lxxviii 19).
Christ, by refusing, demonstrates that he will perfect and fulfil the old type,
the carnal Israel. Satan's banquet is frequently compared with that in Tasso,
Jerusalem Delivered x 64, with which Armida tempts her lovers. T. H. Banks,
PMLA lv (1940) 773–6, considers that Christ is tempted not so much to eat
as to claim his own godhead by accepting as his due the offering of the
fruits of the earth: the temptation lies not in the luxury but in the fact that
the gift is presented (332–6) as Nature's tribute to her Lord.

Grisamber-steamed; all fish from sea or shore,
345   Freshet, or purling brook, of shell or fin,
And exquisitest name, for which was drained
Pontus and Lucrine bay, and Afric coast.
Alas how simple, to these cates compared,
Was that crude apple that diverted Eve!
350   And at a stately sideboard by the wine
That fragrant smell diffused, in order stood
Tall stripling youths rich-clad, of fairer hue
Than Ganymede or Hylas, distant more
Under the trees now tripped, now solemn stood
355   Nymphs of Diana's train, and Naiades
With fruits and flowers from Amalthea's horn,
And ladies of the Hesperides, that seemed
Fairer than feigned of old, or fabled since

ii *344. Grisamber*] ambergris, used in cooking as well as perfumery. The form was a fairly common one in the seventeenth century.

ii *345. Freshet*] small stream.

ii *347. Pontus*] the Black Sea. Pliny ix 19–20 remarks on the swiftness with which all kinds of fish come to perfection in this sea, and says that it is particularly famous for tunny fish.      *Lucrine bay*] a lagoon near Naples, famed for its oysters, which Horace mentions, *Epodes* ii 49, *Satires* II iv 32.

ii *349. crude*] raw, uncooked.      *diverted*] seduced.

ii *353. Ganymede*] See *Elegia VII* 21n.     *Hylas*] Apollonius Rhodius, *Argonautica* i 1207–39, tells how a nymph falls in love with the beautiful boy, Hylas, as he is drawing water for his master Hercules at her spring, and draws him to the depths.

ii *356. Amalthea's horn*] the cornucopia. Ovid, *Fasti* v 115–28, tells how the nymph Amalthea owned a she-goat which suckled the infant Jupiter on Mt Ida, 'but she broke a horn on a tree and was shorn of half her charm. The nymph picked it up, wrapped it in fresh herbs, and carried it, full of fruit, to the lips of Jove. He, when he gained the kingdom of heaven . . . made his nurse and her horn of plenty into stars.'

ii *357. ladies of the Hesperides*] See *Comus* 980–1n. M. here uses 'Hesperides' as a name for the garden of the Hesperides, as does Shakespeare, *Love's Labour's Lost* IV iii 341.

ii *358–61.* Hughes[2] 256–7 reads these lines as M.'s confession of his indebtedness to the grail romances, particularly Malory's *Morte d'Arthur*, an indebtedness suggested by Tillyard 319. Pope 116–19 sees M. associating Christ's prowess in overcoming temptation with feats of knight-errantry (see i 9n), and notes that John Knox, in his exposition upon the temptations of Christ, had put a formal, quasi-chivalric challenge into Christ's mouth. Cp. M.'s mention of his reading in 'those lofty Fables and Romances, which recount in solemne cantos the deeds of Knighthood founded by our victorious Kings; & from hence had in renowne all over Christendome' (Columbia

Of faëry damsels met in forest wide
360　By knights of Logres, or of Lyonesse,
Lancelot or Pelleas, or Pellenore,
And all the while harmonious airs were heard
Of chiming strings, or charming pipes and winds
Of gentlest gale Arabian odours fanned
365　From their soft wings, and Flora's earliest smells.
Such was the splendour, and the tempter now
His invitation earnestly renewed.
　　What doubts the Son of God to sit and eat?
These are not fruits forbidden, no interdict
370　Defends the touching of these viands pure,
Their taste no knowledge works, at least of evil,
But life preserves, destroys life's enemy,
Hunger, with sweet restorative delight.
All these are spirits of air, and woods, and springs,
375　Thy gentle ministers, who come to pay
Thee homage, and acknowledge thee their Lord:
What doubt'st thou Son of God? Sit down and eat.
　　To whom thus Jesus temperately replied:
Said'st thou not that to all things I had right?
380　And who withholds my power that right to use?

iii 304, Yale i 891). Lewalski 223–4 makes the point that by including beautiful women in the temptation Satan goes against his previous decision (ii 225–7): the inclusion extends the Christ / Adam parallel, since undue susceptibility to woman was Adam's particular sin.

ii *360. Logres*] Loegria: England east of Severn and south of Humber. *Lyonesse*] between Land's End and the Scillies: now submerged.

ii *361. Lancelot*] 'Head of all Christian knights', as Sir Ector calls him in Malory, *Morte d'Arthur* xxi 13, the lover of Guinivere; besotted by wine, he was twice led to sleep with the fair Elaine, thinking her Guinivere.　*Pelleas*] lover of Ettare. Some traditions make him one of the four knights of the Round Table to achieve the Grail.　*Pellenore*] King of the Isles, eventually killed by Sir Gawain. Lewalski 225 thinks the allusion should be to his son Percival, who was offered after a three-day fast a banquet with 'all manner of meetes that he cowde thynke on' by a fair gentlewoman (actually 'the mayster fyende of helle' in disguise). He was saved from serious sin with the lady only by making the sign of the cross, which caused the scene to vanish (*Morte d'Arthur* xiv 9–10).

ii *364.* Cp. *PL* iv 162–3.

ii *365. Flora*] goddess of flowers.

ii *369. fruits forbidden*] The temptation of Eve is again recalled, see ii 324n.

ii *370. Defends*] forbids.

Shall I receive by gift what of my own,
When and where likes me best, I can command?
I can at will, doubt not, as soon as thou,
Command a table in this wilderness,
385    And call swift flights of angels ministrant
Arrayed in glory on my cup to attend:
Why shouldst thou then obtrude this diligence,
In vain, where no acceptance it can find,
And with my hunger what hast thou to do?
390    Thy pompous delicacies I contemn,
And count thy specious gifts no gifts but guiles.
        To whom thus answered Satan malcontent:
That I have also power to give thou seest,
If of that power I bring thee voluntary
395    What I might have bestowed on whom I pleased,
And rather opportunely in this place
Chose to impart to thy apparent need,
Why shouldst thou not accept it? but I see
What I can do or offer is suspect;
400    Of these things others quickly will dispose
Whose pains have earned the far-fet spoil. With that
Both table and provision vanished quite
With sound of harpies' wings, and talons heard;
Only th' importune tempter still remained,
405    And with these words his temptation pursued.
        By hunger, that each other creature tames,
Thou art not to be harmed, therefore not moved;
Thy temperance invincible besides,

ii *381–6.* Cp. *Ps.* lxxviii 19: 'They said, Can God furnish a table in the wilderness?' Martz (187) detects a hint of the communion table. Lewalski 218 agrees, and adds: 'Christ's own "table in the wilderness" alludes typologically to such future manifestations of his proper "banquet" as the angelic repast which is to celebrate his victory over Satan at the conclusion . . . the feeding of the multitude in the wilderness in reprise and fulfilment of the manna type, and the Eucharistic banquet.'

ii *391. no gifts*] M. in the *Apology*, decrying the traces of Roman Catholicism in the Anglican liturgy, speaks of 'enemies . . . whose guifts are no guifts, but the instruments of our bane' (Columbia iii 354, Yale i 939).

ii *401. far-fet*] far fetched.

ii *402–3.* Recalling the stage direction to *Tempest* III iii 83, 'enter Ariel like a harpy; claps his wings upon the table; and with a quaint device, the banquet vanishes'; also *Aen.* iii 225–8, where harpies snatch away the Trojans' meal.

ii *404. importune*] importunate, persistent.

ii *408. besides*] in other respects as well.

For no allurement yields to appetite,
410  And all thy heart is set on high designs,
High actions; but wherewith to be achieved?
Great acts require great means of enterprise,
Thou art unknown, unfriended, low of birth,
A carpenter thy father known, thyself
415  Bred up in poverty and straits at home;
Lost in a desert here and hunger-bit:
Which way or from what hope dost thou aspire
To greatness? whence authority deriv'st,
What followers, what retinue canst thou gain,
420  Or at thy heels the dizzy multitude,
Longer than thou canst feed them on thy cost?
Money brings honour, friends, conquest, and realms;
What raised Antipater the Edomite,
And his son Herod placed on Judah's throne;
425  (Thy throne) but gold that got him puissant friends?
Therefore, if at great things thou wouldst arrive,
Get riches first, get wealth, and treasure heap,
Not difficult, if thou hearken to me,
Riches are mine, fortune is in my hand;
430  They whom I favour thrive in wealth amain,
While virtue, valour, wisdom sit in want.
To whom thus Jesus patiently replied;
Yet wealth without these three is impotent,
To gain dominion or to keep it gained.
435  Witness those ancient empires of the earth,
In highth of all their flowing wealth dissolved:
But men endued with these have oft attained
In lowest poverty to highest deeds;
Gideon and Jephtha, and the shepherd lad,
440  Whose offspring on the throne of Judah sat
So many ages, and shall yet regain
That seat, and reign in Israel without end.

ii 416. *hunger-bit*] Cp. *Job* xviii 12: 'His strength shall be hunger-bitten.'
ii 422. Cp. Horace, *Epistles* I vi 36–7: 'Of course a wife and dowry, credit
and friends, birth and beauty, are the gift of Queen Money.'
ii 423–4. Josephus, *Antiquities* xiv 1 mentions Antipater's great wealth and
rise to power, and stresses as the main reason for Herod's obtaining control
over Judaea his promise of money to Mark Antony.
ii 426–7. Cp. Mammon's advice to Guyon, *F.Q.* II vii, to gain honour
through riches, and Horace's ironic O *cives, cives, quaerenda pecunia primum
est, Epistles* I i 53.
ii 429. *Riches are mine*] Cp. *Hag.* ii 8: 'The silver is mine, and the gold is
mine, saith the Lord of hosts.'

  Among the heathen, (for throughout the world
  To me is not unknown what hath been done
445 Worthy of memorial) canst thou not remember
  Quintius, Fabricius, Curius, Regulus?
  For I esteem those names of men so poor
  Who could do mighty things, and could contemn
  Riches though offered from the hand of kings.
450 And what in me seems wanting, but that I
  May also in this poverty as soon
  Accomplish what they did, perhaps and more?

ii *439. Gideon*] his reply, when commanded by God to lead Israel against the Midianites was 'O my Lord, wherewith shall I save Israel? behold my family is poor in Manasseh, and I am the least in my father's house', *Judges* vi 15. Lewalski 252 argues that he is not merely a type of poverty here but also of Christ's repudiation of kingship (see *Judges* viii 23). *Jephtha*] champion of Israel against the Ammonites: he had been disinherited and banished in his youth, *Judges* xi 2–3. The Fathers and later exegetes saw his sacrifice of his daughter as typifying Christ's sacrifice on the cross. Lewalski 253 thinks he is used here to emphasize the sacrificial aspect of kingship. *shepherd lad*] David. God 'took him from the sheepfolds: from following the ewes', and 'brought him to feed Jacob his people', *Ps* lxxviii 70–1. 'Christ sees himself as second David because he also expects to obtain the throne of Israel after overcoming great difficulties' (Lewalski 252).
ii *443–9*. Hughes² 267 refers to Tasso, *Del Poema Eroico*, where it is maintained that, while the first earthly honour previously belonged to the Roman worthies like the Curtii, Decii and Marcelli, the heroic spirit of such men is merely 'a shadow and a figure' of the divine love which Christ brought into the world.
ii *446. Quintius*] Lucius Quinctius Cincinnatus, a historical figure, though details of his career were derived from popular poetry. In 458 B.C., according to tradition, when Minucius was besieged by the Aequi, Cincinnatus was appointed dictator, dispatched to the rescue, defeated the Aequi, resigned his dictatorship after fifteen days and returned to farm beyond the Tiber. *Fabricius*] Gaius Fabricius Luscinus, hero of the war with Pyrrhus, consul 282 and 278 B.C. There are several stories of his poverty, austerity and incorruptibility: he rejected bribes from Pyrrhus and also the offers of Pyrrhus' would-be poisoners. *Curius*] Manius Curius Dentatus. He conquered the Samnites and Sabines (290 B.C.) and Pyrrhus (275 B.C.). The rhetorical accounts of his incorruptibility and frugality derive largely from Cato, who idealized him. *Regulus*] Marcus Atilius Regulus: captured by the Carthaginians in the first Punic War (255 B.C.), he was sent to Rome with terms. On his advice they were rejected. He insisted on returning to Carthage with the answer, and died in captivity. The story of his death by torture was a national legend, and is celebrated by Horace, *Odes* III v, but is probably untrue. Augustine, *De Civitate Dei* v 18,

Extol not riches then, the toil of fools,
The wise man's cumbrance if not snare, more apt
455   To slacken virtue, and abate her edge,
Than prompt her to do aught may merit praise.
What if with like aversion I reject
Riches and realms; yet not for that a crown,
Golden in show, is but a wreath of thorns,
460   Brings dangers, troubles, cares, and sleepless nights
To him who wears the regal diadem,
When on his shoulders each man's burden lies;
For therein stands the office of a king,
His honour, virtue, merit, and chief praise,
465   That for the public all this weight he bears.
Yet he who reigns within himself, and rules
Passions, desires, and fears, is more a king;
Which every wise and virtuous man attains:
And who attains not, ill aspires to rule
470   Cities of men, or headstrong multitudes,
Subject himself to anarchy within,
Or lawless passions in him which he serves.
But to guide nations in the way of truth
By saving doctrine, and from error lead
475   To know, and, knowing worship God aright,
Is yet more kingly, this attracts the soul,
Governs the inner man, the nobler part,
That other o'er the body only reigns,
And oft by force, which to a generous mind
480   So reigning can be no sincere delight.
Besides to give a kingdom hath been thought
Greater and nobler done, and to lay down

linked together Regulus, Quintius and Fabricius as examples of virtue surpassing that of most Christians.

ii *453. toil*] snare.

ii *458. for that*] because. M. makes it clear that it is not the cares and responsibilities of kingship that Christ fears.

ii *466–8.* Cp. *Prov.* xvi 32 which, as Hughes[2] 271 points out, Leone Ebreo cites in the *Dialoghi d'Amore* when outlining the familiar neo-Platonic case that the hero is the man who vanquishes himself, and in whom 'sensuality has quite ceased to disturb virtuous reason'. Horace, *Odes* II ii 9–12 makes a similar point: 'You will rule a broader realm by subduing a greedy heart than you would by joining Libya to distant Gades.'

ii *480. sincere*] pure.

ii *481–2.* Perhaps echoing Seneca, *Thyestes* 529: *Habere regnum casus est, virtus dare* (To have a kingdom is chance; to give one, virtue).

Far more magnanimous, than to assume.
Riches are needless then, both for themselves,
485     And for thy reason why they should be sought,
To gain a sceptre, oftest better missed.

## THE THIRD BOOK

So spake the Son of God, and Satan stood
A while as mute confounded what to say,
What to reply, confuted and convinced
Of his weak arguing, and fallacious drift;
5     At length collecting all his serpent wiles,
With soothing words renewed, him thus accosts.
I see thou know'st what is of use to know,
What best to say canst say, to do canst do;
Thy actions to thy words accord, thy words
10     To thy large heart give utterance due, thy heart
Contains of good, wise, just, the perfect shape.
Should kings and nations from thy mouth consult,
Thy counsel would be as the oracle
Urim and Thummim, those oraculous gems
15     On Aaron's breast: or tongue of seers old
Infallible; or wert thou sought to deeds
That might require the array of war, thy skill
Of conduct would be such, that all the world
Could not sustain thy prowess, or subsist
20     In battle, though against thy few in arms.
These godlike virtues wherefore dost thou hide?
Affecting private life, or more obscure
In savage wilderness, wherefore deprive
All earth her wonder at thy acts, thyself

ii *483. magnanimous*] Hughes[2] 258–9, seeing M.'s Christ as a Christianiza-
tion of the Aristotelian magnanimous man, refers to *De doctrina* ii 9 (Colum-
bia xvii 240–3) where Christ's rejection of the world in *Matt.* iv is cited as
an example of magnanimity.

iii *14. Urim and Thummim*] As R. J. Beck, *N & Q* n.s. iv (1957) 27–9, remarks,
none of the half-dozen references to these oracular gems in the Old Testa-
ment makes their exact nature clear, and other authorities (e.g. Josephus,
*Antiquities* iii 8–9, Philo, *Life of Moses* ii) are contradictory. *Num.* xxvii 21
shows that they were used in divination, and *Exod.* xxviii 30 that they were
in Aaron's breastplate. Urim means 'light' and Thummim, 'truth', the
plurals being intensitive.

iii *16. sought to*] called upon for.

25    The fame and glory, glory the reward
        That sole excites to high attempts the flame
        Of most erected spirits, most tempered pure
        Ethereal, who all pleasures else despise,
        All treasures and all gain esteem as dross,
30    And dignities and powers all but the highest?
        Thy years are ripe, and over-ripe, the son
        Of Macedonian Philip had ere these
        Won Asia and the throne of Cyrus held
        At his dispose, young Scipio had brought down
35    The Carthaginian pride, young Pompey quelled
        The Pontic king and in triumph had rode.
        Yet years, and to ripe years judgment mature,
        Quench not the thirst of glory, but augment.
        Great Julius, whom now all the world admires

iii *25–30.* Cp. Cicero, *De officiis* I viii 26: 'It is in the greatest souls and in the most brilliant geniuses that we usually find ambitions for civil and military authority, for power and for glory, springing up'; also M.'s reference in the *Defensio Secunda* to 'what itself conquers the most excellent of mortals . . . glory' (Columbia viii 218–9), and *Lycidas* 70–2.

Pope 67–9 notes that M. breaks with tradition by including the temptation to vainglorious presumption ('glory') among the kingdoms-of-the-world temptations: a seventeenth-century reader would have expected it to be the temptation presented on the pinnacle of the temple, since this was the view taken by all orthodox theologians. Glory following wealth is, however, the order of temptations in *F.Q.* ii, where the persuasions of Mammon give way to Philotime (Vainglory).

iii *27. erected*] elevated, exalted: an obsolescent sense: *PL* i 679 is the last instance of it recorded in *OED*.

iii *31. Thy years are ripe*] According to *Luke* iii 23, Christ's baptism took place when he was about thirty.

iii *31–4.* Alexander won the battle of the Issus (333 B.C.) when he was twenty-three, and he was twenty-five when, at Arbela, he overthrew the Persian empire founded by Cyrus.

iii *34–5.* Scipio drove the Carthaginians from Spain when he was twenty-seven (207 B.C.). He was thirty-two when he won his greatest victory, at Zama.

iii *35–6.* Satan exaggerates. Pompey was forty when he overthrew Mithridates (66 B.C.), and forty-five when he celebrated his triumph in Rome.

iii *37. to*] in addition to.

iii *39–42.* Plutarch, *Life of Caesar* xi 3 tells how Caesar, as a young man, burst into tears on reading the exploits of Alexander, and when asked the reason, replied: 'Do you not think it is matter for sorrow that while Alexander, at my age, was already king of so many peoples, I have as yet achieved no brilliant success.'

*40*  The more he grew in years, the more inflamed
     With glory, wept that he had lived so long
     Inglorious: but thou yet art not too late.
        To whom our Saviour calmly thus replied.
     Thou neither dost persuade me to seek wealth
*45*  For empire's sake, nor empire to affect
     For glory's sake by all thy argument.
     For what is glory but the blaze of fame,
     The people's praise, if always praise unmixed?
     And what the people but a herd confused,
*50*  A miscellaneous rabble, who extol
     Things vulgar, and well weighed, scarce worth the
          praise,
     They praise and they admire they know not what;
     And know not whom, but as one leads the other;
     And what delight to be by such extolled,
*55*  To live upon their tongues and be their talk,
     Of whom to be dispraised were no small praise?
     His lot who dares be singularly good.
     The intelligent among them and the wise
     Are few, and glory scarce of few is raised.
*60*  This is true glory and renown, when God,
     Looking on the earth, with approbation marks
     The just man, and divulges him through heaven
     To all his angels, who with true applause

iii *47–51.* Cp. Seneca, *Epistles* cii 17: 'There is this difference between re-
nown and glory: the latter depends upon the judgments of the many, but
renown on the judgments of good men'; and Cicero, *Tusculan Disputations*
v 36: 'Popular glory is not to be coveted for its own sake nor obscurity
feared ... Can anything be more foolish than to suppose that those whom
individually one despises as illiterate mechanics, have ideas of value col-
lectively? The wise man will ... reject the distinctions bestowed by the
people'; also Giles Fletcher, *Christ's Triumph over Death* 31: 'Fraile Multi-
tude, whose giddy lawe is list, / And best applause is windy flattering, / Most
like the breath of which it doth consist, / No sooner blowne, but as soone
vanishing, / As much desir'd, as little profiting, / That makes the men that
have it oft as light / As those that give it ...'
   Hughes[2] 260 finds in Alessandro Piccolomini's *Della Institution Morale*
vi 9 and viii 17, a foretaste of M.'s Christ's almost Hobbesian exaggeration
of the aristocratic element in the Aristotelian magnanimous man's renun-
ciation of the world.
iii *56.* An echo of Jonson, *Cynthia's Revels* III iii 15–6 'of such / To be dis-
prais'd is the most perfect praise'. Jonson is himself echoing Seneca, *De
remediis fortuitorum* vii 1: *Malis displicere laudari est.*
iii *62. divulges*] makes known.

Recount his praises; thus he did to Job,
65   When to extend his fame through heaven and earth,
As thou to thy reproach may'st well remember,
He asked thee, Hast thou seen my servant Job?
Famous he was in heaven, on earth less known;
Where glory is false glory, attributed
70   To things not glorious, men not worthy of fame.
They err who count it glorious to subdue
By conquest far and wide, to overrun
Large countries, and in field great battles win,
Great cities by assault: what do these worthies,
75   But rob and spoil, burn, slaughter, and enslave
Peaceable nations, neighbouring, or remote,
Made captive, yet deserving freedom more
Than those their conquerors, who leave behind
Nothing but ruin wheresoe'er they rove,
80   And all the flourishing works of peace destroy,
Then swell with pride, and must be titled gods,
Great benefactors of mankind, deliverers,
Worshipped with temple, priest, and sacrifice;
One is the son of Jove, of Mars the other,
85   Till conqueror Death discover them scarce men,
Rolling in brutish vices, and deformed,
Violent or shameful death their due reward.
But if there be in glory aught of good,
It may by means far different be attained
90   Without ambition, war, or violence;
By deeds of peace, by wisdom eminent,
By patience, temperance; I mention still
Him whom thy wrongs with saintly patience borne,

iii 67. Cp. *Job* i 8: 'And the Lord said unto Satan, Hast thou considered my servant Job, that there is none like him in the earth, a perfect and an upright man, one that feareth God, escheweth evil?'

iii 81. *titled gods*] The Roman emperors were generally accorded the title 'divine' by the Senate. Cp. also *Acts* xii 21–2: 'Herod . . . made an oration unto them. And the people gave a shout, saying, It is the voice of a god, and not of a man.'

iii 82. *benefactors*] Cp. *Luke* xxii 25: 'The kings of the Gentiles . . . are called benefactors.'

iii 84. Alexander was made out to be the son of Jupiter Ammon, and Scipio of Jupiter Capitolinus (see *PL* ix 508–10): Romulus was called son of Mars.

iii 86. *brutish vices*] Alexander was an alcoholic, and his early death in 323 B.C. was often attributed to this.

iii 91–2. *wisdom . . . patience, temperance*] Cp. *2 Pet.* i 6 'And [add] to knowledge temperance; and to temperance patience'.

Made famous in a land and times obscure;
95 Who names not now with honour patient Job?
Poor Socrates (who next more memorable?)
By what he taught and suffered for so doing,
For truth's sake suffering death unjust, lives now
Equal in fame to proudest conquerors.
100 Yet if for fame and glory aught be done,
Aught suffered; if young African for fame
His wasted country freed from Punic rage,
The deed becomes unpraised, the man at least,
And loses, though but verbal, his reward.
105 Shall I seek glory then, as vain men seek
Oft not deserved? I seek not mine, but his
Who sent me, and thereby witness whence I am.
   To whom the tempter murmuring thus replied.
Think not so slight of glory; therein least
110 Resembling thy great Father: he seeks glory,
And for his glory all things made, all things
Orders and governs, nor content in heaven
By all his angels glorified, requires
Glory from men, from all men good or bad,
115 Wise or unwise, no difference, no exemption;
Above all sacrifice, or hallowed gift
Glory he requires, and glory he receives
Promiscuous from all nations, Jew, or Greek,
Or barbarous, nor exception hath declared;
120 From us his foes pronounced glory he exacts.

iii *98. unjust*] Socrates was condemned for corrupting the youth and malig-
ning the gods of the state. He could easily have escaped, but chose to die
rather than act in a lawless way (his reasons for the choice are recorded in
full in Plato's *Crito*). Lewalski 240, quoting Justin Martyr, *First Apology* v,
points out that behind Christ's words is a tradition of commentary which
saw Socrates' death for truth's sake as a foreshadowing of Christ's, and his
teaching as prefiguring Christ's doctrine.
iii *101. young African*] Scipio, who landed in Africa in 204 B.C. and forced
the Carthaginians to recall Hannibal from Italy.
iii *106–7. not mine, but his / Who sent me*] Cp. *John* vii 18: 'He that speaketh
of himself seeketh his own glory: but he that seeketh his glory that sent him,
the same is true', and viii 50: 'I seek not mine own glory.'
iii *111. for his glory all things made*] Cp. *Rev.* iv 11, where the elders falling
down and casting their crowns before 'him that sat on the throne' cry:
'Thou art worthy, O Lord, to receive glory and honour and power; for
thou hast created all things, and for thy pleasure they are and were created.'
iii *119. barbarous*] non-Hellenic.

To whom our Saviour fervently replied.
And reason; since his word all things produced,
Though chiefly not for glory as prime end,
But to show forth his goodness, and impart
*125* His good communicable to every soul
Freely; of whom what could he less expect
Than glory and benediction, that is, thanks,
The slightest, easiest, readiest recompense
From them who could return him nothing else,
*130* And not returning that would likeliest render
Contempt instead, dishonour, obloquy?
Hard recompense, unsuitable return
For so much good, so much beneficence.
But why should man seek glory? who of his own
*135* Hath nothing, and to whom nothing belongs
But condemnation, ignominy, and shame?
Who for so many benefits received
Turned recreant to God, ingrate and false,
And so of all true good himself despoiled,
*140* Yet, sacrilegious, to himself would take
That which to God alone of right belongs;
Yet so much bounty is in God, such grace,
That who advance his glory, not their own,
Them he himself to glory will advance.
*145* So spake the Son of God; and here again
Satan had not to answer, but stood struck
With guilt of his own sin, for he himself
Insatiable of glory had lost all,
Yet of another plea bethought him soon.
*150* Of glory as thou wilt, said he, so deem,
Worth or not worth the seeking, let it pass:
But to a kingdom thou art born, ordained
To sit upon thy father David's throne;
By mother's side thy father, though thy right

iii *121. fervently*] The adverb distinguishes this reply from Christ's others;
he grows heated because his Father's name is called in question.

iii *138. recreant*] The primary meaning is 'confessing oneself overcome or
vanquished'. M. in the *Doctrine and Discipline of Divorce* (1643) uses the word
for the first time, according to *OED*, in the sense 'unfaithful to duty, false,
apostate', as here.

iii *140. sacrilegious*] Cp. *De doctrina* ii 4 (Columbia xvii 116–7): 'Sacrilege
... consists in ... the appropriation to private uses of things dedicated to
God.'

iii *146. had ... answer*] had no answer.

iii *154. By mother's side thy father*] The genealogy of Christ in the gospels

*155*   Be now in powerful hands, that will not part
        Easily from possession won with arms;
        Judaea now and all the promised land
        Reduced a province under Roman yoke,
        Obeys Tiberius; nor is always ruled
*160*   With temperate sway; oft have they violated
        The Temple, oft the Law with foul affronts,
        Abominations rather, as did once
        Antiochus: and think'st thou to regain
        Thy right by sitting still or thus retiring?
*165*   So did not Maccabeus: he indeed
        Retired unto the desert, but with arms;

(*Matt.* i 1–16, *Luke* iii 23–38) is traced through Joseph back to David and beyond. David is referred to as Christ's 'father' (ancestor) in *Luke* i 32, and Christ is frequently addressed as 'son of David' in the gospels (cp. *Rev.* xxii 16: 'I Jesus ... am the root and the offspring of David'). It is not asserted in the gospels that Mary was of the house of David, though the assumption that she was was common in the seventeenth century. Jewish law did not, in any case, recognize descent through the mother, so Satan's qualification is a slighting one: after all, he suggests, Christ is not son of Joseph; perhaps, then, not descended from David.

iii *157–60*. Judaea was annexed to Syria by Quirinius, Roman governor of Syria, in A.D. 6. Tiberius (A.D. 14–37) retained Pilate as governor from 25–36, in spite of various acts of tyranny (cp. *Luke* xiii 1: 'the Galileans, whose blood Pilate had mingled with their sacrifices'). Josephus, *Antiquities* xviii 3, tells how Pilate planted armed soldiers, disguised as Jews, in the mob at Jerusalem, and when the mob began to abuse him the soldiers 'laid about them with much greater vigour than Pilate had commanded', killing many who had not been abusive as well as those who had.

iii *160. oft*] Satan is exaggerating. Pompey, however, had violated the Holy of Holies in Jerusalem in 63 B.C.

iii *163. Antiochus*] In 169 B.C. Antiochus Epiphanes stole all the holy vessels from the Temple, the altar, candlesticks and hangings, scaled off the gold facing of the building, and forced the Jews to build shrines for idols and pollute the temple by sacrificing swine and unclean beasts. *1 Macc.* i 20–63 and Josephus, *Antiquities* xii 5, have accounts of the desecration.

iii *165–70*. The national resistance to Antiochus Epiphanes began in 166 B.C. in the obscure town of Modin and centred round Judas Maccabeus, a Levite, whose heroic struggle with Antiochus resulted in the founding of the Asmonaean dynasty. Lewalski 262 notes that in traditional biblical exegesis Judas' defeat of Antiochus was regarded as a type of Christ's conquest over Antichrist.

iii *166. Retired unto the desert*] Cp. *1 Macc.* v 24–8: 'And Judas ... passed over Jordan and went three days' journey in the wilderness ... and Judas and his army turned suddenly by the way of the wilderness unto Bosora.'

And o'er a mighty king so oft prevailed,
That by strong hand his family obtained,
Though priests, the crown, and David's throne
        usurped,
*170*  With Modin and her suburbs once content.
If kingdom move thee not, let move thee zeal,
And duty; zeal and duty are not slow;
But on occasion's forelock watchful wait.
They themselves rather are occasion best,
*175*  Zeal of thy Father's house, duty to free
Thy country from her heathen servitude;
So shalt thou best fulfil, best verify
The prophets old, who sung thy endless reign,
The happier reign the sooner it begins,
*180*  Reign then; what canst thou better do the while?
        To whom our Saviour answer thus returned.
All things are best fulfilled in their due time,
And time there is for all things, Truth hath said:
If of my reign prophetic writ hath told,
*185*  That it shall never end, so when begin
The Father in his purpose hath decreed,
He in whose hand all times and seasons roll.
What if he hath decreed that I shall first
Be tried in humble state, and things adverse,
*190*  By tribulations, injuries, insults,
Contempts, and scorns, and snares, and violence,
Suffering, abstaining, quietly expecting
Without distrust or doubt, that he may know

iii *171. kingdom*] kingship.

iii *172–4. occasion's forelock*] Proverbially occasion (opportunity) had a forelock which had to be grasped because she was bald behind. In *F.Q.* II iv 12, where the proverb is acted out, Guyon grasps it.      *zeal and duty . . . are occasion best*] Here Satan slightly changes the meaning of 'occasion' from 'opportunity' to 'reason, cause'—an equally well-established meaning in the seventeenth century.

iii *175. Zeal of thy Father's house*] Christ's disciples, *John* ii 17, regarded his expulsion of the money-changers from the Temple as a fulfilment of the prophecy in *Ps.* lxix 9: 'The zeal of thine house hath eaten me up.'

iii *178. endless*] Cp. *Isa.* ix 7: 'Of the increase of his government and peace there shall be no end.'

iii *183. time . . . for all things*] Cp. *Eccles.* iii 1: 'To every thing there is a season, and a time to every purpose under the heaven.'

iii *187.* Cp. *Acts* i 7: 'It is not for you to know the times or the seasons, which the Father hath put in his own power.'

What I can suffer, how obey? Who best
195  Can suffer, best can do; best reign, who first
Well hath obeyed; just trial ere I merit
My exaltation without change or end.
But what concerns it thee when I begin
My everlasting kingdom, why art thou
200  Solicitous, what moves thy inquisition?
Know'st thou not that my rising is thy fall,
And my promotion will be thy destruction?
    To whom the tempter inly racked replied.
Let that come when it comes; all hope is lost
205  Of my reception into grace; what worse?
For where no hope is left, is left no fear;
If there be worse, the expectation more
Of worse torments me than the feeling can.
I would be at the worst; worst is my port,
210  My harbour and my ultimate repose,
The end I would attain, my final good.
My error was my error, and my crime
My crime; whatever for itself condemned,
And will alike be punished; whether thou
215  Reign or reign not; though to that gentle brow
Willingly I could fly, and hope thy reign,
From that placid aspect and meek regard,
Rather than aggravate my evil state,
Would stand between me and thy Father's ire,

iii *194-6. Who best . . . Well hath obeyed*] Cp. *Matt.* xx 26-7:'Whosoever will
be great among you, let him be your minister; And whosoever will be
chief among you, let him be your servant'; also Mucius Scaevola's boast,
Livy ii 12, before thrusting his hand into the flames: 'Both to do and to
endure valiantly is the Roman way.' Among the various classical authorities
for the maxim that the most obedient servant makes the best master are
Plato, *Laws* iv 715, 762, Aristotle, *Politics* iii 4, Cicero, *De Legibus* iii 2 and
Seneca, *De Ira* ii 15.

iii *204-22.* Arnold Stein, *ELH* xxiii (1956) 117-21, quoting this 'masterly
exhibition of dramatic art', claims that the language and rhythm reveal
Satan's 'real self' overcoming the 'dramatic self'. Stein thinks that Satan is
ready 'to turn weakness into strength', to create a new drama and a new
protagonist who will be Saviour to Satan, though in fact 'no offer is made,
and no pause to permit a counter-offer'–a fact which tells against those who
interpret the speech as merely another stratagem of Satan's, a histrionic ap-
proach which, as H. J. Laskowsky, *Thoth* iv (1963) 24-9, sees it, he tries when
sophistry has failed. Lewalski 258 reads the speech as mere 'rhetorical
craft': an attempt to corrupt Christ by urging him to hasten to his own
kingdom (see iii 223-4).

220    (Whose ire I dread more than the fire of hell)
     A shelter and a kind of shading cool
     Interposition, as a summer's cloud.
     If I then to the worst that can be haste,
     Why move thy feet so slow to what is best,
225    Happiest both to thyself and all the world,
     That thou who worthiest art shouldst be their king?
     Perhaps thou linger'st in deep thoughts detained
     Of the enterprise so hazardous and high;
     No wonder, for though in thee be united
230    What of perfection can in man be found,
     Or human nature can receive, consider
     Thy life hath yet been private, most part spent
     At home, scarce viewed the Galilean towns,
     And once a year Jerusalem, few days'
235    Short sojourn; and what thence couldst thou observe?
     The world thou hast not seen, much less her glory,
     Empires, and monarchs, and their radiant courts,
     Best school of best experience, quickest in sight
     In all things that to greatest actions lead.
240    The wisest, unexperienced, will be ever
     Timorous and loth, with novice modesty,
     (As he who seeking asses found a kingdom)
     Irresolute, unhardy, unadventurous:
     But I will bring thee where thou soon shalt quit
245    Those rudiments, and see before thine eyes
     The monarchies of the earth, their pomp and state,
     Sufficient introduction to inform
     Thee, of thyself so apt, in regal arts,

iii *221–2*. Frye 237 maintains that *PL* iii 385–6 shows that this is the direct opposite of Christ's true nature: cp. however *Isa.* xxv 4–5: 'For thou hast been . . . a shadow from the heat . . . even the heat with the shadow of a cloud.' Rachel Trickett, *E & S* (1978) 35 cites *Macbeth* III iv 110–12.

iii *234. once a year*] Cp. *Luke* ii 41: 'Now his parents went to Jerusalem every year at the feast of the passover.'

iii *242. he who . . . found a kingdom*] Saul. In *1 Sam.* ix 1–x 1, Kish, Saul's father, loses his asses, and Saul, looking for them, comes to Samuel who, forewarned by God, anoints him with the words, 'Is it not because the Lord hath anointed thee to be captain over his inheritance?' Saul's 'novice modesty' shows itself in his initial reaction, ix 21. Lewalski 265 thinks Satan is implying that Christ may, if he is backward like Saul, be, like Saul, at length rejected by God for disobedience.

iii *245. rudiments*] initial stages.

iii *247. inform*] train.

And regal mysteries; that thou may'st know
250    How best their opposition to withstand.
With that (such power was given him then) he took
The Son of God up to a mountain high.
It was a mountain at whose verdant feet
A spacious plain outstretched in circuit wide
255    Lay pleasant; from his side two rivers flowed,
Th' one winding, the other straight, and left between
Fair champaign with less rivers interveined,
Then meeting joined their tribute to the sea:
Fertile of corn the glebe, of oil and wine,
260    With herds the pastures thronged, with flocks the hills,
Huge cities and high-towered, that well might seem
The seats of mightiest monarchs, and so large
The prospect was, that here and there was room
For barren desert fountainless and dry.
265    To this high mountain-top the tempter brought
Our Saviour, and new train of words began.
Well have we speeded, and o'er hill and dale,
Forest and field, and flood, temples and towers
Cut shorter many a league; here thou behold'st

iii *249. regal mysteries*] either 'state secrets' or 'the skills of government'.
'Mystery' could mean either 'secret' or 'skill' in the seventeenth century.
A contrast is suggested with *Matt.* xiii 11: 'It is given unto you to know the
mysteries of the kingdom of heaven.'
iii *250. their*] that of the 'monarchies' (l. 246).
iii *252. a mountain high*] Cp. *Matt.* iv 8: 'an exceeding high mountain',
*Luke* iv 5: 'an high mountain'. Though the Bible does not specify which
mountain it was, the candidate most favoured by tradition was Mt Quaran-
tania, which rises from the plain of Jericho. It seems likely that M. has Mt
Niphates in mind: he had made Satan alight on this in *PL* iii 742. Strabo,
*Geography* XI xii 4, describing the Taurus range, writes 'it rises higher, and
bears the name Niphates, and somewhere here are the sources of the Tigris'.
The source of the Tigris is, in fact, on the southern slope of Niphates:
there was a tradition that it was identical with that of the Euphrates (cp.
Boethius, *De Consol.* v 1 *Tigris et Euphrates uno se fonte resolvunt*). This would
fit M.'s 'from his side two rivers flowed' (l. 255).
iii *256. winding ... straight*] Strabo XI xii 3, distinguishing the Euphrates
from the Tigris, says that the Euphrates flows 'with winding stream'.
Pliny vi 31 says that 'Tigris' is the Persian word for 'arrow', and that it
is so called because of its swift, straight course.
iii *257. champaign*] open, flat land; here Mesopotamia.
iii *258. meeting*] The Tigris and Euphrates meet and flow into the Persian
Gulf.

270  Assyria and her empire's ancient bounds,
     Araxes and the Caspian lake, thence on
     As far as Indus east, Euphrates west,
     And oft beyond; to south the Persian bay,
     And inaccessible the Arabian drouth:
275  Here Nineveh, of length within her wall
     Several days' journey, built by Ninus old,
     Of that first golden monarchy the seat,
     And seat of Salmanassar, whose success
     Israel in long captivity still mourns;
280  There Babylon the wonder of all tongues,
     As ancient, but rebuilt by him who twice
     Judah and all thy father David's house
     Led captive, and Jerusalem laid waste,
     Till Cyrus set them free; Persepolis,

iii *270-3*. On Niphates Christ and Satan stand at the tip of a huge horn of land (representing the Assyrian empire as it was at the zenith of Assyrian power, about 722-636 B.C.). The horn widens and curves away southwards and eastwards, ending at the Indus, the great river which flows south into the Arabian Sea. The horn's southern (convex) side runs from the tip along the Euphrates and then along the northern shores of the Persian Gulf and the Arabian Sea. Part of its concave side is formed by the Araxes, which flows eastward from central Armenia into the Caspian. Whiting 124 thinks that M. was using Tables iv-vii of Ptolemy's *Geographia* (1605).

iii *274. drouth*] desert. Usually a variant form of 'drought'. *OED* records no other instance of the word in M.'s sense in modern English.

iii *275-9. Nineveh*] The great capital of Assyria (cp. *Jonah* iii 3 'an exceeding great city of three days' journey') lies in the middle of the tip of the horn of land which Christ and Satan survey, about 250 miles south-east of Niphates. Ninus was its eponymous founder. Shalmaneser (Salmanassar) captured Samaria and carried the ten northern tribes of Israel into captivity *c.* 722 B.C. and, *2 Kings* xvii 6, 'placed them in Halah and Habor by the river of Gozan and in the cities of the Medes'.

iii *280-3*. Babylon, on the Euphrates, about 600 miles from Niphates on the convex side of the horn, was originally built by Belus and Semiramis, father and wife of Ninus, and was rebuilt by Nebuchadnezzar from 604 B.C. onwards (*Dan.* iv 30), after which it became one of the wonders of the ancient world. Nebuchadnezzar twice sacked Jerusalem and led its inhabitants into captivity: once in the reign of Jehoiakim (*c.* 596 B.C.), and again in 586 in the reign of Zedekiah (*2 Kings* xxiv 13-5 and xxv 11, *2 Chron.* xxxvi 6-20). J. E. Parish, *N & Q* ccix (1964) 337, notes that 'the wonder of all tongues' is a pun: M. in *PL* xii 342-3 had identified Babylon with the Babel of *Genesis*.

iii *284-7*. Cyrus was founder of the Persian empire, and united the Medes and the Persians by the capture of Ecbatana, capital of Media, a city whose massive fortifications are described in *Judith* i 2-4. (Looking south-east

285    His city there thou seest, and Bactra there;
       Ecbatana her structure vast there shows,
       And Hecatompylos her hundred gates,
       There Susa by Choaspes, amber stream,
       The drink of none but kings; of later fame
290    Built by Emathian, or by Parthian hands,
       The great Seleucia, Nisibis, and there
       Artaxata, Teredon, Ctesiphon,
       Turning with easy eye thou may'st behold.
       All these the Parthian, now some ages past,

from Niphates, Ecbatana would be seen about 250 miles beyond Nineveh).
Then, in 538 B.C., he took Babylon and freed the Israelites from the power of
Belshazzar (*Dan.* v, *Ezra* i 1–8). His summer capital, Persepolis, was in
southern Persia (more or less in line with Nineveh, viewed from Niphates,
but 600 miles beyond). Bactra was capital of the Persian province of Bactria,
now Balkh in Afghanistan, near to the furthest end of the concave side of the
horn, viewed from Niphates, and about 1500 miles away. Hecatompylos
(which means 'hundred-gated') was a city in Parthia, but its site is not
known.

iii *288–9.* Susa (Shushan), winter-palace of the Persian kings, stood on the
banks of the Choaspes. From Niphates it would lie in the same direction as
Persepolis, but about 300 miles nearer. Herodotus i 188 says that when
Cyrus marched he carried with him water from the Choaspes 'whereof
alone, and of none other, the king drinks. This water of the Choaspes is
boiled, and very many four-wheeled waggons drawn by mules carry it in
silver vessels'; M. is also indebted here to Athenaeus, *Deipnosophists* xii
515: 'Agathocles . . . says that in Persia there is water called "golden" . . .
and none may drink of it save only the king and his eldest son.'

iii *290. Emathian*] Macedonian.

iii *291–2. Seleucia*] Founded by Alexander's general Seleucus Nicator, after
Alexander's death. It lay on the Tigris, about 350 miles up river, near the
modern Baghdad, and was called 'the great' to distinguish it from other
Seleucid foundations of the same name.    *Nisibis*] On a tributary of the
Euphrates, in Mesopotamia, only about 100 miles south-east of Niphates.
*Artaxata*] The ancient capital of Armenia, on the Araxes.    *Teredon*] Near
the confluence of the Tigris and Euphrates.    *Ctesiphon*] On the east bank
of the Tigris, opposite Seleucia: for some time it was the Parthian capital.
Cp. Josephus, *Antiquities* xviii 9: 'Ctesiphon, a Greek city, near Seleucia,
where the king [of Parthia] wintered every year, and where the greatest
part of his treasures are deposited.' Starnes and Talbert (305) suggestively
quote Stephanus, *Ctesiphon . . . magnitude est adeo, ut Parthorum multitudinem
et apparatum omnem recipiat* (Ctesiphon . . . so great in size that it can contain
the Parthian host and all its equipment).

iii *294–7.* About 250 B.C. Arsaces invaded Parthia, then a province of the
Seleucid empire which had its capital at Antioch on the Orontes. He was

295   By great Arsaces led, who founded first
      That empire, under his dominion holds
      From the luxurious kings of Antioch won.
      And just in time thou com'st to have a view
      Of his great power; for now the Parthian king
300   In Ctesiphon hath gathered all his host
      Against the Scythian, whose incursions wild
      Have wasted Sogdiana; to her aid
      He marches now in haste: see, though from far,
      His thousands, in what martial equipage
305   They issue forth, steel bows, and shafts their arms
      Of equal dread in flight, or in pursuit;
      All horsemen, in which fight they most excel;
      See how in warlike muster they appear,
      In rhombs and wedges, and half-moons, and wings.
310       He looked and saw what numbers numberless
      The city gates outpoured, light-armed troops

expelled by Seleucus II about 238, but his brother Tiridates, who took the
name Arsaces, recaptured Parthia and founded the Arsacid line of Parthian
kings. The Parthian empire remained very limited in extent until the final
decay of the Seleucid empire after the death of Antiochus Epiphanes in 165
B.C. 'Luxurious' is not an adjective deserved by the Seleucid kings generally
though Antiochus Epiphanes certainly deserved it: Satan is allowing his
reputation to colour that of his predecessors, or is perhaps thinking of the
reputation of the city of Antioch, which had in its suburbs the park of woods
and waters known as the paradise of Daphne, the beauty and lax morals of
which were celebrated all over the western world.
iii *301-2*. The Scythians were the barbarians who lived north-east of the
Caspian and north of the Aral Sea. They eventually overran the province
of Sogdiana, the area round the mouth and lower reaches of the Oxus,
which flows into the south-east corner of the Aral Sea. The watcher from
Niphates could, theoretically, look to his left across the waist of the
Caspian to the Aral Sea beyond. Even by the shortest possible route the
distance from Ctesiphon to this area would be over 1200 miles.
iii *306*. The Parthians were notoriously skilful mounted archers, and were
particularly noted for the accuracy with which they could fire backwards
while in retreat.
iii *309. rhombs*] lozenge-shaped or diamond-shaped formations.
iii *311-40*. M. seems to recall several details from Ammianus Marcellinus,
who has a most vivid account of the battle with the Parthians near Maranga,
in which Julian was killed, xxv i 11-19: 'All their companies were clad
in iron, and all parts of their bodies were covered with thick plates, so fitted
that the stiff joints conformed with those of their limbs . . . their entire
bodies were covered with metal. . . . Hard by the archers (for that nation
has especially trusted in this art from the very cradle) were bending their

          In coats of mail and military pride;
          In mail their horses clad, yet fleet and strong,
          Prancing their riders bore, the flower and choice
     315  Of many provinces from bound to bound;
          From Arachosia, from Candaor east,
          And Margiana to the Hyrcanian cliffs
          Of Caucasus, and dark Iberian dales,
          From Atropatia and the neighbouring plains
     320  Of Adiabene, Media, and the south

flexible bows. . . . Behind them gleaming elephants, with their awful
figures and savage, gaping mouths. . . . If they perceived their forces were
giving way, as they retreated they would shoot their arrows back like a
shower of rain and keep the enemy from a bold pursuit.' xxv iii 11: 'They
sent forth such a shower of arrows that they prevented their opponents
from seeing the bowmen.' Perhaps the details came to M. by way of Mon-
taigne, *Essays* ii 9, who paraphrases Marcellinus (Florio's translation):
'They had (saith he) their horses stiffe and strong, covered with thick hides
and themselves armed from head to foot, with massie iron plates so arti-
ficially contrived, that where the joynts are, there they furthered the mo-
tion, and helped the stirring. A man would have said, they had been men
made of yron.' Lewalski 120–2 regards these lines as a reworking of a *topos*
common in biblical epic, the detailed description of a pagan metropolis.
Nearest to M.'s picture, in her opinion, is the view of Memphis in Girolamo
Fracastoro's *Joseph* (printed in Du Bartas² 818).
iii *316–21*. The components of the great horn of land which Christ is viewing
are named anti-clockwise, beginning at the south-east corner with Aracho-
sia, a province west of the Indus, in modern Baluchistan, then moving north-
wards to Candaor in Afghanistan, then west from Afghanistan to Margiana
(modern Khorasan) and Hyrcania, which lies a little further west, skirting
the south-east shore of the Caspian, and, further west still, Iberia, a region
of the Caucasus west of the Caspian and north of Araxes (Purchas, *Pilgrimes*
iii 110 speaks of the 'palpable darkness' of this thickly wooded region).
Moving south across Araxes again we come to Atropatia, the northern
province of Media, and then, to the west, Adiabene, one of the plains around
Nineveh. Travelling away from Niphates again to the south, we come to
Susiana, the most southerly Parthian province, bordering on the Persian
Gulf, and Balsara, a port on the Chatt-el-Arab (united Tigris and Eu-
phrates), the modern Basra. The juxtaposition of 'Hyrcanian' and 'Cauca-
sus' was probably suggested to M. by a recollection of Virgil, *Aen.* iv 365–7.
iii *326*. Cp. the approaching army in Euripides, *Phoenissae* 110, 'the glare of
brass flashes all over the plain', and Plutarch's description of the Parthians
at Carrhae, *Life of Crassus* xxiv: 'They dropped the coverings of their ar-
mour, and were seen to be themselves blazing in helmets and breastplates,
their Margianian steel glittering keen and bright and their horses clad in
plates of bronze and steel.'

Of Susiana to Balsara's haven.
He saw them in their forms of battle ranged,
How quick they wheeled, and flying behind them shot
Sharp sleet of arrowy showers against the face
325  Of their pursuers, and overcame by flight;
The field all iron cast a gleaming brown,
Nor wanted clouds of foot, nor on each horn,
Cuirassiers all in steel for standing fight;
Chariots or elephants endorsed with towers
330  Of archers, nor of labouring pioneers
A multitude with spades and axes armed
To lay hills plain, fell woods, or valleys fill,
Or where plain was raise hill, or overlay
With bridges rivers proud, as with a yoke;
335  Mules after these, camels and dromedaries,
And waggons fraught with utensils of war.
Such forces met not, nor so wide a camp,
When Agrican with all his northern powers
Besieged Albracca, as romances tell;
340  The city of Gallaphrone, from thence to win
The fairest of her sex Angelica
His daughter, sought by many prowest knights,
Both paynim, and the peers of Charlemagne.

iii *327. clouds of foot*] Echoes *Aen.* vii 793: *nimbus peditum.*

iii *328. Cuirassiers*] heavy cavalry armed with the cuirass (metal armour extending from neck to waist).

iii *329. endorsed*] both in the sense 'carrying on their backs' and in the sense 'confirmed, strengthened', (to 'endorse' meant to write on the back of a document, indicating its validity). Ben Jonson has the same word play in his epigram on the Earl of Newcastle's horsemanship, *Underwood* liii 11–12: 'Nay, so your Seate his beauties did endorse, / As I began to wish myselfe a horse.'

iii *337–43.* In Boiardo, *Orlando Innamorato* I x–xiv, Agrican, King of Tartary, brings 2,200,000 men to Albracca, the stronghold of Gallaphrone, King of Cathay and father of Angelica, whom Agrican loves. Roland and the French paladins are involved, and Lewalski (267) considers that the parallel 'identifies Parthia with great and misused military force, for the *Orlando Innamorato* records that many of Charlemagne's knights were enticed to this siege through Angelica's deceit and thereby defaulted in their proper service to their king'.

iii *342. prowest*] most valiant: a favourite superlative of Spenser, who uses it coupled with 'knight' or 'knightly' six times in *F.Q.*

iii *343. paynim*] pagan: another favourite Spenserian word, used twentyfive times in *F.Q.*

Such and so numerous was their chivalry;
345   At sight whereof the Fiend yet more presumed,
And to our Saviour thus his words renewed.
      That thou mayst know I seek not to engage
Thy virtue, and not every way secure
On no slight grounds thy safety; hear, and mark
350   To what end I have brought thee hither and shown
All this fair sight; thy kingdom though foretold
By prophet or by angel, unless thou
Endeavour, as thy father David did,
Thou never shalt obtain; prediction still
355   In all things, and all men, supposes means,
Without means used, what it predicts revokes.
But say thou wert possessed of David's throne
By free consent of all, none opposite,
Samaritan or Jew; how couldst thou hope
360   Long to enjoy it quiet and secure,
Between two such enclosing enemies
Roman and Parthian? Therefore one of these
Thou must make sure thy own, the Parthian first
By my advice, as nearer and of late
365   Found able by invasion to annoy
Thy country, and captive lead away her kings
Antigonus, and old Hyrcanus bound,
Maugre the Roman: it shall be my task
To render thee the Parthian at dispose;
370   Choose which thou wilt by conquest or by league.
By him thou shalt regain, without him not,
That which alone can truly reinstall thee
In David's royal seat, his true successor,

iii *344. chivalry*] cavalry.
iii *347-9. I seek not . . . thy safety*] It is not my aim to arouse your courage
without making provision for your safety.
iii *358. opposite*] opposing.
iii *359. Samaritan or Jew*] The Jews of Judaea and Galilee did not regard the
Samaritans as pure Jews, since Samaria had been colonized by alien races.
Jews had 'no dealings with the Samaritans' (*John* iv 9).
iii *366-7.* Satan is inaccurate. The Parthians were allies of Antigonus: with
their support he overran Judaea and captured Jerusalem. He took prisoner
his uncle, the seventy-year-old Hyrcanus II, and Herod's brother Phasaelus,
killed the latter and cut off the ears of the former to disqualify him from
priestly office, carrying him off to Seleucia. After a three-year reign Anti-
gonus was defeated and captured by Herod, who bribed Antony to have him
executed (37 B.C.). These events are related in Josephus, *Antiquities* xiv 13–16.
iii *368. Maugre*] in spite of.

Deliverance of thy brethren, those ten tribes
375 Whose offspring in his territory yet serve
In Habor, and among the Medes dispersed,
Ten sons of Jacob, two of Joseph lost
Thus long from Israel; serving as of old
Their fathers in the land of Egypt served,
380 This offer sets before thee to deliver.
These if from servitude thou shalt restore
To their inheritance, then, nor till then,
Thou on the throne of David in full glory,
From Egypt to Euphrates and beyond
385 Shalt reign, and Rome or Caesar not need fear.
To whom our Saviour answered thus unmoved.
Much ostentation vain of fleshly arm,
And fragile arms, much instrument of war
Long in preparing, soon to nothing brought,
390 Before mine eyes thou hast set; and in my ear
Vented much policy, and projects deep
Of enemies, of aids, battles and leagues,
Plausible to the world, to me worth naught.
Means I must use thou say'st, prediction else
395 Will unpredict and fail me of the throne:
My time I told thee, (and that time for thee
Were better farthest off) is not yet come;

iii 374-6. See ll. 275-9n. The Habor was a tributary of the Euphrates, and the land around it, Gozan, was under Parthian domination in the time of Christ. It lay only about 150 miles south of Niphates, nearer than any of the regions previously mentioned by Satan.

iii 377. *two of Joseph*] The ten tribes included Ephraim and Manasses, named after the sons of Joseph.

iii 384. *From Egypt to Euphrates*] Cp. *Gen.* xv 18, where God makes a covenant with Abraham, promising to give his sons dominion from Nile to Euphrates, also 1 *Kings* iv 21: 'And Solomon reigned over all kingdoms from the river [Euphrates] unto the land of the Philistines, and unto the border of Egypt.'

iii 387. Cp. 2 *Chron.* xxxii 8: 'With him is an arm of flesh; but with us is the Lord our God to help us, and to fight our battles', also Jer. xvii 5: 'Cursed is the man that trusteth in man, and maketh flesh his arm'; M.'s phrase echoes Spenser, *F.Q.* III iv 27 'So feeble is the powre of fleshly arme.'

iii 395. *fail me of the throne*] To 'fail of' means to come short of attaining, but M.'s construction with an imitation of the Latin dative pronoun ('me') is singular: OED gives no instance of it.

iii 396-7. *My time . . . is not yet come*] Cp. *John* vii 6: 'My time is not yet come'–Jesus' reply to his brothers when they tell him to show himself to the world.

When that comes think not thou to find me slack
On my part aught endeavouring, or to need
400 Thy politic maxims, or that cumbersome
Luggage of war there shown me, argument
Of human weakness rather than of strength.
My brethren, as thou call'st them; those ten tribes,
I must deliver, if I mean to reign
405 David's true heir, and his full sceptre sway
To just extent over all Israel's sons;
But whence to thee this zeal, where was it then
For Israel, or for David, or his throne,
When thou stood'st up his tempter to the pride
410 Of numb'ring Israel, which cost the lives
Of threescore and ten thousand Israelites
By three days' pestilence? such was thy zeal
To Israel then, the same that now to me.
As for those captive tribes, themselves were they
415 Who wrought their own captivity, fell off
From God to worship calves, the deities
Of Egypt, Baal next and Ashtaroth,
And all the idolatries of heathen round,
Besides their other worse than heathenish crimes;
420 Nor in the land of their captivity
Humbled themselves, or penitent besought
The God of their forefathers; but so died
Impenitent, and left a race behind
Like to themselves, distinguishable scarce

iii *401. Luggage*] Commonly used in the seventeenth century to mean the baggage of an army.

iii *409-12.* Cp. *1 Chron.* xxi 1-14: 'And Satan stood up against Israel, and provoked David to number Israel . . . And God was displeased with this thing; therefore he smote Israel . . . So the Lord sent pestilence upon Israel: and there fell of Israel seventy thousand men.'

iii *414-9.* Jeroboam divided the northern tribes from Judah and Benjamin and founded the kingdom of Samaria. He set up calves in Bethel and in Dan, in imitation of the two calves worshipped by the Egyptians, and said 'Behold thy gods, O Israel, which brought thee up out of the land of Egypt' (*1 Kings* xii 25-33). Ahab built an altar for Baal, and married Jezebel, a Zidonian princess (*1 Kings* xvi 31-2); Ashtoreth, goddess of the moon, was the Zidonian Venus. For Baal and Ashtoreth (Ashtaroth is the plural form), see *Nativity Ode* 197-201 and *PL* i 419-24.

iii *419. worse than heathenish crimes*] The worship of Baal entailed human sacrifice (cp. *Jer.* xix 5).

425   From Gentiles, but by circumcision vain,
      And God with idols in their worship joined.
      Should I of these the liberty regard,
      Who freed, as to their ancient patrimony,
      Unhumbled, unrepentant, unreformed,
430   Headlong would follow; and to their gods perhaps
      Of Bethel and of Dan? No, let them serve
      Their enemies, who serve idols with God.
      Yet he at length, time to himself best known,
      Rememb'ring Abraham by some wondrous call
435   May bring them back repentant and sincere,
      And at their passing cleave the Assyrian flood,
      While to their native land with joy they haste,
      As the Red Sea and Jordan once he cleft,
      When to the promised land their fathers passed;
440   To his due time and providence I leave them.
          So spake Israel's true King, and to the Fiend
      Made answer meet, that made void all his wiles.
      So fares it when with truth falsehood contends.


## THE FOURTH BOOK

      Perplexed and troubled at his bad success
      The tempter stood, nor had what to reply,
      Discovered in his fraud, thrown from his hope,
      So oft, and the persuasive rhetoric
5     That sleeked his tongue, and won so much on Eve,
      So little here, nay lost; but Eve was Eve,
      This far his over-match, who self-deceived

iii *425. circumcision vain*] Cp. *Rom.* ii 25: 'If thou be a breaker of the law, thy circumcision is made uncircumcision.'
iii *430.* The awkwardly compressed syntax has frequently been commented on, and various unlikely emendations (e.g. 'fall unto' for 'follow; and to') suggested.
iii *431–2.* Cp. *Jer.* v 19: 'Like as ye have forsaken me, and served strange gods in your land, so shall ye serve strangers in a land that is not yours.'
iii *436. Assyrian flood*] Euphrates; cp. Isaiah's prophecy, *Is.* xi 15–16: 'The Lord . . . with his mighty wind shall . . . shake his hand over the river . . . and make men go over dryshod. And there shall be an highway for the remnant of his people, which shall be left, from Assyria; like as it was to Israel in the day that he came up out of the land of Egypt.'
iii *438.* The cleaving of the Red Sea is narrated in *Exod.* xiv 21–2, and that of Jordan in *Josh.* iii 14–17.

And rash, beforehand had no better weighed
The strength he was to cope with, or his own:
10   But as a man who had been matchless held
In cunning, over-reached where least he thought,
To salve his credit, and for very spite
Still will be tempting him who foils him still,
And never cease, though to his shame the more;
15   Or as a swarm of flies in vintage-time,
About the wine-press where sweet must is poured,
Beat off, returns as oft with humming sound;
Or surging waves against a solid rock,
Though all to shivers dashed, the assault renew,
20   Vain battery, and in froth or bubbles end;
So Satan, whom repulse upon repulse
Met ever; and to shameful silence brought,
Yet gives not o'er though desperate of success,
And his vain importunity pursues.
25   He brought our Saviour to the western side
Of that high mountain, whence he might behold
Another plain, long but in breadth not wide;

iv *8. better*] than Eve.

iv *15–17*. Cp. *Il.* xvi 641, where Homer compares warriors round Sarpe-
don's body to flies round a milk can, and Ariosto, *Orlando Furioso* xiv 109,
where the Moors attack the Christians as flies swarm over milking pails
or left-overs of food. Arnold Stein, *ELH* xxiii (1956) 123, sees in M.'s wine
image 'a striking anticipatory symbol of the sacerdotal role not yet entered
in'.

iv *18–20*. Cp. *Il.* xv 618–22: 'They abode firm-fixed . . . like a crag, sheer
and great, hard by the grey sea, that abideth the swift paths of the shrill
winds, and the swelling waves that belch forth against it; even so the
Danaans withstood the Trojans steadfastly, and fled not', and *Aen.* vii
586–90: 'He, like an unmoved ocean-cliff resists; like an ocean-cliff, which,
when a great crash comes, stands steadfast in its bulk amid many howling
waves; in vain the crags and foaming rocks roar about it, and the sea-weed,
dashed upon its sides, is whirled back.'

iv *27. Another plain*] The plain of Latium in central Italy, lying south and
west of the Apennines, which screen it from the north ('Septentrion')
winds, and with Rome, on the Tiber, at its centre. S. Kliger, *PMLA* lxi
(1946) 474–91, connects M.'s panoramic view of Rome and her power with
the literary tradition which saw in Rome the *urbs aeterna*, and more particu-
larly with two examples of this tradition–Anchises's speech in *Aen.* vi and
Claudian's eulogy in *On Stilicho's Consulship* iii. There was a long-standing
Christian attempt, running through Augustine, Lactantius, Tertullian,
Prudentius, Dante and others, to take over this pagan tradition and convert
the *urbs aeterna* into an *urbs sacra*. Kliger sees Christ's stern rebuke of Satan
(iv 147–51) as a drastic rejection of this compromise.

Washed by the southern sea, and on the north
To equal length backed with a ridge of hills
*30*   That screened the fruits of the earth and seats of men
From cold Septentrion blasts, thence in the midst
Divided by a river, of whose banks
On each side an imperial city stood,
With towers and temples proudly elevate
*35*   On seven small hills, with palaces adorned,
Porches and theatres, baths, aqueducts,
Statues and trophies, and triumphal arcs,
Gardens and groves presented to his eyes
Above the height of mountains interposed.
*40*   By what strange parallax or optic skill
Of vision multiplied through air, or glass
Of telescope, were curious to inquire:
And now the tempter thus his silence broke.
　　　The city which thou seest no other deem
*45*   Than great and glorious Rome, queen of the earth
So far renowned, and with the spoils enriched
Of nations; there the Capitol thou seest
Above the rest lifting his stately head
On the Tarpeian rock, her citadel
*50*   Impregnable, and there Mount Palatine
The imperial palace, compass huge, and high
The structure, skill of noblest architects,
With gilded battlements, conspicuous far,
Turrets and terraces, and glittering spires.
*55*   Many a fair edifice besides, more like
Houses of gods (so well I have disposed

iv *40. parallax*] apparent displacement of an object caused by actual change
in the position of the observer.

iv *42. were curious to inquire*] As Pope 112-4 remarks, many commentators
*did* inquire how Satan could have shown Christ all the kingdoms of the world
from a single mountain-top. M.'s telescopic explanation (iv 56-7) had been
anticipated by Cornelius Jansen and Francis Luca. Another popular theory
was that the kingdoms were mere mirages or visions.

iv *49. Tarpeian rock*] The steepest precipice on the Capitoline hill. The
citadel occupied the commanding northern summit of the Capitoline.

iv *50-1. Mount Palatine / The imperial palace*] During the empire a large part
of the Palatine hill was gradually covered by the expanding imperial palace.
What now remains on the Palatine, occupying its centre, are the ruins of
Domitian's palace, which M. would have seen when he visited Rome.
Satan may be referring to Augustus' second palace, rebuilt after the fire of
A.D.3, or to the Domus Tiberiana.

> My airy microscope) thou mayst behold
> Outside and inside both, pillars and roofs
> Carved work, the hand of famed artificers
> 60  In cedar, marble, ivory or gold.
> Thence to the gates cast round thine eye, and see
> What conflux issuing forth, or entering in,
> Praetors, proconsuls to their provinces
> Hasting or on return, in robes of state;
> 65  Lictors and rods the ensigns of their power,
> Legions and cohorts, turms of horse and wings:
> Or embassies from regions far remote
> In various habits on the Appian road,
> Or on the Aemilian, some from farthest south,
> 70  Syene, and where the shadow both way falls,

iv 57. *microscope*] *OED* gives this as the first instance of 'microscope' in a transferred sense: the peculiarity of M.'s 'microscope' is that it can see 'Outside and inside both'. Marjorie Nicolson, *JELH* ii (1935) 1–11, considers that M.'s blindness prevented him from understanding the real nature of the microscope. While microscopes were known in England between 1625 and 1660, they did not come into common use until after 1660. She thinks that M., from vague accounts of the new instrument, misunderstood its function. Kester Svendsen, *MLN* lxiv (1949) 525–7, draws attention to a passage in Leonard and Thomas Digges's *Pantometria* (1591) I xxi, which describes a system of lens arrangement that produces the same effects as Satan's 'microscope'.

iv 59. *hand*] handiwork.

iv 63. *Praetors, proconsuls*] Under the empire there were sixteen praetors (magistrates), each of whom was allowed a year of provincial government following his term of office in Rome. Proconsuls were governors of senatorial provinces.

iv 65. *Lictors*] attendants who accompanied Roman dignitaries and carried bundles of rods to symbolize the officials' power to punish criminals.

iv 66. *cohorts*] tenth parts of a legion.     *wings*] Roman cavalry fought on the flanks of the infantry, and its formations became known as wings. A 'turm' (Latin *turma*) was the tenth part of a wing, about thirty in number. 'Turm' is found in English usage from the fifteenth century.

iv 68–9. *Appian ... Aemilian*] The Via Appia, built by Appius Claudius 312 B.C., was the main road running south from Rome to Brindisi. The Via Aemilia, built by Aemilius Lepidus, went from Rimini to Piacenza.

iv 69–70. *farthest south, Syene*] Assouan, on the first cataract of the Nile, at the extreme south of the Roman sphere of influence. Tacitus, *Ann.* ii 61, speaks of it as one of the former 'limits of the Roman empire'.

iv 70–1. *where the shadow both way falls, Meroe*] Cp. Pliny ii 75: 'In Meroe–this is an inhabited island in the river Nile 5000 stades from Syene, and is the

Meroe Nilotic isle, and more to west,
The realm of Bocchus to the Blackmoor sea;
From the Asian kings and Parthian among these,
From India and the golden Chersoness,
75    And utmost Indian isle Taprobane,
Dusk faces with white silken turbans wreathed:
From Gallia, Gades, and the British west,
Germans and Scythians, and Sarmatians north
Beyond Danubius to the Tauric pool.
80    All nations now to Rome obedience pay,
To Rome's great emperor, whose wide domain
In ample territory, wealth and power,
Civility of manners, arts, and arms,
And long renown thou justly mayst prefer
85    Before the Parthian; these two thrones except,
The rest are barbarous, and scarce worth the sight,
Shared among petty kings too far removed;

capital of the Ethiopian race–the shadows disappear twice a year, when the sun is in the 18th degree of Taurus and in the 14th of Leo. There is a mountain named Maleus in the Indian tribe of the Oretes, near which shadows are thrown southward in summer and northward in winter.' As Whiting 88–9 notes, M. seems to have read the second sentence as if it also referred to Meroe.

iv *72. realm of Bocchus*] Mauretania; Bocchus was king of it at the time of the Jugurthine war: he surrendered his son-in-law Jugurtha to the Romans in 106 B.C.      *Blackmoor sea*] that part of the Mediterranean bordering on Mauretania, the land of the moors or 'blackamoors'. It is called *Africum Pelagus* in Ortelius, but Horace, *Odes* II vi 3–4 calls it *Maura unda*, which may have suggested the name M. uses.

iv *74. golden Chersoness*] In *PL* xi 392 the spelling is 'Chersonese'; here M. may be avoiding rhyme with 'these'. The Malay peninsula was called 'golden' to distinguish it from the 'Tauric Chersonese' (the Crimea): Josephus, *Antiquities* viii 6, says that it was formerly called Ophir, and that Solomon sent a fleet there to bring back gold. 'Chersonese' is from the Greek word for a peninsula.

iv *75. Taprobane*] G. W. Whiting, *RES* xiii (1937) 209–12, produces evidence from Ortelius, *Theatrum Orbis Terrarum* and elsewhere to show that 'Taprobane' usually meant Sumatra. J. D. Gordon, *RES* xviii (1942) 319, notes that Ariosto, *Orlando Furioso* xv 17, mentions *l'aurea Chersonesso* (a form near to M.'s) and Taprobane together in the same stanza.

iv *77. Gallia*] France.      *Gades*] Cadiz.

iv *78. Scythians*] See iii 301–2n.      *Sarmatians*] the barbarians living north of the Scythians, divided from them by the Don: they occupied Poland and Russia west of the Volga.

iv *79. Tauric pool*] Sea of Azov.

These having shown thee, I have shown thee all
The kingdoms of the world, and all their glory.
90   This emperor hath no son, and now is old,
Old, and lascivious, and from Rome retired
To Capreae an island small but strong
On the Campanian shore, with purpose there
His horrid lusts in private to enjoy,
95   Committing to a wicked favourite
All public cares, and yet of him suspicious,
Hated of all, and hating; with what ease
Endued with regal virtues as thou art,
Appearing, and beginning noble deeds,
100   Might'st thou expel this monster from his throne
Now made a sty, and in his place ascending
A victor people free from servile yoke!
And with my help thou mayst; to me the power
Is given, and by that right I give it thee.
105   Aim therefore at no less than all the world,
Aim at the highest, without the highest attained
Will be for thee no sitting, or not long
On David's throne, be prophesied what will.
To whom the Son of God unmoved replied.
110   Nor doth this grandeur and majestic show

iv *90-4*. Tiberius (42 B.C.–A.D. 37) retired from active government in A.D. 26 and took up residence the following year on Capri, attracted to it, according to Suetonius, *Caesars* iii 40 and Tacitus, *Ann.* iv 67, because a landing could only be made on one small beach, and it was otherwise surrounded by sheer cliffs and deep water. Suetonius, iii 43–5, and Tacitus, vi 1, both describe Tiberius' progressive degradation on Capri. Lewalski 122 cites a parallel passage from Beaumont's *Psyche* ix 225–6, 229, in which Satan calls forth Tiberius from the globe wherein he is displaying all the kingdoms to Christ, upbraids him for mismanagement and offers Christ his place.

iv *95. a wicked favourite*] Sejanus. Tiberius grew suspicious of him, and finally denounced him to the Senate which condemned the fallen favourite to death A.D. 31.

iv *102. victor people*] The *1671 Errata* removes a comma from between these words.

iv *103-4*. Cp. *Luke* iv 6: 'And the devil said unto him, All this power will I give thee, and the glory of them: for that is delivered unto me; and to whomsoever I will I give it.'

iv *110-20*. Pope 56–66 remarks that the emphasis on luxury and physical pleasure in these lines is in keeping with the treatment of the temptations by Protestant theologians (see i 355*n*) who, as they regarded the first temptation as one not of gluttony but of distrust in God, were obliged to inter-

Of luxury, though called magnificence,
More than of arms before, allure mine eye,
Much less my mind; though thou should'st add to tell
Their sumptuous gluttonies, and gorgeous feasts
*115* On citron tables or Atlantic stone;
(For I have also heard, perhaps have read)
Their wines of Setia, Cales, and Falerne,
Chios and Crete, and how they quaff in gold,
Crystal and myrrhine cups embossed with gems

pret the kingdoms-of-the-world temptation as an attempt to excite bodily appetite, as well as the longing for honour, wealth, dominion and power. Thus the devil in Bale's *Temptation of Our Lord*, after enumerating the actual regions he is preparing to hand over to Christ, and dwelling on their 'ryches, their honor, their wealth', goes on to persuade him that 'Here are fayre women, of countenaunce ameable, / With all kyndes of meates, to the body dylectable', and Giles Fletcher, *Christ's Victory and Triumph* i 49–59, describes the temptation of the kingdoms allegorically as a house with four stories: on the first are wine and alluring ladies, on the second and third, 'avarice' and 'ambitious honour'.

iv *115. citron tables*] The wood of the African citrus was in great demand among wealthy Romans for table-tops, as Pliny xiii 29–30 relates, partly because it was very hard and spilt wine would not mark it, and partly because it had beautiful graining, either in stripes (tiger wood) or in rounds (panther wood) or in clusters (parsley wood). *Atlantic stone*] The meaning is not certain. 'Atlantic' derives from the Libyan Mt Atlas (and was thence applied to the sea near the W. shore of Africa, afterwards extending to the whole ocean). M. may, then, mean marble from the Atlas mountains, or he may be referring again to the citrus wood, which looked like marble and grew on the slopes of Atlas (cp. Pliny xiii 29: 'adjoining Mt Atlas is Mauretania, which produces a great many citrus trees').

iv *117. Setia*] Sezza, near Rome, mentioned for its wines by Martial xiii 23. *Cales, and Falerne*] Cales, and the Falernian vineyards, were in Campania, near Vesuvius. Cp. Horace, *Odes* I xxxi 9: 'trim the vine with Calenian pruning-knife', and Virgil, *Georg.* ii 96: 'Falernian wine vaults'.

iv *118. Chios*] Island off the Ionian coast, the source of expensive, sweet Greek wines. Horace looks forward to a jar of Chian wine, *Odes* III xix 5.

iv *119. Crystal and myrrhine cups*] Cp. Pliny xxxiii 2: 'out of the same earth we have dug myrrhine (*murrina*) and crystal (*crystallina*), things which their mere fragility rendered costly. . . . Nor was this enough: we drink out of a crowd of precious stones, and set our cups with emeralds', and Juvenal, *Sat.* vi 155–6, who says that two of the things spoilt women will squander their husbands' money on are crystal and myrrhine cups. Of the materials M. mentions only gold would be embossed and decorated with jewels. Pliny thought that the basic material of myrrhine cups was a fossil; Propertius IV v 26 regarded it as porcelain from Parthia. It is now thought

*120*　And studs of pearl, to me should'st tell who thirst
　　　And hunger still: then embassies thou show'st
　　　From nations far and nigh; what honour that,
　　　But tedious waste of time to sit and hear
　　　So many hollow compliments and lies,
*125*　Outlandish flatteries? Then proceed'st to talk
　　　Of the emperor, how easily subdued,
　　　How gloriously; I shall, thou say'st, expel
　　　A brutish monster: what if I withal
　　　Expel a devil who first made him such?
*130*　Let his tormentor conscience find him out,
　　　For him I was not sent, nor yet to free
　　　That people victor once, now vile and base,
　　　Deservedly made vassal, who once just,
　　　Frugal, and mild, and temperate, conquered well,
*135*　But govern ill the nations under yoke,
　　　Peeling their provinces, exhausted all
　　　By lust and rapine; first ambitious grown
　　　Of triumph that insulting vanity;
　　　Then cruel, by their sports to blood inured
*140*　Of fighting beasts, and men to beasts exposed,
　　　Luxurious by their wealth, and greedier still,
　　　And from the daily scene effeminate.
　　　What wise and valiant man would seek to free
　　　These thus degenerate, by themselves enslaved,

that these cups, though they reached Rome via Parthia, came from China and were made of a rare sort of clay.

iv *130. conscience*] Cp. Tacitus, *Ann.* vi 6, where Tiberius writes to the Senate: 'May all the gods and goddesses destroy me more miserably than I feel myself to be daily perishing, if I know at this moment what to write to you.' Tacitus comments: 'Tiberius was not saved by his elevation or his solitude from having to confess the anguish of his heart.'

iv *133. Deservedly made vassal*] It was a favourite theory of M.'s that those who became slaves to their own passions deservedly and frequently allowed themselves to be enslaved politically. Cp. *History of Britain*: 'But when God hath decreed servitude on a sinful nation, fitted by their own vices for no condition but servile, all Estates of Government are alike unable to avoid it'; also *Defensio Secunda*: 'by the wonted judgment, and as it were by the just retribution of God, it comes to pass, that the nation, which has been incapable of governing and ordering itself, and has delivered itself up to the slavery of its own lusts, is itself delivered over, against its will, to other masters' (Columbia x 198 and viii 250–1).

iv *136. Peeling*] pillaging.

iv *142. scene*] stage show, theatrical performance; a common seventeenth-century sense.

*145*  Or could of inward slaves make outward free?
       Know therefore when my season comes to sit
       On David's throne, it shall be like a tree
       Spreading and overshadowing all the earth,
       Or as a stone that shall to pieces dash
*150*  All monarchies besides throughout the world,
       And of my kingdom there shall be no end:
       Means there shall be to this, but what the means,
       Is not for thee to know, nor me to tell.
           To whom the tempter impudent replied.
*155*  I see all offers made by me how slight
       Thou valu'st, because offered, and reject'st:
       Nothing will please the difficult and nice,
       Or nothing more than still to contradict:
       On the other side know also thou, that I
*160*  On what I offer set as high esteem,
       Nor what I part with mean to give for naught;
       All these which in a moment thou behold'st,
       The kingdoms of the world to thee I give;
       For given to me, I give to whom I please,
*165*  No trifle; yet with this reserve, not else,

iv *147–50.* Christ sees himself (and, as Lewalski 279 points out, Christian exegesis up to M.'s day had consistently seen him) as the fulfilment of the two visions in *Dan.* iv 10–12 and ii 31–5: Nebuchadnezzar's dream of the tree that 'reached unto heaven, and the sight thereof to the end of all the earth', and his vision of a stone which smashed the metal image of the kingdoms and 'became a great mountain, and filled the whole earth'.

iv *151.* Cp. *Luke* i 33: 'And of his kingdom there shall be no end.'

iv *153. Is not for thee to know*] Pope 39 remarks that the phrase suggests that M. was working under the influence of the tradition that Christ deliberately withheld from Satan all evidence of his own identity. It is not necessary to assume, however, that Christ is aware of his own identity all along: Allen's theory that he has moments of illumination (see headnote) would explain flashes of confidence like this one.

iv *157. the*] C. W. Brodribb, *TLS* (17 May, 1941) 239–41, and some eight-teenth-century critics, would prefer to read 'thee', thus turning a general statement into a particular one. There is no authority or necessity for this emendation.    *nice*] over-fastidious.

iv *164.* As Pope 67 and Gilbert[2] 606 remark, the glory of Athens is not offered as one of the gifts of Satan, or as one of the kingdoms which he can personally bestow upon Christ. He presents his bargain at the conclusion of the temptation of Rome. Thoroughly as M. castigates classical philosophy and literature, he does not place them under the direct control of the devil.

iv *165–7.* Cp. *Matt.* iv 9: 'All these things will I give thee, if thou wilt fall down and worship me.' Arnold Stein, *ELH* xxiii (1956) 126, considers that

On this condition, if thou wilt fall down,
And worship me as thy superior lord,
Easily done, and hold them all of me;
For what can less so great a gift deserve?
*170*    Whom thus our Saviour answered with disdain.
I never liked thy talk, thy offers less,
Now both abhor, since thou hast dared to utter
The abominable terms, impious condition;
But I endure the time, till which expired,
*175*  Thou hast permission on me. It is written
The first of all commandments, Thou shalt worship
The Lord thy God, and only him shalt serve;
And dar'st thou to the Son of God propound
To worship thee accursed, now more accursed
*180*  For this attempt bolder than that on Eve,
And more blasphemous? which expect to rue.
The kingdoms of the world to thee were given,
Permitted rather, and by thee usurped,
Other donation none thou canst produce:
*185*  If given, by whom but by the King of kings,
God over all supreme? If given to thee,
By thee how fairly is the giver now
Repaid! But gratitude in thee is lost
Long since. Wert thou so void of fear or shame,
*190*  As offer them to me the Son of God,
To me my own, on such abhorred pact,
That I fall down and worship thee as God?
Get thee behind me; plain thou now appear'st
That Evil One, Satan for ever damned.

Satan is not really tempting Christ to accept this price: 'A bargainer like Satan does not expect a customer uninterested in the merchandise to become interested on hearing the full price. . . . If this *is* the Son of God, and is successfully provoked, then Satan may learn, however sadly, the fact.' Lewalski 260, however, regards Satan's move as 'a desperate face-saving maneuver: recognizing that Christ has regarded all his offers as "slight" and valueless, he here attempts to prove their value by citing their high price'.

iv *174–6*. Cp. *Luke* iv 8: 'And Jesus answered and said unto him, Get thee behind me, Satan: for it is written, Thou shalt worship the Lord thy God, and him only shalt thou serve', where Christ is quoting *Deut.* vi 13.

iv *184. donation*] grant, bestowal of property.

iv *191. To me my own*] Pope 37 comments that the phrase is ambiguous. It may mean 'the kingdoms you have offered me for my own', as well as 'my own kingdoms': Christ is not provoked into making a direct claim.

195  To whom the Fiend with fear abashed replied.
     Be not so sore offended, Son of God;
     Though Sons of God both angels are and men,
     If I to try whether in higher sort
     Than these thou bear'st that title, have proposed
200  What both from men and angels I receive,
     Tetrarchs of fire, air, flood, and on the earth
     Nations besides from all the quartered winds,
     God of this world invoked and world beneath;
     Who then thou art, whose coming is foretold
205  To me so fatal, me it most concerns.
     The trial hath endamaged thee no way,
     Rather more honour left and more esteem;
     Me naught advantaged, missing what I aimed.
     Therefore let pass, as they are transitory,
210  The kingdoms of this world; I shall no more
     Advise thee, gain them as thou canst, or not.
     And thou thyself seem'st otherwise inclined
     Than to a worldly crown, addicted more
     To contemplation and profound dispute,
215  As by that early action may be judged,
     When slipping from thy mother's eye thou went'st
     Alone into the Temple; there was found
     Amongst the gravest Rabbis disputant
     On points and questions fitting Moses' chair,
220  Teaching not taught; the childhood shows the man,
     As morning shows the day. Be famous then
     By wisdom; as thy empire must extend,
     So let extend thy mind o'er all the world,
     In knowledge, all things in it comprehend,
225  All knowledge is not couched in Moses' law,
     The Pentateuch or what the prophets wrote,
     The Gentiles also know, and write, and teach

iv *197*. Cp. *Rom.* viii 14: 'For as many as are led by the Spirit of God, they are the sons of God'.
iv *201*. *Tetrarchs*] rulers of fourth parts: here, of one of the four elements.
iv *203*. Satan is called 'the god of this world' in *2 Cor.* iv 4.
iv *215*. See i 209–14*n*.
iv *219*. *Moses' chair*] the chair from which the doctors expounded the law. *Matt.* xxiii 2: 'The scribes and Pharisees sit in Moses' seat.'
iv *221–2*. *Be famous then / By wisdom*] Pope 67 finds M. the first writer to include learning among the temptations.
iv *226*. *Pentateuch*] the first five books of the Old Testament, containing the Mosaic Law.

To admiration, led by nature's light;
And with the Gentiles much thou must converse,
230    Ruling them by persuasion as thou mean'st,
Without their learning how wilt thou with them,
Or they with thee hold conversation meet?
How wilt thou reason with them, how refute
Their idolisms, traditions, paradoxes?
235    Error by his own arms is best evinced.
Look once more ere we leave this specular mount
Westward, much nearer by south-west, behold
Where on the Aegean shore a city stands
Built nobly, pure the air, and light the soil,
240    Athens the eye of Greece, mother of arts
And eloquence, native to famous wits
Or hospitable, in her sweet recess,
City or suburban, studious walks and shades;
See there the olive-grove of Academe,
245    Plato's retirement, where the Attic bird
Trills her thick-warbled notes the summer long,
There flowery hill Hymettus with the sound

iv *228. To admiration*] admirably.

iv *229–35.* Schultz 227, viewing the whole temptation in an ecclesiastical context (see headnote), remarks that Satan's two arguments for philosophy as *ancilla theologiae*–that it would make one socially acceptable, hence escaping contempt, and that it would be useful for refuting heresy–were the arguments constantly used by the conservative side in the learned-ministry controversy.

iv *234. idolisms*] idolatries: first found in Sylvester (Du Bartas 632).

iv *235. evinced*] conquered.

iv *236. specular mount*] lookout mountain; according to *OED*, the first instance of 'specular' (Latin *specula*= watchtower) in the sense 'affording an extensive view'.

iv *240. the eye*] the seat of intelligence or light. *OED* first records this idiom in Hakluyt *Voyages* (1582) of Oxford and Cambridge. It is also found in Justin V viii 4 and Aristotle *Rhet.* III x 7 of Athens and Sparta.

iv *244. Academe*] The Academy was a gymnasium, enlarged as a public park by Cimon, about a mile north-west of Athens. It was planted with olive trees. Plato used to walk there with his pupils, and from it his school of philosophy took its name.

iv *245. the Attic bird*] the nightingale; near the Academy was Colonus, celebrated by Sophocles, *Oedipus at Colonus* 671, as the haunt of nightingales.

iv *247. Hymettus*] A line of hills to the south-east of Athens; the thyme-covered slopes are famous for their honey.

Of bees' industrious murmur oft invites
To studious musing; there Ilissus rolls
250　His whispering stream; within the walls then view
The schools of ancient sages; his who bred
Great Alexander to subdue the world,
Lyceum there, and painted Stoa next:
There thou shalt hear and learn the secret power
255　Of harmony in tones and numbers hit
By voice or hand, and various-measured verse,
Aeolian charms and Dorian lyric odes,
And his who gave them breath, but higher sung,
Blind Melesigenes thence Homer called,
260　Whose poem Phoebus challenged for his own.
Thence what the lofty grave tragedians taught
In chorus or iambic, teachers best

iv 249. *Ilissus*] A little river which rises on the slopes of Hymettus and flows
to the south of the city.

iv 251. *his*] Aristotle's, tutor to Alexander.

iv 253. *Lyceum*] Originally a sanctuary of Apollo Lyceius, the Lyceum was
a park to the E. of the city, beyond the Diocharean Gate (not, then, 'within
the walls'). Aristotle and his pupils used to stroll up and down its walks,
hence the name of their school, the 'peripatetics' (strollers).　*Stoa*]
covered colonnade. The Athenian agora had more than one, but one, on the
north side, was, according to Pausanias I iii 1, XIV vi 3, decorated with
frescoes by famous artists and known as the 'painted stoa': this was where
the founder of the 'Stoics', Zeno, taught.

iv 257. *Aeolian*] The island of Lesbos belonged to the Aeolians, and the songs
of Sappho and Alcaeus were in the Aeolic dialect. In *Odes* III xxx 13–4,
Horace boasts that he introduced the *Aeolium carmen* into Italy.　*charms*]
songs (Latin *carmen*).　*Dorian*] Pindar's odes and hymns are written in the
Dorian dialect.

iv 259. *Melesigenes*] Not used as a title for Homer by any Greek or Latin
poet; presumably M. invented it, referring to the fact that, according to
one tradition, Homer was born near the river Meles in Ionia. It was common
among the ancients to represent Homer as the source of all poetry. Aelian,
*Var. Hist.* xiii 22, says Galaton the painter drew Homer as a fountain with
other poets receiving water from his mouth.　*thence*] from his blindness.
The pseudo-Herodotean *Life of Homer* explained ὅμηρος as a Cumaean
word meaning 'blind'.

iv 260. An epigram in the *Greek Anthology* ix 455, entitled 'What Apollo
would say about Homer' perpetuates the tradition that Apollo envied
Homer's poetry. It reads: 'The song is mine, but divine Homer wrote it
down.'

iv 262. *chorus or iambic*] In Greek tragedy the dialogue is written in iambics,
the chorus in various metres.

Of moral prudence, with delight received
In brief sententious precepts, while they treat
265 Of fate, and chance, and change in human life;
High actions, and high passions best describing:
Thence to the famous orators repair,
Those ancient, whose resistless eloquence
Wielded at will that fierce democraty,
270 Shook the Arsenal and fulmined over Greece,
To Macedon, and Artaxerxes' throne;
To sage philosophy next lend thine ear,
From heaven descended to the low-roofed house
Of Socrates, see there his tenement,
275 Whom well inspired the oracle pronounced

iv 264. *brief sententious precepts*] Cp. Quintilian X i 68, on the style of M.'s
favourite Euripides: *sententiis densus* (thick with maxims).

iv 269. *democraty*] democracy. M.'s form, nearer to the Greek δημοκρατία,
was common in the seventeenth century.

iv 270. *Shook the Arsenal*] E. C. Baldwin, *PQ* xviii (1939) 218–22, refers to
Dionysius of Halicarnassus, *Epistle to Ammoeus* i 15–22, for the information
that Demosthenes 'shook' the great Arsenal or dockyard which Philo
of Eleusis constructed at Piraeus in that, on his advice, the building of it was
suspended from 339–338 B.C. so that public funds might be freed for use
against Philip of Macedon. B. A. Wright, *N & Q* n.s. v. (1958) 199–200,
accepting the fact that it is Philo's dockyard that is meant, interprets 'shook'
as 'brandished, as the symbol of Athenian naval power'.    *fulmined*] sent
forth lightning and thunder: the first recorded use of the verb is *F.Q.* III ii 5.
M. is echoing Aristophanes' satiric identification of Pericles with the Olym-
pian Zeus in *Acharnians* 530: 'He lightened, thundered and confounded
Hellas.' It was Pericles who endeavoured to inspire the Athenians while the
Spartans were ravaging outside their gates, and while the Athenian fleet was
away supporting the Egyptian revolt against the Persian king Artaxerxes,
allied to Sparta.

iv 273. *From heaven descended*] Cp. Cicero, *Tusculan Disputations* V iv 10
'Socrates on the other hand was the first to call philosophy down from the
heavens and set her in the cities of men and bring her also into their homes
and compel her to ask questions about life and morality'. Cicero is referring
to the scientific pretentiousness of pre-Socratic thought (cp. *Phaedo* 96–9,
where Socrates tells Cebes of his youthful enthusiasm for scientific philo-
sophy, and how he eventually decided he must give up investigating
'realities', and investigate 'conceptions' instead). When Satan speaks of the
descent of philosophy from heaven he means something more than Cicero
does, and something he hopes will be more tempting to Christ.    *low-
roofed house*] In Aristophanes, *Clouds* 92, the dwelling of Socrates is pointed
out as a 'little house'.

iv 275–6. Cp. Plato, *Apology* 21, where Socrates at his trial tells how his

Wisest of men; from whose mouth issued forth
Mellifluous streams that watered all the schools
Of Academics old and new, with those
Surnamed Peripatetics, and the sect
280 Epicurean, and the Stoic severe;
These here revolve, or, as thou lik'st, at home,
Till time mature thee to a kingdom's weight;
These rules will render thee a king complete
Within thyself, much more with empire joined.
285 To whom our Saviour sagely thus replied.
Think not but that I know these things, or think

friend Chaerephon asked the Delphic oracle if there were any men wiser than Socrates, and how the oracle replied that there was no one wiser.

iv *276–8.* Cp. Quintilian I x, who calls Socrates the 'fountain' of philosophers.

iv *278. old and new*] There were three phases of Academic philosophy: old, under Plato (d. 347 B.C.); middle, under Arcesilas (d. 271 B.C.); new, under Carneades (d. 128 B.C.).

iv *279. Peripatetics*] See l. 253*n.*

iv *280. Epicurean*] Epicurus, 341–270 B.C., reacting against Plato and Aristotle, based his ethical doctrine not on logic and metaphysics but on sensation – the only touchstone of truth, as he saw it. Thus his moral philosophy is a qualified hedonism. He became the loved and venerated head of a little community of men and women who lived a life of simple pleasure, drinking water and eating barley-bread. The accusations of debauchery which the Stoics brought against this community are probably mere venomous slander. *Stoic*] See *Comus* 706*n*.

iv *286–7.* J. H. Hanford, *SP* xv (1918) 183–4, remarks that M. 'cannot bring himself to say quite flatly that Jesus Christ was ignorant' of pagan philosophy. In fact, Christ's reply is plain evidence of knowledge.

iv *286–321.* M. introduces the temptation of learning, without any precedent, in order to maintain the parallel between the temptations of the first and second Adam (cp. Adam's thirst for unnecessary knowledge, against which Raphael warns him, *PL* viii 66–178). There has been frequent expression of surprise that M. should be false to his earlier affiliations. Irene Samuel, *PMLA* lxiv (1949) 709–23, stresses, however, the constancy of M.'s attitude to learning throughout his life. Not only Raphael's reply to Adam about astronomy and Michael's restriction of the 'sum Of wisdom' (*PL* viii 66–178 and xii 575–87), but also M.'s insistence on the 'plainness and brightness' of truth in *Of Reformation* (Columbia iii 33, Yale i 566), and his commendation of the 'plain unlearned man that lives well by that light which he has' in *Animadversions* (Columbia iii 162–3, Yale i 720) and of the man 'learned without letters' in *Defensio prima* (Columbia vii 69), are quite in harmony, she argues, with Christ's words here. What Christ insists on, as Miss Samuel sees it, is what M. had always insisted on:

> I know them not; not therefore am I short
> Of knowing what I ought: he who receives
> Light from above, from the fountain of light,
> 290  No other doctrine needs, though granted true;

the adequacy of the human spirit, with or without particular books, in the quest for all knowledge essential to the good life. Stein[2] 97 takes the same view as Miss Samuel. Plainly, however, Miss Samuel's argument applies better to ll. 286–90 than to the specific condemnation of Greek philosophy as 'false' and 'built on nothing firm', which follows. This certainly does seem, as G. F. Sensabaugh, *SP* xliii (1946) 258–72, feels, out of key with the ideals and enthusiasms of *Of Education*. Sensabaugh thinks M. did change his educational philosophy between the 1640s and the Restoration, and that this was the result of the process by which he forced his mind into a systematized scheme of Christian thought–a process which produced the *De doctrina*. In this work he ostensibly lifts his whole educational policy from the secular to the religious plane, though there is a tendency, particularly in Book ii, to retain an ethical system drawn largely from classical and Renaissance thought, while asserting the all-sufficiency of Scripture. Perhaps Christ's speech should be read in this light, or as that of a *dramatis persona*, in which case the difficulties of fitting what he says to M.'s own beliefs disappear, and all that is needed is a reason for the placing of this anti-Hellenic speech in the mouth of the historical Christ. The reason is not far to seek. The gradual Hellenisation of Judaea had been in train since Antiochus violated the Holy of Holies (167 B.C.) and forbade circumcision. Hellenisation was part of Herod's policy too.

Schultz 92 notes that 'almost any of the Fathers or their modern imitators could have matched M.'s school-by-school criticism of pagan philosophy', with its 'labour-saving device of rejecting only the *summum bonum* of each sect'. He refers particularly to Clement, *Protrepticus* v–vii, Tertullian, *De praescriptione haereticorum* vii, and Lactantius, *De falsa sapientia* (*Divine Institutes* iii 5–23 – this source is also suggested by J. Horrell, *RES* xviii (1943) 423–4): among more modern works, Philippe de Mornay's *De la vérité de la chrétienne religion*, which Sidney translated, and George Hakewill's *Apology* (see *Natur* headnote). E. Newmeyer, *Bulletin of the N.Y. Public Library* lxvi 485–98, adds to this list Theodore Beza's *Job Expounded*: Beza, following Josephus, maintains that Abraham taught the Egyptians, and that Greek philosophy, derived from Egypt, was therefore a corrupt residue of Abraham's superior learning. Lewalski 120 notes that in Quarles' *Job Militant*, a meditation upon the varieties of false felicity which seduce other men but not Job includes Athenian learning.

iv *288–90*. Lewalski 291–5 shows that in assuming a radical distinction between knowledge (*scientia*), which derives from the study of the things of the world, and wisdom (*sapientia*) which comes only from above, M.'s Christ is defending a Christian commonplace prevalent from Augustine's time through to the seventeenth century.

But these are false, or little else but dreams,
Conjectures, fancies, built on nothing firm.
The first and wisest of them all professed
To know this only, that he nothing knew;
295　The next to fabling fell and smooth conceits,
A third sort doubted all things, though plain sense;
Others in virtue placed felicity,
But virtue joined with riches and long life,
In corporal pleasure he, and careless ease,
300　The Stoic last in philosophic pride,
By him called virtue; and his virtuous man,
Wise, perfect in himself, and all possessing,
Equal to God, oft shames not to prefer,
As fearing God nor man, contemning all
305　Wealth, pleasure, pain or torment, death and life,
Which when he lists, he leaves, or boasts he can,

iv *294. that he nothing knew*] In Plato, *Apology* 21–3, Socrates, having told of the answer of the Delphic oracle (see 275–6*n*), adds that he went round Athens interviewing reputedly wise people, and eventually concluded that he was indeed the wisest, but only because he alone knew that he knew nothing. Lewalski 126–7 quotes from Quarles, *Job Militant* xi a passage on the uselessness of knowledge without wisdom, 'Which made that great Philosopher avow, / He knew so much, that he did nothing know'.

iv *295. The next to fabling fell*] An objection to Plato, as Kermode[4] 328 notes, which is ultimately Platonic. In *Id Plat* 38 M. calls Plato *fabulator maximus*: allegories and myths are frequent in the dialogues.

iv *296. third sort*] the Sceptics, founded by Pyrrho of Elis, *c.* 360–270 B.C. Because they believed the impossibility of knowing things in their own nature, and held that against every statement the contrary might be advanced with equal reason, they thought it necessary to preserve an attitude of intellectual suspense and imperturbability.

iv *297–8. Others . . . riches and long life*] the Peripatetics; Aristotle taught that man's happiness is the activity of soul according to virtue in a mature life, requiring as conditions moderate bodily health and external goods of fortune.

iv *299. he*] Epicurus; a jaundiced view: see l. 280*n*.

iv *300–6.* M. may be influenced in his arguments against Stoicism by Cicero's account and systematic refutation of it, *De finibus* iii–iv. Schultz 92 and 261 lists later denunciations in Cyprian and Lactantius and, in the seventeenth century, Samuel Gardiner, William Rawley, Anthony Burges and others. The Stoics divided humanity into two classes: wise or virtuous, unwise or wicked. The wise man alone, they claimed, is free, rich, beautiful, skilled to govern, capable of giving or receiving a benefit. His happiness is in no way inferior to that of Zeus ('Equal to God'). The so-called goods of life ('Wealth, pleasure') are to him indifferent. He will have self-control

For all his tedious talk is but vain boast,
Or subtle shifts conviction to evade.
Alas what can they teach, and not mislead;
310     Ignorant of themselves, of God much more,
And how the world began, and how man fell
Degraded by himself, on grace depending?
Much of the soul they talk, but all awry,
And in themselves seek virtue, and to themselves
315     All glory arrogate, to God give none,
Rather accuse him under usual names,
Fortune and Fate, as one regardless quite
Of mortal things. Who therefore seeks in these
True wisdom, finds her not, or by delusion
320     Far worse, her false resemblance only meets,
An empty cloud. However many books
Wise men have said are wearisome; who reads
Incessantly, and to his reading brings not
A spirit and judgment equal or superior,
325     (And what he brings, what needs he elsewhere seek)
Uncertain and unsettled still remains,
Deep-versed in books and shallow in himself,
Crude or intoxicate, collecting toys,

even in the midst of pain. Suicide is allowable for him, if the circumstances
should call for it ('life, Which when he lists, he leaves'). Cp. *De doctrina*
ii 10 (Columbia xvii 253) where M. lists as one of the opposites of true pa-
tience, 'a stoical apathy; for sensibility to pain, and even lamentations, are
not inconsistent with true patience; as may be seen in Job and the other
saints, when under the pressure of affliction'.

iv *308. subtle shifts*] It is to the personal characteristics of Chrysippus that the
hair-splitting and formal pedantry of the Stoics can be traced; because of
this they became known as the Dialecticians.

iv *314–5*. So Cicero, *De natura deorum* iii 36, argues that man has a right to
take pride in his own wisdom and virtue as proceeding from himself and
not, like external things, a gift of the gods: 'Our virtue is a just ground for
others' praise and a right reason for our own pride, and this would not be so
if the gift of virtue came to us from a god and not from ourselves.'

iv *321. cloud*] See *Passion* 56n.

iv *321–2*. Cp. *Eccles.* xii 12 'Of making many books there is no end; and
much study is a weariness of the flesh.'

iv *322–30*. Kermode[4] 328 suggests that Seneca, *Epistle* lxxxviii, which treats
of intemperate learning and the tenuous relationship of learning to virtue
may be among M.'s sources: his rejection of the classics is not independent
of classical authority. Augustine's dismissal of the Gentile philosophers,
*De civitate Dei* xviii 41, may also have contributed.

iv *328. crude*] unable to digest.

And trifles for choice matters, worth a sponge;
330   As children gathering pebbles on the shore.
      Or if I would delight my private hours
      With music or with poem, where so soon
      As in our native language can I find
      That solace? All our Law and story strewed
335   With hymns, our psalms with artful terms inscribed,
      Our Hebrew songs and harps in Babylon,
      That pleased so well our victor's ear, declare
      That rather Greece from us these arts derived;
      Ill imitated, while they loudest sing
340   The vices of their deities, and their own
      In fable, hymn, or song, so personating
      Their gods ridiculous, and themselves past shame.
      Remove their swelling epithets thick-laid
      As varnish on a harlot's cheek, the rest,
345   Thin-sown with aught of profit or delight,
      Will far be found unworthy to compare
      With Sion's songs, to all true tastes excelling,

iv *329. worth a sponge*] fit to be expunged, erased.

iv *335. artful terms*] artistic expressions; language that shows technical skill.

iv *336–7.* Cp. *Ps.* cxxxvii 1–3: 'By the rivers of Babylon, there we sat down, yea, we wept, when we remembered Zion. . . . For they that carried us away captive required of us a song . . . saying, Sing us one of the songs of Zion.'

iv *337. declare*] show.

iv *338. Greece from us these arts derived*] Schultz 89–90 and 260–1 notes that Josephus, *Antiquities* I viii 2, had traced learning from Abraham through the Egyptians to the Greeks: Philo of Alexandria had allegorized Moses until he could find the teachings of Plato in the Old Testament: Clement of Alexandria, Eusebius and other Fathers had affirmed the Jewish origin of learning; by the seventeenth century the idea was a commonplace.

iv *344.* Echoing *Hamlet* III i, 'The harlot's cheek, beautied with plast'ring art'.

iv *346–7. unworthy to compare With Sion's songs*] Among previous claims in English for the supremacy of Hebrew poetry Kermode[4] 329 cites Wither, *Preparation to the Psalter*, and Falkland's verses on Sandys's version of the Psalms. Schultz 91, 261 adds similar claims from Daniel Featley, *Characters of Heavenly Wisdom* and Felltham, *Resolves*. Cp. also Sidney, *Defence* (*Works* ed. A. Feuillerat (Cambridge 1923) iii 9) 'the chiefe [poets] both in antiquitie and excellencie, were they that did imitate the unconceivable excellencies of God. Such were David, in his Psalmes, Salomon in his song of songs, in his Ecclesiastes, and Proverbes. Moses and Debora in their Hymnes, and the wryter of Jobe', and M. himself, in *Reason of Church-Government* (Columbia iii 238, Yale i 816): 'But those frequent songs throughout the

Where God is praised aright, and godlike men,
The Holiest of Holies, and his saints;
350   Such are from God inspired, not such from thee;
Unless where moral virtue is expressed
By light of nature not in all quite lost.
Their orators thou then extoll'st, as those
The top of eloquence, statists indeed,
355   And lovers of their country, as may seem;
But herein to our prophets far beneath,
As men divinely taught, and better teaching
The solid rules of civil government
In their majestic unaffected style
360   Than all the oratory of Greece and Rome.
In them is plainest taught, and easiest learnt,
What makes a nation happy, and keeps it so,
What ruins kingdoms, and lays cities flat;
These only with our Law best form a king.
365      So spake the Son of God; but Satan now
Quite at a loss, for all his darts were spent,
Thus to our Saviour with stern brow replied.
Since neither wealth, nor honour, arms nor arts,
Kingdom nor empire pleases thee, nor aught
370   By me proposed in life contemplative,
Or active, tended on by glory, or fame,
What dost thou in this world? The wilderness

law and prophets beyond all these, not in their divine argument alone, but in the very critical art of composition may be easily made appear over all the kinds of Lyrick poesy, to be incomparable.'

iv *347. tastes*] OED records this as the first instance in the sense 'faculty of perceiving what is excellent in art or literature.'

iv *351. Unless*] catches up 'unworthy' (l. 346): pagan thought is not unworthy if it discovers moral truth, inspired by the light of nature. This view finds scriptural support in texts like *Rom.* ii 14–5: 'The Gentiles, which have not the law. . . . Which shew the work of the law written in their hearts.' M. quotes this in support of his contention, in the *De doctrina* (Columbia xv 208–11), that 'it cannot be denied . . . that some remnants of the divine image still exist in us, not wholly extinguished by the spiritual death. This is evident . . . from the wisdom and holiness of many of the heathen, manifested both in words and deeds.'

iv *354. statists*] statesmen.

iv *361–4.* Cp. *De doctrina* ii 17 (Columbia xvii 412–3): 'The observance of the divine commandments is the source of prosperity to nations . . . It renders them flourishing and wealthy and victorious . . . *Deut.* xxviii 1 etc.–a chapter which should be read again and again by those who have the direction of political affairs.'

For thee is fittest place, I found thee there,
And thither will return thee, yet remember
375  What I foretell thee, soon thou shalt have cause
To wish thou never hadst rejected thus
Nicely or cautiously my offered aid,
Which would have set thee in short time with ease
On David's throne; or throne of all the world,
380  Now at full age, fulness of time, thy season,
When prophecies of thee are best fulfilled.
Now contrary, if I read aught in heaven,
Or heaven write aught of fate, by what the stars
Voluminous, or single characters,
385  In their conjunction met, give me to spell,
Sorrows, and labours, opposition, hate,
Attends thee, scorns, reproaches, injuries,
Violence and stripes, and lastly cruel death,
A kingdom they portend thee, but what kingdom,
390  Real or allegoric I discern not,

iv *382–8*. Schultz 54 reviewing the orthodox opposition to divinatory astrology, notes that Satan's pretence to it here stamps it as devilish. It was still widely practised in seventeenth century England, and controversy about it was lively, the anti-astrologists drawing for ammunition upon such biblical texts as *Jer*. x 2: 'Learn not the way of the heathen, and be not dismayed at the signs of heaven.' In 1624 Bishop Carleton published his *Astrologomania*, refuting Sir Christopher Heydon's *Defence of Judicial Astrology*. Eighteenth-century critics regarded Satan's speech as an allusion to the presumption of the Italian astrologer Cardano (1501–76), who cast Christ's horoscope. It is as well, however, to recall M.'s reservation in *De doctrina* ii 5 (Columbia xvii 151): 'All study of the heavenly bodies, however, is not unlawful or unprofitable; as appears from the journey of the wise men, and still more from the star itself, divinely appointed to announce the birth of Christ, *Matt*. ii 1, 2.'

iv *384*. *Voluminous*] forming a large volume, or book.    *single characters*] regarded as single letters in this volume.

iv *385*. *conjunction*] When two stars or planets were in conjunction they were in the same sign of the zodiac, and apparently close together; this was one of the unfavourable astrological 'aspects'.    *spell*] See *Il Penseroso* 170*n*.

iv *387*. *Attends*] L. H. Kendall, *N & Q* n.s. iv (1957) 523, notes approvingly that B. A. Wright in his ed. of M.'s *Poems* (1956) emends to 'Attend', for the sake of grammar. A plural subject and singular verb is, however, quite common in seventeenth-century English, especially when, as here, there is a singular noun in close proximity.

Nor when, eternal sure, as without end,
Without beginning; for no date prefixed
Directs me in the starry rubric set.
   So saying he took (for still he knew his power
395 Not yet expired) and to the wilderness
Brought back the Son of God, and left him there,
Feigning to disappear. Darkness now rose,
As daylight sunk, and brought in louring night
Her shadowy offspring unsubstantial both,
400 Privation mere of light and absent day.
Our Saviour meek and with untroubled mind
After his airy jaunt, though hurried sore,
Hungry and cold betook him to his rest,
Wherever, under some concourse of shades
405 Whose branching arms thick intertwined might shield
From dews and damps of night his sheltered head,
But sheltered slept in vain, for at his head
The tempter watched, and soon with ugly dreams
Disturbed his sleep; and either tropic now
410 'Gan thunder, and both ends of heaven, the clouds
From many a horrid rift abortive poured
Fierce rain with lightning mixed, water with fire

iv *391–2.* Satan is being ironic: an eternal kingdom can have no end, but
neither can it have a beginning.

iv *393. rubric*] manual containing laws or rules; the word derived from the
red colour of captions in law books and liturgical works, which made them
stand out from the surrounding black lettering. So M. imagines stars stan-
ding out against the sky.

iv *402. jaunt*] develops from 'jaunce' (prance of a horse), and means 'a
tiring journey' from its first usage (*Romeo and Juliet* II v 26) until the end of the
seventeenth century, when the 'pleasure-trip' meaning begins to develop.

iv *407–25.* J. M. Steadman, *MP* lix (1961) 81–8, sees M. complying with a
commonplace in the literature of spiritual warfare by including the storm,
as an adversity symbol, to complement the other temptations of prosperity
and demonstrate the dual aspect of the world's assault on the Christian
warrior. Lewalski 311–12 reads the storm as a foreshadowing of the violent
upheavals of nature recorded at Christ's death (*Matt.* xxvii 51–2), and takes
'shrouded' (l. 419) as a reference to Christ's burial and the 'hellish furies'
(l. 422) as suggesting the descent into hell.

iv *409. tropic*] apparently used loosely to mean 'part of the sky' or 'point
of the compass': *OED* does not instance this use, or any appropriate sense.

iv *411. abortive*] destructive of life.

iv *412–13. water with fire . . . reconciled*] Cp. Aeschylus, *Agamemnon* 650–2:
'fire and sea, formerly the bitterest of enemies, swore alliance and for proof

In ruin reconciled: nor slept the winds
Within their stony caves, but rushed abroad
415 From the four hinges of the world, and fell
On the vexed wilderness, whose tallest pines,
Though rooted deep as high, and sturdiest oaks
Bowed their stiff necks, loaden with stormy blasts,
Or torn up sheer: ill wast thou shrouded then,
420 O patient Son of God, yet only stood'st
Unshaken; nor yet stayed the terror there,
Infernal ghosts, and hellish furies, round
Environed thee, some howled, some yelled, some
    shrieked,
Some bent at thee their fiery darts, while thou
425 Sat'st unappalled in calm and sinless peace.
Thus passed the night so foul till morning fair
Came forth with pilgrim steps in amice grey;
Who with her radiant finger stilled the roar
Of thunder, chased the clouds, and laid the winds,
430 And grisly spectres, which the Fiend had raised
To tempt the Son of God with terrors dire.
And now the sun with more effectual beams
Had cheered the face of earth, and dried the wet
From drooping plant, or dropping tree; the birds
435 Who all things now behold more fresh and green,
After a night of storm so ruinous,
Cleared up their choicest notes in bush and spray
To gratulate the sweet return of morn;
Nor yet amidst this joy and brightest morn
440 Was absent, after all his mischief done,
The Prince of Darkness, glad would also seem
Of this fair change, and to our Saviour came,

of it destroyed the hapless Greek fleet.'      *ruin*] 'fall', as well as 'destruc-
tion': both were common seventeenth-century senses.
iv *414. caves*] Cp. *Aen.* i 52–4, where Aeolus keeps the 'struggling winds
and roaring gales' imprisoned in a vast cavern.
iv *415. hinges*] cardinal points of the compass (Latin *cardo*, a hinge).
iv *419. shrouded*] sheltered.
iv *420. only*] alone.
iv *422–3.* Cp. *Richard III* I iv 58–9: 'With that, methoughts, a legion of
foul fiends / Environ'd me about, and howled in my ears.'
iv *426–7.* See *Comus* 188–9, *Lycidas* 187.      *amice*] hood or cape made or
lined with grey fur.
iv *432. more effectual*] than those of the early morning sun.
iv *437. Cleared up*] made clear, brightened.
iv *438. gratulate*] give thanks for.

Yet with no new device, they all were spent,
Rather by this his last affront resolved,
445   Desperate of better course, to vent his rage,
And mad despite to be so oft repelled.
Him walking on a sunny hill he found,
Backed on the north and west by a thick wood,
Out of the wood he starts in wonted shape;
450   And in a careless mood thus to him said.
      Fair morning yet betides thee Son of God,
After a dismal night; I heard the rack
As earth and sky would mingle; but myself
Was distant; and these flaws, though mortals fear them
455   As dangerous to the pillared frame of heaven,
Or to the earth's dark basis underneath,
Are to the main as inconsiderable,
And harmless, if not wholesome, as a sneeze
To man's less universe, and soon are gone;
460   Yet as being oft-times noxious where they light
On man, beast, plant, wasteful and turbulent,
Like turbulencies in the affairs of men,
Over whose heads they roar, and seem to point,
They oft fore-signify and threaten ill:

iv 449. *wonted shape*] Pope 49–50 notes the ambiguity; the phrase may mean 'his own shape (with wings, cloven hooves etc.), with no disguise' or 'his usual disguise': if the second, the old man of i 314 must be regarded as the same man (though in different clothes) as the courtier ('Not rustic as before') of ii 298–300. There was support among artists and writers before M. either for Satan's continuing his disguise to the end, or for his throwing it off before the last temptation. Miss Pope favours the idea that Satan here retains his disguise (i.e. appears as a man), and points to the phrase 'without wing / Of hippogrif' (ll. 541–2).

iv 452. *rack*] *OED* gives this as the only instance of the word in the sense 'crash as of something breaking'. The meaning 'destruction' was common in the seventeenth century, however (cp. *PL* xi 817), and would fit here.

iv 453. *earth and sky ... mingle*] Echoes *Aen.* i 133–4: *caelum terramque ... miscere.*

iv 454. *flaws*] squalls.

iv 455. *pillared*] Cp. *Job* xxvi 11: 'The pillars of heaven tremble.'

iv 457. *main*] universe.

iv 464–83. Satan's emphasis on portents here and elsewhere (e.g. iii 152–3, iv 380–93), and the care with which he dissociates himself from the storm (iv 452–4) and interprets it as intended for Christ (465–6), lead Dick Taylor, *UTQ* xxiv (1955) 359–76, to the conclusion that the storm scene is not a mere exhibition of enraged violence but an essential part of the second temptation – Satan is tempting Christ to take the storm as a portent, a sign

465 This tempest at this desert most was bent;
    Of men at thee, for only thou here dwell'st.
    Did I not tell thee, if thou didst reject
    The perfect season offered with my aid
    To win thy destined seat, but wilt prolong
470 All to the push of fate, pursue thy way
    Of gaining David's throne no man knows when,
    For both the when and how is nowhere told,
    Thou shalt be what thou art ordained, no doubt;
    For angels have proclaimed it, but concealing
475 The time and means: each act is rightliest done,
    Not when it must, but when it may be best.
    If thou observe not this, be sure to find,
    What I foretold thee, many a hard assay
    Of dangers, and adversities and pains,
480 Ere thou of Israel's sceptre get fast hold;
    Whereof this ominous night that closed thee round,
    So many terrors, voices, prodigies
    May warn thee, as a sure foregoing sign.
        So talked he, while the Son of God went on
485 And stayed not, but in brief him answered thus.
        Me worse than wet thou find'st not; other harm
    Those terrors which thou speak'st of, did me none;
    I never feared they could, though noising loud
    And threat'ning nigh; what they can do as signs
490 Betokening, or ill-boding, I contemn
    As false portents, not sent from God, but thee;
    Who knowing I shall reign past thy preventing,
    Obtrud'st thy offered aid, that I accepting
    At least might seem to hold all power of thee,
495 Ambitious spirit, and would'st be thought my God,
    And storm'st refused, thinking to terrify
    Me to thy will; desist, thou art discerned
    And toil'st in vain, nor me in vain molest.
        To whom the Fiend now swoll'n with rage replied:
500 Then hear, O Son of David, virgin-born;

of God's will that he should assume power under Satan's auspices. Taylor
draws attention to the intense contemporary interest in portents around
1666, and thinks it may have influenced M. Though iv 365–6 and 443–6
seem to discredit Taylor's theory, he claims that these passages merely exem-
plify M.'s consistent practice of describing Satan, incident by incident, as at
a loss at the failure of each stratagem (cp. ii 119–20, iii 2–4, 145–8, iv 1–6).
iv 467. *Did I not tell thee*] i.e. in iv 375ff. M. here begins his sentence as a
question but continues it as an affirmation.
iv 481. *ominous*] full of omens.

        For Son of God to me is yet in doubt,
        Of the Messiah I have heard foretold
        By all the prophets; of thy birth at length
        Announced by Gabriel with the first I knew,
*505*     And of the angelic song in Bethlehem field,
        On thy birth-night, that sung thee Saviour born.
        From that time seldom have I ceased to eye
        Thy infancy, thy childhood, and thy youth,
        Thy manhood last, though yet in private bred;
*510*     Till at the ford of Jordan whither all
        Flocked to the Baptist, I among the rest,
        Though not to be baptized, by voice from heaven
        Heard thee pronounced the Son of God beloved.
        Thenceforth I thought thee worth my nearer view
*515*     And narrower scrutiny, that I might learn
        In what degree or meaning thou art called
        The Son of God, which bears no single sense;
        The Son of God I also am, or was,
        And if I was, I am; relation stands;
*520*     All men are Sons of God; yet thee I thought
        In some respect far higher so declared.
        Therefore I watched thy footsteps from that hour,
        And followed thee still on to this waste wild;
        Where by all best conjectures I collect
*525*     Thou art to be my fatal enemy.
        Good reason then, if I beforehand seek
        To understand my adversary, who
        And what he is; his wisdom, power, intent,
        By parle, or composition, truce, or league
*530*     To win him, or win from him what I can.
        And opportunity I here have had
        To try thee, sift thee, and confess have found thee
        Proof against all temptation as a rock
        Of adamant, and as a centre, firm
*535*     To the utmost of mere man both wise and good,
        Not more; for honours, riches, kingdoms, glory

iv *518.* Cp. *Job* i 6: 'Now there was a day when the sons of God came to present themselves before the Lord, and Satan came also among them.'
iv *520. All men are Sons of God*] Cp. *Matt.* vi 9: 'After this manner therefore pray ye: Our Father . . .'
iv *524. collect*] infer.
iv *525. fatal*] in the sense 'fated' as well as 'deadly'.
iv *529. parle*] parley.      *composition*] treaty, truce.
iv *534. adamant*] See *SA* 134n.      *centre*] pivot; the unmoving point around which a body turns.

Have been before contemned, and may again:
Therefore to know what more thou art than man,
Worth naming Son of God by voice from heaven,
540   Another method I must now begin.
        So saying he caught him up, and without wing
Of hippogrif bore through the air sublime
Over the wilderness and o'er the plain;
Till underneath them fair Jerusalem,
545   The holy city lifted high her towers,
And higher yet the glorious Temple reared
Her pile, far off appearing like a mount
Of alabaster, topped with golden spires:
There on the highest pinnacle he set

iv 538–40. Satan's words suggest that the pinnacle episode is to be an at-
tempt to discover Christ's identity, not a temptation to vainglory or pre-
sumption (see iii 25–30n). M.'s handling of this episode represents his most
spectacular break with tradition, as Pope 80–107 demonstrates.

iv 542. *hippogrif*] fabulous creature, front half griffin, rear half horse. It
appears frequently in Ariosto, *Orlando Furioso*, and in IV xviii carries
Astolfo to the moon. See 449n.

iv 545. *towers*] Sandys 156–7, describing Jerusalem, mentions several towers:
'Upon a steepe rocke . . . stood the tower of Baris . . . but Herod . . . built
thereon a stately strong Castle, having at every corner a tower' (156),
'Mariamnes Tower . . . that of Phaseolus . . . in the North wall [of Herod's
palace] on a lofty hill stood the tower Hippic, eighty foure cubits high:
fouresquare, and having two spires at the top', and on the north the outer
wall 'fortified with ninety Towers, two hundred cubits distant from each
other' (157).

iv 548. *alabaster . . . golden spires*] Josephus speaks of the gold and white
appearance of the Temple, *Jewish War* V v 6: 'The outward front of the
temple . . . was covered all over with massive plates of gold, and reflected
at the first rising of the sun a very fiery splendour, and made those who
forced themselves to look upon it turn their eyes away. . . . But it appeared
to strangers, when they were approaching it at some distance, like a mountain
covered with snow, for where it was not gilt, it was exceeding white.'

iv 549. *highest pinnacle*] The nature of the 'pinnacle' (the word is used in
*Matt.* iv 5 and *Luke* iv 9) was, as Pope 85–9 explains, much debated. Some
commentators, like Diodati, held that it was merely a flat roof: thus Christ
was quite free to stand or throw himself down, and the temptation was pure-
ly one of presumption. Others made it a balustrade or a peaked gable or a
spire. Fuller and Chemnitius quote Josephus, *Jewish War* V v 6, who re-
cords that the Temple roof 'had sharp points to prevent any pollution of it
by birds sitting upon it'. Of those who take 'pinnacle' to mean 'point'
or 'spire', however, it appears that only Thomas Bilson goes on to suggest
that Christ's ability to stand upon such a point was a deliberate display of

*550*   The Son of God; and added thus in scorn:
         There stand, if thou wilt stand; to stand upright
         Will ask thee skill; I to thy Father's house
         Have brought thee, and highest placed, highest is best,
         Now show thy progeny; if not to stand,
*555*   Cast thyself down; safely if Son of God:
         For it is written, He will give command
         Concerning thee to his angels, in their hands
         They shall uplift thee, lest at any time
         Thou chance to dash thy foot against a stone.

his miraculous powers. The others explain either that Satan held him to
prevent his falling, or that there was room for a man to stand; and they
often add that Christ could perfectly well have climbed down and escaped
by the stairs. Bilson's view ran counter to the doctrine that Christ was
undergoing temptation as a man, and that a display of his miraculous
powers was just what Satan wanted to provoke. It is clear that M.'s pinnacle
is too small for a man to stand firmly, and that Satan does not hold Christ:
Satan expects him to fall (l. 571), and tells him to stand only 'in scorn'
(l. 550). M.'s view might seem near to Bilson's, therefore. But 'uneasy
station' (l. 584) implies that the standing was not miraculous but a balancing
feat. Perhaps M. remembers Josephus's description of the royal portico to
the south of the Temple, which looked over the ravine of Kedron: 'the
valley was very deep, and its bottom could not be seen if you looked from
above into the depth, the high elevation of the portico stood upon that
height, that if anyone looked down from the top of the roof to those depths,
he would be giddy, while his sight could not reach down to such an abyss',
*Antiquities* XV xi 5. E. Cleveland, *MLQ* xvi (1955) 232–6, thinks the pin-
nacle symbolic of the cross, and Satan's speech (ll. 551–9) a foreshadowing
of the scornful questioning at the crucifixion. Lewalski (309–10) shows that
this symbolism was a traditional feature of biblical commentary. John
Knox, Joseph Hall and others regarded the violent transportation to the
tower as prefiguring the crucifixion, and Satan's words as a foretaste of the
taunts of the crowd.

iv 555. *Cast thyself down*] In the gospel account, *Luke* iv 9–11, Satan intends
Christ to choose; the temptation is to presumption. In M. it is clear Satan
thinks Christ has no choice: he expects him to fall, and is amazed when he
stands (ll. 562, 571). 'Cast thyself down' is therefore sarcastic: Christ's fall,
as Satan sees it, will settle the problem of his identity: if he is not merely
perfect man, but something more, angels will save him: if he is merely
perfect man, he will die.

iv 556–9. *He will give . . . stone*] Frye 237 finds irony in Satan's quotation
from *Ps.* xci 11–12, since the next verse reads: 'Thou shalt tread upon the
lion and adder: the young lion and the dragon shalt thou trample under
feet': Satan is the dragon Christ is to trample upon. The irony is present in
M.'s source, *Luke* iv 10–11, where Satan uses the same quotation.

560     To whom thus Jesus: Also it is written,
         Tempt not the Lord thy God, he said and stood.
         But Satan smitten with amazement fell

iv *560–1. Also it is written, Tempt not the Lord thy God*] Cp. *Luke* iv 12: 'And Jesus answering said unto him, It is said, Thou shalt not tempt the Lord thy God', where Jesus is quoting *Deut.* vi 16: 'Ye shall not tempt [i.e. make trial of, test] the Lord your God.'

As Pope 83, 103, sees it, since Satan has deliberately placed Christ in a position where, as man, he cannot stand (see however, iv 549*n*), there is no question of his 'making trial' of God by casting himself down, so his reply cannot be taken in the usual sense. It must mean 'Tempt not *me*', and must amount to a claim to, or revelation of, his own divinity. Some early commentators, chiefly Church Fathers, had interpreted the reply in *Luke* in this way, but as a doctrine it had never won general acceptance, and Thomas Taylor, among other seventeenth-century exegetes, refutes it.

G. G. Loane, *N & Q* clxxv (1938) 184–5, also thinks that Christ's reply in M. (though not in *Luke*) can be taken to mean 'Tempt not *me*', but considers that it could also be taken in the normal sense (i.e. as meaning 'I cannot cast myself down, because that would be to make trial of God, and we are commanded not to'). It is, then, an ambiguous reply, and Loane finds this odd after Christ's denunciation of the ambiguity of the oracles (i 435). More recently Frye (237) and Lewalski (316) have agreed that the reply, in M., is ambiguous.

Stein[2] 128–9, however, rejects the idea that Christ's reply can mean 'Tempt not *me*': for Christ to reveal his own divinity would be to give in, at last, to Satan's pressure. Instead Stein assumes that Christ does not speak the reply at all: it is spoken by God through Christ: 'the full revelation occurs, the miracle of epiphany, theophany, but not as an act of will, not from the self'. Stein's solution is perhaps unnecessarily ingenious. It could be argued that Christ takes Satan's sarcastic 'There stand' at its face value, stands on his 'uneasy station' by a supreme display of nerve, and gives as his reason for doing so his unwillingness to make trial of God. His reply would then mean the same as it does in *Luke* (and *Deuteronomy*), and would entail no claim to divinity (a claim which the M. who wrote *De doctrina* might wish to avoid). Even if Christ had performed a miracle by standing it would not in itself have been a revelation of his divinity, since miracles can be performed by men, as they had been by Moses and were later by the apostles. Alternatively it could be argued that if a miracle does occur it is not Christ but God who performs it: thus Christ suddenly finds himself able to stand, and makes his reply. This explanation is adopted by Dick Taylor, *Tulane Studies in English* iv (1954) 57–90, and Lewalski 316. But '*uneasy* station' (l. 584) seems decisively against the theory that any miracle occurs.

iv *562. fell*] Pope 11 notes that no other writer states that Satan fell after his final defeat: the traditional accounts follow *Luke* iv 13 in saying that Satan, when he had 'ended all the temptation, . . . departed from him for a season'.

As when Earth's son Antaeus (to compare
Small things with greatest) in Irassa strove
565  With Jove's Alcides, and oft foiled still rose,
Receiving from his mother Earth new strength,
Fresh from his fall, and fiercer grapple joined,
Throttled at length in the air, expired and fell;
So after many a foil the tempter proud,
570  Renewing fresh assaults, amidst his pride
Fell whence he stood to see his victor fall.
And as that Theban monster that proposed
Her riddle, and him, who solved it not, devoured;
That once found out and solved, for grief and spite
575  Cast herself headlong from the Ismenian steep,
So struck with dread and anguish fell the Fiend,
And to his crew, that sat consulting, brought

In visual art, on the other hand, it was quite common for the artist to depict
Satan as reeling or falling. Perhaps M. was influenced by iconography, or by
Fletcher's *Christ's Victory and Triumph* i 49, where the allegorical figure of
Presumption 'tombles headlong' from the tower at the end of the second
temptation, or, as Hughes[2] 256 suggests, by the fall of Malory's fiend in the
*Morte d'Arthur* xiv 9 who, when Sir Percivale has resisted all his wiles, goes
away at last 'with the wind roaring and yelling'.

iv *563–8*. Antaeus was a giant, son of Ge (Earth), who fought with Hercules
(called 'Alcides' after his grandfather Alcaeus, and 'Jove's' because he was
the son of Jove). Antaeus drew strength from his mother every time he
fell, and Hercules had to hold him in the air and strangle him. In the Re-
naissance this contest was frequently treated as an allegory of the victory
of the spirit over the flesh; Hercules was a common type of Christ (see
*Nativity Ode* 227–8*n*). Lewalski 128 finds precedent for M.'s parallel bet-
ween Hercules / Antaeus and Christ / Satan the tempter, in Sedulius,
*Carmen Paschale* ii 199–200. Starnes and Talbert 238 claim that the account
of the incident in Conti (paraphrased in Stephanus) is 'very suggestive'
of M.'s language.

iv *563–4*. *to compare . . . greatest*] Echoes Virgil, *Ecl.* i 24: *Sic parvis componere
magna solebam* (Thus I used to compare great things with small).

iv *564*. *Irassa*] L. R. Farnell, *TLS* (1 Oct. 1931) 754, points out that nowhere
else in ancient literature could M. have found the name Antaeus brought
into connection with the Libyan town 'Irassa' except in Pindar, *Pyth.*
ix 106. Farnell thinks that the piling of divine epithets on Aristaeus in this
ode (64–5) may have suggested the 'swelling epithets' of iv 343.

iv *572–5*. The Sphinx threw itself from the acropolis at Thebes (above the
River Ismenus) when Oedipus gave the right answer, 'Man', to its riddle,
'Which creature goes first on four, then on two, and finally on three legs?'

Joyless triumphals of his hoped success,
Ruin, and desperation, and dismay,
580  Who durst so proudly tempt the Son of God.
So Satan fell and straight a fiery globe
Of angels on full sail of wing flew nigh,
Who on their plumy vans received him soft
From his uneasy station, and upbore
585  As on a floating couch through the blithe air,
Then in a flowery valley set him down
On a green bank, and set before him spread
A table of celestial food, divine,
Ambrosial, fruits fetched from the tree of life,
590  And from the fount of life ambrosial drink,
That soon refreshed him wearied, and repaired
What hunger, if aught hunger had impaired,
Or thirst, and as he fed, angelic choirs
Sung heavenly anthems of his victory
595  Over temptation, and the tempter proud.
True image of the Father whether throned

iv 578. *triumphals*] tokens of triumph: the first recorded instance of the noun in this sense: previously it had meant 'triumph', 'triumphal chariot' or 'triumphal ode'.

iv 581. *globe*] Cp. Fletcher, *Christ's Triumph after Death* 13: 'Out thear flies / A globe of winged Angels, swift as thought', which is the first recorded instance of 'globe' in the sense 'compact body of persons' (one of the meanings of the Latin *globus*).

iv 582. *angels*] Kermode[4] 324 notes that the following passage is M.'s development of a hint in *Matt.* iv 11: 'Angels came and ministered unto him': Fletcher, *Christ's Victory on Earth* 61, also has choiring angels who bring a banquet to Christ.

iv 583. *vans*] wings. M. is the first (here and in *PL* ii 927) to use 'van' to mean 'wing'. 'Fan' is found meaning 'wing' in mid-seventeenth-century poetry: M. adopts the form nearer to the Italian *vanni*. Cp. Fletcher, *Christ's Victory on Earth* 38: 'But him the Angels on their feathers caught / And to an ayrie mountaine nimbly bore.'

iv 589. *Ambrosial*] belonging to heaven or paradise: the first recorded instance of this sense is *Comus* 16.    the tree of life] J. M. Steadman, *RES* n.s. xi (1960) 348–91, draws attention to the multiple significance of this tree: it is the reward of obedience, a meaning given to it as early as the Jerusalem Targum on *Gen.* ii 9; it is a symbol of eternal life, as M. says in *De doctrina* (Columbia xv 114–5); and as it was indigenous to paradise, Christ's participation in its fruits signifies that he has regained the paradise that Adam lost, and parallels Adam's participation in the fruits of the tree of knowledge.

In the bosom of bliss, and light of light
Conceiving, or remote from heaven, enshrined
In fleshly tabernacle, and human form,
600 Wandering the wilderness, whatever place,
Habit, or state, or motion, still expressing
The Son of God, with godlike force endued
Against the attempter of thy Father's throne,
And thief of Paradise; him long of old
605 Thou didst debel, and down from heaven cast
With all his army, now thou hast avenged
Supplanted Adam, and, by vanquishing
Temptation, hast regained lost Paradise,
And frustrated the conquest fraudulent:
610 He never more henceforth will dare set foot
In Paradise to tempt; his snares are broke:
For though that seat of earthly bliss be failed,
A fairer Paradise is founded now
For Adam and his chosen sons, whom thou
615 A Saviour art come down to reinstall.
Where they shall dwell secure, when time shall be
Of tempter and temptation without fear.
But thou, infernal serpent, shalt not long
Rule in the clouds; like an autumnal star
620 Or lightning thou shalt fall from heaven trod down
Under his feet: for proof, ere this thou feel'st
Thy wound, yet not thy last and deadliest wound
By this repulse received, and hold'st in hell

iv 597–8. Cp. *John* i 9 and 18: 'the true Light . . . which is in the bosom of the Father'. *light of light / Conceiving*] taking on light from the Father (Light).

iv .605. *debel*] suppress by war (Latin *debellare*): first recorded in mid-sixteenth century.

iv 611. Cp. *Ps.* cxxiv 7: 'The snare is broken and we are escaped.'

iv 612. *be failed*] is absent, has disappeared.

iv 617. The line is inverted.

iv 619. *autumnal star*] One of the names given to Sirius: here, however, M. seems to mean a comet or meteor (cp. *PL* ii 708–11).

iv 620–1. Cp. *Luke* x 18: 'And he said unto them, I beheld Satan as lightning fall from heaven'; and *Mal.* iv 3: 'Ye shall tread down the wicked . . . under the soles of your feet.'

iv 622. *thy last and deadliest wound*] Cp. *Rev.* xx 10: 'And the devil that deceived them was cast into the lake of fire and brimstone, where the beast and the false prophet are, and shall be tormented day and night for ever and ever.'

No triumph; in all her gates Abaddon rues
625   Thy bold attempt; hereafter learn with awe
To dread the Son of God: he all unarmed
Shall chase thee with the terror of his voice
From thy demoniac holds, possession foul,
Thee and thy legions, yelling they shall fly,
630   And beg to hide them in a herd of swine,
Lest he command them down into the deep
Bound, and to torment sent before their time.
Hail Son of the Most High, heir of both worlds,
Queller of Satan, on thy glorious work
635   Now enter, and begin to save mankind.
    Thus they the Son of God our Saviour meek
Sung victor, and from heavenly feast refreshed
Brought on his way with joy; he unobserved
Home to his mother's house private returned.

iv *624. Abaddon*] Cp. *Rev.* ix 11: 'And they had a king over them, which is the angel of the bottomless pit, whose name in the Hebrew tongue is Abaddon, but in the Greek tongue hath his name Apollyon.' In *Job* xxvi 6 'Abaddon' is used as a name for hell. In his version of Ps. lxxxviii 47 (p. 318) M. translates it as 'perdition'.

iv *628. holds*] strongholds. Cp. *Rev.* xviii 2: 'Babylon the great is fallen, is spirit.'

iv *630.* In *Matt.* viii 28–32 Christ meets two people 'possessed with devils', and the devils cry out 'Art thou come hither to torment us before the time ?' There is a herd of swine nearby, and the devils ask 'If thou cast us out, suffer us to go away into the herd of swine'. Christ does so, and the swine 'ran violently down a steep place into the sea, and perished in the waters'.

iv *636. meek*] Cp. *Matt.* xi 29: 'I am meek, and lowly in heart.'

# Bibliography of References Cited

Unless otherwise stated, the place of publication is London.

ADAMS, ROBERT MARTIN. *Ikon: John Milton and the Modern Critics*. Ithaca, N.Y. 1955.

ALLEN, DON CAMERON. *The Harmonious Vision: Studies in Milton's Poetry*. Baltimore, Md. 1954.

ALLEN². *The Legend of Noah: Renaissance Rationalism in Art, Science, and Letters*. Urbana, Ill. 1963.

ALCIATI, ANDREA. *Emblemata*. Lyons 1600.

ARTHOS, J. *On a Masque Presented at Ludlow Castle*. Ann Arbor, Mich. 1954.

BACON, FRANCIS. *The Philosophical Works*, ed. Ellis and Spedding, re-ed. John M. Robertson. 1905.

BARKER, ARTHUR E., ed. *Milton: Modern Essays in Criticism*. New York 1965.

BATESON, F. W. *English Poetry*. 1950.

BRETT, R. L. *Reason and Imagination*. Oxford 1960.

BROADBENT, JOHN B. *Some Graver Subject: An Essay on 'Paradise Lost'*. 1960.

BROADBENT². 'Milton's Hell', *ELH* xxi, 1954.

BROOKS, CLEANTH and HARDY, J. E. *Poems of Mr John Milton*. 1957.

BROWNE, WILLIAM. *Poems*, ed. G. Goodwin. 1894.

BUSH, DOUGLAS. *Milton: Poetical Works*. 1966.

CLARK, D. L. *John Milton at St Paul's School*. New York 1948.

COLUMBIA. *The Works of John Milton*, ed. F. A. Patterson *et al*. New York 1931-8.

CONTI, NATALE. *Mythologiae, sive explicationis fabularum, Libri decem*. Lyons 1653.

COWLEY, ABRAHAM. *Poems*, ed. A. R. Waller. Cambridge 1905.

CURRY. *Essays in Honour of Walter Clyde Curry*, ed. H. Craig. Nashville, Tenn. 1954.

DAICHES, DAVID. *Milton*. 1957.

DAICHES². 'The Opening of *Paradise Lost*', in *The Living Milton*, ed. Frank Kermode. 1960.

DARBISHIRE, HELEN, ed. *The Early Lives of Milton*. 1932.

DARBISHIRE², ed. *The Poetical Works of John Milton*. 2 vols. Oxford 1952-5.

DARBISHIRE³, ed. *The Manuscript of Milton's 'Paradise Lost' Book I*. Oxford 1931.

DAVIE, DONALD. *Articulate Energy: An Inquiry into the Syntax of English Poetry.* 1955.

DAVIE[2]. 'Syntax and Music in *Paradise Lost*', in *The Living Milton*, ed. Frank Kermode. 1960.

DIEKHOFF, J. S. 'The Text of *Comus*', *PMLA* lii, 1937.

DORIAN, D. C. *The English Diodatis.* New Brunswick, N.J. 1950.

DRAYTON, MICHAEL. *Works*, ed. J. William Hebel. Oxford 1961.

DRUMMOND, WILLIAM. *The Poems*, ed. W. C. Ward. 2 vols. n.d.

DU BARTAS. *Devine Weekes and Workes*, tr. Joshua Sylvester. 1613.

DU BARTAS[2]. *Devine Weekes and Workes*, tr. Joshua Sylvester. 1621.

EMPSON, WILLIAM. *Milton's God.* 1961.

EMPSON[2]. *Some Versions of Pastoral.* 1950.

EMPSON[3]. *The Structure of Complex Words.* 1952.

EVANS, W. M. *Henry Lawes.* New York 1941.

FICINO, MARSILIO. *Opera omnia.* Basel 1576.

FINLEY, J. H. 'Milton and Horace', *Harvard Studies in Classical Philology* xlviii, 1937.

FIXLER, M. *Milton and the Kingdoms of God.* 1964.

FLETCHER, HARRIS F. *The Intellectual Development of John Milton.* Vol. i: *The Institution to 1625: From the Beginnings Through Grammar School.* Vol. ii: *The Cambridge University Period 1625-32.* Urbana, Ill. 1956-61.

FLETCHER[2]. *Milton's Rabbinical Readings.* Urbana, Ill. 1930.

FLETCHER[3], ed. *Milton's Complete Poetical Works in Photographic Facsimile.* Urbana, Ill. 1943.

FREEMAN, ROSEMARY. *English Emblem Books.* 1948.

FRENCH, J. MILTON, ed. *The Life Records of John Milton.* New Brunswick, N.J. 1949-58.

FRYE, NORTHROP. 'The Typology of *Paradise Regained*', *MP* liii, 1956.

GILBERT, ALLAN H. *On the Composition of 'Paradise Lost': A Study of the Ordering and Insertion of Material.* Chapel Hill, N.C. 1947.

GILBERT[2]. 'The Temptation in *Paradise Regained*', *JEGP* xv, 1916.

GRIERSON, H. J. C., ed. *The Poems of John Milton.* 1925.

HANFORD, JAMES HOLLY. 'That Shepherd, Who First Taught the Chosen Seed', *UTQ* viii, 1939.

HANFORD[2]. *A Milton Handbook.* New York 1947.

HANFORD[3]. *John Milton, Englishman.* 1950.

HARDING, D. P. 'Milton and the Renaissance Ovid', *Illinois Studies in Language and Literature*, xxx, 1946.

HARTWELL, K. E. *Lactantius and Milton.* Cambridge, Mass. 1929.

HERRICK, ROBERT. *The Poetical Works of Robert Herrick*, ed. L. C. Martin. Oxford 1956.

HORWOOD, A. J., ed. *A Commonplace Book of John Milton*. Camden Society. 1876.

HUGHES, MERRITT Y., ed. *John Milton: Complete Poems and Major Prose*. New York 1957.

HUGHES². 'The Christ of *Paradise Regained* and the Renaissance Poetic Tradition', *SP* xxxv, 1938.

JERRAM, C. S., ed. *The 'Lycidas' and the 'Epitaphium Damonis'*. 1878.

JONSON, BENJAMIN. *Works*, ed. C. H. Herford and P. and E. Simpson. Oxford 1925–50.

KELLEY, MAURICE. *This Great Argument: a Study of Milton's 'De Doctrina Christiana' as a Gloss upon 'Paradise Lost'*. Princeton, N.J. 1941.

KERMODE, FRANK. 'Adam Unparadised', in *The Living Milton*, ed. Frank Kermode. 1960.

KERMODE². 'The Banquet of Sense', *Bulletin of the John Rylands Libr.* xliv, 1961.

KERMODE³, ed. *The Living Milton*. 1960.

KERMODE⁴. 'Milton's Hero', *RES*, iv, 1953.

KLIBANSKY, RAYMOND, and others. *Saturn and Melancholy*. 1964.

KROUSE, F. M. *Milton's Samson and the Christian Tradition*. Princeton 1949.

LOVEJOY, ARTHUR O. *The Great Chain of Being: A Study of the History of an Idea*. New York 1960.

LEWALSKI, B. K. *Milton's Brief Epic*. Providence, R. I. 1966.

MACKELLAR, W., ed. *The Latin Poems of John Milton*. Cornell Studies in English, No. xv. New Haven, Conn. 1930

MARLOWE, CHRISTOPHER. *Works*, ed. C. F. Tucker Brooke. Cambridge 1910.

MARTZ, L. *The Paradise Within*. New Haven, Conn. 1964.

MASSON, DAVID, ed. *The Poetical Works of John Milton*. 1890.

MASSON². *The Life of John Milton*. 1881.

NELSON, L. *Baroque Lyric Poetry*. New Haven, Conn. 1961.

NICOLSON, MARJORIE H. 'Milton and the Conjectura Cabbalistica', *PQ*, vi, 1927.

NICOLSON². 'A World in the Moon', *Smith College Studies in Modern Languages*, xvii, 1936.

NICOLSON³. *The Breaking of the Circle: Studies in the Effect of the 'New Science' Upon Seventeenth Century Poetry*. Evanston, Ill. 1950.

NICOLSON⁴. *Science and Imagination*. Ithaca, N.Y. 1956.

NORWOOD. *Studies in Honour of Gilbert Norwood*, ed. M. E. White. Toronto 1952.

OVID. See under SANDYS².

PANOFSKY, ERWIN. *Meaning in the Visual Arts*. New York 1955.

PANOFSKY². *Studies in Iconology*. New York and Evanston, Ill. 1962.

PARKER, W. R. *Milton's Contemporary Reputation*. Columbus, Ohio. 1940.

PARKER². *Milton's Debt to Greek Tragedy in 'Samson Agonistes'*. Baltimore, Md. 1937.

PARROTT. *Essays in Dramatic Literature. The Parrott Presentation Volume*, ed. H. Craig. Princeton, N.J. 1935.

PATRIDES, C. A. ed. *Milton's 'Lycidas': The Tradition and the Poem*. New York 1961.

POPE, E. M. *'Paradise Regained', The Tradition and the Poem*. Baltimore 1947.

PRINCE, F. T. *The Italian Element in Milton's Verse*. Oxford 1954.

RAJAN, B. *'Paradise Lost' and the Seventeenth Century Reader*. 1962.

RAJAN², ed. *John Milton: 'Paradise Lost' Books I and II*. 1964.

RANDOLPH, THOMAS. *Works*, ed. W. C. Hazlitt. 1875.

READ. *Studies for William A. Read*, ed. N. M. Caffee and T. A. Kirby. Baton Rouge, La. 1940.

RICKS, CHRISTOPHER. *Milton's Grand Style*. Oxford 1963.

RIPA, CESARE. *Iconologia*. Rome 1603.

ROBINS, HARRY F. *If This Be Heresy: A Study of Milton and Origen*. Illinois Studies in Lang. and Lit., No. li. Urbana, Ill. 1963.

ROBSON, W. W. 'The Better Fortitude', in *The Living Milton*, ed. Frank Kermode. 1960.

RØSTVIG, MAREN-SOFIE. *The Happy Man: Studies in the Metamorphoses of a Classical Ideal*. Vol. i: *1600–1700*. Oslo 1962.

RØSTVIG². *The Hidden Sense*. Oslo 1963.

SAMLA. *SAMLA Studies in English*, ed. J. Max Patrick. Gainesville, Fla. 1953.

SAMUEL, IRENE. *Plato and Milton*. Ithaca, N.Y. 1947.

SANDYS, GEORGE. *A relation of a journey*. 1615.

SANDYS². *Ovid's Metamorphosis. Englished Mythologiz'd and Represented in Figures* by G[eorge] S[andys]. 1632.

SCHULTZ, HOWARD. *Milton and Forbidden Knowledge*. New York 1955.

SCOTT. *Fred Newton Scott Anniversary Papers*, Chicago, Ill. 1929.

SCOULAR, KITTY W. *Natural Magic: Studies in the Presentation of Nature in English Poetry from Spenser to Marvell*. Oxford 1965.

SELDEN, JOHN. *De Dis Syris*. 1617.

SHAWCROSS, J. T. 'The Establishment of a Text of Milton's Poems through a Study of *Lycidas*'. *Bibliographical Society of America Papers* lvi, 1962.

SHAWCROSS². 'Certain Relationships of the Manuscripts of *Comus*'. *Bibliographical Society of America Papers* liv, 1960.

SIMS, JAMES H. *The Bible in Milton's Epics*. Gainesville, Fla. 1962.

SMART, JOHN, ed. *The Sonnets of Milton*. Glasgow 1921.

SPAETH, SIGMUND. *Milton's Knowledge of Music*. Ann Arbor, Mich. 1963.

STARNES, DEWITT T. and TALBERT, ERNEST WILLIAM. *Classical Myth and Legend*. Chapel Hill 1955.

STEIN, ARNOLD. *Answerable Style: Essays on 'Paradise Lost'*. Minneapolis, Minn. 1953.

STEIN[2]. *Heroic Knowledge*. Minneapolis, Minn. 1957.

STEPHANUS, CAROLUS. *Dictionarium historicum, geographicum, poeticum*. Geneva 1621.

SVENDSEN, KESTER. *Milton and Science*. Cambridge, Mass. 1956.

SYLVESTER'S DU BARTAS. See DU BARTAS.

TAYLOR, GEORGE C. *Milton's Use of Du Bartas*. Cambridge, Mass. 1934.

TAYLOR[2]. *A Tribute to George Coffin Taylor*, ed. A. Williams. Chapel Hill, N.C. 1952.

TILLEY, M. P. *A Dictionary of Proverbs in England in the Sixteenth and Seventeenth Centuries*. Ann Arbor, Mich. 1950.

TILLYARD, E. M. W. *Milton*. 1930.

TILLYARD[2]. *The Miltonic Setting, Past and Present*. Cambridge 1938.

TILLYARD[3]. *Studies in Milton*. 1951.

TODD, H. J., ed. *The Poetical Works of John Milton*. 1801.

TUVE, ROSEMOND. *A Reading of George Herbert*. 1952.

TUVE[2]. *Images and Themes in Five Poems by Milton*. Oxford 1957.

VERITY, A. W. ed. *Milton: 'Paradise Lost'*. Cambridge 1910.

VISIAK, E. H., ed. *Milton's 'Lament for Damon'*. 1935.

WARTON, THOMAS, ed. *Poems upon Several Occasions... by John Milton*. 1791.

WHITING, GEORGE W. *Milton's Literary Milieu*. New York 1964.

WHITING[2]. *Milton and this Pendant World*. Austin, Texas 1958.

WILSON KNIGHT, G. *The Burning Oracle*. Oxford 1939.

WIND, EDGAR. *Pagan Mysteries in the Renaissance*. 1958.

WIND[2]. *Bellini's Feast of the Gods*. Cambridge, Mass, 1948.

WOODHOUSE, A. S. P. 'Theme and Pattern in *Paradise Regained*', *UTQ*. xxv, 1956.

WRIGHT, B. A. '"Shade" for "Tree" in Milton's Poetry', *N & Q* cciii, 1958.

WRIGHT[2], ed. *Milton's Poems*. 1959.

YALE. *The Complete Prose Works of John Milton*, ed. Douglas Bush *et al.* New Haven, Conn. 1953–.

# Index of Titles and First Lines

*Titles are given in italic type.*